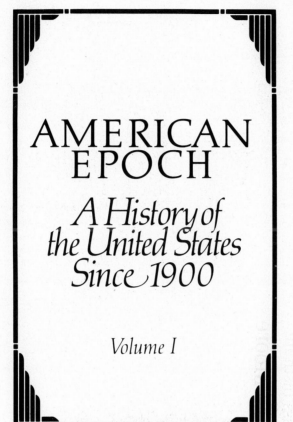

AMERICAN EPOCH

*A History of
the United States
Since 1900*

Volume I

AMERICAN EPOCH

VOLUME I: An Era of Economic and Social
Change, Reform, and World Wars, 1900–1945

VOLUME II: An Era of Total War and
Uncertain Peace, 1936–1985

SIXTH EDITION

AMERICAN EPOCH

A History of the United States Since 1900

VOLUME I: AN ERA OF ECONOMIC AND SOCIAL CHANGE, REFORM, AND WORLD WARS 1900–1945

ARTHUR S. LINK

George Henry Davis '86 Professor of American History and
Editor and Director of The Papers of Woodrow Wilson
Princeton University

WILLIAM A. LINK

Associate Professor
University of North Carolina at Greensboro

WILLIAM B. CATTON

Professor Emeritus
Middlebury College

ALFRED A. KNOPF *NEW YORK*

Arthur S. Link Dedicates This Book to His Grandchildren

Arthur Stanley Link III
Percy Anne Link
Margaret Dorothy Link

THIS IS A BORZOI BOOK PUBLISHED BY ALFRED A. KNOPF, INC.

Sixth Edition
987654321

Library of Congress Cataloging-in-Publication Data

Link, Arthur Stanley.
  American epoch.

  Includes bibliographies and indexes.
  Contents: v. 1. An era of economic and social change,
reform, and world wars, 1900–1945 — v. 2. An era of
total war and uncertain peace, 1936–1985.
  1. United States—History—20th century. I. Link,
William A. II. Catton, William Bruce, 1926–
III. Title.
E741.L56 1986   973.9   86–21458
ISBN 0-394-36204-7 (v.1)
ISBN 0-394-36205-5 (v. 2)

Cover design by Nadja Furlan-Lorbek

Manufactured in the United States of America

PREFACE

-»» «««-

This sixth edition of *American Epoch* continues, as the earlier editions have done, to present what is one of the most exciting stories in history—the saga of the people of the United States from the War with Spain to the present—with all its marvelous complexity and kaleidoscopic change. As the end of the twentieth century nears, the meaning of events and developments, particularly since 1945, assumes greater clarity. When the last chapter in the fifth edition was written in mid-1979, the United States was still suffering from a crisis of confidence due to the traumas of the Vietnam War and Watergate. The optimism voiced in that last chapter has been largely justified. Americans today are still beset by difficult problems, and always will be. But they have come out of the mood of doubt and despair of 1979 with renewed hope. They have also regained their characteristic faith in their political institutions and their belief that it is possible for a democracy to deal with the problems of our time.

I extend a warm welcome to a new collaborator, William A. Link, Associate Professor of History at the University of North Carolina at Greensboro. He has completely rewritten the economic, social, and cultural chapters, the chapter on progressivism, those on American foreign policy from 1961 to 1985, and the chapters on the Carter and Ford administrations. He has also added a chapter on the Reagan administration. He has greatly enriched *American Epoch* with new insights on the progressive transformation, sections on changes in the American family and women's roles over eighty-five years, the findings of the new labor historians, and discussions of popular culture and sports and the politics and diplomacy of the past twelve years. In addition, he has rewritten all other chapters in order to make the sixth edition shorter than its predecessor.

When I wrote the first edition of this book, it was my supreme ambition to give as much attention to social, economic, and cultural history as to political and diplomatic history. Along with my subsequent collaborators, I have continued to work toward this goal. I think that we have finally achieved it in this sixth edition. Each section of the book begins with social, economic, and cultural overviews that provide the essential context for a history of the politics and diplomacy of what are more or less discrete periods. However, in the narrative chapters, we also try to show how social, cultural, and economic events impinge upon and intersect with particular political and diplomatic events and developments. For example, the chapter on the American people since the Second World War paints in broad strokes the experiences of American blacks since 1945. However, the postwar civil rights movement, with all its profound impact upon judicial interpretation, legislation, and domestic politics, is related closely to the political history of the postwar period.

In our discussion of the Cold War and American–Soviet competition since 1945, we have tried to present this difficult subject with as much fairness and objectivity as possible. We have learned much from the so-called "revisionists," but we obviously do not agree with the more extreme of them who place most of the blame for Soviet–American tension and conflict upon the United States. We have a special section on the "revisionists" in the bibliography. Many of the books listed therein not only offer important insights but are a good antidote to mindless anti-Sovietism, and we urge students to read them.

Not only have statistics and the narrative been updated, but also the "Suggested Additional Reading." We have tried to include all important works on twentieth-century American history, and the omission of any important book was inadvertent.

We owe a very special debt to Christopher J. Rogers, History Editor in the College Department of Alfred A. Knopf, Inc. He urged us to prepare this sixth edition and gave unstinting encouragement through all stages of its writing and production. We thank him sincerely. We also thank our project editor, Fred H. Burns, for shepherding this book to completion. A number of people provided invaluable aid in preparing the manuscript for publication: Richard C. Ellis, Jo Gainey, Joseph W. Hickey, and Sara S. Lindley. The typing of the manuscript was speeded by the support of the Academic Computer Center of the University of North Carolina at Greensboro, particularly of Diane Case. This book has also benefited from the work of several skilled editors. We are indebted to our copyeditor at Alfred A. Knopf, William Bischoff, who substantially improved the book's clarity and elegance, and to two other fine editors, Margaret D. Link and Susannah Jones Link, whose efforts made this book more readable.

ARTHUR S. LINK
Princeton, New Jersey

CONTENTS

—»» ««—

CHARTS

————————— ⇒⟫ ⟪⇐ —————————

MAPS

—————— →》》 《《← ——————

AN ERA OF ECONOMIC CHANGE, REFORM, AND WORLD WARS 1900–1945

In which the American people experience both the benefits and the disadvantages of rapid industrial growth, attempt substantial political and economic reform, and contribute decisively to Allied victory in two world wars.

Chapter 1

—>>> <<<—

Patterns of Economic Development, 1900–1920

Early twentieth-century Americans were almost blithely confident about their political, economic, and cultural institutions, and with good reasons. By 1900, the United States benefited from rich and varied natural resources, a transportation system to exploit them, abundant investment capital, a skilled labor force, and the presence of aggressive business entrepreneurs. Economic growth had widespread consequences, some beneficial, some baneful. It stimulated outmigration from rural areas and in the process put heavy strains upon traditional social organization. It drew millions of people from the countryside and from rural Europe and molded them into a new industrial proletariat. It also imposed a new and alien work regime. Not least important, it spurred the growth of towns and cities as dominant residential and work centers.

1. Origins of the American Industrial Revolution

At the end of the nineteenth century, the historian Henry Adams, scion of a long line of presidents, congressmen, and diplomats, described the United States of a century earlier as an almost static world. "Old landmarks," he wrote of the eastern seaboard, "remained nearly where they stood before"; the "same bad roads and difficult rivers, connecting the same small towns, stretched into the same forests" as a half century previously. Nature was "rather man's master than his servant," and Americans struggling with the "untamed continent" were scarcely "more competent to their task than the beavers and buffalo which had for countless generations made bridges and roads of their own."

Adams's virtually pristine United States was a society on the verge of fundamental change: within fifty years, an industrial revolution was permanently reshaping the country. Industrialization was, however, a complex process. It did not occur uniformly across the country. By 1850, industrial manufacturing was firmly rooted only

3

in the urban North and Middle West. Moreover, the hallmark of the industrial revolution—mass production—affected different industries at different times. The earliest fully industrialized form of manufacturing was that of cotton textiles, which pioneered industrial forms of production, management, and labor relations beginning in the 1790s. Modeled on English factory organization, New England's cotton textile factories made a quick transition from domestic manufacturing—which had local markets and was based on home production by women—into a system that involved a workplace outside of the home, regular factory-work discipline, power-driven machinery, and managerial hierarchies.

Yet the case of cotton textiles was far from typical. In most manufacturing enterprises, the transition from artisan-based production took place slowly. In part this was because other manufacturing lacked textiles' preexisting factory technology and organization. Thus, another success story of early industrial New England—shoe manufacturing—followed a different path from the one blazed by textiles. Industrialization of shoe production took place through reorganization of the work process rather than through factory production. Before industrialization, small-scale independent shoemakers, or cobblers, themselves financed the production of shoes and sponsored their local distribution. By 1850, in a new system (the so-called "putting-out" system), merchant-entrepreneurs distributed shoes over wider areas and had assumed control over production. With merchant control came other changes: a growth in the size of operations; the spread of the domestic system over much of rural New England; and the specialization of shoemaking into several component parts or phases. When a factory system finally came to New England shoe manufacturing in the 1860s, therefore, the work process had already been industrialized.

2. Railroads and Economic Growth

It is impossible to comprehend the origins of the twentieth-century American economy without understanding the central importance of railroads. By 1900, with about a quarter of a million miles of track, the American railroad system was the largest and most efficiently managed in the world, and few parts of the nation did not feel its influence directly. But railroads were more than mere symbols of the country's coming of age: they were the chief engine of economic growth. They dramatically lowered transportation costs and made possible continuous, regular movement of goods and people across long distances. They also fostered the creation of a truly national market system and linked agriculture and industry together as never before had been possible. As transcontinental carriers and major real-estate developers, they were the most important agents of western expansion and settlement. Moreover, as the first "big" business, railroads developed new methods of capital formation and investment, originated bureaucratic managerial hierarchies, and set up the first kinds of corporate interstate business organization.

Railroads underwent an early stage of development in the three decades preceding the Civil War, when entrepreneurs—most of them from the Atlantic states—began to assemble governmental backing, capital investment, and business organization necessary to support their new enterprises. In 1860, these early lines had laid some 31,000 miles of track and extended to the Mississippi River. By 1900, the American railroad system included almost 260,000 miles of track.

As important as their physical expansion was the railroads' development of bureaucratic organizations during the last half of the nineteenth century. As railroads grew, they became large enterprises; as they became large, those firms that were most efficiently organized survived a merciless competition. Whole systems thus emerged that tightened control over costs but also extended service through more elaborate business organizations staffed by rational and efficient managers.

By the 1890s, both as a result of the railroads' development and because the period of their rapid expansion had now ended, the capital market was favorable to investment in other sectors of the economy. The completed national transportation network had further consequences. It encouraged the growth of an integrated communication system, also completed by the end of the nineteenth century through extensive construction of telegraph lines. Railroads had a striking effect on the nation's sense of time. Their emphasis on regularity and schedule was influential in shaping modern attitudes, and it was at the instigation of railroads that a national system of regional time zones was adopted in 1883. Still another important contribution to economic growth made by railroads was that they served as a model for the subsequent development of corporations.

3. The Emergence of the Modern Corporation

The most important characteristic of the early twentieth-century American economy was the rise of corporations as the prevalent form of interstate commerce and

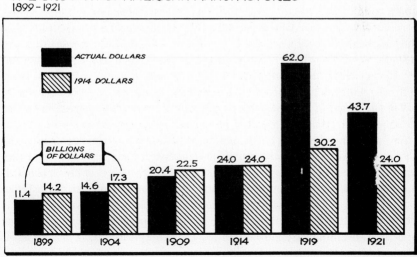

THE GROWTH OF AMERICAN MANUFACTURES
1899–1921

ACTUAL DOLLARS

1914 DOLLARS

BILLIONS OF DOLLARS

62.0

43.7

30.2

24.0 24.0

24.0

22.5

20.4

17.3

11.4 14.2 14.6

1899   1904   1909   1914   1919   1921

industrial manufacturing. This movement in industry, finance, and transportation transformed an economy of relatively small competitive producers into one dominated by an oligarchy of giant combinations. Ever since the corporation first emerged, journalists, publicists, and politicians have frequently denounced it with the pejorative and stereotypical description "big business"—a creation of Wall Street monopolists intent on controlling whole industries, raising prices, and reaping huge profits. "Big business," so many contemporaries thought, endangered the very foundations of American society.

Like all stereotypes, this view contains both truth and distortion. The post–Civil War years are filled with examples of entrepreneur-capitalists—railroad financier Jay Gould and oilman John D. Rockefeller are prominent examples—who made huge fortunes through manipulation and intrigue, and did so openly and often with the willing cooperation of state and federal governments. But, as products of the increasing size and complexity of the economy, corporations were in many respects an irresistible historical development. By 1900, it was simply impossible to compete without due attention to national markets and without the introduction of mass-production technology. Nor was it possible to achieve a rationalized integration of production and distribution without innovations in business organization.

Corporations before 1865 were prominent mainly in transportation, insurance, banking, and to a lesser degree in textiles. Yet by the end of the 1890s, they were the dominant form of industrial organization and had displaced proprietorship and partnership as the chief instrumentality for combining capital and labor. Corporations accounted for 66 percent of all manufactured goods by 1899; ten years later, that proportion had increased to 79 percent.

The emergence of corporations out of the intensely competitive atmosphere of the 1870s and 1880s was a key development in the evolution of American business. The integration of production and distribution brought about by individual firms occurred mainly in food processing and tobacco and, before 1890, did not extend to other types of manufacturing. In those areas, firms sought a national system of production and distribution through merger or amalgamation. One early form of business combination was the "trust," an extralegal arrangement by which competing manufacturers pooled properties to achieve industrywide control. The trust gained national notoriety when the Ohio oil refiner John D. Rockefeller organized the Standard Oil Trust in 1879—superseded by the Trust Agreement of three years later. Dominated by Standard, the Trust Agreement was signed by forty-odd oil companies, which together controlled over 90 percent of the country's refining capacity and an equal proportion of its pipelines. In turn, the member companies were issued trust certificates equal to the value of their assets.

Similar trusts and holding companies were organized in mining, sugar, and other industries. Yet the use of the trust to achieve industrywide control had been abandoned by 1900 for several reasons. To begin with, trusts were not always able to stifle competition and maintain control over most of an industry's market. More important, the spread of trusts ran against a pervasive ideological current in American political thought: strong antimonopoly feelings, especially against monopolies blessed with governmental approval. Consequently, the trusts faced sweeping legislation which specifically prohibited combinations in restraint of trade and instituted the first forms of business regulation. The most important of these laws were the Interstate Commerce Act of 1887 and the Sherman Antitrust Act of 1890. In addition, many states enacted similar legislation (see pp. 51–53).

During and after the depression of the 1890s, another form of interstate enterprise—the holding company—began to replace the trust. A crucial new factor was a legal and political climate favorable to industrial combination. In 1895, the Supreme Court ruled in the *E. C. Knight* case that the Sherman Antitrust Act did not apply to interstate manufacturing, signaling that the Court would not apply the Sherman Act to industrial mergers. With the election of a pro-business president, William McKinley, in 1896, the way was clear for virtually unrestricted amalgamations. To these elements was added another key factor: the participation of Wall Street investment bankers in sponsoring the organization of corporate mergers.

No one person better embodied the movement of bankers into transportation and industry than J. Pierpont Morgan. During the depression that lasted from 1893 to 1897, Morgan reorganized through consolidation several mammoth new transportation systems. Morgan's firm, J. P. Morgan & Company, was so successful in rehabilitating bankrupt railroads that he began to extend his control into manufacturing. His chance came when a bitter rivalry between Andrew Carnegie and other producers of finished steel threatened to plunge the entire industry into a price war. Morgan intervened with a plan to combine 60 percent of the iron and steel producers into a single corporate giant, the United States Steel Corporation. Thereafter, Morgan played a central role in the organization of combinations in other industries by raising needed capital through the sale of stocks and bonds that launched the new corporations on their way. Through his representatives on boards of directors and his control of sources of credit, Morgan continued to exert an unparalleled degree of influence in American industry.

Between 1897 and 1903 American manufacturing became more concentrated than ever before. While only 12 important combinations, with a total capitalization of under $1 billion, took place between 1879 and 1897, in 1899 alone some 185 combinations occurred, with a total capital of over $3 billion. By 1904, a comprehensive survey of corporations found that 305 industrial combinations, with an aggregate capital of $7 billion, controlled two-fifths of total manufacturing capital. Corporate amalgamations had risen to an even more spectacular level in transportation: six groups controlled 95 percent of the nation's mileage.

The merger movement of 1899–1904 catapulted the corporation to the center of the American economy. The concentration of operations and capital resources which these amalgamations allowed led to the increasing integration of production and distribution and, with it, to the rise of managerial cadres capable of long-range planning and decision making. There were a number of success stories: Standard Oil and United States Steel both dominated their industries not only because of control of the market but also because of superior managerial hierarchies. Yet mergers did not automatically win the day. The National Biscuit Company (Nabisco), for example, was formed in 1898 out of three regional holding companies. Within three years of the organization of this "biscuit trust," however, its managers found that simply buying out the competition did not insure dominance or even necessarily survival. Instead, as Nabisco managers put it, it was essential to improve the "internal management of our own business" in purchasing raw materials at low-cost bulk, cutting production expenses, and systematizing the company's distribution system.

4. The United States and the World Economy, 1897–1914

In association with the profound changes transforming the American domestic economy, the volume and character of foreign trade underwent significant modifications. Between 1897 and 1914, foreign trade steadily expanded, and at a faster pace than at any time since the Civil War. From almost $1.4 billion in 1900, exports increased to nearly $2.5 billion fourteen years later; meanwhile, imports rose from $850 million to $1.8 billion. As important as the expansion in the volume of international trade was a shift in the character of exports and imports. Since colonial times, America had been active in the international economy primarily through its exports of agricultural commodities. As late as 1900 agricultural products constituted 60 percent of the nation's exports, manufactured products only 35 percent. Thereafter, however, industrial manufacturing assumed greater importance, and by 1914 it accounted for nearly half of all American exports. At the same time, development of new domestic industries lessened demand for foreign manufactured goods and stimulated demand for raw materials such as rubber, tin, and manganese.

U.S. FOREIGN TRADE
1900 – 1948

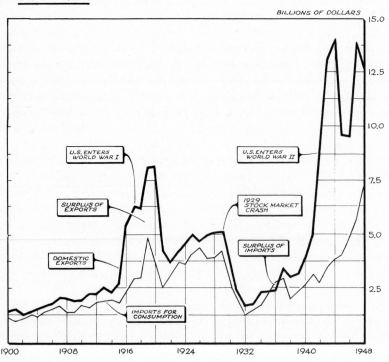

The expansion of international trade before the First World War foreshadowed the day when the United States would assume a commanding position in the world economy. Even while trade grew, however, the center of international finance remained in London; the United States before 1915 retained its traditional status as debtor nation to Europe. In 1897 Europeans held American securities—over half of them in railroads—valued at almost $3.5 billion. By 1914 European investment in the United States, direct and indirect, had more than doubled; although partly offset by greater American investment abroad, the nation's balance of payments still ran heavily in the red.

For most of the nineteenth century, American investments rarely left home. Almost every available dollar went into the heavy capital requirements of building railroads, settling the West, and financing industrialization. On the eve of the Spanish–American War, Americans had invested only about $685 million abroad. Such investments had increased to about $3.5 million in 1914. A large portion, $692 million, went to Europe, and another $246 million to the Far East. But the greater share remained in the Western Hemisphere. While American capitalists invested some $867 million in Canadian mines, industries, and railroads, an era of political stability under Mexico's President Porfirio Díaz attracted almost an equal amount —$854 million—into railroads, mines, ranches, and oil wells south of the border. By 1914, American investments totaled $200 million in Cuba (by then an American quasi-protectorate); $136 million in other Caribbean islands; $93 million in Central America; and $366 million in South America.

5. Workers in the Industrial Age

The period between the depression of the 1890s and the First World War was, generally speaking, a time of steady economic progress for American workers. Except for a brief interlude in 1908, employment remained robust for most of the period. At the same time, real earnings of workers engaged in manufacturing increased 37 percent, while average hours in industry declined from 59.1 a week in 1897 to 55.2 in 1914.

Yet generalizing about American workers as a whole distorts significant differences among them. In fact, there was no single working class. Rather, there were a variety of working classes, as the boundaries of class sometimes conflicted with those of race and ethnicity and at times superseded them. The American work force was a patchwork of women, children, native Protestants, Catholic immigrants, and nonwhites. Until the 1890s, for example, the majority of anthracite coal miners were English-speaking; by 1919, some 90 percent of them were non-English-speaking immigrants from southeastern Europe. By the same date, of about 14,000 steelworkers employed in the Carnegie plants of Pittsburgh, some 12,000 were recent, southeastern European immigrants.

Still another factor that makes generalizing about American workers difficult was their extreme geographical mobility. What evidence has survived about early twentieth-century workers indicates that mobility—whether among European immigrants in search of jobs or native Americans "tramping" for regular or seasonal employment—was a basic fact of life. Of the workers employed at Ford Motor Company's Highland Park, Michigan, automobile assembly plant during March 1913, for example, about half left work. Most of these were "five-day" men who were absent for five or more consecutive days and were dropped from the payroll. Worker mobility had important implications. On the one hand, it meant an extraordinary adaptability to the economy's demand for labor; on the other, mobility made working-class cohesiveness difficult to achieve.

This was also a perilous time for American workers. For most of them, employment in mills, factories, and railroad yards was extremely hazardous and frequently life-threatening. In 1907, one survey found that at least half a million Americans annually were killed, crippled, or seriously injured while on the job; as late as 1913, another survey revealed that 25,000 workers were killed and 700,000 seriously injured. Work was not only dangerous, it continued to demand long hours. Even in 1920, the average skilled worker was employed for about fifty hours a week, and in certain industries this figure was even higher.

In spite of the period's prosperity, moreover, a large portion of the work force straddled a thin line between survival and starvation. Surveying the industrial scene in 1915, the United States Commission on Industrial Relations noted that "a large part" of industrial workers subsisted "in a condition of actual poverty." It estimated that at least one-third, and possibly one-half, of all workers employed in manufacturing and mining annually earned "less than enough to support them in anything like a comfortable and decent condition." The fact that so large a proportion of workers were impoverished had grave social consequences: poor children died at three times the rate of middle-class children; as many as a fifth of all children in large cities experienced hunger and malnutrition; and poor children were greatly undereducated as compared to their middle-class counterparts.

As important as the persistence of poverty was the effect of industrialization and the subsequent rise of the corporation on worker autonomy. The concentration of control over manufacturing invariably affected workers. On the one hand, it increased employment through the expansion of production and the establishment of factories. On the other hand, it was precisely the larger, amalgamated firms that were most interested in achieving cost reductions by reorganizing the work process, reducing the traditional privileges of certain workers, especially autonomous craftsmen. In this way, the bigger companies increased worker productivity by introducing systematic and scientific management. All of these changes added on-the-job pressures, restructured the nature of labor relations in the twentieth century, and dealt a severe blow to the fortunes of craft unions.

6. The Rise of Scientific Management

The trend to scientific management was tied to the emergence of mass-production manufacturing. As we have seen, the factory system had already been in existence for almost a century; between 1880 and 1930, however, it expanded significantly, partly because of the utilization of electricity. First introduced in the 1880s, within ten years electric power had begun to replace oil and gas for lighting; at the same time, it also became the most widely used form of power for machinery. Moreover, the increasing use of electricity in materials handling—in the use of electric traveling cranes, electric-powered factory railroads, and other forms of conveyance—transformed the workplace.

Scientific management originated as early as the 1880s. Late nineteenth-century scientific managers—Henry R. Towne, A. H. Church, and, above all, Frederick Winslow Taylor—criticized the chaos of the contemporary factory and urged coordination as a means of increasing production and insuring greater labor stability. In particular, scientific managers advocated three changes in the factory environment: the introduction of a cost-accounting system, including a time clock for workers and a greater degree of managerial regimentation; production and inventory controls; and incentive wage plans to stimulate production and reduce labor costs. In each instance, the undisguised objective was to increase the power of managers at the expense of the traditional position of skilled workers.

The most famous of the scientific managers was, as we have said, Taylor. Born to a prominent Philadelphia family, at the age of eighteen he became an apprentice at a local metal-working plant. He rose to foreman and then engineer at Midvale Steel Company and later became its plant manager. By 1900, as the world's leading advocate of scientific management, he served as consultant and independent publicist. Taylor's approach was shaped in particular by his experience at Midvale. In the 1880s, he had introduced changes there in shop management, including systematic accounting in order to control costs, production planning through a planning office, and, most important, an incentive wage system. All of these innovations, Taylor believed, would bring rational management to previously chaotic labor relations.

Taylor was an important figure in the scientific management movement not because he was an original thinker, but because he was an adept popularizer. In 1899, he began a campaign to promote an incentive wage system—known as the "differential piece rate"—as a solution to labor problems. Under this plan, "time and motion" studies would determine the most efficient rate of production and thereby motivate employees to work hard and increase productivity. Soon, Taylor's fame was so great that he resigned his job at Midvale to devote fulltime to converting manufacturers to scientific management. He found a receptive audience in large, often consolidated firms. Even if they did not hire Taylor, few American manufacturers were unaffected by the movement for scientific management, which they generally regarded as a change no less important than the advent of the corporation itself.

Another innovation, also inspired and directed by managers, were various company-controlled welfare systems. The advocates of what came to be known as "welfare capitalism" were inspired by humanitarian motives of uplift. However, they also perceived "welfare capitalism" as another instrument of orderly industrial labor relations. They believed that two features of nineteenth-century work were responsible for chaotic labor relations and low productivity: the prevalence of a system of workers' privileges and the influence of craft unions. Since the beginning of the industrial revolution, workers had retained well-defined areas of autonomy in the workplace. Especially before 1900, the crucial role of artisans and skilled workers in industrial manufacturing meant that, through their craft unions, they were able to affect, and even make, important decisions. In industries that sorely depended on skilled labor, autonomous craftsmen frequently decided tasks, schedules, and even production quotas.

In part, then, "welfare capitalism" sought to displace the traditional role of craft unions. By assuming the welfare functions of the union, managers hoped to root out inefficiency, assert greater control over production, and bring about a new era of labor peace and stability. By the 1890s, some American manufacturers were already viewing a company-run welfare system as a road to greater labor control. In one early example, the H. J. Heinz Company initiated a program during the 1890s in which the company supplied workers' uniforms; provided dressing rooms, washrooms, lockers, and even a roof garden for lunch-hour strolls; and employed a permanent "welfare secretary" to organize annual outings and company recreational activities. The president of National Cash Register (NCR), John H. Patterson, developed a similar welfare system. In the NCR factory outside Dayton, Ohio, Patterson began a company plan during the mid-1890s. It included health and sanitary inspections of the workplace; awarded prizes to the most "efficient" departments; established a worker grievance procedure; and provided a library, reading room, and other cultural amenities for workers. By 1902, Patterson had added a Labor Department which handled grievances, recruitment, worker supervision, sanitation, and shop safety.

The growth of welfare activities under company control accounted for a significant improvement of working conditions. Yet "welfare capitalism," along with scientific management, upped the ante in the tense contest between managers and workers in the American economy. Although both initiatives brought a greater degree of labor stability, higher worker productivity, and added managerial control over work, they achieved these goals at a substantial cost: disruption of the equilibrium in nineteenth-century labor relations, loss of worker autonomy, and partial or total elimination of skilled workers. In the process, the balance was tipped—for the time being—in favor of the managers.

7. The Ford Worker

A pioneer of these innovations in labor relations was the largest early twentieth-century automobile manufacturer, the Ford Motor Company. Between 1908 and 1914, Ford Motor Company, then emerging as the industry leader, expanded employment from 450 to over 14,000 workers. Henry Ford was successful primarily for one reason: his determination to reorganize the work process and to introduce mass-production methods. Although skilled craftsmen and laborers dominated early automobile production, with the introduction of the moving assembly line in 1913–1914, workers now became semiskilled and "deskilled" operatives in a monotonous, but also highly productive, manufacturing process. Using tracks and elevators powered by electricity, Ford workers at the mammoth complex at Highland Park, Michigan, operated at a ferocious pace. According to one contemporary, "each man on each gang has just one small thing to do—and do over and over again." Work at the Highland Park plant reduced life to a "definite number of jerks, twists, and turns," wrote a Ford worker.

The new mass-production system at Highland Park created an enormous demand for labor that was filled by European immigrants. By 1914, 71 percent of all Ford workers were foreign-born and included twenty-two different language groups. Yet the monotony of the work also resulted in labor instability, reflected in a high rate of turnover, "soldiering" (deliberate restriction of output), and absenteeism. In direct response to the problem of instability, Ford hired John R. Lee, from Buffalo, New York, a manager, to design a worker welfare system. Like other company-run programs, Lee's reforms, introduced in October 1913, began regular medical inspections, improved sanitary conditions, and established recreational facilities for workers. More broadly, however, the Lee reforms attempted to strike at the root causes of labor discontent by increasing wages 15 percent, instituting a system of wage classification, establishing a new, regularized scheme of recruitment and employment under the control of an Employment Bureau, and founding an Employee Credit Union to encourage habits of thrift among workers.

A sequel to the Lee reforms was one of the most famous labor programs in American history, Ford's "Five Dollar Day." Introduced in January 1914, the Five Dollar Day's main objective was to attract reliable, stable workers by paying them high wages—twice the going rate—and permitting them to work a shorter, eight-hour day. But it was also an ingenious system of incentive pay that extended Ford's control of his employees. The Five Dollar Day was a profit-sharing agreement. Workers received a minimum daily wage of $2.34; the remaining $2.66 was "profits," paid according to performance on the job—and often at home as well. In April 1914, Ford established a Sociological Department to manage the program and to determine workers' eligibility for these "profits." By reducing, or threatening to reduce, the "profit" share of workers' paychecks, Ford managers offered a highly sucessful wage incentive plan that simultaneously increased job satisfaction and raised the productivity of labor. By no coincidence, the program raised profits as well.

8. The Rise of Organized Labor

Nothing better illustrates the precarious position that workers occupied in American society during the half century between the Civil War and the First World War than the story of labor's attempts to achieve self-protection through organization. It was an age in which the status of workers, especially skilled craftsmen, underwent a steady erosion; it was also a time during which workers engaged in mass-production manufacturing experienced a concerted attempt on the part of management to tighten control and uproot unions. Finally, it was also an age of industrial conflict and violence in which different models for labor relations appeared on the scene.

The most popular form of labor organizing by the end of the 1890s was the trade, or craft, union. The National Labor Union and the Knights of Labor—both oriented toward industrial unionism (a form that groups all workers in a single industry into a single organization)—enjoyed momentary success during the 1870s and 1880s.

Meanwhile, however, the leaders of the Cigar Makers' Union, Samuel Gompers and Adolph Strasser, were building a powerful trade union. Led by Gompers and Strasser, cigar makers joined with other trade and craft unions to form the Federation of Organized Trades in 1881; five years later, it became the American Federation of Labor (AFL). With Gompers as president, the AFL survived the hard times of the 1890s by following a conservative, bread-and-butter approach which eschewed utopianism and was avowedly opportunistic and practical in its objectives. Unlike its predecessors, the AFL was conservative in approach and allowed its affiliates to set their own membership rules. As a result, more often than not craft unions excluded women and blacks, thereby effectively barring them from skilled jobs. Gompers, unlike his trade-union counterparts in western Europe, avoided any association with an independent, labor-dominated political party. By 1897, the AFL claimed 265,000 members, and from this point it fought its way to dominance as the most influential voice in organized labor. Its membership had climbed to 548,-000 by 1900, and it continued to grow until 1904, when it reached 1,676,000.

Several factors accounted for the determined rise of the AFL: superb esprit de corps, able leadership, and a public opinion that was growing less hostile to organized labor. Above all, AFL leadership brought real benefits to skilled workers, and after 1897 Gompers and his colleagues succeeded in winning collective bargaining, higher wages, and shorter hours in most of the building trades and the skilled crafts. Yet, no sooner had the AFL achieved its dominant position than its leadership faced serious challenge in two major industries—anthracite coal mining and steel.

The first test came in the effort of the United Mine Workers of America (UMW), a union affiliated with the AFL, to organize the coal industry. Decisively beaten in 1894, the UMW had only 10,000 members and seemed moribund by 1897. Nonetheless, when its leaders demanded—and were refused—recognition and increased wages from bituminous coal operators, they orchestrated a general strike that affected fields in western Pennsylvania, Ohio, Indiana, and Illinois. The UMW won a decisive victory, gaining recognition, higher wages, and other demands, and emerged from the strike well organized and over 100,000 strong. It now turned its attention to the anthracite coal industry located in five counties of northeastern Pennsylvania and, on September 12, 1900, 150,000 miners walked out of the pits. The UMW, led by its president, John Mitchell, demanded recognition, establishment of a labor–management grievance procedure, and a wage increase. Mitchell waived the demand for recognition and proposed that other issues be arbitrated. When the operators agreed to a 10 percent wage increase and made other concessions in October 1900, Mitchell called off the strike.

Although the UMW gained a major victory and began a thorough organization of the industry, its differences with the operators remained. In 1902, the latter refused to discuss the wage issue with union officials, and Mitchell called a strike that began on May 14. As the strike dragged on into the autumn, coal prices skyrocketed, while residents of eastern cities were on the brink of a fuel famine. Under strong pressure from President Theodore Roosevelt, Mitchell agreed to submit the strike to arbitration, but the operators denounced the union as a lawless body and refused. Roosevelt then moved decisively—if also unconstitutionally—and issued secret orders to the army to move 10,000 troops in preparation for a government seizure of the mines. At the same time, he sent Secretary of War Elihu Root to warn J. P. Morgan, who had close ties with the mine operators, of the impending seizure. Morgan and Root soon devised a mediation plan acceptable to the operators. It established an arbitration commission but provided that no labor official be appointed to it. With Mitchell's approval, Roosevelt appointed the entire commission and included a former railroad union official in the capacity of "sociologist."

With the help of federal intervention—the first ever on the side of organized labor—the UMW had organized the eastern and midwestern bituminous and the entire anthracite coal industry by 1903. Even so, the coal union faced a troubled future and, by the end of the First World War, had suffered staggering defeats. One nagging problem was that of the southern Appalachian fields, which were opened during the 1890s. Operators in that region were unaffected by the strikes of 1897, 1900, and 1902 and militantly opposed concessions to organized labor. At the center of southern Appalachia were the crucial mines of West Virginia. So long as its fields were unorganized, both the UMW and the northern operators suffered intense competition from this low-wage and low-cost area. UMW efforts to organize the state in 1902 failed. As new fields were opened in Virginia, Kentucky, Tennessee, and Alabama, the task of organizing the South became even more urgent. Another attempt by the UMW to organize West Virginia in 1912–1913 brought much bloodshed and, in certain parts of the state, virtual civil war. The effort was only partly successful.

The UMW suffered other defeats on another frontier—Colorado. In 1903–1904, a strike against John D. Rockefeller's Colorado Fuel & Iron Company resulted in a union rout and the deportation of many strikers. When the union made another attempt ten years later, in 1913, the state was beset by a violent civil war, ignited when state troops attacked and burned a tent colony of strikers at Ludlow, killing eleven women and children.

For its part, the AFL's most discouraging and significant reversal in its early history was its failure to organize the steel industry. Before 1890, iron manufacturing was dominated by a single union, the Amalgamated Iron, Steel and Tin Workers, which was affiliated with the AFL and represented the interests of skilled craftsmen. By 1900, however, several new factors had undermined the strength of the Amalgamated. With the development of new technologies in the steel industry, skilled iron workers—the backbone of the Amalgamated—found their skills antiquated and were no longer crucial to the manufacturing process. As mass production became the rule in the huge new steel complexes of the industrial Middle West, steel producers increasingly hired recent immigrants from southern and eastern Europe, who had little interest or stake in the union. Finally, beginning with the violent Homestead strike of 1892, steel officials made a concerted, and generally successful, effort to root the union from the steel mills.

When the steel plants of Andrew Carnegie were merged into the United States Steel Corporation in 1901, the stage was set for a showdown between organized labor and management. Union officials, despite major internal weaknesses, called a strike against all plants of the giant steel corporation on August 10, 1901. Although a majority of workers walked out, the strike lacked the support of unskilled, recent immigrant workers or even the full backing of skilled workers, and the Amalgamated surrendered unconditionally in the end. The corporation agreed to pay union wages, but a wage increase was no longer at issue. What *was* at issue was the presence of the union, which agreed to withdraw from fourteen mills, to "freeze" its membership, and to concede the corporation the right to discharge workers for union activities.

Thereafter, the steel industry consolidated its victory over organized labor. After 1901, it began an aggressive program to woo workers away from the union, including profit sharing, employee-safety, workmen's compensation, and old-age pension plans —all in place by 1910. After another abortive strike in 1909, the Amalgamated lost even more ground as the major steel producers introduced a policy of excluding the union throughout the industry. By the First World War, it appeared that the Amalgamated's conservative, craft-union strategy was no match for the assembled resources of management, whose absolute authority was the product of relentless warfare against the union, use of spies and blacklisting of strikers, domination of local governments, and a welfare program that undermined the union's appeal.

9. A Challenge from Above

The examples of coal mining and steel typfify the fortunes of the AFL between about 1904 and 1914. Indeed, the union, which had been growing at a spectacular rate from 1900 to 1904, then experienced declining membership until 1911. The weakness of the AFL during these years reflected serious challenges to the trade-union movement during the first three decades of the twentieth century. One was a challenge from above—an aggressive campaign on the part of manufacturers to destroy unions. The other came from within the ranks of labor itself and questioned the direction and leadership of the AFL.

For a time at the turn of the century, it seemed that management might reach an accommodation with organized labor. One sign of hope for industrial peace was the organization in 1900 of the National Civic Federation, founded to prove that "organized labor cannot be destroyed without debasement of the masses." Its leaders included industrialists like Mark Hanna and George W. Perkins, bankers like J. P. Morgan, and labor spokesmen like Samuel Gompers and John Mitchell. The federation rendered service for a few years to the labor movement by prevention or mediation of strikes and by giving a high degree of visibility and respectability to Gompers in particular.

Yet the federation represented only a minority of employers, a fact made evident by a mass offensive on their part to destroy unionism altogether and to establish an "open shop," or nonunion pattern, throughout industry. This counterattack began in 1900 in Dayton, Ohio, where employers banded together in an association which, within two years, had driven the unions out of town. Flushed with victory, promoters went from Dayton to other cities to educate employers in other cities about the value of what they called the "American Plan." So successful were these campaigns through employers' associations in Chicago, in Beloit, Wisconsin, and in Sedalia, Missouri, that the leaders of the crusade received appeals for assistance from employers' groups all over the country.

Obviously, what these industrialists and businessmen wanted most was destruction of the labor movement. The National Association of Manufacturers (NAM) took command of the open-shop movement in 1903 and formed the Citizens' Industrial Association to sponsor the organization of employers' associations across the country and to orchestrate a public-relations campaign to win public support for the "American Plan." This campaign defended the right of Americans to work when and where they pleased, depicted labor organizers as agitators and Socialists, and portrayed employers as champions of free enterprise and venerable American liberties. This counteroffensive struck such a heavy blow to the AFL that it actually lost membership between 1904 and 1910.

The entrance of federal courts into labor disputes also adversely affected the fortunes of organized labor. Particularly important was the way courts increasingly interpreted the Sherman Antitrust Act of 1890 to justify antistrike injunctions. This new development began with the Chicago railroad strike of 1894, when the attorney general obtained an injunction against Eugene V. Debs and other leaders of the American Railway Union for conspiring to restrain trade and obstruct the movement of mail. The effect of this doctrine, which was confirmed by the Supreme Court in 1895, was not to outlaw unions as illegal conspiracies per se, but to forbid union practices that might be construed to be unreasonable, or illegal, restraints on trade.

The Sherman Act was used before 1901 less against illegal industrial combinations than against labor's allegedly illegal weapons—mass picketing, the sympathetic strike, the secondary boycott, and blacklisting of goods manufactured by antiunion employers. Two important cases, the *Danbury Hatters* case and the *Buck's Stove and Range Company* case, demonstrated the continued willingness of federal courts to intervene on the side of management. In 1902, the United Hatters of North America called a strike against a hatmaker of Danbury, Connecticut, D. E. Loewe and Company, and declared a nationwide boycott of its products. Company officials struck back by organizing the American Anti-Boycott Association and by suing the United Hatters in 1903 for damages of $240,000 under the Sherman Act. Five years later, the Supreme Court affirmed the rulings of a lower court that the boycott constituted a restraint of trade, and thereupon awarded the company full damages. In the second case, the Buck's Stove and Range Company in 1907 obtained an injunction that ordered AFL officials to end a boycott against its products. When Gompers and the AFL's executive committee ignored the injunction, a federal court sentenced them to jail terms. This injunction was upheld by the Supreme Court in 1914, even though it removed the penalties on a technicality.

10. Left-Wing Unionism

The seeming inability of the AFL to respond to the erosion of the status of workers created a leadership vacuum in the American labor movement. In particular, it opened an unprecedented opportunity for the left wing of organized labor to provide a more aggressive, militant alternative. Left-wing unionism first developed on an important scale, not in eastern urban areas, but in the mining regions of the Rockies.

It was a form of labor radicalism indigenous to the brutality of the American frontier. There a raw kind of industrial absolutism often provoked brutal retaliation by miners, and open class warfare resulted. Out of this environment emerged in 1905 the Industrial Workers of the World (IWW), a coalition formed from the Western Federation of Miners, the American Labor Union, and the Socialist Trade and Labor Alliance. Organized along industrial lines, the IWW openly advocated a fiery brand of revolutionary syndicalism, recruitment of workers en masse, and strikes. Its objectives were abolition of the wage system and establishment of a proletarian commonwealth.

Within a year after its formation, however, the IWW showed signs of disintegration. An unresolved tension existed between leaders of the Western Federation of Miners, who were more concerned with the immediate goals of labor than in building a socialist utopia, and the Marxist head of the Socialist Trade and Labor Alliance, Daniel De Leon. After De Leon was unceremoniously expelled in 1908, the IWW became an unquestioning advocate of lower-class, unskilled workers. In the West, it battled for lumbermen, migratory workers, and frontier miners. In the East, the IWW organized and led unskilled workers ignored by the AFL. The IWW led a strike in Lawrence, Massachusetts, against the American Woolen Company in 1912 and won a wage increase. It took command of rebellious silk workers in Paterson and Passaic, New Jersey, and led them in a successful strike in 1912–1913. Because it emphasized the militant strike, the IWW frequently came into conflict with employers, the police, and the courts. Its militancy also prevented systematic organizational campaigns or participation in the mainstream of labor politics.

Meanwhile, the political counterpart of left-wing unionism, socialism, was struggling for a program and a means of expression. The Socialists were united during the 1890s in the Socialist Labor Party, which De Leon ruled until his inflexible Marxism provoked a rebellion by a moderate element in 1899–1900. Meanwhile, in 1897 the labor leader Eugene V. Debs had founded a rival group, the Social Democratic Party, dedicated to advancing public ownership of railroads, utilities, and industrial monopolies. The anti-De Leon faction in the Socialist Labor Party, headed by Morris Hillquit of New York and Victor Berger of Milwaukee, then joined the Debs group in Indianapolis to launch the Socialist Party of America in 1901.

Although Socialists included Marxists in their ranks, they were so completely dominated by moderates like Debs, Hillquit, and Berger that they were more a left-wing reform group than a revolutionary workers' party. By 1908, the party had a membership of 58,000; within four years, members numbered 126,000. Yet Socialists exerted leadership disproportionate to their small membership. By 1912, Socialist administrations governed Berkeley, California, Milwaukee, Wisconsin, and Schenectady, New York. One of the party's leaders, Victor Berger, sat in the House of Representatives and was soon joined by another Socialist from New York's East Side, Meyer London. And the Socialist presidential candidate, Debs, polled over 897,000 votes in the election of 1912.

Chapter 2

—>>> <<<—

A New Industrial Society

Industrialization left few aspects of life untouched. For much of the nineteenth century, most Americans lived and died by agriculture; even urban wealth depended on mercantile activities tied to farming. The new manufacturing economy brought both costs and benefits, disruptions and opportunities. It lured Americans off farms and into cities; rather than a land of sturdy yeomen, the United States became a nation of city and town dwellers. With urbanization came other changes. New forms of group interaction and leisure arose in a highly commercialized mass culture whose appeal cut across regional, class, and ethnic lines. The new industrial society shattered the traditional unity and homogeneity of rural life. The new industrial society was also highly segmented, as ethnicity, gender, and race increased as important defining characteristics of twentieth-century Americans.

1. The American People: An Overview

Early twentieth-century America was a dynamic society. A world center of commercialized agriculture, then manufacturing, and then finance, it was also the scene of a rapid population expansion. From 1900 to 1920 the population of the United States grew nearly 40 percent, from about 76 million to almost 106 million. Most of this increase was caused by a steady influx of immigrants. During this period, the Pacific states more than doubled in population, while the Middle Atlantic states grew by 43 percent. Urban population nationwide meanwhile rose by 80 percent— a rate of increase more than six and a half times that of rural areas.

Although the United States remained a predominantly white, Protestant society, growth brought a greater degree of diversity. In 1920, 88 percent of all Americans were classified as white; at the same time, some 400,000 Orientals and 10 million blacks resided in the United States. Although most Americans were native born, under the increased impact of European immigration the foreign-born population rose from almost 10 million in 1900 to 14 million twenty years later. Also apparent in this American "melting pot" were demographic and regional characteristics. The overwhelming proportion of recent immigrants inhabited cities, especially in the urban manufacturing belt that extended from New England to the Middle West. Here nearly 83 percent of foreign-born Americans lived. Below the Mason–Dixon

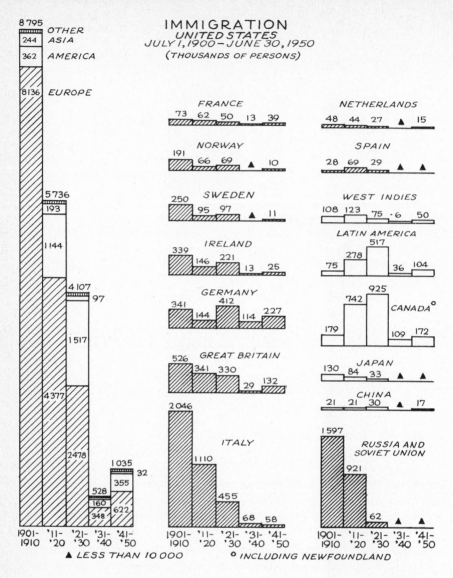

IMMIGRATION
UNITED STATES
JULY 1, 1900 – JUNE 30, 1950
(THOUSANDS OF PERSONS)

▲ LESS THAN 10 000   ° INCLUDING NEWFOUNDLAND

Line, a large proportion of American blacks—85 percent in 1920—lived in the rural South, with the highest concentrations in a "black belt" stretching from Virginia to Texas.

In general, living conditions improved distinctly during the progressive era. As medical knowledge expanded through experience and research, most Americans became better nourished, less afflicted by parasites, and less susceptible to epidemic diseases than their ancestors. Although reliable statistics for the period are scarce, surviving data indicate that the death rate decreased between 1900 and 1920 from 17 to 12.6 per thousand for whites and from 25 to 17.7 per thousand for nonwhites. This improvement was made possible in part by a sharp decline in deaths from

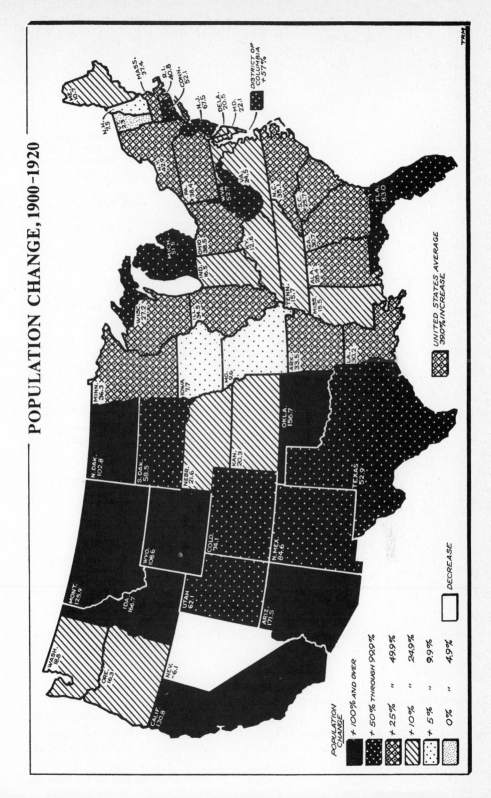

POPULATION CHANGE, 1900–1920

MASS.
37.4

R.I.
40.8

CONN.
52.1

N.J.
67.5

DELA.
20.5

MD.
22.1

DISTRICT OF
COLUMBIA
+ 57%

ME.
10.7

N.H.
7.5

VT.
2.3

N.Y.
42.9

PA.
38.4

W.VA.
52.7

VA.
24.5

N.C.
35.1

S.C.
25.7

FLA.
83.0

GA.
30.7

ALA.
28.4

MICH.
51.5

OHIO
38.5

IND.
16.5

KY.
12.6

TENN.
15.7

MISS.
15.5

LA.
30.2

WISC.
27.2

MINN.
36.3

IOWA
7.7

MO.
9.6

ARK.
33.5

OKLA.
156.7

TEXAS
52.9

N.DAK.
102.8

S.DAK.
58.5

NEBR.
21.6

KAN.
20.3

COLO.
74.1

N.MEX.
84.6

WYO.
108.6

UTAH
62.1

ARIZ.
171.5

MONT.
125.9

IDA.
166.7

WASH.
16.8

ORE.
16.3

NEV.
-6.1

CALIF.
130.8

UNITED STATES AVERAGE
39.0% INCREASE

POPULATION
CHANGE

+ 100% AND OVER

+ 50% THROUGH 99.9%

+ 25%   "   49.9%

+ 10%   "   24.9%

+ 5%   "   9.9%

0%   "   4.9%

DECREASE

TRM

21

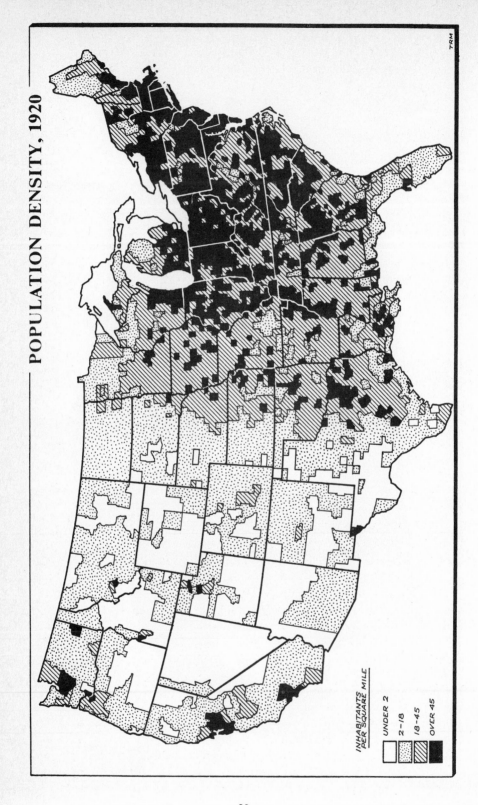

INHABITANTS
PER SQUARE MILE

UNDER 2
2–18
18–45
OVER 45

TRM

22

typhoid fever and tuberculosis, and in part by the near-total elimination of smallpox and malaria.

In spite of a clear improvement in the general American health environment, problems remained. By the First World War, health officials still had far to go in reducing diseases and eradicating parasites. Especially in rural areas, disease and malnutrition vividly demonstrated the backwardness of the American countryside and the superiority of urban over rural living. For both rural and urban Americans, moreover, ill health was closely connected to the larger, still unresolved, problem of poverty.

In another respect, conditions for Americans improved substantially. The most striking phenomenon of the first years of the twentieth century was a general increase in wealth and income. Adjusted for inflation, national income increased from $480 per capita in 1900 to $567 in 1920. About 42 million Americans were employed in the latter year, and, generally speaking, the early twentieth century was a period of high employment and steadily increasing standard of living. Yet the benefits of increased wealth and prosperity were not distributed evenly: this was an era of flamboyant wealth but persistent poverty.

Although diverse in ethnic and racial composition, and plagued by ancient problems of ill health and poverty, early twentieth-century Americans were enjoying economic conditions that compared favorably with any other society in the world and represented a distinct advance over the material condition of their parents and grandparents. Yet simply saying that Americans lived in a society which was improving does not do justice to the complete, but also complex, mosaic of early twentieth-century life.

2. The Rise of the City

By 1920, a striking transformation of the social and physical environment was well under way. Most early nineteenth-century Americans lived on isolated farms and in small villages; a century later, they inhabited bustling towns and expanding metropolitan areas. In turn, the rise of towns and cities as the dominant economic, political, social, and cultural centers remade the American landscape. Urban centers before 1860 reflected a basic reality: towns and cities were usually extensions of the countryside which, strictly speaking, lacked an independent identity. Since they were heavily dependent on the agricultural commodities of outlying agricultural areas, their primary activities involved trade rather than manufacturing. As a result, early nineteenth-century American cities were small in both physical size and population. Without transit systems and built around narrow, often impassable streets, they were confined to the "walking city," defined by an approximate distance of two and a half miles from city center to city perimeter. Consequently, residential patterns were mixed; the wealthy and the poor tended to live in close proximity, with no clear lines distinguishing residential from commercial sectors.

During the last half of the nineteenth century, the social and physical environment of the American city was transformed. The greatest force for change was the

THE NATIONAL INCOME, 1909-1926

TOTAL–1926– $78 649 MILLIONS

IN "1913" DOLLARS – $46 392 MILLIONS

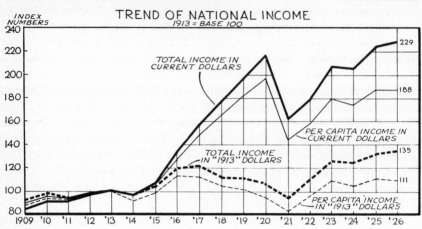

INDEX
NUMBERS

TREND OF NATIONAL INCOME
1913 = BASE 100

TOTAL INCOME IN CURRENT DOLLARS

PER CAPITA INCOME IN CURRENT DOLLARS

TOTAL INCOME IN "1913" DOLLARS

PER CAPITA INCOME IN "1913" DOLLARS

229

188

135

111

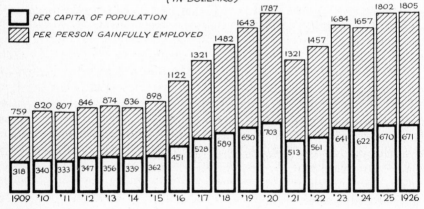

NATIONAL INCOME PER CAPITA AND PER WORKER
(IN DOLLARS)

☐ PER CAPITA OF POPULATION

▨ PER PERSON GAINFULLY EMPLOYED

rapid increase in urban population, itself a product of immigration both from rural areas of the United States and from Europe. Between 1830 and 1930, some 35 million Europeans left their native lands for the United States, and the majority of them settled in urban areas. Between 1860 and 1910, they were joined by approximately 21 million rural Americans who left their home communities. Although urbanization began before the Civil War, it gained its greatest intensity after 1870. By then, large metropolitan centers of population had come into existence in the Northeast, Middle West, and Far West. The onetime colonial cities of the eastern seaboard continued to grow in population. New York, the nation's largest city in 1860, had more than quadrupled its population—to 5.2 million—by 1920. During the same period, moreover, major new population centers arose, especially in the West and Middle West. In 1860, the most important cities of the Middle West were Cincinnati and St. Louis. By 1920 they had been surpassed in population by Chicago and Detroit; with 2.7 million inhabitants, Chicago was second in size only to New York. Chicago increased in importance because it was a regional transportation center; as early as 1880, it connected 15,000 miles of railroad track to the Northwest and the upper Mississippi Valley. It also grew because it became a national manufacturing and distribution center in meatpacking, men's clothing, iron and steel, and agricultural implements.

The case of Detroit, by 1920 the fourth largest city in the nation, provides another instance of metropolitan expansion. Founded in the 1830s, Detroit grew thereafter as a Great Lakes center of food processing, copper smelting, and iron making. In 1880, with a population of about 116,000, it ranked eighteenth among American cities. The coming of the automobile industry, and especially the construction of Henry Ford's huge plants at the satellite industrial centers of Highland Park and River Rouge, largely accounted for Detroit's rapid growth during the first three decades of the twentieth century. By 1920, it had a population just shy of one million. But every region in the country saw the emergence of large cities. On the West coast, both San Francisco and Los Angeles recorded more than 500,000 inhabitants in 1920. In the Pacific Northwest, Seattle and Portland competed for regional supremacy. And, although the South remained the nation's most rural region, metropolitan centers existed in New Orleans, Atlanta, and Birmingham.

The rise of large cities was only part of the process of urbanization. Metropolitan centers tended to attract European immigrants. Rural American immigrants, however, were more likely to move to the large number of big towns and midsized cities that sprang into existence in the last third of the nineteenth century. The growth of such towns and cities was even more startling than that of metropolitan America. In 1860, the federal census recorded 400 communities in the United States with between 2,500 and 50,000 people; by 1910, such communities had increased to 2,200 in number.

These towns and cities brought the message of urban life to a once agrarian nation. Tied to metropolitan areas through trade and transportation links, these smaller urban centers duplicated in miniature the residential and commercial patterns of large cities. They were, moreover, especially important in the nation's rural heartlands, replacing pastures and cornfields. In the prairie West, for example, Wichita, Kansas, more than trebled its population between 1900 and 1920, from about 25,000 to 72,000; in the Far West, Spokane grew from 37,000 to 104,000; and in the South, Roanoke, Virginia, grew from 22,000 to 51,000. Through the network connecting metropolitan centers to subordinate but pervasive towns and smaller cities, early twentieth-century America became an indisputably urban nation.

3. The New Urban Environment

Urbanization spawned a new physical environment. When most immigrants came to the cities, they entered an alien world. They were likely to find it a dynamic society filled with opportunity. If they were willing to work long hours and submit to an industrial work discipline, and especially if they possessed some skills, then there were—at least in good times—available jobs paying ready cash. Yet newcomers to cities probably encountered other features of urban life which seemed strange and difficult to comprehend.

Perhaps the most apparent difference between rural and urban life was the constant presence of light—powered, by 1900, increasingly by electricity. Electricity not only provided illumination for home and work, but power for industrial machinery, streetcars, and elevators. The introduction of electricity occurred after Thomas Edison's invention, in 1880, of the incandescent lamp and its successful marketing later on. In 1882, thirty-eight central electrical stations existed; sixteen years later, this figure had increased to 3,000. By the turn of the twentieth century, the city's bright lights symbolized the aggressive modernity of urban America.

Rapid population growth brought about other physical and environmental differences between city and country. The rise in urban population stimulated greater demand for housing which, in turn, encouraged a profusion of real-estate entrepreneurs. Before the Civil War, limited transportation constricted available real-estate space; subsequent growth thus depended on improved transportation. Nineteenth-century cities were interconnected by narrow roads, frequently made of dirt, and urbanites depended on ferries to traverse rivers. By 1920, most towns and cities had begun to construct bridges and to pave roadways with brick, macadam, and concrete. Especially important in bridge building was the technological breakthrough of steel suspension, which allowed structures like the Brooklyn Bridge (1883), Pittsburgh's Seventh Street Bridge (1884), and Richmond, Indiana's Whitewater River Bridge (1889), to traverse large bodies of water.

Better roads and bridges made possible an even more critical prerequisite to urban spatial expansion—the development of urban mass transit. Encouraged by real-estate entrepreneurs who recognized the potential of easy access to outlying residential suburbs, privately run means of mass conveyance appeared as early as the 1820s in omnibus wagons and then, by the 1850s, in horse-drawn railways running on iron tracks. In the late 1880s, electric streetcars appeared in American cities, first in Montgomery, Alabama (1886), and a year later in Richmond, Virginia. Moving on iron tracks and powered by electricity from overhead wires, streetcars were fast, comfortable, and inexpensive to install and maintain. For these reasons, they soon became the most popular form of urban transit. By 1895, 850 lines existed nationally; within five years only 2 percent of the nation's trolleys were horse-drawn, as compared to 78 percent ten years earlier. Not until the more widespread use of automobiles after the Second World War did the age of the streetcar end.

Popular in towns and small cities, streetcars were often inadequate for the congested streets of metropolitan areas. The nation's most populous cities led the way in establishing rapid transit systems. By 1900, Chicago had constructed an elevated railway connecting the city's center with outlying suburbs. Similarly, New York City built an elevated, steam-powered system that ran along Sixth and Ninth avenues and carried 175,000 passengers daily during the 1880s. Because the "El" could no longer serve the expanded needs of the boroughs of Greater New York, however, construction began in 1904 on an extensive underground railway system.

The improvement of urban transit stimulated the outward expansion of residential and work areas. Suburbanization, largely the product of improved transportation, profoundly changed the character of urban America. It fostered a residential building boom lasting from the 1880s to the post–World War II period. With suburbs, in general, came increasing efforts to identity the environment with a pastoral past through landscaping and urban parks, playgrounds, and cemeteries. Pre-Civil War cities, spatially very confined, tended to be aggregate mixes of residence, work, cultures, and races. Suburbs, and the escape from the "walking city," reflected an increasing degree of internal segregation by economic status, ethnicity, and race. By 1920, a similar pattern prevailed across urban America: a downtown core of manufacturing, trade, and banking enterprises, often accompanied by poor residential areas; a belt of highly segregated middle-class and upper-middle class neighborhoods; and an outlying ring of satellite industrial manufacturing communities.

As cities grew outward, they also grew upward, and a symbol of urban pride was the presence of tall buildings dominating the horizon. These skyscrapers, a response to the scarcity of prime real estate in the downtown core, were also manifestations of sophisticated new building design and construction. Especially the use of steel beams made possible added height. Much of the innovation in urban buildings first occurred in Chicago, where the architect William Le Baron Jenny constructed the nation's first skyscraper in the ten-story Home Insurance Building, completed in 1885. By the 1890s, the architects of the so-called "Chicago School," such as Louis Sullivan, were popularizing skyscrapers elsewhere. In 1894, the seventeen-story Manhattan Life Insurance Company was erected as New York City's first skyscraper. It was followed by even larger structures: the American Surety Building (1895), twenty stories; the St. Paul Building (1896), twenty-six stories; the Park Row Building (1898), thirty stories; and, above all, the Woolworth Building, fifty-five stories.

4. Rural Life in the Industrial Age

Not without considerable justification were the years 1899–1920 known as the "golden age" of American agriculture. In this period, farm prices rose 72 percent, and in comparison to the prices of manufactured goods, they either increased or at least held their own. The prosperity of rural America was partly the result of significant increases in productivity. Between 1870 and 1900, total farm output increased by 135 percent, while worker productivity—especially in the highly mechanized wheat and corn belts of the Middle West and prairie states—rose 60 percent. In addition, in direct response to high prices, the amount of cultivated land continued to rise, from about 879 million acres in 1910 to 956 million acres a decade later. During the same period, gross farm income rose from $7.5 billion to $15.9 billion, while the value of farm land rose nearly 400 percent. When the Country Life Commission reported on rural conditions in 1909, it concluded that the American farmer had never been "as well off as he is today."

Yet prosperity masked the underlying decline of the countryside. Powerful forces worked to alter traditional ways of life and, ultimately, to hasten its disintegration. Rural decline was partly a product of the rise of urban centers; cities and towns displaced isolated farm communities as attractive, dynamic centers of opportunity even as they aggressively asserted national political and cultural leadership. Urban population expansion and spatial growth were the result of larger, more important developments: the new primacy of the city and the erosion in the status of American farmers.

The most obvious manifestation of rural America's waning was the exodus from the countryside, a long-term, pervasive trend that culminated during the first half of the twentieth century. In 1800, about 94 percent of all Americans inhabited rural communities of fewer than 2,500 persons; a century later, in 1900, that proportion had declined to 60 percent. Twenty years later—a milestone in American history —the federal census reported that a majority of the population lived in urban areas. Few rural communities escaped the exodus, but it was most prominent in those areas, such as the grain-growing and dairy regions of the Northeast and Middle West, where mechanization diminished the demand for labor at the same time that urbanization attracted young farmers off the land.

In no other period of American history was the contrast between the traditional and the modern more apparent than in the late nineteenth-century clash between the new, vibrant urban world and the isolated, stagnant rural environment. While towns and cities were centers of opportunity, the American countryside—in spite of a general increase in prices and income—experienced basic structural problems. The increase in farm prices helped perpetuate two long-standing agricultural practices: frequent migration to richer soil and an almost complete disregard for the land. Because it was abundant, pioneers since the seventeenth century had cleared and then exploited farm land. Once the land was exhausted, they moved west. Abuse and misuse of the soil were the rule rather than the exception among American farmers, and the soil they tilled consequently suffered disastrous erosion. By 1910, large expanses of land—some 200 million acres—had been tilled until barren.

A similar predicament arose from tenancy and sharecropping, forms of land tenure in which farmers rented land for a fixed payment or a share of their crop. To varying extents, it was a national problem. Drawn into the market system because of high agricultural prices, tenant farmers abounded in the Middle West and especially in the cotton-growing South. The increase of tenancy aggravated existing problems of overproduction, land exhaustion, and high mobility. In the South, tenants and sharecroppers were locked in a cycle of debt and poverty that induced them to cultivate more and more cotton. In the period between the Civil War and the First World War, the South, largely because of the spread of tenancy and sharecropping and the system's emphasis on cash-crop production, changed from a net food-exporting region into a net food-importing region. Although poverty was less acute outside the South, tenancy was a social problem wherever it existed. Its extent actually sank in the Northeast and on the Pacific Coast during this period; but in the heart of agricultural America—the Middle West—it stubbornly persisted and even expanded.

Rural America's decline in less material respects resulted from a clash of life-styles. As railroad expansion and town growth projected urban values, the hardships of country living appeared less and less attractive, especially to the young. There was nothing new about these hardships. The monotony, isolation, and hard work of rural life had been the fate of generations of Americans and their European ancestors. What was new was the availability of an alternative which, by comparison, cast these hardships in a new light. Modernization only hastened the process of rural disinte-gration. Scientific agriculture, better crop methods, and increased use of tractors and other farm machinery were commonplace by the 1920s. Farm work became less burdensome and more productive, but it also required a smaller labor force. Tele-phones and, later, radios diminished the isolation and monotony of rural living, but they also hastened the spread of urban values. Better roads and the prevalence of the automobile interconnected the countryside, but they also made contact with towns and cities—and escape from farm communities—that much easier.

Early twentieth-century America, although retaining links to the past, was a distinctly new world. Yet the magnitude of this transformation should not be exaggerated. To begin with, as has been already suggested, the United States—even in 1920—remained a collection of vastly different localities within regions, and the spread of the urban–industrial system, while rapid in some areas, seemed to have hardly occurred in others. Thus, while much of rural New England and the Middle Atlantic states were littered with abandoned homes and churches, southern farmers did not emigrate northward en masse until after the First World War. And, while it is essential to remember geographical and sectional diversity, an understanding of early twentieth-century America also requires attention to the increasing impor-tance of ethnic, racial, and gender differences.

5. The Beginnings of Urban Mass Culture

No better evidence of the changes brought by urbanization and industrialization exists than the spread of new forms of cultural interaction. "Culture"—broadly defined, the means by which any group achieves self-identity and expression—has existed as long as humanity itself. Age-old expressions of oral popular ritual, magic, religion, and folklore show how universal culture in the broad sense has been. Yet insofar as culture has found permanent expression in "higher" forms—in literature and the fine arts, for example—for most of human history it has been available only to those with a large income and a good education.

A distinctively new feature of the environment of industrializing America was the emergence of cultural forms geared to mass audiences and produced mainly for profit. These exhibited several characteristics. First, mass culture originated in cities and was fostered by the congregation there of people with surplus income and leisure. Second, these cultural expressions tended toward standardization; they followed prescribed formulas readily identifiable by nationwide audiences. Third, they conformed generally to the same practices as those governing large-scale business enterprise. By 1920, the most important forms of mass culture were thus commercially run, tended to follow industrial forms of production and distribution, and had introduced new labor–management relationships.

Especially prominent in the new entertainment culture were commerical spectator sports. By the 1890s, by far the most important commercialized sport (but not the only one) was baseball, already a national pastime. After two decades of amateur development in northeastern and middle-western cities, baseball became commercial in the 1880s; by the end of the century, it had grown into the nation's most popular spectator sport. In 1902, professional baseball attracted an audience of 3.5 million; by 1911, this figure had risen to 6.5 million. In spite of a decline in attendance just before and during the First World War, in 1920 it reached an unprecedented peak of 9 million fans.

While baseball evolved into a popular form of urban mass entertainment, it also developed a sophisticated, mature industry structure. Steady increases in attendance reflected the intrinsic appeal of a game that recreated a rural-pastoral scene in an enclosed, urban environment. It was a form of leisure that was easily understood, open to a large consumer market, and one that required only a modest price of admission. Those entrepreneurs who promoted the sport, moreover, strove relentlessly to increase attendance. They introduced various gimmicks, such as free tickets for women and young fans. They also began to expand the game's appeal to working urbanites by initiating doubleheaders and by beginning a campaign to overcome laws outlawing Sunday games.

Baseball owners also pioneered the construction of ornate palaces to accommodate their teams, to create a fantasy environment of spectator sports, and to house larger and larger numbers of fans. Just as the period between 1880 and 1920 became the age of the skyscraper, so too did it witness a building boom in fireproof sports parks that took advantage of technological advances in steel frames and concrete construction. In 1903, Pittsburgh owner Barney Drefuss built what he described as a "baseball palace." Named Forbes Field, it was located in the city's best residential section and had three levels, elevators, telephones, and electric lights. Similar modern structures soon appeared in Chicago, Cleveland, and Boston. By 1923, New York boasted three "baseball palaces" of its own: the Polo Grounds, housing the New York Giants; Yankee Stadium; and Ebbets Field, home of the Brooklyn Dodgers. In the same year, of the sixteen major league baseball franchises, fifteen had twentieth-century parks which held between 18,000 (St. Louis) and 65,000 (Yankee Stadium) people.

As baseball developed into a mature industry, it also increasingly searched for new sources of internal stability. Through extensive recruitment networks and the construction of a "farm" system of minor-league teams, the sport was assured a steady supply of capable players. Although players controlled the game during its early days, dominance by 1900 had shifted to owners who, through a new contract system that bound players indefinitely, controlled the labor supply and restricted ruinous salary competition. Several furious trade wars between the older National League and a number of upstarts, including the American League, led to periods of instability but, by 1920, the two leagues had pooled their interests into what was, in effect, a legalized monopoly.

Other forms of urban mass culture came into existence for similar reasons. One of the most significant forms of the new entertainment industry was motion pictures, which began as an important popular cultural form during the first third of the twentieth century. Like baseball, its origins were mainly urban, its appeal was national, and its organization was highly commercial and followed prevalent corporate business forms.

From their beginnings in the 1890s, motion pictures were linked to the rise of urban popular culture. The first national mass medium of communication, "movies" depended on technological advances in photography, yet their commercial success was also contingent on mass marketing and a carefully framed appeal to working-class and middle-class audiences. Thomas A. Edison pioneered the development and distribution of a kineotoscope, a peep-show viewer which ran for about a minute and a half. A former employee of Edison's, W. K. L. Dickson, subsequently developed a more popular viewer, the mutoscope, which flipped postcard-shaped cards instead of film and was marketed through the American Mutoscope and Biograph Company. Along with European inventors, Edison and Dickson had made available the large-scale motion picture by 1900. Movies soon found urban audiences, first in stage theaters—where they often were shown after vaudeville acts—and then in independent, working-class storefront theaters that charged a small admission, usually a nickel. Movies fast became the most popular leisure-time activity among early twentieth-century Americans. According to one early filmmaker, profits increased by 600 percent between 1905 and 1907. A year later, New York City possessed 600 nickel theaters, which had a daily attendance that ran as high as 400,000.

Vivid evidence of the subsequent growth of the market for films was the construction of more elaborate, ornate "movie palaces." Filmmaking meanwhile changed so as to satisfy middle-class as well as working-class audiences. Although the early pioneers of the industry had emphasized technical equipment over moviemaking, directors such as David W. Griffith and producer–entrepreneurs like William Fox and Adolph Zukor concentrated on full, feature-length films. In revolutionizing film technique and directing the first American film extravaganzas, *The Birth of a Nation* (1915) and *Intolerance* (1917), Griffith made filmmaking into a highly technical, aesthetic enterprise. He also attracted new, primarily middle-class, audiences and created an appetite for visual entertainment.

Fox and Zukor, both Hungarian Jewish immigrants, exploited the potential for motion pictures and had helped to initiate an extensive reorganization of the industry by 1920. Along with other New Yorkers like Marcus Loew, they helped to create a national system to distribute projection equipment and stimulated the construction of movie houses. Realizing the potential for a wider market, they produced and promoted a growing number of feature-length films which were distributed around the world. They also encouraged the relocation of the industry to southern California because its year-round warm weather and cheap labor—approximately half the cost of labor in New York—permitted faster and less expensive film production.

The same period that saw the rise of baseball and motion pictures also witnessed the building of amusement parks. Like other highly commercialized forms of entertainment and cultural interaction, amusement parks tapped urban markets which were made more accessible by transportation improvements. Going to amusement parks, like other facilities of twentieth-century popular culture, was essentially an exercise in escapism which required little education and social standing. Indeed, a large market existed among patrons who were "low brow" but could afford the admission price.

One of the nation's first centers of urban amusement-park entertainment was Coney Island, located on the southwestern end of Long Island, nine miles from central Manhattan. In the post–Civil War period, the area had grown as a beach resort, and in the 1880s it had gained a certain notoriety for its various amusements —saloons, shows, bands, fortune tellers, and the like. Coney Island's potential as a popular culture center, however, awaited good, inexpensive transportation from metropolitan New York. Before 1890, various forms of transportation were available —mainly ferries and railroads—but by 1895, the advent of the cheap electric trolley reduced the fare from Manhattan to Coney Island from forty cents to a nickel. Transportation was not only cheaper, it was also quicker; express trains from the Brooklyn Bridge could reach Coney Island in about thirty minutes.

Transportation improvements opened up unprecedented opportunities in the late 1890s for those aggressive cultural entrepreneurs ready to exploit them. Between 1895 and 1905, the nation's earliest amusement parks were constructed in Coney Island. In 1895, Captain Paul Boyton built Sea Lion Park there; it was followed in short order by Steeplechase Park, erected by George Tilyou in 1897 and named for a roller coaster encircling it; Luna Park, created by Elmer Purdy and Frederic Thompson in 1903; and, a year later, Dreamland, built by William H. Reynolds.

Exploiting the full potential of separate, enclosed amusement parks, these entrepreneurs carefully shaped a form of entertainment that would attract working-class audiences but would also, through an imposing physical presence, appeal to the urban middle classes. For workers, cheap transportation and equally inexpensive admission fees made Coney Island amusements a common feature of summertime entertainment. But the sense of grandeur and magnificence conveyed by the parks also lured middle-class audiences. Their emphasis was escapist. They were places where the workaday world was left behind, where beach bathing and amusements suggested freedom from late-Victorian social restrictions. Even the architecture of the amusement parks expressed a fantasy of luxury, the exotic, and the magical. As the creator of Luna Park, Frederic Thompson, wrote in 1907, amusement parks were designed to create a "different world, a dream world, perhaps a nightmare world— where all is bizarre and fantastic . . . gayer and more different [*sic*] from the every-day world."

6. Women and the Family in Transition

The shift in human and material resources caused by industrialization and urbanization had come into full effect by 1920. Yet these changes were only part of other new aspects of the social scene, for modernization was beginning to influence the fabric of life for rural and urban Americans alike. Two apparently contradictory trends accompanied change and the breakdown in traditional ways of life. One reflected the importance of nationalizing influences. It was the increasing integration of hitherto isolated Americans. They came into contact with centralized, cosmopolitan currents and were drawn together in common bonds of culture and group identity that appeared to transcend formidable barriers of race, culture, and section. Another trend, working in the opposite direction, was the fragmentation of Americans into occupational, cultural, racial, and gender groups, each of which increasingly demanded autonomy.

Nothing better illustrates the fundamental transformation of American life between 1850 and 1920 than the new position of the family. For millenia, the family had served a primarily economic function, and in colonial and early national America it continued to be a unit of production first and foremost. By 1900, however, the American family had undergone important and basic changes. As both agriculture and industry experienced startling increases in productivity, and as production moved out of the home, the family became more a unit of affection than of production. In turn, the family's new function had other ramifications—above all, reduced family size and increased attention to childbearing and education.

Because of the importance of their economic function, American families tended to be large before about 1800. In the seventeenth and eighteenth centuries, it was not unusual to find families that were composed of eight, nine, or even ten children, and the first federal census in 1790 recorded the average American household size as about six. Like most preindustrial, agricultural societies, a powerful incentive sustained large families: the need for a large labor supply within the family unit. At the turn of this century, a new trend in the character of family structures was clear. The birth rate underwent a steady decline during the nineteenth century —the deepest decline in American history. By 1880, it had stabilized at a dramatically lower rate of reproduction than in 1800. All told, between 1800 and 1900, total fertility declined by about 50 percent. By 1900, women giving birth would, on the average, spend a decade less than their grandmothers raising their children.

Smaller family size was the product of several converging influences. In one respect, it was a manifestation of growing urbanization, for both the scarcity of space and the smaller demand for child labor tended to work against large families in urban communities. Yet during the same period a sharp decline in births also occurred in rural areas, which suggests that the decrease in family size and the new character of American families may not have simply been the product of socioeconomic factors. Indeed, a compelling supplementary explanation lies in the growing assertiveness of women within the family. Women may have been expressing a basic form of autonomy by limiting the time they spent on bearing and rearing children. Whatever the explanation, it is clear that such a dramatic decline in the birth rate could come only through deferring marriage or through the more prevalent use of birth control later popularized by the crusading Margaret Sanger. Both suggest dramatically new gender roles.

The fact that the family was a very different entity by the early years of the twentieth century indisputably affected the position of women in American society. With a diminished role as producer, with smaller childbearing risks and more years at home free of children, women now possessed unprecedented opportunities for work and other extradomestic activities. Yet pressures persisted to reconcile these new opportunities with the strong tradition that woman's place was in the home.

7. Early Twentieth-Century Women at Work

The increased presence of women in the work force was not new to the twentieth century. Early textile and shoe factories employed women in large numbers, and, throughout the nineteenth century, women entered the work force in manufacturing, teaching, and the professions. By 1900, rapid economic growth had generated new opportunities for women and partly undermined their traditional subordinate position within the family. Women composed a quarter of all workers employed in nonagricultural jobs in 1910; ten years later women were represented in all but 35 of the 572 occupations listed by the federal census.

Where women worked depended heavily on their class, ethnic, and racial status. Most desirable—and most accessible to native-born, middle-class, and white women —were jobs in the professions. After 1870, graduates of women's colleges and coeducational institutions looked for alternatives to marriage by filling professional ranks. These middle-class women found certain professions, such as engineering and the law, difficult to enter because of restrictions imposed by professional organizations or by statute. In 1891, for example, there were only 291 female lawyers in the United States. Other professions opened their doors with slightly less hesitation. For instance, medical schools, which had previously barred women, began to admit them during the 1880s and 1890s. In spite of this advance, however, major medical schools initiated a restrictive quota system during the early years of the twentieth century that held the number of women admitted to about 5 percent. Opportunities were more abundant in professions clearly dominated by women, such as teaching, nursing, and social work. Both social work and nursing were relatively new professions adapted specifically for women. By 1920, there were 144,000 nurses, of whom 96 percent were female and 40,000 social workers, of whom 67 percent were female.

Requiring less education and carrying less status, and thus less attractive to middle-class women, were jobs in manufacturing, retailing, and domestic service. Yet for the great mass of women, these were the jobs most available during the nineteenth and early twentieth centuries. Domestic service was an occupation widely considered by women as the least desirable type of employment—and rightly so. Domestics received low wages—not much more than subsistence. But worse than low wages was the demeaning nature of the work and the loss of freedom. Typical domestics had little time of their own, with usually only one afternoon off a week. They worked about eleven to twelve hours a day. In the one-third of American households that employed servants, work was arduous and labor-intensive. Most work was done without mechanical conveniences. That domestic service remained, until the first decades of the twentieth century, the largest single category of female employment testifies to the necessities of survival that poor, immigrant, and black women confronted.

In other respects, working women faced formidable obstacles. Into the early twentieth century, the main reason why employers hired women was clear: they could pay them substantially lower wages than those received by men doing the same work. In manufacturing, women workers were usually unskilled, underpaid machine operatives. In other occupations, which became defined as women's work, there developed structural differences in pay. Even such professional occupations as nursing, teaching, and social work became lower paid and enjoyed lower status because of women's predominance in them.

Just as important, the entrance of women into the industrial work force did not alter a traditional pattern: when they married, women permanently left the work force to become wives and mothers. The pattern was evident from the early stages of industrialization. In the textile mills of Lawrence, Massachusetts, for example, only 30 out of 1,000 women employed in 1830 were married or widowed; fifty years later, in 1881, another survey of 15,000 women in twenty-two cities across the nation discovered that only 10 percent were in this category. Even in 1900, this figure had changed only slightly: about 85 percent of American working women were single. That the great majority of women in the pre-1920 work force were single implied another important characteristic: they were also young. In 1889, for example, a survey of Virginia teachers found that 55 percent of white females and 70 percent of black females were under the age of twenty-five, as compared with 35 percent for white males and 32 percent for black males.

The persisting conflict between marriage and work had important ramifications. It meant that turn-of-the-century women seeking a profession usually had to forego marriage and children. Of the women graduating from college before 1910, for example, only a quarter ever married. Because women who married seldom stayed at work, they were highly transient, and this characteristic reinforced the built-in wage and occupational bias against them. Why pay women as much as male workers or grant them access to male-dominated occupations, employers reasoned, if they would probably leave their jobs on marriage? As transient and underpaid workers, women generally did not enjoy the protection of organized labor; indeed, they frequently faced hostility from male union members. Although the Knights of Labor opened its doors to women during the 1870s and 1880s and actively recruited them, the AFL did little to represent their interests. Most union members, moreover, regarded women as temporary interlopers who debased the general condition of work, lowered the wage level, and more properly belonged in the home.

8. Origins of the "New" Immigration

Much more than Europeans, Americans in the nineteenth century were constantly on the go, from countryside to city and, frequently, from city to city. The relative abundance of land and the existence of jobs encouraged another type of geographical mobility: the influx of millions of immigrants from across the Atlantic and from French Canada. The rush of alien peoples into the United States from 1830 to 1930 was one of the most important developments in American history. European immigrants provided cheap, abundant labor to construct railroads, build canals, mine coal and ores, and work in industrial manufacturing. As immigration interacted with urbanization, moreover, a large majority of immigrants settled not in the countryside but in the cities.

Increasingly prominent were the so-called "new" immigrants. They were "new" because they were unlike previous generations of newcomers, the overwhelming majority of whom were from northwestern Europe, primarily England, Scotland, Ireland, Germany, and Scandinavia. In contrast, the "new" immigrants brought with them different cultural traditions; by the 1880s, an increasing number of immigrants came from southern and eastern Europe. During the 1890s, almost 52 percent of immigrants to the United States came from there; in the next decade, that proportion increased to 72 percent. Italians, Slavs, Magyars, Jews, and Greeks were especially prominent in this tide.

Although the term "new immigrant" suggests a similarity among all these groups, in reality they were united only by their differences from native-born Americans. Each possessed distinct traditions that emphasized religious and language differences. Poles and Italians, though both groups consisted of faithful Roman Catholics, differed significantly in their approach to church organization and liturgy. Some of the "new" immigrants, like the eastern European Jews, migrated as whole family units; others, such as Italians and Greeks, tended to arrive as single males.

Even so, common reasons explain why millions of immigrants poured out of southern and eastern Europe, not only into the United States, but also into Brazil, Argentina, and Canada. In the case of the 2 million Jews who entered the United States between 1881 and 1915, the reasons were primarily religious. Emigrating from Russia, Austria–Hungary, and Rumania, Jews left their native lands because of a rising tide of persecution that swept through these countries during the last third of the nineteenth century. In Russia and Russian Poland, they were confined to a "pale of settlement," an area of 386,000 square miles extending from the Baltic to the Black Sea. After 1881, the czarist government pursued a deliberate policy of persecution by prohibiting Jews from owning or renting land outside of urban areas. Moreover, after 1900 the Russian government carried out periodic *pogroms* — violent attacks on the Jewish community inspired by the authorities and carried out by mobs—against them. Jewish immigrants came to America with unique group characteristics. They came as family units. They were highly literate. Because of centuries of persecution, they had little attachment to the land or an agricultural way of life. And many of them came with well-developed skills as artisans, merchants, and workers.

But for the majority of "new" immigrants, the most important reasons for leaving home were economic. Large areas of the eastern and southern European countryside were afflicted by extreme social pressures. Traditional agriculture was breaking down as much of rural Europe became incorporated into the world economy and as manufacturing accentuated urbanization at the expense of more traditional ways of life. Added to these elements was another factor: overpopulation and growing pressure on available land resources. In Italy, for example, an increase in the birth rate, coupled with a decline in mortality, produced a population increase of more than 6 million between 1880 and 1910 alone. Smaller increases in the rest of southern and eastern Europe had a devastating effect as well. Overpopulation tended to decrease the size of farms—and thus income and food supply—while also increasing the number of tenant farmers and landless agricultural workers.

For many rural Europeans, the only alternative to starvation lay in emigration. In Italy, the government openly used—alone among western nations—emigration as an instrument of national policy to rid itself of excess population and to increase the flow of immigrants' receipts from abroad. European immigration was also made easier by a network of recent arrivals, who regularly communicated about conditions in the United States through letters and word of mouth and kept their former countrymen informed about the specific details of travel. In the United States, immigrant self-help organizations and immigrant entrepreneurs, such as the Italian *padrones* (or labor brokers), provided another communication link with European homelands.

Religious and economic factors pushed emigrants across the Atlantic, but they were also "pulled" by economic opportunities generated by the American industrial revolution. In this sense, emigration was less a flight from hardship and oppression than it was a positive, conscious decision made by individual Europeans. Indeed, in the years of the "new" immigration, greatly improved transportation facilities, along with increased opportunities in urban centers, made possible a high degree of geographical mobility. In what modern social scientists and historians have described as the "birds of passage" syndrome, Italian, Greek, and Austro–Hungarian Slavic immigrants were frequently young males who traveled alone and stayed only temporarily in the United States. At the turn of the century, it was estimated that 78 percent of Italian immigrants and 95 percent of Greek immigrants were male: the frequent pattern was migration to America in the spring, a stay until autumn, and a return home during winter. Until the First World War, a constant traffic in humanity swirled back and forth across the Atlantic.

Even more striking evidence of the immigrants' determination and specific objectives is the fact that they settled in great numbers in industrial centers. In spite of the availability of land in the Middle West, South, and Far West, "new" immigrants avoided farming more than any other previous generation of newcomers. Instead, in another conscious choice, they settled where other immigrants of their nationality had previously settled, worked where their national groups worked—in the heart of the industrial manufacturing belt in the Northeast and Middle West. Correspondingly, "new" immigrants only rarely settled where jobs in industry were scarce. Thus a large proportion of immigrants arriving between 1880 and 1920— about 80 percent—remained in these regions.

9. The "New" Immigrant in America

Post-1880 immigrants to the United States probably experienced a combination of bafflement and exhilaration. Compared with the poverty they left behind, they found an opportunity for work and, with luck and persistence, a chance for advancement up the occupational ladder. Recent historians have shown a high degree of social mobility among "new" immigrants that varied according to locale and the skills and advantages the immigrants brought with them. Those settling in New York tended to improve their status rapidly because of its extraordinary growth and its relative openness to diverse ethnic groups. But mobility was not uniform among either individuals or ethnic groups. As individuals, immigrants possessed varying amounts of drive, ambition, and good luck, which often had much to do with success or failure. Differences in mobility also had much to do with ethnic group differences. In New York, eastern European Jews and Italians arrived en masse during and after the 1880s, but because Jews arrived as families, settled permanently, and were usually both literate and skilled, they rapidly improved their status. Arriving usually as single males, Italians were frequently illiterate and unskilled, so they began at the bottom of the occupational ladder.

The most serious challenge faced by most immigrants, however, was cultural adaptation rather than economic success. Especially for post-1880 immigrants, the world around them was at best indifferent and at worst hostile. Many "new" immigrants originally believed that their stay in the United States would be only temporary, but well before the First World War most decided to stay—and make a difficult accommodation to American ways of life. Many of the old-country traditions were soon abandoned. Economic advancement meant shedding the clothes and hats, the haircuts and beards, and especially the language of their native land, for assimilation was the key to success. Even so, immigrants still felt the pull of their homelands in the extensive transatlantic networks and in the ethnic communities scattered across urban America.

A common lament about the "problem" of "new" immigrants was that, in contrast to earlier generations of newcomers, differences in language and culture made homogenization in the American melting pot nearly impossible. Yet agencies—both within and without the immigrant community—facilitated a remarkable acculturation. It was remarkable because, within a generation, the great majority of new immigrants considered themselves Americans first and Europeans second. It was a process that occurred with little or no governmental regulation, for federal authorities took no part in easing the transition to the new world. Instead, private groups, among them immigrant-run mutual assistance societies, helped immigrants to find work, provided moral support, sponsored insurance and college education plans, and even extended a form of unemployment and life insurance to their members.

Other groups, usually run by native-born Americans, sought to "Americanize" immigrants by teaching them English, educating them about American social and political institutions, and in the process preparing them for full status as citizens. At settlement houses such as Jane Addams's Hull-House in Chicago or James B. Reynolds's University Settlement in New York City, middle-class reformers provided relief, employment information, and language and vocational classes.

That America was able to absorb this transfusion of different national strains without a violent reaction testified to its ability to incorporate diversity into an urban–industrial society. Yet everywhere the process of social assimilation was increasingly regarded with suspicion by many native-born Americans; they believed that the "new" immigrants were an inferior people, incapable of understanding American ideals. One manifestation of this nativism was the organization of the American Protective Association in 1887. It was an anti-Catholic organization whose main purposes were to institute compulsory, Protestant-oriented public education, to impose temperance on alcohol-imbibing ethnic groups, and to restrict the political power of immigrant Catholics. Another manifestation of anti-immigrant sentiment was the growth of political support to reverse America's traditionally open immigration policy and especially to restrict the arrival of Asians and southern and eastern Europeans. So strong was support for restriction among social reformers, labor leaders, and nativists that the influx had been reduced to a trickle by 1921 (see pp. 216–217).

10. American Blacks in the Age of Jim Crow

As a legacy of three centuries of slavery and racial oppression, Americans during the early twentieth century were increasingly forced to confront what contemporaries described as the "Negro problem." At issue was how to forestall racial conflict, even warfare, in a modernizing, industrial society. There is little question that most white Americans concerned with the "Negro problem" believed in the principle of white supremacy. The result can be accurately characterized as the most obvious contradiction in American society: a society that offered increased opportunity for Europeans and women, yet denied opportunity to blacks; a society that boasted of political democracy yet curtailed the essential democratic rights of a tenth of its population; a society that preached progress yet institutionalized racial oppression. These uniquely American paradoxes were not resolved during the early twentieth century; indeed, the social and political status of blacks, by and large, worsened, and their economic condition improved only slightly.

Since the emancipation of all southern slaves in 1865, blacks had recorded some progress. They had dramatically reduced their illiteracy rate from 95 percent in 1865 to 45 percent in 1900. During the next two decades, illiteracy among blacks decreased at an even more rapid rate, to 30 percent in 1910 and to 23 percent in 1920. Before the First World War, a large proportion of American blacks, some 86 percent, lived in the South; of them, about four out of five lived in rural areas. It is thus not an insignificant measure of progress that the percentage of southern rural blacks owning land increased steadily. By the start of the new century, blacks owned about 12 million acreas of farm lands in the region.

Aside from improvements in literacy and landowning, however, there was little to encourage and much to discourage early twentieth-century blacks. In spite of considerable educational advances, blacks in the South attended schools that had been segregated, and inferior, since Reconstruction. The gap between white and black schools grew larger during the first two decades of the twentieth century. Although white schools in southern towns and cities, as well as the countryside, saw real gains in terms of length of session, quality of facilities, and availability of schools, blacks attended schools that remained close to their pre-1900 status. In a crucial area of growth—the inauguration and spread of secondary education—the extent of the black–white differential was unmistakably clear. In 1910, for example, in the South there were only eighty-eight public black high schools, with 4,288 pupils enrolled, as compared with 1,791 public white high schools with 102,616 pupils enrolled. Meanwhile, in spite of improved economic conditions through greater land ownership, most southern blacks faced a future of grinding poverty.

Nor did the political environment provide much relief. Civil War and Reconstruction did not change southern racial attitudes which held that, whether under slavery or freedom, it was natural and right that blacks be subordinate to whites. Black political power, achieved through the vote from the late 1860s to the early 1890s, had kept white racial antagonism at bay. By 1900, however, this equilibrium was permanently disrupted, and a genuine crisis in race relations ensued. After the late 1880s, a rapid rise in lynchings of black men occurred. Urban race riots in Wilmington, North Carolina (1898), Atlanta, Georgia (1906), and Springfield, Illinois (1908), suggested that violence rather than cooperation might characterize the future of race relations. By 1900, moreover, the status of southern blacks had taken another turn for the worse as state after state in the South, through poll taxes and literacy requirements, effectively ended black voting and established one-party, white Democratic rule. By the First World War, the southern post-Reconstruction experiment in black political participation had ended, and more than nine out of ten southern blacks had lost access to the polls.

The end of black political power paved the way for the institution of "Jim Crow," or state-enforced, *de jure* segregation in wide areas of southern life. First came state and local legislation which required that public transportation be segregated. In 1896, these statutory requirements were upheld in a landmark decision by the Supreme Court, *Plessy* v. *Ferguson*, which allowed "separate but equal" facilities in transportation. The case was crucial because it provided a working model for legal segregation in housing, restaurants, entertainment, and hotels. In instances where separate facilities were required by law, there was at least an attempt to portray them as equal. In actual fact, however, only rarely did separate mean equal —quite apart from the intrinsically humiliating nature of legally mandated segregation.

In a sense, the spread of Jim Crow represented an attempt by the early twentieth-century South to come to terms with change and modernization while retaining a system of racial subordination. *De jure* segregation was, moreover, a response to the new requirements of the urban South, whereby stratification by race and class was built into the new social and physical environment. Although closely tied to urbanization in this way, legally enforced segregation could not long survive the consequences of widespread socioeconomic change. The future would see the migration of millions of southern rural blacks to northern cities and the reemergence there of black political power. Then would come a growing sensitivity to the *national,* as opposed to regional, import of politics and culture that tended to focus on the gross injustices of segregation. Finally, the federal government, through the judiciary and executive, would intervene to rectify racial injustices. But all these changes lay in the future, and for the moment, the more immediate question was how to confront this assault on the status of blacks without further worsening their condition.

11. Accommodation and Protest

In the greatest challenge to their position in American society since the Civil War, early twentieth-century blacks employed two radically differing responses to *de jure* segregation and the spread of racism. The first and probably most common response had already been practiced by southern rural blacks since slavery: accommodation and acceptance combined with resistance and job sabotage. In reality, few blacks in the rural South had an alternative, for to survive in a system in which they had virtually no political or economic independence, they had to accept white terms. Yet they were able also to assert their interests in subtle ways and to undermine the system as best they could. A second response, less common but important for the long term, was to challenge the legality of segregation through the political process and the courts.

One of these approaches was each championed by two giants of their time, Booker T. Washington and William E. B. Du Bois. Born a slave in Franklin County, Virginia, in 1856, Washington was a model of self-help and racial accommodation. He was educated at Hampton Institute, a Virginia school founded by the northern missionary educator Samuel Chapman Armstrong. At Hampton, Washington became a devotee of Armstrong's formula for black uplift: hard work and self-help through an "industrial" education. Hampton-style "industrial" education taught blacks such as Washington concrete skills like carpentry, joinery, and blacksmithing, but its main emphasis was on habits and values. At Hampton, wrote Washington in his autobiography, *Up From Slavery*, he learned that "it was not a disgrace to labour." Rather, he learned "to love labour, not alone for its financial value, but for labour's own sake and for the independence and self-reliance" it brought. In 1881, Washington founded Tuskegee Institute, in Tuskegee, Alabama; thereafter, he captured regional and national attention as an advocate of industrial education. In 1895, in a famous address later known as the "Atlanta Compromise," Washington maintained that industrial education had a broad value as a way to stabilize race relations in a turbulent era. Responding to the spread of political disfranchisement and Jim Crow, Washington counseled southern blacks to eschew politics, to accept segregation for the time being, and to concentrate on self-help and uplift. As he put it in his famous phrase: "In all things purely social we can be as separate as the five fingers, and yet one as the hand in all things essential to mutual progress."

The "Atlanta Compromise" found immediate favor among both blacks and whites. With its emphasis on education and its apparent accommodation to segregation, the compromise was hailed by moderate southern whites as a solution to the poisonous atmosphere of race relations then prevailing in the South. Because it seemed to legitimize racial inequality while also providing for black progress, the compromise appealed to a spectrum of white opinion. The appeal to black Southerners was more subtle. Part of it was political: through associations with southern whites and especially northern Republicans like Theodore Roosevelt, Washington by 1905 had constructed a powerful patronage apparatus known as the "Tuskegee machine." Moreover, as he stressed to blacks, while the "Atlanta Compromise" appeared to accommodate, it also provided for eventual black equality. It was simply a matter of timing and strategy; because of the racial crisis, Washington argued, it was far better to invest in a long-term, realistic policy of uplift. It is significant that Washington never approved of either black disfranchisement or *de jure* segregation, and in several important instances he provided secret financial support for legal challenges to both.

The contrast between Washington and his leading rival for black leadership, Du Bois, was striking. While Washington was a former slave born in the South, Du Bois was descended from free Negroes in Massachusetts and was trained in Germany and at Harvard University, where he earned the Ph.D. in history. By 1910, he had formulated a program of black action in direct opposition to the "Atlanta Compromise." In *The Souls of Black Folk* (1903), he stressed that Washington's program of industrial education, accumulation of wealth, and conciliation also required that blacks abandon political power, equal civil rights, and the type of higher education available to whites. Blacks had submitted to racism without receiving any tangible benefits in return. "Manly self-respect," Du Bois wrote, was "worth more than lands and houses"; a "people who voluntarily surrender such respect, or cease striving for it, are not worth civilizing." How could blacks make economic progress, asked Du Bois, if they were a "servile caste" whose most talented members possessed no chance for higher development?

Rather than accommodation, Du Bois favored a militant, aggressive challenge to segregation and disfranchisement. His strategy was for both the short and long term. Blacks should reject the erosion of their civil and political status but also provide for its eventual return through rigorous forms of higher education designed to develop a "talented tenth" of black leadership. Du Bois, whose appeal was more limited than Washington's, enjoyed less support among black masses than among northern black intellectuals and sympathetic whites. Du Bois gave expression to a twentieth-century tradition of black militancy when, in June 1905, he and a small group of supporters met at Niagara Falls, Canada, and adopted a platform demanding political and economic equality and announcing their determination to begin a new war for emancipation. Meeting the following year at Harper's Ferry, West Virginia, the site of John Brown's raid, the Niagara movement, as the Du Bois group was called, reaffirmed its position.

The Niagara movement culminated in February 1909, on Lincoln's birthday, when the young black militant and a distinguished group of white educators, clergymen, editors, and social workers met in New York to consider the crisis in race relations. A year later they formed the National Association for the Advancement of Colored People (NAACP). It pledged to work for the abolition of all forced segregation, equal justice for blacks, and enlarged educational opportunities for black children. The only black official of the NAACP during this early period was Du Bois, who was director of publicity and research and editor of the association's monthly magazine, *The Crisis*.

For much of the twentieth century, blacks alternated between accommodation and protest, using them to resist and ultimately to undermine the Jim Crow system. In the South, although Washington's approach appeared to legitimize racial inequality, it was also an opening wedge for some improvements in public schools during the first half of the twentieth century. It appeared for a time that Du Bois' militancy had little relevance to the harsh realities of the South, yet it subsequently provided the basis for a revolution in race relations.

Chapter 3

———————— →⟩⟩ ⟨⟨← ————————

The Progressive
Transformation

Between the depression of the 1890s and the First World War, many of the same historical forces that remade traditional mores also worked to change American social and political institutions. The political convulsion somewhat loosely described by historians as the progressive movement re-formed both politics and governance. In general, progressives were united by the belief that nineteenth-century public institutions were unable to solve the problems generated by industrialization and urbanization. Progressives were convinced that the American system of government was in a crisis apparent everywhere: in a breakdown of what they considered responsible government in city, state, and nation; in the exploitation of labor, particularly women and children; in the growth of industrial and financial concentration; and in the emergence of large combinations in business that profoundly affected Americans but eluded their control.

Progressivism bridged the gap between the broad, evangelical-supported movements of the nineteenth century—common-school reform, abolitionism, and temperance—and the pressure-group politics of the twentieth century. But progressivism was unique. There was actually no such thing as *a* progressive movement, for it had so many contradictory impulses, so many variations on the theme of reform that it defies any attempt at straightforward definition. No single, organized campaign existed at any level which united diverse efforts at political, social, and economic reform. Indeed, it often seemed that these efforts worked at crosspurposes, for some reformers emphasized democracy and uplift while others aimed at control and new forms of coercion.

The key to understanding progressivism lies in the fact that it was a conglomeration of movements. The movement for political reform, for example, first appeared at the local and state level during the 1890s as an antimachine movement designed to eradicate traditional political practices. It emerged simultaneously on another, apparently unrelated level. This was a diverse campaign to realign community ties and traditional social practices by making public institutions more responsive and by increasing governmental intervention to foster social justice, education, and public health. Not until about 1905 did these reform movements acquire a unified sense of purpose and become a far-flung movement at the national level.

The nature of this progressive coalition meant that reformers agreed only on general goals. United by a common vision of the future and by a similar ideology, they rejected much of the social and political heritage of the nineteenth century. United by a shared vision of the general nature of the social and political crisis, in equally general terms they sought a remedy in an increased role for government in politics and social life. Although they were not socialists, progressives eventually decided that the solution to the most urgent issues of their time was to substitute collective for individual decisions in broad matters of social and economic policy. Progressives wanted to rationalize decision making in order to make it more efficient. The new, "progressive," polity was, however, democratic only in the ideosyncratic way that reformers themselves defined "democracy." Much of their criticism and many of their policy solutions came down to rechanneling power from grass-roots democracy toward a bureaucratic system in which decisions and policy came from above.

1. Background to Reform

Progressivism's diversity has tempted historians to emphasize its contradictions and ambiguities at the expense of similarities and even to discard altogether the term progressivism as an organizing historical concept. Several considerations, however, suggest that this approach is mistaken. Although reform was diverse, it is possible to identify some of its general characteristics. Although it attracted rural support, reform was rooted for the most part in the new industrial and urban centers, while its leadership and political constituency was primarily middle class. It attracted the support of various professional and other middle-class groups most associated with industrial growth and urban expansion. These included middle-class, generally married and nonworking women; small businessmen and bankers; editors, professors, and clergymen; "new" professionals in engineering, the law, and medicine; and, in rural America, farmers tied to modern scientific agriculture. In the last two decades of the nineteenth century, these groups had begun to exert cultural and political leadership through the activities of civic organizations and through increasing involvement in pressure-group politics. Reform, it should be emphasized, was not a grass-roots, mass movement. Progressives from time to time worked creatively and effectively with the leaders of organized labor on all levels of government. In some large cities, they also allied themselves with ethnic groups and big-city bosses. But they rarely had a solid base of popular, mass support.

Early twentieth-century reform was also tied to a realignment of political values and attitudes among urban, middle-class Americans. For reasons discussed later, this realignment tended to energize this group in such a way as to cut across existing regional and partisan lines. As a result, one feature of progressivism that distinguished it from other nineteenth-century social movements was its truly national character; reform appeared almost simultaneously in urban localities in the 1890s across the nation. Just as it cut across regional lines, the progressive movement also transcended an even stronger tie—loyalty to party. Within both political parties, indeed, reformers were prominent in local, state, and national politics. And although neither the Democratic nor the Republican party was identifiable as the "party of reform," both experienced serious internal turmoil because of it.

These shared characteristics do not, of course, explain the drive behind reform and reformers. Because of progressivism's sheer diversity, it is difficult to provide such an explanation. Early historians viewed reform as a struggle between democratic, popular forces and monied, antidemocratic interests. Subsequent historians have also emphasized the social basis of reform, whether as a "status revolution" led by a declining, older middle class, or as part of an "organizational revolution" led by a dynamic, new middle class. Yet these interpretations have proved inadequate when tested in specific cases, for the moving forces in reform were as complex and as varied as progressivism itself.

A useful way to look at the emergence of progressivism is to examine, first, the conditions that made it possible and, second, the factors that account for the timing of its emergence. It is a truism that progressive reform could not have existed without a constituency in the urban middle classes. Yet it is also true that this constituency needed a means of expression and a rationale for action. In the literature of exposure and the growth of a national, urban press devoted to investigating social and political problems, middle-class audiences increasingly became sensitized to problems of the social and political order. Henry George's *Progress and Poverty* (1879) and Edward Bellamy's *Looking Backward* (1888) were both utopian in approach, concluding that the new industrial system was fundamentally wrong. George's and Bellamy's indictments were general rather than specific. Both writers advocated general, and rather simple, solutions to late nineteenth-century social problems. George's panacea was a "single tax" on the unearned increment in the value of land, and Bellamy advocated the development of a sense of "nationalism." By the 1890s, a growing number of writers and journalists—typified by Henry Demarest Lloyd, author of a scathing exposé of the Standard Oil Trust, *Wealth Against Commonwealth* (1894)—were more specific in their attacks and, by implication, were suggesting the need for definite reforms. Newspapers and the popular press created a market for the literature of exposure, making American urbanites increasingly aware of social problems.

The popularity of George, Bellamy, and Lloyd typified a new style of journalism called muckraking—a form of investigative reporting which exposed corruption in public life. Muckrakers arrived with the spread of inexpensive magazines such as *Cosmopolitan, Munsey's,* and *McClure's,* which catered to a wide audience among the urban middle classes. The indisputable leader of the three was *McClure's,* established by S. S. McClure, an ebullient if erratic Irishman who decided to publish articles of contemporary significance. To one young writer, Ida M. Tarbell, McClure assigned the task of writing a history of the Standard Oil Company, which appeared in serial form in 1902 and ran for fifteen months. *McClure's* managing editor, Lincoln Steffens, reported on political corruption in St. Louis, Minneapolis, Cleveland, New York, Chicago, Philadelphia, and Pittsburgh. The third one of *McClure's* great muckrakers was Ray Stannard Baker, a young midwestern journalist who explored labor conditions, railroad practices, and race relations. Muckrakers in general saturated the reading public with revelations of social and political problems.

Equally important to reform was a rationale for action, a justification for rational and scientific solutions of social problems. For most of the nineteenth century, interventionism remained alien to American thinking because it ran contrary to cultural and intellectual traditions. Interventionism grew in popularity for two reasons. One was the increased activity of urban evangelical Protestants—known by the 1890s as adherents of the "social gospel"—who became convinced that the church and, if need be, the government should intervene to solve the ills of the industrial system. Another was the growth of a group of intellectuals—generally university-oriented professionals active in the new disciplines of the social sciences —who constructed a rationale for governmental and group intervention in the social order. By the 1890s, economists like Richard T. Ely, sociologists like Lester F. Ward, and political scientists like Woodrow Wilson were beginning to challenge success-fully the philosophical foundations of the laissez-faire state—Social Darwinism and classical economics—and the whole cluster of values and attitudes associated with individualism.

Reform began during the crisis that gripped urban and rural America in the 1890s. The crisis extended to the political system, which seemed increasingly unable to deal with the demands of major segments of American society. In the South and West, agrarians experienced such frustration with two-party politics that they orga-nized a pressure group, the Farmers' Alliance; then they took the extraordinary step of forming a third party, the People's Party, in 1892. By the end of the decade, the Populists were no longer a factor in elections, but they left a permanent mark on a political system wherever they were active. In other areas of the country, cultural issues—particularly anti-Catholicism and Protestant-led campaigns to restrict immi-gration, extend naturalization requirements, and end public subsidies to parochial education—shook traditional partisan alliances and seemed to demonstrate the political system's inability to resolve divisive conflicts.

The most important crisis of the 1890s, however, was the suffering and misery caused by the severe depression of 1893–1897. Human distress, abundant in the absence of a government social-safety net, dramatized for increasing numbers of urban Americans the wide contrast between the rich and the poor. More important, it also raised the specter of violent social conflict. The economic crisis also demon-strated the inability of local and state governments to solve the problems of an industrial society. This in turn galvanized urban middle-class groups, previously special-interest organizations, into supporting reform. It aroused them, in moral indignation, to look for new solutions and to discard nineteenth-century means of governance, decision making, and social policy, since all of them seemed to be aggravating rather than alleviating the crisis. The atmosphere of the 1890s prompted a close, hard look at the industrial system. Reformers tended to see social problems as endemic rather than isolated, national rather than local. The solution, perforce, had to be changes that embraced the entire nation and society at large. In sum, in response to the intensity of the crisis of the 1890s, different reform groups attained a shared sense of purpose about the necessity for their proposed social and political reconstruction.

2. Municipal Reform

In politics, the first important manifestation of the progressive movement came in a nationwide drive to restructure urban government. Middle-class reform groups of various stripes had existed in major American cities since the Civil War, and by the late 1880s they had begun to organize themselves into something resembling modern pressure groups. They rallied behind the causes of civil-service reform, good government, and an end to corruption. These urban reformers believed that the nineteenth-century system of politics was not working. Most of the problems, they claimed as early as the 1870s, resulted from party government and domination by professional "machine" politicians. Reformers admitted that this system was democratic, but they charged that participatory politics meant disorganization, waste, and corruption. At the same time, reformers claimed, urban politics was unrepresentative. Instead of being governed by impartially chosen leaders, most cities were run by tightly organized, hierarchical political machines directed, often dictatorially, by a "boss." Rising from the ranks, holding no office, and commanding a "ring" of thousands of workers, the boss was the invisible governor of the nation's largest cities. This machine survived, reformers maintained, through officeholding—more specifically, through the benefits of officeholding in the form of graft and patronage.

Much of what reformers had to say was correct. Mass democratic politics—a national tradition of decentralized home rule and the pervasive ideological preference for minimal government—had permitted the creation of a system of urban politics that was at once highly responsive to people and highly inefficient. In this system, local government was not expected to do anything but provide for public safety and distribute the few favors and privileges it might possess. For most of the nineteenth century, this arrangement had served quite well. It was well adapted to an era of intensely competitive party politics. Acquiring power meant patronage, and patronage meant jobs for the party faithful and money for the party apparatus. Urban "machines" were also highly responsive to the electorate and often provided political representation and social services not otherwise available. Most voters in nineteenth-century cities probably did not ask whether the system was corrupt but whether it did something for them. And the machine made a point of doing something for them, whether by helping immigrants or by providing coal and food when constituents needed them. Finally, urban machines were vigorous supporters of cultural pluralism; at the local, state, and national levels they defended the autonomy of Catholic and foreign-language groups. While party government satisfied the poorer third of urban communities, it also gratified business interests by providing an atmosphere conducive to growth. Decentralized, minimal governance supplied a loose and flexible apparatus which fostered expansion. Entrepreneurs faced few barriers and experienced considerable encouragement from urban machines.

As long as machine politics satisfied these groups, the pleas of good-government reformers were cries in the wilderness. However, by 1895 several new political and economic developments had upset this system and seemed to confirm the reformers' analysis of the problem of urban politics. One new element was that urban growth was rendering the partisan political system obsolete. Growth tended to fragment metropolitan areas along geographic, class, and ethnic lines. By the late 1880s, the resultant groups had begun to involve themselves in pressure-group politics. Another new factor was political. In what political scientists characterize as an "electoral realignment," Americans changed their political behavior during the 1890s by abandoning traditionally strong allegiances to parties and by decreasing their voting.

But the most acute challenge to the nineteenth-century urban political system was the depression that followed the Panic of 1893. City after city witnessed mismanagement of revenues in the midst of budgetary crisis and an inability to attack staggering problems of poverty, undermining the machines' broad political support. The governments of a number of cities were so impecunious that there was an almost total breakdown of basic services. Well-organized and offering a clear program for change, good-government reformers led reversals of the status quo in major American cities during the depression years. The first urban reformer to assemble a viable political coalition was Hazen S. Pingree, who was elected mayor of Detroit in 1890, and who served in that office until 1897. In 1894, urban reformers formed the National Municipal League, which laid its agenda before a national audience and held annual good-government conferences. Within two years, the Tammany machine in New York had been overthrown by a reform coalition led by William L. Strong. In Chicago, issues of graft and the corrupt selling of franchises led to formation of the Municipal Voters' League in 1895 and, two years later, to the election of a reform mayor, Carter Harrison. By the late 1890s, these spasmodic revolts had become more widespread and broader in their support and leadership.

By the turn of the twentieth century, the long-isolated good-government groups of the nineteenth century had expanded their constituencies through coalition building and had so broadened their objectives that they had become the advance guard of political progressivism. Tom L. Johnson, a dynamic and colorful reformer, was elected mayor of Cleveland in 1901 on a platform demanding equal taxation and the three-cent fare on trolley lines. Assembling an impressive array of capable young administrators, Johnson made the tax and fiscal system more equitable and then began a campaign to lower trolley fares. Still more problems with the trolley lines led him to the conclusion that public ownership was the necessary alternative. The "municipal socialism" of Johnson and other reformers like Sam "Golden Rule" Jones of Toledo was spectacular and attention getting, but in its essential elements it was not unlike what occurred in metropolitan and other urban communities across the United States.

The early municipal reformers of the 1890s soon found, in fact, that simply winning elections would not effect real change and root out the system of machine politics. Indeed, in a number of cities such as New York and Chicago, reformers, in winning office, raised expectations which they could not fulfill, and they soon lost power to the old machines. A major policy objective of nineteenth-century progressives—civil service reform—brought little real change; other attempts to limit partisan influence and eliminate corruption were similarly unsuccessful. Forced to broaden their program, reformers eventually shaped a permanent alteration of the political system. They favored ending legislative control of urban government by expanding home rule, thus severing the connections between urban machines and state-house organizations. They favored replacing the decentralized system of urban government—most commonly, a board of aldermen headed by a weak mayor—with a more centralized system headed by a strong mayor. Reformers endorsed a new, rationalized system of revenue appropriation and expenditure as well as specific restrictions on franchises for public utilities and transit systems. Finally, reformers favored restricting partisan influence in voting through such innovations as at-large voting, nomination by primaries, and the secret ballot.

To this cluster of administrative changes should be added the most important innovation in municipal government: introduction of the commission and city-management forms of government. Both plans sought to do away with the old aldermanic system entirely and replace it with nonpartisan government by qualified, expert administrators. The commission plan abolished the mayor–council system of administration—and the segmented boards and officials that went with it—and centralized new administrative authority in professionalized departments. Much discussed during the 1890s, the commission form was first used when a hurricane and tidal wave devastated Galveston, Texas, on September 8, 1900. The disaster took over 6,000 lives and wiped out about $17 million in property. After the city government, corrupt and incompetent, could not face the crisis, business groups and advocates of good government joined forces to submit a plan to the Texas legislature which would rewrite Galveston's charter and establish a government composed of five commissioners elected, after 1903, by popular vote. The Galveston plan soon spread to other Texas cities, and, in 1907, Iowa adopted a more elaborate version of the Texas model. The Iowa statute permitted cities of over 25,000 to adopt the commission form and, at the same time, incorporated the initiative, referendum, and recall as part of city politics. It also provided for the election of commissioners in nonpartisan elections. Since Des Moines was the first city in Iowa to make use of the plan, it was became known as the "Des Moines Idea." More than 100 cities had adopted commission government by 1910; by 1922, the number was nearly 500.

Popular in medium-sized cities, the commission form of city government never made much headway in large cities, where the complexities of politics and administration moved reformers to centralize power in the mayor's office. Moreover, experience soon demonstrated that the commission form had inherent weaknesses. It failed really to concentrate responsibility for administration in a rationalized fashion, since there was no guarantee that the commissioners would be expert managers or that they would coordinate their administration with other commissioners. Municipal reformers therefore developed a refinement of the commission form—the city-manager plan, first adopted in its complete form by Dayton, Ohio, in 1913. City-manager government vested all authority in a board of commissioners, elected on a nonpartisan basis, who made laws and policies for the city. These commissioners appointed a city manager, who was expected to be a trained expert in administration and to serve as manager of all departments. Quickly growing in popularity, city-manager government had been adopted in more than 300 cities by 1923.

In retrospect, it is clear that the municipal reform movement had a lasting effect on American urban government. Originating in special-interest groups who were not satisfied by the nineteenth-century system and who sought specific policy changes, reformers were brought together by the collective realization during the 1890s of the prevailing system's inadequacies. In particular, suddenly it appeared that corruption—in a sense basic to urban politics—was a degenerative force that had to be uprooted. Yet municipal reform also went beyond a short-lived political uprising to achieve fundamental changes in the political system. These changes were designed to destroy the partisan basis of urban politics, to open up the system to well-organized pressure groups, and to restructure urban government so as to provide for bureaucratic, "expert" control. Measured against these objectives, municipal reform was spectacularly successful. It undermined old-style party politics and, especially in the small cities and large towns which instituted the commission and city-manager forms of governments, it brought new, reform-minded leadership to urban America. But on other counts it fell short of its objectives. Progressive reformers met formidable opponents in the big-city machines, a number of which were able to adapt municipal reform to increase their constituencies and buttress their control. At the same time, a basic contradiction persisted between the reformers' announced objective of democratizing the system and the reduced democratic participation they actually brought about.

3. Progressivism and State Politics

Little of the early twentieth-century United States escaped the influence of urban reform, and it soon began to have an impact on state politics. The victories of urban progressive reformers brought new modes of political behavior and leadership to statewide attention. Simultaneously, progressives began to build state organizations, exert power in state elections, and affect the actions of state legislatures. As was the case in municipal reform, they were extremely effective coalition builders. Urban and middle-class in leadership, they found issues which could expand their appeal and make their constituency broad-based.

In most states, the political system had changed little since the age of Andrew Jackson. From the 1830s to the 1890s, most Americans took a keen interest in state elections, manifesting it in the hoopla of torchlight parades, barbecues, and enthusiasm that accompanied elections as well as in the extremely high rate of voter participation. As was true for urban government, the focus was on elections and parties rather than policy making and administration, and state governments from Maine to California were dominated by well-greased political organizations whose main purpose was to retain power. These statewide machines, like city machines, distributed contracts, franchises, and immunities. They received in return favors and cash. State organizations also used patronage to build powerful organizations. In some cases, these statewide organizations were linked to urban bosses, who sometimes headed the state machine. In largely rural states, machines were based on small-town and rural political organizations. This system, which emphasized minimal government, worked well enough throughout most of the nineteenth century, and it satisfied most Americans, who generally tolerated the kind of special favor and corruption it gave rise to. Yet, by 1900, the nineteenth-century polity seemed less suitable to the complexities of coalition and pressure-group politics. In state after state, the political system was unable to meet the demands of the new interest groups emerging in the late 1880s—for example, farmers, Protestant nativists, and prohibitionists—who found that the party system and the organization shut them out. These groups all existed throughout the 1890s without joining forces. What brought them together was the urban-based reform leadership which was able to create and maintain a statewide coalition.

Between 1901 and 1910, various reform groups won control of state governments across the country. In the Middle West, the dominant Republican party was convulsed by a series of spectacular revolts from within its ranks from 1900 to 1908. Under insurgent leaders like Robert M. La Follette of Wisconsin and Albert B. Cummins of Iowa—elected governor in 1900 and 1901—the midwestern states were transformed from bastions of conservative Republicanism into strongholds of reform. Reformers depended on considerable rural support in these states, but in the Northeast the progressive revolt, as exemplified by Charles Evans Hughes's election as governor of New York State in 1906 and 1908, was more urban in both constituency and leadership. Nor was state progressivism confined to these regions, for reform movements swept the South and the Pacific states as well.

Here, clearly, was no minor phenomenon but a political revolt of national proportions and momentous consequences. It is no exaggeration to say that the progressive coalitions sweeping to power across the country were so successful that a thoroughgoing revolution occurred. The power of the old political organizations had either been shattered or at least curtailed, and the nature of politics and policy making had been remade. Along with changes in the structure of government and method of election which greatly reduced the power of political parties, moreover, reformers also introduced new functions for state governments which increased their regulatory power in unprecedented fashion. The chief reason why reformers were able to effect these long-lasting changes was that they appealed to a broad range of the electorate and crystallized its disaffection with traditional politics.

In particular, progressives in the states succeeded in creating and energizing an antimachine coalition by exposing two fundamental characteristics of the nineteenth-century system—corruption and special privilege. By 1906, reformers, using sophisticated means of exposure, had demonstrated that corruption was so extensive as to virtually constitute a way of life in state legislatures across the country. In New York State, a legislative investigation of the insurance industry discovered an apparently corrupt relationship between the dominant Republican political organization and company executives. Similarly, in other states, reformers were able to prove that railroad interests had dominated state legislatures through the liberal use of graft, favors, and campaign contributions. The issue of business influence in state politics provided a rallying point of agreement for urban reformers and disaffected agrarians. In many states, legislatures enacted measures to reduce the power of railroads and corporations in political life through stringent corrupt-practices laws. In 1907 and 1909, Congress prohibited corporations, insurance companies, banks, and railroads from contributing to campaign funds in federal elections. Even more important, reformers confronted the problem of business influence on political power by expanding the sphere of governance itself. They empowered states to regulate and intervene in social and economic life in the public interest. Particularly in the Middle West and South, where longstanding resentment existed against railroads and corporations, reformers allied with agrarians were able to create new state commissions with the power to regulate railroads and even to set their rates inside state borders. At the height of the state progressive revolt, between 1905 and 1907, some fifteen new commissions were established, while the powers of others already in existence were greatly strengthened. And, although the original jurisdiction of state regulatory power was confined to transportation, soon it was expanded to include finance, insurance, and utilities.

It is fair to say that the greater portion of popular enthusiasm for reform was probably confined to these attempts to reduce the power of business in state political life. Yet reformers were also determined to destroy the system that made extensive business domination possible: they wanted to destroy partisan influence and, where possible, to uproot the power of state machines. Invariably, the first objective of reform leadership was the inauguration of the direct-primary system of nominating candidates and party officials. This innovation aimed at the old caucus and convention system which seemed to perpetuate rule by bosses. The direct primary originated in Pennsylvania in the 1840s, but it was not used on the local level until the 1890s, and then mainly in the South. After 1900, however, it became of central importance to state progressives. Mississippi passed the first compulsory statewide primary law in 1902; Wisconsin followed the next year. By 1916, the spread of the primary was so rapid that only Rhode Island, Connecticut, and New Mexico lacked some form of it.

Other innovations, usually accompanying legislation about primaries, were designed to alter the institutional structure of state politics. The short ballot, popular in many western states, struck at partisan control by reducing the number of elected officials. The direct election of senators was instituted to combat partisan power in state legislatures, which had previously elected senators and often regarded them as heads of the state parties. In many states, reformers were able to obtain this reform indirectly by requiring senatorial candidates to be nominated in primary elections and candidates for the state legislature to swear that they would vote for these popularly nominated senatorial candidates. In spite of strong opposition, the United States Senate approved the Seventeenth Amendment for direct election of Senators in 1912; the amendment became part of the Constitution on May 31, 1913.

Still other changes at the state level attempted to strengthen the influence of pressure groups while reducing that of political parties. Especially popular in the West was the recall, a device that gave voters a way of removing unsatisfactory elected officials. First used on the municipal level in Los Angeles in 1903, the recall was adopted on the state level in Oregon in 1908. Nine other states, most of them western, followed suit from 1911 to 1915. Closely related to the recall were other progressive innovations—such as the initiative and referendum, which gave voters the power to enact and veto legislation, in effect, without the consent of the legislature. The initiative and referendum originated and was most common in the West, and had been adopted by twenty-one states by 1915.

4. Social Reform and Social Control

Coming into existence simultaneously with, and to some extent connected to, political reform was a far-reaching transformation of social policy. Like political reform, it began largely during the 1890s, in the social crisis of that decade. It, too, was led mostly by middle-class reformers, and its values were urban–industrial in nature. As was the case in politics, social reformers believed that nineteenth-century governance and the absence of interventionist social policy had led to social disintegration in both urban and rural America. What they envisioned as reform, therefore, involved a social "reconstruction" in which public institutions, governmental and private, would assume functions previously performed by the church, family, and community.

Social reformers, as diverse as the progressive movement itself, were united only by their consensus in perceiving a social crisis and the need for drastic change. Frequently they disagreed about methods. How should the state act as a provider of welfare? To what degree should social policy be governmental, rather than private? To what extent should reform respond to community desires, rather than shape and direct them? And should reform be a voluntary or coercive process? In general, the divided mind of progressivism was revealed in a basic conflict over reform. The question was whether society should be reconstructed in a planned, generally bureaucratic, process, with stress on social efficiency and rationality, or whether reform should take place from below, through individuals and community organizations.

The conflict between these "hard" and "soft" approaches is exemplified in the shared objectives, yet contrasting methods, of two of the most important architects of social reform, Edward Alsworth Ross and Charles Horton Cooley. Pioneers in the new academic discipline of sociology, both Ross and Cooley provided intellectual rationales for interventionist governance and an activist social policy. Both believed that reformers, working with professional sociologists, could successfully reconstruct and manage society and eventually solve most of its problems. Rejecting laissez-faire governance, they maintained that new, industrial conditions demanded rational, human control of social development.

Yet they differed fundamentally over the means to effect the necessary changes. By the First World War, Cooley had become a major figure among those American sociologists whose approach can be best described as a "soft" type of social reform. In his major works, *Human Nature and the Social Order* (1903), *Social Organization* (1909), and *Social Progress* (1918), Cooley endorsed active, rational management of the social environment. Disagreeing with a previous generation of Social Darwinists, he argued that evolution was best expressed not in unrestrained competition but in social improvement through human management. Society was an "organic" entity, not simply a collection of individuals. Hence the objective of sociologists and social reformers should be to strengthen interpersonal relationships and the organic bonds of society. Cooley's analysis of the need for social reform went further. Above all, he stressed that social unity in an industrial society could come only by tightening bonds on the community level in "primary" groups such as churches, families, and neighborhoods. He would then transplant what he called a primordial "we-feeling" to "secondary" groups such as schools, civic organizations, and welfare agencies. This, clearly, was a program for social reform, but for reform through voluntary and noncoercive institutions.

Ross was one of the giants of twentieth-century sociology. Like Cooley, he believed that changed economic conditions necessitated new types of intervention and more active direction of social development. Writing in the aftermath of the convulsive 1890s, Ross published *Social Control* in 1901. Industrialization, he said, had torn away traditional community restraints and produced strains with which nineteenth-century institutions could not cope. It was necessary to protect the majority against the "lawlessness, the insolence, and the rapacity of over-grown private interests," he wrote; and the restoration of order and stability could only come through the increase of state power. Economic change had tended to fracture society into divergent interest groups. The task of "social control" was to "assimilate and reconcile its members and weaken the ties that bind men into minor groups." Moreover, the leadership and direction of social reconstruction, Ross said, should come from trained experts and "the wise," who would guide social development toward a harmonious future.

Although the difference in approach between Ross and Cooley is apparent in retrospect, it was less clear in the early years of the twentieth century. No less than political reformers, social reformers were a diverse coalition of sharply varying groups with different problems and different approaches. As a working coalition, a degree of unity was possible because of agreement on common goals, although the shared agenda masked internal differences and even contradictions. Moreover, social reformers borrowed liberally from both the "soft" and the "hard" sides of the progressive tradition. At times they stressed community development with voluntary participation and cooperation. At other times they advocated governmental intervention and coercion to bring about lasting change.

5. The Social Gospel and the Settlement House

The earliest manifestation of progressive social reform—the social-justice movement —approached matters more like Charles Horton Cooley than Edward Alsworth Ross. In its vanguard were church workers who became associated with urban problems after the Civil War. The Salvation Army, founded by William Booth in London in 1878, spread to the United States in 1880. By 1890, Washington Gladden, a Congregationalist minister of Springfield, Massachusetts, and Columbus, Ohio, was advocating a "social" form of Christianity which would help to alleviate the tense social atmosphere of the industrial age. Numerous urban churches, meanwhile, began to expand their social involvement by sponsoring missions, charity organizations, and relief agencies. Urban Protestant efforts to make the church an agency of reform gained greater momentum during the 1890s, when a whole generation of Protestant ministers began to espouse institutional and environmental solutions of social problems. George D. Herron, a Congregationalist minister of Minneapolis, Minnesota, and Burlington, Iowa, and professor of "applied" Christianity at Grinnell College, favored establishing a "new social machinery" in which "love and conscience" would be standards of behavior. In 1895, Herron helped to found a utopian community in Georgia, which published a national journal of reform, *The Social Gospel.*

This "social gospel" was now a wide movement among urban Protestants. Its most famous exponent was Walter Rauschenbusch. Born to a long line of New York Baptist preachers, he was educated at the University of Rochester and in Germany. In 1886, at twenty-five years of age he took his first pastorate in New York. There he encountered the harsh realities of poverty and misery and there he became committed to reformed Christianity. In his most important works, *Christianity and the Social Crisis* (1907) and *Christianity and the Social Order* (1915), Rauschenbusch maintained that it was the responsibility of all Christians to build the Kingdom of God on earth here and now. Human improvement, even perhaps perfection, was possible through structural changes in the economic and social system.

By the late 1880s, social gospelers were frequently in alliance with a different class of social workers—most of them young, middle-class women's college graduates—who lived and worked in urban settlement houses. Social service provided an attractive opportunity for these women. Work in settlement houses did not violate Victorian gender roles. In its emphasis on family, education, and culture, social work extended feminine qualities to an urban setting. The earliest and most successful settlement houses were led and staffed by women—the College Settlement in Lower East Side New York and Hull-House in Chicago (both founded in 1889), and the approximately 400 other settlement houses established across the country during the next three decades. Much of the work of settlement houses involved cultural uplift and amelioration. Social workers thus ran kindergartens and taught classes in English and in vocational skills such as cooking, sewing, and carpentry; they constructed playgrounds; they staged community events; and they helped the urban poor to obtain jobs. At the same time, they conducted intensive surveys of labor conditions, the causes of poverty, and means of alleviating social distress. As time passed, moreover, they became departmentalized: some concerned themselves with the care of immigrants, others with juvenile delinquency, and still others with the problems of working men and women.

By the First World War, both social-gospel and settlement-house reformers had traveled a long road from an emphasis on individual moral reform and charity to advocacy of a more systematic use of the state's police power to rearrange economic relationships. Experience seemed to demonstrate the need for a changed environment in order to solve social problems, and by the 1890s these social-justice reformers were supporting a number of measures to improve the urban environment. One prominent center of poverty was the tenement house, which reformers attempted to regulate through the adoption of stricter building and housing codes. They also favored a strong, concerted effort at city planning to relieve crowded streets and housing. Just as important, they supported the spread of public parks to beautify the city and sponsored organized recreation and sports in playgrounds as ways to better the urban milieu.

6. Child Labor and Protective Legislation

Many of these social-justice reforms were achieved through efforts undertaken by private charities or through greater involvement on the part of municipal governments. Yet the more ambitious reformers became, the more they became determined to uproot poverty and heal social divisions through use of governmental power. They thus began to advocate that the state and federal governments should guarantee the welfare of its citizens by protecting the disadvantaged. First would come legislation based on intensive investigation. Then would follow welfare agencies staffed by social workers. What reformers came to support, in effect, amounted to a modern welfare state.

Particularly repugnant to reformers was the still prevalent use of child labor in American manufacturing, mining, and agriculture. Reformers saw children as individuals who were in a distinct stage of human development that required special attention and nurture. Reformers drew on a traditional, middle-class Victorian conception of the sanctity of the home. They also drew on the new ideas of psychologists such as Sigmund Freud and G. Stanley Hall, who stressed childhood and adolescence as formative periods in individual development. Social reformers maintained that children should not be made to work but should rather be equipped for future harmonious interaction and responsible political behavior through institutions such as the public school. And these changes, in turn, meant ending child labor.

In 1901, social justice reformers initiated a campaign to outlaw child labor on two fronts. First came the Southeast, with the introduction of bills in the legislatures of the Carolinas, Georgia, and Alabama. Then New Jersey, New York, and Illinois adopted strong legislation in 1903–1904. In 1904, the southern and northern wings of the movements came together in the National Child Labor Committee, which had twenty-five branch committees in twenty-two states by 1910. The accomplishments of child-labor reformers constituted perhaps the greatest single triumph of the social-justice movement. In 1900, twenty-four states and the District of Columbia made no provision for a minimum working age; fourteen years later, every state but one had established such a limit, usually fourteen, while many states had prohibited children between fourteen and sixteen from working at night and in dangerous occupations.

In spite of these successes, reformers found action at the state level inadequate. It was questionable how far the Supreme Court would be willing to allow the states to go in regulating interstate trade. Moreover, in many states, especially in the cotton-textile states of the Piedmont Southeast, child-labor legislation was watered down and provided no enforcement machinery. It became clear that effective regulation demanded federal child-labor legislation. In 1914, the National Child

Labor Committee sponsored the introduction of a bill in Congress that prohibited the shipment in interstate commerce of goods manufactured in whole or in part by children under fourteen and of products of mines or quarries where children under sixteen were employed. In spite of strong opposition from the NAM and southern textile interests, the bill was passed by Congress and signed by President Woodrow Wilson in the summer of 1916.

Another major objective of social-justice reform was the passage of protective legislation for working women. This goal had the support of labor reformers, settlement-house workers, and civic-minded women; each of these groups believed that women needed a special, protected status in the work force. A broad range of laws was passed to exclude women from employment in certain types of jobs, set minimum wages, and shorten their hours. In 1893, Illinois enacted the first enforceable eight-hour law for women, but the state supreme court nullified the statute two years later. In the East, New York in 1896 and Massachusetts in 1900 limited women's hours to sixty a week; comparable legislation was soon passed by Nebraska, Michigan, Colorado, Oregon, Washington, and Tennessee. Most importantly, the statutes were upheld, first by state courts and then by the Supreme Court in *Muller* v. *Oregon* (1908). The latter decision established an important precedent. It permitted thirty-nine states to pass hours legislation for the first time, or to strengthen existing laws, between 1909 and 1917; four subsequent challenges to women's-hours legislation between 1908 and 1915 survived the Supreme Court's scrutiny. Moreover, the Court for the first time admitted the need to assemble facts through sociological inquiry in order to establish the reasonableness or unreasonableness of labor legislation.

Enacting a separate minimum wage for women workers, however, proved more difficult. Australia and Great Britain, by enacting statutes of this kind from 1896 to 1909, provided inspiration and a model for American reformers. So also did numerous governmental and private investigations in the United States. They demonstrated that many women's pay was inadequate to maintain a decent standard of living. By 1911, minimum-wage legislation for women had become part of the program of both the National Consumers' League and the Women's Trade Union League. This coalition won its first legislative victory in 1912, when the Massachusetts legislature created a wage commission with the power to recommend minimum wages for women and to make public the names of employers who did not abide by them. In the next year, eight midwestern states went further and empowered wage commissions to establish binding minimum-wage rates. Yet the campaign for a female minimum wage began to lose momentum in 1913, and over the next ten years only six other states, the District of Columbia, and Puerto Rico passed similar legislation.

A final objective of social-justice reform was the creation of a public system of industrial-accident insurance. Although such programs had long since existed in western Europe, in the United States the common-law "fellow servant" and "assumption of risk" rules—which shifted responsibility for injury and resultant costs to workers—still prevailed. The obvious injustice involved led to a movement to change this legal doctrine. By 1910, most states had modified rules in favor of the injured workers, yet it remained their responsibility to sue for recovery of damages.

Maryland, Montana, and the federal government experimented from 1902 to 1909 with crude and limited systems of accident insurance, but this represented all that had been accomplished up to the latter date. Then, largely as a result of intense public and private investigation between 1909 and 1913—which revealed the gross inadequacies of the traditional scheme of compensation for work-related injury—a wave of states enacted new legislation. Ten states established insurance systems in 1911, and twenty states, three territories, and the federal government followed suit from 1912 to 1916.

7. Social Reform and Social Purity

Among urban social reformers an important goal was the purification of the city environment. Purification meant not just improving the physical environment of housing, parks, and playground. It also included improving the moral environment. In the crisis atmosphere of the 1890s, middle-class urban America was swept by an enthusiasm for moral uplift. In numerous cities, church and civic groups led local campaigns against visible signs of moral decay: saloons, gambling, prostitution, and violations of the traditional proscription of doing business on Sunday. Yet, much more than in the case of social-justice reform, social purity required imposing Protestant, middle-class standards by means of governmental coercion.

The most prominent concern of the social-purity reformers was, of course, the pervasiveness of the saloon. In spite of temperance campaigns throughout much of the nineteenth century, reformers could see little progress by the 1890s. In 1900, only three states had legal prohibition, and with the spread of working-class, urban communities there also came the saloon. Consumption of alcohol remained a serious social problem; indeed, between 1860 and 1900, per capita consumption of alcohol nearly doubled. In 1895, reformers formed a new organization, the Anti-Saloon League of America, whose purpose was to mount an aggressive campaign with the single goal of prohibition. Organizing at the grass roots, the Anti-Saloon League orchestrated efforts to ban alcohol, either by local option, legislative statute, or constitutional amendment. By 1918, prohibitionists had won thirty-one prohibition referendums which endorsed statewide prohibition, and, with the adoption of the Eighteenth Amendment in January 1919, the entire nation became dry within a year. Although much of the subsequent support for prohibition came from rural areas, leadership and vital backing also came from towns and cities which had activist reformers engaged in campaigns against vice. Before nationwide prohibition in 1919–1920, a large number of cities had adopted it by local ordinance: Portland, Spokane, Seattle, Albuquerque in the West; Birmingham and Raleigh in the South; and Worcester, Massachusetts, in the North.

Closely tied to these efforts to eliminate drunkenness and the host of social problems that accompanied it were efforts to eradicate urban prostitution. Here again, the impetus for reform came largely from the cities. In 1900, New York led the way with the formation of the Committee of Fifteen, a private commission whose purpose was to investigate and expose immorality and then press for legislative solutions. By 1910, this group and others were responsible for a series of exposés on prostitution and the white-slave trade. In Chicago, Mayor Fred Busse appointed a thirty-member vice commission to investigate prostitution in 1910. A year later, it published *The Social Evil in Chicago,* a long investigation which advocated "repression" and "annihilation" of prostitution. Meanwhile, a flood of publications—many of them luridly sensational in nature—appeared detailing the so-called problem of white slavery. They included George Kibbe Turner's film *Traffic in Souls* (1913), Clifford Roe's *Horrors of the White Slave Trade* (1911), and David Graham Phillips's novel *Susan Lenox: Her Fall and Rise* (1917). Before the First World War, antiprostitution crusaders had gone national and could boast of the passage of the Mann Act (1910), which prohibited the interstate transportation of women for immoral purposes. By 1916, some 102 cities and three states had investigated vice through commissions like those in New York and Chicago. Based partly on the results of these investigations, almost every state in the Union by 1920 had passed legislation outlawing soliciting; over thirty, meanwhile, empowered state courts to close brothels upon the filing of citizens' complaints.

8.   Social Reform and the Progressive State

Although reform laid the foundations of what we would today call the welfare state, progressives wanted more: they sought a wholesale revamping of social policy. Sharing the general objectives of the social-justice reformers, this diverse group of social-policy reformers favored restructuring old relationships and involving centralized state power in a variety of aspects of social life. The motives of many of these social reformers were disinterested and humanitarian, but to many others the achievement of social harmony in an industrial society would require the type of manipulative "social control" advocated by E. A. Ross. This kind of social reform differed from social-justice reform in important respects. While social-justice crusaders were concerned with individuals—in particular the protection of those women, children, and workers who lacked bargaining power—these other reformers were more concerned with institutions which could effect long-term changes in individuals' behavior by shaping their environment. Social-policy reformers were therefore also more concerned with an institutional objective—making institutions "efficient" in their administration and transforming them into instruments of long-term social change. The emphasis of social-policy progressives on institutions suggests another characteristic: unlike social-justice crusaders, they drew disproportionately from the ranks of reforming professional groups.

    The best example of this type of reform movement was in the field of public education. As was the case in other kinds of reform, the leadership arose, and pioneer changes first took place, in urban areas. In the nineteenth century, major cities— New York, Boston, St. Louis, and Chicago—were the first to develop tuition-free, tax-supported "common," or elementary, schools; by the 1880s, they were also beginning to develop comprehensive systems which offered schooling from kindergarten through adolescence.

Much of this growth in the public school system occurred during the first two decades of the twentieth century. In 1900, there were kindergartens in about 250 cities and 6,000 public high schools, with 500,000 enrolled pupils; twenty years later, there were 8,000 separate kindergartens, with 511,000 children enrolled, and 14,000 public high schools, with some 2 million students.

Not only did urban school reformers expand facilities, they also began after 1880 to increase central administrative control over the public schools. Civic groups, such as the Public Education Association of New York and the Public Education Society of Philadelphia, joined with professional administrators in the school systems to push for less popular involvement and greater central, bureaucratic control through supervision of the schools. By 1920, urban educational reformers had largely succeeded in converting a decentralized system into a rationalized bureaucracy.

After 1900, the transformation of urban public education went forward rapidly. As urban educators publicized their innovations through the national periodical press, and as they began to press for statewide changes in the school system, they began to attract allies from the rural schools. In particular, the centralization of administration in urban schools seemed especially relevant for rural schools, but it was also their biggest challenge. By 1920, however, reforming professionals and their allies had the initiative in rural school systems across the country. In the South, one of the nation's most rural areas—and its poorest—reformers conducted a campaign of publicity and exposure beginning with the formation of the Southern Education Board in 1901. By 1914, every state in the region was either controlled or strongly influenced by reform-oriented professionals, who undertook long-lasting changes in the administrative structure of public education. Most of them attempted to increase central state control by enhancing public financial involvement, which about doubled between 1900 and 1910. With greater control over the purse strings, southern school reformers introduced other administrative innovations. They centralized control over whole counties and increased the power of superintendents and visiting supervisors. They also initiated early attempts to consolidate isolated, small schools and transport pupils at public expense. And, ultimately, they introduced legislation providing for compulsory education, with effective enforcement machinery.

For reformers, changing the administration of schools was only a means to the end of changing the stuff of learning. Beginning in the 1890s, a chorus of voices was calling for a new, progressive, conception of public education. The philosopher John Dewey (who taught at the University of Chicago and at Columbia Teachers' College) led the way. He was joined by a host of child psychologists, sociologists, and university-based curriculum reformers who advocated expanding the agenda of education to include more than it had previously. Rather, the progressive school would prepare children and adolescents for participation in life. It would give vocational education to urban pupils and agricultural education to rural pupils. It would also prepare them hygienically, morally, and politically for what reformers considered responsible behavior in a modern, industrial society.

It is no exaggeration to say that, by the 1920s, social-policy reformers had effected a significant transformation of the public schools. It is clear, from hindsight, that the changes which they brought about put less emphasis on social justice than on social control and the overall efficiency of an industrial society. Social-policy reformers were determined to use schools to shape and form the future. If children could be molded into responsible, productive citizens through curricular changes, then the progressive school would become an essential instrumentality to insure stability in a modern society.

Similar in leadership and goals were other social-policy reform groups that sought to change public-health institutions. A thoroughgoing reorganization of the medical profession, for example, produced a general rise in standards, the professionalization of medical schools, and the establishment of hospitals all during the progressive era. These changes were the product of several factors. By the 1890s, advances in basic science and research had begun to demonstrate that disease, rather than being carried by "miasmas," or noxious vapors, was the product of bacteria and other microorganisms. If they had an identifiable epidemiological origin, diseases could at least be prevented through antiseptic procedures. The American Medical Association, which was reorganized in 1901, and which grew from 8,400 to 70,000 members in the next ten years, provided leadership in changing the status of medical professionals. Finally, philanthropists, especially John D. Rockefeller, committed huge financial resources to improve medical research and to sponsor the spread of sanitary procedures. Instrumental in leading the professionalization of medicine and spreading the gospel of sanitation was the Rockefeller Institute for Medical Research, founded in 1901.

Under such leadership, major public health campaigns began during this period. They were closely related to other types of political and social reform movement in leadership, organization, and general goals. As was the case for other types of reform, reform crusaders discovered a "problem" of public health which had long existed —disease, malnutrition, and parasitic infection. What shocked their modern sensibilities was the fact that local, state, and national governments did next to nothing to protect public health against such scourges. Boards of health before the 1890s served a mainly advisory function, only intervening once a genuine crisis—usually an epidemic—had already begun. Health reformers favored changing this system fundamentally and instituting a new social policy—making local governments in particular active in prevention, regulation, and intervention.

Public-health reform began as part of the far-flung anxiety among the urban middle class over the apparent breakdown of the social and political order during the 1890s. Rapid growth in American cities had taken place with little regard for community health. It was the exception to find cities which had adequate water and sewer and garbage disposal systems, and, throughout the nineteenth century, periodic outbreaks of epidemic diseases occurred. In a number of urban communities, the intense focus of reformers during the 1890s on local government served as a spur to transform its public-health function. As a result, by 1920 municipal governments had developed aggressive departments of health whose responsibilities now included vaccination, inspection of the milk supply, supervision of a safe system of water and sewage, and control of disease-carrying insects. These changes brought almost immediate results in dramatic declines in infant mortality, the near elimination of common epidemic diseases such as cholera, smallpox, and typhoid, and a general improvement in health conditions for urban Americans.

Reformers soon discovered that changing the urban health environment was linked to the situation on the farm: impure food and milk were dangerous to everyone. Public-health reform came to the American countryside from two sources. One was the United States Public Health Service (PHS). The other was the Rockefeller-financed Sanitary Commission for the Eradication of Hookworm in the Southern States, formed in 1909. Both agencies found a shocking degree of ill health in rural areas. In the South, the PHS and Rockefeller investigators worked to solve two age-old regional problems—widespread affliction by the parasite called hookworm and the high incidence of pellagra, a disease caused by nutritional deficiency. Both had simple remedies—hookworm, through a dose of the poison, thymol; pellagra, through the mineral, niacin. However, the eradication of both hookworm and pellagra required basic institutional changes in local government to safeguard, through permanent public-health agencies, the health of all people.

By the 1920s, the objectives of social-policy reformers in public health were far from realized. Yet they had achieved notable success in altering the old-fashioned health governance prevailing at the local, state, and federal levels. Few communities were now free from the authority of municipal, county, or state health officials, many of whom possessed coercive powers to regulate local life in an unprecedented way. And these health officials held tenure based on their expertise rather than their political appeal to a constituency.

9. Reform and Woman Suffrage

Many social reformers considered still another reform—enfranchising women—a goal of paramount importance. Supporters of woman suffrage argued that the United States could never be a truly democratic society if it denied the vote to half its citizens. They pointed to increases in the number of women in the work force as proof that women desperately needed the ballot in order to protect their economic interests. They wanted suffrage, however, above all because, as one authority has written, it would be "a vital step toward winning human dignity, and the recognition that they too were endowed with the faculty of reason, the power of judgment, the capacity for social responsibility."

The movement for woman suffrage began in 1848 and, during the following half century, found devoted leaders in Lucretia Mott, Elizabeth Cady Stanton, and Susan B. Anthony. However, the real power and momentum of the movement awaited the emergence of the new middle-class generation and the awakening of a large group among the male population to the indignity and injustices of denying the vote on account of gender. Nonetheless, by 1900 only the states of Wyoming (1890), Colorado (1893), and Idaho and Utah (1896) had granted suffrage to women.

What had been a somewhat desultory campaign turned into a crusade in 1900 with the election of Carrie Chapman Catt as president of the National American Woman Suffrage Association, which had been founded in 1890 by the merger of two hitherto rival organizations. The fight for women's rights now spread from the West to the East and became a significant part of the general movement for reform.

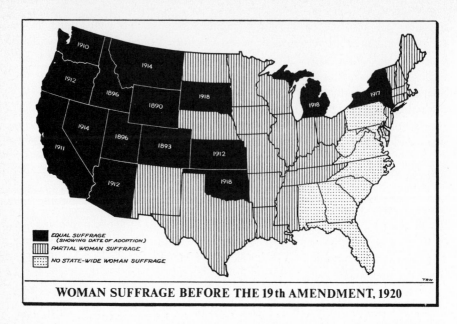

WOMAN SUFFRAGE BEFORE THE 19th AMENDMENT, 1920

Women not only spoke and organized, but they also mounted suffrage parades in all the large cities. More militant groups—such as the Equality League (later the Women's Political Union), the Congressional Union for Woman Suffrage, and the National Woman's Party—demonstrated, picketed, heckled political candidates, and occasionally went to jail, where they carried on hunger strikes in imitation of their British counterparts.

It was evident by 1910–1911, when the states of Washington and California adopted woman suffrage, that the movement was becoming irresistible. Arizona, Kansas, and Oregon fell into line in 1912. The next year, Illinois granted women the right to vote in presidential elections; Montana and Nevada joined the suffrage ranks in 1914; and the key state of New York fell to women crusaders in 1917. By this date, pressure for a federal suffrage amendment was also virtually irresistible. Under the prodding of President Wilson, the House of Representatives, on January 10, 1918, approved an amendment forbidding the states to deny suffrage on account of gender; and the Senate, in response to a personal appeal from Wilson, concurred on June 4, 1919. This Nineteenth Amendment became a part of the Constitution on August 26, 1920, after Tennessee completed the thirty-sixth ratification.

Meanwhile, along with political equality had come a comprehensive revision of state laws. These now permitted women to own, inherit, and bequeath property; divorce statutes now protected women's economic rights and their right to custody of children.

The millennium had not come for American women by 1920. They were still grossly discriminated against in employment and wages. Many of them still lived in semislavery to fathers and husbands. But the goal of general political equality had been won, and that must be counted as one of the most important milestones in the progress of democracy.

Chapter 4

--->>> <<<---

National Progressivism from TR to Taft

Although reform of nineteenth-century American social and political institutions began at the local level, it was primarily at the national level that progressivism acquired a clear degree of unity and single-mindedness. It was a logical step to make. Reformers saw problems and their solutions in national, even international, terms. As advocates of greater central administrative control through increased public state power, they favored increasing the role of the federal government—even if it occurred at the expense of localities and of the states. Well before 1910, the uprising of municipal and state reformers brought a large core of congressmen of both parties to Washington who had received their political baptism in new forms of progressive politics and who pressed a new policy agenda. To these considerations must be added still another: the growth of executive power under two presidents, Theodore Roosevelt and Woodrow Wilson, both of whose careers intertwined with the fortunes of national reform.

As the twentieth century began, the dominant party in national politics—the Republicans—advocated generous assistance to business and opposed most forms of public regulation. Democrats under the leadership of William Jennings Bryan carried on the Jacksonian antimonopoly and antirailroad traditions but stopped short of support for governmental intervention in the economy. Within less than a decade, however, the impact of progressive politics virtually remade the national political scene. By 1910, reformers who sought to expand the federal government's role in society and the economy constituted a powerful part of the Republican party, while Democrats were united and confident under new, reform-minded leadership. Not only did national progressivism bring new leaders to the fore, it also initiated a spate of policy changes. This began with a redefinition of the federal government's purposes and its relationship to the states, the implications of which extend into our own time.

1. Theodore Roosevelt and the Progressive Movement

Theodore Roosevelt, an extraordinary leader of national progressivism, came to the presidency by tragic accident and presided over the national destiny during a crucial period in American history. Highly intelligent and keenly self-disciplined, Roosevelt's personality was a complex mixture of contradictory, even baffling, characteristics. Guided by a strong strain of idealism—sometimes even humanitarianism—that manifested itself in his interest in international peace and a paternalistic concern for the downtrodden, Roosevelt was also a canny opportunist who adapted his policies to the changing configurations of political power. Out of this frequently ambiguous but always interesting personality came a style of leadership that galvanized national reformers.

Born to a well-to-do mercantile and banking family, Roosevelt was reared in the genteel traditions of New York. He was afflicted with a frail body and weak eyes but, while still young, became determined to invigorate himself physically and overcome his weakness through an exhausting regimen and iron self-discipline. These childhood experiences confirmed in his mind the virtues of what he called the "strenuous life"; whether as cowboy, Rough Rider, or big-game hunter, Roosevelt demonstrated his physical prowess and absolute fearlessness.

From his social environment and especially from his father, he acquired a compulsion to do good for people less fortunate than himself. Most people of his class donated money to settlement houses or home missions. For Roosevelt, however, real social service lay in politics, and, after graduation from Harvard in 1880, he won election to the New York Assembly. Part of his motivation must have been the strong moral sense which he acquired from his Dutch Reformed religion and its emphasis on day-to-day righteousness. In any event, Roosevelt usually viewed political contests as struggles between the forces of good and evil, and, like Wilson and Bryan, he became a preacher at large to the American people.

Background, training, temperament, and personal associations all combined to produce TR's fundamentally cautious, conservative approach to politics. Roosevelt believed in justice for all classes and therefore legislation in the general interest. As a patrician, he rejected the vulgarity and materialism of the newly rich, yet he refused to condemn whole classes or to hold the economic system alone responsible for society's ills. Roosevelt's conservatism was manifested in his insistence on continuity and his abhorrence of those who advocated violent change. Believing that progressive adaptation to new circumstances was impossible without order and social stability, he feared a mob as much as what he called "the malefactors of great wealth."

If Roosevelt's approach to politics was idealistic in theory, in practice he was a hardheaded realist. He was facinated with power—compelled by a need to acquire and use it—and he did not hesitate to compromise his objectives to maintain it. Thus, as governor of New York, he frequently cooperated with the state Republican boss, in spite of important differences, because he recognized political realities. When he became president in 1901, he found political power in the Republican party concentrated in state organizations and exercised by their representatives in Congress. He did not attempt to destroy the party hierarchy; rather, he worked with and through it. The important point is that Roosevelt not only accepted the existing power structures as he found them in New York and Washington but, in manipulating his party for his own and the national interest, he became a master politician.

In using power, however, Roosevelt also learned to love it. As the years passed, this characteristic verged on egomania, and the strength of his own opinions overshadowed the sense of balance that was present during his younger years, sometimes causing him—especially as president—to consider himself above the law and the conventions of more ordinary men and women. Yet his confidence was as much a source of strength as of danger, and gave him the assertiveness essential to leadership. Judgments of Roosevelt vary, and will continue to vary, but no one should make the mistake of not taking him seriously. Among presidents, he will surely remain high in importance in his effect on the art of government and the diplomacy of his country.

2. Roosevelt and the Republican Party, 1900–1904

When Republican leaders laid their plans for the election of 1900, President William McKinley was the natural choice as the party's nominee. But the death of Vice-President Garret A. Hobart in 1899 created an unusual opportunity for Thomas C. Platt, Republican boss of New York State. Platt had nominated Theodore Roosevelt, hero of the Spanish–American War, for governor of New York in 1898. Elected easily, Roosevelt attacked corruption vigorously, championed social-welfare legislation, and was consequently soon at odds with Platt. Hobart's death offered a dignified way to remove Roosevelt from New York politics.

When Platt first presented his plan, Mark Hanna, McKinley's main political adviser, responded coldly. Did Platt and his allies not realize, he supposedly asked, that there was "only one life between this madman and the White House?" But Hanna finally gave in to Platt. Roosevelt, seeing through Platt's scheme, expressed grave misgivings about an apparent consignment to oblivion, but his friends suggested that he would become the logical presidential candidate in 1904. Consequently, when the nomination was offered to him, he could think of no alternative but to accept. The election, which once more pitted McKinley against William Jennings Bryan, resulted in a Republican victory by an even greater margin than the party had gained four years earlier.

Hanna's misgivings about nominating Roosevelt were confirmed in September 1901, when an assassin mortally wounded McKinley in Buffalo. "That damned cowboy," as Hanna described him, was now president. Yet neither the worst fears of Hanna nor the best hopes of reform-minded Republicans were confirmed. The locus of the power in the Republican party—and, for that matter, in the federal government—resided with Congress, not the presidency. And, inside Congress, power mainly lay with a group of Republican congressmen known as the "Old Guard," so named because of their long position of party leadership. Their preeminent leader was Mark Hanna, senator from Ohio; nearly his equal was Senator Nelson W. Aldrich of Rhode Island, the avowed spokesman of Wall Street. Allied with Hanna and Aldrich in the upper house were John C. Spooner of Wisconsin, William B. Allison of Iowa, and Orville H. Platt of Connecticut. The Old Guard were as firmly entrenched in the House of Representatives, where after 1902 the Speaker, Joseph G. Cannon of Illinois, ruled with rural wit and an iron hand.

Almost as soon as he was inaugurated, advice came to Roosevelt to move slowly. It was unnecessary counsel. Roosevelt was in no position to challenge the Old Guard, so he determined to work with them for a time and immediately announced that he would continue McKinley's policies and retain his cabinet. Building support for his nomination in 1904, Roosevelt was not yet ready to take on the GOP's strongest faction, and by 1902, he had assured Old Guard leaders that he would leave the protective tariff system and monetary structure essentially undisturbed. In return, the Old Guard gave him freedom of action in other areas.

Meanwhile, antirailroad and antitrust agitation was beginning to have a significant impact on the Middle West in the form of a revolt within the Republican party against the policies of Hanna and Aldrich. In 1900, the most important of the "insurgent," or anti-Old Guard, Republicans, Robert M. La Follette, was elected governor of Wisconsin on a platform favoring the direct primary and stronger railroad regulation; in Iowa, Albert Baird Cummins became the state's dominant political leader on a similar platform. Roosevelt realized far better than Aldrich and his friends the necessity of appeasing midwestern opinion. His first move was to instruct the attorney general in February 1902 to begin proceedings to dissolve the Northern Securities Company, a gigantic railroad combination which J. P. Morgan had recently formed.

Yet midwestern insurgents were not easily propitiated. They demanded drastic tariff reductions, aggressive federal railroad regulation, and a more vigorous policy toward large corporations. Roosevelt traveled through the Middle West in August 1902. The following year, when he returned to the region in April, it was clear that he understood and sympathized with midwestern discontent. Roosevelt's first hard fight in Congress for reform legislation occurred in early 1903, when he requested (in a bill creating the Department of Commerce and Labor) the establishment of a Bureau of Corporations possessing full power to investigate business practices. Confronting strong opposition from Congress, Roosevelt won his measure through an appeal to public opinion.

3. The Emergence of a Progressive President

By 1904, Roosevelt had a clear strategy for winning his chance to be president in his own right. He gradually retired Hanna as chief dispenser of patronage and made his own alliances with dominant state organizations—especially in the South. After Hanna died in early 1904, Roosevelt received the Republican nomination in June without even a show of opposition. The Democrats, twice defeated under Bryan, nominated an obscure and ineffectual politician, Judge Alton B. Parker of New York. The campaign was a drab affair, enlivened only by Parker's charge, near the end of the campaign, that Roosevelt was blackmailing Wall Street into supporting the Republican ticket. The charge was false, and voters ignored it, for they elected Roosevelt by the largest popular majority ever given a presidential candidate up to that time.

Events soon proved that Roosevelt was no hostage to Wall Street. On the contrary, with the clearest mandate granted any president since Lincoln, he was exhilarated and strengthened in his determination to be a real national leader. His annual message of 1904 suggested a new position, but it was his address before the Union League Club of Philadelphia, delivered in January 1905, that blazoned his new commitment to reform. Great industries and wealth, he warned, had to submit to public control; specifically, the public interest demanded effective railroad regulation.

Pressure mounted on Roosevelt to support such causes as railroad regulation, the direct election of senators, and control of corporations through vigorous antitrust prosecutions. Not merely acceding to these pressures, but haunted by a fear that failure to address popular demands would provoke revolution, he took personal control of national reform during the summer and autumn of 1905. He began with an attack on meatpackers and a thorough investigation of the industry. When Congress met in December 1905, he proposed laws for stringent railroad regulation and pure food and drugs, for making campaign contributions public, and for additional conservation.

The more vigorously Roosevelt asserted his leadership, the more successes he won. He pushed through pure food and drug legislation and a meat-inspection act; he forced passage of a railroad bill in 1906; and he advanced conservation through executive action alone. Moreover, he attacked the so-called trust problem vigorously, not only by dissolution suits, but, perhaps even more effectively, through a number of searching exposures by federal agencies. At the same time, Roosevelt was also discovering the limits of his leadership. He recognized the intensity of the midwestern demand for tariff reduction, but he never considered it a paramount issue. Consequently, he never challenged the Old Guard on this issue during his presidency. He also knew that the country needed currency reform and more effective regulation of the banking system, but he never pressed these issues before Congress and the country.

By 1907, Roosevelt's ability to lead national reform from what he described as the "bully pulpit" of the White House was constricted by several circumstances. During late 1907, a severe panic was followed by a deep recession. By then, moreover, Roosevelt faced a congressional opposition which had regrouped and was determined to block any major policy initiatives. And because of his decision, announced soon after the election of 1904, not to seek reelection, Roosevelt increasingly became a lame-duck president. Nonetheless, in 1908, Roosevelt began to articulate a new, national program that went well beyond the limited accomplishments of 1904–1907. In a special message to Congress on January 31, 1908, he outlined his objectives in broad strokes, perhaps sensing that this was a last opportunity to leave some sort of legacy. Outraged by the Supreme Court's nullification of the federal Employer's Liability Act of 1906, Roosevelt demanded new legislation; he also urged the states to adopt accident compensation systems. Moreover, he condemned the courts for using injunctions to protect property in labor disputes and urged Congress to empower the Interstate Commerce Commission to make a physical valuation of railroad property and supervise the financial operation of the railroads. Finally, he suggested closer supervision of corporations, either through federal licensing "or in some other way equally efficacious," and he denounced the influence of "very wealthy men of enormous power in the industrial, and therefore in the social, lives of all our people." He looked forward to the day "when greed and trickery and cunning shall be trampled . . . by those who fight for the righteousness that exalteth a nation."

4. Taft and Republican Infighting

In 1908, the Republican renomination was Roosevelt's for the asking. But, as we have said, in 1904 he had promised not to run again, and he stuck by his promise. However, he exercised the right to choose his successor as Republican standard-bearer. He decided against the capable secretary of state, Elihu Root, because of his Wall Street connections and selected instead Secretary of War William Howard Taft. A loyal Roosevelt supporter in the cabinet, Taft had a distinguished record as federal judge, governor general of the Philippines, and secretary of war. Roosevelt's blessing assured him of a first-ballot nomination in the Republican convention held in Chicago in June 1908. Running against Bryan—the Democratic nominee for the third and final time—Taft won an easy victory. More significant during the same election was the noticeable rise in the number of Republican insurgents elected to Congress.

Roosevelt left the United States soon after Taft's inaugural to hunt big game in Africa and then to go on an extended tour of Europe. His departure was applauded in financial circles, where many wished luck to the lions. Conservatives generally were sure that Taft would align himself with the Old Guard in Congress; insurgents were just as sure that he would come to their aid. As it turned out, neither group was entirely right or wrong. It would be unkind to say that Taft took the presidency under false pretenses. On the eve of his magistracy, he considered himself a progressive, and he genuinely shared Roosevelt's belief in the supremacy of the public over the private interest. He believed in railroad regulation, was ruthlessly opposed to industrial monopolies, and honestly wanted to continue Roosevelt's policy of preserving the national heritage of natural resources. In a normal period, he might have been a beloved president.

The years of Taft's presidency, however, were anything but normal. Civil war within the Republican party impended and could have been averted only by bold presidential leadership. Unhappily, Taft was temperamentally unfit to assume the role assigned him. He could not lead in a time of trouble because leadership in such circumstances required wholehearted commitment and abandonment of the judicial quality dominant in his character. Philosophically, Taft was a reformer, but he could not get on with progressive leaders in Congress because he found them too harsh in their denunciations, too impatient, and too willing to experiment with untried measures.

The new president was forced to choose between congressional Old Guard leaders and the insurgent Republican bloc at the very outset—that is, at the beginning of the special session which convened in March 1909 to consider tariff revision. As the Republicans now had a majority of only forty-seven in the House, insurgent leaders concluded that the time had come to combine with Democrats to unhorse the tyrannical leadership of Speaker Joe Cannon. But Cannon appealed to Taft for help and promised support for the president's legislative program in return. Taft faced a dilemma: he did not like Cannon, yet he needed his cooperation. Taft made his first mistake by endorsing Cannon and hinting that the insurgents should end their campaign. Although the defection of southern and Tammany democrats—not Taft's opposition—frustrated the insurgents' plans, many insurgent Republicans deeply resented what they said was Taft's betrayal.

This incident only marked the beginning of the split between GOP insurgents and Taft. Instead of repairing the damage resulting from the speakership fight, Taft soon blundered again, this time in a battle over tariff revision during the spring of 1909 (for further details of this conflict, see pp. 173–74). Although Taft sincerely desired substantial tariff reductions, he erred by refusing to intervene in the legislative fight and by failing to rally public opinion behind reform. When he finally did act, moreover, he did so in such a way as to convince midwestern insurgents, the leading advocates of tariff reduction, that he had deserted them and surrendered to special privilege. Taft won a few noteworthy concessions, but the bill that was signed —the Payne–Aldrich Act—represented a substantial victory for manufacturing interests. By this time—the late summer of 1909—the Republican Middle West was in a rebellious mood.

No sooner had public agitation over the tariff quieted than a worse catastrophe completed the alienation of the insurgents. This was the Ballinger affair, which grew out of a feud between the secretary of the interior, Richard A. Ballinger, and the chief of the Forestry Service in the Department of Agriculture, Gifford Pinchot. The root of the conflict lay in the fact that Pinchot was a conservationist and Ballinger was not. Ballinger was charged with conspiring with the Morgan–Guggenheim syndicate to validate withdrawals of Alaskan coal lands from the public domain. Pinchot, believing the accusation, urged an Interior Department official, Louis R. Glavis, to present his evidence to the president, while he, Pinchot, publicly denounced Ballinger as a traitor to the cause of conservation.

When Glavis presented his indictment, however, Taft accepted Ballinger's rebuttal and authorized the secretary to dismiss Glavis for insubordination. Pinchot refused to stop his attack and forced his own removal from the Forestry Service in January 1910. By then, the controversy had developed into a national cause célèbre, the climax of which occurred when Democrats and insurgent Republicans in Congress insisted upon an investigation of the Interior Department. A committee cleared Ballinger, but the trenchant questions asked by Louis D. Brandeis, who represented Glavis, exposed Ballinger, not as a corrupt public official, but as an opponent of conservation and a champion of far-western demands for rapid distribution of the remaining public domain.

The final blow dividing Taft from the insurgents occurred in early 1910, when progressive House Republicans tried again to strip Speaker Cannon of dictatorial control over legislation in the House. With support from Democrats, insurgents, led by George W. Norris of Nebraska, deposed the Speaker from the Rules Committee in March and deprived him of the power to appoint members of standing committees. Although Taft secretly approved—knowing well what a liability Cannon was

—because he made no show of support for the insurgents, Taft appeared to be on Cannon's side.

The misunderstanding about Taft's position in the speakership fight occasioned a complete break between the administration and the insurgents. The rebels quarreled with Taft over the terms of a bill to strengthen the powers of the Interstate Commerce Commission; they accused him of conspiring with Wall Street when he proposed a postal savings system. Convinced that the insurgents were maneuvering in every possible way to destroy him politically, and goaded by incessant and often unfair attacks, Taft turned fiercely against the progressives and joined the Old Guard in a powerful anti-insurgent campaign. Taft, Aldrich, and Cannon conferred in March 1910 and formulated a plan of attack. It involved the use of money and patronage to build up strong midwestern conservative organizations and to defeat insurgent bids for renomination.

In a bitter fight for their political lives, the insurgents virtually declared their independence from the party dominated by Taft, Aldrich, and Cannon. It was a crucial battle; its outcome affected the future of the GOP, not only in the Middle West but in the nation as well. The railroad, industrial, and financial interests of the Midwest supported the administration almost solidly, but the popular vote in every state endorsed the insurgent cause. Nothing was more indicative of the inevitable doom of the Taft administration than the failure of its attempt to purge the insurgents. Insurgents were already talking about organizing a new party if Taft was renominated; already midwestern eyes were turning to Theodore Roosevelt for leadership.

5. The Changing Fiscal Structure

No public questions were potentially more explosive and at the same time more frequently discussed after the Civil War than tariff and tax policies. A series of tariffs passed after the War of 1812 established them as the main source of federal revenue, and an elaborate system of protection was created for American manufacturing, mining, and even agriculture. Along with excise taxes and the sale of federal lands, tariff duties made up the overwhelming proportion of federal revenues, and, until the 1890s, federal budgets sometimes even ran surpluses. At the same time, throughout the post–Civil War period, much of the wealth produced by the Industrial Revolution enjoyed virtually complete immunity from taxation because there was no income tax.

The Democrats had made a fumbling effort at tariff and tax reform during the second Cleveland administration. The outcome, the Wilson–Gorman Tariff of 1894, revised duties only slightly downward and left the protective structure essentially untouched. But a coalition of western and southern Representatives forced an amendment into the tariff bill which levied a 2 percent tax on all net incomes of individuals and corporations over $4,000. The nineteenth-century fiscal system easily survived this challenge, however, both judicially and legislatively. In a strained opinion, a bare majority of the Supreme Court ruled the income tax unconstitutional in 1895. Meanwhile, the year after McKinley's decisive victory in the presidential election of 1896, the new Congress enacted a tariff that substantially increased duties on agricultural raw materials such as wool and hides, as well as on manufactured products. The upshot of this log rolling was the Dingley tariff, the highest tariff in American history up to that time. Manufacturing interests and western agricultural producers were able to forestall any attempt at general revision for twelve years after adoption of the Dingley Act. Meanwhile, conservatives kept an equally firm hand on tax policy. Congress imposed a moderate estate tax during the Spanish–American War, but it was repealed in 1902, and the federal government reverted to its usual practice of obtaining revenue almost entirely from consumption taxes. They were customs duties and excise taxes on tobacco and alcoholic beverages, levies which fell most heavily on the lower and middle classes.

Nonetheless, forces were at work to undermine political support for the nineteenth-century fiscal system in general and the high protective tariff in particular. The passage of the Dingley Act coincided with the beginning, in 1897, of a rash of industrial combinations (see pp. 7–8), lending credence to the charge often made by Bryan and other Democrats that tariff protection stimulated the growth of monopolies and supercorporations. Widespread discussion of the increasing concentration of income and wealth alarmed the middle class and fostered the conviction that only income and inheritance taxes could reverse a process that seemed to threaten the future of American democracy. Another factor behind antitariff sentiment was the cost of living, which increased by nearly one-fourth between 1897 and 1907. The average consumer saw a close relation between high prices and high tariffs, although there was often no connection between the two.

A still more important political factor was the emergence of antitariff feeling among insurgent Republicans in the GOP heartland—the Middle West. In 1901, after a hard-fought battle, Iowa Republicans nominated the reformer Albert B. Cummins for governor and wrote into their platform his proposal to remove all duties on articles manufactured by so-called trusts. Thereafter the "Iowa Idea," as Cummins's suggestion was called, became a stock feature of most midwestern state Republican platforms. Although the movement for downward revision was soon nationwide and included many small businessmen, the midwestern insurgents remained the most consistent advocates of tariff reform in the GOP.

Roosevelt recognized the potential danger of popular discontent and was often tempted to take leadership of the movement for tariff reform. He failed to do so for three reasons. First, he agreed with his Old Guard friends that such a step would disrupt the Republican party. Second, he struck a bargain in late 1904 with Cannon in which he agreed to jettison tariff revision in return for the Speaker's promise to clear the road for a railroad regulation bill. Third, and most important, Roosevelt considered the tariff a question of expediency rather than principle. However, both Roosevelt and Taft agreed in 1908 that the tariff issue could no longer be deferred, and, at their insistence, the Republican platform included a plank declaring "unequivocally" for revision. Both men by then had also endorsed graduated federal estate, gift, and income taxes.

When Taft called Congress into special session in March 1909, momentum toward reform of the fiscal system seemed to be building. An administration bill, sponsored by Sereno E. Payne of New York, chairman of the House Ways and Means Committee, included new raw materials on the tariff list but substantially reduced rates on iron and steel products, agricultural implements, sugar, and lumber. The measure also included a federal inheritance tax ranging from 1 to 5 percent. Although Democrats opposed the bill for partisan reasons, it passed the House. An altogether different fate awaited it in the Senate, where Aldrich and his Finance Committee took the Payne bill in hand and reported it in April 1909—but without the provision for an inheritance tax and with 847 amendments, the majority of which actually effected increases. Instead of lowering the Dingley rates, as the Rhode Island Senator claimed, the Aldrich bill increased the ad valorem duties from 40.21 to 41.77 percent. But Aldrich faced powerful opposition from the midwestern insurgents. They waged an open fight against the Finance Committee's amendments and joined with Democrats in substituting an income tax for the discarded inheritance tax.

Backed by strong administration support, the Aldrich bill passed in July 1909. In an important concession, Aldrich accepted a 2 percent tax on net corporate income and agreed to the passage of an income tax amendment to the Constitution. Yet the final version of the "reform" tariff bill, the Payne–Aldrich Act, constituted a significant victory for the Old Guard, for it maintained duties on hides, iron ore, and lumber, and increased duties on a number of manufactured products. The tariff debate had immediate repercussions. It demonstrated the gulf between Taft and the insurgents and enabled the Democrats, in the election of 1910, to capture the House of Representatives for the first time since 1892. After 1910, moreover, insurgent Republicans bolted party lines to join with Democrats on a number of issues. This coalition combined to pass three tariff bills, all vetoed by Taft: a farmers' free list, which removed duties from about 100 articles that the farmer bought; a wool and woolens bill; and a bill reducing duties on iron and steel products, cotton goods, and chemicals. During 1911 and 1912, the insurgent Republican–Democratic coalition extended its influence to the states, where it helped to ratify the Sixteenth, or income tax, Amendment, which Congress had submitted in 1909 and which became part of the Constitution in February 1913.

Although the tariff and other taxes on consumption still generated most of the federal government's revenues by 1913, the adoption of the income tax amendment in 1913 and the enactment of a modest income tax in the same year began truly revolutionary changes in federal fiscal policy. The unprecedented expansion of government during the First World War, and then the establishment of a welfare state during the 1930s, both depended on a shift from consumption-oriented taxation to a graduated income tax.

6. Origins of Federal Railroad Regulation

Two other issues assumed importance in national politics during the Roosevelt and Taft presidencies—railroad regulation and antitrust policy. Both railroads and corporations were familiar popular symbols of the political power of large economic units.

In the late nineteenth century, the urban, largely middle-class progressive constituency believed that that the traditional polity was not equipped to resist domination by outside economic interests. Because the disproportionate power of "big business" appeared to corrupt the polity, national reformers favored asserting the public interest by changing the nature of government itself. For two centuries of American history, both local and central government had had a very limited role in social and economic life. The basic function of government was to preserve public safety and distribute what favors the state possessed. Local, state, and national reformers together wanted to change this minimal role for governance; they wanted to make the state an active instrument of intervention to foster not just public order, but to further the common, national interest. Almost inevitably, the two most obvious manifestations of the national economic system—railroads and the newly formed supercorporations—soon became the target of this new conception of government and of its reformulation of economic policy.

Railroad regulation was not, however, new to the progressive era. During the 1870s and 1880s, a number of midwestern and southern state legislatures first attempted regulation by statute or commission, and, while some of these efforts succeeded, others failed completely. The general inability of state regulation to curtail railroad abuses soon became apparent. The Supreme Court's decision in the *Wabash* case of 1886 forbade states to regulate *interstate* rates, thus demonstrating that real regulation lay beyond state jurisdiction. By the time of the *Wabash* decision, considerable political support already existed in favor of a federal railroad policy. The Interstate Commerce Act of 1887, a response to the *Wabash* decision, represented the first attempt to establish a national regulatory policy. The act proscribed railroad practices such as pooling, discrimination, rebating*, and charging more for a short than for a long haul. But the Interstate Commerce Act also went beyond simply listing illegalities. It also required, in principle, that interstate passenger and freight rates should be reasonable and just, be levied according to published rate schedules, and be subject to the scrutiny of a new agency, the Interstate Commerce Commission (ICC).

As it turned out, during the first years of its existence, the ICC was no match for the railroads. When the agency attempted to eradicate the prevalent practice of rebating, years of adjudication were necessary to establish the commission's authority to compel testimony. Even more important in weakening the ICC was the Supreme Court, which, in a series of cases, limited the commission's coercive power and reduced it to a fact-finding, advisory body. By 1900, therefore, the whole problem of federal railroad regulation still concerned the extent of the ICC's power, and the debate that followed was over legislation to amend the Interstate Commerce Act. The Elkins Antirebate Act of 1903 was adopted, ironically enough, in response to the pleas of raiload managers themselves, many of whom saw federal intervention as a solution to the rebating evil. It had grown to such proportions that it threatened to bankrupt many of the railroads.

The framers of the Elkins Act carefully avoided giving the ICC any authority over the rate-making process, but, after considerable public agitation, Theodore

*The return by railroads of a portion of freight charges to large shippers.

Roosevelt intervened in December 1904 by recommending that the ICC be empowered, upon complaint of shippers, to fix maximum rates, subject to review by the courts. Implementing the president's wish, the House of Representatives passed the Esch–Townshend bill by a strong majority. The Old Guard Senate leaders, in a delaying action, were able to require an investigation by the Senate Commerce Committee. This committee led a far-flung campaign in support of the railroads' stand against regulation. The committee maintained that to permit a federal agency, rather than the marketplace, to set rates would result in inefficiencies and disruptions in the ability of railroads to make a profit and maintain a strong national transportation system.

Although the railroads, in retrospect, may have had the force of logic and economic facts behind them, their case did nothing to blunt the widespread, national antirailroad sentiment and public pressure for greater regulation. Roosevelt pressed his own campaign in support of regulation during the summer and fall of 1905, and, at his urging, the House passed a new measure, the Hepburn bill, in February 1906. It was less than what many advocates of regulation wanted, but it did directly address the railroad problem by empowering the ICC, on complaint by shippers, to lower rates.

In spite of all-out opposition led by Aldrich, the Senate approved the Hepburn bill in June 1906. Under Roosevelt, the new act survived largely intact, even though it was amended to grant the courts the right to review the ICC's decisions on rates. Although some reformers believed that he had compromised too much on this issue, it is clear that the president won a major victory. The Allison amendment to the act—sponsored by William B. Allison of Iowa but written by Aldrich—provided that the courts could issue interlocutory, or suspensive, injunctions against the ICC's decisions, but it also stipulated a speedy appeal process and instructed courts to consider the commission's decisions with the presumption always in its favor. In effect, judicial nullification of the Hepburn Act was rendered impossible.

The dimensions of Roosevelt's accomplishment become even clearer when we examine the Hepburn Act's general provisions. By taking ultimate control over rates out of private hands and giving it to a governmental agency, the Hepburn Act pioneered a new regulatory role for the federal government. But the act went beyond these rate-making powers. It also granted the commission wider jurisdiction over express- and sleeping-car companies, switches and spurs, and pipelines; eliminated the free-pass system; and required, after 1908, that railroads divest themselves of outside properties. The latter provision was aimed directly at the anthracite coal industry, which was controlled by nine eastern railroads.

The passage of the Hepburn Act in 1906 did not end the campaign for regulation. Although chastened, railroad managers resisted federal regulation with determination and, by 1908, had begun a deliberate policy of challenging ICC decisions and thereby crowding the circuit-court dockets. It was clear, in other words, that with a determined opposition from the railroads, the ICC, even with the extensive powers granted it by the Hepburn Act, could not control the national transportation system. Yet the railroads' policy of dogged resistance won them few friends and did little to challenge the apparent relevance of antirailroad rhetoric. Then, because of the railroads' desperate need for capital, managers effected a general rate increase in 1909.

The railroads' resistance to regulation and the general rate increase of 1909 inflamed public opinion and increased political pressures for another expansion of the ICC's powers. In the summer of 1909, the Taft administration drafted a new bill which would significantly enlarge the commission's rate-making power and—in response to the problem of crowded court dockets—would also establish a commerce court with original jurisdiction in appeals from ICC rulings. Although it greatly expanded federal regulatory powers, the bill encountered strong opposition from insurgent Republicans, who suspected Taft of prorailroad sympathies and criticized the measure because it made no provision for allowing the ICC power to make a physical valuation of railroad property as a basis for setting rates. Introduced in the House in January 1910, the administration bill—now known as the Mann bill—was virtually rewritten by the insurgent–Democratic coalition. In key amendments, it struck out the provision permitting mergers of competing lines, added arrangements for physical valuation and equality in charges for long and short hauls, and brought telephone and telegraph lines under the ICC's jurisdiction. Meanwhile, insurgents were less successful in the Senate, where Taft was able to attract Democratic support in exchange for his approval of statehood acts for New Mexico and Arizona.

Even so, the bill that emerged from the conference committee and was signed by Taft as the Mann–Elkins Act represented a victory for the regulatory reformers. In its most important provisions, the act empowered the ICC to suspend general rate increases and revise rates on its own initiative, and it created a commerce court to hear appeals against the commission's decisions. Railroads were prohibited from acquiring competing lines, and the ICC's jurisdiction was extended to the "common carriers": telephone, telegraph, cable, and wireless companies.

Only one other component was missing for full supervision of the railroads: the grant to the ICC of the power to make a physical valuation of railroad property. Such valuation, its advocates contended, would enable the commission to fix rates according to the true value of railroad property, rather than on the basis of the price of railroad stocks and bonds. The insurgent–Democratic congressional coalition won this last objective during the closing months of the Taft administration. The Physical Valuation Act of 1913 required the Interstate Commerce Commission to report the value of all property owned by every common carrier subject to its jurisdiction, including the original cost, the cost of reproduction new, and the cost of reproduction less depreciation. When completed, the act declared, such valuations were to be accepted as prima facie evidence of the worth of railroad property.

The passage of this series of laws, from the Hepburn Act in 1906 to the Physical Valuation Act of 1913, capped the steady expansion of federal regulatory power over the nation's mammoth transportation industry. Transformation of the ICC from an essentially advisory body into an agency with almost unlimited powers of intervention was possible because of an important political event: the coalescence of a national progressive coalition, composed of insurgent Republicans from the Middle West and reform-minded, generally Bryanite, Democrats. Both groups represented constituencies who placed antirailroad legislation high on their agenda of economic policy; both had concluded that the new, twentieth-century reality of large-scale economic units required regulation and equally large-scale governmental intervention. The long-run effects of this first and most important example of early federal regulatory policy are subject to considerable debate. Some critics argue that railroad regulation was actually in the interest of the lines and rarely served the public interest; others claim that regulation served political purpose but in reality destroyed the railroads' ability to raise capital and to effect the rate increases called for by market conditions. At the same time, other critics say, ICC regulation by the 1920s had promoted a general shift of resources away from railroads to the trucking industry.

Whatever the final verdict on these questions, the enlargement of the ICC's power constituted a significant step in the evolution of American politics and government. It wedded both parties to some form of regulation on a permanent basis. Indeed, after the passage of the Hepburn Act the question was not whether regulation should occur, but how much was beneficial to the American economy. The broader issue of railroad regulation involved a first, but by no means final, step away from the traditions of nineteenth-century governance, in which government served a barebones function, toward a type of governance that emphasized intervention and regulation.

7. Federal Antitrust Policy, 1890–1913

Closely connected with the rise of a national political coalition that favored railroad regulation was the growing political pressure against large industrial combinations. As was the case in the earliest forms of railroad regulation, the first attempts at restricting the power of large companies through antitrust legislation occurred at the state level. At least fourteen states and territories had written antitrust provisions into their constitutions by 1890, while thirteen others had adopted antitrust laws. Almost without exception, these were western and southern states, where a strong antimonopoly and antirailroad tradition had existed since the mid-nineteenth century.

These sporadic, uncoordinated, and generally ineffective actions by the states led to political pressures for a national antitrust policy. It was embodied in the Sherman Antitrust Act of 1890, which prohibited "every contract, combination in the form of trust or otherwise, or conspiracy, in restraint of trade or commerce among the several States, or with foreign nations." The Sherman Act also provided punishment for such misdoing and stipulated that persons injured by illegal combinations or conspiracies might sue to recover threefold damages and the cost of the suit. No statute ever enacted by Congress reflected more accurately an overwhelming popular demand. Yet the Sherman law, after several prosecutions by the Benjamin Harrison administration, fell into neglect and general contempt, mainly because attorneys general during the Grover Cleveland and McKinley administrations had little interest in further prosecutions—at least not against trusts. A case in point was *E. C. Knight* v. *United States* (1895), in which the government challenged the monopoly recently acquired by the American Sugar Refining Company of Philadelphia. Instead of vindicating the Sherman law, Cleveland's attorney general, Richard Olney, presented the government's case in such a manner that the Supreme Court thought it had to declare that the act did not apply to combinations in manufacturing. The consequences of Olney's calculated subversion were far-reaching, and the effect was to cripple the federal antitrust law.

Clearly, only vigorous presidential leadership could make the Sherman Act effective. Realizing the political popularity of the antitrust issue, Theodore Roosevelt also genuinely believed in affirmation of a common, national interest which, through the federal government, could restrain large industrial combinations from damaging the public welfare. By way of direct attack, the Justice Department under Roosevelt instituted eighteen proceedings in equity, obtained twenty-five indictments, and participated in one forfeiture proceeding. In his first prosecution—a suit to dissolve the Northern Securities Company in 1902—Roosevelt signaled his resolve to enforce the Sherman Act, and the Supreme Court later decided the case against the holding company. Later that year, Roosevelt also ordered prosecution of the Swift, Armour, and Nelson Morris companies—the so-called Beef Trust— for organizing the National Packing Company to acquire control of independent packing firms in the Middle West. Although the Supreme Court rendered a unanimous verdict against the trust in 1905, the packers continued to defy the government, and not until 1920 was competition effectively restored to the meat industry. The climax of Roosevelt's campaign came with sweeping indictments by the Justice Department of the Standard Oil Company in 1907 and of the American Tobacco Company a year later. These two cases, the most important in the history of antitrust litigation before 1945, did not reach final settlement until 1911.

In spite of this vigorous beginning, Roosevelt's antitrust program was limited and specific in its objectives. Unlike some who favored restricting the size of all corporations, Roosevelt never feared bigness in industry—unless bigness was accompanied by monopolistic control and a disposition to defy the public interest. He therefore never moved against two large combinations, United States Steel and International Harvester, because he lacked good evidence that they were monopolies or that they were illegally suppressing competition. Although the Taft administration later abandoned this distinction between "good" and "bad" trusts and instituted dissolution proceedings against these two corporations, the Supreme Court confirmed Roosevelt's judgment in both cases.

Roosevelt's aggressive program of publicity and prosecution was carried forward at an even more brisk pace by President Taft and his attorney general, George W. Wickersham. When Congress refused to enact Taft's proposal for a federal incorporation law, a corporation commission, and legislation against stock watering, Taft moved in a wholesale way against combinations. All told, he instituted forty-six proceedings for dissolution, brought forty-three indictments, and began one contempt proceeding. His two most important cases—those against United States Steel and International Harvester—ended in failure. His two most important victories, over Standard Oil and American Tobacco, were scored in proceedings that Roosevelt had initiated. The government, after five years of legal warfare, won complete victory in 1911 with the Supreme Court's order for the dissolution of the gigantic oil and tobacco monopolies. The Court implicitly repudiated the *Knight* decision and made it plain that the holding company device could not be used to evade the Sherman Act.

8. The Supreme Court and Economic Policy

In the American constitutional system, Congress proposes and the Supreme Court disposes. The phrase is of course hyperbole, but it points up a problem that frequently perplexed those who favored extending the boundaries of governmental power. Unlike their counterparts in some other countries, American reformers in state and nation were never free to develop a full system of administrative regulation. For one thing, they were bound by a written Constitution that could be construed as prohibiting regulation and interventionist governance. For another, they were restrained by the fear that a conservative Supreme Court, which insisted on having the final word, would not tolerate the extension of governmental power that they desired.

By 1900, the Supreme Court had established the right to review all *state* attempts at railroad regulation. This power the Court had assumed through one of the most important judicial revolutions in American history. It began when Roscoe Conkling, while arguing the case of *San Mateo County* v. *Southern Pacific Railroad* before the Supreme Court in 1882, asserted that the congressional committee that framed the Fourteenth Amendment had intended to confer federal citizenship upon corporations. As Conkling had been a member of the committee and produced its secret journal, the Court listened carefully to his argument, although it did not take judicial cognizance of it. In *Santa Clara County* v. *Southern Pacific Railroad* (1886) and the *Minnesota Rate* case (1889), however, the Court accepted Conkling's reasoning and declared that corporations were federal citizens, entitled to protection by the Fourteenth Amendment against state action which deprived them of property or income without due process of law. Finally, in *Smyth* v. *Ames* (1898), the Supreme Court reached the last stage in its judicial revolution. Nebraska had established maximum legal rates which railroads could charge within the state. Overturning the Nebraska statute, the Court reaffirmed the federal citizenship of corporations, declared that rates had to be high enough to guarantee a fair return to railroads, and warned state legislators that the courts existed, among other reasons, to protect property against unreasonable legislation.

In none of these cases did the Supreme Court deny the right of the states to regulate railroads and other corporations. It only insisted that state regulation be reasonable and fair and not invade the jurisdiction of Congress. Until a body of doctrine defining due process regarding state regulation had been built, however, the effect of the Court's new departure was to create a twilight zone of authority. Judges of numerous federal district courts could prevent the states from acting; and the states had no recourse but to await the verdict of the high tribunal in such cases.

Advocates of regulation charged that the courts had usurped the administrative function of the states and imposed their own notion of due process and reasonableness on state commissions. They resented even more bitterly the systematic manner in which the Supreme Court narrowed the authority of the ICC and even reduced that statute to an unenforceable platitude. In view of the absence of any specific delegation of rate-making authority to the ICC by the Interstate Commerce Act, the Court could probably not have ruled otherwise. Impatient reformers, however, found the Supreme Court a more vulnerable scapegoat than Congress.

Progressives were on more solid ground when they denounced the Court's nullification of the income tax provision of the Wilson–Gorman Tariff of 1894. By a five-to-four decision in *Pollock* v. *Farmers Loan and Trust Company* (1895), the Court reversed precedent by declaring that the income tax was in part a direct tax on land and would therefore have to be apportioned among the states according to population. It was easily the most unpopular judicial ruling since the *Dred Scott* decision of 1857. For one thing, the income tax decision effectively blocked the movement for fundamental change in tax policy until a constitutional amendment could be adopted. For another, the Court's majority had obviously made a political rather than a judicial statement. Coming as it did in the same year in which the Court upheld the conviction of Eugene V. Debs and other officials of the American Railway Union for violating the Sherman law, the income tax decision only deepened the popular conviction that the highest tribunal in the land had become the tool of railroads, corporations, and millionaires.

Popular distrust was further intensified in 1895, when the Supreme Court, in the case of *E. C. Knight*, seemingly emasculated the Sherman Act's prohibition against industrial monopoly. That the Court was actually willing to interpret the Sherman law liberally was demonstrated in a series of important antitrust cases from 1897 to 1899. In the *Trans–Missouri Freight Association* case (1897), the justices affirmed that the Sherman law applied to railroads and outlawed a pool operating south and west of the Missouri River. The Court reaffirmed this judgment in the *Joint Traffic Association* case of the following year. And in the *Addyston Pipe Company* decision (1899), the justices made it clear that the Sherman law applied also to manufacturers who combined in pools to eliminate price competition.

Thus by the turn of the century, the Supreme Court had firmly established the rule that combinations formed directly to suppress competition in the transportation and distribution of products were illegal. Promoters of industrial combinations and their lawyers, however, continued to assume on account of the *Knight* decision that manufacturing consolidations did not fall under the prohibitions of the antitrust act. This impression the Court finally and completely shattered in deciding the *Standard Oil* and *American Tobacco* cases in 1911.

The *Standard Oil* and *American Tobacco* rulings represented, in fact, a complete accommodation of legal doctrine to prevailing antitrust sentiment. But even more important was the fact that they marked the end of a long struggle within the Court itself over the basic meaning of the Sherman Act. Did that statute forbid all restraints of trade, or did it prohibit only unreasonable, that is, direct and calculated, restraints? The Supreme Court's majority had consistently ruled before 1911 that the Sherman law proscribed all restraints, reasonable and unreasonable. However, Justice Edward Douglass White had vigorously dissented in the *Trans–Missouri*

Freight Association case, declaring that the framers of the antitrust law had intended to outlaw only unreasonable restraints. He reiterated his position over the years and won converts to it. He finally won a majority to his side in the *Standard Oil* and *American Tobacco* cases and, as chief justice, he wrote the "rule of reason" into American legal doctrine. The Sherman law, he declared, prohibited only unreasonable restraints of trade. Actually, the rule of reason was the only standard by which the antitrust law could be enforced, as the Court had tacitly admitted years before. Hence the promulgation of the rule of reason represented the greatest victory thus far accomplished in the long fight to destroy monopoly in the United States.

Chapter 5

--- ->>> <<<- ---

Woodrow Wilson
and Reform, 1910–1916

American political reform came into existence on the local and state level during the 1890s and achieved a degree of national coherence and unity under the presidency of Theodore Roosevelt. After internal divisions among Republicans weakened national progressivism, however, the years from 1910 to 1916 were a time of fulfillment for American reform. In 1912, Roosevelt attempted to rally progressives of all parties under the banner of a third party, but, because Democrats now possessed a reform leader of their own in Woodrow Wilson, Roosevelt failed to attract solid reform support or to build a permanent party structure. Instead, as another consequence, Democrats captured the presidency and Congress.

But Roosevelt did more than make possible a Democratic victory in 1912. By championing an ambitious program of federal regulation, he also defined the major dilemma confronting American reformers. The progressives' divided mind partly reflected traditional partisan differences, partly the clear theoretical distinctions articulated by Roosevelt and Wilson during the campaign of 1912. Could national regeneration be achieved, as Wilson and most Democratic reformers maintained, merely by destroying special privilege and restoring "equal rights" for all classes? Or could the promise of American life be fulfilled only through an aggressive program of federal intervention and participation in economic and social affairs, as Roosevelt and others contended? This dialogue between Rooseveltian and Wilsonian reformers did not end in 1912. Rather, it continued during the first Wilson administration to shape the form and character of federal legislation.

1.   The Struggle for Party Control

Numerous warnings that Republicans faced a violent, internecine power struggle were apparent in all parts of the country during the spring and summer of 1910. The most portentous was the growing intensity of the insurgent revolt in the Middle West. After the disaster of 1910, Taft tried to make peace with midwestern Republican insurgents in order to save the GOP from disaster in 1912. But the insurgents, now determined to seize control of the party and prevent Taft's renomination, rebuffed the president's overtures and began to search for a leader of their own.

Another sign of Republican distress was the estrangement between Roosevelt and Taft, which was fully evident when the former president returned from Europe in June 1910. Partly the outgrowth of incidents like the Ballinger affair, it was also a consequence of Roosevelt's growing conviction that Taft had allowed the Old Guard to maneuver him in such a way that a revolt by insurgents was now inevitable. However, Roosevelt tried hard to heal factional divisions, and it was only after he felt rebuffed by Taft that he set out upon a speaking tour in the summer of 1910. It evoked an enthusiastic response and captapulted Roosevelt into leadership of the anti-Taft rebellion.

Republican insurgents were determined to win in 1912, and to win with their own ticket and platform. Many signs in 1910 and early 1911 pointed to Senator Robert M. La Follette of Wisconsin as their leader, especially after prominent insurgents formed the National Progressive Republican League in January 1911 to campaign for the senator's nomination. A small and dedicated group of idealists supported La Follette, but most Republican progressives preferred Roosevelt. Convinced that his party faced defeat if Taft headed the ticket, and persuaded that La Follette could never be nominated, Roosevelt at last announced his candidacy in February 1912. The ensuing struggle was bitter. In the thirteen states holding presidential primaries, Roosevelt captured 278 delegates, as compared to 48 for Taft and 36 for La Follette. But Taft controlled the southern states, had the support of Old Guard strongholds such as New York, and dominated the Republican National Committee. Consequently the Taft forces organized the national convention that met in Chicago in June, awarded themselves 235 of the crucial 254 contested delegates, and proceeded ruthlessly to renominate the president on the first ballot.

Meanwhile, over 300 Roosevelt delegates returned to Chicago in August 1912, formed the Progressive party, and nominated Roosevelt for president. Roosevelt, declaring that he felt like a bull moose, came in person and delivered his acceptance speech, "A Confession of Faith." The convention also endorsed a party platform it called a "Contract with the People." That document erected mileposts that reform-minded Americans would follow for the next fifty years. It approved a broad program of social justice reform—minimum wages and protective legislation for women, child-labor legislation, workmen's compensation, and social insurance. It also endorsed a large agenda of political reform: the initiative, referendum, and recall, the recall of state judicial decision, nomination of presidential candidates by preferential primaries, and woman suffrage. Finally, it demanded the expansion of the existing federal regulatory structure by the creation of powerful new agencies —a federal trade commission and a federal tariff commission—to regulate business and industry; the proposed agencies were to have many of the same powers as the ICC.

Meanwhile, a different, but no less important, power struggle was taking place among Democrats. Bryan's announcement soon after the elections of November 1910 that he would not be a candidate for a fourth nomination encouraged a host of new political leaders. Woodrow Wilson, a political scientist, former university president, and recently elected governor of New Jersey, quickly emerged as the frontrunner. Most of his support came from the party's progressive wing, which divined unique qualities of leadership from Wilson's ability to persuade an unwilling New Jersey legislature to pass a series of reform measures.

Wilson's apparent success made the meteoric rise of his chief rival, Champ Clark of Missouri, Speaker of the House of Representatives, all the more surprising. Clark's candidacy was a strong one for two reasons. While Wilson was an outsider and newcomer, Clark was an old-line politician who had served in the House since the 1890s. By 1912, he had amassed considerable support within the party for the nomination. He inherited most of Bryan's following in the West, made alliances with a number of eastern and southern state organizations, and won the the support of William Randolph Hearst and his chain of newspapers. Even as Wilson conducted an energetic primary campaign and won not quite one-fourth of the delegates, Clark negotiated shrewdly and harvested a crop nearly twice as large. To make matters worse for Wilson, Oscar W. Underwood of Alabama, chairman of the House Ways and Means Committee, entered the contest and won more than one hundred southern delegates who probably would otherwise have supported Wilson.

When the Democratic convention assembled in Baltimore in June 1912, nothing less than control of the federal government was at stake. The convention was a bitter affair from the beginning. The outcome of preliminary contests over organization seemed to suggest Clark's impending victory. Clark took a commanding lead in early balloting; then ninety Tammany-controlled New York delegates went to him on the tenth ballot, giving him a majority—but not the then necessary two-thirds margin. Yet the expected and seemingly inevitable Clark landslide did not materialize; in fact, Clark lost votes during the next few ballots. A long and grueling battle followed, in which Wilson's managers gradually undermined Clark's strength and finally gained a two-thirds majority for the New Jersey governor on the forty-sixth ballot.

The Democratic platform, heavily influenced by Bryan, denounced the Payne-Aldrich tariff, promised its downward revision, demanded new antitrust legislation, and favored the establishment of a decentralized banking system free of Wall Street control. It held out the hope of early independence to Filipinos. Finally, it supported the amendments for the income tax and the direct election of senators, and it favored exempting labor unions from prosecution under the Sherman law. Although it was neither as reform-oriented nor as nationalistic as the Progressive party's "Contract with the People," the Democratic platform did promise to overturn many Republican policies.

2. The Campaign of 1912

Once in every generation or so, a presidential election offers such clear alternatives that it appears, to contemporaries and historians alike, to embody its era and its conflicting ideals. Such was the case in 1800 and again in 1860. It was also the case in 1912, when the four parties and presidential candidates offered programs that well reflected existing divisions of political sentiment. Just as voters understood that Taft's reelection would mean a continuation of Old Guard leadership and policies, so, too, they realized that Eugene V. Debs, the Socialist candidate, and his party offered what was then thought to be a revolutionary program for the gradual nationalization of resources and major industries.

More important, however, was the unusual dialogue between the two political giants of their time, Theodore Roosevelt and Woodrow Wilson. Born within a year of each other, both were highly disciplined intellectuals who were also men of action. In 1912, both also considered themselves progressives, yet they reflected in their respective programs and philosophies a significant ideological divergence in national progressivism. Roosevelt's program, the New Nationalism, represented the consummation of a philosophy that had been long been maturing. In essence a paternalist, Roosevelt believed that power and decision making should be lodged at the top— among those best able and qualified to make policy. He also believed that a society needed social integration and unified purpose to survive in the global competition of nations. Like the publicist Herbert Croly, Roosevelt urged reformers to examine their basic political assumptions and to realize that the historic American democratic tradition was intensely individualistic and thus no longer adequate for an urban– industrial society. In practice, Roosevelt declared, this meant that progressives had to abandon laissez faire for democratic collectivism and be willing to use the federal government as a regulator and protector of business, industry, and workers. It meant, in brief, that progressives had to abandon their hostility to strong government and espouse instead a New Nationalism that would achieve democratic ends through nationalistic means.

In expounding this philosophy, Roosevelt advocated a policy toward corporate enterprise that was entirely opposed to the American tradition of individualism. Americans should recognize that concentration and bigness in industry were inevitable trends in modern societies. At the same time, Americans should also subject large corporations to comprehensive control through a powerful trade commission. Most American workers, especially women and children, were powerless to protect themselves; hence, stronger state and federal governmental power was essential to improve their lot—among other things, by establishing minimum wages for women, workmen's compensation, federal prohibition of child labor, and expanded public-health services.

A recent convert to progressivism, Wilson possessed no such well-constructed program. His alternative to Roosevelt's New Nationalism was instead derived from several sources. Unlike Roosevelt, he believed that the dynamism of American society came from below—from struggle and creative competition. He therefore believed that federal authority should be limited to the destruction of artificial barriers to the full development of individual energies; it should not involve the restructuring of social and economic relationships or the protection of special classes. Wilson was also steeped in the traditions of the Democratic party. He opposed large economic units in industry and transportation and was a strong supporter of antitrust measures. Acting like a traditional Democrat, Wilson began his campaign by promising to destroy the Republican system of tariff protection as a first step toward

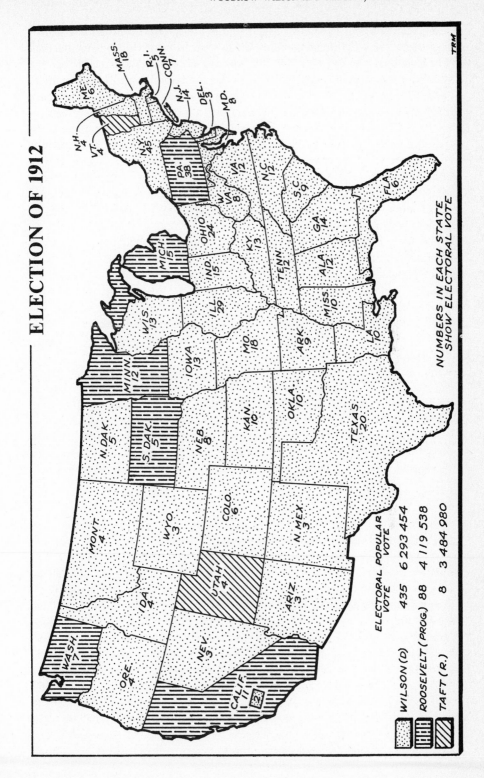

ELECTION OF 1912

NUMBERS IN EACH STATE
SHOW ELECTORAL VOTE

	ELECTORAL VOTE	POPULAR VOTE
WILSON (D)	435	6 293 454
ROOSEVELT (PROG.)	88	4 119 538
TAFT (R.)	8	3 484 980

restoring competition. When this issue failed to arouse audiences, he followed the suggestion of Louis D. Brandeis and moved to what he made the fundamental issue of the campaign—emancipation of business and labor from monopolistic control. Lashing out at Roosevelt's proposals for social legislation and control of corporations, he warned that the New Nationalism could end only with big business controlling the federal government and enslaving workers. In a program which he called the New Freedom, Wilson in contrast promised to destroy monopoly and unleash the potential energies of businessmen by restoring conditions under which competition could flourish. This he would do, specifically, by instituting tariff reform, freeing credit from Wall Street control, and strengthening the Sherman Antitrust Act so as to outlaw unfair trade practices and break up interlocking directorates. On social and economic justice, Wilson was more ambiguous, and he offered no definite program comparable to Roosevelt's.

The most striking aspect of the campaign was Roosevelt's failure to split Democratic ranks and create a solid reform coalition. The results, therefore, were obvious long before election day. Wilson polled 6.3 million popular votes; Roosevelt, 4.1 million; Taft, 3.5 million; and Debs, 897,000. Although Wilson received slightly less than 42 percent of the popular vote, his victory in the Electoral College was overwhelming because of the multiple division of popular votes. The disruption of the GOP, moreover, gave the Democrats a large majority in the House and a small but workable majority in the Senate.

The election of 1912 seemed to have demonstrated that the American people were in an overwhelmingly progressive, if not rebellious, mood. Had progressive Republicans and progressive Democrats been able to unite behind a single ticket and platform, progressivism's triumph would have been even more spectacular. As it was, the Democrats would control the federal government chiefly because of the disunion among their opponents. The future of the progressive movement in the United States would depend on Wilson's ability to bring the reform movement to fulfillment and unite the two divergent wings.

3. Woodrow Wilson and the Progressive Movement

No leader in American history before 1910 had such a meteoric rise to political prominence as Woodrow Wilson. Born in a Presbyterian manse in Staunton, Virginia, on December 29, 1856, he grew to boyhood in a South convulsed by the Civil War and Reconstruction. After graduation from Princeton University in 1879, Wilson studied law at the University of Virginia and tried unsuccessfully, in 1882 and 1883, to practice law in Atlanta. Disillusioned by the sharp practices of Atlanta lawyers, he entered the new Johns Hopkins University in Baltimore and won a doctorate in political science and history in 1886. He taught successively, from 1885 to 1902, at Bryn Mawr College, Wesleyan University, and Princeton University. He found an outlet for his political energies in lecturing and writing, and above all in analyzing the weaknesses inherent in the structure of the national government. The basic cause of the failure of leadership in the American political system, he asserted in his most famous work, *Congressional Government* (1885), lay in the separation of executive from legislative responsibility and leadership.

Wilson's election as president of Princeton University in 1902 provided him with his first opportunity to practice these principles. Visualizing himself as a prime minister, he put into operation a reorganized curriculum and a new method of undergraduate instruction—the preceptorial system of discussion in small groups. As he emerged as an educational leader of national prominence, he also became increasingly articulate as a spokesman of Democratic conservatism.

Wilson probably would not have allowed his suppressed political ambitions to revive had events continued to go well for him at Princeton. He attempted in 1906 and 1907 to reorganize the social life of undergraduates by abolishing their eating clubs and substituting quadrangles, or residential colleges, in their stead. Students and alumni were so bitterly opposed that the trustees felt compelled to withdraw their approval of the plan. This first reversal was so humiliating that Princeton's prime minister nearly resigned. But the really crushing blow, the event that made Wilson willing to embark on an uncertain political career when the opportunity arose in 1910, was his defeat in a personal controversy in 1909 and 1910 with the trustees and dean of the graduate school over the establishment and control of a graduate college.

While the graduate college controversy was at its height in the spring of 1910, George Harvey, editor of *Harper's Weekly,* persuaded the leading Democratic boss of New Jersey, James Smith, Jr., to nominate Wilson for the governorship. Wilson accepted the nomination chiefly because the situation at Princeton had become personally intolerable to him. Once in politics, however, he refused to play the role that Harvey and Smith had cut out for him. Sensing that the progressive movement in his state was at high tide, he came out squarely in favor of the reform program and, with support of insurgent Republicans, won a startling victory in November 1910. As has already been said, he seized control of the state Democratic party, pushed a comprehensive reform program through a heretofore boss-dominated legislature, and then undertook a nationwide campaign for the White House.

For the four years that followed his election to the presidency in 1912, Wilson occupied the same position with regard to national reform that Theodore Roosevelt had occupied from 1905 to 1909. Changed circumstances and personality differences, however, made Wilson's role in the movement's development considerably different from Roosevelt's. Unlike Roosevelt, Wilson had never been identified as a reformer before 1910. In Trenton, and later in Washington, he was given leadership of state and national movements ripe for fulfillment. The chief thing required of him was to act as the catalytic agent of his time—to rally and strengthen his forces, to synthesize ideas and proposals, and then to use his incomparable powers of articulation and leadership to translate these ideas into statutory realities.

Roosevelt had never really mastered the powerful and entrenched Old Guard machine in Congress. By appealing to the country he had forced Congress to act, but he never actually led the legislative branch of the government. In contrast, Wilson found a congressional situation in 1913 that afforded a unique opportunity for a strong executive. There was no established Democratic bloc in control of Congress; indeed, a large number of Democratic congressmen had been elected for the first time in 1910 and 1912. After wandering in the wilderness for twenty years, moreover, Democratic congressional leaders were determined to make good and to cooperate for the success of their program and party. As president, Wilson had the rare opportunity to be the best and most effective kind of leader in the American system—the parliamentary leader of a cooperative congressional majority. A strong believer in party government and responsibility. Wilson prepared a legislative program, personally guided legislators in drafting measures, and mediated between various factions when disputes arose over principles and details.

Wilson's first and most important contribution to reform and American government was his strengthening and extension of the power of the presidency. By his own example, he demonstrated that the president has it in his power, not only to represent the majority opinion, as Roosevelt had done, but also to destroy the wall between the executive and legislative branches. His second contribution was a more immediate one—the manner in which he used this leadership to bring the national progressive movement to legislative consummation.

From all accounts, Wilson exercised a magnetic type of leadership. Among friends and associates, he was usually warm and intimate. He was in most circumstances an excellent administrator who gave the greatest possible rein to subordinates. But he commanded loyalty by superior intelligence and by appealing to principles and moral purposes rather than by personal friendship. Wilson's leadership succeeded as long as his intelligence and eloquence survived the hazards of an increasingly demanding presidential career. Even so, his leadership was impaired by certain defects, the most striking of which was a tendency to value his own intuitive and moralistic judgments over conclusions deduced from an analysis of sometimes unpleasant facts. Moreover, he too often assumed that others were as high-minded as he; consequently, he was sometimes a poor judge of men. Finally, his strong activism and urge to achieve his own solutions sometimes prevented him from making necessary compromises.

4. The New Freedom

The first item on Wilson's legislative agenda was tariff revision, for Democratic promises would ring hollow so long as the Payne–Aldrich Act remained in force. On the day of his inauguration, March 4, 1913, Wilson called a special session of Congress and, on April 8, he went in person before the two houses. In the process, he broke the precedent established by Jefferson, asserted personal leadership in legislation, and focused national attention on Congress.

The measure that Oscar U. Underwood, chairman of the Ways and Means Committee, presented to the House on April 22, 1913, fulfilled Democratic promises of tariff reform. It was not a free-trade bill. Rather, it attempted to place American industries in a genuinely competitive position with regard to European producers. All products manufactured by so-called trusts, such as iron and steel products and agricultural machinery, were placed on the free list, while most raw material, clothing, food, shoes, and other such items were either put on the free list or given only incidental protection. The general average of the Underwood duties was about 29 percent, as contrasted with the 37 to 40 percent general level of the Payne–Aldrich Act. Finally, to compensate for the anticipated loss of revenue, the Ways and Means Committee added a provision levying a graduated but slight tax on incomes.

Although the House passed the Underwood bill by a thumping majority on May 8, the battle for tariff reform had only begun. By insisting on duty-free sugar and wool, the bill had antagonized Democratic senators from Louisiana, Montana, and Colorado, states which produced these raw materials—and a change of three Democratic votes in the upper house could convert a Democratic majority into a minority. Responding to a dangerous situation, Wilson took unusual measures. He first applied heavy personal and political pressure on wavering Democrats; then, on May 26, he issued a statement to the country denouncing the swarms of lobbyists who, he said, infested Washington and were hard at work to defeat tariff reform.

In response to Wilson's indictment of the lobbyists, La Follette and other progressives in the Senate instituted a searching inquiry into lobbying and compelled senators to reveal personal property holdings that might be affected by tariff legislation. Subjected to such penetrating publicity, the opposition of Democratic senators, except for the two Louisianians, vanished, thus clearing the way for the bill's passage. In fact, by putting food and other farm products on the free list, the Senate Finance Committee, headed by Furnifold M. Simmons of North Carolina, actually reduced the Underwood rates by 4 percent. At the same time, a threatened rebellion of progressive senators of both parties forced the Finance Committee to raise levies on incomes from a maximum of 4 percent to a maximum of 7 percent. The Senate approved the tariff bill on September 9, 1913; the House conferees accepted the Senate amendments; and Wilson signed the revised Underwood–Simmons bill on October 3.

Fortunately for Wilson, he emerged from this first and crucial test stronger than before. As he signed the Underwood–Simmons Act, a controversy was raging which had been provoked by his attempt to reorganize the national banking and currency systems. There had long existed a consensus for changing these systems, which had performed badly in the financial crisis of 1907. In its aftermath, Roosevelt had appointed a commission headed by Nelson W. Aldrich to study banking reform. Aldrich's group recommended the establishment of a large central bank, with branches, under the control of private banks. But different political groups demanded different kinds of legislation. The banking community and conservative Republicans almost unanimously supported the Aldrich commission's plan. The Democrats, however, condemned it in their platform in 1912, but they were divided about alternatives. The party's Bryanite wing demanded a reserve system and currency supply owned and controlled by the government. They pointed to the revelations of the Pujo Committee, which investigated the so-called Money Trust in early 1913, to prove that only decisive public control could destroy the existing concentration of credit resources in Wall Street. On the other hand, conservative Democrats, fearful of Bryan's monetary heresies, proposed a decentralized reserve system, free from Wall Street domination, but owned and controlled by private interests.

Amid such confusion Wilson tried to steer a middle course and develop a consensus. He commissioned Carter Glass of Virginia, chairman of the House Banking Committee, to prepare a preliminary bill. A leader of the conservative Democratic faction, Glass drafted a measure that would have established a system consisting of as many as twenty reserve banks, under private control and without central direction. At Wilson's insistence, Glass added a provision for a central governing board, on which bankers would have minority representation, to coordinate the far-flung system.

The publication of the original Glass bill set off a controversy in administration circles that threatened for a time to disrupt the Democratic party. Secretary of State Bryan, Secretary of the Treasury William G. McAdoo, and Robert L. Owen, chairman of the Senate Banking Committee, led progressive Democrats in demanding public ownership and control of the reserve and currency system. Agrarian spokesmen in the House opposed the Glass bill for different reasons–because it would neither destroy the Money Trust nor furnish credit to farmers. Confronted by a seemingly impossible situation, Wilson decided that bankers should be denied representation on the proposed Federal Reserve Board and that Federal Reserve currency should be the obligation of the United States. At Bryan's urging, he permitted the agrarian faction to amend the Glass bill to provide short-term credit facilities for farmers. On the other hand, private banking interests would own and largely control the Federal Reserve banks and have a voice in an advisory commission that would counsel the Federal Reserve Board. Under Wilson's mediation, progressive, agrarian, and conservative Democratic factions joined in an acceptable compromise. And, despite the vigorous opposition of banking interests, the Glass bill passed the House in September. After some revision, the Senate passed it on December 19, and Wilson signed it four days later.

The Federal Reserve Act established twelve Federal Reserve banks owned by member banks and controlled by boards of directors, the majority of whom were chosen by member banks. As the central banks of their various districts, reserve banks held a portion of member banks' reserves and performed other central banking functions. The act also created a new currency, Federal Reserve notes, issued by the reserve banks to member banks against collateral consisting of commercial and agricultural paper and a 40 percent gold reserve. This Federal Reserve currency was flexible, that is, it would expand or contract in volume in direct relation to the needs of the business community. Uniting and controlling the entire system in a limited fashion was a Federal Reserve Board of seven members, appointed for long terms by the president with the consent of the Senate.

It was the great merit of the Federal Reserve Act that it provided the means to mobilize the major part of the banking reserves of a region, indeed of the entire country. It also created a new and flexible, yet absolutely sound, currency; effectively destroyed the concentration of credit resources in a few financial centers; and reinforced private control on the local level, tempered by a degree of public supervision and national coordination. Some reformers like La Follette denounced the Federal Reserve Act because it did not provide for comprehensive federal control or ownership and operation of the national banking system. Yet the framers of the measure never intended to implement such far-reaching policy. In the spirit of

Wilson's New Freedom, they conceived of a system in which private and public interests would work harmoniously, reconciled by the Federal Reserve Board.

5. The Turning Point in Wilsonian Progressivism

The Federal Reserve Act marked the high tide of the New Freedom. Throughout 1913 and early 1914, Wilson remained committed to limited reform and was determined not to involve the federal government in advanced welfare programs. Not all of his supporters in Congress and elsewhere agreed with him, however, for many agrarian, labor, and social justice reformers held a different conception of the proper role of the federal government. Like Theodore Roosevelt, they championed measures that would use federal authority to benefit underprivileged special classes. Wilson invoked New Freedom concepts to thwart these demands.

Wilson was so strong a defender of New Freedom principles that he obstructed or refused to encourage a large part of the reform program. He thus blocked the AFL's campaign to obtain immunity for labor unions from the application of antitrust law to their strike activities (see p. 94). Using the same rationale, Wilson in the spring of 1914 successfully opposed a bill establishing a system of long-term rural credits financed and operated by the federal government. When the National Child Labor Committee's child-labor bill passed the House in the same year, he refused to fight for its approval by the Senate because he considered it unconstitutional. And he refused to support a woman-suffrage amendment because he thought suffrage qualifications should be determined by the states.

Three other examples illustrate Wilson's ambiguous position on national reform. The first was his momentary obstruction of the movement to reduce the number of immigrants coming to American shores. Restriction, or outright exclusion, of immigration had long been an objective of the AFL, many sociologists, and social workers. The instrument supported by these groups, the literacy test, was embodied in the Burnett immigration bill that passed Congress on January 2, 1915. Wilson vetoed the measure, and his veto held then. But two years later, in January 1917, Congress overrode his veto of a similar bill.

The second example, perhaps the most revealing of all, concerns Wilson's position on race relations. By 1915, Wilson had gained a partly deserved reputation as the person responsible for instituting a national policy inimical to black rights. Soon after taking office in 1913, he permitted his secretary of the treasury and his postmaster general to segregate certain black and white workers in their departments. After provoking a storm of protest from northern blacks and northern whites, after considerable unfavorable national publicity, and after several meetings with the Boston black militant William Monroe Trotter, the administration went no further in segregating the federal government after late 1914. But the damage, at least as far as civil-rights advocates were concerned, had already been done, and an incident in 1915 did little to improve Wilson's reputation. David W. Griffith in that year released *The Birth of a Nation,* the first great spectacular in American film history. An adaptation of Thomas Dixon's novel *The Clansman,* it was also a celebration of a southern, white-supremacist view of American history, and it portrayed blacks in derogatory stereotypes. When Dixon tricked Wilson into permitting a private showing of *The Birth of a Nation* at the White House, Wilson won no friends among advocates of social justice for blacks. Ironically, Wilson later wrote that he had always regarded *The Birth of a Nation* as "a most unfortunate production."

Although it seemed by late 1914 that Wilson's commitment to reform had reached its limits, his attitudes toward it were undergoing a steady evolution. The first important movement occurred in the early months of 1914, as Wilson and congressional leaders set about to prepare antitrust legislation. Advanced progressives demanded establishment of an independent trade commission empowered with a kind of freewheeling authority to oversee business activities and suppress unfair trade practices. Yet Wilson insisted upon a solution consistent with the New Freedom doctrine of limited intervention. His original antitrust program was embodied in two measures, the Clayton bill and the Covington interstate trade commission bill. The former enumerated and prohibited a series of unfair trade practices, outlawed interlocking directorates, and allowed private parties to obtain damages in antitrust suits won by the government. The Covington bill created an interstate trade commission to supplant the Bureau of Corporations. The new commission would exert no independent regulatory authority but, as the Bureau of Corporations had done, would act merely as a fact-finding agency for the executive and legislative branches.

The confusing dissent that greeted the administration's bills was so great that it seemed that there might be no legislation at all. The AFL opposed the Clayton bill because it failed to provide immunity from antitrust prosecution for labor unions. Reformers in both parties denounced it as futile, because the measure attempted to enumerate every conceivable restraint of trade. Because it made no attempt to destroy large-scale enterprise in finance and industry outright, agrarian radicals from the South and West claimed that the Clayton bill betrayed Democratic electoral promises. Wilson's informal adviser, Louis D. Brandeis, then came forward in April 1914 with a plan designed to satisfy the diverse components of the Democratic coalition. It involved the virtual abandonment of the provisions in the Clayton bill that tried to prohibit unfair trade practices by the statutory method. Brandeis proposed instead to outlaw unfair trade practices in general and then to establish a federal trade commission endowed with enough authority to suppress restraints of trade whenever they occurred. Brandeis's solution had been embodied in a trade commission bill introduced earlier by Representative Raymond B. Stevens of New Hampshire.

Although Brandeis's proposal envisioned at least something like the kind of business regulation advocated by Roosevelt and at least implicitly condemned by Wilson in 1912, it seemed to be the only practical answer to an otherwise insoluble problem. Thus Wilson at once made the Stevens bill the cornerstone of his new antitrust policy, and administration leaders in Congress sidetracked the Covington bill and pressed the Stevens measure instead. His faith in the efficacy of a strong commission complete, Wilson now acquiesced in and presided over the weakening of the rigorous provisions of the Clayton bill; he signed the measure on October 15, 1914. Meanwhile, the president had bent all his energies toward obtaining congressional approval of the Stevens trade commission bill. After a hard battle he won a decisive victory, because the Federal Trade Commission Act that he approved on September 26 committed the federal government to a policy of vigorous regulation of all business activities. In sweeping terms, it outlawed—but did not attempt to define—unfair trade practices. Moreover, it established a Federal Trade Commission to supersede the Bureau of Corporations. The new commission was armed with authority to move swiftly and directly against corporations accused of suppressing competition—first by issuing cease-and-desist orders and then, if that failed, by bringing the accused corporations to trial.

Wilson similarly turned to Rooseveltian solutions of antitrust issues. Rejecting agrarian radical demands for a relentless campaign against bigness per se, Wilson and his attorneys general instead continued the Roosevelt–Taft policy of moving only against combinations that seemed obviously to have been made in restraint of trade. For example, they continued Taft's case against United States Steel, in spite of that corporation's offer to settle out of court. What was new in the antitrust story under Wilson was the eagerness of officials of several important combinations to accept government-dictated reorganizations in order to avoid prosecution. The American Telephone & Telegraph Company, the New Haven Railroad, and the Southern Pacific Railroad, among others, accepted consent decrees proposed by the Justice Department in 1913 and 1914. The Federal Trade Commission was hampered at first by incompetence and internal dissension. It had little to do during the period of American belligerence, 1917–1918, since antitrust prosecutions were then generally suspended. But it finally came to life under new leadership in 1919–1920 in a victorious campaign to destroy the old Beef Trust.

Wilson's acceptance of the Federal Trade Commission bill during the congressional discussions of 1914 was also an important turning point in the history of national progressivism. It was the first important sign that he might be willing to abandon his doctrinaire New Freedom concepts and surrender to rising demands of the progressive coalition for bold social and economic legislation in other fields. Any such surrender, however, would have to come in the future, for adoption of the Clayton and Federal Trade Commission acts in the autumn of 1914 seemed to signal the completion of the president's reform program. In a public letter to Secretary McAdoo on November 17, 1914, Wilson asserted that the legislation of the past eighteen months had destroyed the Republican system of special privilege and ended the antagonism between business and the public. The future, he added, would be a time in which businessmen would adapt themselves to changed conditions and the nation would enter a new era "of cooperation, of new understanding, of common purpose." In brief, the active phase of national reform was now over.

6. The Triumph of New Nationalism

As it turned out, Wilson's forecast of future political developments was somewhat naive. By the time that the president wrote his letter to McAdoo, the Progressive party had virtually disappeared in the congressional elections of November 1914. The outbreak of war in Europe a few months earlier had diverted American attention from the campaign and evoked a general disposition to stand by Wilson. Even so, the Democratic majority in the House was reduced from seventy-three to twenty-five, and Republicans swept back into power in such key states as New York, Pennsylvania, Illinois, and New Jersey. Indeed, a general Republican victory in 1916 seemed probable.

It was obvious by January 1916 that Theodore Roosevelt would abandon his third party and rejoin the GOP to drive the Democrats from power—which he could probably do if he succeeded in bringing most Progressives back into the Republican fold. By the beginning of 1916, therefore, Wilson faced an urgent political necessity: to find some means of attracting at least a large minority of former Progressives and thereby converting a normal Democratic minority into a majority in the forthcoming presidential election. To execute this strategy, however, Wilson and the Democrats had to discard two long-standing party positions—limited government and state rights—and convince still suspicious Progressives that they offered the best hope of genuine economic and social reform.

This crucial political transition required the abandonment of much of the ideological foundation of the New Freedom, as well as two generations of Democratic dogma. Not shrinking from the task, Wilson shifted ground quickly and easily. Political expediency—the need to win a second term as the candidate of a minority party—was important, but it is probably also accurate to say that changed convictions, growing out of his own experience during the past two years, were as much responsible for Wilson's shift. Beginning in January 1916, he embarked upon a new course of action; and because his new departure seemed to offer the only hope of maintaining their power, most Democrats in Congress followed him.

The first sign of this metamorphosis was Wilson's nomination of Louis D. Brandeis to the Supreme Court in January 1916. Reformers in both parties were delighted, for Brandeis was one of the country's leading exponents of social and economic reform. Wilson called the sponsors of the controversial rural credits bill to the White House shortly thereafter and told them that he would support their measure. He was as good as his word, and the Federal Farm Loan Act passed Congress in May. A few months later, after the presidential campaign had begun, spokesmen of the social-justice forces informed Wilson that they regarded the pending child-labor and federal workmen's compensation bills as the acid tests of his commitment to reform. Wilson had said not a word up to this point in advocacy of these measures. Now he applied heavy pressure on Democratic leaders in the Senate and obtained passage of these two bills in August.

The extent of Wilson's commitment to advanced progressivism can best be understood when we perceive the long-run significance of the Child Labor Act of 1916. By this measure, Congress for the first time used its power over interstate commerce in an important way to control conditions under which employers might operate their industries. Did this signify the beginning of a new and enlarged federal regulation under the commerce clause, as the NAM spokesman declared, "of any commodity produced in whole or in part by the labor of men or women who work more than eight hours, receive less than a minimum wage, or have not certain educational qualifications"? Progressives hoped and conservatives feared that it did. In any event, it seemed that a constitutional way had been found to extend federal control over all phases of the manufacturing process.

Nor did the foregoing measures alone represent the full extent of Wilson's espousal of the program embodied in the Progressive platform of 1912. Echoing a proposal that Roosevelt had made in 1912, Wilson in 1916 sponsored and obtained passage of a bill to establish an independent tariff commission, allegedly to remove the tariff issue from politics. Moreover, in language that Roosevelt might have used, Wilson publicly reversed historic Democratic policy and approved the principle of selective protection for certain infant industries. He supported and won passage of a series of measures launching the federal government on a new program of aid to the states for education and highway construction. Finally, he sponsored—but did not obtain adoption until January 1918—of the Webb–Pomerene bill to permit American manufacturers to combine for the purpose of carrying on export trade.

Thus it was that political necessity and changed political convictions compelled a president and party who had taken office in 1913 for the purpose of effectuating a limited reform program to sponsor and enact the most far-reaching and significant economic and social legislation in American history before 1933. Looking back in 1916 on the development of the progressive movement since 1912, observers might well have been puzzled by the extensive changes that had taken place. On the one hand, Wilson and his party had effectively abandoned the New Freedom, and the president could portray Democrats as the party of reform, indeed as "Progressive." Meanwhile, Theodore Roosevelt, the great advocate of the New Nationalism in 1912, had by 1916 abandoned his platform to the Democrats and was striving to defeat the party that had carried out his proposals.

7. The Campaign of 1916

Not since 1910 had the American political scene seemed so confused as during the early months of 1916. Wilson's policy toward the European war (see pp. 118–123) had nearly disrupted the Democratic party. On the other hand, Republicans were even more divided than their opponents on foreign-policy issues and, by the spring of 1916, Democrats had closed ranks behind Wilson. The key to the future was the alignment of former Progressives—whether they would follow Roosevelt back into the Republican party or would be won to the Democratic party by Wilson's espousal of advanced progressive measures.

The chief task before the Republicans was to find a candidate and write a platform that would hold the East without alienating the progressive, antiwar Midwest and West. At the Republican National Convention that opened in Chicago in June 1916, the party managers rejected Roosevelt, who had made a hard fight for the nomination, and chose instead Charles Evans Hughes, former governor of New York and now an associate justice of the Supreme Court. Meanwhile, the Democrats assembled a week later in St. Louis. They dutifully approved the platform prepared by Wilson and his advisers. It promised a program of advanced social legislation and endorsed a neutral foreign policy. On June 15, the delegates cheerfully renominated Wilson.

The campaign that followed was full of strange surprises, but soon a clear pattern of issues emerged. Hughes tried to avoid a straightforward discussion of American neutrality in the First World War and was unable to attack the Democratic reforms of the past three years without seeming reactionary. He finally concentrated his main fire on Wilson's Mexican policy (see pp. 116–118) and alleged Democratic ineffi- ciency. Everywhere that he spoke, he made votes for Wilson by his petty criticisms and failure to offer any constructive alternatives.

Because of a threatened railroad strike, Wilson was unable to enter the campaign until September. He averted the strike by forcing through Congress the Adamson Act, which established the eight-hour day as the standard for all interstate railroad workers. Once this crisis had passed, Wilson, on September 23, began a series of speeches that left Republicans dazed. Hughes, thinking that he had finally discov- ered an issue, denounced the Adamson Act as a craven surrender to the railroad workers. Wilson replied that the eight-hour day was the goal for which all workers should strive. Hughes denounced the Democrats for lacking a constructive program. Wilson replied by pointing to the most sweeping reform program in the history of the country.

Hughes's straddling and Wilson's bold defense of progressivism caused such a division on domestic issues as the country had not seen since 1896. The left wing of the progressive movement, including many Socialists, single taxers, sociologists, social workers, and intellectuals and their journals, moved en masse into the Wilson ranks. Most of the leaders of the Progressive party repudiated Roosevelt and came out for Wilson. The railroad brotherhoods, the AFL, and several powerful farm organizations worked hard for the Democratic ticket. Finally, virtually all important independent newspapers and magazines came to Wilson's support. Thus a new political coalition which included practically all independent progressives came into being during the campaign of 1916 as a result of Wilson's and the Democratic party's straightforward espousal of reform legislation.

To interpret this campaign solely in terms of domestic issues, however, would be to miss its chief development: the fusion of progressivism with the peace cause. Unhesitatingly, Wilson took command of the peace issue. He charged that the Republicans were a war party and that Hughes's election would mean almost certain war with Germany and Mexico. By implication he promised to keep the country out of war. So overwhelming was the response in the Midwest to the peace appeal that the Democratic orators took up the battle cry. "He kept us out of war" became a constant refrain of Democratic campaign speeches and the chief theme of Demo- cratic campaign literature.

Early returns on election night revealed that Hughes had made nearly a clean sweep of the East and the eastern Middle West. But the tide turned suddenly in Wilson's favor as returns from the trans-Mississippi West came in. To the core of the Solid South, Wilson added New Hampshire, Ohio, Kansas, Nebraska, North Dakota, Montana, Wyoming, Colorado, New Mexico, Arizona, Utah, Nevada, Idaho, Washington, and California—for a total of 277 electoral votes and a majority of 23. He received 9.1 million popular votes, as against 8.5 million for Hughes. It was a gain for Wilson of nearly 3 million popular votes over the vote that he had received in 1912.

The causes of Wilson's victory became apparent soon after the returns were

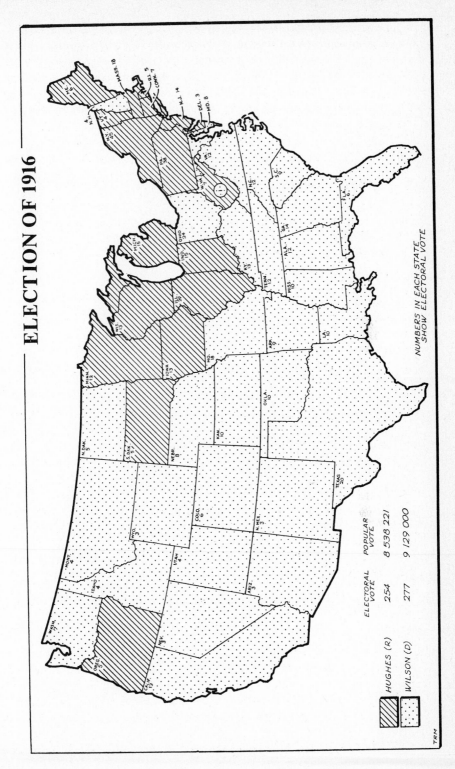

ELECTION OF 1916

NUMBERS IN EACH STATE
SHOW ELECTORAL VOTE

	ELECTORAL VOTE	POPULAR VOTE
HUGHES (R)	254	8 538 221
WILSON (D)	277	9 129 000

TRM

counted. Democratic promises of continued peace, prosperity, and progressive policies won most independents, a large minority of former Progressives, women voters
in the suffrage states, and some Socialist voters. The defection to Wilson of some
400,000 persons who had voted Socialist in 1912 was alone sufficient to give the
president a majority in key states like California. These advanced progressives, when
added to the normal Democratic minority, gave Wilson a bare majority and enabled
the Democrats narrowly to control Congress for another two years.

Chapter 6

—————— ⋙ ⋘ ——————

The Perils of
World Leadership, 1898–1917

Between the end of the Napoleonic Wars in 1815 and the outbreak of the Spanish–
American War in 1898, the American people enjoyed a large degree of freedom
from the concerns of the outside world. Yet powerful forces were at work to draw
the United States into active participation—for the first time in American history—in
world affairs. The American economy was moving toward world dominance, and the
nation's government could not ignore the increasing interdependence of the world
economy. The strategic economic position of the United States would also make it
hard to avoid involvement in any future European war. Technological advances were
drawing the world closer and diminishing the military importance of America's
oceanic defensive barriers. In sum, for both strategic and economic reasons, the
United States would find isolation from developments in Europe, Asia, and Latin
America increasingly difficult.

1. Imperialism and the Conquest of the Philippines

When the Spanish–American War officially ended with the Treaty of Paris in
December 1898, the United States acquired a formal, overseas empire extending
from the Caribbean far into the Pacific. Although Americans always considered
themselves anti-imperialistic people, imperialism came easy. Throughout the nineteenth century, a chorus of voices clamored for a "manifest destiny" which demanded that much of the western hemisphere come under American suzerainty.
Americans, penetrating native societies through the twin invasions of Protestant
missionaries and traders, had been deeply involved in the Hawaiian Islands and
China since the middle of the nineteenth century. Not least important, the acquisition of empire abroad was also consistent with the triumph of racism at home.

When the Senate approved the Treaty of Paris in 1899 and when McKinley won
a landslide victory over Bryan a year later, the United States embarked on its first

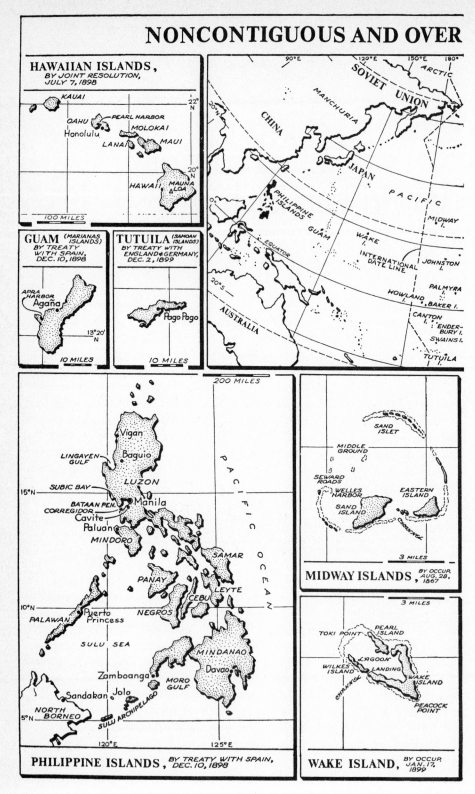

NONCONTIGUOUS AND OVER

HAWAIIAN ISLANDS, BY JOINT RESOLUTION, JULY 7, 1898

KAUAI
OAHU — PEARL HARBOR
Honolulu — MOLOKAI
LANAI — MAUI
HAWAII — MAUNA LOA
22° N
20° N
100 MILES

GUAM (MARIANAS ISLANDS) BY TREATY WITH SPAIN, DEC. 10, 1898

APRA HARBOR
Agaña
13° 20'
10 MILES

TUTUILA (SAMOAN ISLANDS) BY TREATY WITH ENGLAND & GERMANY, DEC. 2, 1899

Pago Pago
10 MILES

90°E 120°E 150°E 180°
SOVIET UNION
ARCTIC
CHINA
MANCHURIA
JAPAN
PACIFIC
PHILIPPINE ISLANDS
GUAM
WAKE
MIDWAY
INTERNATIONAL DATE LINE
JOHNSTON
EQUATOR
HOWLAND
BAKER I.
PALMYRA
CANTON
ENDERBURY I.
SWAINS I.
AUSTRALIA
TUTUILA
20°S

200 MILES
Vigan
LINGAYEN GULF
Baguio
SUBIC BAY
LUZON
BATAAN PEN.
CORREGIDOR
Manila
Cavite
Paluan
MINDORO
SAMAR
PANAY
LEYTE
CEBU
NEGROS
PALAWAN
Puerto Princess
SULU SEA
MINDANAO
Davao
Zamboanga
MORO GULF
Sandakan
Jolo
NORTH BORNEO
SULU ARCHIPELAGO
15°N
10°N
5°N
120°E
125°E
PACIFIC OCEAN

PHILIPPINE ISLANDS, BY TREATY WITH SPAIN, DEC. 10, 1898

SAND ISLET
MIDDLE GROUND
SEWARD ROADS
WELLES HARBOR
SAND ISLAND
EASTERN ISLAND
CHANNEL
3 MILES

MIDWAY ISLANDS, BY OCCUP. AUG. 28, 1867

3 MILES
TOKI POINT
PEARL ISLAND
LAGOON
WILKES ISLAND
LANDING
WAKE ISLAND
CHANNEL
PEACOCK POINT

WAKE ISLAND, BY OCCUP. JAN. 17, 1899

102

SEAS EXPANSION, 1867-1914

150°W 120°W 90°W 60°W
OCEAN
ARCTIC CIRCLE
CANADA
ALASKA
UNITED STATES
OCEAN
MEXICO
PUERTO RICO
PANAMA CANAL ZONE
EQUATOR
HAWAIIAN ISLANDS
CHRISTMAS I.
JARVIS I.

BAKER, CANTON, CHRISTMAS, ENDERBURY,
HOWLAND, JARVIS, JOHNSTON, PALMYRA,
AND SWAINS ISLANDS CLAIMED UNDER
GUANO ACT OF AUGUST 18, 1856 AND
LATER ACTS OF CONGRESS.

2000 MILES   TRM

PANAMA CANAL ZONE,
BY TREATY WITH PANAMA, NOV. 18, 1903

10 MILES
ATLANTIC OCEAN
Colon
GATUN DAM
GATUN LAKE
PANAMA
CANAL
Balboa
Panama
PANAMA
PACIFIC OCEAN
9°N

PUERTO RICO AND VIRGIN ISLANDS,
PUERTO RICO BY TREATY
WITH SPAIN, DEC. 10, 1898
VIRGIN ISLANDS BY TREATY
WITH DENMARK, AUG. 4, 1916

San Juan
ST. THOMAS
CULEBRA
ST. JOHN
Ponce
VIEQUES
18°N
ST. CROIX
100 MILES

WRANGEL I.
ARCTIC OCEAN
Barrow
PT. BARROW
ARCTIC CIRCLE
COLVILLE
BROOKS RANGE
MACKENZIE R.
CHUKOTSKI PEN.
Ft. Yukon
BERING STRAIT
YUKON R.
Dawson
Klondike
SEWARD PEN.
Fairbanks
Nome
NORTON SOUND
YUKON R.
Whitehorse
ST. LAWRENCE I.
ALASKA RANGE
MT. McKINLEY 20300
St. Michael
MT. LOGAN 19850
Skagway
ST. MATTHEW I.
Bethel
Anchorage
Juneau
NUNIVAK I.
Seward
Yakutat
Sitka
Ketchikan
SEA
Naknek
GULF OF ALASKA
PRIBILOF IS.
BRISTOL BAY
Kodiak
KODIAK I.
QUEEN CHARLOTTE IS.
ALASKA PEN.
UNIMAK I.
OCEAN
UNALASKA I.
UMNAK I.
Dutch Harbor
PACIFIC
ALEUTIAN IS.
165°W
150°W
400 MILES

ALASKA, BY TREATY WITH RUSSIA, MARCH 30, 1867

103

experiment in imperialism. Yet it soon became apparent that it was easier to acquire a colonial empire than to govern it. In the Philippines, an insurrection had been in progress against the Spanish rulers since 1896, and, when Admiral George Dewey won his stunning victory at Manila Bay in 1898, a well-organized Philippine resistance force under Emilio Aguinaldo already existed. Aguinaldo had been aided by Dewey—transported, in fact, from Hong Kong to Luzon—and believed that the American government would help create a Philippine Republic. In June 1898, Aguinaldo therefore issued a declaration of independence based on the American declaration of 1776.

The Philippine desire for independence, however, soon clashed with a formidable obstacle—strong political pressures in the United States to make the Philippines an American colony. By December 1898, American intentions were becoming clear. The presence of Americans in the Philippines, wrote McKinley in a presidential proclamation of December 21, 1898, was permanent; its main purpose was "benevolent assimilation"—"substituting the mild sway of justice and right for arbitrary rule." Acting on the basis of McKinley's proclamation, General Elmwell S. Otis, the American military commander in the Philippines, pressed Aguinaldo to disband his military force, provoking a confrontation in February 1899. This ignited a full-scale war of conquest. To many Filipinos, fighting one of the earliest nationalist guerilla "wars of liberation," the issue soon became one of independence versus foreign domination. So stubborn did Philippine resistance become that McKinley eventually had to send some 70,000 troops to the islands, and his military commanders soon were waging ugly counterinsurgent warfare against civilians and soldiers alike. Even after Aguinaldo was captured in March 1901, pockets of resistance remained, and the war dragged on for the next two years.

The American conquest was achieved, indeed, only at considerable cost. It required a type of antiguerilla warfare—conducted by veterans of the American Indian wars, who frequently had little regard for "savage" lives—which caused heavy losses: over 15,000 Filipinos and about 4,200 Americans dead on the battlefield, along with a much larger number of civilians—probably in the hundreds of thousands—who died either directly or indirectly as a result of the war. The Philippine war also took place in spite of mounting public opposition to it and to imperialism in general in the United States. Anti-imperialists organized an Anti-Imperialist League in 1898 which drew a diverse membership, including such different political types as William Jennings Bryan, Massachusetts Senator George F. Hoar, and "Pitchfork" Ben Tillman of South Carolina as its leaders. Opposing annexation and the acquisition of empire, they had begun to organize public criticism of the Philippine war by 1900.

McKinley, and then Roosevelt, thus needed to legitimize the American presence in the Philippines and to shape an imperial policy acceptable to domestic opinion. A civilian administration, headed by William Howard Taft as civil governor, supplanted military rule in July 1901. A year later, Congress passed an Organic Act for the Philippines and established a government for the islands that survived until 1916. While the act reflected the conviction that the Filipinos were not yet ready for autonomy, it also bespoke an intention to give them the opportunity to learn the difficult ways of American democracy.

The results of able administration, generous appropriations by Congress, and the determination of American leaders to lay a solid foundation for self-government were evident by 1913. By then, Filipinos constituted four out of the nine members of the commission governing the islands, 71 percent of the classified employees in the civil service, 92 percent of the teachers, and all governors of the Christian provinces. In addition, the Phillipine government had established a strong system of schools and other public services, dispensed impartial justice, and carried out land reform.

In spite of the apparent successes of "benevolent assimilation," the Democrats continued to support Philippine independence during every presidential campaign after 1900. Woodrow Wilson was elected President in 1912 on a platform that reiterated this position, and the new Organic Act for the Philippines that Congress passed on August 29, 1916, also known as the Jones Act, granted the islands virtual dominion status.

2. The United States and Caribbean Supremacy

Another strategic legacy of the Spanish–American War was the extension of American power and interests into the Caribbean. The United States in 1898 gained control of a colony—Puerto Rico—without resistance from the inhabitants. In Cuba, now also under American domination, the United States faced a troublesome situation in some ways similar to that in the Philippines. Long coveted for its economic and strategic value, Cuba was the scene of increasing American investment during the 1890s. In the same decade, however, a nationalist revolt against Spain attracted widespread support across the island.

Once in military control of the island, McKinley and Secretary of War Root were determined to establish a permanent American presence by making Cuba an American protectorate. The Platt Amendment to the army appropriations bill of 1901 spelled out this relationship by providing for American naval bases in Cuba and by authorizing the United States to intervene in Cuba to maintain orderly government. Agreeing to the Platt Amendment under duress, the Cubans incorporated it into their constitution in 1902 and signed a treaty with the United States in 1903 which embodied its provisions. This left a dangerous legacy as a justification for further intervention and as a humiliating reminder of Yankee arrogance. Invoking the Platt Amendment, Roosevelt sent troops to Cuba in 1906, where they remained three years. The State Department thereafter intervened frequently on a diplomatic level, and American troops were briefly sent into the republic to preserve order in 1911 and 1917.

Another product of the same ideological, strategic, and economic factors that motivated the United States to expand its influence in the Caribbean was the building of an isthmian canal. Once the canal was built, moreover, its defense through absolute naval supremacy in the Caribbean became a cardinal feature of American foreign policy. After the British withdrew the larger units of their West Indian squadron in 1904–1905, the United States was in fact the dominant power in the region. A diplomatic obstacle, however, blocked what had become a widespread national objective by 1900. Under the terms of the Clayton–Bulwer Treaty of 1850, the United States and Great Britain had each agreed not to build a canal without the other's participation. Eager to placate the Americans, the British relinquished their construction rights in the first Hay–Pauncefote Treaty, negotiated at Washington in 1900, in exchange for American agreement never to fortify the canal. When the Senate, in 1901, refused to approve the treaty without an amendment providing for fortification, the British then conceded that right in the second Hay–Pauncefote Treaty.

A more troublesome problem was finding a route through a cooperative host country. Although Roosevelt, Congress, and a presidential commission all favored a Nicaraguan route, a French company—the New Panama Canal company—offered to sell its rights and abandoned property in Panama to the United States at the bargain price of $40 million. Congress then approved the Panamanian route, but the problem remained of securing the approval of Colombia to whom the Isthmus of Panama belonged. After long negotiations, Secretary of State John Hay concluded a treaty with the Colombian chargé, Tomás Herrán, in January 1903. It authorized the United States to build a canal across the Isthmus of Panama in return for payment of $10 million and an annual rental of $250,000. The Hay–Herrán Treaty was approved by the Senate in March 1903. The Colombian government, however, balked. Public opinion in that country opposed the treaty because it violated the nation's sovereignty in the proposed Canal Zone. Colombian leaders were also reluctant because the French company's concession would expire in 1904; all its rights and property, including the $40 million payment, would then revert to Colombia.

Colombia's rejection of the Hay–Herrán Treaty enraged Roosevelt, who described Colombia as a country of "inefficient bandits." Roosevelt now made plans to seize the Isthmus based on the flimsy basis of a Colombian–American treaty of 1846 which guaranteed the neutrality and free transit of the Isthmus. Fortunately for Roosevelt, the New Panama Canal Company's representative in the United States, Philippe Bunau-Varilla, was making an outright American invasion unnecessary. Working through his agents in Panama, he organized a Panamanian "revolution" against Colombia. Roosevelt was deeply involved in the scheme, for when Bunau-Varilla informed the president and secretary of state of the impending "revolution," Bunau-Varilla was able to deduce that the United States would not permit Colombia to suppress it. Roosevelt dispatched the *U.S.S. Nashville* to Colón, on the Atlantic side of the Isthmus, where it arrived on November 2, 1903. On the following day, the army of patriots rebelled at Panama City, on the Pacific side, and the commander of the *Nashville* landed troops at Colón and forbade the Colombian troops there to cross the Isthmus and suppress the rebellion. In fact, the Colombian commander agreed to take his troops back to Colombia in return for a generous gift from Bunau-Varilla's agent.

At 11:35 A.M. on November 6, 1903, the American consul in Panama City informed the State Department that the revolution had succeeded. At 12:51 P.M. the same day, Secretary Hay instructed the consul to extend de facto recognition to the new Panamanian government. Fearing that the revolutionists would demand a share of the $40 million, Bunau-Varilla persuaded Roosevelt to receive him as the minister from Panama. He signed a treaty with Secretary Hay on November 18 that conveyed to the United States, in perpetuity, a zone ten miles wide. In return, the United States agreed to pay $10 million in cash and an annual rental of $250,000. The leaders of the new republic had no choice but to ratify this treaty. The American government took possession of the Canal Zone in May 1904 and began to prepare to excavate the great ditch. The canal finally opened in August 1914.

Strident nationalism impelled Roosevelt to build the Panama Canal, even if it was accomplished at the expense of a weaker nation's sovereignty. Control of the canal had important long-term consequences. Its defense became a cornerstone of American Caribbean policy. This meant, in turn, that policy makers increasingly saw insuring the political stability of the countries of this region as a way of forestalling European domination there. The Monroe Doctrine, which since its inception had been a passive, defensive policy, thus came to justify an aggressive program of hemispheric domination.

On the day before the Senate approved the Hay–Bunau-Varilla Treaty, the Hague Court of International Justice rendered a verdict with significant implications for American policy in the Caribbean. In December 1902, Great Britain, Germany, and later Italy instituted, with the State Department's approval, a blockade of Venezuela because its dictator, Cipriano Castro, refused to acknowledge his nation's indebtedness to European creditors. The European intervention expanded, however, when German naval vessels bombarded Fort San Carlos and destroyed a Venezuelan town in January 1903. Suspicious of German intentions and fearing the outcry of American public opinion, Roosevelt informed the German ambassador that he would be obliged to use his own Atlantic fleet if the Germans made any moves to take territory in Venezuela or elsewhere in the Caribbean. The crisis was resolved when all parties agreed to submit to the arbitration of the Hague Court. That tribunal then ruled that those very powers which had used force against Venezuela—Germany, Great Britain, and Italy—were entitled to first claim on Venezuelan payments to creditors. In other words, the court apparently gave legal sanction to international interventions to enforce payment of debts.

Roosevelt knew, after the Venezuelan blockade affair, that the United States could not tolerate European armed intervention on a major scale in the Caribbean, yet he also realized that he commanded insufficient naval power to ward it off. One way of reconciling American security needs with European economic interests was suggested in 1902 by the British prime minister, Arthur Balfour: European powers would renounce intervention if the United States assumed responsibility for making it unnecessary. Or, put another way, the United States could forestall one kind of foreign domination of Latin America by imposing another—its own. Two years later, in 1904, when the Dominican Republic defaulted on its foreign debt of $32 million, Roosevelt began to develop a new Caribbean policy along these lines. To prevent European intervention, American representatives signed a protocol establishing an American receivership over the Dominican customs. Under this arrangement, American receivers collected the revenue, turned over 45 percent of it to the Dominican government, and applied the balance to liquidation of the foreign debt.

The Dominican incident marked an important change in American policy. It appeared to work, to bring stability, peace, and prosperity to the island republic—and to prevent European intervention. It also provided Roosevelt with an opportunity to proclaim a new Latin American policy—the Roosevelt Corollary to the Monroe Doctrine. Roosevelt gave an intimation of his corollary in a public letter to Secretary Root in May 1904, and articulated it more fully in his annual message in the following December. In order to forestall European intervention in Latin America—the basic principle of the Monroe Doctrine—the United States would police flagrant instances of "wrongdoing or impotence." The Roosevelt Corollary was based on false assumptions and bad history, for no American statesman, not even Theodore Roosevelt, had ever before interpreted the Monroe Doctrine as forbidding temporary European intervention to compel Latin American states to pay debts or discharge international obligations. Roosevelt was simply invoking the sanction of a historic doctrine to justify two major tenets in American foreign policy: one, that the United States would tolerate no further European intervention in the Caribbean region; the other, that the Caribbean Basin was now an area of exclusively American hegemony.

3. Theodore Roosevelt and Imperial Diplomacy

The years between 1901 and 1909 saw a steady growth in international tension in Europe and the Far East. Germany's simultaneous determination to dominate the Continent and challenge Britain's naval supremacy brought about a diplomatic revolution in Europe by forcing Britain to seek rapprochement, first with France and then, in 1907, with Russia. In the Far East, both the rise of Japan and Russia's determination to control Korea and Manchuria upset the traditional balance of power. This environment of international, great-power tension provided additional opportunity for Roosevelt to exert America's newly found diplomatic influence.

While Roosevelt used military force to expand American control of the Caribbean, in Europe he used diplomacy and statesmanship. In 1905, a crisis occurred in Morocco, when, in order to prevent French domination of that North African nation, the German emperor, or kaiser, demanded an international conference to define its status. When the French refused, the kaiser appealed to Roosevelt. Although reluctant to intervene, Roosevelt realized that war might be imminent, and he persuaded England and France to attend a conference. The kaiser had won the first round, but the Germans faced a solid Anglo-French bloc, which usually had the support of the American delegate, when the conference met at Algeciras in southern Spain in early 1906. The General Act of Algeciras, signed in April 1906, although superficially a victory for commercial freedom, ultimately permitted the French to close the door on non-French trade in Morocco. At the moment, however, when a general war seemed probable, Roosevelt had intervened decisively and helped Europeans to find a peaceful solution.

A viable far eastern policy posed an even greater challenge, partly shaped by growing Japanese–American economic and military competition in the region. Thus, American policy makers sought to protect the vulnerable Philippines by

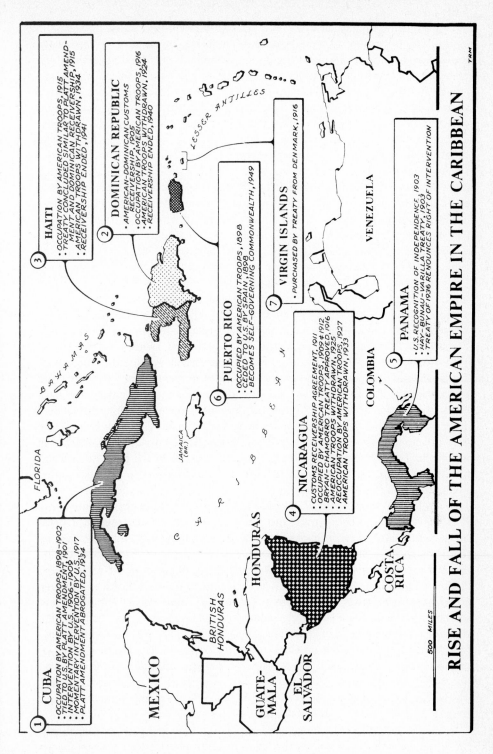

RISE AND FALL OF THE AMERICAN EMPIRE IN THE CARIBBEAN

① CUBA
· OCCUPATION BY AMERICAN TROOPS, 1898–1902
· TIED TO U.S. BY PLATT AMENDMENT, 1901
· INTERVENTION BY U.S., 1906–1909
· MOMENTARY INTERVENTION BY U.S., 1917
· PLATT AMENDMENT ABROGATED, 1934

② DOMINICAN REPUBLIC
· AMERICAN-DOMINICAN CUSTOMS RECEIVERSHIP, 1905
· OCCUPATION BY AMERICAN TROOPS, 1916
· AMERICAN TROOPS WITHDRAWN, 1924
· RECEIVERSHIP ENDED, 1940

③ HAITI
· OCCUPATION BY AMERICAN TROOPS, 1915
· TREATY CONCLUDED SIMILAR TO PLATT AMENDMENT AND DOMINICAN RECEIVERSHIP, 1915
· AMERICAN TROOPS WITHDRAWN, 1934
· RECEIVERSHIP ENDED, 1941

④ NICARAGUA
· CUSTOMS RECEIVERSHIP AGREEMENT, 1911
· OCCUPIED BY AMERICAN TROOPS, 1909 #1912
· BRYAN-CHAMORRO TREATY APPROVED, 1916
· AMERICAN TROOPS WITHDRAWN, 1925
· REOCCUPATION BY AMERICAN TROOPS, 1927
· AMERICAN TROOPS WITHDRAWN, 1933

⑤ PANAMA
· U.S. RECOGNITION OF INDEPENDENCE, 1903
· HAY-BUNAU-VARILLA TREATY, 1903
· TREATY OF 1936 RENOUNCES RIGHT OF INTERVENTION

⑥ PUERTO RICO
· OCCUPIED BY AMERICAN TROOPS, 1898
· CEDED TO U.S. BY SPAIN, 1898
· BECOMES SELF-GOVERNING COMMONWEALTH, 1949

⑦ VIRGIN ISLANDS
· PURCHASED BY TREATY FROM DENMARK, 1916

MEXICO

FLORIDA

BAHAMAS

GUATE-MALA

EL SALVADOR

BRITISH HONDURAS

HONDURAS

JAMAICA (BR.)

CARIBBEAN

COSTA RICA

COLOMBIA

VENEZUELA

LESSER ANTILLES

500 MILES

TRM

stalling Japanese expansionism in Asia. Americans were even more interested in China, largely because of a long-standing emotional investment by missionary, medical, and educational workers during the second half of the nineteenth century. Secretary of State John Hay's Open Door notes of 1899 and 1900 became fundamental to American policy. They insisted both on open access for American trade and missionaries to China and on China's territorial integrity. Most Americans now regarded their government as China's sole defender against allegedly rapacious European and Japanese imperialism. For most Chinese, however, the Open Door simply exchanged one sort of foreign exploition for another.

Another threat to peace in the late 1890s and early 1900s was Russian expansion into Manchuria and Korea. In order to halt Russian expansion, the British concluded an alliance with Japan in 1902. And, when war broke out between Japan and Russia in 1904, Americans tended to sympathize with Japan. Convinced that Japan was playing America's game by curbing and offsetting Russian dominance in the Far East, Roosevelt supported the Japanese, even to the extent of warning Germany and France that he would not countenance their going to the support of Russia. Japan had won a series of spectacular victories on land and sea by the spring of 1905; however, Japan was so exhausted that it appealed secretly to Roosevelt in April to mediate. Convinced that final Japanese victory would restore a balance of power, Roosevelt invited the belligerents in June to a peace conference, which opened in Portsmouth, New Hampshire, in August. The result—the Treaty of Portsmouth of 1905—attained Roosevelt's objectives. Russia remained an important Pacific power; but Japan now stood as an effective counterpoise. Whether this configuration would protect American interests in the Far East depended on many factors, the most important of which was Japan's future conduct. Subsequently, Roosevelt mounted other efforts to channel Japanese policy in an advantageous direction. Even before the Portsmouth Conference, in July 1905, he sent Secretary of War Taft, then in Manila, to Tokyo to conclude an executive agreement by which the United States recognized Japan's suzerainty over Korea and Japan disavowed any designs on the Philippines.

Nonetheless, events were developing in the United States that threatened to impair good relations between the two countries. The most dangerous trouble was brewing in California on account of heavy Japanese immigration into the state. As the first step in an anti-Japanese campaign, the San Francisco board of education adopted an order in October 1906 requiring the segregation of all Asian school children. The Japanese, regarding this as an affront to their national honor, lodged a formal protest. It was a dangerous situation, but Roosevelt acted cautiously to soothe Japanese ire while effectively ending immigration from Japan. At his invitation, the mayor and board of education of San Francisco came to the White House in February 1907. Roosevelt promised to use diplomacy to stop Japanese immigration; in return, the school board revoked the segregation order. Then Roosevelt negotiated, in 1907 and 1908, the so-called Gentlemen's Agreement with the Japanese, in which they promised to issue no more passports to peasants or workers coming directly to the continental United States.

In order to disabuse the Japanese of any notion that he had acted out of fear, Roosevelt decided in the summer of 1907 to send an American fleet of sixteen battleships on a cruise around the world—by way of the Pacific. While the fleet was still at sea, the Japanese opened negotiations for what resulted in the Root–Takahira Agreement, signed in November 1908. Japan and the United States undertook to help maintain the status quo in the Pacific, to respect each other's territorial possessions, and to support jointly the Open Door in China and the independence and territorial integrity of that country.

4. Taft and Dollar Diplomacy

Roosevelt's policy in Asia, Europe, and Latin America effectively determined the strategic interests and principles of American foreign policy for the next quarter century. In Asia, American policy centered on protecting the Philippines and warding off Japanese expansion in China. In Europe, it involved the mediation of old-world rivalries. And in Latin America, it meant defending the approaches to the Panama Canal by imposing the military and political dominance of the United States in the Caribbean Basin. The traditional American policies of isolation and noninterference had clearly ended. The two men who became president after 1909 each placed a distinct stamp on the nature of this world involvement, yet the terms of the foreign-policy debate were established by Roosevelt.

Although Taft abandoned Roosevelt's policy of participation in European politics and blundered into partial reversal of Roosevelt's policy of maintaining Japanese good will, he and his secretary of state, Philander C. Knox, could not reverse Roosevelt's policy of protecting American supremacy in the Caribbean. In fact, they went beyond the type of intervention that Roosevelt and Root had practiced and devised a new policy, "dollar diplomacy," to strengthen American power in the approaches to the canal. "Dollar diplomacy" involved using private American banking resources to displace European concessionaires and creditors, and hence to strengthen American influence in the region.

"Dollar diplomacy" thus raised the stakes of American intervention in the Caribbean. In Central America, Knox attempted in 1909 to persuade American bankers to assume a debt owed to British bankers. Two years later, the Honduran government refused to permit the establishment of an American customs receivership. These early initiatives were part of a growing intervention in Central American affairs. When the Nicaraguan dictator José Zelaya threatened to move against American mining concessons and made plans to offer an option on a canal route to the Japanese, the American government helped to stage his overthrow and, in 1911, to install a pro-American president, Aldolfo Díaz. Knox then widened American intervention by sponsoring the involvement of American banks and by establishing control over the Nicaraguan customs houses. When anti-Díaz sentiment grew into a full-fledged revolt in 1912, moreover, Taft sent 2,700 marines to suppress the uprising. So bitter was anti-Díaz and anti-American feeling that the marines occupied the country for many years.

The objectives of "dollar diplomacy" were as ambitious in the Far East. In 1909, when a consortium of European bankers signed a contract with the Chinese government to build the Hukuang Railway in central and southern China, Knox, invoking the Open Door principle, demanded that American bankers be permitted to participate. An American banking syndicate, formed by J. P. Morgan & Company, was admitted to the consortium, along with Japanese and Russian bankers, in May 1911. But for various reasons the project never prospered, and President Wilson announced the withdrawal of the American group in March 1913. Meanwhile, Knox pressed forward in a more reckless move with his ill-fated proposal, made in late 1909, for the internationalization of Manchurian railways in order to offset growing Japanese and Russian influence in the province. The British, who were at this time encouraging Japanese expansion in Manchuria to keep them at a safe distance from their own sphere of influence, promptly rebuffed Knox's suggestion. The Japanese regarded it as an attempt to undermine their influence in an area already tacitly acknowledged by Roosevelt as within their orbit. In short, Knox's proposal angered the British, drove the Japanese and Russians into an anti-American bloc, and even alienated the American banking group.

The historian must conclude that, on the whole, Taft's record in foreign affairs was even more barren than in domestic politics. The most important outcome of "dollar diplomacy" in Latin America was an armed intervention in Nicaragua that lacked strategic necessity, failed to bring peace to that country, and intensified anti-American feeling in all of Central America. In the Far East, the result of "dollar diplomacy" was an embitterment of Japanese–American relations without any real benefit to the United States. For the failure of his foreign policy, Taft had only himself and his secretary of state to blame.

5. Woodrow Wilson and New Freedom Diplomacy

Wilson's inauguration in 1913 promised to usher in a more idealistic era in American foreign relations. Most Democrats since 1901 had consistently condemned militarism, imperialism, and interventionism in foreign policy. They instead advocated world involvement along liberal-internationalist lines. Wilson's appointment of William Jennings Bryan as secretary of state indicated a new departure, for Bryan had long been the leading opponent of imperialism and militarism and a pioneer in the world peace movement.

The early foreign-policy initiatives of the Wilson administration confirmed these impressions. Wilson and Bryan worked to challenge and perhaps even to dismantle the traditional imperialistic basis of European diplomacy. Under Bryan's sponsorship, treaties were signed with twenty-nine nations to provide for the submission of all disputes to international commissions. The signatories agreed, moreover, to a one-year "cooling off" period before resorting to war. Further evidence of New Freedom idealism was the administration's withdrawal of the American banking group from the six-power loan consortium in China because it would allegedly lead to intolerable interference in Chinese affairs. A few weeks later, as if to emphasize his determination to cut loose from all such imperialistic conspiracies, Wilson recognized the new Republic of China without first consulting other powers.

Still another example of Wilson's conscious retreat from selfish nationalism occurred in the Anglo–American dispute provoked when Congress, in August 1912, exempted American ships engaged in coastwise trade from payment of tolls for using the Panama Canal. Facing a British objection that the exemption violated the Hay–Pauncefote Treaty's promise of equal rates for ships of all nations, Wilson in January 1914 urged repeal of the exemption provision. Despite opposition from some Democrats and the Hearst press, Congress passed a repeal bill in June 1914. The determination of both Wilson and Bryan to do the moral if unpleasant thing in foreign affairs was evidenced, finally, in a reparation treaty negotiated with Colombia and signed in April 1914. The United States expressed "sincere regret" for anything that had occurred to impair good relations between the two countries. It also agreed to pay $25 million to Colombia for the loss of Panama, gave the government of Colombia free use of the canal, and assured Colombian citizens of equality of treatment with Americans in the Canal Zone. Roosevelt's allies in the Senate blocked ratification in 1914 and again in 1917, but Wilson's intentions had been clearly demonstrated.

The Wilson administration's record in its relations with Japan from 1913 to 1917 demonstrates that good intentions alone do not always suffice to settle international disputes. The possibility of new difficulties was raised during the campaign of 1912, when Democrats and Progressives launched a campaign in California for a law prohibiting ownership of land by Japanese. Instead of perceiving the dangers, Wilson conferred with California leaders and even volunteered a method of excluding Japanese from land ownership without violating the Japanese–American commercial treaty of 1911. Acting on the president's suggestion, the California Assembly in April 1913 enacted an alien bill prohibiting, in an indirect manner, Japanese land ownership.

A crisis suddenly developed when news of the California's Assembly's action reached Japan. Then the California Senate exacerbated the tension by adopting an alien land bill that was openly anti-Japanese. A rising war fever in Japan brought Wilson to his senses and compelled him to act. He first addressed a public appeal to the Californians, urging them not to make their alien land bill openly discriminatory. Next he sent Bryan to Sacramento to plead for caution. Wilson's and Bryan's supplications did not budge the California leaders from their determination to humiliate the Japanese people. The legislature in May 1913 approved a bill excluding from land ownership those persons "ineligible to citizenship"—words hateful to the Japanese. Governor Hiram Johnson signed the measure in spite of last-minute appeals from Wilson and Bryan.

For a brief moment it now seemed possible that Japan and the United States might be heading for war. The Japanese ambassador lodged a strong protest with the State Department, and Japanese public opinion was at a dangerous level of anger. So explosive was the situation that the Joint Board of the Army and Navy warned Wilson that war with Japan was "not only possible, but even probable." It urged him to transfer American warships in Chinese waters to the Philippines to counter a possible Japanese surprise attack. Although war was averted, relations remained gravely unsettled as the First World War began.

General European war, moreover, provided irresistible opportunities for the

Japanese to expand their influence in China, and they joined the war on the Allied side by seizing the German naval base and concession in Shantung Province in northern China. The Japanese then further attempted to impose a treaty on China which would have made it a virtual satellite. Wilson and Bryan responded vigorously in diplomatic notes to the Japanese and Chinese governments in the spring of 1915, declaring the United States would not recognize any agreement that violated the Open Door and the political and territorial integrity of China. As a result of combined Anglo–American pressure, Japan for the time being abandoned its efforts to make China a protectorate.

Subsequent efforts on the part of Wilson to combat Japanese expansionism, however, necessitated a clear policy reversal for New Freedom diplomacy. When the Japanese attempted to enhance their economic position in China by offering capital for development, Wilson responded by reversing his position on an international bankers' loan and, in November 1917, he endorsed American participation in a four-power banking consortium. The era of Japanese–American hostility, which began in 1913, took a turn for the better when the two countries signed the Lansing–Ishii Agreement in 1917. In it, the United States recognized that Japan had "special interests" in China; in return, Japan reaffirmed its support for the Open Door and the territorial and administrative independence of China. Ambiguous though it was, the Lansing–Ishii Agreement served to stabilize relations between the two countries for the duration of the First World War.

In spite of Wilson's rejection of Rooseveltian diplomacy and his articulation of liberal-internationalist principles, the realities of world affairs which he inherited from his predecessors had not changed. Nor had the basic objectives of American foreign policy. Consequently, Wilson often found it difficult to uphold New Freedom diplomacy, particularly in the Caribbean area.

Wilson inherited a foreign policy aimed primarily at protecting the future Panamanian lifeline, a policy which could not be reversed without abandoning what seemed to be the cornerstone of the American security system. Although Bryan and the Democratic party had solemnly condemned "dollar diplomacy" as insidious financial imperialism, circumstances compelled the new secretary of state to use these instruments. Bryan had hoped to free the Caribbean area from the snares of foreign concessionaires and bankers by having the United States government— rather than banks—assume and refinance the external debts of small Latin American states. When Wilson rejected this proposal as too "radical" for Congress to approve, Bryan continued to use private capital to consolidate American influence over this vital area. These two factors—the strategic imperative of defending the Panama Canal and Bryan's and Wilson's desire to extend American influence—help to explain why there was no essential change in the Latin American policies of the United States in 1913. But the motives behind Wilson's and Bryan's extension of the Roosevelt–Taft policy lay deeper. As missionaries of democracy and freedom, Wilson and Bryan sincerely wanted to help underdeveloped, supposedly inferior neighboring peoples to develop liberal-democratic institutions modeled on the American economic and political system. Although theirs was an intervention to enlighten and liberate, it had the effect of extending American diplomatic and military involvement in Central America and the Caribbean area.

The formulation of Wilson's program in Nicaragua shows how all these factors combined to shape and control policy. Because Bryan realized that withdrawing American troops would invite civil war and the inauguration of a bitterly anti-American regime in an area close to the canal, he continued to support the unpopular Knox-sponsored Díaz government. Having concluded that it was necessary to control the government of Nicaragua, Bryan attempted to make it an American protectorate. Under the terms of the Bryan–Chamorro Treaty, the United States received an option on the Nicaraguan canal route for $3 million. Yet the treaty—in a clause resembling the Platt Amendment—also permitted the United States to intervene in Nicaragua to preserve order, protect property, and maintain Nicaraguan independence. Although the Senate approved the treaty in February 1916 without the provision authorizing American intervention, the deletion made no difference in State Department policy, which continued to be one of active interference in Nicaraguan politics.

The conclusion of this treaty, moreover, was only the beginning of a policy of further intervention in the Caribbean. In two instances, in the Dominican Republic and Haiti, Wilson used *realpolitik* methods to obtain what he considered to be New Freedom goals—to save the Dominican and Haitian peoples from anarchy and starvation. In the summer of 1916, the Dominican Republic approached a condition of anarchy, and Wilson was advised by the State Department that only full-scale military occupation would save it from chaos. He intervened first by trying to persuade the warring chieftains to lay down their arms and agree on a provisional president, and permit the United States to assume control of the Dominican constabulary. Dominican leaders consented to the first two proposals but refused to make their country a virtual American protectorate. Wilson, deciding that the time for drastic action had come when the leader of the strongest rebel band launched a new revolution in 1916, ordered American marine and naval forces to seize the capital city of Santo Domingo. When the Dominicans still refused to ratify the proposed treaty, the American naval commander established a military government in late November 1916.

Haitians had also indulged frequently in the habit of revolution, but they had contrived before 1915 to pay their external debts and escape foreign intervention and control. The political situation grew so anarchic by 1915, however, that the State Department concluded that American control of Haitian customhouses was the only possible way to remove the incentive to revolution. An excuse for intervention presented itself when a new revolution exploded in June 1915. American marines and bluejackets seized Port-au-Prince on July 28, and the commanding American naval officer took control of the government on August 9. He then compelled the National Assembly to elect a pro-American as president. The State Department, moreover, now imposed a treaty—revised to provide not only American supervision of Haitian finances but also establishment of a native constabulary under American control—upon the puppet regime.

To such extremes was the Wilson administration driven in its Caribbean and Central American policy. One feature that prevented that policy from becoming imperialistic—at least in the sense of establishing more colonies—was the idealism that prompted Wilson and especially Bryan to adopt it. Accepting the precepts of

Latin American policy as set down by Roosevelt, Wilsonian diplomacy advocated a form of intervention which was justified by reverence for liberal international order. For most Latin Americans, intervention, whatever its rationale, was still intervention—an attempt by Yankees to dominate the hemisphere. This basic conflict—between an ideology of freedom and a policy of domination—would pose new challenges in Mexico, where the new force of revolutionary nationalism would sorely test Wilsonian diplomacy.

6. Woodrow Wilson and the Mexican Revolution

When Wilson was inaugurated in 1913, Mexico had already experienced two years of revolution, during which the regime of Porfirio Díaz had been overthrown by Francisco I. Madero. Madero challenged the special privileges of the upper classes, and this brought on civil war and provoked the head of the army, Victoriano Huerta, to seize control of the government in February 1913 and to murder the deposed president. In spite of appeals from representatives of American investors in Mexico to accord immediate de facto recognition to Huerta's government, Wilson hesitated because of personal revulsion against Huerta and his "government of butchers." Meanwhile, an uprising was developing in northern Mexico, led by the governor of Coahuila, Venustiano Carranza.

In mid-June 1913, Wilson began a policy of isolating Huerta and encouraging his opponents. He offered to mediate between Carranza and his Constitutionalist followers and Huerta, and he sent John Lind, former governor of Minnesota, as emissary to Mexico. Although Wilson assumed that Mexicans would welcome his assistance, all factions, Constitutionalists as well as *Huertistas,* bitterly resented his interference and applauded when Huerta rejected Wilson's offer of mediation. Thus rebuffed, Wilson announced a policy of "watchful waiting." But when Huerta dissolved the national congress and began a full-fledged dictatorship in October 1913, Wilson was so angered that he abandoned his policy immediately. He first informed foreign powers that he would employ "such means as may be necessary" to depose Huerta and then pressured Huerta's major European supporter, Great Britain, to abandon him.

In November 1913, Wilson sent an agent to Carranza's camp at Nogales with an offer of cooperation and support. The president was surprised and indignant when Carranza replied that the Constitutionalists did not want American support, would oppose with arms the entry of American troops into Mexico, and would proceed to establish their own government in their own way. All that the Constitutionalists desired from the American government, Carranza said, was the privilege of buying arms and ammunition in the United States. Although rebuffed, two months after the Nogales conference Wilson lifted the arms embargo that Taft had imposed.

By the spring of 1914, although Wilson was deeply committed to Huerta's overthrow and to support for the revolution, there appeared to be no way to effect these objectives short of war with both the *Huertistas* and the Constitutionalists.

Then a trivial incident provided a pretext for intervention on the Constitutionalist side. When a *Huertista* colonel arrested several American seamen at Tampico in April 1914, the commander of the American fleet off Veracruz demanded a twenty-one gun salute to the American flag. Huerta agreed, but only if, in a face-saving gesture, an American warship returned a simultaneous volley. Responding to the crisis, Wilson went before Congress, ostensibly for authority to compel respect for American honor but in reality to humiliate Huerta. Before Congress had had a chance to act, however, word came that a German merchant ship was about to arrive at Veracruz with a load of ammunition for Huerta, and Wilson seized the opportunity to order the occupation of that port city to prevent the unloading of the cargo. After sharp resistance from students at the Mexican naval academy provoked heavy casualties, Veracruz was in American hands on April 22.

Far from strengthening Wilson's hand with the Constitutionalists, the Veracruz occupation brought the United States close to war and was denounced by Carranza as wanton aggression. Wilson, who had no intention of going to war with Mexico, accepted Argentine, Brazilian, and Chilean mediation as a way out of the crisis. While this mediation proceeded, Huerta's power waned, and he abdicated on July 15, 1914, after taking one parting shot at the "puritan" in the White House. Carranza and his armies entered Mexico City on August 20.

Although Wilson's immediate objective of a Constitutionalist victory was thus realized, he soon faced an even greater crisis—an internal power struggle between Carranza and his most successful general, Francisco "Pancho" Villa. By the autumn of 1914, a full-scale war had erupted, but within six months Villa, defeated by Carranza's forces, was reduced to control of his home province, Chihuahua. In October 1915, Wilson extended de facto recognition to the Carranza government. In response, Villa began a new campaign to provoke American intervention. In January 1916, a band of *Villistas* stopped a train at Santa Ysabel (fifty miles west of Chihuahua City), removed seventeen Americans, and shot sixteen of them on the spot. When this massacre failed to cause American reprisal, Villa made a bold raid on Columbus, New Mexico, in March 1916, burning the town and killing nineteen inhabitants.

Wilson immediately ordered army commanders in Texas to assemble an expedition for the pursuit of Villa. With the apparent consent of the leaders of the de facto government, Wilson sent a punitive expedition, under the command of Brigadier General John J. Pershing, across the border on March 18. The dispatch of the punitive expedition would have provoked no crisis if Villa had been quickly apprehended. However, Villa cunningly led his pursuers deep into Mexico. By early April, the American expedition had penetrated more than 300 miles into northern Mexico, but Villa still remained at large. At this point the expedition halted and gave all appearances of becoming an army of occupation.

Wilson refused to withdraw Pershing's forces because he believed that Carranza was either unable or unwilling to control the bandit gangs that menaced the American border. At the same time, Wilson aroused the suspicion of Mexican leaders, who thought that he intended to occupy northern Mexico permanently. As this suspicion grew, Carranza gave less attention to pursuing Villa and more to preparing for an inevitable showdown with the United States. A skirmish between American and

Mexican troops occurred at Parral in April in which forty Mexicans were killed. Such a wave of anger swept over Mexico that Carranza could do nothing less than demand prompt withdrawal of the expedition. Accusing the United States of warlike intentions, he ordered his field commanders to resist American forces if they moved in any direction other than toward the border. In June, when an American patrol tried to force its way through a Mexican garrison at Carrizal in northern Chihuahua, a battle ensued in which the Mexicans lost thirty soldiers but killed twelve and captured twenty-three Americans. War was averted only when it subsequently became apparent that the American forces had been guilty of an aggressive attack.

The Carrizal affair brought an end to this troublesome phase of Mexican–American relations. Both sides agreed to the appointment of a joint high commission to consider all aspects of relations, but it broke up without agreement. In January 1917, Wilson yielded and withdrew all American forces from northern Mexico.

7. The World War and American Neutrality, 1914–1917

On the eve of the most frightful war in history up to that time, Americans believed that they were still living in a secure international community, in which a benevolent British sea power and a fine world balance of power operated almost automatically to protect the Monroe Doctrine without a huge American military establishment. Then things suddenly changed in 1914, and, with the established international community in shambles, Americans found themselves at a crossroads in their history.

The sudden threat and then the outbreak of war in Europe in late July and early August 1914 compelled the Wilson administration to take immediate steps. Most Americans, although holding Germany and Austria (the Central Powers) responsible for the war's outbreak and sympathizing with the British and the French (the Allies), strongly wanted to avoid participation. Supported by a vast majority of the population, Wilson issued a proclamation of neutrality on August 4 and also began steps to prevent an economic panic. To protect the nation's gold reserve, Washington adopted a policy of discouraging loans by American bankers to the belligerents.

British naval superiority soon shaped American neutrality. With control of the seas, the British began extending, slowly but inexorably, far-reaching controls which prevented neutral trade with the Central Powers. By late February 1915, when the British system of maritime controls was severely tightened, the Admiralty had mined the North Sea, laid down a long-range naval blockade of Germany and neutral Europe, and seized American ships containing certain noncontraband materials, particularly food, en route to Italy, Holland, and other European neutrals for transshipment to Germany. The crucial question during this early period of the war was whether the United States would accept the British maritime system, some aspects of which probably exceeded the bounds of international law, or whether it would insist to the point of war on freedom of trade with Germany in all noncontraband materials. Wilson's first impulse was to insist on full American commercial rights, but his options were severely limited. On second thought, he decided to acquiesce and to restrict the State Department to protests reserving American rights for future adjudication.

This decision was virtually inevitable. Wilson believed, as did many Americans, that German methods were morally reprehensible and that the triumph of imperial Germany, militaristic and expansive as it was, would sooner or later threaten American security. Yet condoning the British blockade also drew the United States into a close trading relationship with the Allies. The British did control the seas, and their maritime measures were essentially grounded from the beginning on traditional law and custom. Under British control of the Atlantic, American direct trade with Germany and Austria declined from $169 million in 1914 to $1.2 million in 1916, while American trade with the Allies rose from $825 million to $3.2 billion. In short, the United States became virtually an Allied warehouse, from which munitions, food, and other vital raw materials flowed in an increasing stream.

The Allied–American war trade was not the only consequence of American acquiescence in British sea measures. The system of international exchange began to collapse as Allied, and particularly British, purchases began to assume enormous proportions in the spring and summer of 1915. By March 1915, in an important change, Bryan allowed the House of Morgan to extend a $50 million commercial credit to the French, thus opening the door for further credits. When the State Department, in September 1915, permitted an Anglo–French commission to raise an unsecured public loan of $500 million, the United States began to become an arsenal of credit as well as of war materials. By 1917, Allied governments had borrowed an additional $1.8 million from *private* bankers to finance the war trade.

When, during early 1915, Germany used a new weapon, the submarine, to challenge British control of the seas, and when the Allies responded by interdicting all trade with the Central Powers, Wilson was compelled to reexamine American neutrality. Acquiescence in the British blockade imperiled relations with the Germans; acceptance of the submarine blackade impaired relations with the Allies and perhaps would contribute to a German victory. In other words, in these circumstances impartiality and neutrality were virtually impossible. Not surprisingly, the submarine issue soon posed the greatest dilemma. Although the German Admiralty announced a submarine blockade on February 4, it lacked a sufficient number of U-boats to make it effective. Consequently, by March the Germans were using submarines to inaugurate a general terror campaign of sinking, without warning, unarmed British passenger vessels in the North Atlantic. The great German–American crisis of 1915 revolved entirely around the alleged right of Americans to travel in safety on these British liners.

Earlier, in February 1915, Wilson had addressed a note to Berlin announcing a policy of "strict accountability" for the loss of American ships and lives. When a submarine sank without warning the British liner *Falaba* on March 28, 1915, with one American drowned, Wilson began a policy designed to protect American rights without provoking a serious crisis in relations with Germany. While Bryan favored warning Americans not to travel on belligerent ships, the counselor of the State Department, Robert Lansing, and the advisory Joint Neutrality Board recommended a firm antisubmarine stand. Before Wilson reached any decision, however, an even more severe crisis erupted with the sinking, on May 7, 1915, of the great

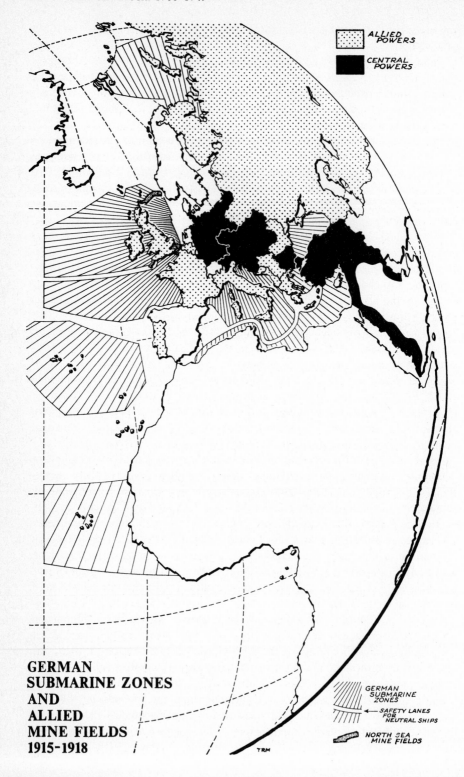

ALLIED
POWERS

CENTRAL
POWERS

**GERMAN
SUBMARINE ZONES
AND
ALLIED
MINE FIELDS
1915-1918**

GERMAN
SUBMARINE
ZONES

SAFETY LANES
FOR
NEUTRAL SHIPS

NORTH SEA
MINE FIELDS

TRM

British passenger liner *Lusitania* off the coast of Ireland, with the loss of 1,200 lives, including 128 Americans. Americans were horrified, but few of them favored war, and Wilson shared their disinclination to fight. In a series of three diplomatic notes to the German government, he instead pressed a campaign to end the sinkings of unarmed passenger liners. So emphatic was Wilson that Bryan, eager to avoid any prospect of war, resigned rather than sign the second *Lusitania* note.

The sinking of another passenger liner, the *Arabic*, on August 19, forced a showdown. For the time being at least, the Germans were unwilling to risk war with the United States, and the German emperor in late August ordered the abandonment of warfare against passenger liners. This "*Arabic* pledge" temporarily ended the submarine controversy and constituted a major victory for Wilsonian diplomacy. It also prompted Wilson to reinvigorate American diplomacy. He began a vigorous campaign to reassert neutral rights against the total British blockade. Moreover, beginning in the autumn of 1915, he began a long series of attempts to end the war through his personal mediation.

To this task Wilson delegated an inordinate responsibility to his trusted adviser and confidant, Colonel Edward M. House. A fundamentally devious man, House fancied himself a persuasive diplomatist with his own vision of a world order which combined *realpolitik* with Wilsonian internationalism. Yet his deviousness led him to negotiate by telling the Allies and Wilson what they wanted to hear, even if the message that he delivered to each differed fundamentally. House went to Europe in January 1915, without success. By autumn, he favored a bolder move which would combine his (and, he supposed, Wilson's) pro-Allied sympathies with a mediation plan. In brief, House's plan, which unfolded in a European trip in late 1915 and early 1916, envisioned Anglo–American cooperation in both mediation and a postwar settlement. Wilson would call for a peace conference. If Germany refused, or if it agreed but proved intransigent at the conference, the United States would probably enter the war on the Allied side. The agreement was embodied in a document signed by House and the British foreign secretary, Sir Edward Grey, on February 22, 1916. It has henceforth been known as the House–Grey Memorandum.

Meanwhile, a controversy was brewing back in the United States that nearly wrecked House's peace negotiations. In January 1916, Secretary of State Robert Lansing proposed a modus vivendi, or working arrangement, which would establish rules governing maritime warfare. Repeating the German argument that any armed merchant ship was offensively armed in relation to a submarine, Lansing suggested that the Allies disarm their merchant ships and warned that the American government was considering classifying armed merchantmen as warships. During 1915, the British had not only armed merchant ships but had also ordered them to attack submarines, and Wilson and Lansing began to wonder whether it was fair to require submarines to surface before attacking. Coming just when House was in London, Lansing's suggested modus vivendi struck like a bolt from a clear sky. Grey remarked bitterly that the United States was proposing nothing less than the destruction of the entire British merchant marine. House, perceiving the threat that the modus vivendi posed to the entente he sought with Great Britain, urged that the proposal be held in abeyance. But, before Lansing could act, the German government, on

February 10, 1916, announced that its submarines would sink armed merchantmen without warning beginning at the end of the month.

Instead of acquiescing—which his modus vivendi suggested—Lansing declared on February 15 that the United States would *not* warn its citizens against traveling on ships armed for limited defense. News of these developments provoked a panic in the House of Representatives. Democratic members of the Foreign Affairs Committee agreed unanimously to demand action on a resolution, sponsored by Representative Jeff McLemore of Texas, warning Americans against traveling on armed ships, while Senator Thomas P. Gore of Oklahoma introduced an identical resolution in the upper house. Although Wilson succeeded after a bitter struggle in Congress in having the Gore and McLemore resolutions tabled, because he refused for security reasons to explain his policy, many Democrats began to suspect that he meant to take the country into war.

Renewed friction with Germany soon shifted attention away from the armed-ship controversy. On March 24, a German submarine torpedoed an unarmed channel packet, the *Sussex,* with eighty casualties. After some deliberation, Wilson on April 18 delivered an ultimatum to Berlin: the United States would sever relations unless Germany abandoned its unrestricted submarine operations against all shipping, belligerent and neutral, armed and unarmed. Wilson's ultimatum brought to a head a controversy over submarine policy then going on in Germany between the military and civilian branches of the government. Discussion convinced the emperor that the Admiralty had too few submarines for a blockade successful enough to justify bringing the United States into the war. He announced submission to the president's demands on May 1; three days later, the German foreign secretary informed the State Department that henceforth submarine commanders would observe the rules of visit and search before sinking merchant vessels. But the note ended by reserving Germany's freedom of action and maintaining the right to intensify the submarine campaign if the United States did not compel the British to observe international law concerning neutral trade.

8. The Preparedness Controversy, 1914–1916

The German–American crisis of 1915–1916, and the possibility of war that it posed, gave impetus to advocates of greater preparedness, or military strength. Preparedness supporters pointed out that, because of its military weakness, the United States was virtually powerless to affect the outcome of the European war. Wilson and most of the Democratic party—which traditionally opposed militarism and standing armies —resisted a massive military buildup. But, in an important move with domestic and international implications. Wilson endorsed a preparedness program on November 4, 1915. This scheme would have substantially increased the regular army, scrapped the National Guard, and created a volunteer, Continental Army of 400,000 men.

A group of some thirty to fifty Democrats in Congress, most of them Southerners and Westerners, formed an antipreparedness bloc to wrest control of policy from Wilson. Through a member of their group, House Majority Leader Claude Kitchin of North Carolina, antipreparedness congressmen were able to pack the House Military Affairs Committee when Congress met in December 1915. Largely through their efforts, the army reorganization bill adopted in March 1916 represented a compromise. It increased the regular army to 11,327 officers and 208,338 men; integrated the National Guard into the national defense structure and increased its authorized strength; and permitted the War Department to establish volunteer summer training camps. The naval expansion bill, passed by Congress in August, went even further, and provided for the completion of a large five-year building program in three years.

The final victory belonged to the antipreparedness congressmen when it came to finding ways to finance the military buildup. Conservatives proposed to meet the entire cost by a bond issue and increased consumption taxes, but the antipreparedness coalition insisted that the wealthy pay the full bill. The measure reported by Kitchin's committee and adopted by the House in July doubled the normal income tax; raised the maximum surtax from 6 to 10 percent; levied a 1 to 8 percent tax on gross receipts of munitions manufacturers; imposed a new federal estate tax ranging from 1 to 5 percent; and repealed special consumption taxes that had been imposed in 1914. In the Senate, midwestern progressives like George W. Norris of Nebraska and Robert M. La Follette of Wisconsin forced even further changes, and the resulting Revenue Act of 1916 represented a frank effort to "soak the rich." It was Bryanism finally triumphant in federal tax policy.

9.   The United States Enters the War

Following the *Sussex* pledge, German–American relations improved noticeably, and events soon afterward cast a dark shadow over relations between the United States and Great Britain. Sir Edward Grey made it plain during the spring and summer of 1916 that the Allies would not welcome Wilsonian mediation as long as they had any hope of a military victory. To Wilson and House this was a crushing blow, almost a betrayal. They began to suspect that the Allies desired a vindictive peace, not a righteous settlement. Moreover, American opinion was profoundly shocked by the British Army's ruthless suppression of the abortive Irish Easter Rebellion of April 1916. Tension rose during the summer and autumn as the British intensified their economic warfare in a supreme effort to control all neutral commerce.

Once the election of 1916 was over, Wilson embarked on a new, high-risk strategy to end the war. The only way to preserve peace and safety, he realized, was to end hostilities altogether. Because this was difficult in the face of British resistance to peace negotiations, Wilson sought a peace through cooperation with the German government, which, since the end of the *Sussex* crisis, had been urging him to lead a drive for peace. In fact, civilian and military leaders in Berlin had concluded that the success of their recent campaign in Rumania had created a situation favorable to a peace move. They drafted terms that would have assured Germany mastery of Europe. They agreed that Wilson should be used only to force the Allies to the peace table and then be ignored during the peace conference. Finally, they resolved to begin all-out submarine warfare if their initiative failed. When Wilson did not move quickly enough, they invited their enemies to a peace conference on December 12. Wilson backed up the German overture six days later by calling upon the belligerents to state their war aims. In secret negotiations, the British sent word that they were willing to negotiate on liberal terms, but the Germans were evasive and then informed Wilson that they did not want his presence at the peace table. Defining American objectives in January 1917, Wilson endorsed a "peace without victory," without indemnities and annexations.

The kind of settlement that Wilson outlined was possible only if the German leaders were willing to accept a draw and cooperate in forcing the Allies to moderate their own extreme objectives. But, by then, the Germans had abandoned any hope of negotiations. They gave their answer to Wilson's appeal on January 31, 1917: after February 1, submarines would sink *all* ships, belligerent and neutral, without warning, in a broad zone extending around Great Britain, France, and Italy, and in the eastern Mediterranean. The German government would allow one American ship to sail weekly between New York and Falmouth, England, provided that the ship was suitably marked.

In response, Wilson broke diplomatic relations with Germany on February 3, 1917. By late February, all doubts as to German intentions were removed when Wilson received a message from Ambassador Walter H. Page in London. It was a dispatch transmitting a message, intercepted and deciphered by the British, from the German foreign secretary, Arthur Zimmermann, to the German minister in Mexico City. In the event that Germany and the United States went to war, Zimmermann's message read, the minister should propose to the Mexican government an alliance by which Mexico would join the war against the United States and receive as reward "the lost territory in Texas, New Mexico, and Arizona." Moreover, the minister should request President Carranza to invite Japan into the new anti-American coalition.

The day after he learned of the Zimmermann telegram, Wilson requested congressional authority to arm American ships and employ other measures to protect commerce. But there was stubborn resistance to granting Wilson authority to wage an undeclared naval war, and, despite the surge of anger that followed when Wilson released the Zimmermann telegram on March 1, a small group of southern and western senators—described by Wilson as a "little group of wilful men"—refused to abdicate the war-making authority.

From this point, events led exorably to war. Wilson announced on March 9 that he would put guns and naval crews on merchant vessels; German submarines on March 18 sank three American merchantmen with great loss of life. The demand for war, which had heretofore been largely confined to the East, now spread to the South and West. On April 2, Wilson asked a joint session of Congress for a declaration of war. After recounting German aggressions against American neutrality, he tried to find moral justification for leading Americans into this "most terrible and disastrous of all wars." The world, he declared, had to be made safe for democracy and led to a universal dominion of righteousness through a concert of free peoples. There was opposition in both houses from antiwar progressives, but the

Senate approved the war resolution on April 4, and the House concurred two days later.

What caused American entry into the war? Opponents of the war claimed in 1917 that a cabal of businessmen, bankers, and munitions manufacturers had driven the country to it—a charge repeated by many historians since then. This pro-Allied group, through a sly propaganda campaign, had deceived Americans into believing that the Allies were fighting for noble objectives. Wilson's policy had never been truly neutral, but from the outset had favored the Allies and encouraged a dangerous economic investment in their cause.

This explanation contains elements of truth, but it obscures the complex causes of the decision for war in 1917. In the final analysis, it was Wilson, influenced by public opinion and his own conception of right and duty, who made the important decisions that shaped American policy. In the beginning, he pursued a course of more or less strict neutrality that favored the Allies because the British controlled the seas. Then, as the British rejected his leadership in his drive for peace, the conditions seemed ripe for independent mediation with German cooperation. Indeed, it is reasonable to assume that there would have been no war between Germany and the United States had the German government stayed at least technically within the bounds of the *Sussex* pledge. The German leaders knew this, just as they knew that their plan for all-out submarine warfare would drive the United States to war. But after much doubt and conflict among themselves, they rejected American friendship and cooperation and invited war because they did not trust Wilson and had concluded that their only hope lay in a deperate bid for all-out victory. In German hands, in the final analysis, lay the decision for war or peace in 1917.

Chapter 7

—»» ««—

The United States and the First World War, 1917–1918

The American people entered the First World War not really knowing what the struggle was about or the objectives for which their new friends and enemies were fighting. Wilson attempted to give a moral and altruistic meaning to American participation, to depict intervention in terms of the strong and pure democracy putting on the breastplate of righteousness to do battle for the Lord. Americans responded with astonishing enthusiasm. The hastily accomplished industrial and military mobilization produced the food, materials, ships, and manpower that tipped the balance and broke the deadlock on the western front in 1918.

1. An Army to Save the Allies

Neither Wilson nor his military advisers understood the weakness of the Allied military situation in the spring of 1917. Since 1914, Americans had assumed as a matter of course that the Allies would win. Even after it was evident that the United States would enter the war, most Americans visualized their contribution only in terms of shipping, naval support, credit, and materials. Allied war missions to Washington soon counseled differently.

Wilson and his advisers were shocked when British and French generals revealed that their governments were reaching their last reserves of manpower. Drawing on an Army War College plan for raising a large army, administration and army officials agreed that "Selective Service," or conscription, offered the only rational and democratic method. Even so, the selective service bill, presented to Congress soon after adoption of the war resolution, ignited a bitter contest in the House of Representatives. Wilson insisted that selective service was essential to victory. In the end he had his way, although there was a hard struggle over age limits and the sale of alcoholic beverages at or near army camps. In the measure that Wilson signed in May 1917, the House won its fight to set the minimum age at twenty-one instead of nineteen, as the army demanded, and the Anti-Saloon League won another victory over Demon Rum.

Secretary of War Newton D. Baker enlisted state and local officials in making the first registration on June 5, 1917, a nationwide demonstration of patriotism. On that date 9,586,508 men between the ages of twenty-one and thirty-one registered with local civilian boards without commotion, riot, or organized resistance. In August 1918, Congress expanded the age limits to include all men between eighteen and forty-five. All told, draft boards registered 24,234,021 men, of whom 6,300,000 were found to be fit for service and 2,810,296 were inducted into the army. In addition, volunteer enlistments in the army, navy, and marine corps brought the total number of men and women under arms by November 1918 to 4,800,000.

For commander of the projected American Expeditionary Force (AEF) the president and secretary of war turned to Major General John J. Pershing, who had recently commanded the punitive expedition in Mexico. He arrived in June 1917 in Paris and established AEF headquarters at Chaumont, southeast of the French capital. While Allied military leaders argued that available American troops should be integrated into the existing structure and subordinated to Allied field commanders, Pershing insisted on preserving the identity and integrity of his command and even demanded a share of the front. The French command gave him the small and quiet Toul sector east of Verdun to defend with his initial force of 14,500 men.

The Germans began a series of heavy blows in October 1917 that pointed up the urgent need of large American reinforcements and forced the Allied governments to unite effectively for the first time. Following a near rout of the Italian armies by the Germans and Austrians at Caporetto, Italy, in October 1917, came the triumph of the Bolsheviks in Russia. This raised the possibility that Russia would soon withdraw from the war. The Allied prime ministers assembled in extraordinary conference at Rapallo, Italy, in November 1917 and created a Supreme War Council to sit at Versailles and coordinate and direct military operations. During the next few months, Pershing and President Wilson were subjected to heavy pressure by British and French leaders to permit American troops, even troops inadequately trained, to be amalgamated into their armies. Pershing refused, promising that he would have an army of a million men in France by the end of 1918. Yet it seemed that the Germans might win the war before the arrival of Pershing's reinforcements. The imperial German army hit hard at the British Fifth Army in the Somme Valley in March 1918 and rolled it back. The Allied leaders and President Wilson elevated Marshal Ferdinand Foch to the post of supreme commander five days later, and Pershing offered his four divisions for use anywhere on the front. The Germans renewed their offensive against the British in early April, captured enormous quantities of booty and 60,000 prisoners—but failed to break the British lines. The German forces then turned hard against the French in May and pushed to Château-Thierry on the Marne, only fifty miles from Paris. Foch sent the American Second Division and several regiments of marines to bolster French colonial troops in this sector, and American troops for the first time participated in an important way. For most of June, they pushed the Germans back across the Marne at Château-Thierry and cleared the enemy out of Belleau Wood.

The German General Staff began its last great drive—to break through the

THE UNITED STATES ARMY
IN WORLD WAR I

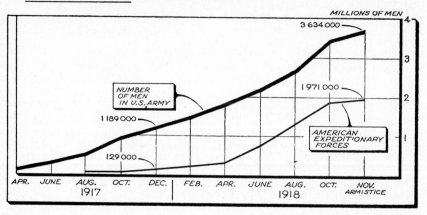

Marne pocket between Rheims and Soissons and reach Paris—in mid-July 1918. Some 85,000 Americans were engaged in this battle. The German thrust was quickly parried, and the force of the German drive was spent. Foch then began a counter-offensive against the weak western flank of the German line from the Aisne to the Marne, between Rheims and Soissons. In this engagement, which lasted until August 6, eight American divisions and French troops wiped out the German salient. British and French armies, reinforced by new American divisions, shortly afterward began offensives that did not end until they neared the Belgian frontier in November.

American soldiers began to pour into France in large numbers while Foch was mounting his offensive mainly with British and French troops. The American First Army, 550,000 strong, and under Pershing's personal command, was placed in front of the St. Mihiel salient at the southern end of the front in August. The Americans pressed forward in the morning of September 12; within three days they had wiped out the German salient and captured 16,000 prisoners and 443 guns. It was the first independent American operation of the war.

The tide was turning rapidly. Pershing had 1.2 million men, 2,417 guns, and 324 tanks by September 26 and was eager, as he afterward said, "to draw the best German divisions to our front and to consume them." He now hurled his force against the German defenses between Verdun and Sedan. His goal was the Sedan–Mézières railroad, the main supply line for the German forces in this sector. Both sides threw every available man into the battle that raged all during October. The German lines began to crumble on November 1; Americans reached the outskirts of Sedan and cut the Sedan–Mézières railroad on November 7. The American victory in this so-called Meuse–Argonne offensive destroyed a major portion of the German defenses and, coupled with British and French successes in the central and northern sectors, brought the war to an end.

Americans tempted to exaggerate their country's contribution to the victory will be less inclined to boast when they recall that only 112,432 Americans died while in service, as compared with 1.7 million Russians, 1.4 million Frenchmen, and

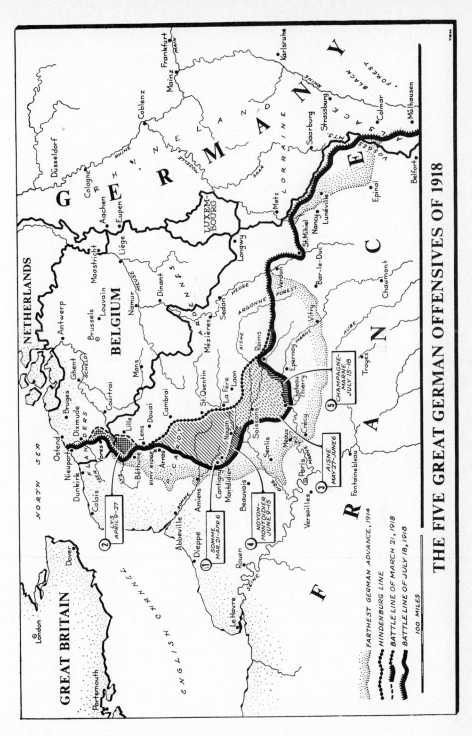

THE FIVE GREAT GERMAN OFFENSIVES OF 1918

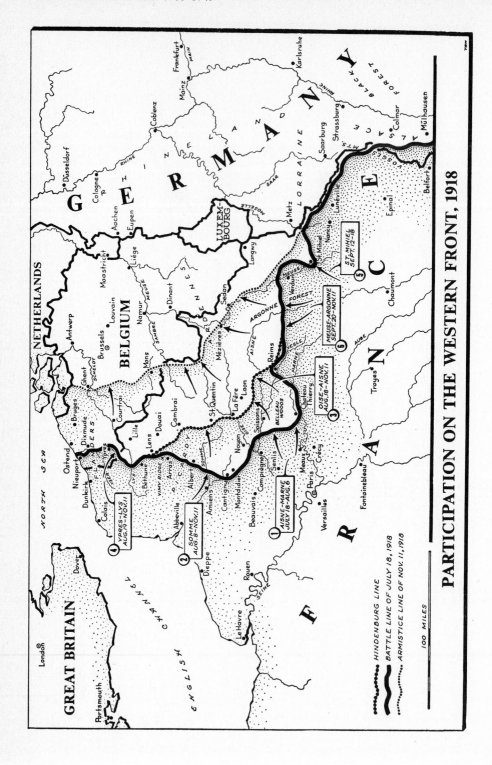

PARTICIPATION ON THE WESTERN FRONT, 1918

900,000 Britons. Belated though it was, the American contribution came in the nick of time to enable the Allies to withstand the last great German assault. On April 1, 1918, at the beginning of the German drive and before the American buildup in France, the Germans had a superiority of 324,000 infantrymen on the western front. By June American reinforcements gave the Allies a majority in manpower. By November the Allied preponderance was more than 600,000 men, enough to overwhelm the German defenses. Americans could rightly say, therefore, that their contribution had at least been decisive.

2. The United States Navy and the War

As U-boats set out in February 1917 to destroy all seaborne commerce, the most dangerous threat to the Allied cause came first not on land but on the seas. The German Admiralty had calculated that sinkings at the rate of 600,000 tons a month would bring England to her knees within six months, and it seemed for a time that the promise of the U-boat champions would be fulfilled. All told, submarines destroyed more than 6.5 million tons of shipping during 1917, while all American, Allied, and neutral shipyards combined built only 2.7 million tons. "They will win, unless we can stop these losses—and stop them soon," Admiral Jellicoe, first sea lord of the admiralty, told the American liaison admiral in London, William S. Sims, in mid-April 1917.

The adoption of the war resolution found the American navy ready and eager to join the battle. Secretary Josephus Daniels and his staff conferred with British and French admirals in April 1917 and mapped out a preliminary division of duty. The American navy would defend and patrol the western hemisphere, while the British fleet would carry the brunt of the antisubmarine campaign in waters around the British Isles with what help the American navy could spare. American assistance was not long in coming. The first six destroyers reached Queenstown, Ireland, in early May; there were thirty-five American destroyers stationed at that base by July; and 383 American craft were overseas by the end of the war.

The British system of defense against submarines in April 1917 consisted of dispersing sea traffic widely and then channeling merchant ships through heavily patrolled waters around the British Isles. The system created a positive deathtrap for merchantmen, as there simply were not enough ships to patrol the area. To the obvious alternative—the convoy system—British naval planners and masters of merchant ships objected, arguing that convoys were slow and merchant ships could not stay in formation. But, as the submarine toll mounted, a minority in the British Admirality joined Secretary Daniels and Admiral Sims in virtually demanding the use of convoys. Even after the feasibility of the plan had been demonstrated in the latter part of May 1917, the British Admiralty contended that it did not have enough warships to use the system generally. The American reinforcement of destroyers turned the tide in July, however, and convoys for merchant ships were begun. The intensified antisubmarine campaign and inauguration of the convoy system were the two decisive factors that brought the U-boats under control. Shipping losses fell from

881,027 tons in April to half that figure in December 1917; and losses never ran above 200,000 tons a month after April 1918.

The American navy's next task was to transport and supply the AEF. The Navy Department had seven troop and six cargo ships, totaling 94,000 tons, on hand in July 1917. By November 1918, it had created a Cruiser and Transport Force of 143 vessels, aggregating 3.3 million tons, which carried 911,047 soldiers to France. In addition, every available British transport was pressed into service in the Atlantic Ferry when the need for American manpower grew acute in 1918. Slightly more than 1 million soldiers were carried by British vessels. The troop carriers were so fast and so closely guarded by naval escorts that only two of them, both British vessels, were sunk on the eastbound voyage.

The American navy, with more than 2,000 vessels and 533,000 officers and men in service at the end of the war, had attained unparalleled size and fighting effectiveness. By November 1918, American ships were patrolling the far reaches of the western hemisphere and cooperating with Japanese and British forces in the Far East, while 834 vessels and 200,000 men were either serving in European waters or else transporting troops and supplies to France. By insisting on the adoption of the convoy system, American naval strategists had made a significant contribution to operations that assured an Allied–American victory at sea. By throwing its destroyers into the campaign against the submarines, the American navy perhaps turned the tide against the U-boats. And by transporting nearly half the AEF and almost all the army's cargo to France, the navy made possible the defeat of Germany in 1918 instead of 1920, as the Allied leaders had originally anticipated.

3. Wartime Tax Policy

Americans entered the First World War without the slightest idea of the costs of participation. Although predictions as to long-run costs were impossible, two facts became apparent almost at once. First, the structure of international exchange would collapse and the European Allies would be in desperate straits unless Britain and France received huge credits, not a piddling few hundred million dollars. Second, the Revenue Act of March 1917, which had increased taxes only slightly, was inadequate to meet war needs.

Without opposition a somewhat dazed Congress approved the first War Loan Act in April 1917. It authorized the Treasury to issue $2 billion in short-term notes and $5 billion in bonds, $3 billion of which should be lent to the Allies. Congress added subsequent authorizations as the needs of the American and Allied governments grew, so that the government had borrowed $23 billion on a long-term basis by 1920. Out of the $33.5 billion that is estimated as the cost of the war by 1920, therefore, some $23 billion was charged to future generations, about $10.5 billion raised by contemporary taxation. Determining how much should be borrowed and how much should be raised by taxes set off protracted struggles in Congress. Conservatives of both parties favored consumption taxes, borrowing, and perhaps slight increases in income taxes. Progressives believed that the wealthy classes, who had allegedly driven the country to war, should bear most of the cost through extraordinary income, inheritance, and excess profits taxes.

Between these two extremes stood Wilson, the secretary of the treasury, and a large majority of Congress. Congress enacted a new War Revenue bill, signed by Wilson in October 1917, which imposed a graduated excess profits tax ranging from 20 to 60 percent; increased the normal income tax to 4 percent for individuals and 6 percent for corporations; and increased the maximum surtax to 63 percent. The measure, moreover, increased excise taxes and imposed new ones on luxuries, services, and facilities. Finally, it increased the estate tax to a maximum of 25 percent.

The War Revenue Act of 1917 imposed 74 percent of the financial burden of the war on large individual and corporate incomes alone. Even so, radicals in the Senate denounced the bill as a betrayal of the people because it failed to confiscate all incomes over $100,000. Mounting expenditures during the early months of 1918 convinced Wilson and McAdoo that their critics had at least been partly correct, and in May 1918 Wilson urged Congress to impose additional levies on incomes, profits, and luxuries. Congress's response, the Revenue Act of 1918, approved by Wilson in February 1919, increased the prevailing tax burden by almost 250 percent and put four-fifths of the load on large incomes, profits, and estates. The normal tax on individual net incomes up to $4,000 was increased to 6 percent, while all net incomes above $4,000 had to pay a normal tax of 12 percent. An additional surtax ranging up to 65 percent brought the total levy on the largest incomes to 77 percent. In addition, the excess profits tax was increased to a maximum of 65 percent.

The effect of the war revenue legislation can best be seen by comparing the fortunes of the wealthy classes with those of other groups during the war period. The average annual real earnings of workers in manufacturing, transportation, and coal mining were 14 percent higher in 1917 than in 1914 and 20 percent higher in 1918 than in 1914. A rapid increase in agricultural prices also brought new prosperity to farmers. The real income, after taxes, of all persons engaged in farming was 25 percent higher in 1918 than in 1915. It is instructive to contrast these spectacular economic gains by the large majority of low-income receivers with the fortunes of the upper classes during the war period. To be sure, there were notable cases of "swollen" profits among certain industries, particularly munitions, shipbuilding, and steel; and the number of persons reporting incomes—before taxes—of between $50,000 and $100,000 increased from 5,000 in 1914 to 13,000 in 1918. But the gains of the wealthy classes as a whole were in good measure due to inflation and were far less important than a few sensational figures would indicate. Total disbursements to owners in manufacturing, measured in terms of *real* income, increased hardly at all from 1913 to 1916. Real income from property increased about 30 percent in 1917 and then fell back in 1918 almost to the level of 1916. But since the recipients of this income from property paid about seven-eighths of the total personal income taxes in 1917 and 1918, it is evident that they suffered a sizable economic loss as a result of the war.

The picture of the American upper classes fattening on the nation's misery during wartime is, to say the least, overdrawn. The effect of wartime policies was to lighten the relative share of the tax burden carried by the overwhelming majority of Americans, and to increase the burdens of that small minority who had paid only slight taxes before 1916. Thus reformers could boast in 1918 that their leaders were putting democracy to work at home with a vengeance while American soldiers were fighting to save democracy in Europe.

4. The Mobilization of Industry and Agriculture

Preliminary groundwork for industrial mobilization had been laid before the United States entered the war. Congress, in the preparedness legislation of 1916, had established a Council of National Defense, composed of six cabinet members, and the council's working body, the advisory commission, made up of business, industrial, railroad, and labor representatives. The council was armed with limited authority, but it proceeded to take a complete inventory of America's industrial plant and then to establish a Munitions Standards Board in March 1917.

This board was soon reorganized as the General Munitions Board and was given control over the purchase and supply of ammunition for the armed forces. But the new agency never established its authority over the armed services and the Allied purchasing commissions, and it was evident by the early summer of 1917 that only a central authority, with far-reaching controls, could bring order out of the prevailing chaos. The Council of National Defense abolished the General Munitions Board in July 1917 and created in its place the War Industries Board (WIB) to serve as a clearing house for purchases, to allocate raw materials and control production, and supervise labor relations.

The WIB made rapid progress in many fields of industrial mobilization, but it failed to coordinate military purchases because it lacked direct authority over the War and Navy departments. It seemed that the war effort at home was collapsing. The winter of 1917–1918 was terribly severe. Heavy snows blocked the railroads so frequently that there were fuel shortages in the East and a decline in steel production. Rumors of inefficiency led the Senate Military Affairs Committee to begin a searching investigation in December 1917 of the mobilization effort. The inquiry revealed a near breakdown in railroad transportation, confusion in the War Department, and failure to provide adequate shelter and clothing for soldiers in cantonments.

The exposures of the Senate Military Affairs Committee led Republicans to demand establishment of a coalition war cabinet to take direction of the war effort out of the president's hands. In response, Wilson drafted a measure—the so-called Overman bill—conferring on himself practically unlimited power to organize and direct the nation's resources. As Congress did not adopt the Overman bill until May, the president summoned Bernard M. Baruch, a Wall Street broker with much experience in the WIB, to the White House in March 1918 and made him chairman. Acting under his emergency war powers, Wilson also granted sweeping new authority to the agency to conserve resources, advise purchasing agencies as to prices, make purchases for the Allies, and, most important, determine priorities of production and distribution in industry.

Gathering about him one hundred of the ablest businessmen in the country, Baruch soon established the WIB as the most powerful agency in the government, with himself as economic dictator of the United States and, to a large extent, of the Allied countries as well. And before many months had passed the board had harnessed the gigantic American industrial machine, mainly by instituting strict controls over the use of scarce materials, particularly steel, and had brought such order into the mobilization effort that criticism of it almost vanished.

An urgent need in the spring of 1917 was to increase the flow of food from the United States to provide the margin between life and death for the British, French, and Italian armies and peoples. In May 1917, Wilson announced the inauguration of a food control program under Herbert Hoover, recently director of the Belgian Relief Commission. Hoover's agency at first acted without legal authority as a subcommittee of the Council of National Defense. After lengthy and bitter debate, Congress, in adopting the Lever Act, endowed Wilson with sweeping control over the production, manufacture, prices, and distribution of foodstuffs, fuel, fertilizers, and farm implements. Wilson created the Food Administration on the day that the Lever bill became law and delegated full authority to Hoover.

The most urgent task in the summer of 1917 was the production and control of wheat. Bad weather and an epidemic of black stem rust had caused a sharp decline in the American crop in 1916. The domestic supply was nearly exhausted by January 1917, and the price of wheat was skyrocketing. The Lever Act fixed a minimum price of $2.00 a bushel in order to stimulate production; and the Food Administration, in August 1917, offered to buy the 1917 crop at $2.20 a bushel and established the United States Grain Corporation to purchase and distribute wheat. But 1917 was another poor wheat season, and stocks of bread grains abroad fell below the danger point in early 1918. Only through cooperation from American housewives and the severest economies and controls was Hoover able to find enough wheat to carry Britain and France through the winter. Nature was more bountiful in 1918, and the bumper wheat crop of that year assured a plentiful supply of bread. The Food Administration's second major objective was increased production of hogs, as pork was another important staple in the Allied diet. When Hoover's agency began its work in the spring of 1917, the slaughtering of hogs was running 7 to 10 percent below the figure for the corresponding period in 1916. The Food Administration solved the problem in November 1917 by setting hog prices so high that farmers (and hogs) outdid themselves and nearly doubled production in 1918 and 1919.

For overall accomplishment with a minimum of confusion and direct controls, the Food Administration rivaled the reorganized WIB under Baruch's direction. By appealing to American pride and patriotism, Hoover persuaded people to tighten their belts on meatless and breadless days. Consequently, the United States was able to export 12.3 million tons of food in 1917–1918 and 18.7 million tons in 1918–1919, as compared with an average for the three prewar years of about 7 million tons.

5. Shipping and Railroads

The British prime minister, David Lloyd George, told a group of Americans in London a few days after the United States entered the war: "The absolute assurance of victory has to be found in one word, ships, in a second word, ships, and a third word, ships." And so it seemed, as submarines took a fearful toll—nearly 900,000 tons of shipping—in that gloomy April of 1917. But the Wilson administration promised "a bridge of ships" and chartered the Emergency Fleet Corporation, a subsidiary of the United States Shipping Board, on April 16, 1917, to build ships faster than submarines could sink them.

The government's shipbuilding program began with great fanfare but soon ran afoul of adversities. In the end it was the most important failure of the American war effort. Because of violent quarrels between the heads of the Shipping Board and the Emergency Fleet Corporation, little progress had been made by July 1917. The president removed them both and gave full power to Edward N. Hurley, energetic chairman of the Federal Trade Commission. Moving with great speed, Hurley began construction of new shipyards along the Atlantic coast; they contained ninety-four shipways and were supposed to produce 15 million tons of shipping. But the Emergency Fleet Corporation had delivered only 465,454 tons of new shipping by September 1918, while the first ship from the corporation's largest shipyard—at Hog Island, near Philadelphia—was not delivered until December 3, 1918.

Meanwhile, the Shipping Board had moved in more fruitful directions to assemble an American merchant marine. It seized and put into service ninety-seven German ships in American harbors, totaling more than 500,000 tons. In August 1917, Hurley commandeered for the Shipping Board the 431 ships, totaling 3 million tons, then under construction in private shipyards, and in March 1918 he seized over half a million tons of Dutch shipping then in American ports. Through purchase, seizure, and requisition, the Shipping Board by September 1918 had acquired the large fleet without which the AEF could never have been transported and supplied.

During most of 1917, a voluntary Railroads War Board assumed control of the railroad system. It worked in cooperation with the Council of National Defense to divide traffic and move troops and army supplies. Struggling under an extraordinary burden and lacking any unified control, the railroads seemed near collapse in December 1917, when snows blocked lines and cold weather froze switches and impeded

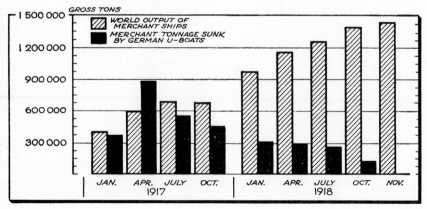

SUBMARINE SINKINGS AND SHIPBUILDING
JANUARY, 1917 TO NOVEMBER, 1918

the operation of terminals. Conditions in the eastern freight yards and ports were so chaotic by Christmas that Wilson in December 1917 placed all railroad transportation under the control of a United States Railroad Administration headed by William G. McAdoo. By controlling traffic on a rational, nationwide scale, spending more than $500 million for long-needed improvements and equipment, and subordinating passenger traffic to war needs, the Railroad Administration created an efficient national transportation system that met fully the demands of the military effort of 1918.

6.   Government and Labor During Wartime

In no area of public policy was the Wilson administration's determination to reinforce democracy at home during wartime better illustrated than in the field of labor policy. Rejecting proposals to conscript labor and refusing to allow the machinery of the labor market to regulate wages and hours, Wilson and his advisers began a comprehensive program to guarantee full utilization of manpower without depriving workers of hard-fought rights and living standards.

Like most wartime policies, the labor program evolved slowly in response to need, experience, and the administration's maturing social conscience. The War and Navy departments had the most immediate and the largest interest in uninterrupted production and could wield direct power over manufacturers and contractors. They moved quickly into the field of labor relations during the first months of the war. The Department of Labor, under Secretary William B. Wilson, was active on a daily basis in preventing or mediating strikes and protecting such rights of labor as the eight-hour day. It also established the United States Employment Service, which, before the end of the war, had registered over 5 million workers and placed 3.7 million of them in war-related industries.

Even so, by early 1918 it was evident that there was still a need for unified policies and national direction of the labor program. Hence the president established the National War Labor Board (WLB) in April 1918, as a supreme court for labor controversies. Under the joint chairmanship of Frank P. Walsh, a distinguished labor lawyer, and former President William H. Taft, the WLB heard 1,251 cases affecting 711,500 workers. Lacking any statutory authority, the board enforced its rulings through the president's war powers. For example, when the Smith & Wesson Arms factory at Springfield, Massachusetts, refused to accept the WLB's decision, the War Department simply commandeered the plant. On the other hand, when some workers in the munitions factories in Bridgeport, Connecticut, threatened to strike rather than accept the board's award, Wilson wrote a sharp letter to the machinists' union at Bridgeport, telling members that they could either work or fight.

This, then, was the administrative machinery that mobilized American manpower and inaugurated a far-reaching social experiment. In general, the government threw its war power to the side of organized labor, virtually guaranteeing the right of collective bargaining where it already existed and encouraging it generally. In fact, intervention of the federal government had a wide-ranging impact. Under federal protection, total membership in the AFL grew from 2.1 million in 1916 to 3.3 million in 1920. The administration compelled the adoption of the eight-hour day wherever it was possible to do so without disrupting industrial operations. Consequently, the work week declined from an average of 53.5 hours per week in 1914 to 50.4 hours in 1920, while the proportion of wage earners in manufacturing who worked 48 hours or less a week rose from 11.8 percent in 1914 to 48.6 percent in 1919. The War and Navy departments and various labor boards worked diligently to improve conditions of labor and prevent exploitation of women and children by manufacturers with government contracts. When the Supreme Court in 1918 invalidated the Child Labor Act of 1916, Congress responded immediately by levying a prohibitive 10 percent tax on products manufactured in whole or in part by children under fourteen. Federal administrators attempted to guarantee all workers under their jurisdiction a living wage, that is, an income sufficient to provide a minimum of health and decency. In the face of a 50 percent increase in the cost of living from 1914 to 1918, such a program helped to keep wages abreast of the rising level of prices. Because of full employment and the vigilance of the war labor agencies, the average annual real income of labor increased 14 percent above the prewar level in 1917 and 20 percent above that level in 1918.

These efforts involved such federal intervention as few progressives had dreamed of before 1917. Under the spur of war necessity, an advanced element in the administration had demonstrated that public control of hours, wages, and working conditions could be effected without enslaving workers or causing undue hardship on management. The experiment was abandoned after the war, to be sure, but a precedent for future action in another dire emergency had been established.

7. Public Opinion and the War

At the outset there was a profound division in public sentiment over American participation in the war. It is impossible to estimate the extent of opposition to the war resolution soon after its adoption. Probably a majority reluctantly accepted it as the only solution, but there were millions of Americans—Socialists, extreme radicals, many progressives, and hundreds of thousands of German and Irish Americans—who still believed that American intervention was the work of an unneutral president and great evil forces that abetted him.

To convert this hostile opinion, Wilson, only a week after the adoption of the war resolution, created the Committee on Public Information with George Creel, a progressive journalist from Denver, as its head. One of Creel's first official acts was the establishment of a voluntary press censorship that worked remarkably well. He next turned to the more difficult task of making Americans war-conscious; before the war had ended he had mobilized 150,000 lecturers, writers, artists, actors, and scholars in the most gigantic propaganda campaign in American history.

As a consequence, an official line was sold to the American people. One side of the propaganda glorified American participation in terms of an idealistic crusade to advance the cause of freedom and democracy throughout the world—a concept that the president reiterated in 1917 and 1918. The other side portrayed the German menace in striking colors, in terms of the Hun attempting to despoil Europe and extend his dominion to the Western Hemisphere. Although the Creel committee rejected the cruder atrocity stories, it appropriated and spread many of the official Allied atrocity charges.

The Creel committee's efforts to make Americans war- and security-conscious came at a time when they were already distraught over rumors of disloyalty, espionage, and sabotage. The result of Creel's propaganda, and even more of the agitation of volunteer organizations such as the National Security League, was to stimulate an outbreak of the mob spirit such as the country had never before witnessed. Most of the hysteria, which increased greatly after the German offensive began in March 1918 and lists of American casualties lengthened, was turned against German Americans, all things German, and antiwar radicals. Each state had a committee of public safety, with branches in every county and city, and in many areas these committees were not much better than vigilante groups. It was they who conducted reigns of terror against German Americans, especially in Montana, Minnesota, and Wisconsin. La Follette, as the leader of antiwar senators who voted against the war resolution, was burned in effigy in Madison, expelled from the Madison Club, and publicly censored by most of the faculty of his beloved University of Wisconsin. The climax came when the Minnesota Public Safety Committee demanded his expulsion from the Senate.

As one historian has shrewdly observed, the majority of Americans in their hatred of things German lost not only their tolerance but their sense of humor as well. Statues of heroes like Von Steuben and Frederick the Great were taken from their pedestals. Many states forbade the teaching of German or church services conducted in German. Sauerkraut was renamed "liberty cabbage," German measles, "liberty measles." The crowning blow came when Cincinnati ruled pretzels off free lunch counters in saloons.

8. Civil Liberties During Wartime

All governments try to protect themselves against enemies from within as well as from without during extreme crises. To Wilson and other administration leaders it was an absurd situation when the federal government could force men to fight and give their lives for their country and yet could not punish persons who attempted to obstruct the war effort or gave aid and comfort to the enemy, albeit without violating the law against treason. Their answer to opponents of the war was the Espionage Act, enacted in June 1917. It provided imprisonment up to twenty years and/or a fine up to $10,000 for persons who willfully made false reports to help the enemy, incited rebellion among the armed forces, or attempted to obstruct recruiting or the operation of the draft. A mild measure of censorship appeared in a section empowering the postmaster general to deny use of the mails to any printed matter which, in his opinion, advocated treason, insurrection, or forcible resistance to the laws of the United States. Postmaster General Albert S. Burleson of Texas had been a staunch supporter of Wilson's policies. But he was neither tolerant nor discriminating in judgment, and he used his new power to prevent the mailing of most Socialist publications. He banned the *American Socialist* from the mails soon after the passage of the Espionage Act. Two other leading Socialist publications, *The Masses* and Victor Berger's daily *Milwaukee Leader,* fell under the Texan's mail ban in August and October 1917.

In effect the Espionage Act became a tool to stamp out dissent and radical— never conservative—criticism. As one authority has observed, "It became criminal to advocate heavier taxation instead of bond issues, to state that conscription was unconstitutional though the Supreme Court had not yet held it valid, to say that the sinking of merchant ships was legal, to urge that a referendum should have preceded our declaration of war, to say that war was contrary to the teachings of Christ. Men have been punished for criticizing the Red Cross and the Y.M.C.A." A movie producer, Robert Goldstein, was sentenced to prison for ten years for showing a film about the American Revolution that allegedly incited hostility toward an associate of the United States. The most famous case involved Eugene V. Debs, the leader of the Socialist party. Debs expressed his frank revulsion at the war in a speech before a Socialist convention in Canton, Ohio, in June 1918. He was speedily brought to trial and sentenced to a term of ten years in federal prison.

In all fairness, it should be said that the administration was not responsible for the excesses of this legal witch hunt. Indeed, President Wilson courageously headed off a movement to have so-called traitors tried and punished by military courts. The excesses were the outcome largely of the hysteria and maelstrom of hatred that converted district attorneys, judges, and juries into persecutors of a dissenting minority. For example, Debs' indictment was brought by a zealous federal district attorney in Ohio; the Justice Department had decided not to seek Debs's indictment after the incident at Canton. Federal judges in the North had often stood forthrightly, although usually to no avail, during the Civil War in defense of free speech and assembly against encroachments by military commanders. However, most, but not all, federal courts provided no effective defense during the First World War against the momentary madness of the majority. None of the sedition cases reached the Supreme Court until after the war was over. But in *Schenck* v. *United States* (1919), Justice Oliver Wendell Holmes, speaking for a unanimous court, and following well-established precedents, upheld the Espionage Act. Schenck had admittedly counseled resistance to the draft. In ordinary times, Holmes said, such action would have been legal. In wartime, however, Congress had the power to prevent utterances that might constitute a "clear and present danger" and provoke evils that Congress had a right to prevent.

The government's power over thought and utterance was inevitably gradually enlarged, not diminished, as the war progressed. The Trading-with-the-Enemy Act of October 1917 empowered the president to censor all international communications and gave the postmaster general some control over the foreign-language press in the United States. Congress moved again in April and May 1918 in reaction to two developments that had shaken the country during preceding months.

The first of these was the government's suppression of the Industrial Workers of the World, the left-wing union which, as we have seen, flourished mainly among western lumbermen, miners, and agricultural workers. The IWW conducted a violent campaign during the first eight months of 1917 against the copper companies, especially the Anaconda in Montana and Arizona. The production of vital copper began to decline precipitately, and the Justice Department moved swiftly. Federal agents raided IWW offices throughout the West on September 5, 1917, and arrested the union's leaders. Nearly one hundred of them were subsequently tried, convicted, and imprisoned.

The second development was the mounting of war hysteria during the preceding winter, especially in states like Montana and Minnesota, where the IWW and German Americans were an important element. The Montana legislature met in special session in February 1918 to consider the crisis; and Governor Samuel V. Stewart signed a criminal-syndicalism act on February 21. It prohibited any language calculated to bring the American Constitution, form of government, flag, or armed forces into disrepute or contempt.

Spurred by appeals from the West, Congress succumbed to the clamor for legislation against sabotage and sedition. The Sabotage Act, approved in April 1918, was aimed at the IWW and made willful sabotage of war materials, utilities, and transportation facilities into federal crimes. The Sedition Act, signed by Wilson in May 1918, was modeled after the Montana statute and was supported chiefly by senators from the Rocky Mountain states. The Espionage Act had empowered the government to punish seditious utterances only if it could prove that injurious consequences would result directly from such utterances. The Sedition Act, in contrast, extended the power of the United States over speech and printed opinion, regardless of consequences. It forbade disloyal, profane, scurrilous, or abusive remarks about the form of government, flag, or uniform of the United States, or any language intended to obstruct the war effort in any way. In addition, the postmaster general was empowered to deny the use of the mails to any person who, in his opinion, used the mail service to violate the Sedition Act.

All told, 2,168 persons were prosecuted and only 1,055 were convicted under the Espionage and Sedition acts, 65 for threats against the president and just 10 for actual sabotage. But this reckoning gives little indication of the extent to which suppression of dissent was carried out by state courts, committees of public safety, and private groups who lynched, whipped, tarred and feathered, or otherwise wreaked vengeance on labor radicals, German Americans, or any persons suspected of disloyalty. Wilson, movingly and eloquently, issued a public statement on July 26, 1918, against the mob spirit and lynching, but largely in vain. In retrospect, the war hysteria seems one of the most fearful prices that the American people paid for participation in the First World War.

Chapter 8

-»» «««-

A Separate Peace
and Domestic Adjustment,
1918–1920

In retrospect, it is obvious that the participation of the United States in the First World War made for a compelling new reality: the continued preponderance of British and French power, and the future peace of the world, depended on American support. Although Wilson and others realized this fact in 1919 and 1920, most Americans were unprepared to assume the responsibilities of world leadership. That the Paris Peace Conference brought not a Wilsonian millennium but in part an old-style settlement turned many crusaders in the United States into cynics. Yet disillusionment about the shortcomings of the Treaty of Versailles does not alone explain American withdrawal from world leadership. Historic and powerful isolationist sentiments revived in full force once the war was over and provided an ideological frame of reference to which opponents of the treaty could appeal. Suppressed anti-British animosities found a more virulent expression, while some national groups remained dissatisfied with portions of the treaty. But the most decisive development accounting for the failure of the treaty was the manner in which the question of a peace settlement was subordinated, by Democrats and Republicans alike, to partisan ambitions.

1. The Armistice and Preliminaries to the Peace Conference

As a result of the weight of the Allied–American offensive on the western front which began in July 1918, General Erich Ludendorff, one of the German supreme commanders, demanded on September 29 and October 1 that the imperial authorities obtain an immediate armistice. Headed by a new chancellor, Prince Max of Baden, the civilian German government directly appealed to Wilson on October 3 for peace negotiations based on his liberal peace program. As early as 1916, Wilson had begun to outline the objectives of the war and the nature of the postwar settlement. Drawing on the support and ideas of intellectuals and humanitarians in western European nations and his own country, Wilson proposed a program to end antagonistic balances of power and postwar indemnities or annexations and to establish, as new principles of international relations, self-determination for subject nationalities, collective security, open diplomacy, freedom of the seas, and disarmament.

Wilson came to support a liberal peace program only gradually. In May 1916, in a speech before the League to Enforce Peace, he endorsed American participation in a postwar association to maintain the freedom of the seas and the territorial integrity of its members. In January 1917, he next conjoined the league concept to the liberal peace program in his "Peace without Victory" speech before the Senate; a year later, on January 8, 1918, he further elaborated on this program in a speech before a joint session of Congress. Wilson's ideas were enumerated in fourteen points, including the general postwar objectives of open diplomacy, freedom of the seas, removal of artificial trade barriers, reduction of armaments, "impartial adjustment of colonial claims," and national self-determination. In Point 14, Wilson presented the capstone of his settlement—a league of nations "affording mutual guarantees of political independence and territorial integrity to great and small states alike." The Fourteen Points at once became a war manifesto, endorsed by western European and American liberal, labor, and socialist groups. But the manifesto also had a powerful appeal inside Germany, for it promised not sheer destruction but the welcoming of a democratized Reich into a new concert of power. For this reason, Prince Max made his appeal to Wilson for a settlement based on the Fourteen Points and subsequent Wilsonian pronouncements.

Yet the German civilian authorities could negotiate a peace only with the cooperation of the military commanders, who at this point hoped to win a respite to prepare a defense of the Fatherland. Wilson, however, insisted on German evacuation of occupied parts of Belgium and France as a precondition to negotiations; he added that he would deal only with a legitimate civilian government, not with Germany's military masters. By late October, Wilson was suggesting to Prince Max that a German Republic would fare better at a peace conference than would an imperial Germany. When the Allies agreed to the terms of the armistice on November 4, Germany verged on collapse, incapable of waging even a purely defensive war. On November 8, the kaiser fled to Holland and later abdicated; three days later, Allied and German representatives, meeting in a railroad car in Compiègne Forest, signed articles providing for withdrawal of German forces to the Rhine, surrender of matériel and 150 submarines, and withdrawal of the German surface fleet to the Baltic.

Although the war had ended, the fight for the postwar settlement had only begun. Wilson's scheme faced several serious impediments. From the beginning of American participation in the war, the British and the French supported only parts of the liberal peace program and never fully endorsed it. Wilson had believed in 1917 and 1918 that these Allied–American differences could be overcome since, by war's end, the Allies would be so near collapse that he would command extraordinary leverage at any peace conference. The early end of the war and the sudden collapse of German military power changed all of this and left Wilson with fewer cards to play in a postwar settlement. As important were political developments in the

United States (some of them of Wilson's own making) that undermined his ability to negotiate with the Allies and win unified domestic support for a peace settlement.

Wilson made his first mistake even before the guns were silenced on the western front, at the close of a hotly contested congressional campaign in the autumn of 1918. Instead of asking voters to elect candidates who would support him regardless of party affiliation, Wilson made a frankly partisan appeal on October 25 which declared that a return of a Republican majority in either house of Congress would mean "a repudiation of my leadership" in Europe. It was an invitation to disaster which could only impair his domestic and international standing at a crucially important juncture. Not only did his injection of foreign affairs into domestic politics disrupt bipartisan support for the conduct of the war and the peace settlement, but Wilson had declared that he would stand repudiated in the eyes of the world if Americans did not vote the Democratic ticket. Although Wilson's appeal probably had little effect on the outcome of the elections, other factors—resentment against high wartime taxes, disaffection of western wheat farmers about ceilings on wheat prices, and the normal inclination of a majority of the electorate to vote Republican —accounted for a GOP victory that resulted in Republican control of both houses of Congress.

Wilson's second mistake occurred in his choice of peace commissioners accompanying him to Paris. Other considerations aside, political necessity demanded appointment of a peace commission that was broadly representative, for Wilson would fail in the critical period after the peace conference if he could not command the support of the Senate and a large minority of Republicans. Wilson understandably ignored the Senate, because he knew that, if he appointed any senators at all, he would have to include Henry Cabot Lodge of Massachusetts, who would soon be the new chairman of the Foreign Relations Committee. Personal relations between the president and Senator Lodge were already so bad that Lodge's appointment was out of the question. On the other hand, it is difficult to understand why Wilson ignored certain other prominent Republicans, notably William H. Taft, who would undoubtedly have worked loyally with him in Paris. The answer lies perhaps in Wilson's growing realization that the important work would, perforce, have to be done by the heads of government at the conference, and in his belief that he would need a group of advisers whom he could trust absolutely. But by refusing to include prominent Republicans, Wilson offended most moderate Republicans and lent credibility to the charge then current that he intended to maintain a personal monopoly on peacemaking.

2. The Versailles Treaty

Wilson, the peace commissioners, and a large body of technical experts sailed from New York aboard the *U.S.S. George Washington* on December 4, 1918. The situation in Europe did not, however, portend easy sailing. Britain was in the throes of a parliamentary campaign that found Prime Minister Lloyd George and his Conservative-dominated coalition hostage to the aroused passions of the electorate.

The French were in a state of postwar shock and clamoring for fearful retribution. Italians expected compensation for their losses by annexing large parts of former Austro–Hungarian territory. Germany was torn by revolt, and the old Austro–Hungarian Empire had already crumbled. Moreover, the meeting place of the conference, Paris, was a hotbed of anti-German sentiment.

At the same time, consideration of long-term issues was handicapped by a pervasive fear of Bolshevism; as has often been said, Bolshevism was the ghost that stalked the peace conference. As for Russia itself, the situation in that country was in so much flux on account of a civil war raging between the Bolsheviks and their enemies, the Whites, that it would be difficult if not impossible for Wilson and Allied leaders to try to provide self-determination for the Russian people. All through the early months of 1918, Wilson vetoed fantastic Anglo–French proposals for intervention in Russia to reestablish the eastern front. Under intense Allied pressure, Wilson, in August 1918, reluctantly dispatched about 4,000 to 5,000 troops to join British forces at Murmansk to guard military supplies there against possible capture by the Germans. He also sent a force of some 7,000 men under General William S. Graves to Vladivostok to keep the door of escape open for a sizable Czech army fleeing eastward from the Bolsheviks. More important, this force was also to keep an eye on the Japanese, who sent some 73,000 troops into Siberia. Beyond this limited action Wilson would not go, and throughout the peace conference he continued to reject proposals for Allied–American intervention in Russia.

When Wilson arrived in Europe in early 1919, therefore, the atmosphere had changed for the worse, and the treaty, signed by representatives of the Allied governments at Versailles Palace, on June 28, 1919, reflected these new realities. What did Wilson accomplish at the Paris Peace Conference? How did his liberal peace program fare? The answer is that Wilson accomplished less than he fought for and more than his critics later admitted, for the Versailles treaty was a compromise between the Fourteen Points and the demands of the Allied, and especially French, governments.

The foremost problem was security against future German aggression. Foch and the French premier, Georges Clemenceau, proposed to tear the west bank of the Rhine from Germany and create a buffer state under French control, a demand which Wilson, with Lloyd George's assistance, successfully resisted. Instead, France had to be satisfied with the return of Alsace-Lorraine, which was in accord with the principle of self-determination and the Fourteen Points; the permanent demilitarization and a fifteen-year occupation by Allied forces of the west bank of the Rhine; and Anglo–French and Franco–American treaties of mutual defense against Germany. It was this promise of the defensive security treaties that persuaded Clemenceau to abandon his demand for the creation of a buffer state in the Rhineland. The German army and navy were so severely limited in size that a future German war of aggression was to be impossible. On the whole, Wilson, Lloyd George, and Clemenceau succeeded in erecting an intelligent defensive structure which, if maintained in full vigor, might have preserved European peace. Certainly it did not violate the Fourteen Points in any important way.

Wilson found, moreover, that the British, Japanese, and Italians were determined that Germany should not recover her overseas colonies. In the face of their

INTERVENTION IN RUSSIA, 1918

inflexible position, he gave in, but only after he obtained important concessions. Japan received title to German economic rights in Shantung Province in exchange for a promise to return that province to Chinese political control. Former German colonies were not awarded outright to new masters, but were made mandates of the League of Nations and given in responsible trusteeship to Great Britain, France, the Dominions, and Japan. Whether this arrangement represented the "absolutely impartial adjustment of all colonial claims" that Wilson had demanded in Point 5 would in large measure depend upon the development of the mandate system. In fact, approval of the mandate system heralded the end of western colonialism.

A third major problem was the creation, without undue violation of the principle of self-determination, of a Polish state with access to the sea and composed of former German and Austrian territory inhabited mainly by Poles. Poland was given a corridor to the Baltic, while Danzig, its outlet to the sea, became a free city under League of Nations administration.

Another important issue—how much Austrian territory Italy should receive— involved the validity of the secret Treaty of London of 1915. It had brought Italy into the war and promised her the Trentino, the Austrian Tyrol, and a strip of the Dalmatian coast. Impressed by the argument that control of the Brenner Pass in the Tyrol was absolutely essential to Italian security, Wilson agreed that this area, which contained some 200,000 German-speaking people, should go to Italy. The Italians also demanded a long strip of the Dalmatian coast, including the important port of Fiume. Wilson strongly objected and appealed to the Italian people. Maintaining that Fiume was the only possible outlet to the sea for the new state of Yugoslavia, he pointed to the Treaty of London, which awarded the port to Yugoslavia. He won his case by main force. He also prevented the Italians from winning the Dalmatian coast. It went to Yugoslavia as well.

Wilson made his most important concession in still another issue, reparations. During the prearmistice negotiations, he agreed that Germany should pay all civilian damages incurred by the Allied countries during the war—this alone would be a staggering sum. At the conference, he further conceded that Germany should also be forced to bear the cost of separation allowances and pensions for Allied veterans. Although he was ill at the time and acted through Colonel House, the president later approved Article CCXXXI of the treaty, in which Germany acknowledged legal responsibility for all losses incurred by the Allied governments and peoples during the war. Wilson agreed, besides, that the Allies might occupy the Rhineland until the potentially astronomical reparations bill was finally paid. Nor was this all. In compensation for wanton destruction of French mines by the retreating German armies, France was given at least temporary ownership of the mines in the Saar province of Germany. The territory was to be governed by a League of Nations commission for fifteen years, after which the people of the Saar might vote to rejoin Germany. The treaty also compelled the Germans to pay to Britain, France, and Belgium twenty billion gold marks' worth of reparations in kind—merchant shipping, coal, livestock, and the like, before 1921. In Wilson's defense, it should be said, first, that he argued consistently in favor of setting a fixed sum for the reparations bill and adjusting it to Germany's capacity to pay. Second, he knew that the reparations terms were impossible and would have to be revised in the near future

—as indeed they were. Finally, he gave in to the terms of the reparations provisions of the treaty only after a long struggle and under duress.

In Wilson's mind, the first, last, and overriding issue was the establishment of an international organization to create a concert of world power and preserve the peace. From the outset of the conference, he insisted that the Covenant, or constitution, of the League of Nations be firmly embedded in the treaty, and that the treaty's execution be entrusted to the League. Clemenceau was not opposed to the League, but he contended that the organization would be helpless to maintain peace unless it had a powerful army and navy at its command. Convinced that such a proposal was politically impossible, Wilson and the British delegates created a League whose effectiveness would depend upon the wholehearted support of its leading members. As Clemenceau thought that he had obtained security for his beloved France by other means, he was willing to let Wilson write any kind of covenant he desired.

Critics, both contemporaries and historians, have castigated Wilson for bargaining away his liberal peace program at Paris in order to win a League of Nations. They were only partly correct. Wilson's chief failures—on the colonial question and on reparations—were perhaps inevitable. But the damage done was not irreparable, given forceful American leadership in the League of Nations and the reparations commission. He knew that the treaty was not perfect, but he was sure that time would heal many wounds and that the United States could obtain modifications within the League of Nations. Moreover, he hoped that the new international order would be one in which a reformed capitalism, purged of predatory imperialism and led by the United States, would offer an irresistible alternative to the Bolshevik demand for a new order through class warfare and proletarian dictatorship.

Not content with exaggerating his failures, Wilson's critics have also minimized his difficulties. He did not write the treaty alone but in collaboration with three astute and determined negotiators. Wilson could have withdrawn from the conference, as on one occasion he seriously threatened to do. But the results of American withdrawal would have been even worse than an imperfect settlement. Furthermore, Wilson's difficulties at Paris were compounded by virulent opposition to his peace program in the United States. Senator Lodge, for example, did not lighten the president's burdens by writing to Clemenceau that Wilson did not speak for the American people, who, Lodge declared, desired a harsh and punitive settlement.

3. The Treaty Fight

Before the Paris Peace Conference ended, it had already become evident that Wilson would face strong Senate opposition if he insisted on incorporating the Covenant of the League in the treaty. Returning briefly to Washington in February 1919 to meet criticism, he learned that many senators objected because the Covenant contained no explicit recognition of the Monroe Doctrine, did not specifically exclude internal affairs from the jurisdiction of the League, and made no provision for the right of a member nation to withdraw. Back in Paris, Wilson obtained changes in the Covenant to meet all these criticisms. He returned to the United

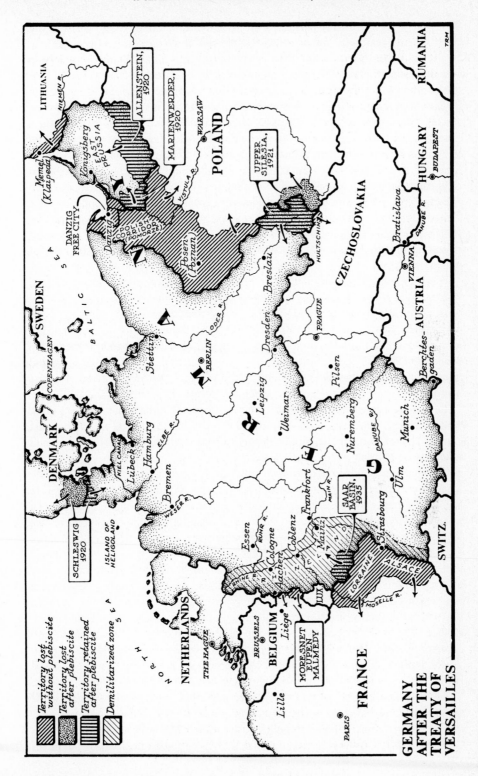

GERMANY
AFTER THE
TREATY OF
VERSAILLES

Territory lost
without plebiscite

Territory lost
after plebiscite

Territory retained
after plebiscite

Demilitarized zone

States in July and formally presented the treaty to the Senate. "Our isolation was ended twenty years ago," he declared. "There can be no question of our ceasing to be a world power. The only question is whether we can refuse the moral leadership that is offered, whether we shall accept or reject the confidence of the world." These poetic phrases, however, suggested a unanimity that did not exist. No one could yet say how large a part of the population critics of the treaty represented, but they were already well organized and exceedingly vociferous. Leading that opposition was a small group of extreme isolationists in the Senate, chief among whom were Hiram W. Johnson of California, William E. Borah of Idaho, and James A. Reed of Missouri. These irreconcilables, as they were called, believed that membership in the League violated a wise and historic policy, and they pledged themselves to keep America free from European entanglements. Even more bitterly opposed were German Americans, who saw the treaty as a betrayal of the prearmistice agreement; Italian Americans, angered by Wilson's refusal to award Fiume to Italy; and, most importantly, Irish Americans, alienated because they thought that Wilson had not pressed the cause of Irish independence at Paris.

Perhaps this opposition might have been overcome if the supporters of a liberal international order had endorsed the treaty and the League wholeheartedly. Unfortunately for Wilson, such a solid phalanx did not materialize. Many cautious liberal internationalists—such as Elihu Root and Henry L. Stimson, who put their faith in international law and arbitration—feared that Wilson was going too far too fast in breaking with ingrained American traditions. Others, independent progressives and radicals who had followed Wilson during the war and shared his dream of a new world order, drew back in revulsion when the terms of the treaty were published. "The European politicians who with American complicity have hatched this inhuman monster," exclaimed *The New Republic,* the leading liberal internationalist journal, "have acted either cynically, hypocritically, or vindictively." *The Nation* and other liberal journals were equally bitter.

In the Senate, a distinct alignment was already evident by midsummer of 1919. There were sixteen bitter-end isolationists, mainly Republicans, who would vote against the treaty in any form so long as it contained the Covenant. They were a small minority, but they dominated the Foreign Relations Committee and were able to influence its chairman, Lodge, by frequent threats to bolt the Republican camp. In contrast, at least forty-three of the forty-seven Democrats would follow Wilson's lead, while the great majority of the forty-nine Republicans favored ratification after making certain reservations to safeguard American interests. Most of these were so-called strong reservationists. Considerably more than the necessary two thirds in the Senate, in other words, favored ratification of the treaty and membership in the League. The main task of statesmanship in the months ahead would be to find common ground upon which this preponderant majority could stand.

By September 1919, opponents of the treaty were beginning to win the battle for public opinion. Earlier, in July, sentiment ran strongly in favor of the treaty. Thirty-two state legislatures and thirty-three governors endorsed the League, while a poll indicated that an overwhelming majority of the nation's newspapers held a similar opinion. But opponents stalled ratification while waging a national anti-League campaign. Wilson began to realize that the situation was passing out of his control, and he decided on bold steps. On September 3, he announced that he would not oppose interpretive reservations that did not impair the integrity of the Covenant or require new diplomatic negotiations. At the same time, he decided to take his case to the American people.

No act of his public career so dramatically demonstrated Wilson's sincerity as his decision to undertake this campaign. His health had been poor ever since he had a near breakdown at Paris in April and May. In the late summer of 1919, he was weak and exhausted, and his physician warned that a long speaking tour might take his life. He gladly took the risk, however, thinking that he could arouse a groundswell of support for the League which would overwhelm his senatorial opponents. He traveled more than 8,000 miles through the Middle and Far West for three weeks in September and delivered some thirty-seven addresses. Yet the effects of strain began to tell on Wilson even before the tour was half over. He began to have blinding headaches and to show signs of exhaustion, and, after one of his longest and most important speeches at Pueblo, Colorado, on September 25, he collapsed. His physician then canceled the remaining speeches and ordered the presidential train to return to Washington. On October 2, Wilson suffered a stroke that paralyzed the left side of his face and body, and for days his life hung in the balance.

With Wilson disabled, the Senate moved toward a vote on ratification, and, on September 10, 1919, the Foreign Relations Committee reported the Versailles Treaty with forty-five amendments and four reservations. When the Democrats, joined by twelve Republican "mild reservationists," defeated all the amendments, Lodge presented for his committee a list of fourteen reservations. The most important reservation (the second) asserted that the United States assumed no obligations under Article X of the Covenant to preserve the territorial integrity or political independence of any country, to interfere in international controversies, or to use its armed forces to uphold any article of the treaty without a joint resolution of Congress. The Senate approved twelve of Lodge's reservations, including the second, and added two others.

Bedridden and convinced that accepting Lodge's reservations would subvert the League, Wilson rejected the advice of Colonel House, Gilbert M. Hitchcock of Nebraska, Democratic leader in the Senate, and other League supporters to compromise on Lodge's terms or else accept the senator's reservations entirely. On November 18, in a public letter to Hitchcock—actually drafted by Hitchcock—Wilson denounced the Lodge reservations as a nullification, not a consent to ratification, of the treaty, and he virtually ordered Democratic senators to vote against them. On the following day, in a resolution to consent to ratification with the Lodge reservations, the irreconcilables combined with a solidly Democratic bloc to defeat ratification by fifty-five to thirty-nine; a Democratic resolution to consent to ratification without any reservations failed immediately thereafter by a vote of fifty-three to thirty-eight.

From these two votes it was clear that more than two-thirds of the Senate— seventy-seven senators—favored some form of ratification, and during the next six months there was considerable support for compromise. French and British leaders eagerly pressed for ratification; Sir Edward Grey (now Viscount Grey of Fallodon) was dispatched as special ambassador, and he stated flatly that the Allies would accept the Lodge reservations without requiring a reopening of negotiations. At the same time, leaders of twenty-six internationalist organizations representing some 20 million members demanded in January and February 1920 that Lodge and Wilson compromise. But the weary man in the White House paid scant heed to their pleas —if, indeed, he knew much about them. On January 8, 1920, in a public letter to Democrats assembled at a Jackson Day dinner in Washington, Wilson asserted that the overwhelming majority of Americans desired prompt ratification without crippling reservations. If, however, the Senate refused thus to ratify, then the presidential election of 1920 would be a "great and solemn referendum" in which the voters would decide the issue. It was one of the greatest tactical errors of Wilson's public career. Heretofore he had taken pains to avoid any show of partisanship in the treaty fight. By making ratification a partisan issue, he made it inevitable that most Republicans in the Senate would follow their majority leader. Moreover, public opinion now turned decisively against him. In the face of what seemed to be an overwhelming demand at home and abroad for ratification, the Senate agreed to reconsider and began debate anew in mid-February 1920. While Democratic leaders tried desperately to find common ground with the Republicans, the president, now improved in health and mental vigor, hurled blast after blast at the Lodge reservations and even intimated that he would refuse to ratify and proclaim the treaty if the Senate adopted them. The treaty came up for vote on March 19, and twenty-three Democrats joined the irreconcilables to defeat approval by a vote of thirty-five nays to forty-nine ayes.

The blame for the failure of ratification cannot be placed exclusively on any one group or person. Certainly Lodge and his Republican allies shared a large measure of responsibility; had they been less interested in the election of 1920, they might have been more willing to meet League supporters halfway. The irreconcilables, using every possible device to defeat ratification, share part of the blame. The unscrupulous propaganda that some of them put forth helped to confuse the public about the implications of American membership in the League. Finally, Wilson himself was partly responsible. Perhaps because of his hatred of Lodge, perhaps because he believed to the end that the people would force the Senate to his terms, and certainly because his stroke had impaired his judgment, he also refused to compromise. He ignored the advice of his best counselors and threw away the only possible chance for ratification.

4. Demobilization and Postwar Labor and Inflation Troubles

All postwar periods in American history have been times when partisanship runs strong and passions generated by the war drive people to acts of violence. So it was during the years following the armistice, as war hysteria found new victims in "Reds," foreigners, Jews, blacks, and Catholics. As if further to confuse the domestic scene, labor unrest during 1919 and 1920 was at its highest peak since the 1890s. Politically, the postwar era was marked by extraordinary partisanship. Centering at first on the struggle over ratification of the Versailles treaty, this partisan conflict culminated in 1920, when a reunited Republican party smashed the Wilsonian progressive coalition and swept into control of the federal government. The election results were convincing evidence that the people were determined to put an end to the division of control in the federal government and to return, as the Republican candidate in 1920 said, to "normalcy," to the good days of prosperity and peace.

Demobilization followed quickly on the heels of the armistice of November 11, 1918. While the AEF was brought home and quickly demobilized, various war agencies wound up their affairs. The War Industries Board, for example, abandoned its control of industry once the fighting ceased; it refused to believe that any problems of demobilization existed that the business world could not solve. By February 1919, however, it was apparent that the readjustment to a peacetime economy would not be smooth, for the economy was beset by inflation, the prospect of unemployment, and the potential for industrial conflict. Summoning governors and mayors to the White House in March, Wilson warned of future dangers, and he established an Industrial Board to coordinate an anti-inflation effort. But this agency possessed neither statutory authority nor prestige and was disbanded in May 1919. Broadly speaking, indeed, the administration's efforts to meet problems of inflation, business readjustment, and industrial conflict were either too little or too late.

On the other hand, the period 1919–1920 was not as chaotic or unproductive as the foregoing words suggest. Some specific problems of demobilization demanded immediate attention; moreover, several items on the reform agenda remained unfulfilled. In both instances, the focus of attention shifted to Congress. After the armistice, it provided funds to liquidate the war effort at home, care for wounded servicemen, bring the AEF home, and provide relief for Europe. It extended—and even increased—wartime levels of taxation on business and the upper classes with a War Revenue bill in February 1919.

Dismantling the system of government control over the transportation system and shipbuilding industry also required congressional action. While McAdoo recommended a five-year experiment in public operation and Congress deliberated during the summer of 1919, the Plumb Plan (suggested by Glenn E. Plumb, a lawyer for the railway brotherhoods) to nationalize the railroads and give the workers a share in their management and profit gained the support of the AFL and the railroad workers. Congress responded with the Transportation Act of 1920, drafted largely by two midwestern progressive Republicans, Representative John J. Esch of Wisconsin and Senator Albert B. Cummins of Iowa, and approved in February 1920. The Transportation Act was perhaps the most significant measure of the immediate postwar era because it marked the complete fulfillment of the movement for thoroughgoing federal control of railroads. Stopping only short of nationalization, the act gave the ICC complete control over rates, even those set by state commissions, and authorized the ICC to supervise the sale of railroad securities and expenditure of the proceeds. It also permitted railroads to pool traffic in the interest of economy and empowered the ICC to consolidate existing lines into a limited number of systems.

Another issue was the disposition of the huge fleet of merchant vessels which the Shipping Board had purchased, confiscated, or built during and after the war.

Although no one wanted to junk a merchant marine that totaled some 15 million tons by 1920, Congress was unwilling to inaugurate a permanent program of public operation. A compromise solution—the Merchant Marine Act of 1920—directed the Shipping Board to sell as many vessels as possible to corporations of predominantly American ownership and authorized the federally owned Emergency Merchant Fleet Corporation to open new shipping lines and operate surplus vessels. As it turned out, the Shipping Board's low prices on easy terms and guarantees against operational losses to private firms lured considerable private capital into the shipping industry and kept a sizable merchant marine afloat in the 1920s. By 1930 the privately owned American merchant marine totaled over 7 million tons.

Four measures—the General Leasing and Water Power acts of 1920 and the woman suffrage and prohibition amendments—rounded out the postwar legislative program and revealed that the reform spirit was by no means dead. The General Leasing Act empowered the secretary of the interior to lease public lands containing mineral and oil deposits to private parties on terms that safeguarded the public interest. The Water Power Act established a Federal Power Commission, composed of the secretaries of war, the interior, and agriculture. The commission could license the building and operation of dams and hydroelectric plants on navigable rivers and nonnavigable streams in the public domain. We will reserve our discussion of national prohibition for a later chapter. The point here is that Congress acted promptly and, it thought, effectively to implement what many progressives hailed as the greatest triumph for morality since the abolition of slavery. As we have seen, another important objective of the progressive movement—woman suffrage—also came to fruition at this time.

Although leaders in Washington and in the states feared that mass unemployment would result from demobilization in early 1919, the anticipated crisis never occurred. What followed instead was an economic boom well under way by the summer of 1919, in which industrial production rose above the wartime peak by October. Yet the postwar boom brought another consequence: insatiable consumer demand and inflation, as prices rose by 77 percent in 1919 and 105 percent in 1920 above prewar levels. Combined with other forces, postwar inflation ignited an unprecedented outbreak of labor–management conflict. In all, 2,665 strikes took place in 1919. They involved more than 4 million workers, as organized labor fought to preserve wartime gains and embarked on ambitious new projects of unionization. A wave of strikes began four days after the armistice, when the Amalgamated Clothing Workers in New York and Chicago struck for the forty-four-hour week and a 15 percent wage increase. Victory for the union was followed by adoption of the new wage and hours scale in the entire clothing industry. In rapid succession other strikes ensued: a general strike in Seattle and strikes by textile workers in New England and New Jersey, telephone operators in New England, telegraph operators throughout the country, the printers' union, the longshoremen of New York, and switchmen in the Chicago railroad yards. Practically all these strikes, and hundreds of others, succeeded, and organized labor was able not only to hold its own against rising prices but also to win an increase in real income.

Yet the outbreak of industrial unrest occurred while Americans became alarmed by the threat of world revolution. Most of the strikes of 1919 were waged successfully in spite of a growing popular suspicion that they were being provoked by Communist agents and would culminate in a general labor uprising. But organized labor's most important effort in 1919—the AFL's drive to win collective bargaining in the steel industry—ran afoul of the so-called Red Scare.

The United States Steel Corporation had stood since 1901 as the chief barrier to unionization of the basic industries. Encouraged by the friendly attitude of federal authorities and what it thought was a sympathetic public opinion, the AFL national convention directed its executive committee in June 1918 to undertake "one mighty drive to organize the steel plants of America"—the first attack in a new general offensive against the mass industries. The AFL's president, Samuel Gompers, appointed a National Committee for Organizing the Iron and Steel Industry on August 1, with William Z. Foster, a left-wing syndicalist, as secretary. Foster and his committee organized the steelworkers all during late 1918 and early 1919; the reorganized steelworkers' union claimed a membership of 100,000 by June 1919 and was ready to test its strength in battle.

When the head of United States Steel, Judge Elbert H. Gary, refused to negotiate, some 343,000 workers went on strike on September 22. There followed a struggle which was characterized by widespread violence resulting in the deaths of eighteen strikers, the use of federal and state troops to prevent picketing, and the suppression of civil liberties in all strike districts except West Virginia. But the most important battle was the struggle for public opinion, which management won by painting strikers as Bolsheviks and tainting organized labor with the false issue of Communism. By November 1919, the tide had turned against labor, and the struggle dragged on into January 1920, when the AFL surrendered unconditionally.

Two other major strikes during the autumn of 1919 gave further evidence of deep social unrest. In Boston, a policemen's union affiliated with the AFL went on strike in September 1919 for higher wages and redress of other grievances. A volunteer force was unable to control the gangs of looters that menaced the city, and Governor Calvin Coolidge called out the Boston companies of the National Guard and took personal command. The strike was quickly broken; the rebel policemen were dismissed; and a new police force was assembled. And when Gompers appealed to Coolidge to persuade the Boston authorities to reinstate the strikers, the governor replied with a rebuke that made him at once nationally famous: "There is no right to strike against the public safety by anybody, anywhere, anytime."

The last important labor action of the immediate postwar era—the short-lived bituminous coal strike of November 1919—was notable in that it provoked the first test of strength between the federal government and the new president of the United Mine Workers of America (UMW), John L. Lewis. Of all workers in the country, bituminous miners probably had the best grounds for discontent. The UMW had concluded a no-strike agreement—the so-called Washington Agreement —with the United States Fuel Administration in August 1917. Although anthracite miners later received substantial wage increases, bituminous miners received none. Meeting in Indianapolis in September 1919, the UMW adopted a bold program demanding immediate abrogation of the Washington Agreement, a six-hour day and five-day week, and wage increases up to 60 percent. And when the operators refused to negotiate until the Washington Agreement had expired, Lewis called a nationwide bituminous strike for November 1. Meanwhile, Attorney General A. Mitchell Palmer had tried vainly to persuade the UMW to cancel the strike order, which, he claimed, was in violation of the Lever Act, by whose authority the Fuel Administration had been created in 1917.

Faced with a complete shutdown of the mines, Palmer obtained one injunction on November 8 from the federal district court in Indianapolis ordering Lewis and other UMW officials to cease all strike activity. Shortly afterward Palmer obtained another injunction commanding union officials to cancel their strike order by November 10. "We cannot fight the government," Lewis declared as he called off the strike. Nonetheless, the miners refused to go back to work until the government, a month later, ordered an immediate 14 percent wage increase and established an arbitration commission to consider the union's demands. The commission, after extended hearings, awarded the miners another 27 percent increase in pay without changing the hours of work.

5.   The First Red Scare

No development better reflected the fears and insecurities about enemies—domestic and foreign—than the growth of the fear of a Bolshevik uprising in the United States during 1919 and 1920. This first "Red Scare" could not have taken place without the crisis atmosphere that prevailed during the postwar period—the sudden end of the war, the rapid demobilization, the onset of rapidly accelerating inflation, and, above all, the fierce labor conflict. But it also depended on the apparent success of an alien revolutionary ideology that threatened to spread foreign political ideas to American shores. Indeed, the triumph of the Bolshevik revolution in Russia in November 1917, the ensuing spread of revolution in postwar Germany, Hungary, and other parts of Europe, and especially the formation in Moscow in March 1919 of the Third International, or Comintern, dedicated to leading world revolution, inspired a wave of anti-Bolshevik hysteria in the United States.

Sentiment against revolutionary Communism soon fused with other powerful forces: xenophobic passions aroused by the war and the suppression of dissent; antiunion feelings; and a conspiratorial view of American society and politics that depicted impersonal changes as the product of personal collusion. As early as December 1918, Victor Berger, a Socialist congressman from Milwaukee, was tried for conspiracy under the Sedition Act, convicted, and sentenced to prison for twenty years. Released on bail—the government dropped all charges in 1922—Berger was denied his seat in Congress in 1919 and again in 1920. During the following months, anti-Bolshevik hysteria spread further. When Seattle workers staged a general strike in February 1919 that paralyzed industry, transportation, and utilities, Mayor Ole Hanson asserted that the strike was part of a nationwide IWW and Bolshevik plot to begin a workers' uprising. Meantime, committees of the United States Senate and the New York legislature began investigations of Bolshevik activities, while the Justice Department rounded up fifty-three alien Communists on the West Coast on February 11, 1919, and shipped them to New York for deportation. A week later a naturalized citizen was quickly acquitted in Indiana for killing an alien who had shouted, "To hell with the United States!"

The climax came with the discovery in April 1919 of a plot to assassinate governors, judges, cabinet members, and other public officials. A large bomb was found in Mayor Hanson's mail on April 28. The following day the maid of a Georgia senator had her hands blown off when she opened a package in the senator's Atlanta home. Immediate investigation in the New York Post Office uncovered sixteen bomb packages addressed to such persons as Attorney General Palmer, Postmaster General Burleson, Justice Oliver Wendell Holmes, Jr., J. P. Morgan, and John D. Rockefeller. Some twenty other explosive devices were discovered in the mails elsewhere. In addition, later in the spring the residences of Attorney General Palmer, two judges, and others were partially destroyed, with loss of two lives, by bombs in eight cities. The guilty parties, probably a few anarchists, were never apprehended.

Popular retaliation came quickly and indiscriminately. The California legislature outlawed membership in organizations that advocated use of violence. In the wake of the investigations of its Lusk Committee, the New York legislature enacted similar, if less drastic legislation. Some four hundred soldiers and sailors invaded the offices of the New York *Call*, a Socialist daily, and beat up several May Day celebrants. In other parts of New York, and in Boston and Cleveland, May Day paraders clashed with servicemen and police. The most serious outbreak occurred in the lumber town of Centralia, Washington, on Armistice Day 1919. Members of the newly organized American Legion, a veterans' organization, attacked the local headquarters of the IWW, and four of the attackers were killed in the ensuing fracas. In swift reprisal, enraged townspeople lynched one of the defenders. Police officials raided IWW headquarters throughout the state and arrested more than one thousand leaders of the union. And eleven IWW members involved in the Centralia affair were soon afterward convicted of murder and sentenced to long prison terms.

Scare headlines and sensational newspaper reports magnified the events and stimulated a widespread public alarm. Any threat would have had to come from the newly organized Communist parties, the alleged spearheads of the revolution. One of them, the Communist Labor party, breaking away from the national Socialist convention in Chicago, was formed in August 1919. It had between 10,000 and 30,000 members by the end of the year. Another, the Communist Party of America, was organized in September and had a membership of between 30,000 and 60,000 by the end of 1919.

The danger of social upheaval in 1919 now seems exceedingly remote in view of the extreme weakness of these parties of the Left. The Wilson administration, however, acted as if the menace were dire and launched a vigorous campaign against alleged Communists. The organizer and leader of this campaign was the attorney general and presidential aspirant, A. Mitchell Palmer of Pennsylvania. It is very possible that the sick president knew nothing about Palmer's plans and subsequent actions. Palmer not only set the entire Federal Bureau of Investigation to work ferreting out Communists and boring into their organizations, but he also urged Congress to adopt a measure that went so far as to punish persons guilty even of inciting sedition.

When Congress refused to enact Palmer's sedition bill, the attorney general struck out on his own private campaign. The Labor Department had rounded up some 249 known Russian Communists and shipped them to Finland in December 1919. But Palmer was after bigger game. Without informing the secretary or assistant secretary of labor of his plan, Palmer obtained warrants from a subordinate official in the Labor Department for the arrest of some three thousand alien members of the Communist and Communist Labor parties. Thousands of federal agents and local police launched a gigantic simultaneous raid on Communist headquarters throughout the country on the night of January 2, 1920. Some four thousand people, many of them American citizens who were not Communists, were hurried off to jails and bull pens in thirty-three major cities in twenty-three states. Persons visiting prisoners in Hartford, Connecticut, were arrested on the grounds that they too must be Communists.

Eventually one-third of the victims were released for lack of evidence. American citizens suspected of membership in a Communist party were turned over to local authorities for indictment and prosecution under state syndicalism laws. But for the aliens it was a different story. Outraged by Palmer's procedure, Assistant Secretary of Labor Louis F. Post took charge of the deportation proceedings to assure due process. Only 556 aliens, all of them proved members of the Communist party, were deported.

Palmer, although continuing to warn of enormous Red plots, executed no more raids. The scene now shifted to the states, with investigations by the Lusk Committee of the New York Assembly and the subsequent expulsion of five Socialist members of the legislature in April 1920 for no crime except Socialist party membership; the arrest and conviction of two anarchists, Nicola Sacco and Bartolomeo Vanzetti, for the alleged murder of a paymaster in a South Braintree, Massachusetts, shoe factory; and the growth everywhere of demands for conformity. As we will see in a later chapter, the postwar era bequeathed a heritage of hatred and hysteria that permeated and disturbed every aspect of life and thought during the 1920s.

6. A Crisis in Race Relations

The Red summer was also a time of trial for American blacks, who were victims of another sort of postwar intolerance—the worst outbreak of racial conflict in American history. Its causes lay in wartime and postwar social conditions. The beginning of the First World War resulted in a sharp decline in immigration—from about 1.2 million in 1914 to 327,000 in 1915—which, in turn, caused a scarcity of unskilled labor. The availability of jobs, especially once the United States entered the war in 1917, initiated a development of long-term importance: the first large-scale migration of blacks from the southern countryside to northern and midwestern industrial centers. The nearly half-million blacks who went to the Middle West and North found no warm welcome awaiting them. Forced to crowd into the worst areas, they became the object of the suspicion and hatred of white unskilled workers, most of them immigrants themselves, who resented Negro competition and detested black mores.

At the same time, black participation in the war raised expectations on the part of blacks and heightened fears on the part of whites. Some 400,000 Negroes served in the armed forces, about half of them overseas, where they were accorded an equality unknown in their native South. Many white Southerners, terrified at the prospect of so many black men equipped to use firearms and affected by the ways of equality, were prepared to use the rope and the faggot to remind black veterans that the Great Crusade had been no war for racial democracy in the South.

While the war stimulated black migration to midwestern and northern cities and so nationalized the potential for racial conflict, it also raised black expectations. Growing in militancy, black leaders were beginning to demand higher wages, immunity from violence, and a larger voice in politics. Most important, participation in the war effort had given Negroes a new sense of pride in their own race. The National Association for the Advancement of Colored People, now under the control of more militant leaders, was especially active during the war. One of the NAACP's leaders, William E. B. Du Bois, convoked a Pan-African Congress in Paris during the peace conference to speak for blacks throughout the world.

These tensions exploded into full-scale violence in the South as white men resorted to traditional weapons to intimidate black communities. Lynchings increased from thirty-four in 1917 to sixty in 1918, and to more than seventy in 1919. Ten Negro veterans, several of them still in uniform, were lynched in 1919; fourteen blacks were burned publicly. Southern white terrorism also found expression in a form more ominous than these individual acts of violence—in the rapid spread, especially through the Southwest, of the newly revived Ku Klux Klan, about which more will be said later. The Klan grew during 1919 from insignificance into a thriving organization of more than 100,000 members with cells in twenty-seven states. Defying law enforcement officials, hooded Klan night riders flogged, tarred, and hanged their victims in many southern and southwestern communities.

Even worse travail awaited black Americans in the outbreak of the most fearful race riots in American history. They began in July 1919 in Longview, Texas, and spread a week later to the nation's capital, where mobs composed principally of white servicemen pillaged the black section. The worst riot broke out in Chicago in July 1919, after an altercation between whites and blacks on a Lake Michigan beach. Mobs roamed the slum areas of the city for thirteen days burning, pillaging, and killing, with the National Guard unable to subdue them. When it was all over, 15 whites and 23 blacks were dead; 178 whites and 342 blacks were injured; and more than 1,000 families were homeless. During the next two months, major riots broke out in Knoxville, Omaha, and Elaine, Arkansas. The final count by the end of 1919 revealed some twenty-five riots, with hundreds dead and injured and property damages running in the millions.

Blacks and liberal whites were dismayed and reacted in varied ways. The NAACP and other militant black organizations advised resistance and undertook a public campaign against lynching that culminated in the passage by the House of Representatives of the first federal antilynching bill in 1921. This measure was endorsed by twenty-four governors and an overwhelming majority of northern opinion, but it was defeated by a southern filibuster in the Senate. The most significant reaction in the South was the first substantial awakening of the southern conscience in racial matters, exemplified by the organization in Atlanta of the Commission on

Interracial Cooperation in 1919. The commission would become the spearhead of a growing southern liberal movement in the 1920s and 1930s.

7. The Election of 1920

It was clear by early 1920 that any passable Republican candidate would win the presidency, and the retirement and death of the commanding figures dominating the party since 1900 opened the way for a fight for the nomination. The frontrunner, General Leonard Wood, inherited most of the following of Theodore Roosevelt, who had died in 1919. Wood was also independent of party bosses, intensely nationalistic, and favored universal military training. Other candidates were Governor Frank O. Lowden of Illinois, Senator Hiram W. Johnson of California, Herbert Hoover, and a number of favorite sons, including the nondescript Senator Warren G. Harding of Ohio.

When the Republican convention met in June 1920, the Wood and Lowden forces battled to a deadlock during the first four ballots. Fearing an impasse, the chairman of the convention, Henry Cabot Lodge, adjourned the convention on June 11. In the interim, a group which included National Chairman Will H. Hays, Lodge, Senator Frank B. Brandegee of Connecticut, and the New York editor, George Harvey, decided—in a now legendary "smoke-filled" room—to nominate Harding as an alternative, dark-horse candidate. When the Wood and Lowden forces were unable to agree, the convention nominated Harding on the tenth ballot. For vice-president, the convention, rejecting the Lodge–Brandegee candidate, Senator Irvine L. Lenroot of Wisconsin, nominated instead Governor Calvin Coolidge of Massachusetts. The platform proclaimed a repudiation of Wilsonianism. It condemned Wilson's League, but approved membership in the World Court and international agreements to preserve peace. It promised a return to traditional GOP domestic policies—high tariff and low taxes—and an end to further federal social legislation. Finally, it pledged to support restriction of immigration and aid to farmers.

Meanwhile, primarily because Wilson himself acted like a presidential candidate, confusion reigned in Democratic ranks. Most affected were the aspirations of the frontrunner and Wilson's son-in-law, William G. McAdoo, who "withdrew" from the campaign on June 18 out of filial respect. Other candidates included the attorney-general and leading Red-baiter, A. Mitchell Palmer, McAdoo's strongest rival, and Governor James M. Cox, a leading favorite-son candidate. As events turned out, Wilson had no influence over the convention's choice. He had made plans to have his name presented and his nomination effected by acclamation once a deadlock occurred. But this stratagem was never executed because a group of the president's close friends met in San Francisco in early July and agreed that a third nomination would kill both Wilson and the Democratic party. The Irish bosses who controlled the delegations from Massachusetts, New York, New Jersey, Indiana, and Illinois held the balance of power and, in the end, named the candidate. The McAdoo and Palmer forces fought to a standstill for thirty-seven weary ballots. Palmer released his delegates on the thirty-eighth ballot; but as most of them went

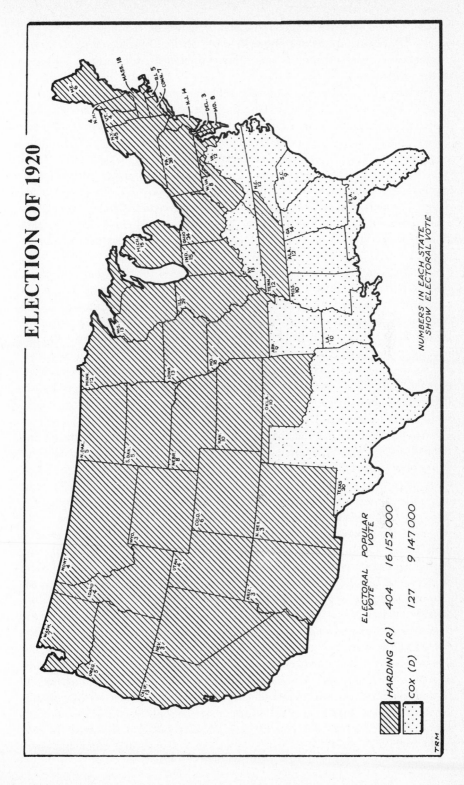

ELECTION OF 1920

NUMBERS IN EACH STATE
SHOW ELECTORAL VOTE

	ELECTORAL VOTE	POPULAR VOTE
HARDING (R)	404	16 152 000
COX (D)	127	9 147 000

to Cox, a McAdoo drive fizzled, and Cox was named on the forty-fourth roll call on July 5. Cox's choice for running mate was Franklin D. Roosevelt of New York, assistant secretary of the navy. Roosevelt was a prominent Wilsonian and supporter of the League.

Although the convention adopted a deliberately ambiguous statement on the League—endorsing it but also leaving the door open for reservations—Cox and Roosevelt campaigned as pro-League candidates. Harding's managers decided that the less their candidate said the better. Harding made no long tours like Cox; rather, he stayed home in Marion, Ohio, and greeted delegations on his front porch. It was impossible to judge from his sonorous homilies just where Harding stood on any specific issue. Isolationists were certain that he would keep the country out of the detested League. In contrast, a group of thirty-one distinguished pro-League Republicans, including Charles Evans Hughes, Elihu Root, and Herbert Hoover, assured voters that Harding's election was the first necessary step in ratification with reservations.

Harding's ambivalent speeches and the statement of the thirty-one so confused the voters that it is doubtful if the League was even an important issue in the campaign. It was evident long before election day that the Republicans were capitalizing on an accumulation of grievances going back all the way to the progressive legislation of 1916 and the adoption of the war resolution. The disparate elements opposed to Democratic policies—Irish and German Americans, blacks, industrialists and businessmen in rebellion against high taxes and policies favorable to labor, champions of civil liberty, independent progressives outraged by the treaty and the Palmer raids, and midwestern and Plains farmers then undergoing a severe depression—all moved en masse into the Republican camp.

The result of the combination of such dissident elements with the normal Republican majority was a smashing electoral triumph. Harding received 16.2 million popular votes, or 61 percent of the total; he won all the states outside the South, for an electoral vote of 404; and he even broke the Solid South by carrying Tennessee. With only 9.2 million popular and 127 electoral votes, Cox was the worst-beaten Democratic candidate since Stephen A. Douglas. The Republican sweep in the senatorial and congressional contests—there would be Republican majorities of 22 in the Senate and 167 in the House in the next Congress—was nearly as impressive as Harding's own majority.

This landslide did not signify a repudiation of the League, but it revealed the confusion and growing popular apathy over that issue. It did not signify a repudiation of progressivism or any great collapse of idealism among the people. It instead signified the triumph of the combined forces of dissent and protest. Wilson had created a Democratic majority in 1916 composed principally of Southerners, middle and far western antiwar progressives and farmers, independents, and workingmen throughout the country. Wilson's policies after 1916 consistently alienated independents, antiwar progressives, and most important, western farmers. By destroying the Wilsonian coalition in 1920, these groups not only registered their protests against Wilson's alleged betrayal of their interests, but also destroyed the only political alliance capable of carrying on progressive policies in a systematic way.

Chapter 9

—>>> <<<—

Patterns of Economic Development, 1920–1940

The decade between 1919 and 1929 witnessed both growth and higher living standards to a degree previously unknown in American history. Because of managerial and technological innovations, spectacular gains were recorded in productivity. Whole new industries came into existence which, by the end of the 1920s, were dominating the American economy. Yet the economic progress of the 1920s disguised significant problems. Although growth brought visible improvement, it also brought losers. The most important were farmers, who experienced a painful agricultural depression and who participated in a massive outmigration from rural America. In addition, New England cotton textiles and coal mining were plagued by labor violence and high unemployment. In general, prosperity, more urban than rural, was more typical of some industries than of others. More dangerous was the fact that the resources of commercial banks were used to finance a speculative boom in real estate and the stock market. These signs, however, are more apparent in retrospect. On the brink of the worst depression in their history, Americans were basking in the golden glow of prosperity.

1. The American People, 1920–1940: An Overview

Between the two world wars, revolutionary changes affected the growth, distribution, and composition of the American people. The decline in the birth rate, which had begun a century before, rapidly accelerated after 1915. It fell from 30.1 per thousand in 1910 to 27.7 in 1920, and then it dropped to 21.3 in 1930. Overall, population increased during the 1920s by 16.1 percent, as compared to 21.2 percent for the period 1900–1910. With the onset of the depression, the birth rate fell even further, hovering between 18.5 and 19.0 per thousand during the last half of the 1930s. For the entire decade of the 1930s, the rate of increase was only 7.2 percent. Offsetting the declining birth rate to some degree, however, was a phenomenal improvement in the health of the American people. The death rate in areas furnishing reliable statistics fell from 17.2 per thousand in 1900 to 13 per thousand in 1920, and to 10.8 per thousand in 1940. Life expectancy for both sexes increased from 47.3 years in 1900 to 62.9 years in 1940.

Americans in 1940 were still predominantly white and native-born. Nonwhites represented 10 percent of the total population, as compared to 12 percent in 1920. The severe restriction and selection of European immigration effected by the legislation of the 1920s (see pp. 216-217) had already begun markedly to alter the composition of the white population. Foreign-born persons in the United States in 1940 constituted only 9 percent of the total population, whereas 15 percent had been foreign-born in 1910. Total net immigration declined from a prewar peak of 3 million for the period 1911-1915 to about 69,000 for the entire decade of the 1930s. Since these totals include Canadians and Mexicans unaffected by restrictions, they fail to convey the full impact that the quota system enacted in the twenties had on immigration from Europe.

The most important internal demographic change of this period was the increasing movement from the countryside to the cities. The American farm population suffered a loss of more than 10 million by internal migration from 1920-1940. It was so tremendous a movement that total farm population sustained a net loss of over 1 million during the two decades, in spite of a high birth rate among farm people. One of the most important changes in the American social fabric during the first four decades of the twentieth century can be described in the following sentences. In 1900, nearly 60 percent of the American people lived in the country and in small towns under 2,500. By 1940, 44 percent of the people lived in rural areas, while only 23 percent actually lived on farms.

The depopulation of the countryside accelerated urban growth. The five cities of 1 million inhabitants or over alone absorbed more than one-third of the total urban increase of 14.6 million during the decade 1920-1930, while satellite cities surrounding the metropolises grew at twice the speed of nonsatellite cities of similar size. This movement was momentarily reversed during the early thirties, but the exodus to the cities began again with the return of prosperity between 1935 and 1937. In 1940 the Census Bureau could count 140 so-called metropolitan districts, in which 48 percent of the people lived. This represented an increase of 9.3 percent for the decade of the 1930s alone. Another significant internal population change was a steady migration of blacks from the South to the North and Middle West, a movement which had begun on a large scale around 1915. In 1920, 85 percent of all Negroes lived south of the Mason–Dixon line, barely different from the 92 percent on the eve of the Civil War. By 1940, about 76 percent of blacks lived in the South, and this drop reflected the beginning of a movement that would grow enormously after 1940.

Following the First World War, Americans enjoyed a period of steady economic growth and increases in living standards. The postwar boom of 1919-1920 was followed by a sharp economic downturn, but recovery was in full swing by 1922 and evident everywhere until 1927, when a slight recession was followed by a boom lasting until 1929. In a period known as the "New Economic Era," Americans seemed to be enjoying the best of all possible worlds: high production, low prices,

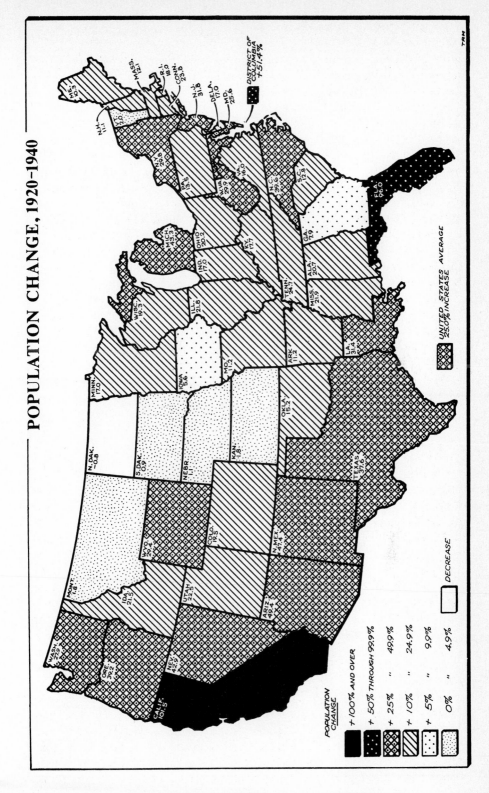

POPULATION CHANGE, 1920–1940

N.H. 11.1
V.T. [handwritten]
MASS. 12.1
R.I. 18.0
CONN. 23.8
N.J. 31.8
DELA. 17.0
MD. 25.6
DISTRICT OF COLUMBIA +51.4%

ME. 10.3

PA. 13.5

MICH. 43.3
OHIO 20.2
IND. 17.0
KY. 17.7
W.VA. 29.9
VA. 16.0
N.C. 29.6
S.C. 12.8
GA. 7.9
ALA. 20.7
TENN. 24.7
MISS. 21.9
FLA. 96.0

WIS. 19.3
ILL. 21.8
MO. 11.2
IOWA 5.6
MINN. 17.0
ARK. 1.2
LA. 31.4
OKLA. 15.2
TEXAS 37.6

N.DAK. −0.8
S.DAK. 0.9
NEBR. 1.1
KAN. 1.8
COLO. 19.5
WYO. 23.4
N.MEX. 47.4
UTAH 22.5
ARIZ. 49.4

MONT. 1.8
IDA. 21.5
NEV. 42.5
CALIF. 101.5
ORE. 39.2
WASH. 25.9

UNITED STATES AVERAGE 25.0% INCREASE

DECREASE

POPULATION CHANGE

+ 100% AND OVER
+ 50% THROUGH 99.9%
+ 25% " 49.9%
+ 10% " 24.9%
+ 5% " 9.9%
0% " 4.9%

T.R.M.

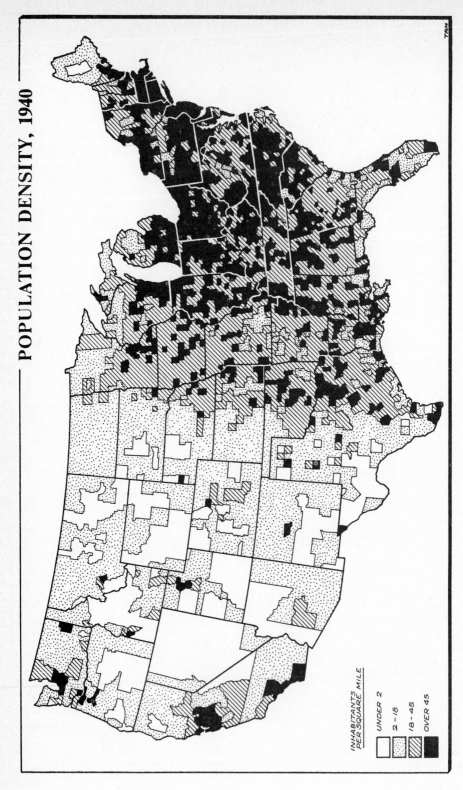

POPULATION DENSITY, 1940

INHABITANTS
PER SQUARE MILE

UNDER 2
2 – 18
18 – 45
OVER 45

and increasing wages. Although time would prove such hopes overconfident, the 1920s were nonetheless a time of steady improvement for most Americans; per capita income, adjusted for inflation, rose from $620 in 1919 to $681 ten years later. The spectacular increase in the material well-being of the American people during the first decades of the twentieth century becomes apparent when we recall that the adjusted per capita income in 1900 was $480. Yet these generalizations fail to indicate internal maladjustments that made the prosperity of the period ephemeral for large elements of the population. We can, therefore, obtain a more meaningful picture of the state of the nation during the New Economic Era by examining the important changes that occurred from 1923 to 1929 in the relative economic status of major groups.

Farmers suffered from a sharp drop in agricultural prices in 1920 and 1921, and, in spite of some recovery after 1921, prices never regained the relative balance that they had enjoyed in 1914 and 1919. The share of agriculture in the national income had been 22.9 percent in 1919; it was 12.7 percent in 1929. In contrast, the condition of most workers in industry substantially improved in almost all aspects during the 1920s. Over the decade 1919–1929, annual real earnings rose 26 percent; it was perhaps the largest decennial increase up to that time. During the period of greatest expansion—1923 to 1929—the number of wage earners increased only about 0.5 percent, but average hourly wages increased 8.0 percent and average real earnings increased 11.0 percent, while the average work week decreased from 47.3 to 45.7 hours.

A basic stimulant of prosperity in the 1920s was expansion in the construction industry after 1918. Stable costs and a continued high demand enabled the industry

EMPLOYMENT AND PAYROLLS OF PRODUCTION WORKERS
IN MANUFACTURING
1920-1940
BUREAU OF LABOR STATISTICS INDEXES, WITHOUT SEASONAL ADJUSTMENT, 1947-1949 = 100

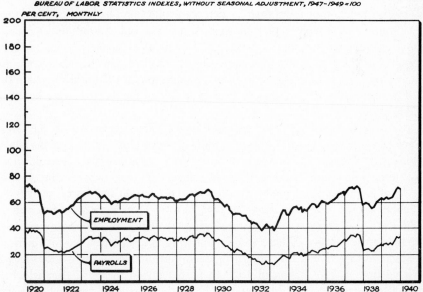

to record one large gain after another from 1922 to 1928, when it began to slacken. The estimated value of construction, based on the value of materials used, rose from a little over $12.0 billion in 1919 to a peak of nearly $17.5 billion in 1928. Manufacturing, meanwhile, enjoyed an even more significant expansion. The number of manufacturing establishments declined between 1919 and 1929 through consolidation and the elimination of small producers—from 274,598 to 210,959. Moreover, the number of industrial workers declined from 9 million to 8.8 million. On the other hand, there was an increase of 64 percent in manufacturing output, chiefly because of a 40 percent increase in labor's productivity. The following table illustrates the general character of the shifting pattern of production (see page 169).

These are statistics of dollar volume of production which partially obscure the important growth of certain segments of the economy. Thus the actual production of automobiles increased 255 percent from 1919 to 1929; chemical products increased 94 percent; rubber products, 86 percent; printing and publishing, 85 percent; and iron and steel products, 70 percent. Output of leather, food, tobacco, and textile products increased at a slower pace. On the reverse side, production of coal and railroad equipment sharply declined.

Despite their robust economy, Americans enjoyed an unevenly divided prosperity. Because an increasing share of national income went to industry and finance, workers lost ground in relative terms, while farmers suffered an absolute retrogression. Indeed, the evidence seems indisputable that maldistribution of wealth hampered the ability of Americans to purchase the goods they produced. Corporate profits and dividends rose 62 and 65 percent, respectively, from 1923 to 1929, but workers enjoyed an increase of only 11 percent in real income. That is, the prosperity decade, rather than resulting in a stable consumer economy, did not alter a skewed distribution of wealth—a generalization dramatically revealed by the following analysis. There were nearly 27.5 million families in the United States in 1929. Almost 6.0 million families, or more than 21 percent of the total, had incomes less than $1,000; nearly 12.0 million, or more than 42 percent, had incomes under $1,500; nearly 20.0 million, or some 71 percent, had incomes under $2,500, the sum estimated as being necessary for a decent living standard. On the other hand, the 36,000 wealthiest families received an aggregate income in 1929 nearly equal to the total income received by the more than 11.6 million families receiving less than $1,500 a year.

Since we will relate in some detail in later chapters the course of the Great Depression, the slow progress toward economic recovery, and other changes affecting industry, wage earners, and farmers in the 1930s, a few summary generalizations about economic trends in the 1930s must suffice. The years between the onset of the Great Depression and 1940 were a time of retrogression and despair such as the American people had rarely known in their history. These years were followed by painful and slow recovery. Briefly stated, recovery from the depression was under way before the massive defense spending of 1941 opened a new era in American economic history. The gross national product, measured in constant 1953 dollars, declined from $175.9 billion in 1929 to $123.4 billion in 1933, after which it gradually increased to $205.7 billion in 1940. At the same time, per capita after-tax

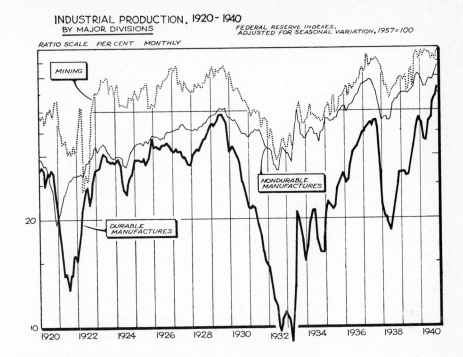

INDUSTRIAL PRODUCTION, 1920-1940
BY MAJOR DIVISIONS

FEDERAL RESERVE INDEXES,
ADJUSTED FOR SEASONAL VARIATION, 1957= 100

RATIO SCALE   PER CENT   MONTHLY

income, measured in 1953 dollars, declined from $1,059 in 1929 to $728 in 1933 but recovered steadily to $1,130 by 1940.

2. New Technologies and New Industries

Increased production in the 1920s was stimulated by innovations in industrial management and technology. Of all the causes of American industrial development in the twentieth century, the technological revolution was most basic and therefore most significant, for the age of mass production could never have come without the techniques it provided. Like other economic developments of the 1920s and 1930s, the technological revolution had its roots deep in the American past and its greatest impact after 1920.

Neither new forms of industrial management nor new technology of work production were unique to the 1920s; indeed, both were developed during the years immediately before the First World War. As we have already seen (see pp. 10–11), Frederick Winslow Taylor and other scientific and systematic managers had introduced changes to rationalize the work process and increase production—generally at the expense of traditional workers' prerogatives. By the 1920s, so successful were the Taylorites and their emulators that almost every branch of industry and business had adopted some form of scientific management. Equally important were the continued introduction of mass production by the assembly-line technique and production of interchangeable parts by automatic precision machinery. Although interchangeable parts had been in use since the eighteenth century, the assembly line in its modern form was first developed by Henry Ford. From 1908 to 1913, Ford used a stationary assembly line. In 1913 and 1914, however, he reorganized the assembly process in a revolutionary way—by introducing the moving assembly line, which reduced labor required for putting together an automobile chassis from fourteen to less than two man-hours. In the effort to increase production during the First World War, the assembly-line technique was applied to shipbuilding, the manufacture of airplane engines, and the production of munitions. The new method was well established in many branches of industry by the early 1920s. The introduction of these mass-production methods was accompanied by increased mechanization and conversion from steam to electric power. Between 1919 and 1929, mechanization—as measured by horsepower per worker—increased 50 percent in manufacturing and 60 percent in mining. Meanwhile, by 1929 some 70 percent of industrial production was powered by electricity.

The technological revolution in American industry in turn depended on a new factor—research. Stimulated by the war, many corporations by 1920 had established independent research laboratories. By 1927, at least 1,000 corporations were carrying on either independent or cooperative research for the improvement of product or service, reduction of production costs, development of by-products and new products, and the like. Data on total expenditures in 1927 are unavailable, but 208 firms reported expenditures aggregating nearly $12 million. This was a significant beginning, but industrial research was still in its infancy. By 1937, for example, American industrialists were spending $180 million annually for research; four years later the figure stood at $510 million.

Technology spread so rapidly that many observers thought that they were living in an age of miracles. In many respects, they were correct. Perhaps the most far-reaching economic change during the 1920s was a rise in productivity of 40 percent in manufacturing and 26 percent in agriculture between 1919 and 1929, as compared with gains of 7 percent in manufacturing and 6 percent in agriculture between 1899 and 1909. Although investment in technology—and productivity—slowed perceptibly following the stock market crash in 1929, general output per man-hour continued to increase—by about 20 percent during the 1930s. The added importance of technology had still another effect: an intensified focus by managers on productivity and the concommitant acceptance of the theory that conditions affecting worker health, comfort, and safety directly influence production and productivity. Most factories constructed during the 1920s followed modern safety standards, while older factories were modernized in this regard. A study of industrial accidents about 1928 found that only 10 percent of them were caused by lack of mechanical safeguards.

Highly productive and technology-intensive, new industries arose as the dynamic movers of the postwar economy. They stimulated demand for other goods and services and were at the cutting edge of a new, consumer-oriented economy. But they were also dynamic in another sense: they were prime movers in changing living habits and social attitudes that were taking shape by 1929 and would come to a fuller development after 1945.

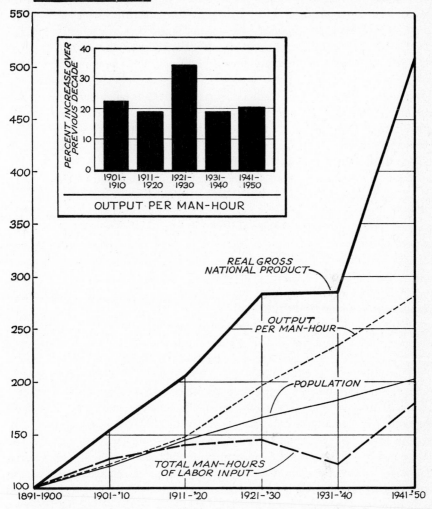

THE INCREASE OF PRODUCTIVITY IN THE UNITED STATES, 1891–1950, *BY DECADES*

None of these new, technology-intensive industries had a wider effect on the American economy than the automobile industry. Like many other new industries, it underwent its most important period of development in the decade before the First World War (see pp. 12–13). Europeans experimented for almost a century with self-propelled carriages, until Carl Benz, a German, built the first automobile powered by a gasoline engine in 1884. Charles and Frank Duryea of Springfield, Massachusetts, and Henry Ford of Detroit built the first successful gasoline-driven carriages in the United States in 1892–1893. There were some 8,000 automobiles in the United States by 1900. Some 181 companies entered the field during the next quarter century, but three major concerns—Ford, General Motors, and Chrysler—accounted for 83 percent of the output by 1930.

Indisputably the leading force in automobile manufacturing was Henry Ford. After experimenting with earlier versions of a low-priced car, he introduced the Model T in the autumn of 1908. By concentrating on this single unlovely but enduring model, and by introducing the assembly line process and scientific management, Ford realized his dream of producing automobiles for the masses. The price of Ford cars dropped after the introduction of the assembly line from $950 to $290. Ford's closest rival in the fierce struggle for supremacy was the General Motors Corporation, organized by William C. Durant in 1908. It fell under the control of the DuPont and Morgan interests in 1921 and produced a wide number of lines, ranging from the luxurious Cadillac to the low-priced Chevrolet. Another, much smaller competitor was the Chrysler Corporation, organized in 1923, which acquired Dodge Brothers in 1928 and Plymouth in 1929.

By 1929, from a small prewar enterprise, the automobile had become a leader in American manufacturing. It was a leader in productivity increases; during the 1920s, automobile manufacturers recorded a general productivity increase of 255 percent. The industry set a pattern of labor relations in which manufacturers hired nonunion workers and instituted a system of penalities and incentives to discourage inroads by unions. Its industry structure was competitive in both price and—especially—advertising, but it was also oligopolistic in structure since three firms manufactured the vast majority of automobiles. It was, by 1929, the largest single manufacturing industry in the United States, as production increased from 4,000 in 1900 to 4.8 million in 1929. Thereafter, automobile production declined to 1.1 million in 1932, but, by 1937, had risen to 4 million. By 1940, there were nearly 32.5 million cars, trucks, and buses in operation throughout the nation.

The industry in 1940 employed about 400,000 workers and paid them $646 million in wages, while it manufactured a product with an aggregate value of $4.1 billion. It is no exaggeration to say that automobile manufacturing was largely responsible for the intense economic activity of the 1920s. According to one estimate, it gave employment, directly or indirectly, to 3.7 million people by 1929. Use of the automobile stimulated the construction and maintenance of hard-surfaced highways, operation of garages and filling stations, maintenance of tourist camps, operation of fleets of motor trucks and buses, and the like. County, state, and federal authorities were spending nearly $2.5 billion annually by the end of the 1930s for the construction, maintenance, and financing of highways and bridges alone.

Other new industries resembled automobiles in their effect on the economy. Most of these were in an infant stage of development prior to the First World War, but thereafter they developed so rapidly through infusions of capital and technology that they began to have a significant effect on the economy. The electric power industry from 1900 to 1929 rose from comparative insignificance to major importance. Production increased from 6 billion to nearly 117 billion kilowatt-hours; capital invested in the industry grew to nearly $12 billion, total income to nearly $2 billion. Growth slowed in the 1930s, but in 1940 production was nearly 180 billion kilowatt-hours; capital invested stood at $15.5 billion; and total income was nearly $3.0 billion. Only 16 percent of American homes were electrified in 1912; nearly 79 percent used electric power by 1940. Almost overnight the manufacture of electric turbines, motors, supplies, and appliances grew into an important industry.

Although most inventions necessary to produce radio receivers and transmitters had been perfected before the First World War, radio became a dynamic new industry only when the federal government lifted its ban on the private ownership of sets in 1919. The spread of radio into American homes between 1920 and 1940 was nothing less than astounding. The General Electric and Westinghouse companies organized the Radio Corporation of America in 1919 and began to manufacture radio parts on a small scale. Radio soon became a virtual obsession of the American people, and the production of sets rapidly increased. In 1921 sales of radio parts totaled a mere $10.6 million. In 1939 the industry produced nearly 11 million radios

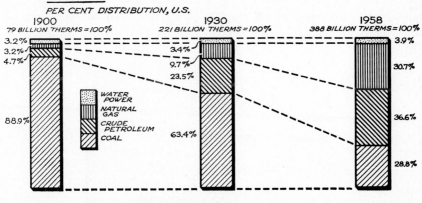

SOURCES OF ENERGY IN THE UNITED STATES
1900–1958

PER CENT DISTRIBUTION, U.S.

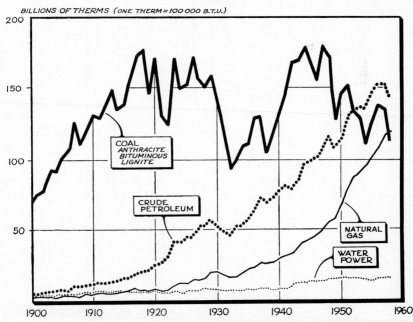

with a total product value of $276 million. And census reporters discovered the following year that 28.5 million American families, or 80 percent of the total number, had radio sets—an increase of 100 percent since 1929.

Two final examples of new industries rising in importance in the postwar period were aviation and motion pictures. Two Americans, Wilbur and Orville Wright, were the first to build and fly successfully an airplane at Kitty Hawk, North Carolina, on December 17, 1903. However, the aviation industry only developed once the United States entered the First World War and began a large-scale program to train pilots and, through an Aircraft Production Board, to construct thousands of aircraft. Although the United States possessed twenty-four plants with the capacity to produce 21,000 planes annually in 1918, the government hastily canceled its orders after the Armistice, and the entire industry nearly collapsed. The industry began to recover and even experienced significant growth during the 1920s. It was aided by two important acts of Congress: in 1925, when Congress authorized the Post Office Department to award contracts for carrying mail to private aircraft companies; and in 1926, when, in the Air Commerce Act, Congress permitted commercial air service and vested control of it in the Commerce Department. By 1930, the aviation

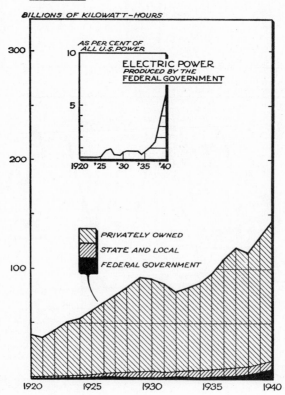

ELECTRICAL POWER PRODUCTION
IN THE UNITED STATES
1920–1940

BILLIONS OF KILOWATT-HOURS

AS PER CENT OF ALL U.S. POWER

ELECTRIC POWER *PRODUCED BY THE* FEDERAL GOVERNMENT

PRIVATELY OWNED

STATE AND LOCAL

FEDERAL GOVERNMENT

industry was firmly established, with 122 airlines in operation over routes covering nearly 50,000 miles. Technological progress was painfully slow until the sluggish and inefficient Ford trimotor aircraft gave way to the all-metal twin-engined Douglas DC-3 in 1936. It at once became the workhorse of the airlines. By 1940 the industry had consolidated to carrying 3,185,000 passengers over routes totaling 94,000 miles.

As we have already seen (see pp. 31–32), the motion-picture industry was already well established on the eve of the First World War. By the 1920s, it was undergoing a period of rapid expansion, testified to by the spread of huge production studios to southern California, the popularity of the star system of film acting, and the construction of new movie houses across the country. Rapid technological developments, the most important of which were sound movies, brought the industry to full maturity by the end of the 1920s. By 1930 the motion-picture industry had a capital investment of some $2 billion and gave employment to 325,000 persons. Motion pictures had become so important a part of American social life that even the depression did not halt the growth or diminish the prosperity of the industry.

The rise of these new industries after 1920 had a wide-ranging effect on American life. Because they depended heavily on technology and capital investment, they were the leaders in the largest decennial rise in productivity in American history. In the process, these growth industries generated opportunity through profits available for reinvestment in other sectors of the economy, through jobs for American workers, and through an overall growth in the demand for goods and services. Perhaps even more remarkable, however, was the effect that technology-intensive industry had on American lifestyles. By 1940, the automobile had become a cultural symbol of power, prestige, and mobility and freedom. Electric power made possible an array of changes in the way Americans lived, not only in lighting, but also in a variety of household appliances. The growth of commercial aviation made rapid transportation and the interconnection of the diverse economies and cultural habits of Americans a possibility. At the same time, the quick rise of radio and motion pictures, both as industries and as cultural media, began to remake the entertainment habits and mores of Americans in other important ways.

3. The Corporate Economy, 1919–1940

The emergence of new technologies and new industries would not have been possible without the spread of the corporate form of business enterprise. It was no accident that each of the major new technology-intensive industries flourished under corporate modes of business organization. By 1929, more than three-fifths of employment in industrial research was concentrated in the electrical, chemical, metals, and rubber industries. Corporations of course integrated mass production and mass distribution. But they also allowed for a truly national means of conducting business which permitted corporations to diversify their product lines and to adapt to regional differences in their marketing. For example, chemical firms like Du Pont and Monsanto all diversified from a narrow base in which they produced primarily one product. Similarly, General Electric—which had previously concentrated on electric power—successfully expanded its production into appliances and radios. Finally, corporations provided a means by which, by attracting investment capital, expensive technology could be introduced and research financed to provide future technology.

Following the recession ending in 1922, a consolidation movement began in industry comparable to a similar movement at the turn of the twentieth century. By 1929, the leading 200 corporations controlled 49 percent of all corporate wealth and received 43 percent of corporate income. For various reasons—mainly the depression and a political climate unfavorable to large-scale enterprise—the merger movement virtually ceased, and concentration in industry was slightly reversed in the 1930s. Five percent of corporations received 85 percent of total corporation income in 1930. The figure declined to 81 percent in 1935 and stood at not quite 84.5 percent four years later.

A major source of capital for industrial expansion came from the savings of middle-class investors rather than from the investment of a few promoters and industrial leaders—which had been the case in the nineteenth century. The medium for this extensive investment, and for industry access to it, was the stock market. Yet the expansion of stock holding also changed the nature of ownership of factories, banks, railroads, and insurance companies. Only 4 million people owned corporate stock in 1900. That number had grown to 20 million thirty years later. The spread of stock ownership had another important consequence: the separation of ownership from control in industry and a managerial revolution in which control passed from single owners or partners, and even from boards of directors, to a salaried bureaucracy, trained in production and distribution. In fact, American industry was so thoroughly bureaucratized by 1929 that the large majority of routine decisions were made by plant managers and shop foremen even in privately held corporations.

The American industrial economy had obviously become highly consolidated by the end of the 1930s, but not to the degree that the bare statistics might imply. Actually, there were few examples of industrial monopoly remaining by 1940, while many important industries, notably textiles, clothing, furniture, and bituminous coal, remained fiercely competitive. In many branches of industry where consolidation occurred, oligopoly—control by a few large producers—was more common than monopoly. For example, in 1937–1938 ten large companies controlled approximately 88 percent of the total productive capacity of the steel industry; three corporations controlled 90 percent of the automobile output; four meat-packing concerns produced 70 percent of the product of that industry; the four largest rubber companies turned out 80 percent of the automobile tires; and four tobacco companies produced 85 percent of the cigarettes.

This trend toward oligopoly, however, did not necessarily signify a diminution of competition. On the contrary, it meant restoration of competition in several important branches of industry. In 1901, for example, United States Steel controlled about 60 percent of the nation's steel ingot capacity. That corporation grew steadily, but its rivals grew even faster, and in 1937 United States Steel controlled only 40 percent of the industry's total steel ingot capacity. At the time of its dissolution in 1911, the Standard Oil Company of New Jersey enjoyed a virtual monopoly over the refining of petroleum in the United States. The dissolution of the holding company into its constituent corporations was followed by the gradual emergence of these companies as independent concerns. Meanwhile, tremendous new amounts of capital entered the oil-refining field, and all the former members of the Standard Oil Trust combined did only about 50 percent of the nation's oil business in 1930. In retailing, also, the rise of mail-order houses and chain stores, which did 25 percent of the retail business in 1935, gave a powerful stimulus to competition in the distribution field.

Other examples could demonstrate that oligopoly actually strengthened competition in many branches of industry in which little competition had existed before 1910. The important phenomenon in this regard, however, was the manner in which competition itself changed during the three decades before 1940. Historic price competition remained in many branches of industry and was always a potential threat in others. But producers in a given branch of industry tended more and more to follow the price leadership of the largest manufacturer and to concentrate on improving and advertising their products.

Industrial growth during the period 1919 to 1929 was accompanied by a rapid accumulation of financial resources. Bankers, security promoters and salesmen, and other financial managers had never before been so numerous or prosperous and had never received such a large share of the national income. Nor had the financial structure of the country ever seemed more solvent. Between 1919 and 1929, total bank capital and surpluses almost doubled, while total banking resources increased from $47.6 billion to $72 billion. Other financial institutions grew at an even faster rate. For example, life insurance companies, which had now emerged as the chief depositories of the people's savings, grew in resources much faster than the banks. Life insurance income and policies in force increased nearly 300 percent from 1919 to 1929, and the aggregate resources of life insurance companies grew from $6.8 billion to $17.5 billion.

Along with expansion came consolidation through the growth of large banking institutions, either through mergers or branch banking. Federal and state legislation had prevented branch banking in the nineteenth century, but by 1920 these laws were amended to allow banks to extend their operations to international and domestic markets. In 1900, fewer than 100 American banks operated in more than one office. By 1919, 464 banks had 1,082 branches; a decade later, these figures had more than doubled, to 816 banks and 3,603 branches. In essence, the banking industry was undergoing the same process of reorganization affecting other kinds of American business: the emergence of larger units of production and distribution through consolidation and rationalization. As a result, multiunit banks' share of banking resources had risen from 16 percent in 1919 to 46 percent in 1929.

Bank consolidation brought yet another change: a diversification of function. The chief function of commercial banks in the past had been to make short-term loans to care for the needs of industry, commerce, and agriculture. The high prosperity of the period from 1922 to 1929 caused corporations to rely increasingly upon profits and upon proceeds from the sale of securities for expansion or even for current needs. As a consequence, bank loans during the prosperity decade did not increase in pace with the rising level of economic activity, and there was no inflation either of bank credit or of the money supply. Coming at a time when banking resources were greatly expanding, this phenomenon caused the managers of large commercial banks to look elsewhere than to business and industry for ways to use idle money. Consequently, they increased bank purchases of stock and bonds by two-thirds and expanded bank loans against real estate by about 350 percent. Most important, they allowed surplus funds to be used to finance reckless speculation. Loans to brokers against stocks and bonds stood at a total of $8.5 billion by late 1929.

The role of commercial banks in abetting stock speculation did not end at this point, for practically all large commercial banks established investment affiliates, hired thousands of salesmen, organized speculative campaigns, and did a flourishing business so long as the upward surge continued.

Meanwhile, the great financial leaders—Kuhn, Loeb & Company, the House of Morgan, and their allies—not only survived but also prospered and grew larger during the New Economic Era. They continued to dominate the financial operations of the railroads, in spite of the efforts of the Interstate Commerce Commission to break their control. They led in organizing and underwriting utility holding companies. They continued to play a major role in marketing securities and wielded influence through interlocking directorships in industrial corporations. And yet events and developments of the twenties changed and greatly weakened their dominance. That weakening came about from competition in the money markets as new financial centers emerged and old ones grew in power. Corporations were too independent and prosperous to remain under the financiers' tutelage. Finally, there was too vast a growth of financial machinery to allow continued domination by one or two firms.

Although banking and finance experienced rapid expansion during the 1920s, significant structural weaknesses were apparent by the end of the decade. The total number of banks declined from 29,767 in 1919 to 25,568 in 1929, primarily because of bank failures in rural areas and in Florida following the collapse of a land boom there in 1926. All told, 5,714 banks closed their doors during the 1920s. Because of its weaknesses, the financial structure could not withstand the series of domestic and international shocks to the economy between 1929 and 1933. We need only sketch the outlines of the troubled financial structure during the 1930s, since we will return to this subject later (see pp. 228–229, 246–248). First came the frightening attrition of the depression and the near collapse of the banking structure in 1933. By 1935, federal reorganization and massive assistance had saved the system and provided new safeguards for the future. Meanwhile, the American people were slowly rebuilding their ravaged financial resources. By 1940 there were only 15,076 banks in operation (as compared with 25,568 in 1929), but they had total resources of nearly $80 billion (as compared with $72 billion in 1929).

4. Work in the Interwar Years

In the decade following the end of the First World War, the trends in labor relations which were earlier apparent (see pp. 16–17) spread to wider reaches of industry. Because of the weakness of organized labor, management was able to systematize the work process and eliminate many of the traditional privileges of workers. Systems of scientific and systematic management made it possible to institute greater supervision over workers and inaugurate a much more tightly articulated corporate hierarchy. Moreover, as part of the same process which brought these innovations, managers also introduced a system of welfare capitalism; work conditions and job status were improved to bolster labor stability and to foster industrial peace.

Changes in the work process that were designed to raise productivity usually accompanied the spread of mass production. Between 1919 and 1929, while the number of wage earners in manufacturing decreased, productivity, as we have seen, greatly increased. Employers achieved increased production in part through a larger supervisory force. Between 1910 and 1930, engineers employed in American industry increased in number from 77,00 to 217,000, managers from 126,000 to 313,000. In increasing pressure on workers to produce and in reducing their control over the work process, the goal of managers was clear: to inaugurate a new era of labor stability and to insure that industrial conflict—and unions—would not interrupt production. These motives became even clearer with the inauguration in the early 1920s of an antiunion campaign. State manufacturers' associations and the National Association of Manufacturers began a crusade in 1920 to restore the "open shop" —a term originating in a meeting of twenty-two manufacturers' associations in Chicago in 1921—and to eradicate organized labor through the "American Plan."

These new labor policies were accompanied by attempts on the part of factory managers to increase on-the-job satisfaction through welfare capitalism and employee-representation plans. Frequently introduced in tandem with scientific management, welfare capitalism spread rapidly during the 1920s. Like the reorganized work process, it sought to insure labor stability and forestall the need for unions. Some firms offered home-ownership plans providing workers with aid to locate and finance homes. Many other businesses provided opportunities for stock ownership; in 1927, 800,000 workers in 315 firms owned stock worth more than $1 billion. Another popular form of welfare capitalism was company-sponsored pension and insurance plans. By the end of the 1920s more than 6 million workers were covered by group insurance plans valued at $7.5 billion. Nor was this all. In probably the most important innovation, employers voluntarily began programs to improve working conditions and to insure greater worker safety. Welfare capitalism did not come cheaply; for United States Steel in the 1920s, it cost about $10 million a year.

With scientific management and welfare capitalism came still another innovation in labor relations: the spread of employee representation plans. They were partly derived from various plans promoting "industrial democracy" in American business which arose in the wake of the violent Colorado coal strike of 1913–1914. Under the leadership of John D. Rockefeller, Jr., his Colorado Fuel & Iron Company began a labor relations program whose chief feature was the formation of a company union dominated by management. Under the sponsorship of the National War Labor Board, this idea gained currency during the First World War, and, following the war, some 317 companies introduced plans by which workers elected representatives to speak before management on their behalf.

These changes in worker–management relations tended to follow the spread of large-scale business enterprise and to be associated with the highly productive, technology-intensive new industries. One study conducted in the 1920s found that of the firms employing under 500 persons, only about 7 percent had industrial-relations departments. At the same time, half of those firms with more than 2,000 employees had them. It was thus no mere coincidence that corporate-run manufacturing, in championing these changes, was also able to diminish the power of workers and to succeed remarkably well in thwarting—and even reducing—the strength of organized labor.

5. The Decline of Organized Labor, 1920–1932

Scientific management, welfare capitalism, and employee-representation plans were partly responsible for the era of industrial peace that began after 1920. In some declining industries, such as textiles and coal mining, union officials acquiesced in wage incentive plans so as to boost productivity and forestall layoffs. Especially when management accepted the principle of collective bargaining, labor leaders went to unusual lengths to prove that cooperation was more profitable than conflict. For example, the Amalgamated Clothing Workers of America assumed responsibility for shop discipline, encouraged efforts to increase efficiency, and even lent money to clothing manufacturers in distress. In the wake of these developments, tensions between management and organized labor lessened appreciably after 1921. The average number of strikes per year declined from 3,503 for the period 1916 to 1921 to 1,304 during the years 1922 to 1925, and to 791 from 1926 through 1930. Put another way, in 1919, 4 million workers went on strike. Ten years later, only 300,000 were involved in strikes.

Yet this era of labor peace was achieved at the expense of the power of organized labor, especially the AFL. Under its president, William Green, who succeeded Samuel Gompers on his death in 1924, the AFL became increasingly conservative, and it accepted welfare capitalism if accompanied by union recognition and the right of collective bargaining. In spite of a growing restiveness in the ranks of workers, labor leaders steadfastly refused to provide aggressive leadership. Thus, while the AFL declined to launch movements to organize industry-wide unions and thereby abandon its trade-union approach, it also faced a challenge from the Communist party which, under William Z. Foster, began a serious campaign in 1922 to organize workers. Although the AFL leadership fought hard and successfully to uproot Communists, in a number of industries such as cotton textiles and automobiles workers were attracted to their militant style of union leadership.

It is little wonder, therefore, that liberal critics of the AFL and the railroad brotherhoods charged that organized labor had ceased to speak for the great mass of workers and had become a bulwark of the established order. It was little wonder, also, that the power of organized labor not only did not grow but instead steadily declined during the 1920s. Trade-union membership fell generally from 5 million in 1920 to 2.9 million in 1932, while membership in the AFL fell from 4 million to 2.5 million. Part of this loss resulted from the AFL's failure to consolidate gains during the First World War; part of it was caused by the employers' counteroffensive; and a small part stemmed from losses incurred by unemployment during the depression. But the most important factor was timid leadership.

The violent experiences of workers in coal mining and textiles during the decade 1920–1930 stand in striking contrast to the generalizations of the foregoing discussion. These two industries remained highly competitive, unstable, and plagued by overproduction and dislocations resulting from the movement, especially by textile manufacturers, into the low-wage area of the South. Frontier social conditions still prevailed to a large degree in mining areas and mill towns. Low wages and attempts by employers to preserve their autocratic rule stimulated efforts at unionization. And these organizational campaigns were accompanied by the kind of violent warfare that had often characterized the American industrial scene before the First World War.

The United Mine Workers of America emerged from the bituminous coal strike of 1919 superficially defeated but actually strengthened by the award of the Bituminous Coal Commission and by simultaneous negotiations with the anthracite operators. Along the frontier of the bituminous industry in West Virginia and eastern Kentucky, however, an outbreak occurred that ended in disastrous defeat for the UMW. The union's attempt to organize mines in West Virginia in 1919 and 1920 provoked fierce resistance by operators and pitched battles between striking miners and imported guards. The governor declared martial law in the strike area, and state and federal troops momentarily stopped the fighting. Then violence again erupted in 1921, after the miners organized an army of 4,000 men and began to invade the strike zone. The uprising quickly collapsed when President Harding dispatched 2,100 troops to the area, and state authorities arrested the strike leaders on charges of treason, murder, and conspiracy.

The West Virginia civil war marked the beginning of a decade of conflict in the troubled coal fields. Negotiations for new contracts with bituminous and anthracite operators failed in early 1922, and John L. Lewis, president of the UMW, called miners out in the greatest coal strike in American history to that time. There was no violence until the Southern Illinois Coal Company, in Williamson County, Illinois, imported strikebreakers and attempted to resume operations in June 1922. The killing of two strikers by mine guards brought swift retaliation at Herrin, when enraged miners slaughtered nineteen strikebreakers. Tempers subsided after the Herrin Massacre, and a test of endurance between the UMW and the operators then followed. In the late summer the operators gave in.

Although Lewis forced the operators to renew their contracts in 1924, the UMW soon experienced a series of catastrophic developments. Increased competition from nonunion operators in the South and West forced northern and midwestern operators to cut wages. At the same time, left-wing and Communist leaders in the UMW began an attempt in 1926 to destroy Lewis's allegedly dictatorial and corrupt control. Although the movement failed, it seriously weakened the UMW and led to the formation of two rival unions, a reorganized UMW and the Communist-controlled National Miners' Union. Lewis preserved a semblance of collective bargaining in the coal industry by accepting wage reductions during contract negotiations in 1927. But, by 1929, the once proud UMW was so weakened, both from within and from without, that it would be helpless to cope with problems raised by the depression.

Tensions and conflicts also plagued the textile industry during the 1920s. New England manufacturers, pleading southern competition and depressed economic circumstances, cut wages about 20 percent in 1921. When they attempted to raise hours and impose another 20 percent wage cut early in the following year, a series of strikes by the United Textile Workers and left-wing unions ensued that forced a restoration of the old wage and hour scales. In Passaic, New Jersey, the large woolen textile mills in that city cut wages 10 percent in September 1925. A United Front Committee under Communist leadership began a strike in January 1926. It quickly spread to all the large mills. After the Communists withdrew from leadership in the strike, the United Textile Workers of the AFL took control and brought it to a successful conclusion in March 1927.

Northern textile workers were able to stave off wage reductions after 1921 by such means. But the rise of southern manufacturers to dominance in the industry, and the movement of New England mills to the South in the 1920s, posed a serious long-range menace to union wages in the North. Obviously, safety for northern workers lay in eliminating the sectional wage differential—by unionizing southern mills and imposing a uniform national wage scale.

The United Textile Workers, after a brief and successful attempt to organize the southern mills in 1919, invaded the South again in 1927 and 1928. They found the mass of workers bitter and resentful over long hours, low wages, the "stretch-out," and above all, high profits for mill owners. They also found complete dominance by mill owners, who, in alliance with local police and state officials, were ready to use any means to prevent unionization. It is not surprising that one of the bloodiest outbreaks of labor violence in recent American history ensued.

The disturbances began in March 1929, when more than 5,000 rayon textile workers in Elizabethton, Tennessee, struck against a low wage scale. Local vigilante groups combined with company guards, state troops, and the courts to drive the organizers of the United Textile Workers from the mills. A month later the Communist-controlled National Textile Workers' Union began a strike against the largest cotton mill in Gastonia, North Carolina, the center of the textile industry. The strike collapsed after the conviction, in October 1929, of seven of the Communist leaders for the second-degree murder of the Gastonia chief of police. At the same time, a United Textile Workers strike in Marion, North Carolina, ended with the slaughter of five and the wounding of nineteen unarmed pickets by a sheriff's posse. The United Textile Workers made their most formidable effort in the autumn of 1930 at the Riverside and Dan River mills in Danville, Virginia. The owners stubbornly refused either to bargain with the union or to submit to arbitration, and the strikers had to surrender to avoid starvation.

Although the decade ended with declining union power and tense labor-management relations in coal and textiles, in other respects governmental and public opinion began to turn in favor of organized labor. Federal endorsement, in principle, of collective bargaining between railroads and their employees occurred during the 1920s. The Transportation Act of 1920 created a Railroad Labor Board that demonstrated its ineffectiveness after it failed to prevent a nationwide strike of railway shopmen in 1922. In 1926, in the Railway Labor Act, Congress strengthened the mediation and arbitration machinery and, more important, virtually compelled railroads to eschew company unionism and deal exclusively with the independent brotherhoods. Another example of changing federal labor policy was the Senate's refusal in 1930 to confirm the nomination of Circuit Court Judge John J. Parker to the Supreme Court. Among other things, his opponents pointed out that Parker had upheld the use of injunctions to prohibit organizers from attempting to unionize workers who had signed a yellow-dog contract—that is, an agreement between employer and employee in which the worker agreed not to join a union as a condition of employment. Finally, Congress in March 1932 adopted the Anti-Injunction Act sponsored by Representative Fiorello La Guardia of New York and Senator George W. Norris of Nebraska. This measure made yellow-dog contracts unenforceable in federal courts; forbade issuance of injunctions against a number of hitherto outlawed union practices; and guaranteed jury trials in cases involving violations of criminal injunctions. Together, these instances, although not suggesting a revolution in federal policy, heralded more important changes after 1932.

Chapter 10

-->>> <<<-

American Society and Culture, 1920–1940

The period between the Armistice and the beginning of the Second World War was a time of rapid social and cultural change. The industrial revolution had already affected two generations of Americans, and the resulting changes in lifestyles, work, and cultural interaction were at least partly clear by the end of the war. Even so, the remaking of American society and culture after 1920 constituted a change of a different kind. In a delayed, "ripple" effect, economic change fostered an array of cultural responses known broadly as "modernism." Its extent ranged widely, from the pervasive alienation of intellectuals to the nationalization of popular culture in motion pictures and the new broadcasting media, and to changes in sexual practices and moral standards. Yet the triumph of modernism was not entirely unqualified, for it evoked strong, yet also ambivalent, resistance among large numbers of Americans.

The period between the world wars was a time of growth and change in other respects. Americans poured out money to improve and expand public schools and construct the most extensive system of higher education in the world. Although facing strong secularizing forces, American Protestantism continued to prosper and even expanded its role in American society. Moreover, the period after 1920 was also characterized by important changes in the status of women at home and at work, changes which set the stage for an even more extensive transformation after 1945. And, while it was a period of growing racial intolerance, it was also an era of unprecedented cultural independence among the newly urbanized blacks in northern cities.

1. The Prohibition Experiment

Nothing better illustrates the tone of American culture during the 1920s than the unique social experiment that undertook to prohibit the manufacture and sale of alcoholic beverages in the United States. Historians and contemporaries alike have long regarded prohibition as a curious aberration. Actually, it arose from central currents in American culture. Beginning in the late eighteenth century, most of the western world consumed significantly greater quantities of alcohol, especially of distilled gin, vodka, and whiskies, than previously. So serious was the resultant social problem that contemporaries described early nineteenth-century America as "the alcoholic republic."

In response to this urgent social problem, temperance reformers had long been active in nineteenth-century American society, and eventually they advocated complete prohibition. By the end of 1914, fourteen states had adopted prohibition; within four years, over three-fourths of Americans lived in either "dry" states or counties. Rather than the product of sudden impulse or wartime hysteria, prohibition was an important component of social reform and demonstrated better than any other aspect of that movement the progressive faith in the efficacy of legislation to accomplish fundamental social change.

On the other hand, the main national advocate of prohibition, the Anti-Saloon League, might never have won the Eighteenth, or prohibition, Amendment without the entrance of the United States into the war. Many champions of local option and state rights had consistently opposed such far-reaching extension of federal authority as national prohibition would involve. But Anti-Saloon spokesmen succeeded in identifying prohibition with patriotism: conservative voices were momentarily stilled. Consequently, the dry leaders were able to carry the government and people from one step to another in their relentless campaign.

To begin with, the Anti-Saloon lobbyists forced adoption of an amendment to the Selective Service Act of 1917 forbidding the sale of alcoholic beverages at or near army camps and naval bases. Secondly, the Lever Act of 1917—an effort to conserve needed grain—prohibited the use of grain for distilling and brewing and empowered the president to ban manufacture of other alcoholic beverages. Thirdly, Congress, on December 18, 1917, passed and submitted to the states the Eighteenth Amendment. It prohibited, one year after ratification, the manufacture, sale, or transportation of alcoholic beverages in the United States. Fourthly, Congress in October 1919 passed, over Wilson's veto, the Volstead Act. It extended the wartime ban on distilling and brewing and defined alcoholic beverages as those containing more than one-half of 1 percent alcohol by volume. Finally, Congress prohibited the manufacture or sale of any such beverages after the Eighteenth Amendment had gone into effect in January 1920.

Meanwhile, all the states except Connecticut and Rhode Island approved the Eighteenth Amendment. Nebraska—the home of William Jennings Bryan, one of the prime leaders of the prohibition crusade—appropriately provided the decisive thirty-sixth ratification on January 16, 1919. Nationwide prohibition went into force a year later; but, since the country had in effect been dry since the summer of 1917, there were few protest demonstrations. Bryan held a victory celebration in New York in March 1920 and announced that the liquor issue was as dead as slavery. The first prohibition commissioner later promised that no liquor would be manufactured, "nor sold, nor given away, nor hauled in anything on the surface of the earth or under the earth or in the air."

Of course, it did not turn out that way. Strict enforcement was impossible unless the government put a million agents in the field and sternly suppressed personal liberty. Partial enforcement was possible only if a large majority of the people were determined to exterminate the liquor traffic. There was probably a considerable decline in drinking and the sale of liquor in rural and strongly Protestant areas, where public opinion generally supported state and federal enforcement authorities. In fact, prohibition was accompanied by a sharp decline throughout the country in the measurable results of drinking—arrests for drunkenness and deaths from alcoholism.

The difficulties of enforcement were, however, enormous from the outset. The politically dry majority in Congress followed the advice of the Anti-Saloon League throughout the 1920s in making appropriations and tightening enforcement laws. Even so, such provisions were hopelessly inadequate without the full support of local officials and public opinion. There were only 1,520 agents in the Prohibition Bureau in 1920 and 2,836 ten years later. As a consequence, enforcement was spasmodic, largely ineffective in areas where public opinion was hostile to the Eighteenth Amendment, and often violent and corrupt because of the bad character and strong-arm methods of many agents.

The two chief obstacles to enforcement were the determined resistance of large and important segments of the population and the fanaticism of dry leaders. Probably a majority of people in states with large foreign-born populations—like Massachusetts, New York, New Jersey, Maryland, Illinois, Ohio, and Wisconsin—would have voted against prohibition in a national referendum. Certainly the overwhelming majority in the large cities, native and foreign-born alike, thought that they had an inalienable right to drink. Consequently, neither local or state officials nor the masses of people in these states and cities supported enforcement. Instead, they rallied behind organizations like the Association Against the Prohibition Amendment and political leaders like Governor Albert C. Ritchie of Maryland and Governor Alfred E. Smith of New York, who worked for the repeal of the Eighteenth Amendment.

Prohibition might have succeeded had dry leaders realized that most opposition to the Eighteenth Amendment stemmed from the ban on the sale of beer and light wine. Immediately after ratification of the Eighteenth Amendment, the legislatures of Wisconsin, Massachusetts, New York, Maryland, and New Jersey adopted laws outlawing saloons and sale of hard liquors but permitting sale of light beer. Instead of accepting this slight deviation from perfection, Anti-Saloon lobbyists forced adoption of the Volstead Act and successfully challenged the constitutionality of the beer laws of these states. Inevitably officials and masses of people in the "wet" states not only refused to respect prohibition but began a relentless war against the dry regime.

The consequences of prohibition—that "noble experiment" in federal social control—were as remarkable as the difficulties that the effort raised. For one thing, prohibition brought in its wake a series of social innovations among the wet minority. Speakeasies instead of saloons, hip flasks at football games, bathtub gin, and the increasing popularity of the cocktail party—these were some of the examples of defiance of the Eighteenth Amendment. Another phenomenon of the Prohibition Era was an increase in drinking by women. Saloons before the war had been exclusively male preserves in which no respectable woman would be seen. In contrast, mixed drinking in the home and speakeasy became the rule after 1919—another sign of the emancipation of women.

The most disastrous consequence of prohibition was the tremendous surge of bootlegging—the illicit production and sale of alcoholic beverages—that followed adoption of the Eighteenth Amendment. Bootlegging in turn encouraged organization of underworld gangs that went into rackets of various kinds, bought control of city governments, and seriously threatened democratic government in American cities during the 1920s and early 1930s. Prohibition alone was not responsible for this development. Organized vice and gambling had long been prevalent in American cities, and gangsterism, racketeering, and organized blackmail developed almost in direct proportion to the spread of the automobile and the ease with which criminals could purchase weapons of wholesale slaughter like the submachine gun. Even so, bootlegging was the chief livelihood and source of income of the gangs.

The truth of this generalization can be demonstrated by a brief account of the rise of the Capone gang in Chicago, the most important underworld association of the 1920s. The story begins in 1920, when young Alphonse, or Al, Capone moved to Chicago after serving a brief apprenticeship in the underworld of New York City. He was soon not only master of his own gang but also the leading bootlegger and gambling and vice operator in the Chicago area, with a gross income by 1927 of $60 million a year. Ironically, most of Capone's income from bootlegging came from the sale of beer. With a private army of from 700 to 1,000 gangsters, he ruthlessly crushed rivals who dared to challenge his sovereignty, and Chicago witnessed pitched battles and mass gang killings that made his name a byword. Capone was toppled from his high eminence only when a Treasury agent worked his way into the organization and obtained evidence that led to the gangster's conviction and imprisonment in 1931 for federal income tax evasion.

Opposition to the Eighteenth Amendment, sporadic and unorganized at the beginning of the 1920s, mounted after New York repealed its enforcement laws in 1923 and the Democratic party in the eastern states assumed leadership of the antiprohibition movement. Republicans continued from 1920 to 1932 to support the "noble experiment," as Herbert Hoover characterized the prohibition effort, without any important division in their ranks. On the other hand, Democrats were so badly split over prohibition, among other issues, that they practically ceased to be a national party in the twenties.

The end of the "noble experiment" came not long after an apparently sweeping popular endorsement of it in the presidential election of 1928. Soon after his inauguration, President Hoover appointed a commission headed by former Attorney General George W. Wickersham to investigate the problems of enforcement. The commission's report, presented in 1931, revealed what most informed Americans already knew—that the whole process of enforcement had broken down, and that it was virtually impossible to impose dryness upon a determined minority. Moreover, the conviction grew and was shared by many persons who originally had approved the experiment that prohibition simply was not worth the political and social costs —among others, the disruption of the Democratic party, subversion of the right of the states to control social customs, widespread contempt for law bred by prohibition, and, most important, the stimulus that it gave to organized crime and bootleg-ging.

By 1932, problems of relief and recovery from the depression overshadowed all other issues. In that year a reunited Democratic party came out frankly for repeal of the Eighteenth Amendment and resumption of state control over the liquor traffic. The deed was quickly done after the smashing Democratic victory in November. The lame-duck session in February 1933 passed and submitted to the people the Twenty-first Amendment. It repealed the Eighteenth Amendment and prohib-ited the transportation of liquor into any dry state or territory. The same Congress also legalized the sale of light beer in March 1933. Three-fourths of the states had ratified the Twenty-first Amendment by the following December, and the "noble experiment," so auspiciously begun, was over.

2. The Sexual Revolution and the Changing Status of Women

Perhaps the most astonishing aspect of the changes in manners and moral standards which occurred after 1918 was the rapidity with which forces that had long been eroding a historic code of standards suddenly destroyed it among influential ele-ments. In its ethical aspects, the traditional system taught respect for parental authority, idealized the husband–father as master of the family, and required premarital chastity and marital fidelity. This code provided the basic guide to life for most Americans before the First World War. It was often violated, to be sure; but it was accepted as an ideal standard that was practically and morally sound.

The postwar rebellion against this moral and social system manifested itself in the first self-conscious youth revolt in American history. Adolescents, congregating in larger numbers in high school and colleges, began to challenge traditional rules governing sexual relations. Some barriers broke down because of wartime disruption; other forces kept them down during the 1920s and 1930s. More extensive use of automobiles extended the possibilities of love making far beyond the sitting room. But even more important was the phenomenal spread of the teachings of Sigmund Freud, a Viennese psychoanalyst, whose writings were popularly misinterpreted to mean that the main cause of maladjusted personality was the suppression of sexual desire, and that a free expression of the libido, or sexual energies, promoted mental health.

Whatever the causes, the breakdown of traditional moral standards was wide-spread. F. Scott Fitzgerald's *This Side of Paradise,* a story of undergraduate life at Princeton, and Charles C. Wertenbaker's novels about students at the University of Virginia undoubtedly drew exaggerated pictures. But sexual promiscuity and drinking among college students became to a degree fashionable. High school students, too, indulged in new freedoms on a shocking scale.

If there was any single most striking social phenomenon of the 1920s and 1930s, it was a growing obsession with sex. Highbrows read James Branch Cabell's erotic novels and applauded Eugene O'Neill's powerful dramas based on Freudian themes. Larger audiences were titillated by a new form of literature—the confession magazines, which featured lurid stories about fallen women or high school girls who had "gone wrong." The most successful of these new periodicals, *True Story,* began with a small circulation in 1919 and approached the 2 million mark seven years later. Motion pictures also emphasized sexual themes. The maidenly Mary Pickford was supplanted as "America's sweetheart" by the voluptuous Clara Bow—the "It" girl of the 1920s—and by the equally voluptuous Jean Harlow in the 1930s.

Another manifestation of changing moral standards was the spread of new kinds of ballroom dancing. Decorous forms such as the waltz gave way to the fox trot, the Charleston, and, late in the thirties, the jitterbug. To defenders of older forms, modern dancing provided further evidence of the general breakdown of sexual standards, and church groups launched heroic but vain attacks upon what they called the "syncopated embrace." The modern dance, exclaimed the Reverend John William Porter of Kentucky in his tract, *The Dangers of the Dance* (1922), was based on the sexual instinct. "If this be not true, why is it that women do not dance with women, and men with men? . . . The mix-up is the magnet. A man dancing with a man is about as satisfactory as near-beer to the old drunkard."

An even more important change in American society occurred in the status of women. The adoption of the Nineteenth Amendment gave women the franchise, and the 1920s and 1930s saw women not only voting but also holding political offices. Although employers still discriminated grossly against women in wages and salaries, women continued to enter the work force after 1920. There was a sharp decline in the number of women employed in farming, and virtually no increase in the number in domestic service. On the other hand, employment of middle-class women in industry, public schools, service industries, and business enterprise expanded rapidly. By 1940, the 14.2 million working women constituted 25 percent of the nation's entire working force, as contrasted with about 18 percent in 1900.

The majority of middle-class married women who remained in the home experienced radical change after 1920. More readily available electrical appliances, central heat, and processed food products reduced the time and drudgery of housework for most urban women. Gas and electricity replaced wood and coal as primary sources of energy, and these fuels lessened or eliminated the tasks of chopping and carrying wood and cleaning the ever-present soot and dirt from fireplaces and stoves. Running water, hot and cold, freed housewives of other responsibilities, as did the widespread availability of refrigerators and gas and electric stoves. Equally significant were innovations in cleaning technologies: vacuum cleaners and washing machines resulted in tremendous reductions of human energy expended at home. These changes in the home environment added up to gains in productivity which matched those in industry. Housework, like factory work, entered an age of mechanization.

Expanding opportunities for middle-class women largely accounted for the revolution in feminine attitudes and manners that began in the early 1920s. Masculine supremacy had been based upon man's economic leadership in the family. That primacy rapidly deteriorated as unmarried women moved into apartments of their own and went into school teaching or office work. Wives gained independence either by going to work or threatening to do so. As they became more nearly autonomous, women married later, had fewer children, and were more willing to dissolve the marriage bonds. Between 1914 and 1940, the divorce rate nearly doubled.

Outward signs of the change were especially disturbing to those who believed in the old way of life. As the barriers fell on all sides, women began to smoke cigarettes and, what seemed worse to traditionalists, demanded and asserted the right to drink with men. As women went to work in large numbers they began to discard historic badges of femininity. The first casualty of feminine independence was the traditional dress that covered the neck and arms and carefully hid the ankles. The average skirt was about six inches from the ground in 1919. From this time on the ascent was spectacular, until the skirt had reached the knees or even above by 1927.

Changes in the status of women reflected a new role for the family itself. As part of a long-term trend that began in the nineteenth century, families by the 1920s were no longer primarily units of production. Instead, they tended to be units defined by love and affection; if they were not, the recourse of divorce was increasingly conceivable. Smaller families and greater assertiveness on the part of women both inside and outside of the home had broad consequences. The general acceptance of a new code which exalted happiness as the supreme objective of marriage, permitted divorce, and gave women and children more equality with men in family relationships signified the emergence of new social bases of American life.

3. Blacks in the Postwar Years

One of the most important changes in twentieth-century America was the migration of millions of rural southern blacks to northern cities between the First World War and the 1970s. Black migration brought important changes. It made national what had once been southern problems—racial conflict and poverty—and raised a host of new issues for Americans to confront for the rest of the century. Yet the Great Migration also provided new opportunities for blacks. In northern cities, blacks gained power, self-awareness, and autonomy—the open expression of which had long been denied them in the South. Northern urban blacks used the vote to exercise an increasing influence on local, state, and national politics. Moreover, although black communities had long existed in northern cities, their rapid expansion provided greater opportunities for cultural power and autonomy.

From the forums of northern cities, moreover, the continuing debate about the road to black uplift continued. W. E. B. Du Bois, editor of *The Crisis*, favored political power, elite education, and legal challenge to segregation as the chief tools of improvement. Militant in style, Du Bois and his followers also favored alliance with liberal whites and a program in which integration was the ultimate objective. But attitudes in the black community were changing rapidly in the 1920s. Much of Booker T. Washington's appeal lay in his exaltation of self-help; although he endorsed accommodation with whites, Washington stressed an independent black leadership. Ironically, the most militant and controversial black leader of the postwar era, the black nationalist, Marcus Garvey, claimed descent from Washington and carried Washington's program to a radical extreme. Born in Jamaica, Garvey had a checkered career as printer, journalist, and politician in the Caribbean. In 1912, he traveled to London, where he came under the influence of then emerging Pan-Africanist thinkers. Returning to Jamaica two years later, Garvey founded the Universal Negro Improvement Association (UNIA) as an organization devoted to "lifting the masses" based on Washington's Tuskegee model of self-help.

Unsuccessful and strapped for funds in Jamaica, Garvey met greater success when he moved to New York in 1916. In spite of NAACP hostility, Garvey was soon attracting large crowds in black Harlem to his rallies. There he preached a message of racial pride and urged blacks to follow him back to Africa to build a "free, redeemed and mighty nation." Within two years, the UNIA had grown so strong that it threatened the security of more established civil-rights groups. Claiming 4 million followers in 1920 and 6 million in 1923, Garvey proclaimed himself provisional president of an African empire in 1921 and raised funds for a Black Star steamship line to carry his people home. Garvey appealed to the same group that had followed Washington—southern rural blacks. The South thus had the largest UNIA chapters, with Louisiana possessing the largest state membership.

Yet Garvey's form of black nationalism ran afoul of potent opposition. Governmental officials feared his radicalism, and J. Edgar Hoover's FBI thoroughly infiltrated the UNIA. By 1924, Garvey had alienated most black leaders in the country and his empire had begun to crumble. In 1923, Garvey was convicted in federal court of using the mails to defraud and was sentenced to the Atlanta penitentiary for a five-year term. He was subsequently deported. American blacks, obviously, would not go back to Africa, but the fact that so many of them rallied to Garvey's standard provided strong evidence that black racial self-respect was growing.

The fusion of self-help and militant resistance to white authority was reflected in other new developments in the black community. Especially in urban centers in the Middle West and Northeast, black artists enjoyed unprecedented successes. Ragtime, derived partly from folk musical traditions and partly from experiences in late nineteenth-century bordellos and honky-tonks, was developed by black musicians into a form with a national following. During and after the migration, however, an even greater cultural market existed in the North for the exotic new musical forms of jazz and the blues in St. Louis and Chicago. By the end of the 1930s, white musicians were strongly influenced by black popular music.

Harlem emerged as a capital of the new black renaissance. As a result of massive black immigration after the First World War, it contained the world's largest black urban population by the 1920s, and there blacks exercised unprecedented political power and cultural autonomy. Harlem also became home to a host of new black writers. Some of them were native New Yorkers, like the poet Countee Cullen, who attended high school in New York and was graduated from New York University. Another poet, one who became Cullen's protégé, was Langston Hughes: he emigrated from Cleveland to Harlem. Along with other Harlem intellectuals, such as Jean Toomer, Claude McKay, and and Alain L. Locke, these writers presented a new view of blacks' place in American culture.

4. Modernism and American Thought

A significant cultural phenomenon in the postwar years was the rise of a self-conscious class of American intellectuals. What distinguished postwar intellectuals from earlier generations was their alienation from the main currents of American culture. A new type of cultural radicalism had its beginning during the First World War among the small colony of bohemians located in Greenwich Village in New York. At the same time, other intellectuals endorsed a critique of what they thought were the fundamental assumptions of American culture.

These rebels were alienated, above all, by what they thought was the cant, hypocrisy, and low cultural level of American life. Young intellectuals of the early 1920s, like the literary critic Harold Stearns, objected to the "morbid perversities" of American life—the small-town anti-intellectualism, the "shoddy, cheap" newspapers that gave more space to baseball than to the theater, the demand for conformity, the emphasis upon utilitaran virtues, the "democracy of mountebanks." They felt rejected, unwanted, and pressured to conform. If they were impecunious, they sought fellowship in Greenwich Village; if they had an independent income, they moved to the Left Bank in Paris to find freedom and cultural refreshment with fellow expatriates.

H. L. Mencken, the chief intellectual rebel of the decade, illustrates the dimensions of this cultural revolt. A native of Baltimore, Mencken received his literary training as a reporter for the Baltimore *Sun,* wrote an excellent study of the American language, and briefly edited a "little" magazine, *The Smart Set,* with George Jean Nathan. Then, in collaboration with Alfred A. Knopf, Mencken and Nathan began publication in 1922 of *American Mercury,* a monthly addressed to like-minded dissenters. Mencken's observations on the American scene were barbed and pungent, and *American Mercury* soon became the Bible of the cultural radicals. Mencken ridiculed idealism, democracy, organized religion, prudery, cant, prohibition, and ignorance. For example, to him, morality and Christian marriage were absurdities; patriotism was imbecilic; the American people were mainly a vast collection of peasants, boobs, and hillbillies.

Other writers of the 1920s expressed a similar pessimism about American society and identified themselves as part of a new tradition of modernism in the arts. Some of the new novelists used the war as a setting. A spate of war novels and plays depicted the misery of trench warfare and its moral and spiritual bankruptcy. John Dos Passos's *Three Soldiers* (1921) portrayed life as reduced to a primeval struggle, chaotic and without moral rules. Ernest Hemingway's *A Farewell to Arms* (1929) summarized a decade of revulsion against wartime idealism.

Preoccupation with sex, which they often glorified as the primal drive, was characteristic of all these writers. There was, however, considerable difference in emphasis. To writers like Theodore Dreiser and Sherwood Anderson, sex was only one of the important drives that determined behavior. But there was a group who were concerned with sexual themes almost to the point of obsession. One of these was James Branch Cabell, author of *Jurgen* (1919), *Figures of Earth* (1921), and *Something About Eve* (1927), novels whose vivid symbolism drew the fire of professional defenders of American morality. More subtle was F. Scott Fitzgerald, a superb storyteller and one of the most talented writers of his generation. In *This Side of Paradise* (1920), *The Beautiful and The Damned* (1922), and *The Great Gatsby* (1925), Fitzgerald chronicled the moral and spiritual dissolution of the Lost Generation, to whom, as he said, all gods were dead, all wars fought, all faiths shaken.

Other writers found a similar degree of moral confusion and hypocrisy pervading American life. Sherwood Anderson, in *Winesburg, Ohio* (1919), *Poor White* (1920), *Many Marriages* (1923), and other novels and stories, attempted to unmask what he considered the perversities of the small-town Middle West. In stories about small-town and country people of the Middle West and South, Ring Lardner and Erskine Caldwell were morbidly fascinated by the diseased in mind and body. As the decade drew to a close, a southern rebel, Thomas Wolfe, published *Look Homeward, Angel* (1929), the expression of a tortured young soul in rebellion against the materialism of his mother and the narrow provincialism of his home town of Asheville, North Carolina.

Even more harsh and almost captious in depicting the drabness of small-town midwestern life, the provincialism and smugness of the business booster, and the moral sham and materialism of his time was Sinclair Lewis. His *Main Street* (1920), *Babbitt* (1922), *Arrowsmith* (1925), *Elmer Gantry* (1927), and *Dodsworth* (1929) presented caricatures of types of middle-class Americans and, in 1930, won for their author the first Nobel Prize in literature ever awarded an American.

In other areas of intellectual life, the effects of modernism were more subtle. University-based social scientists lost the moral certainty exhibited by their predecessors before the First World War. In particular, they were affected by two common influences: cultural relativism and logical positivism. Both rejected guiding Victorian intellectual assumptions. Cultural relativism questioned the superiority of European culture and institutions, while logical positivism required that all conclusions be subjected to systematic proof and verification. Historians abandoned their preoccupation with political institutions and advanced scholarship deep into the frontiers of intellectual, social, and economic history. Sociologists broke loose from the subjective method, developed new, objective criteria, and launched new studies of ecology, urbanization, population, and race relations. The study of anthropology in the United States became an integral part of university curricula rather than merely an avocation of museum scholars. Social psychology became an independent discipline. A host of economists abandoned preoccupation with economic "laws" and set to work to analyze, describe, and dissect the American economic system (see pp. 54–55).

After 1920, social scientists became more neutral in tone than their predecessors, more specialized, and more oriented toward their professional colleagues than to the public at large. Yet many social scientists provided devastating critiques of contemporary American society. The grandfather of modern anthropology, Franz Boas, rejected the way Victorian anthropologists ranked civilizations by order of superiority and advanced a notion of cultural relativism which was to be based on thorough field investigation. Retreat from the absolute certainty of the Victorian age similarly characterized the work of a group of "debunking" American historians. Progressive historians like Vernon Louis Parrington and Charles A. Beard questioned the motives of the revered heroes of American history, while other historians, such as James Truslow Adams, ridiculed the Puritans' supposedly repressive attitudes toward sex.

In retrospect, it is clear that modernism transformed American intellectual life. By the end of the First World War, if not before, intellectuals were united by a common awareness of the modern world and a revulsion toward the traditionalism of most Americans. For some, modernism meant a countercultural flamboyance in flouting taboos for its own sake; for others, it meant deriding, to use Mencken's word, the "boobery" of American culture. Yet alienation and the loss of certainty about values and the progress of the modern world led still other intellectuals toward experimentation and innovation in private life as well as in politics.

5. School and Church in the Interwar Era

The impact of modernism was also felt in schools and churches. Educational institutions at all levels grew very rapidly in the 1920s and, although growth was slowed by the depression, schools were, by 1940, indisputably the most important vehicles of the socialization of youths and determinants of status. Churches, traditionally important institutions in shaping American culture, responded differently to the impact of modernism. Secularization occasioned a decline in the relative importance of American Protestantism, which, with the emergence of popular culture, began to lose its dominant position in group interaction. But many Protestants embraced modernism and incorporated it into a new, liberal form of Christianity.

Progress in expanding and improving free education had been steady and substantial from the Civil War to 1920. The prosperity of the twenties, however, stimulated such achievement as had not been recorded in any earlier comparable period. Then came heavy blows in consequence of diminished revenues during the depression, followed by slow but steady recovery to new heights in the late 1930s. The following generalizations illustrate the main trends. The number of pupils enrolled in public schools from 1920 to 1940 increased from 21.6 million to nearly 25.5 million. Total expenditures for education grew during the same two decades from $1 billion to $2.3 billion, the number of teachers from 680,000 to 875,000, and expenditure per pupil from $53.52 to $88.09. Illiteracy declined during the same period from 6 percent of the total population to 3 percent, and among nonwhites (mainly blacks) from 23 percent to 11.5 percent.

Free elementary education was available on a wide scale by 1920, and, except for expansion in kindergartens and in schools for black children, progress accomplished in the elementary field from 1920 to 1940 came more from improved instruction, longer terms, and the like, than from any great expansion in sheer numbers. State departments of education assumed responsibility for licensing teachers and began to require completion of a four-year college course as a prerequisite for a teaching certificate. Progressive education, as advocated earlier by John Dewey and others, found wider acceptance, and schools of education broke away from the formal classical tradition. Traditionalists bemoaned the change, but increased emphasis upon experimentation and participation by children, as well as widespread use

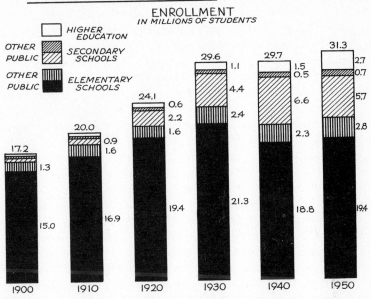

AMERICAN PUBLIC EDUCATION:
A HALF CENTURY OF GROWTH, 1900–1950

ENROLLMENT
IN MILLIONS OF STUDENTS

HIGHER EDUCATION

OTHER PUBLIC — SECONDARY SCHOOLS

OTHER PUBLIC — ELEMENTARY SCHOOLS

	1900	1910	1920	1930	1940	1950
Total	17.2	20.0	24.1	29.6	29.7	31.3
Higher			0.6	1.1	1.5	2.7
	1.3	0.9	2.2	4.4	0.5	0.7
		1.6	1.6	2.4	6.6	5.7
					2.3	2.8
Elementary	15.0	16.9	19.4	21.3	18.8	19.4

of workshops, laboratories, and other material equipment, became indispensable instruments of mass education.

Americans meanwhile made even greater gains in secondary and higher education. Public secondary school enrollment increased nearly 300 percent, from 2.2 million to 6.6 million from 1920 to 1940. With growth came curricular changes as high schools ceased to prepare children exclusively for college. Only 16 percent of high school pupils studied Latin in 1934, as contrasted to nearly 50 percent in 1910. Music, manual training, home economics, typewriting, agricultural science, and other vocational subjects, most of which had not even been offered in 1910, were beginning to overshadow the so-called classical offerings. Accelerated by the Smith–Hughes Act of 1917, which provided federal support for agricultural and technical studies, vocational education became available for high school students who would not go to college. Prosperity and—especially—increased high school enrollment stimulated an unprecedented expansion of American colleges and universities. Between 1920 and 1940, the number of students enrolled in college rose from 598,000 to 1.5 million, the number of instructors from 48,600 to 147,000.

Growth raised serious new problems concerning the role of higher education and inevitably compelled college and university leaders to modify methods and objectives. In short, colleges and universities ceased to prepare students almost exclusively for the professions and became also training schools where young men and young women prepared for careers in industry, business, and other walks of life. This fact did not signify any diminution of advanced professional training, research, and writing. On the contrary, graduate schools grew even more rapidly than undergraduate institutions: the number of students enrolled in graduate schools increased from

16,000 in 1920 to 106,000 in 1940. Meanwhile, the growth of medical, law, and other professional schools was substantial if not as spectacular.

Protestant and Roman Catholic churches and Jewish synagogues continued to grow in membership and wealth during the decades between the religious censuses of 1916 and 1936. Church membership in the United States increased more rapidly than the population—from a total of 41.9 million to 55.8 million, or by a third, while population increased by 27 percent. But these are only rough figures and do not reveal the significant exceptions. Growth was extraordinarily rapid from 1916 to 1929; church membership increased hardly at all during the depression years from 1929 to 1940. Spreading urbanization and use of the automobile occasioned the end of many small rural churches and the consolidation of others, and church construction proceeded at a much slower pace than the growth in the general population. It was a time of such precipitate relative decline as to lead certain observers to conclude that the church in America was a dying institution.

As much as any other cultural institution, moreover, American Protestant churches faced a crucial adaptation. During the previous century, American society had become indisputably more secularized, and with their authority eroded, churches were forced to confront crucial new questions. Was it possible to reconcile scientific materialism with the view that the Bible was the central authority? How were the conclusions and implications of Charles Darwin's writings compatible with the Biblical account of creation? And what was the role of the church in a modern industrial society?

By the end of the First World War, modernists were aggressively asserting a new view of Christianity. They enthusiastically endorsed the Social Gospel, believing that an earthly millennium and the Kingdom of God were attainable through human action. They thus envisioned that churches would serve as the cutting edge of social change and human perfection. They were modernists in another respect, for they advocated viewing the Bible as a divinely inspired but essentially human work which, for its proper understanding, required historical and literary scholarship (the "higher criticism") and adaptation to modern requirements.

Modernists and liberals—who favored making the church a vehicle of social reform—probably constituted a majority of clergymen during the 1920s, at least in the Methodist and Congregationalist churches. Social Gospelers were active in the Federal Council of Churches, and this ecumenical organization served as a podium for leading Protestant liberals such as Shailer Mathews and Harry Ward. Liberals were active as well in establishing the *Christian Century,* which, emerging in the 1920s as the leading journal of liberal Christianity, confronted contemporary political, educational, and economic issues.

Nor was reformism confined to American Protestantism. The Roman Catholic Church officially espoused the cause of reform when American bishops took command of the inchoate social justice groups within the Catholic Church during the First World War and then, in 1919, supported a platform entitled *Social Reconstruction: A General Review of the Problems and Survey of Remedies.* Prepared by Msgr. John A. Ryan, a prophetic sociologist at the Catholic University of America, *Social Reconstruction* was a ringing document that endorsed unionization, collective bargaining, and worker participation in industrial ownership and management. Soon afterward, the bishops established the National Catholic Welfare Council and a special committee of the American hierarchy to coordinate the church's social thought and social ministry. Such was the beginning of wha vould become a vast enterprise by the end of the 1930s.

During the 1930s, the Social Gospel came under a blistering critique known as neo-orthodoxy, or reformed Biblical theology. Drawing on the work of Swiss theologians Karl Barth and Emil Brunner, neo-orthodoxy indicted liberalism for glorifying man instead of God and for forgetting that man's sin produced recurrent crises in history. The neo-orthodox theologians were modernists in higher criticism, but they were thoroughly orthodox in their emphasis upon the sovereignty of God, the sinfulness of man, and the power of God's grace. The leader of American neo-orthodoxy was Reinhold Niebuhr of Union Theological Seminary in New York. His *Moral Man and Immoral Society* (1932), *Reflections on the End of an Era* (1934), *Beyond Tragedy* (1937), and *The Nature and Destiny of Man* (1941–1943) criticized shallow liberalism and hailed the return in the United States to the church's historic knowledge of God and man.

Liberal Protestants were deeply influenced by neo-orthodoxy. Harry Emerson Fosdick, pastor of the Riverside Church in New York, repudiated humanism in a notable 1935 sermon, calling instead for a return to Biblical theology. In addition, there was renewed interest during the 1930s in the writings of Luther and Calvin; the discovery of the Danish existentialist Søren Kierkegaard; and stronger emphasis on the Atonement and the concept of the church as the Body of Christ.

By the Second World War, neo-orthodoxy had left a permanent imprint on American Protestantism. Repudiating the utopianism of thinkers such as Walter Rauschenbusch, it converted many liberal Protestants to a view of the church as an institution confronting evil and the complex social and political problems resulting from it in an immoral society. As the depression and the rise of European fascism seemed to demonstrate the truth of neo-orthodoxy, it gained currency and even began to affect the general currents of liberal thought.

6. Radio and Popular Culture, 1920–1940

As we have already seen, the pattern of popular culture was already well established by the First World War (see pp. 29–32). This new enterprise sought to provide mass entertainment—leisure-time amusement for a large urban market—rather than uplift or education. Established and then run along industrial–corporate lines, popular cultural activities such as spectator sports, amusement parks, and motion pictures were run for profit, and they only required that the consumer come prepared with the price of admission.

After the First World War, these forms of mass entertainment grew even more rapidly as both baseball and movie making entered a golden age. Filmmakers such as Cecil B. DeMille, John Ford, and King Vidor mastered the art of the silent film. The star system centered attention on actors and actresses like Douglas Fairbanks, Rudolph Valentino, Gloria Swanson, and Clara Bow, whose following was promoted by studios through fan magazines and intense press coverage. Motion pictures achieved striking technical improvements and diversified their subject matter and dramatic themes. In the 1930s, the introduction of sound stimulated an even greater expansion of the industry. The depression drove several major studios—Paramount, RKO, and Fox—into bankruptcy, but after reorganization and further consolidation, the motion-picture industry experienced almost no drop in the American public's demand for its products. Many of the silent movie stars faded with the coming of sound, replaced by the stars of the 1930s. They included actors James Cagney, Humphrey Bogart, John Wayne, and Edward G. Robinson and actresses Jean Harlow, Bette Davis, and Joan Crawford.

The two decades after the First World War were a golden age as well for major-league baseball, which began a long period of stability after a series of internal crises. Rising attendance prompted the Federal League in 1913 to challenge the supremacy of the established American and National leagues. This threat was warded off only when the established leagues incorporated the leading Federal League owners into their own organizations and cynically left minor owners out in the cold. Antitrust suits challenging the monopoly of the two leagues were pressed by some of the Federal League owners. But in 1922, Justice Oliver Wendell Holmes, Jr., writing for the majority of the Supreme Court, maintained that baseball was immune from antitrust legislation because it was a sport, not a business.

Another problem faced by baseball was the influence of gambling and corruption. There had long been rumors that bribery and corruption were endemic, but the baseball world was nevertheless stunned by the "Black Sox" scandal, in which eight Chicago White Sox players took bribes in return for throwing the World Series of 1919. To forestall public outrage at what might have been the tip of the iceberg, baseball owners endorsed a new agreement in which an outside commissioner, federal judge Kennesaw Mountain Landis, would restore the game's pristine reputation. As commissioner of baseball, Landis exerted dictatorial powers, and he soon imposed stability on the game. By the time of his death in 1944, Landis had established a strong commissioner's office, with powers to investigate, suspend players, levy fines, and censure wrongdoers—all in the interest of baseball, as he defined it.

Although he was a tyrant, Landis ushered in a new era of prosperity and steady growth for baseball. The most obvious success story was, of course, the New York Yankees: between 1921 and 1939, they won nine world championships and twelve pennants. Most clubs enjoyed less spectacular success; they owed their stability to steady increases in attendance through the 1920s. On the average, attendance rose 50 percent during the decade; in 1930, it increased to a high of 10 million fans. For the 1920s as a whole, fifteen out of sixteen clubs reported a profit.

A major factor in the marketing of mass culture was radio broadcasting. One of the most rapidly growing new industries during the 1920s (see pp. 173–174), commercial radio broadcasting began in East Pittsburgh, Pennsylvania, where station KDKA aired the results of the presidential election in November 1920. During the next ten years, radio broadcasting underwent a period of innovation, experimentation, and then maturation. Only loosely regulated before 1925, radio stations spread quickly across the country. These pioneer broadcasters were owned and operated by such diverse institutions as colleges and universities, department stores like Gimbel's in Philadelphia (WIP), and the Ford Motor Company in Detroit (WWI). Many if not most early radio stations came under the control of either newspapers or radio manufacturers like General Electric and Westinghouse. These stations soon began to provide a wide selection of programming in addition to news reporting. In November 1920, the Texas A&M University station, WTAW, broadcast the first college football game; within two years, football was regularly aired by radios, along with other sports such as boxing and baseball. In 1922, WJZ in Newark, New Jersey, aired a stage production; in the same year, WGY of Schenectady, New York, produced the first radio drama. Still another type of programming in existence by 1925 was music, and radio played a key role in expanding the market for recorded popular music during the decade. At the same time, in 1921, the Chicago station KYW began broadcasting opera; in 1925, the RCA Victor Hour began live performances of light classical music.

By mid-decade, through the large-scale involvement of giant corporations such as AT&T, General Electric, Westinghouse, and United Fruit, a nationwide system of communications programming existed. What followed after 1925 were attempts to increase profits, raise the number of programs, and extend markets by establishing national networks. The organization of the National Broadcasting Corporation (NBC) in 1926 and the Columbia Broadcasting Corporation (CBS) a year later reflected an important new organizational development: the dominance of corporations over broadcasting. There had previously been regional networks which provided a loose web of programming; but the advent of nationwide networks rapidly transformed radio broadcasting. By the end of the decade, both NBC and CBS were transmitting nationally oriented programs closely linked to advertising. In the next ten years, radio quickly established itself as an important new form of mass culture. Radio personalities such as Paul Whiteman, Billy Jones, and Will Rogers were coast-to-coast household names. Programs like *Amos and Andy,* begun in 1929, achieved unprecedented popularity and created a new dramatic form, the situation comedy. Soon other nationally broadcast series followed: *The Adventures of Sherlock Holmes, Fu Manchu Mystery,* and *The Shadow,* all of which originated during the early 1930s.

With national networks, radio made a decisive move toward commercialism. Although the issue of whether paid commercials should support radio broadcasting was frequently debated, by the end of the decade advertising had begun to make a major impact. In turn, the commercialization of radio depended on another development: the creation of rating services which measured the preferences of American listeners. In the early 1930s, the first attempt to measure the size of audiences began with the Cooperative Analysis of Broadcasting, which telephoned listeners in thirty cities and provided a statistical breakdown of the result. This approach was superseded by more sophisticated measurements in the rating systems devised by C. E. Hooper in 1935 and by the A. C. Nielsen Company in 1949.

7. Antimodernism and the Cultural Counterrevolution

Although the impact of modernism on lifestyles, gender roles, and intellectual life was widespread during the 1920s, not all Americans readily accepted the changes that it represented or welcomed the disintegration of traditional ways of life. Indeed, the First World War represents a watershed in American history. After 1920, strong, mass-supported movements arose which rejected modernism and reaffirmed traditional cultural values. Rejecting secularization, they reaffirmed the authority of the Bible and, more broadly, the position of religion in American culture. Antimodernism was also directed toward obvious manifestations of change—cities, new immigrants, blacks, and purveyors of a new morality.

One prominent manifestation of the antimodernist mindset was Protestant fundamentalism. Although a number of different conservative evangelical groups flourished after the 1870s, fundamentalism coalesced as a unified social movement during the First World War. In part because modernists began to challenge conservatives, in part because the European conflict seemed to be a struggle between Christian democracy and a German modernist secular state, the war years marked the beginning of fundamentalism's overt involvement in American cultural politics that lasted until the end of the 1920s and was revived in the 1970s.

Soon conservatives were organizing themselves into a national network. William B. Riley, a Chicago evangelist, helped to organize a Philadelphia Prophecy Conference in 1918 and, a year later, the World's Christian Fundamentals Association (WCFA). The latter became the leading superpatriotic Protestant organization, but it was also concerned with antimodernist and antievolutionist causes. By the spring of 1919, the WCFA was expressing a new fundamentalist self-awareness. It published a national magazine, *The Fundamentals,* and provided liaison with conservatives across the country. Moreover, after the end of the war, it sponsored a new activism by conservatives along two main fronts. Within major Protestant denominations, conservatives waged campaigns to uproot modernist theology and reaffirm absolute Biblical authority.

On the other front, in public schools, fundamentalists attempted to prevent the teaching of Charles Darwin's evolutionist theories. It was fitting that William Jennings Bryan, spokesman of rural, Protestant America, should have taken leadership in a movement that drew most of its recruits from rural areas. The spread of scientific materialism and especially of belief in the material origins of man presented a personal challenge to Bryan. Investigation convinced him that evolutionary teaching caused students first to lose faith in the inspiration and inerrancy of the Scriptures and later to repudiate Christianity altogether. What Bryan dreaded most was the possibility of atheistic evolutionists' being graduated from the colleges, invading public schools as teachers, and undermining the Christian faith of American school children.

Bryan, beginning in 1921, began a struggle to purge evolution from the public-school curriculum and to persuade denominations to condemn it. His campaign had significant reverberations in the Middle West, but it met with strong popular support and a measure of success only in the South. Leadership and support for the movement in that region came largely from Baptists and Presbyterians. There was, however, no uniformity of religious opinion in the so-called Bible Belt. Baptists, for example, were badly split by the evolution issue, while the Episcopal Church and the Methodist Episcopal Church, South, taught theistic evolution and refused to be drawn into the controversy.

But Bryan's call to battle in 1921 was answered by a large number of southern fundamentalists. There was, for example, the Reverend J. Frank Norris of Fort Worth, Texas, the *enfant terrible* of the southern Baptist Church, who established a reign of terror against science teachers at Baylor University in Waco. He also published a weekly newspaper, *The Searchlight,* devoted to exposing atheists and evolutionists. There was also the Reverend T. T. Martin, an itinerant Baptist evangelist, who wrote *Hell in the High Schools,* one of the leading antievolution tracts. They and their cohorts carried on vigorous campaigns in most southern and southwestern states from 1921 to 1925. At the same time, liberal leaders in church, school, and journalism met the fundamentalists head on, fought courageously for academic freedom, and, on the whole, won the first round.

By 1925, the antievolutionists had experienced qualified success in Florida, North Carolina, and Texas. In Tennessee, however, they were completely triumphant. In 1923, the University of Tennessee dismissed a professor of genetic psychology for using James Harvey Robinson's *Mind in the Making,* while it fired five other professors at the end of the college year for teaching evolution. An antievolution bill was introduced in the Tennessee legislature two years later, and Bryan and a powerful Baptist lobby descended upon Nashville. The legislature and governor surrendered by approving a measure forbidding any teacher in the state's schools and colleges to teach any theory denying the Biblical account of creation or asserting that man had evolved from a lower order of animals.

The American Civil Liberties Union at once offered to finance defense of any Tennessee teacher who would test the constitutionality of the statute. A young high school biology teacher in Dayton, John Thomas Scopes, volunteered, and a test case was begun in May 1925. When the state's counsel invited Bryan to join the prosecution, he accepted joyfully, while the famed trial lawyer, Clarence Darrow of Chicago, joined the defense counsel. The stage was set for a major courtroom battle.

When the trial opened in Dayton in July 1925, Bryan was greeted by huge crowds and ovations. He responded by promising a campaign to amend the Constitution to prohibit the teaching of evolution anywhere in the United States. The presiding judge, John T. Raulston, refused to admit expert testimony concerning the validity of the Darwinian hypothesis, and the affair became a verbal duel between the agnostic Darrow and the fundamentalist Bryan. It was soon clear that Scopes had violated the law. The Supreme Court of Tennessee later rescinded the small fine that Raulston had imposed but upheld the conviction and the antievolution law. On July 26, 1925, a few days after the Scopes trial, Bryan died from exhaustion and overeating at the scene of his defense of the faith.

The Scopes trial and Bryan's death stimulated a momentary revival of the antievolution crusade—especially after formation of the Supreme Kingdom, the Bible Crusaders, the Bryan Bible League, and other fundamentalist organizations. The Supreme Kingdom, modeled after the Ku Klux Klan, was dedicated to winning an antievolution constitutional amendment. It functioned in sixteen states, published a monthly magazine, *Dynamite,* and established a rest home in Florida for "those who grow old in the war against evolution." The Bible Crusaders, under T. T. Martin, was the best organized and most formidable of all the antievolution organizations. It formed mobile squadrons that went from one state capitol to another. It descended upon the Mississippi legislature in 1926, for example, and obtained passage of an antievolution law before liberal forces in the state could counterattack. It struck next at Louisiana, was turned back, and then moved to North Carolina. The fight that ensued was bitter and prolonged, but liberal spokesmen fought hard and prevented passage of an antievolution bill in 1927.

Defeat in North Carolina seemed to break the back of the entire fundamentalist crusade. In one state after another—Georgia, Kentucky, Florida, South Carolina, and Oklahoma—antievolutionists met with defeats. They had one last, curious triumph in Arkansas. After the Arkansas legislature several times had refused to adopt an antievolution bill, fundamentalists obtained passage of their measure in 1928 by using the initiative to bypass the legislature. For the first time in the history of the world, the sovereign people by direct legislation decreed that Darwin was wrong!

Thus ended one of the most significant and also one of the most tragic social movements in American history. Southern Protestants who participated in the antievolution crusade thought that they were fighting to preserve the best features of the American heritage—a belief in the spirituality of the universe and in the God-like character of man. Instead, they tended to align organized religion with bigotry and ignorance instead of freedom and learning. In several states and many communities, fundamentalists instituted witch hunts and inquisitions, the effects of which were felt for many years. On the other hand, the antievolution movement had one beneficial effect. Its great challenge to academic freedom revealed the South's intellectual backwardness and compelled the rising body of southern liberals to take a firm stand against intolerance and obscurantism. Their victory in most states was therefore all the more significant, for similar issues would plague the 1970s.

8.   Nativism and Intolerance

The revolt against change—and a spirit of intolerance, bigotry, and chauvinism—was manifested in other ways. There was fear of Reds, an intensification of anti-Semitism, organized campaigns against Roman Catholics, and legislation to end immigration from southern and eastern Europe. Fear of Communism came out in different ways. Following policy established during the Wilson administration, Republican administrations refused to enter into diplomatic relations with the Soviet Union. The New York legislature, in order to prevent the dissemination of revolutionary propaganda, in 1921 required all nonchurch private schools to obtain approval of their curricula by the Board of Regents. When the Socialist party's Rand School refused to apply for a license, the state began proceedings to close that institution. California state officials carried on a ruthless campaign from 1919 to 1924 to destroy the Industrial Workers of the World. During those five years, 504 persons were arrested, and 264 alleged subversives were tried under the state's criminal syndicalism law for committing sabotage and advocating the violent overthrow of the government.

The most controversial case involved two obscure Italian-born anarchists, Nicola

Sacco and Bartolomeo Vanzetti. Arrested in 1920 for the alleged murder of a paymaster in South Braintree, Massachusetts, Sacco and Vanzetti were tried the following year by a judge, Webster Thayer, who publicly vented his contempt for anarchism and allowed the state's attorney to make the defendants' radicalism a cornerstone of his case. Sacco and Vanzetti were convicted and sentenced to death, but radical and liberal groups throughout the United States and Europe believed that the two men had been sentenced not for murder, but for anarchism. In spite of mass demonstrations abroad and fervent appeals at home, Governor Alvan Tufts Fuller permitted Sacco and Vanzetti to die in the electric chair in August 1927.

Anti-Semitism, previously a latent menace, was exacerbated by the identification of many Jewish radicals, first with opposition to the war, and then with the Communist party and other radical groups. It was also intensified by the fact that many Jews were recent immigrants, as yet not "Americanized" during a decade when a great majority demanded unquestioning adoption of American manners and customs. It was, moreover, nurtured and used as a rallying cry by leaders of the Ku Klux Klan, who resurrected discredited charges of an international Jewish conspiracy to control the world. These charges were echoed by Henry Ford's newspaper, the *Dearborn Independent*, until Ford, threatened with court action, repudiated the accusation.

Another development reflecting intolerant nationalism—and another form of antimodernism—was the rise of the Knights of the Ku Klux Klan, the American counterpart of European fascism. The Klan was called to life by William J. Simmons, a former lay preacher and history teacher, under a blazing cross on Stone Mountain near Atlanta on Thanksgiving Day 1915. It was modeled after the hooded organization that had terrorized the South during Reconstruction. Simmons had established a few chapters in Georgia and Alabama by the end of 1919, but loss of membership seemed to threaten his organization with early extinction.

Two expert organizers, Edward Y. Clarke and Elizabeth Tyler, rescued the Klan from oblivion early in 1920. Simmons had constructed an empire headed by himself as imperial wizard, but with only a few thousand subjects of dubious loyalty. Recognizing the rich financial opportunity at hand, Clarke and Tyler increased the initiation fee to $10 and established an imperial promotion department, known as the imperial kleagle. The kleagle included door-to-door solicitors and heads of state promotion departments.

The Klan gained 100,000 new members in 1920 by a vigorous recruiting campaign. The impractical Simmons was removed as imperial wizard in 1922 and replaced by Hiram W. Evans, a Texas dentist with a bent for making money. Spectacular growth followed, first in the Southwest and then rapidly in California and Oregon. Klan organizers meanwhile gained a large following in the Middle West. In Indiana, the leading klansman, David C. Stephenson, captured control of the Republican state organization, cowed the state's two United States senators into submission, and helped to elect his henchman, Ed Jackson, to the governorship in 1924. At the peak of its strength in 1925, the Klan claimed 5 million members, chiefly in the Southwest, Far West, and Middle West. At one time or another and to a varying degree, it controlled or had powerful influence in the governments of Texas, Oklahoma, Arkansas, California, Oregon, Indiana, Ohio, Maine, and other states.

Klan membership was drawn largely from lower middle-class old American stock, mainly in towns and cities, who were intensely suspicious of anything foreign or different and responded enthusiastically to bombastic expressions of patriotism. Its chief appeal outside the South was anti-Catholicism. In the Middle and Far West, the Klan promised to destroy parochial schools, thwart the Catholic hierarchy's alleged plot to capture the United States, and prevent the Pope from moving the Holy See to Georgetown.

The Klan was not officially anti-Semitic, but in practice it was almost invariably so, because Jews were not only not Protestants but were also, for the most part, from southern and eastern Europe. However, the Klan stood openly for white supremacy and for keeping the Negro "in his place." Indeed, the most important impetus for the rise of the Klan in the South was fear among whites of returning black veterans and the troubled condition of race relations from 1919 to 1921.

Aside from its anti-Catholic program, the Klan's strongest attraction was its ritual and secrecy and the fact that for a time it was a going concern. Americans have always been a nation of joiners with a strong penchant for high-flown ritual. The Klan also allowed its members to wear weird-looking white robes and hoods; and any ordinary person could pay his ten dollars, become an exalted Knight of the Ku Klux Klan, and parade in exciting anonymity.

Because the imperial headquarters exercised absolutely no control over the klaverns, or local chapters, Klan tactics varied from community to community. The coming of the Klan to the Southwest in 1920–1921, for example, was accompanied by a wave of murders, floggings, kidnappings, and other outrages. And thus it went, though on a lesser scale, wherever the Klan penetrated. Klan leaders piously protested that criminals using the Klan costume were always responsible for the outrages. Klan opponents replied that the Klan was essentially a lawless, terroristic organization, whose chief purpose was the subversion of orderly constitutional government.

Fascism was triumphant in Italy at the end of the 1920s, and the forces of reaction were gathering strength in Germany. In the United States, on the other hand, the Ku Klux Klan stood exposed and discredited, its membership reduced to perhaps 100,000. For this failure of fascism in the United States the American people had to thank their traditions, a free press, and courageous leaders all over the country. Progressive editors, politicians, clergymen, and other public spokesmen everywhere recognized the Klan for what it was. They took the Klan's measure and threw themselves into what seemed in the beginning a losing fight. They triumphed in the end because they fought to preserve traditions that the overwhelming majority of Americans, even most klansmen, cherished.

Chapter 11

--->>> <<<---

Harding, Coolidge,
and Postwar Politics

American historians used to assume that the return of Republican rule in 1921 concluded an era of national reform and inaugurated a period of conservative control of the federal government. This decade was then followed by the revival and redemption of progressivism under Franklin D. Roosevelt. Reexamining national politics during the 1920s, recent scholars have demonstrated that this view is over-drawn. To be sure, Harding and Coolidge and their allies in Congress represented an alternative to reform policies articulated by leaders of both parties for the previous two decades. Conservative Republicans believed that the well-being of the American people depended on their economic well-being, and they pursued policies which minimized governmental intervention and maximized economic growth. They also believed that American prosperity depended on the upper classes and sponsored tariff and tax policies to promote growth. Finally, they brought federal administrative agencies into close cooperation with the business community and opposed measures that would have discouraged investment or carried the government into new areas of regulation.

But to stop at this point would be to distort the nature of American politics in the 1920s. The dominance of the presidency by conservative Republicans did not represent a complete popular repudiation of reform. Conservative Republicans gained and held power in the executive branch first, because Republicans were still the natural majority party and, second, because the war and especially the postwar crisis had deeply divided Wilson's national progressive coalition. Moreover, conservative Republicans never controlled other levels of American government as they did the presidency. Indeed, for much of the decade, elements of the national reform coalition continued to influence, even to control, Congress, to thwart executive leadership, and to enact a varied legislative program—the most ambitious parts of which met presidential vetoes. On the state and local level, more importantly, progressive reformers persisted in movements for administrative centralization, rationalization, and efficiency, as well as for a steady expansion of state educational and social services. Social reformers, rather than withering away in the 1920s, remained active and achieved notable successes.

The political developments of the period 1920–1928 refuse to accommodate themselves to sweeping generalizations or pat theories. As we shall see, in spite of numerous conflicts, crosscurrents, and elements of confusion, progressivism survived as an articulate expression of social and economic aspiration and even widened its horizons.

1. The Harding Presidency

The inauguration ceremonies of March 4, 1921, provided a striking contrast. As the incumbent and president-elect rode to the Capitol together, there sat Wilson, aged and infirm, a living mind in a dying body; at his side was Warren G. Harding, majestic in countenance but awed and still dazed by his nomination and election as president. Harding was born at Blooming Grove, Ohio, on November 2, 1865. Owner and editor of the Marion, Ohio, *Star,* he then served two terms in the state senate and one as lieutenant governor, was his party's unsuccessful candidate for governor in 1910, and won election to the United States Senate in 1914. He was his party's keynoter in the national convention of 1916. Realizing his own limitations, he was skeptical about running for the Republican presidential nomination. But ambition overcame his scruples. He permitted his friend, Harry M. Daugherty, to conduct an undercover campaign. Harding was popular with the delegates, and he accepted the nomination when it came to him almost by default in June 1920.

A man of average mental endowment can fulfill the duties of the presidency if his will power and character fortify his determination to rule wisely. It was an unkind fate that made Harding president, for he had only average talents, little will power, and a striking inability to discriminate between right and wrong. Easygoing and affable, he possessed an uncanny ability to draw men utterly unworthy of his confidence into his personal circle. The opportunity to honor old friends and enjoy them as drinking and poker companions warmed his heart. He thus selected Daugherty as attorney general over widespread opposition, while he named another crony, Senator Albert B. Fall of New Mexico, as secretary of the interior. On the whole, however, Harding assembled a cabinet of highly qualified administrators. Charles Evans Hughes was secretary of state. Andrew W. Mellon, Pittsburgh industrialist and banker, was secretary of the treasury. Former Senator John W. Weeks of Massachusetts was secretary of war. And Henry C. Wallace, Iowa farm editor, was secretary of agriculture; Herbert Hoover was secretary of commerce; and James J. Davis, a Pennsylvania labor leader, was secretary of labor.

During his brief tenure, Harding presided over the government of the United States with outward dignity. In contrast to Wilson, however, Harding was a weak president, unable to command his party forces in Congress. Although he worked slavishly, his undisciplined mind was incapable of mastering the details of important questions, and he stayed in a constant state of confusion. Hence he abdicated leadership of legislative and foreign policies to Congress and his cabinet. He wanted most of all to be loved by everyone, and two of his own acts reveal the generous side of his nature. The first was the pardoning, in 1921, of Eugene V. Debs, who had spent three years in the Atlanta penitentiary and polled over 900,000 votes as Socialist candidate for president in 1920. The second was his bringing the heads of the steel industry to the White House in 1922 and persuading them to institute the eight-hour day.

Meanwhile, some of the president's subordinates were engaging in a mad scramble for bribes and as much loot as they could lay their hands on. Scandal was inevitable; indeed, the brief Harding regime soon established a record of fraud and corruption unparalleled since the Grant era. Jesse Smith, an old-time friend of Daugherty's who had moved to Washington with the attorney general, soon became the liaison between the Department of Justice and violators of the prohibition laws, income tax evaders, and "fixers" of all kinds. Rumors of Smith's behavior reached Harding, who told Daugherty that his friend had to go back to Ohio. Tormented by exile, Smith soon returned to Daugherty's Washington apartment and killed himself there on May 20, 1923.

Smith's suicide was the first event in a chain that culminated in exposure of several enormous scandals. The first to come to light involved the Veterans' Bureau, established by Congress in August 1921, under the direction of Charles R. Forbes. Harding had a profound concern for disabled veterans, especially for those afflicted with mental illness and tuberculosis. Forbes was a bustling, energetic person with a convincing tongue, by all appearances an efficient administrator. He supervised the building of hospitals and the expenditure of hundreds of millions of dollars, and Harding was pleased. Unhappily, Forbes could not resist the temptation to make money on the side, and he stole or squandered nearly $250 million before he left office.

Daugherty learned about the corruption in the Veterans' Bureau late in 1922 and passed the bad news on to Harding. Harding learned part of the truth from Forbes himself and permitted him to go abroad and resign in February 1923. Rumors soon reached the Senate, which began an investigation on March 2. Twelve days later the legal adviser to the Veterans' Bureau, Charles F. Cramer, committed suicide, breaking the case, and the Senate committee pressed on to expose the full extent of defalcation in the bureau. Forbes was convicted of defrauding the government in 1925 and sentenced to a two-year term in Leavenworth penitentiary.

Meanwhile, Secretary of the Interior Albert B. Fall had persuaded Harding in 1921 to transfer control over naval oil reserve lands at Elk Hills in California and Teapot Dome in Wyoming from the Navy Department to his own jurisdiction. On April 7, 1922, Fall secretly leased Teapot Dome to the Mammoth Oil Company, owned by Harry F. Sinclair. The secretary also leased Elk Hills to the Pan-American Petroleum Company, owned by Edward L. Doheny. News of the leases leaked out at once. Responding to an early Senate inquiry, Fall declared that he had leased Teapot Dome to Sinclair in the interest of national preparedness and was about to lease Elk Hills to Doheny. The Senate Public Lands Committee, spurred on by Thomas J. Walsh of Montana, began an inquiry in October 1923 that was continued the following year by a special commission. These investigations revealed that Sinclair had given Fall $223,000 in government bonds, $85,000 in cash, and some cattle for his ranch at the time that the lease for Teapot Dome was negotiated. The commission also found that Doheny had "lent" $100,000 to Fall when the lease on Elk Hills was signed.

In 1927, the government won its suit to cancel the leases, while Doheny, Sinclair, and Fall were tried for conspiracy to defraud the government. They were acquitted, although Sinclair spent terms in jail for contempt of Congress and jury tampering. Fall was convicted of bribery in October 1929, fined $100,000, and sentenced to a year's imprisonment. After many delays the former secretary went to jail in July 1931.

Attorney General Daugherty was suspected of complicity in several frauds. But all during the furor raised by the revelations of the oil scandal in 1923 and 1924 he not only refused to resign but also turned the FBI on senators and other public leaders who were unearthing details of the corruption. Then a scandal involving the return of the American Metal Company to its German owners by the Alien Property Custodian, Thomas W. Miller, broke in early 1924. It was then revealed that a highly placed New York Republican who engineered the deal had paid $50,000 to Miller and $224,000 to Jesse Smith, and that Smith had deposited $50,000 of the loot in an account that he held jointly with Daugherty. President Coolidge dismissed Daugherty when he refused to testify before a Senate committee of investigation in March 1924. Daugherty was brought to trial in New York in 1926 but again refused to testify, saying that his personal relations with President and Mrs. Harding made it impossible for him to do so. After deliberating nearly three days, the jury failed to convict because it feared that Harding's good name was at stake. The following year Miller was tried, convicted, and sent to jail.

Early in 1923, Harding made plans to conduct a speaking tour through the West and to take a vacation in Alaska. Before he left, however, he had learned of at least some of the corruption of his cronies—enough, at least, to fill him with a presentiment of impending doom. "My God, this is a hell of a job," he was reported to have declared. "I have no trouble with my enemies. . . . But my damned friends, my God-damn friends . . . they're the ones that keep me walking the floor nights!"

Already suffering from a heart condition and hypertension, Harding was physically exhausted and mentally depressed all during the long trip across the continent. The trip to Alaska brought no rest, and, in San Francisco, he suffered a stroke and died on August 2, 1923. As the funeral train bearing Harding's body made its way slowly across the country, millions of Americans paid their respects to the man they thought he had been.

It was not long, however, before Americans learned the details of the various scandals, read the accusations of Harding's alleged mistress, Nan Britton, and heard absurd rumors that Harding had been poisoned by his wife. In consequence, the deflation of Harding's reputation came at once, not slowly. The people forgot his simplicity and kindliness and remembered only that he had appointed thieves and sheltered scoundrels. And, during a later period, when the Republican leadership of the twenties stood discredited in the public mind, Harding's word, "normalcy," became a term of opprobrium, and the scandals of the Harding era, compounded with those of the Great Depression, became a heavy liability to the GOP.

2. The Anomaly of American Politics, 1921–1928

Those business leaders and men of wealth who poured nearly $8 million into the Republican campaign coffers in 1920 soon realized part of the expected return on their investment. Through powerful conservative Republicans in the Senate they had a decisive voice in shaping federal policies, both administrative and legislative. The time seemed ripe for complete fulfillment of the business-sponsored program. It called for economy, drastic tax reductions and sound financing, a return to tariff protection, control of federal regulatory agencies by appointees friendly to business interests, and an end to quasi-socialistic experiments launched during the war.

As it turned out, primarily because of a deep recession beginning in late 1920 that depressed farm prices, agrarian congressmen revolted and blocked Harding's legislative program. In May 1921, a group of midwestern farm spokesmen, led by Senators William S. Kenyon of Iowa and Arthur Capper of Kansas—joined by the powerful American Farm Bureau Federation—agreed on a program. Subsequently, these "farm bloc" Midwesterners, in alliance with southern Democrats, not only enacted their program but blocked the administration's tax cuts. After the congressional elections of 1922, the Midwesterners organized a new and stronger bloc and adopted a platform that appealed as much to independents and workers as it did to farmers. Insurgent leaders insisted that they were merely protesting against conservative Republican policies, not contemplating a campaign to unite the disparate progressive elements in a third party. Even so, this rebelliousness among farmers and organized workers suggested the possibility of a nationwide independent movement in 1924.

Another important sign of incipient rebellion was the sudden revival of the Nonpartisan League after 1919. Organized among wheat growers of North Dakota in 1915, the Nonpartisan League endorsed state ownership and operation of farm credit agencies, warehouses, and grain elevators. It also demanded minimum wages and public control of railroads, banks, and private businesses. Capturing the state government of North Dakota in 1916, league organizers moved into Minnesota, Iowa, Montana, Idaho, and other states in 1917 and 1918. The league joined with a number of farm radicals in 1920 to form the Farmer–Labor party, and it became the major anti-Republican party in Minnesota, South Dakota, and Washington State.

In February 1922, these and other farm and labor groups organized the Conference of Progressive Political Action (CPPA), which first endorsed congressional and senatorial candidates in the autumn elections. Encouraged by the success of farm-bloc Republicans and Farmer–Labor candidates, Senator Robert M. La Follette of Wisconsin became the CPPA candidate for the Republican presidential nomination and, failing that, the candidate of an independent third party. Division within Republican ranks provided an opportunity for Democrats. If they could find a strong leader and unite behind a program which could attract disaffected Republicans, then they might rebuild their party into a powerful coalition. Such had been the case in 1916; such would be the case in 1932.

In 1923 and 1924, however, Democrats were literally incapable of engaging in coalition building. Indeed, although the Democratic party had been badly divided in 1920, it was so fragmented by internal division four years later that it had ceased to be a national party. Southerners demanded vigorous enforcement of prohibition. Northerners, representing "wet," or antiprohibition, constituencies in the cities, demanded repeal. Southerners, along with Midwesterners, either supported or feared the Ku Klux Klan. Most northern Democrats were Catholics or foreign-born citizens, and they were opposed to all that the Klan stood for. These two wings remained hopelessly divided on many other issues. Southerners still supported the League of Nations; the northern Irish bosses wanted to forget it. Southerners demanded radical aid to farmers but were unfriendly to labor, uninterested in social reform, and indifferent or hostile to the interests of blacks. Northern Democratic organizations opposed radical farm support but sponsored advanced labor legislation and were beginning to develop strength among black voters.

The unabridgeable gulf separating southern and northern Democrats was revealed at the Democratic National Convention that met in New York City for seventeen days in late June and early July 1924. Former Secretary of the Treasury William G. McAdoo came to the convention with the support of the South and the West, and he had the support—which he repudiated—of the Klan. Endorsement by the Klan and his association, as one of Edward L. Doheny's lawyers, with the Teapot Dome scandal sorely hurt McAdoo. His chief rival was Alfred E. Smith, New York governor and a Catholic opponent of prohibition and the Klan, who enjoyed the support of urban delegations from the East and Midwest. Soon the convention was in deadlock, for neither the Smith nor McAdoo forces could marshall the necessary two-thirds of the delegates. Then, on the one-hundred-and-third ballot, the weary convention turned to John W. Davis, a former ambassador to Great Britain and a distinguished corporate lawyer. As Davis's running mate, and as a gesture of conciliation to the party's agrarian wing, the convention chose Governor Charles W. Bryan of Nebraska, brother of William Jennings Bryan.

The Democrats found it as difficult to agree upon a platform as upon a candidate. The worst fight centered around a resolution condemning the Klan as un-American, which the Smith leaders introduced solely to embarass McAdoo and the Southerners. It failed by a vote of 543 to 542. Nor could Northerners and Southerners agree on Prohibition: the platform merely scolded the Republicans for failing to enforce the Eighteenth Amendment. Refusing to endorse American membership in the League of Nations, the convention called for a public referendum on the issue. Except for denouncing the Republican Fordney–McCumber tariff of 1922 and promising independence to the Philippines, the Democratic platform differed little from its Republican counterpart.

Meanwhile, insurgents were attempting to capture the Republican party. The futility of this endeavor had become so apparent by the spring of 1924, however, that La Follette withdrew from presidential primaries in Montana, North Dakota, and Michigan. Control of the party had passed to Harding's successor, Calvin Coolidge—a dour, taciturn man. Coolidge and his conservative allies dominated the Republican convention that opened in Cleveland in June 1924. Only the Wisconsin and South Dakota delegates objected when Coolidge was nominated, almost without opposition, on the first ballot. Rejecting a progressive platform submitted by the

Wisconsin delegation, the convention adopted instead a document promising economy, tax reduction, and limited aid to farmers, and approving American membership in the World Court.

Soon afterward, on July 4, the insurgent Republicans and their CPPA allies, representing organized labor, disgruntled western farmers, Socialists, and independent progressives, met in Cleveland. Agreeing that both major parties were hopelessly corrupt and reactionary, the delegates formally organized the Progressive party, then nominated La Follette for president and Senator Burton K. Wheeler of Montana as his running mate. The new party adopted a brief platform demanding nationalization of railroads, public ownership of water power and development of a great public utilities system, abolition of the use of injunctions in labor disputes, the right of Congress to overrule decisions of the Supreme Court, and the direct nomination and election of the president.

La Follette ran a strenuous campaign, appealing chiefly to midwestern farmers and urban workers. But he was hampered by lack of funds, a gradual withdrawal of AFL support, refusal by most midwestern Republican leaders to support his party, and, most of all, by a considerable increase in farm prices a month before the election. Coolidge took little part in the contest, but the other Republican leaders were generously supplied with funds and campaigned vigorously. Republicans practically ignored Davis and Bryan and concentrated their heavy fire against La Follette, who, they said, was un-American and a front for the (Communist) Third International. Davis tried to campaign on the issues of corruption and Coolidge's big-business associations, but his appeals were lost in the anti-Red clamor.

The question whether La Follette would draw enough votes away from Coolidge to throw the election into the House of Representatives was answered emphatically in the negative on election day, November 4, 1924. Coolidge received 15.7 million popular and 382 electoral votes; Davis, 8.4 million popular and 136 electoral votes; and La Follette, 4.8 million popular votes and the 13 electoral votes of Wisconsin. Outwardly the results constituted a thumping endorsement of the Coolidge policies of laissez faire and do-nothingism. Actually, few presidential elections in American history have meant so little. La Follette had frightened numerous voters away from Davis over to Coolidge by portraying the Democratic candidate as a creature of Wall Street. But it was not La Follette's candidacy that caused the Democratic debacle. The Democratic hopes were wrecked in 1924 by internal dissension, failure to adopt a bold program, Davis's inherent weakness as a leader of the forces of discontent, and the failure to appeal to urban, Catholic, and immigrant voters. The fact that only 52 percent of the electorate went to the polls was striking proof of Democratic inability to rally the people behind either a candidate or a platform.

The following four years were a prosperous interlude, during which Coolidge asserted no leadership in legislation and set about quietly to gain control of the regulatory agencies. The Republicans controlled the Sixty-ninth Congress from 1925 to 1927 by large majorities and the Seventieth Congress during the following two years by a slight margin, but they were constantly at war with one another and with Coolidge. The farm bloc in Congress regrouped after La Follette's death in 1925 and put across two measures in 1927 and 1928—the McNary–Haugen farm relief bill and a measure for governmental operation of the Muscle Shoals dam—both of which were nullified by Coolidge's vetoes (see pp. 217–220).

We have reviewed in outline the anomalous pattern of American national politics from 1920 to 1928. The pattern was anomalous because conservative administrations, seemingly endorsed overwhelmingly by the American people in 1920 and 1924, were counterbalanced by progressive coalitions in Congress that perpetuated a reform tradition in legislative policy. How this came about will become more apparent as we discuss the legislative problems and policies of the period in detail.

3. Tariff and Tax Battles of the Twenties

The first item on the Republican agenda after the election of 1920 was upward revision of the tariff to meet the demands of midwestern agrarian congressmen, who were then in panic over declining farm prices. In the lame-duck session of the Sixty-sixth Congress in the winter of 1920–1921, eastern Republicans gladly joined Midwesterners in adopting an emergency tariff bill that imposed high duties on imported meat and major farm staples. Wilson vetoed this measure in March 1921, warning that farmers needed new markets for their products, not futile tariff protection. When the Sixty-seventh Congress met in special session in April, however, midwestern leaders obtained the immediate reenactment of the emergency tariff bill, and Harding signed it in May.

Meanwhile, House Republican leaders reported a bill in June 1921 that incorporated the emergency increases and established modestly increased duties for most industrial products. Deliberating over the bill until April 1922, the Senate Finance Committee reported the House bill with 2,000 amendments, and, after some wrangling, it was enacted by both houses and signed by Harding in September 1922. This, the Fordney–McCumber Tariff Act, reaffirmed the traditional Republican policy of economic nationalism. But it was also a victory for the newly formed farm bloc, for duties on farm products—including reindeer meat and acorns—were higher than the Payne–Aldrich rates, while agricultural implements, wagons, and boots and shoes remained on the free list. For the rapidly expanding chemical industry, the act provided the protection that it needed to withstand competition from German dyes. For makers of silk and rayon textiles, toys, chinaware, cutlery, guns, and other items produced more cheaply by the Japanese and Germans, the measure offered almost prohibitive duties. However, for the great mass of industrial products, the act provided only enough protection to equalize differences between the costs of production at home and abroad. The average ad valorem rate for all schedules was 33 percent, as contrasted to the 26 percent of the Underwood–Simmons Tariff act of 1913.

Even more important than tariff increases were a series of drastic tax cuts. The architect of the Republican tax reduction program was Treasury Secretary Mellon, head of an empire in oil, finance, and aluminum—the personification of the American self-made man. His economic philosophy was epitomized by his Hamiltonian theory of prosperity. Low taxes on wealth and noninterference by government in the economy, he believed, would bring general increases in wealth benefiting all classes. Soon after Harding's inauguration, Mellon proposed the reduction or repeal of the excess profits tax and the extremely high surtaxes enacted under the War Revenue Act of 1918 (see p. 133). The House of Representatives and the Senate Finance Committee approved a bill embodying Mellon's program. In the Senate itself, however, midwestern Republicans joined Democrats to write a tax measure of their own. Commanding a solid majority, these "wild asses of the desert," as the Republican insurgents were derisively called at the time, defied the House of Representatives, the president, and the secretary of the treasury and warned that there would be no tax legislation at all unless their bill prevailed. The president signed their measure in late November 1921.

The Revenue Act of 1921 was significant, not only because it attested to the power of the combined farm bloc and the Democratic minority, but even more because it showed how pervasive the appeal of progressive tax theories remained. The measure repealed the excess profits tax entirely—liberals and conservatives alike agreed that it was an unnecessary burden on business during peacetime. But the insurgent senators won all their demands in the critical battle over the income tax. The 1921 act continued the rates under the Revenue Act of 1918 for the balance of 1921, set the maximum surtax thereafter at 50 percent, increased the tax on net corporation incomes from 10 to 12½ percent, and left estate taxes unchanged.

As a result of the tax reduction of 1921, ordinary federal revenues decreased during the following year by $1.5 billion. Even so, Mellon reduced the national debt by almost $2 billion and rejoiced to report a surplus of $310 million on hand at the end of the fiscal year. He reopened the tax battle in December 1921 by urging Congress to cut the maximum surtax on incomes from 50 to 25 percent, decrease proportionately the normal tax on small incomes, and reduce drastically the federal estate tax. However, insurgent Republicans and Democrats in Congress once again gained the initiative. Their Revenue Act of 1924 cut the maximum surtax from 50 to 40 percent and halved the normal tax on small and middle incomes. To compensate for these reductions, they increased the maximum estate tax from 25 to 40 percent and imposed a new gift tax. President Coolidge and Secretary Mellon were disgusted, but the president signed the measure in June 1924.

Despite its successes, the Democratic–insurgent coalition was eventually forced to surrender control of fiscal policy to Mellon. The low expenditures and high tax receipts brought by prosperity continued to create budget surpluses. Only an enormous increase in expenditures for public works, housing, and farm relief could have justified keeping the high tax structure. The Revenue Act that Congress adopted in February 1926 reduced the normal tax on small incomes, slashed the maximum surtax from 40 to 20 percent, abolished the gift tax, and cut the estate tax in half. One further tax measure—the Revenue Act of 1928, which left income taxes undisturbed but slightly reduced corporation and consumption taxes—rounded out Mellon's fiscal program. He had failed only to obtain complete repeal of the federal estate levy.

4. Agricultural Policy, 1920–1928

The most important domestic economic problem of the 1920s was the agricultural depression that began in the summer of 1920 and continued intermittently until 1935. The farmers' happy world came tumbling down when foreign demand decreased sharply in 1920 and the government withdrew price supports from wheat in May 1920. By the autumn of 1921, the price of wheat had dropped to approximately 40 percent of its highest price in 1920, that of corn to 32 percent, and that of hogs to 50 percent. Farm prices recovered slightly between 1921 and 1929, but they were never high enough to make agriculture really profitable. Total net farm income declined from $10 billion in 1919 to $9 billion in 1920 and $4 billion in 1921. It increased to $7 billion from 1923 through 1929. Farmers received 16 percent of the national income in 1919 and only 8.8 percent a decade later.

The first sharp drop in agricultural prices coincided with the return of the Republican party to national power and, as we have seen, stimulated the formation of the farm bloc in Congress. By operating as a nonpartisan pressure group, the farm bloc took control of agricultural policy between 1921 and 1924 and pushed through the most aggressive agricultural program in American history to that time. The adoption of high tariff protection for agricultural products was only one item on the farm bloc's wish list. A more urgent goal in 1921 was legislation subjecting meat packers and stockyards to rigorous federal control. As the result of an investigation by the Federal Trade Commission in 1919, the meat-packing industry came under intense scrutiny, and there was widespread demand for federal ownership and operation of the stockyards. Shortly afterward, Attorney General A. Mitchell Palmer compelled the packers to accept a consent decree ending their control over the stockyards. In August 1921, moreover, farm bloc congressmen helped to enact a Packers and Stockyards Act. It empowered the secretary of agriculture to issue cease-and-desist orders to preserve competition among packers and to compel commission merchants and stockyards to charge only reasonable rates.

This was not all that the farm bloc won during the hectic special session of 1921. Congress extended for three years the life of the War Finance Corporation, established in 1918 to supply capital for war industries, and authorized it to lend up to $1 billion to stimulate the export of agricultural commodities. The lending operations of the Federal Farm Loan System were expanded by increasing the capital of the Federal Land Banks, established in 1916. The farm bloc also obtained passage of the Grain Futures Act, which gave the secretary of agriculture sweeping control over the grain exchanges. But the agrarians' most important triumph in the early twenties was the enactment in March 1923 of the Agricultural Credits Act—the culmination of a searching inquiry into the farm problem by a joint congressional commission established in 1921. This measure established twelve Intermediate Credit Banks, capitalized by the Treasury and operated in conjunction with the Federal Land Banks, to make loans to organized groups of farmers for periods running from six months to three years.

All these agricultural measures of 1921–1923 were based on a single, guiding assumption: that farm prices would soon experience a full recovery. When that

THE ECONOMIC FORTUNES OF AMERICAN FARMERS:
CASH INCOMES AND PRICES
1910-1940

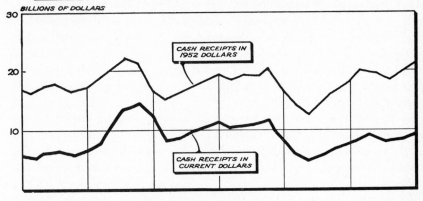

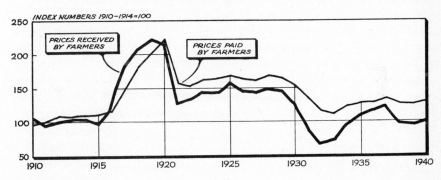

recovery did not occur, farm leaders began to consider even more ambitious measures. The chief task was to prevent farm surpluses from depressing domestic agricultural prices. Among all the numerous suggestions, the most ambitious and popular was the McNary–Haugen plan. It was the invention of George N. Peek and Hugh S. Johnson, two farm machinery manufacturers of Moline, Illinois, whose business had been hard hit by the depression of 1920–1921. They would achieve a "fair exchange value" for farm products by segregating the exportable surplus so that the domestic market would not be affected by world prices. For example, the United States during the 1920s annually produced about 800 million bushels of wheat, of which 650 million bushels were consumed at home. If the world price was $1.00 a bushel, then in a free market American farmers would receive $800 million for the wheat crop. Let us assume, however, that the Peek–Johnson plan was in operation. In this event, a federal board would buy the entire wheat crop at a price that would yield a fair exchange value, presumably the world price plus the tariff on wheat, which after 1924 would have totaled $1.42 a bushel. Farmers would thus receive a gross of $1.1 billion for 800 million bushels of wheat. The board would sell the surplus of 150 million bushels abroad at the world price of $1.00, and its loss of 42 cents a bushel, or a total of $63 million, would be assessed against the farmers in the form of an "equalization fee." Thus under the plan farmers would receive a net of $1 billion for the crop, instead of $800 million if the wheat had been sold in a free market at world prices.

The Peek–Johnson proposal seemed such an easy and sensible way of assuring equitable farm prices that it was embodied in the McNary–Haugen bill in 1924. Violently opposed by eastern Republicans and President Coolidge, the measure was defeated by the House in June 1924. This first defeat, however, only spurred farm leaders to redouble their propaganda and seek new allies. Midwesterners won the support of southern farm organizations in 1926 by including cotton, tobacco, and rice in the proposed system; and the southern–western coalition pushed a revised McNary–Haugen bill through Congress in February 1927. Coolidge replied with a caustic veto message denouncing the measure as unconstitutional special-interest legislation. Reenacted in May 1928, the McNary–Haugen bill drew a second angry presidential veto.

Unsuccessful in committing the federal government to an aggressive farm program, the agrarian interests failed only because the eastern, business wing of the GOP had the president on their side. Actually, by 1929 the American Farm Bureau Federation and other organizations had succeeded in promoting a new unity among farm leaders throughout the country. More important, they had compelled the conservative majority in the Republican party to approve a federal farm program that included strict control of grain exchanges, stockyards, and packing houses, support for agricultural cooperatives, and credit facilities on every level.

5. Immigration Restriction and the Power Controversy

One of the oldest objectives of a certain segment of the progressive movement was exclusion of Asian immigration to the West Coast and restriction of the numbers of Europeans who came to the United States. Rightly or wrongly, leaders of organized labor believed that large-scale immigration depressed the domestic labor market and impeded the progress of unionization. Many sociologists and social workers believed that the immigration of eastern and southern Europeans created grave social problems. Finally, most new immigrants were either Catholics or Jews, and their coming aroused fear among Protestant Americans, especially in the rural areas, of a Catholic and Jewish inundation.

Restrictionists sought to accomplish their objective at first by imposing a literacy test in 1917; it was designed to exclude large number of peasant immigrants from eastern Europe. But the literacy test was only a slight deterrent, since immigrants who went to the trouble to seek a new home were also willing to learn enough to pass a simple test in reading and writing in their own language. Some 1.2 million immigrants poured into American ports between 1920 and 1921, and American consuls warned that millions more were preparing to leave war-ravaged areas.

Labor leaders and social workers found many new allies in 1920 and 1921. Some leaders of Communist and other left-wing groups were eastern Europeans, and employers—who heretofore had usually opposed restriction—now endorsed new legislation. The Ku Klux Klan was meanwhile beginning a campaign that sought to reduce the political and cultural influence of Jews and Catholics. It is only fair to say, however, that the restrictionists probably would have succeeded without the assistance of extreme nativists, for the preponderant majority already desired to end the historic policy of free and almost unlimited immigration.

Congress thus acted with dispatch in 1921. The House approved a bill sponsored by Representative Albert Johnson of Washington to suspend immigration for one year. It was amended in the Senate to limit the number of immigrants to 3 percent of the various foreign-born elements in the United States in 1910 and approved by Congress in the closing days of the lame-duck session. When Wilson refused to sign the bill, congressional leaders quickly pushed it through the special session, and Harding approved the measure in May 1921. The number of immigrants declined in consequence from 805,228 for the fiscal year ending June 30, 1921, to 309,556 during the following fiscal year.

The reduction effected was obviously drastic, but restrictionists, and especially champions of religious and nationalistic bigotry, were still not satisfied. Congress responded in 1924 with a new and comprehensive immigration statute that satisfied even the exclusionists. Known as the National Origins Act, it prohibited Oriental immigration and limited the total number of European immigrants to 2 percent of the foreign-born according to the census of 1890. The latter stipulation reduced the total number of immigrants to 164,000, discriminated heavily in favor of Great Britain, Ireland, and Germany, and cut the flow of Italians, for example, to less than 4,000 a year. The act also provided that immigration should be further reduced to a maximum of 150,000 after July 1, 1927, apportioned on a basis of the national origins of the American people in 1920. The application of the new quota system based upon the national origins of the American people was postponed beyond 1927 because of the difficulty of determining what those origins were. But, on July 1, 1929, the quotas finally went into effect. President Herbert Hoover drastically reduced the quotas in 1931, so that more foreigners left the United States than entered in 1932. The number of immigrants in any one year during the thirties never exceeded 100,000, while the total net immigration for the entire decade was only 68,789.

A less ambiguous sign that the progressive legacy was still a powerful one in national politics was a controversy concerning private or public control over the electric-power industry. Reformers supported a policy of governmental intervention at the local, state, and federal level. They sought either municipal ownership and operation of electric power facilities or effective state regulation of the industry. And they advocated committing the federal government to the operation of important power projects.

Although still young in the 1920s, the electrical industry rose spectacularly. Production of electric power increased from 6 billion to 117 billion kilowatt-hours between 1902 and 1929. Expansion had been accompanied by consolidation of small operating companies into large systems, and of large systems into even larger, holding-company aggregations. By 1930, eleven well-defined holding-company groups controlled 85 percent of the installed capacity of the industry.

Attempts to regulate the vast electrical industry, the second most important in

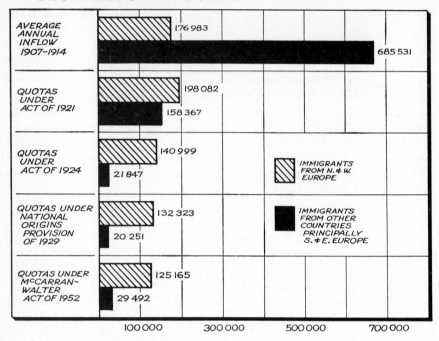

EFFECTS OF THE QUOTA ACTS
ON SOURCES OF IMMIGRATION

the country, closely resembled the experience of railroad regulation. The establishment of public utility commissions with rate-making authority in Virginia in 1901 and in Georgia, Wisconsin, and New York in 1907 marked the beginning of the movement on the state level. In spite of public apathy caused by high-pressure utilities propaganda and a downward trend in rates, many state commissions exercised a reasonable degree of control over rates and services. On the other hand, probably a majority of the state commissions were timid and incompetent, controlled more often than not by the utilities themselves. Regulatory reformers in the 1920s thus not only sought to strengthen state commissions but also supported municipal ownership of power plants and distribution facilities. By 1930, Los Angeles, Seattle, Tacoma, and some 2,000 other cities and towns owned their own generating plants or distribution facilities.

Like the railroads decades before, power companies during the 1920s fought to protect their position, preserve immunity from effective regulation, and prevent public ownership. They waged a gigantic advertising campaign that cost between $28 million and $35 million a year to influence public opinion and indirectly control the editorial policies of hundreds of newspapers. They sometimes bought control of leading dailies. "Information bureaus" working in practically every state on orders from the textbook committee of the National Electric Light Association brought pressure on school boards to force abandonment of civics texts that condemned stock watering and exorbitant rates or mentioned the benefits of regulation or public ownership. Moreover, power companies quietly hired a number of college professors for public lectures, subsidized the General Federation of Women's Clubs, influenced bankers through judicious use of deposits, bribed leaders of farm organizations, and worked relentlessly to control local and state politicians and commissions.

The first serious attempt at federal regulation was the adoption of the Water Power Act of 1920, enacted after a long controversy over policy for the licensing of dams on public lands, reservations, or navigable rivers. This measure created a Federal Power Commission, composed of the secretaries of War, Interior, and Agriculture. The commission was empowered to license hydroelectric projects on sites within the jurisdiction of the federal government. Such leases ran for fifty years, but the government might purchase the entire property at net cost at the expiration of the lease. In addition, the commission was authorized to regulate the rates, services, and financial operation of companies operating under its license, unless such companies were already subject to state regulation.

The Federal Power Commission licensed 449 projects with 2.5 million installed horsepower capacity between 1920 and 1930. Because of inadequate staff and the pressure of private interests, however, it did practically nothing to protect the public interest. At President Hoover's request, Congress created a new and independent Federal Power Commission in 1930. But Congress refused to endow the Commission with additional authority because it feared that Hoover would pack the new agency with men friendly to the power interests. As Hoover soon justified congressional suspicions, effective federal regulation was postponed until the inauguration of an administration less concerned with protecting private enterprise in the production of electricity.

More significant than these largely ineffective efforts at federal regulation was the development of an organized campaign during the 1920s to commit the federal government to large hydroelectric projects in the Tennessee Valley, the Columbia River watershed, the Southwest, and on the St. Lawrence River. These regional developments, progressives asserted, would guarantee cheap, abundant power for millions of consumers and establish standards for rates throughout the country. Before 1928, only one of the proposed projects was begun—Hoover, or Boulder, Dam—but around another proposed development centered one of the most critical battles of the twenties. This was the struggle for control of a large, federally owned dam and nitrogen plant at Muscle Shoals, Alabama, which in time became the focus of the entire controversy over public ownership and operation of power plants.

Congress in 1916 empowered the president and War Department to construct a plant to manufacture nitrates and thus make the United States independent of German and Chilean supplies. Two nitrate plants, with a combined annual capacity of more than 40,000 tons, were built in 1918 at a cost of over $80 million at Muscle Shoals, on the Tennessee River in Alabama. At the same time, the War Department began construction at this site of the gigantic Wilson Dam to provide electric power for the nitrate plants. The war's end found the nitrate plants completed but not yet in production and the dam about three-quarters finished.

Soon after Harding's inauguration, the new secretary of war announced that he would urge Congress to appropriate funds to complete the dam if some private company would lease the Muscle Shoals properties and guarantee a fair return on the government's investment. A number of power companies and industrial corporations submitted bids during the next two years, but it was the proposition made by Henry Ford, the automobile manufacturer, that excited the greatest enthusiasm. He offered to lease the Muscle Shoals facilities for one hundred years, to pay an annual rental of $1.5 million, and to produce at least 40,000 tons of nitrates annually for cheap fertilizers.

Ford's proposal was enthusiastically supported by the Harding and Coolidge administrations and the farm groups, and the House of Representatives in March 1924 approved a bill authorizing acceptance of Ford's bid. The Muscle Shoals offers had been referred in the Senate to the Agriculture Committee, headed by George W. Norris of Nebraska. Norris had already concluded that Ford, the power companies, and other industrialists were deceiving the people in an attempt to steal one of the nation's greatest natural assets—the potentially enormous hydroelectric resources of the Tennessee Valley. As early as 1922 an alternative had begun to take shape in Norris's mind: the creation of a public corporation to control the waters of the Tennessee Valley—and afterward of other such watersheds—for flood control and the production of vast quantities of cheap electric power.

Norris's first move was to push a bill through Congress in 1922 for completion of Wilson Dam; his second move involved persuading the Senate Agriculture Committee, in May 1924, to approve a bill for governmental operation of the Muscle Shoals properties. When the Nebraskan presented his measure to the Senate in December 1924, Senator Oscar W. Underwood of Alabama countered with an alternative bill for private operation. The Senate approved the Underwood bill in January 1925; two weeks later a conference committee met to iron out differences between the Senate and House measures. Just when it seemed that the Senate would approve the conference report, Norris, on February 19, made what was probably the most important parliamentary point of order in American history. He objected that the conference committee had improperly added new provisions to the Muscle Shoals bill. The point of order was sustained, and Norris was able to prevent a vote by threat of filibuster when the conference committee reported a proper bill on February 26, 1925. Norris did not relax his vigilance during the next two years. Indeed, he won new allies among the southern senators, and he got the Senate's approval in March 1928 of his bill for governmental operation of the Muscle Shoals power plant. Insurgent Republicans and Democrats in the House soon afterward adopted a measure that in many respects went even further than the Norris bill. It provided for creation of a federal corporation to operate Wilson Dam and the nitrogen plants, as well as for construction of an additional dam at Cove Creek, Tennessee, to insure flood control and a steady flow of water through the Muscle Shoals turbines. It was this House measure that Congress approved in the latter part of May 1928.

Spokesmen for a large part of the business community appealed to Coolidge to prevent such a far-reaching experiment in socialism. Coolidge did not disappoint his friends; he gave the Muscle Shoals bill a pocket veto. In spite of President Hoover's open opposition, Norris and the progressive coalition adopted a second Muscle Shoals bill in February 1931. Hoover replied with in a veto message that was a ringing defense of private enterprise.

6. The Supreme Court and Public Policy, 1918–1929

In the first third of the twentieth century, the Supreme Court played an increasingly important role in the formulation of public policy. Between 1908 and 1917, it had validated a whole series of laws expanding the welfare and regulatory functions of state and federal government. But, with the child labor case of 1918, discussed below, and especially after the appointment of a new, conservative majority between 1921 and 1930, headed by former President William Howard Taft, the Court began to limit the scope of governmental intervention.

At the same time, the Court between 1919 and 1929 was no great defender of the American tradition of civil rights. In *Schenck* v. *United States,* a unanimous Court agreed that the government had the right to suppress sedition during wartime, on the ground that sedition constituted, to quote Justice Holmes's famous words, a "clear and present danger" to national security (see p. 140). In *Abrams* v. *United States* (1919) and other cases, Holmes and Louis D. Brandeis tried to persuade their colleagues to accept a narrow interpretation of the "clear and present danger" doctrine, but without success. In *Gitlow* v. *New York* (1925) and *Whitney* v. *California* (1927) the Court—with Holmes and Brandeis again eloquently dissenting—upheld criminal anarchy and syndicalism laws of New York and California. The effect of these decisions was to give federal and state officials practically unlimited discretion in determining what constituted a "clear and present danger."

The Court exhibited more boldness in protecting racial and religious minorities. In 1923 it overturned state wartime statutes forbidding the use of foreign languages in schools. In a momentous decision two years later—*Pierce* v. *Society of Sisters*—the Court unanimously outlawed a Klan-sponsored Oregon statute to destroy parochial schools by requiring all children between eight and sixteen to attend public schools. Finally, when the Texas legislature excluded blacks from the Democratic primary and soon afterward authorized the Democratic state committee to exclude black voters, the Court, in 1927 and again in 1932, nullified the statutes on the ground that they violated the Fourteenth and Fifteenth amendments.

It would be an exaggeration to say that the Supreme Court deliberately set out to overturn a whole body of progressive state and federal statutes concerning regulation and welfare. But on two important frontiers of the social justice movement, the Court not only called a halt to reform but also nullified previous gains. The first controversy involved the constitutionality of the Child Labor Act of 1916. By a five-to-four decision in *Hammer* v. *Dagenhart* (1918), the Court declared that the act involved an unconstitutional invasion of the police power of the states. Congress could not use its power over interstate commerce to regulate the conditions of labor. Congress in 1919 levied a prohibitive tax on products manufactured in whole or in part by children, and the Court, in *Bailey* v. *Drexel Furniture Company* (1922), again applied its veto. Congress, the majority declared, could not use the taxing power to accomplish an unconstitutional regulation.

The Court's inflexible opposition to any form of federal regulation of hours, wages, and conditions of labor—for such opposition was clearly implied in the child labor decisions—was discouraging enough to social justice reformers with ambitious plans for extensive federal regulation through the commerce power. Even more disheartening was the Court's destruction of all state efforts to regulate the wages of women workers. The case of *Adkins* v. *Children's Hospital,* involving the constitutionality of a District of Columbia minimum wage statute for women, came before the new conservative Supreme Court in 1923. Brandeis's disciple, Felix Frankfurter, defended the statute by marshaling economic and social data to prove a direct connection between the wages that women received and their health and morals. Justice George Sutherland, speaking for the majority, dismissed this argument as irrelevant. He also resurrected the decision in *Lochner* v. *New York* (1905) to affirm that state efforts to regulate the wages of grown women violated their freedom to make a labor contract.

Another long and bitter controversy erupted when the Court denied that the labor provisions of the Clayton Act of 1914 had conferred any substantial new benefits and privileges on labor unions. The question, in essence, was whether the Clayton Act gave unions immunity from prosecution for, and injunctions against, methods of industrial warfare—the secondary boycott, the blacklist, and mass picketing, among others—which the federal courts had earlier outlawed under the Sherman Antitrust Act. The Supreme Court in a number of decisions in the 1920s ruled that the Clayton Act had neither conferred upon labor unions immunity from prosecution for violating the antitrust laws nor legalized labor practices that were illegal before the Clayton Act was adopted. Although the majority correctly interpreted the intentions of the framers of the Clayton Act (see pp. 94–95), Justices Holmes, Brandeis, and John H. Clarke dissented and lent authority to the AFL's contention that organized labor had been unjustly deprived of the benefits of its "Magna Carta."

Continuing a policy begun in the 1880s, the Supreme Court during the 1920s insisted on wielding the power to review state regulation of economic enterprises. Generally speaking, however, Supreme Court policy concerning state regulation was neither capricious nor reactionary. The high bench readily acknowledged the right of states to regulate businesses clothed with a public interest. At the same time, it insisted that such regulation be nondiscriminatory and according to due process of law. Railroad regulation, both state and federal, had become in practice thoroughly institutionalized by the 1920s. But state regulation of public utilities was not as well developed by precedent and experience, and there was considerable confusion over the proper constitutional basis for rate making. State commission usually determined rates on a basis of original cost. During the prosperous twenties, on the other hand, public utility companies contended that the cost of replacing the properties was the proper basis. Although the Court usually accepted the latter contention before 1933, it did not evolve any definite formula to determine the basis for a fair return.

As for federal regulation, there occurred a marked expansion of the federal power during the 1920s, in spite of the conservative temper of those who determined Republican policies and controlled the Supreme Court. In *Massachusetts* v. *Mellon* (1923), the Court upheld the system of federal grants-in-aid to the states and repudiated Massachusetts's argument that such grants unduly infringed the police power of the states because of conditions attached to acceptance of the grants. The result of the decision was a significant erosion of state sovereignty. Moreover, in all cases in which the United States could demonstrate that the regulated activity was interstate in character, the Supreme Court sanctioned an expansion of federal authority. In *Stafford* v. *Wallace* (1922), for example, the Court upheld the Packers and Stockyards Act, which subjected the meat-packing industry to strict federal control. While nullifying the Grain Futures Act in 1923—because Congress had used the taxing power to regulate grain exchanges—the Court declared that Congress might use its commerce power to accomplish the same result. When Congress established the Federal Radio Commission and gave it complete control over the airways, the Court agreed in 1933 that such regulation was proper and constitutional.

Chapter 12

-»>> «<-

Herbert Hoover and the Great Depression, 1929–1933

The Great Depression brought an end to a long era of economic growth that began in the late 1890s. There had been momentary recessions in 1907, 1913, and 1921, to be sure, but these reversals had never been severe enough or long enough to shake the confidence in the system or to generate any serious nationwide discontent. The depression that began in 1929 did not destroy the faith in the value of capitalism or of democratic institutions. However, it traumatized Americans, caused widespread suffering and profound discontent among all classes in all sections, and revived a belief in the need for strong governmental intervention and regulation, especially at the national level.

1. The Election of 1928

Because of internal conflicts over the Klan, race and religion, and prohibition, the Democrats ceased to be an effective national party between 1924 and 1928. That these same tensions would weaken the Democratic party during the campaign of 1928 became apparent long before the national convention met in Houston, Texas, in June 1928. Governor Alfred E. Smith of New York had emerged as the only Democrat of presidential stature and had won most of the nonsouthern states during the preconvention campaign of 1928. But he had failed to win any popular support in the South on account of his Roman Catholicism, Tammany connections, and avowed opposition to prohibition. All signs pointed to a southern rebellion of large proportions if the northern and western majority insisted on nominating the New York governor and endorsing repeal of the Eighteenth Amendment.

After praying, drinking, and struggling in the Houston convention, Southerners concurred in Smith's nomination only after the northern leaders gave up their demand for a platform plank favoring repeal of prohibition. Without this concession, the southern politicians warned, they could not hold their constituents in the party. Ignoring these warnings, Smith notified the convention that, although he would enforce the prohibition laws if elected, he also reserved the right to advocate and work for repeal of the Volstead Act and perhaps also of the Eighteenth Amendment.

Meanwhile, the Republicans had met at Kansas City during the same month and nominated Secretary of Commerce Herbert Hoover, the ablest member of the Harding–Coolidge administrations and a preeminent champion of individualism and regulated and orderly private enterprise. During the ensuing campaign, Hoover reiterated his opposition to support of agricultural prices, public power projects, and special-interest legislation on organized labor's behalf. Time and again, he repeated his conviction that only a continuation of the Harding–Coolidge policies could make prosperity permanent. "We in America today are nearer to the final triumph over poverty than ever before in the history of any land," he exclaimed in his acceptance speech. "The poorhouse is vanishing from among us. We have not yet reached the goal, but, given a chance to go forward with the policies of the last eight years, we shall soon, with the help of God, be in sight of the day when poverty will be banished from this nation."

Although a distinguished advocate of civil rights and social legislation, Smith conducted a campaign that was thoroughly conservative in tone. Almost exclusively, he discussed the evils of prohibition and bigotry; at the same time, he attempted to convince voters that a Democratic victory would not endanger prosperity. Yet Smith's candidacy was doomed almost from the start. His attacks on prohibition cost him more votes in the South and Middle West than they gained in the East. The fact that he was a devout Roman Catholic stirred bigots and Protestant leaders who feared the aggrandizement of Catholic power. In the South, the campaign to defeat the Democratic nominee assumed the proportions of a religious crusade. Throughout the region, Protestant clergy and laity, led by Bishop James Cannon, Jr., of the Methodist Episcopal Church, South, were up in arms, chiefly because of Smith's opposition to the Eighteenth Amendment.

Cannon's organization broke the Solid South and carried Virginia, North Carolina, Tennessee, Florida, Kentucky, Oklahoma, and Texas for Hoover. The prohibition issue undoubtedly played some role in the outcome, but Smith's Catholicism was the dominant factor. Outside the South, Smith carried only Massachusetts and Rhode Island. He won 15 million votes as compared to Hoover's 21.4 million votes. Yet there were perhaps signs of things to come in the election returns of 1928. First, Smith carried the nation's twelve largest cities—in contrast to Cox's and Davis's failure in the metropolitan areas in 1920 and 1924—and ran impressively in all counties in which Catholics and recent immigrants figured significantly. Second, Smith ran far better in the midwestern farm states, particularly in the wheat belt, than any Democrat had done in a presidential election since 1916.

The prevailing prosperity was also a factor in the election. There was still acute unrest in farm areas, especially in the western Middle West. In Minnesota, Nebraska, North Dakota, Wisconsin, and Washington, insurgent Republicans were elected by large margins. These were signs for the future, to be sure. But a large majority of Americans in the autumn of 1928 apparently endorsed the leadership and policies which had seemingly brought prosperity and which offered the promise of even better times ahead.

2. Origins of the Great Crash

When Hoover won his decisive victory in November 1928, it seemed to many Americans that an economic millennium lay just around the corner. All seemed well with the Republic. The government was in safe hands, and a great engineer and administrator, pledged to abolish poverty and carry on policies that had made the United States prosperous, would soon occupy the White House. And yet, more discerning eyes could detect hidden weaknesses in the economy, even apart from the dangerous stock market boom. In themselves, these weaknesses did not set off the depression. But once the stock market collapse destroyed business confidence and caused huge withdrawals of capital, the subsidiary economic strains combined to prolong and intensify the severity of the depression.

The first and perhaps the most important structural weakness of the 1920s was the unstable nature of the international economy, stemming from a complex of difficulties reviewed in another chapter (see pp. 296–298). The fundamental weakness of the new international exchange system—Europe's financial dependence upon the United States—proved fatal once American credit dried up. The long depression in agriculture that began in 1920 impoverished American farmers and caused them to operate at a net capital loss during most of the decade (see p. 214). The effects of this agricultural depression were apparent in the decline in farm incomes, values, and purchasing power, and in the failure of thousands of country banks. Farmers dragged the rest of the nation with them in their decline when nothing really effective was done after 1929 to halt the downward plunge of farm prices. Another fundamental problem was the lack of any proper balance between private and public control of financial institutions and practices. A rigid gold standard kept the government from expanding the money supply when it would have been advantageous to do so. Finally, there were no state or federal agencies with power to prevent stock market excesses and malpractices that abetted speculation.

In other ways, too, the American political economy was badly out of joint by 1929. Large segments of American industry were concentrated and bureaucratized and able to maintain prices at artificially high levels for a time after the depression began. Abnormally high industrial profits and a federal tax policy that favored the rich also aggravated an unequal distribution of incomes that gave 26 percent of the national income to the top 5 percent of income receivers in 1929. These internal maladjustments were beginning to impair the health of the economic system at least two years before the stock market crash occurred. Even so, the development that threw the financial machinery out of gear and released the cumulative forces of dissolution was the stock market boom that ended in the crash of October 1929.

One of the most startling aspects of the wild bull market was the suddenness with which it developed. In response to increased business activity and rising profits, trading on the New York Stock Exchange increased from 236 million shares in 1923 to 451 million in 1926. At the same time, the average price of 25 representative industrial stocks rose from $108 to $166 a share—an increase of about 54 percent. This increase, actually, reflected only the normal response of the market to higher earnings in industry. Then a tremendous upward surge of the market began in 1927. Brokers' loans—that is, loans with stock for collateral—increased from a little over $3 billion in January 1927 to nearly $4.5 billion by the end of December. The volume of shares traded on the New York Stock Exchange rose from 451 million in 1926 to 577 million in 1927.

Obviously a boom was developing, and conservative bankers, sensing a disastrous inflation of stock prices, urged caution. During the early weeks of 1928 it seemed briefly that the market might break. Instead, it held firm when Treasury officials and President Coolidge declared that the volume of brokers' loans was not too great, and that the country had never been more soundly prosperous. By March 1928, the wild bull market had begun. During the next eighteen months, despite some fluctuation, stock market prices surged ahead. By early 1929, the boom was out of control; industrial issues then sold at more than sixteen times their earnings, although traditionally the safe ratio was ten to one.

The boom had reached such irrational proportions by the summer of 1929 that some kind of readjustment, if not a collapse, was inevitable. Between 1925 and early October 1929, the market value of all stocks listed on the New York Stock Exchange increased from $27 billion in 1925 to a peak of $87 billion on October 1, 1929. The average price of common stocks increased nearly 300 percent, and the volume of trading on the exchange rose from 454 million shares in 1925 to 1.1 billion shares in 1929. But prices could not rise forever, and the financial structure was so precarious that even a slight recession would set off a panic. On September 26, 1929, the Bank of England raised the rediscount rate, or the interest rate for banks, to 6.5 percent in order to halt the outward flow of gold and protect the pound in international exchange. The withdrawal of at least several hundred million dollars from New York to London caused prices to decline on September 30; but the market rallied during the next two weeks. Dissolution and withdrawal began on October 15, gradually at first, as large operators unloaded discreetly. Then total panic seized the stock market on October 24, 1929, "Black Thursday," when nearly 13 million shares changed hands. Prices fell so rapidly that tickers could not keep pace with their descent.

The panic subsided momentarily in the afternoon of "Black Thursday" when J. P. Morgan & Company and other large banks formed a $240 million pool and bought heavily to buoy the market and protect their loans and investments. "The fundamental business of the country, that is, production and distribution of commodities," declared President Hoover on October 25, "is on a sound and prosperous basis." Although Hoover's reassurance was echoed a hundred times in the inner circles of Wall Street, the bottom dropped out of the market again on October 29. Nearly 16.5 million shares changed hands in the wildest trading in the New York Stock Exchange's history to that time, and the average price of fifty leading stocks declined almost forty points under the pressure.

3. The Depression Begins

The decline in stock values—a loss of some $40 billion during the last four months of 1929 alone—set off interacting forces that ultimately resulted in the near collapse of the American economy. Prosperity depended on world trade, investment in capital plant and equipment, the construction industry, and automobile manufacturing. It also depended on business confidence—a belief that, in the future, goods could be sold and investments would yield a good return.

By 1932, these foundations of prosperity had been severely weakened. The stock market crash caused the first shock wave by undermining the confidence of the business community, weakening financial institutions, slowing down industrial expansion, and causing a diminution in American purchases and investments abroad. The practical withdrawal of the American dollar props from under the international economy in turn precipitated a severe financial crisis in Europe in 1931. Europeans met this crisis only by adopting policies which virtually destroyed the system of international exchange. The European collapse in turn caused further strain on American banks and deepened the industrial and business depression. Meanwhile, the Federal Reserve Board reduced the money supply by raising the discount rate between 1930 to 1932, and by doing so made even moderate recovery almost impossible.

Soon, moreover, all sectors of the economy experienced the deepening depression. Banks, major industries, and transportation were all affected. There were 659 bank failures, involving deposits of nearly $250 million, in 1929. In the following year, 1,352 banks, with deposits of $853 million, failed. In 1931, when the European financial crisis intensified the severity of the depression, a total of 2,294 banks, with aggregate deposits of nearly $1.7 billion, closed their doors. In 1932, 1,456 banks, with deposits of nearly $750 million, failed. The two basic industries of construction and automobiles declined alarmingly, and twenty-five representative industrial stocks fell from an average closing price of $366.29 a share in 1929 to $96.63 a share in 1932. This plummeting provoked an even more serious crisis among the railroads. Already beginning to feel the effect of competition from the trucking industry in 1929, they staggered under heavy blows, and great systems, with an aggregate of some 45,000 miles, passed into receivership from 1929 to 1933.

The cumulative momentum of the depression can perhaps best be illustrated by the statistics on industrial production and unemployment. By the last quarter of 1930, industrial production in the United States was 26 percent below the peak level of 1929. By midsummer 1932 the production curve had declined 51 percent below the level of the peak year. In response, unemployment grew rapidly: 3 million in April 1930; 4 million in October 1930; almost 7 million in October 1931; nearly 11 million a year later; and from 12 million to 14 million, or one-fourth of the work force, during the first months of 1933. Moreover, workers fortunate enough to find or retain employment suffered severely from wage reductions, especially after 1931. Total labor income from 1929 to 1933 fell from $53 billion to $31.5 billion; manufacturing wages, from nearly $12 billion to approximately $7 billion. American farmers, already in economic straits by 1929, lost more in cash income and general economic standing during the depression years than any other important group.

THE PROGRESS OF THE GREAT DEPRESSION, 1929-1933

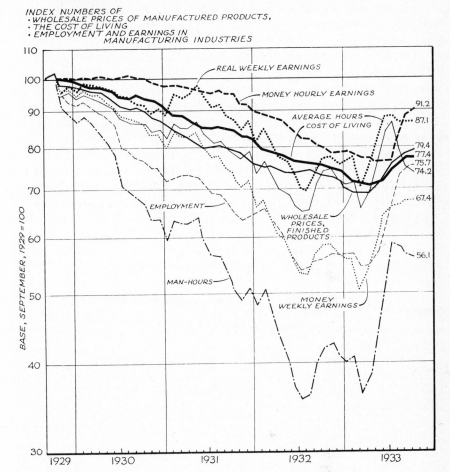

INDEX NUMBERS OF
• WHOLESALE PRICES OF MANUFACTURED PRODUCTS,
• THE COST OF LIVING
• EMPLOYMENT AND EARNINGS IN
      MANUFACTURING INDUSTRIES

Gross farm income shrank from more than $11.9 billion to $5.3 billion between 1929 and 1932.

The dimensions of the economic collapse are perhaps apparent from the following summary view. National income declined from $87.8 billion in 1929 to $40.2 billion in 1933; adjusted for the cost of living, per capita income declined from $681 to $459. Salaries decreased 40 percent, dividends nearly 57 percent, and manufacturing wages 60 percent. The total picture of these years of the locusts, therefore, is one of extreme deflation everywhere except in the debt structure. As the American people struggled to save their financial system, interest payments on long-term debts declined only 3.3 percent from 1929 to 1933.

The depression affected almost all aspects of life. Americans sometimes acted curiously under the impact of shattered hopes. They practically stopped buying new automobiles, to be sure, but they stubbornly refused to give up their old ones, and gasoline consumption increased slightly from 1929 through 1933. Jewelry sales declined precipitately; but women would not give up silk and rayon hosiery or even radios, for soap operas were just coming into vogue. Nor was the tobacco industry affected by depression. Cigarette consumption, in fact, rose steadily during the depression years, as if the nervous strains engendered by distress demanded a form of release.

One of the most unfortunate social effects of the depression was its impact on family relationships and marriage and birth rates. Tens of thousands of families were forced to double up in homes and apartments, and tensions between fathers and sons increased as the latter found it impossible to find work. Young people out of work married later and had fewer children. Thus the number of marriages declined from 1,233,000 in 1929 to 982,000 in 1932, while the birth rate declined from 21.3 per thousand in 1930 to 18.4 in 1933.

Schools and colleges were profoundly affected. Americans struggled successfully to maintain school plants, equipment, and salaries until 1932. By the end of the 1933–1934 school year, however, state and local school systems were beginning to feel a fiscal crunch. Expenditures for school purposes fell from more than $1.8 billion to $1.5 billion, or about 18 percent, from 1930 to 1934. But in many states the decrease exceeded 30 percent, and in Michigan and Mississippi it was 41 and 52 percent, respectively. Colleges and universities experienced even greater adversity. Total enrollment in institutions of higher learning declined 8.5 percent throughout the country between 1931 and 1934. Generally speaking, state colleges and universities were hardest hit, suffering a 31 percent drop in income from state appropriations, as compared with a 19 percent drop in income from endowments owned by private institutions.

But the most important—and lasting—social consequence of the depression was a shift in responsibility for alleviating social distress from private groups to public agencies. Early in the depression, city and state governments formed emergency relief administrations and took over relief and public health services from charitable agencies. In spite of optimism, excellent administration, and the cooperation of federal authorities, the cities and states could not meet the relief emergency after 1931. Staggering under unbearable financial burdens, forced to default on obligations and pay public employees in scrip, cities and states simply could not borrow the money necessary to meet the elementary needs of the unemployed. Appeals for private support yielded only paltry sums; "give-a-job" campaigns, "block-aid" programs, and so on, were largely futile.

The impossibility of using only private, city, and state resources to meet the crisis had been amply demonstrated by social workers and statisticians by the winter of 1932. The destitute congregated in cardboard shacks in so-called Hoovervilles on the edges of cities across the nation. Hundred of thousands of the unemployed roamed the country on foot and in boxcars in futile search of work. There was perhaps little outright starvation, but there was much hunger; and the malnutrition rate among patients admitted to certain community health centers in New York and Philadelphia increased 60 percent. Nor were hunger and malnutrition primarily urban phenomena, for five-cent cotton meant a lean diet of salt pork and hominy for southern poor whites and blacks, and unemployment in the mining areas brought destitution unequaled on a large scale anywhere in the cities.

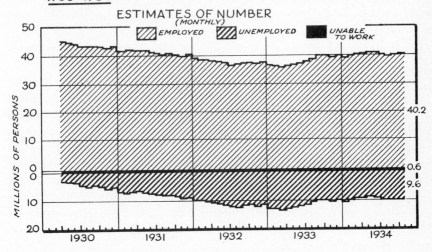

EMPLOYMENT AND UNEMPLOYMENT
IN THE UNITED STATES
1930-1934

ESTIMATES OF NUMBER
(MONTHLY)

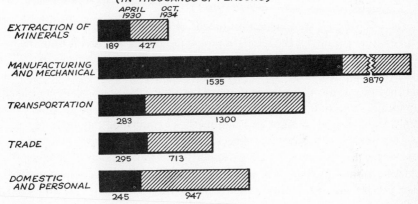

ESTIMATES OF UNEMPLOYED IN SPECIFIED INDUSTRIES
(IN THOUSANDS OF PERSONS)

4. Rumblings of Social Discontent

Many Americans were baffled by the inability of a country with abundant resources, the largest force of skilled labor, and the most productive plant in the world to find the formula for economic recovery. It was difficult to understand why millions of people should go hungry in a country groaning under the burden of huge food surpluses. To many Americans, the depression exposed the shortcomings of the economic system and undermined their faith in business leadership.

The discrediting of an economic leadership that had hitherto been warmly admired did not, of course, occur all at once. Until the summer of 1931, probably a majority of the people believed the assurances of Republican spokesmen and financial leaders, who since the stock market crash had predicted that the economic system would eventually right itself. However, the European collapse in 1931 (described below) caused more banks to fail and bread lines to lengthen, and the Senate Banking Committee in the winter of 1931–1932 exposed corruption and malfeasance in the banking community. Consequently, public confidence in the economic leadership of the Hoover administration sagged and then nearly collapsed during the summer of 1932.

By the spring of 1931, critics of the economic system were developing a full-scale indictment of capitalism. In the late summer of 1931, for example, a commission of the Federal Council of the Churches of Christ in America prepared a statement to be read from pulpits on Labor Sunday. It was one of the most sweeping indictments of capitalism and its leadership ever drawn up by a middle-class group. Nor was such pessimism confined to the churches. In fact, many businessmen abandoned faith in the market system and began to doubt the worth of an economy in which there could be so much abundance and misery at the same time. One startling proposal came from Gerard Swope, president of the General Electric Company. He suggested that industrial leaders cooperate to increase production and protect workers against unemployment and poverty. Swope's warning that government would surely assume this responsibility if industry did not was echoed by the banker–industrialist Owen D. Young, and by the president of the United States Chamber of Commerce.

Labor spokesmen were no less disturbed. AFL leaders at first responded to the depression by waiting for the return of prosperity. But, facing unrest from the rank and file by the autumn of 1931, labor leaders could no longer remain silent. The executive committee of the AFL prepared a statement in October 1931 declaring that the prime cause of the depression had been the unequal distribution of wealth and incomes and calling upon President Hoover to convoke a great national economic conference to consider ways and means of combating the foe from within.

These protests and proposals reflected an ideological upheaval that was transforming popular attitudes toward government and the economy. There were few actual examples of violent social upheaval. Hunger marches and a serious riot of the unemployed took place in Dearborn, Michigan, in the spring of 1932, while embattled farmers organized to prevent mortgage owners from profiting by foreclosure (see p. 255). But the only outbreak that threatened to get out of hand was the descent of the so-called Bonus Expeditionary Force of some 12,000 to 14,000 unemployed and homeless veterans on Washington in May and June 1932. They demanded passage of a bill providing immediate full payment of their bonus by the issuance of $2.4 billion in paper money. Then they built a shanty town on Anacostia Flats outside the capital and threatened to sit it out all summer. The Senate, under strong presidential pressure, refused to approve the bonus bill, and about half the marchers went home when Congress appropriated funds to provide transportation for them. But some 5,000 to 6,000 veterans, many with wives and children, remained as gaunt representatives of the millions of destitute in every state and section.

Then a riot occurred when police attempted to clear a throng of bonus marchers out of a construction area in late July. Two veterans were killed, and several policemen were injured; the District commissioners warned that they could not preserve order without extensive use of force. Hoover immediately called upon the army to control the situation. The army chief of staff, General Douglas MacArthur, assembled a formidable small army with machine guns and tanks, dispersed the bonus marchers from Anacostia Flats and, accidentally or deliberately, burned the shanty town. The very "institutions of our Government" would have been severely threatened, MacArthur declared, if Hoover had not acted decisively.

No doubt the general exaggerated the dimensions of the threat. To be sure, there was much talk of revolution if Hoover should be elected again, but it never got beyond street corners. Actually, the wonder is that there were so few organized expressions of discontent like the bonus march, that people suffered so much without losing their sense of humor or falling prey to left-wing or right-wing agitators.

5. Hoover and the Crisis of American Capitalism

No man ever came to the presidency with broader administrative experience than Herbert Clark Hoover. He was a self-made man whose success story should become as much a part of the American legend as Horatio Alger's tales of boys who made good. Born of Quaker parents at West Branch, Iowa, in 1874, Hoover migrated in his youth to Oregon, attended the newly established Stanford University, and was graduated with a degree in mining engineering in 1895. He proved to be resourceful —in fact, a sheer genius—at running large enterprises. Rising from one high position to another, Hoover had won an international reputation and amassed a large personal fortune by 1914. During the First World War, Hoover served ably as head of the Belgian Relief Commission and was then called to direct the Food Administration when his country entered the war. His reputation was so great by 1920 that he was seriously mentioned for the Democratic presidential nomination. The movement foundered when he decided that he was a Republican.

As secretary of commerce from 1921 until 1928, Hoover was the chief spokesman of limited regulation, mass consumption, and welfare capitalism. Never intimate with professional politicians, Hoover received the GOP nomination in 1928 as a result of strong popular support. With extreme confidence that his administration would witness the maturing of humanitarian capitalism, he entered the White House with such widespread approval as few presidents have ever enjoyed. Yet he left office rejected and despised as few presidents have ever been, his name an object of common sneering and a byword for horsedrawn carts and assemblages of human misery.

How can we account for this almost total deflation of a great reputation? Why was it that a great engineer, administrator, and expert in alleviating human suffering completely failed to provide leadership adequate to deal with the crisis? At least part of Hoover's problem was that he was as inept at politics as he was superb at administration. Before 1928, he had never run for or been elected to political office. He had grown accustomed to obedience during a long career of holding appointive positions of command. In his rigorously honest and orderly mind, he had contempt for mere politicians, so when it came to dealing with Congress he was poorly equipped for effective leadership. Indeed, he could not establish leadership over his own party members in Congress, much less over the Democrats.

Hoover's chief handicap, however, was a rigid, unyielding mental quality that made it difficult for him to adapt to new circumstances or to innovate. Out of long experience and careful thought, he possessed firm convictions concerning government and the economy. He was no laissez-faire economist of the classical school. He approved of regulation of business enterprise clothed with the public interest, and he championed order and efficiency in business rather than destructive competition. Yet he also believed fervently that American progress and prosperity depended upon private initiative and striving. Thus he opposed all measures, like federal operation of Muscle Shoals, that would diminish private energies or impede private investment and enterprise. Out of a sincere belief in local government and the inherent goodness of the American people, Hoover just as strongly opposed any measures to transfer responsibility for social alleviation from localities and states to the federal government. Finally, his almost mystical faith in the gold standard prevented him from adopting bold fiscal measures to spur the economy, although it must be added that the Federal Reserve Board might well have thwarted any fiscal innovations if Hoover had proposed them.

Hoover believed in these principles religiously. During his own lifetime, the American system of comparatively free enterprise, powered by private initiative and what he called "rugged individualism," had worked the greatest material miracle of the modern age. Free capitalism, unhampered by binding controls, had brought a good material life within the reach of the average man, and Hoover saw no reason why it should not bring an even higher standard of living in the future. When the stock market crash set off a business recession, he refused to believe that the downswing was anything more than a passing phase in the business cycle, like the Panic of 1907 or the depression of 1921–1922.

Once the recession of 1929–1930 turned into a full-fledged depression in 1931, Hoover was forced to recognize that complete economic ruin would ensue unless the federal government took positive and unprecedented action. Abandoning momentarily the main tenets of his philosophy, he approved ambitious measures to save the economy. Although he never lost confidence in the gold standard, the inherent soundness of American economic institutions, and the altruism of businessmen and bankers, in a number of important areas he laid the basis for the expansion of the federal government's power. Indeed, it is no exaggeration to say that, in his policy proposals after 1931, Hoover established a foundation for the New Deal.

6. The Hoover Policies: Agricultural Stabilization

Disturbed by the rising insurgency in the Middle West and the Far West, Hoover and other GOP spokesmen during the campaign of 1928 promised farm relief and upward revision of the tariff rates on agricultural products. Soon after his inauguration, Hoover called the Seventy-first Congress into special session to redeem these campaign pledges. Farm leaders still contended that only the McNary–Haugen or some other price-fixing plan would give agriculture parity with industry, and they had long since ceased to believe that higher tariff rates would bring higher agricultural prices at home. But the president had his way, and Congress approved his two measures for farm relief—the Agricultural Marketing Act of June 1929 and the Hawley–Smoot Tariff Act of June 1930.

The draft of the Agricultural Marketing bill that Hoover presented to Congress provided a remedy which would not, he explained, undermine the initiative of the individual farmer or involve the government in any schemes of price control. It created a nonpartisan Federal Farm Board and gave it the use of a revolving fund of $500 million. This money would be lent to agricultural marketing cooperatives to enable them to market products efficiently, build warehouses, and hold farm products in the event of a price decline. In order to win the support of the Senate, however, the president made one concession that changed the character of the proposed stabilization program: an amendment authorizing the Federal Farm Board to establish corporations to stabilize farm prices through direct intervention in the market.

The Agricultural Marketing Act launched the most ambitious federal program of agricultural stabilization and support in American peacetime history to that date. The Federal Farm Board, from 1929 to 1931, organized producers of major staples into national cooperatives and established corporations to stabilize farm prices through large-scale market operations. By lending to cooperatives and buying wheat and cotton in large quantities, the board maintained domestic farm prices a little above the world price level until the summer of 1931. But the financial crisis and depression in Europe that same year shrank foreign demand for American agricultural exports, and dumping by Russia, Argentina, and Australia drove prices to fantastically low levels. From this point on, the board was powerless to prevent the collapse of farm prices at home.

The Federal Farm Board recognized its inability to cope with the situation as early as 1931. Having lost some $354 million in market operations by the summer of 1932, the board openly admitted its helplessness. In December 1932, it urged Congress to establish an effective system for controlling acreage and production as the only alternative to continued agricultural bankruptcy. Hoover's ambitious experiment obviously failed; but out of failure came experience and a profound conviction that cooperation and voluntary action would not suffice. The transition from the Hoover stabilization program to the bolder and more advanced New Deal measures was a natural one.

Hoover's program of tariff relief for agriculture was an even greater fiasco than his ill-fated effort at price stabilization. His intentions undoubtedly were excellent, but all the old lobbies and pressures set diligently to work once deliberations on a tariff bill began. The result was the Hawley–Smoot tariff bill of 1930, which provided about 75 increases for farm products and 925 for manufactured commodities. As a device for supporting domestic agricultural prices, the Hawley–Smoot tariff was completely futile, except, perhaps, with regard to meat and dairy products. Its sheerly economic effect on foreign trade was probably unimportant. Its psychological impact abroad, however, was unfortunate, for it seemed to signal an intensification of economic nationalism in the United States just at the moment when the world desperately needed enlightened leadership. One thousand members of the American Economic Association pointed out this elementary fact in an urgent appeal to the president to veto the Hawley–Smoot bill. Their warning was justified but unheeded. Enlightened economic leadership was in short supply elsewhere as well. The British, for example, adopted protection and a system of imperial preferrence in 1932. Germany in the following year embarked upon a program of autarky that severely damaged world trade. The passage of the Hawley–Smoot bill was not responsible for the international economic demoralization that occurred in 1931 and afterward, but it set a bad example for the rest of the world.

7. The Hoover Policies: Combating the Depression

Hoover moved with a new kind of presidential boldness during the first and relatively mild phase of the depression that lasted from October 1929 to the spring of 1931. He met with railroad presidents in November 1929 and obtained their promise to proceed with normal construction. Calling leaders of finance, industry, and trade to the White House, Hoover frankly warned them that a serious recession would follow the stock market crash. The leaders of American business responded to his urgent plead by agreeing to maintain production and to refrain from severe wage reductions, provided labor leaders would cooperate by withdrawing demands for wage increases. Almost immediately, Hoover obtained the full cooperation of labor leaders. He met with leaders in the construction industry and won their promise to maintain current wage and hours standards. Then he called upon governors and mayors throughout the country to join the federal government in increasing expenditures for public works.

It seemed by the spring of 1930 that Hoover's program of cooperation might work. Bankers had reduced brokers' loans from $8.5 billion to $3 billion, while the index of industrial employment, which had stood at 99 in December 1929, dropped only two and a half points during the next four months. A nationwide census of unemployment taken in the following April revealed that only some 3 million workers were unable to find jobs. Congressional action in the spring of 1930, authorizing expenditure of $145 million for river and harbor improvements, $530 million for public buildings, and $75 million for highways, also had a steadying effect. Moreover, employers were honoring their pledges not to cut wages, and workers kept their promise not to strike.

Then, beginning in May and June 1930, employers began slowly to reduce production. From April to November 1930 the index of industrial employment fell from 96.3 to 84.6, and the index of payrolls dropped from 97.7 to 76.8. When unemployment reached about 4 million in October, Hoover appointed a Committee for Unemployment Relief and called upon city and private agencies to redouble their relief efforts. Moreover, he halted immigration and declared that he would ask Congress for larger appropriations for public works.

Meanwhile, Democratic leaders confidently began the congressional campaign of 1930. Aided by a mounting public fear and by a smear campaign against Hoover personally, the Democrats made a much better showing in the November elections than they had done two years before. The election was no landslide or mass repudiation of Hoover's leadership. Yet by giving control of the legislative branch to Hoover's political foes on the eve of a presidential election, it divided responsibility in the federal government and led inevitably to bitter wrangling.

In fact, there were some manifestations of tension between Hoover and Congress even during the lame-duck session of the Seventy-first Congress that sat from December 1930 to March 1931. Reformers, Republican and Democratic, demanded that the president abandon voluntarism and meet the crisis through a federal relief program, partial payment of the veterans' bonus, and development of the Muscle Shoals facilities. Hoover replied that private and local relief resources were still ample and set himself sternly against any projects for direct federal relief. He successfully vetoed the Norris bill for federal operation of Muscle Shoals, but Congress overrode his veto of a bill allowing veterans to obtain half the value of their certificates in cash.

In early 1931, it seemed again that Hoover's policies were bringing about a recovery. Indices of employment, payrolls, and production steadied in February 1931 and then rallied slightly until about the first of June. Bank failures abated; unemployment slackened. To optimistic observers these encouraging developments signified that the recession was nearly over.

Unfortunately, the optimists' analysis proved incorrect, chiefly because of the impact of the European financial panic on the international economy during the spring and summer of 1931. Central European and South American countries had been borrowing heavily in short-term loans since 1927 to compensate for a drying up of the sources of long-term credit. French bankers, who held large sums of German and Austrian short-term notes, demanded immediate payment, partly for political reasons, in March 1931. To avert bankruptcy, Germany and Austria appealed to London and New York for aid. British bankers did what they could, but it was not enough, and the Kreditanstalt of Vienna, the largest bank in Austria, was "reorganized" in May 1931. Its virtual failure stimulated such heavy withdrawals of gold from Germany that the country was unable by June to meet its reparations payments, much less its short-term obligations. Desperately, almost pathetically, the aged president of Germany, Paul von Hindenburg, appealed personally to Hoover for immediate assistance.

Hoover and his advisers, meanwhile, had been contemplating the proposal of a one-year moratorium on all intergovernmental debt and reparations payments. As these obligations would total about $1 billion, any attempt to force payment would bankrupt Germany and cause the entire international economy to collapse. Hoover proposed the moratorium on June 21, 1931, after delaying too long for fear of political repercussions. Britain and Germany accepted at once; but the French government balked for two weeks, and further withdrawals from Germany compelled the German government to adopt severe measures to stave off repudiation.

No sooner had the German crisis passed than French bankers began withdrawing large sums of gold which they had earlier deposited in British banks. The Bank of England negotiated a short-term gold loan in France and the United States on

August 1 and another in the United States at the end of the month. But the withdrawals were so heavy that the Bank of England defaulted on gold payments in September 1931, and the British cabinet took the government off the gold standard. Within six months, only the United States, France, Italy, Belgium, Holland, and Switzerland remained committed to payment in gold.

This financial crisis virtually destroyed the existing system of international exchange and trade and set off a sharp depression in western Europe. More significant for our story was the effect of the European crisis in deepening the depression in the United States. Before the European crisis erupted, British, French, and other European nationals and banks had deposited some $1.5 billion in gold in American banks, and the American banks in turn had lent out most of this money. Europeans demanded payment of most of this gold when their own crisis came in the spring of 1931, and American depositories had to call in domestic loans. American banks held more than $1 billion of German short-term trade paper and bank acceptances. Fear that these obligations could not be paid gave additional cause for American bankers to call loans to amass liquid reserves. The panic in Europe prompted foreigners to unload large quantities of securities on the New York Stock Exchange. Finally, devaluation and demoralization of exchange caused a virtual stoppage of foreign trade, the consequences of which were catastrophic for the commodity markets.

These and other factors combined during the summer of 1931 to destroy all the encouraging progress toward recovery which the American economy had made since January and to plunge the country deeper into depression. Contraction of loans set off panic, hoarding of cash, and runs by depositors; bankers in turn had to contract further. Dumping of securities drove the price of stocks and bonds to new depths. The loss of foreign markets caused agricultural prices to fall to new lows. Above all, fear seized the American business and financial communities. People began hoarding instead of spending; employers cut production and wages; investors tried to recover money instead of investing it. Confidence gave way to despair as this downward spiral accelerated.

It was obvious by the late summer of 1931 that unrestrained liquidation could lead only to total collapse of the American financial structure. Still hoping to defeat the depression by the voluntary cooperation of the business community, Hoover summoned some thirty leading New York bankers and insurance executives to a secret conference in October 1931. He wanted the banks to form an emergency credit pool of $500 million and the insurance companies to agree not to foreclose mortgages when debtors were, in good faith, unable to meet payments. Moreover, he warned that he would call Congress into special session if the financial leaders did not cooperate. The warning sufficed to bring early compliance. The bankers formed the credit pool soon afterward and organized the National Credit Corporation to administer it. Moreover, Hoover met with congressional leaders of both parties in October and won their promise of support in the impending Seventy-second Congress.

Outlining a recovery program when Congress convened in early December, the president proposed drastic reductions in administrative expenditures and an expansion of federal public works; expansion of the lending powers of Federal Farm banks;

creation of a system of home-loan banks to prevent foreclosures; and a gigantic emergency reconstruction corporation to strengthen the entire economy. Fear of national collapse had obviously forced Hoover to abandon old assumptions about the sufficiency of voluntary measures and to support a program that implied more extensive federal intervention than had ever been attempted in peacetime. But he endorsed this position reluctantly. He had accepted the proposal for an emergency reconstruction agency only after the National Credit Corporation had collapsed, and only under heavy pressure from New York bankers and particularly Eugene Meyer, Jr., a member of the Federal Reserve Board and author of the idea.

At first, during the early months of 1932, Democratic leaders in Congress cooperated. The centerpiece of Hoover's recovery program was the Reconstruction Finance Corporation (RFC), chartered by Congress in January 1932, with a capital of $500 million and authority to borrow up to $1.5 billion more in tax-free obligations. The RFC opened offices in thirty cities and set to work immediately to save banks, railroads, building and loan associations, and other financial institutions. In all, the RFC lent $1.5 billion during 1932 to more than 5,000 concerns, restored a large measure of public confidence, and halted the undermining of the financial structure.

Through other measures the president and Congress cooperated to strengthen the financial machinery. The Glass–Steagall Act of February 1932 made government bonds and new classes of commercial paper acceptable as collateral for Federal Reserve notes. This measure not only permitted the Federal Reserve banks to expand the currency but, more important, released $1 billion in gold to meet foreign withdrawals. The Federal Home Loan Bank Act of July 1932 established home loan banks with a total capital of $125 million to enable building and loan associations, savings banks, and insurance companies to obtain cash without foreclosing on home owners. In addition, an act of January 1932 provided more capital for Federal Land banks.

On the whole these were nonpartisan measures, adopted after a minimum of bickering. Conflicting tax and relief proposals, however, engendered bitter controversies between the administration and its congressional opponents. Some congressmen were frank inflationists, who proposed to extend direct aid to the unemployed by printing money. Hoover blocked their efforts at almost every turn. A case in point was the controversy provoked by the agitation for full and immediate payment of the veterans' bonus. The House of Representatives approved a measure in June 1932, sponsored by Wright Patman of Texas, for full payment of the bonus with $2.4 billion in newly printed money. The Senate rejected the Patman bill under threat of a presidential veto.

Other congressional opponents of Hoover demanded adoption of a large-scale public works and direct relief program to be financed through borrowing. In early July 1932, Congress adopted the Garner–Wagner relief bill, which provided direct aid to individuals and underwrote a vast expansion of public works. Hoover vetoed the Garner–Wagner bill on July 11, 1932, calling it "impractical," "dangerous," and "damaging to our whole conception of governmental relations." Congress then followed his advice and adopted a new relief bill five days later which authorized the RFC to lend $300 million to states whose resources were exhausted and an additional $1.5 billion to states and municipalities for self-liquidating public works.

To repeat the old allegation that Hoover fiddled while the country burned would merely add undue dignity to an important part of the American political mythology. Hoover was surely no old-fashioned conservative, willing to let the depression run its full course in the confidence that the automatic machinery of the economy would eventually start the wheels to roll again. On the contrary, his campaign for recovery was grounded ideologically on the assumption that only strong federal leadership and action could carry the country through the storm. His philosophy and politics, especially during 1931 and 1932, represented a turning point, a transition toward a future characterized by increasing federal participation in economic affairs.

It was Hoover's personal misfortune that he lost the confidence of a large majority of the American people at the very time that he was going to greater lengths to combat depression than any president before his time. This was true in part because he had the bad luck to be president during a time of widespread social and economic misery. It was true even more because he saved the financial structure but stubbornly refused to countenance measures for direct federal relief. In the minds of most Americans, Hoover's program seemed inadequate and too heavily weighted in favor of the upper classes. Moreover, the majority of people were beginning to demand, not a holding action, but a thoroughgoing overhaul of the economic machinery.

Chapter 13

--- →》》 《《— ---

The Early New Deal, 1932–1935

Although the Hoover administration seemed to have halted the most destructive attrition of the depression in the summer of 1932, few Americans believed that prosperity lay just around the corner. Indebted farmers, unemployed workers, and bankrupt businessmen demanded strong federal action—stronger than Hoover was willing to provide. Thus, in November 1932, a loose, anti-Hoover coalition voted to entrust direction of the government to a new leader and a party long out of power.

The consequence was a new era in American political history—the age of Franklin D. Roosevelt. A word of warning is perhaps in order at the outset. The key to understanding this period lies in the realization that Roosevelt's policies followed no prearranged plan. Some historians have delineated two distinctly different New Deals: the first, or the early New Deal, which lasted from 1933 to 1935 and was characterized by cautious policies and continuity with Hoover's approach; and the second New Deal, which lasted from 1935 to 1939 and was characterized by the establishment of a social welfare state. This typology does not completely explain the New Deal, for, although Roosevelt changed his legislative agenda in 1935, he never completely abandoned his economic conservatism. Conversely, especially in the relief measures of the early New Deal, Roosevelt began to embrace a new approach to social welfare well before 1935.

1. The Election of 1932

While Republican fortunes declined in direct ratio to the intensity of economic distress after 1930, Democratic leaders looked forward confidently to victory in the presidential election of 1932. Alfred E. Smith of New York, still titular head of the Democratic party, faced a number of other contenders. Franklin D. Roosevelt was easily Smith's most dangerous rival. Elected governor of New York in 1928, Roosevelt was reelected two years later by a 725,000 vote margin. The magic of this majority soon made him the frontrunner for the presidential nomination. But the situation in the state was discouraging, for the New York Democratic organization, Tammany Hall, remained loyal to Smith. As a result, Roosevelt's managers, Louis Howe and James A. Farley, began to build support in the South and West. They succeeded so well that they had amassed a majority of delegates, but not the then necessary two-thirds, by the time that the Democratic convention opened in Chicago in late June 1932.

Smith's only hope of stopping Roosevelt was to form a coalition with other favorite sons, in particular House Speaker John Nance Garner of Texas, who was supported by the California and Texas delegates. The anti-Roosevelt managers maneuvered desperately, but, after Farley won Garner's support on July 1, a Roosevelt landslide on the fourth ballot ensued. Garner was named as Roosevelt's running mate, perhaps as a reward—there is some evidence of a bargain—more certainly because he was from the Southwest and powerful in the party. In a dramatic act —flying to Chicago to accept the nomination—Roosevelt endorsed the platform, item by item. "I pledge you, I pledge myself, to a new deal for the American people," he promised. "This is more than a political campaign; it is a call to arms."

The Republicans, assembling in Chicago, renominated Hoover on the first ballot. Hoover campaigned vigorously but defensively. He recounted his antidepression policies—"the battles on a thousand fronts . . . the good fight to protect our people in a thousand cities from hunger and cold." To the unemployed he declared that he would mobilize all resources rather than permit a single person to starve. To farmers he promised enlarged tariff protection and additional federal credit. To investors he promised maintenance of the gold standard. To the country at large he promised abundance if the Republicans won. And he warned that grass would grow "in the streets of a hundred cities, a thousand towns" if Roosevelt was elected.

Roosevelt campaigned with a sharply contrasting style and message. He said many things about economy and a balanced budget that he must have regretted afterward. But with the help of his advisers—the so-called "Brain Trust"—Roosevelt also gave an intimation of some future New Deal policies. At Topeka, Kansas, he sketched the outline of a crop-control measure; at Portland, Oregon, he promised federal hydroelectric projects. Before the Commonwealth Club of San Francisco he demanded that businessmen work together to assure full production and employment. To millions of investors he promised to bring the stock exchanges under strict control. To the unemployed he declared that he was "utterly unwilling that economy should be practiced at the expense of starving people."

Although nearly any Democrat probably could have won in that autumn of depression, Roosevelt's contagious smile, reassuring voice, and ability to inspire confidence helped to make the election of 1932 one the most impressive mandates in American history. Retaining some support, Hoover received 15.7 million votes and carried Pennsylvania, Connecticut, Delaware, Maine, New Hampshire, and Vermont. In contrast, Roosevelt received 22.8 million votes, carried the electoral votes of the rest of the nation, and helped give the Democrats staggering majorities in both houses of Congress.

2.   Franklin D. Roosevelt and the Reform Tradition

Roosevelt had an almost unprecedented opportunity for strong presidential leadership in 1933. That opportunity arose in part because of the weakness of the Republi-

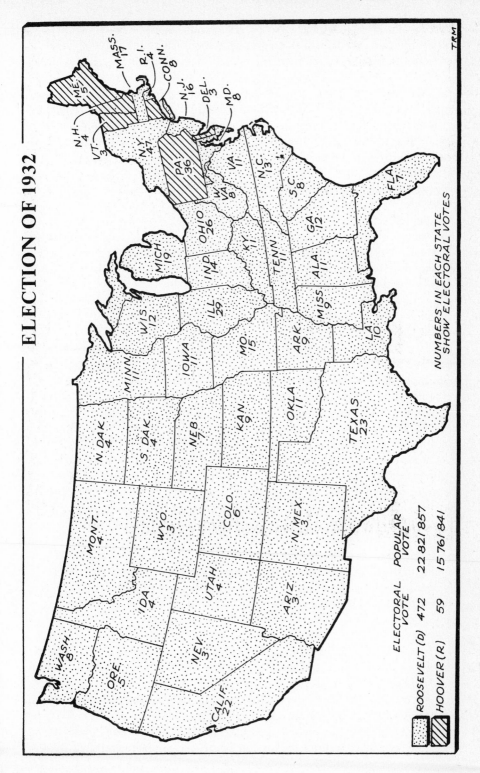

ELECTION OF 1932

TRM

MASS. 17
R.I. 4
CONN. 8
ME. 5
N.J. 16
DEL. 3
MD. 8
N.H. 4
VT. 3
N.Y. 47
PA. 36
W. VA. 8
VA. 11
N.C. 13
S.C. 8
FLA. 7
OHIO 26
KY. 11
TENN. 11
GA. 12
ALA. 11
MICH. 19
IND. 14
ILL. 29
MISS. 9
WIS. 12
MO. 15
ARK. 9
LA. 10
MINN. 11
IOWA 11
OKLA. 11
KAN. 9
TEXAS 23
N. DAK. 4
S. DAK. 4
NEB. 7
MONT. 4
WYO. 3
COLO. 6
N. MEX. 3
IDA. 4
UTAH 4
ARIZ. 3
WASH. 8
ORE. 5
NEV. 3
CALIF. 22

NUMBERS IN EACH STATE
SHOW ELECTORAL VOTES

	ELECTORAL VOTE	POPULAR VOTE
ROOSEVELT (D)	472	22 821 857
HOOVER (R)	59	15 761 841

can opposition and the strength of Roosevelt's congressional forces, in part because of the survival in the 1930s of a reform tradition that came together in 1932. Roosevelt's most urgent task, therefore, was to mold disparate groups into a solid majority coalition.

This task proved deceptively easy in the dark days of early 1933. There was an unusual degree of political unity and consensus, for most Americans demanded action. Once the worst phase of the depression had passed, however, large conservative and business elements deserted the New Deal coalition, and Roosevelt fashioned a new alliance and a new program. Abandoning some of his early policies, in 1935 he built an alliance of farmers and workingmen, added to it social workers and the mass of unemployed, and then began a far-reaching program of federal social welfare and regulatory legislation.

Roosevelt came up the easy way. Born at Hyde Park, New York, on January 30, 1882, the son of James and Sara Delano Roosevelt, Franklin received an upper-class education at Groton and Harvard without demonstrating much ambition or intellectual promise. After graduation from Harvard in 1904, he moved to New York, studied in a desultory way at the Columbia University Law School, married his distant cousin Anna Eleanor Roosevelt in 1905, and two years later settled down to a comfortable career with a prominent New York law firm.

Following the example of his uncle-in-law and fifth cousin, Theodore Roosevelt, Franklin went into politics in 1910. He accepted the Democratic nomination for the New York State Senate in a Hudson Valley district that had gone Republican in every election but one since the Civil War. After hard campaigning and a split in the Republican party, he won his first election. He led a small group of antimachine Democrats at Albany in 1911 in a fight to prevent the election of a Tammany leader to the United States Senate. Success in this first skirmish brought Roosevelt a measure of national publicity. Soon afterward he organized anti-Tammany Democrats in support of Wilson's candidacy for the presidential nomination in 1912.

Roosevelt was appointed assistant secretary of the navy in 1913 by Wilson at the suggestion of Josephus Daniels, who remembered that Theodore Roosevelt had used the same office as a stepping stone to the presidency. The young New Yorker was an able administrator and popular in the second rank of the Wilson circle from 1913 to 1920, even if he agreed more with Theodore Roosevelt than with Wilson and Daniels on issues like preparedness and intervention in the European war. Coming to friendly terms with the new young leaders of Tammany Hall, Roosevelt supported Alfred E. Smith in his first bid for the governorship in 1918. Indeed, Roosevelt won the Democratic vice-presidential nomination in 1920 because he was the leading New York Wilsonian acceptable to Tammany.

Roosevelt lost the election, to be sure, but he gained invaluable experience, friends, and a position of prominence in the Democratic party. Then disaster dimmed his bright future in August 1921, when an attack of polio partly crippled him. He fought to regain his strength and the use of his withered legs, and by 1924 he had recovered sufficiently to nominate Smith for the presidency at the Democratic convention in New York's Madison Square Garden. Four years later, he momentarily discarded his crutches and again placed Smith's name in nomination before the national convention at Houston. Roosevelt, nominated for the governorship of New York soon afterward, surprised friends and opponents by his energy during the campaign of 1928. And, although Smith lost New York by a narrow margin, Roosevelt carried the state by 25,000 votes.

Roosevelt's personality was extraordinarily complex. He was urbane and witty. Despite his patrician upbringing, he had a deep affection for people as individuals. His long illness and fight for recovery softened his social snobbishness and stirred a deep compassion for the physically afflicted and troubled in spirit. He so much wanted people to like him that he often gave the impression of duplicity and rarely had the heart to dismiss a loyal but incompetent friend. On this account he was often a poor administrator, and his refusal to allow subordinates to exercise too much power resulted in frequent administrative snarls.

Roosevelt's religious beliefs underlay all his attitudes toward the individual and society. He believed in a personal God, an absolute ethic, and the essential goodness of mankind. His views on government and what it should do for people stemmed from his belief in decency, justice, and fair play. To his friends he was playful, radiant, and warm, and few could resist his charm. Toward his enemies, on the other hand, he could appear vain, deceptive, petty, and vindictive.

Intellectually, Roosevelt was at once naive and sophisticated. He was not widely read in literature, preferred to obtain information from conversation rather than from study, and gave the impression of relying on intuition more than on hard thinking to solve difficult problems. His was not an original mind, but he demonstrated capacity for learning and for thinking in broad terms and had a flexibility that freed him for experimentation. In economic matters, Roosevelt could assimilate, master, and synthesize complex data. But he was not as competent in economic theory and was often at the mercy of advisers in formulating policy.

In spite of these shortcomings, Roosevelt won widespread affection and loyalty. He was a masterful campaigner, the president for the rest of his life after 1932. His presidency must be judged successful—perhaps the most successful in American history—on several counts. He was able to communicate—either in person, over the radio, or in newsreels—directly with individuals and to infuse his own warmth and confidence into the hearts and minds of all manner of people. He was able to articulate ideals in simple language, and he expressed political values and goals in homely yet moving words. Above all, he possessed an ability to know and understand what a majority of the people wanted.

By the force of this leadership, Roosevelt was responsible for the most significant expansion in the responsibilities and powers of the presidency since Wilson. The domestic crisis of the depression and then the foreign-policy crisis after 1939 concentrated greater power in the White House, and Roosevelt personally supervised the greatest institutional expansion of presidential power to that time. In 1937, based on the recommendations of a blue-ribbon commission headed by Louis Brownlow of the University of Chicago, Roosevelt issued Executive Order 8248. In a historic step in the institutional growth of the presidency, it established the basic structure of the White House staff—a bureaucracy of assistants who increasingly came to run the executive branch. By Roosevelt's death in 1945, the White House staff numbered about fifty, and, although it continued to grow in size thereafter, its structure and administrative functions remained as established under Roosevelt.

3. The Banking Panic and Change in Government

The event that gave the new administration its tremendous emergency power was the virtual collapse of the banking structure during the last months of Hoover's presidency. American banking strength began to give way after the European collapse in the summer of 1931. Banking resources declined from $70.2 billion to $57.3 billion between June 1931 and June 1932, while bank deposits shrank nearly $9 billion. Fear grew into panic in January 1933. The strain of runs and heavy withdrawals was too great for the banks to bear. In late October 1932, the governor of Nevada declared a twelve-day banking holiday in his state to avert the failure of an important chain of banks. When Roosevelt was inaugurated, banks were either closed or doing business under severe restrictions in forty-seven states.

Meanwhile, Hoover sought Roosevelt's approval for policies to stabilize financial institutions and restore public confidence. In private conference and by letter Hoover exhorted the president-elect to announce that he would balance the budget, maintain the dollar at its current value in gold, and cooperate with the European powers in stabilizing currencies and exchange rates. Roosevelt refused, not only because he had already decided to inflate the currency, but also because he suspected that Hoover was trying to transfer some of his own unpopularity to the incoming administration.

Throughout all of this turmoil Roosevelt began constructing an administration. For secretary of state he chose Senator Cordell Hull of Tennessee; as secretary of treasury, William H. Woodin of New York, president of the American Car & Foundry Company and a heavy contributor to the Democratic party. Woodin was succeeded by Henry Morgenthau, Jr., in 1934. The secretaryships of agriculture and of the interior went to two midwestern Republicans, Henry A. Wallace of Iowa and Harold L. Ickes of Chicago. By selecting Frances Perkins, a social worker with long experience in New York City, as secretary of labor, the president-elect honored women and social reformers. The important job of dispenser of patronage, otherwise known as the postmaster general, went to the astute Jim Farley, while the remaining cabinet appointees were an assortment of party hacks and wheelhorses.

Most of Roosevelt's important advisers were not in the cabinet, although a few cabinet members were part of the charmed inner circle made up by Roosevelt's unofficial advisers—the earlier brain trust—now considerably enlarged in number: Raymond Moley, A. A. Berle, Jr., Rexford G. Tugwell, Hugh S. Johnson, George N. Peek, Louis M. Howe, Samuel I. Rosenman, and others. All of them were given posts in various agencies and the White House.

Roosevelt's inauguration took place on a gloomy March 4, 1933. The new president soothed the anxieties of the last three years. "This great Nation," he declared, "will endure as it has endured, will revive and will prosper. So, first of all, let me assert my firm belief that the only thing we have to fear is fear itself." Prepared to assume supreme command, he called on Americans to follow him. People had to be put to work. The banking, credit, and currency systems had to be overhauled and strengthened. And the nation had to learn to use its resources wisely. If Congress failed to provide adequate remedies, he warned, he would ask Congress for "broad Executive power to wage a war against the emergency, as great as the power that would be given to me if we were in fact invaded by a foreign foe."

4. Financial Reform

So desperate was the crisis on March 4, 1933, and so frightened were congressmen and the people, that Roosevelt possessed a power unprecedented in American peacetime history. Had he harbored imperial ambitions, he probably could have obtained dictatorial powers from Congress. Not a fascist, socialist, or communist, Roosevelt was simply an old fashioned American—as he once put, simply "a Christian and a democrat"—with traditional views on the benefits of the system of private enterprise and ownership of property. He believed that capitalism and liberal democracy were both worth saving.

National salvation, Roosevelt believed, lay in quickly overcoming the threat of economic collapse. Two days after taking office, he closed all banks for a four-day period and forbade all gold payments and exports. Meeting in special session on March 9, Congress within four hours enacted the Emergency Banking Act. In this first important piece of New Deal legislation, the administration moved in favor of private ownership and management in banking and finance. It authorized Federal Reserve banks to issue currency against bank assets, empowered the RFC to provide liquid funds to banks by buying their preferred stock, directed Treasury officials to supervise the reopening of banks, and forbade the hoarding and export of gold.

Coupled with the Economy Act, which drastically reduced federal expenditures in an effort to balance the budget, swift Treasury action under the Emergency Banking Act restored the confidence of the business classes. Roosevelt explained what the government was doing and appealed for public confidence in the banking system in his first "fireside chat," or direct radio talk, with the American people on March 12. The response was immediate. By early April, more than $1 billion in currency had flowed back to the banks; hoarders had returned gold to the Federal Reserve banks; and Treasury officials had had to issue only a small amount of new Federal Reserve currency. The worst was over, and now the Treasury began the immense task of strengthening weak banks and eliminating unsound ones. The RFC between March 1933 and July 1935 extended more than $1 billion in aid to 6,468 banks that were deemed essentially sound, while, during the same period, Treasury and state officials liquidated 2,352 ailing banks with aggregate deposits of $2.8 billion.

Congress, meanwhile, began efforts to change the banking system in other ways. The Glass–Steagall Act, or Banking Act of 1933, sought to prevent banks from using the resources of the Federal Reserve system for speculation—chiefly by compelling the absolute separation of commercial banks from their investment affiliates. The Banking Act of 1933 further established the Federal Deposit Insurance Corporation, which, by insuring deposits, restored confidence and prevented runs on banks. The Truth-in-Securities Act of 1933 and the Securities Exchange Act of 1934 left operation of stock exchanges in private hands but compelled all underwriters and brokers to furnish complete information regarding the true value of securities being offered for sale and the arrangements under which the sale was being made. To the Securities and Exchange Commission (SEC), a nonpartisan agency established by the act of 1934, was entrusted the task of preventing and helping to punish misrepresentation and fraud.

After the banking crisis subsided, the administration began to prepare a comprehensive measure to supplant the temporary Banking Act of 1933. The result—the Banking Act of 1935—was the first fundamental revision of the Federal Reserve Act since its adoption in 1913. In contrast to the Wilsonian legislation, which had diffused power within the Federal Reserve system, the Banking Act of 1935 concentrated enormous power in the central board, now called the Board of Governors. The board gained direct authority over the reserve requirements, open-market operations, and discount rates of Federal Reserve banks. In addition, a number of highly technical provisions established new classes of securities and commercial paper against which Federal Reserve currency might be issued.

Roosevelt's contribution to financial reform—the Public Utility Holding Company Act of 1935—gave the SEC complete supervisory control over the financial operations of electric-power holding companies and compelled destruction of the giant utilities empires within five years, but allowed small holding companies which controlled single, integrated operating systems to survive. By 1935, financial reform had accomplished the transformation of financial operations from a private into a quasi-public business.

Two other aspects of early New Deal financial reform remain to be noted. The first was the establishment in June 1933 of the Home Owners Loan Corporation (HOLC). Authorized to borrow up to $2 billion, later increased to $4.75 billion, the HOLC refinanced mortages of home owners in dire peril of foreclosure. The agency lent more than $3 billion to more than 1 million home owners and assumed about one-sixth of the entire urban mortgage load during its three years of life. To stimulate the nearly defunct housing construction industry, Congress established the Federal Housing Administration (FHA) in June 1934. It insured mortgages for new construction and home repairs and played a large role in the resumption of private home construction by providing a system of long-term repayment at low interest rates. Between 1934 and 1940, it insured 2.3 million loans totaling $945 million for home repairs and 554,000 loans totaling $2.3 billion for new construction.

5. The Early New Deal and Economic Recovery

The philosophy underlying Roosevelt's recovery program was a curious mixture of pessimism about the future of the economy and naive faith in the ability of government to work miracles by easy solutions. Roosevelt and his advisers, along with many other Americans, accepted the view that the economy had matured fully in the closing of the agricultural frontier, restriction of immigration, and sharp decline in the birth rate—all of which reflected the loss of self-generating economic forces. The age of expansion and confidence, when businessmen invested in the future and expanded economic frontiers, had apparently ended. More important, the American industrial plant was overbuilt because it produced more than people could consume.

Based on these assumptions, early New Deal economic policy sought to conserve human and natural resources, restore prices to a profitable level, and assure the fair distribution of goods and incomes. This objective could be accomplished, not by stimulating foreign trade and encouraging new investment, but by close cooperation among workers, farmers, businessmen, and government to raise prices, increase purchasing power through shorter hours and higher wages, and limit production to actual needs.

Yet Roosevelt did not take office with any grand plan for recovery. His most ambitious undertakings—the National Recovery Administration and the Public Works Administration—were afterthoughts and improvisations. The administration's original program was aimed chiefly at stimulating recovery by raising the prices of agricultural products by restricting output and by increasing the general price level through controlled inflation. Roosevelt began a policy of controlled inflation in March 1933, when he prohibited redemption of currency in gold coin and the export of gold without the Treasury's approval. Subsequent presidential decrees and acts of Congress assigned exclusive control of gold to the federal government and forbade fulfillment of private and public contracts calling for payment of debts in yellow coin. In effect, Roosevelt took the country off the gold standard at home but retained a gold bullion backing for the currency and allowed limited gold payments in international exchange. At the same time, he allowed gold to decline in value, in the hope of thereby raising the domestic price level.

The dollar had fallen in value by mid-May 1933 to eighty-five cents in gold on international exchanges. Wholesale prices in the United States were rising as a result, and the entire economy seemed on the verge of invigoration. Having apparently set recovery in motion, would Roosevelt now agree to stabilize the gold content of the dollar, or would he embark on a course of frank inflation?

Although this was perhaps the most important question confronting the administration in the late spring of 1933, Roosevelt was caught in an embarrassing dilemma. In Congress, an overwhelming majority favored outright inflation through the issue of paper currency. Abroad, however, an international conference was to meet in London in June 1933 to lower tariffs, stabilize currencies by fixing the price of gold, and find other means to stimulate a revival of international economic activity. Roosevelt had pledged support to the London Economic Conference, yet he was not willing to stabilize the gold content of the dollar and forego the advantages of further inflation.

By the time that the London Economic Conference met, Roosevelt, now converted to the so-called commodity dollar theory, had decided in favor of further inflation. Advocates of the commodity dollar argued that the best hope for sound recovery lay in devaluing the dollar to its 1926 purchasing power. If the dollar's gold value were decreased by 43 percent, these economists further contended, the resulting inflation would stimulate production and help Americans to carry their debt burdens. Before acting, however, Roosevelt waited to see how far the dollar would fall naturally in the exchanges and whether the recovery that had set in would last. The dollar had depreciated about 30 percent by October, and commodity prices had risen 19 percent. Meanwhile, the country had gyrated from depression to near recovery and back to depression again (see the following table).

1933	MANUFACTURING PRODUCTION*	EMPLOYMENT*	PAYROLLS*	WHOLESALE PRICES‡
March	56	58.8	37.1	60.2
April	65	59.9	38.8	60.4
May	77	62.6	42.7	62.7
June	93	66.9	47.2	65.0
July	101	71.5	50.8	68.9
August	91	76.4	56.8	69.5
September	83	80.0	59.1	70.8
October	65	79.6	59.4	71.2

*Monthly average 1923–1925 = 100.
‡1926 average = 100.

Resolved to try any expedient that worked, Roosevelt decided that the time had come to put the commodity dollar theory to work. He announced his decision in a fireside chat on October 22, 1933. Three days later, he instructed the RFC to purchase gold, then selling at $29.80 an ounce, at $31.36 an ounce. Roosevelt gradually increased the price of gold (and correspondingly decreased the dollar's gold value) during the next months until he had finally achieved the commodity dollar. He then persuaded Congress to establish a new gold reserve standard and stabilize the currency. Then, on January 31, 1934, he set the price of gold at $35.00 an ounce and the gold content of the dollar at 59 percent of its pre-1933 value. Not long afterward, he approved a Trade Agreements Act and permitted Secretary Hull to undertake a vigorous campaign to expand foreign trade (for details, see p. 304).

It is impossible to measure precisely the effect of this monetary manipulation. By 1935, the nation was definitely, if slowly, on the road to recovery (see pp. 270–271). However, the increase in the total currency from $9 billion in 1933 to $15.1 billion in 1935 by a cooperative Federal Reserve System and the government itself was probably more decisive in spurring recovery than devaluation had been.

Perhaps the most interesting and revealing fact about the Roosevelt administration when it came into power was its utter lack of any plan for industrial recovery other than devaluation. Its hand, in effect, was forced by organized labor and its congressional spokesmen. In December 1932, Senator Hugo L. Black of Alabama introduced a bill sponsored by the AFL to limit hours of labor in industry to thirty a week. Roosevelt's advisers regarded the Black bill as a dangerous threat to recovery, but they were so engrossed in the banking crisis that they paid it scant attention. But when the Senate passed the measure in early April, Roosevelt directed Secretary Perkins to prepare an administration alternative. After Perkins appeared before the House Labor Committee, it half-heartedly approved the thirty-hour principle and suggested adding provisions for minimum wages and federal control of production. Alarmed by these developments, business leaders prepared an answer. The Chamber of Commerce of the United States had in fact been at work on a recovery plan since 1931. It proposed creation of a national council of industrialists and businessmen who would work through trade associations to control production, raise prices, and stabilize wages. It was the business community's old dream of self-regulation brought to full maturity.

While Congress debated the Black bill, Moley and two other brain trusters, Hugh S. Johnson and Rexford G. Tugwell, worked to reconcile the Chamber of Commerce plan with the principle of federal control. Moley and Johnson presented a draft of their recovery bill to the business leaders when the United States Chamber of Commerce met in Washington in early May 1933. Although it granted substantial concessions to organized labor, the Chamber of Commerce approved it as the only practical alternative to the Black bill, and, with this support, the administration presented its measure—the National Industrial Recovery Act (NIRA)—to Congress on May 15.

The NIRA was one of the most ambitious pieces of legislation ever presented to Congress. Its objectives were to end cutthroat competition, raise prices to a profitable level by limiting production to actual needs, and guarantee a reasonable work week and a living wage to labor. These aims would be accomplished through the adoption of codes covering every conceivable type of economic activity. In the event of irreconcilable disagreement, the president might intervene and impose a code of his own making. Section 7a of the bill—added, incidentally, at the demand of Secretary Perkins and William Green, president of the AFL—affirmed labor's right to organize and bargain collectively. These provisions were included in Title I of the measure. Title II, which appropriated $3.3 billion for a public works program, was incorporated in the measure at the last minute.

The two houses conducted sporadic hearings and debates on the bill for several weeks. A few senators were skeptical; but business, labor, and the administration united in a solid front, and Congress willingly concurred. Roosevelt signed, as he called it, "the most important and far-reaching legislation ever enacted by the American Congress" on June 16, 1933. On the same day, he established the National Recovery Administration (NRA) and named Hugh S. Johnson as administrator.

Johnson plunged into work with great energy and bustle. To provide for the interim, before specific codes could be drawn up, he proposed adoption of a general code, and almost 2.5 million employers with 16 million workers had signed the code within a few weeks. Now began the laborious task of preparing individual codes for every industry and trade in the United States. Theoretically the code-making process involved harmonizing the interests of management, labor, and the consuming public. In actual practice, it was the trade associations, dominated usually by their large members, that wrote the codes. After hasty reviews by the Code Analysis Division and various advisory boards, these codes were adopted as bodies of law governing the industries or trades involved.

From October 1933 to early 1935, when the code-making process was completed, the NRA approved 557 basic codes and 208 supplementary ones. All of them contained provisions confirming labor's right to organize and establishing minimum wage and hours scales. But business leaders, in making these concessions, obtained far-reaching benefits from the government in price stabilization, production controls, and the outlawing of allegedly unfair competition. More important, business leaders won the right to govern themselves. A code authority, almost invariably composed of trade association officials representing the large corporations, administered each code. And businessmen won another long-sought objective—exemption from antitrust prosecution for restrictive practices heretofore deemed illegal by the courts.

This "self-regulation" of industry proceeded smoothly at first, so long as the NRA gave free rein to the trade associations. By the spring of 1934, however, Johnson had assembled his own staff of experts to run the NRA, and they soon concluded that the codes discriminated against small producers, especially in pricing and sales policies. But, because the codes were already written and in force, all that the NRA staff could do was to try to compel code authorities to implement the broad objectives of the NIRA. This effort brought the NRA into increasingly frequent and bitter conflict with business leaders. As if to compound the NRA's perplexities, the inchoate opposition of small businessmen and manufacturers to codes written and administered by larger businesses grew stronger during early 1934. Actually, small business was probably not injured by the codes; the real objection was to the provisions for minimum wages and close supervision of competitive business practices. In response, Roosevelt in February 1934 appointed a National Recovery Review Board, headed by the famed criminal lawyer, Clarence Darrow, to investigate the NRA.

Darrow, instead of trying to evaluate impartially, dealt with the NRA as if he were the prosecutor in a murder trial. Its fortunes fell hard and fast after Darrow's pillorying. Faced with mounting criticism, Roosevelt asked Johnson to resign, abolished the office of the National Recovery Administrator, and, in September 1934, created a National Recovery Board composed of representatives of management, labor, and the public. Any overhauling of the codes themselves, however, had to await congressional action, for the NIRA's life of two years would soon expire. The Supreme Court ended the discussion before Congress could respond to the president's request for extension of the NIRA: the Court declared the measure unconstitutional in May 1935.

Although the NRA brought substantial benefits to workers (discussed in the following section), it failed to achieve many of its original objectives. In the final analysis, the NRA failed because it was based on false assumptions about human nature and the American economy. The framers of the NIRA assumed that businessmen would use self-regulation to promote the general interest. As any serious student of human nature could have predicted, businessmen used the NRA for other purposes, and they fought the NRA when they could not control it. The NIRA was also based on a false assumption: that full production and employment would result from outlawing price competition and either limiting or discouraging full production. Because the NRA discouraged both, it dampened the recovery already under way. The NIRA failed, finally, because it attempted to achieve something like a planned economy without conferring the powers necessary to attain this objective.

It gave no power to the NRA, for example, either to mandate production goals for the entire economy or to compel manufacturers to meet them.

6. Relief and Labor, 1933–1934

In no area of federal action was the essentially emergency character of the New Deal more fully revealed than in its relief policies. The administration, rejecting long-range comprehensive plans, followed Hoover's policies of public works and indirect relief through the cities and states. But, from the outset, Roosevelt was more responsive to the needs of the millions in distress than Hoover had been. Roosevelt devised a pet project to save both human and natural resources—the Civilian Conservation Corps (CCC), authorized by Congress in late March and put into operation in April 1933. The CCC, with an initial grant of $300 million, enrolled 250,000 young men from relief families in some 1,500 camps. They worked under the direction of the War Department at reforestation, flood control, and soil conservation. The CCC had reached a maximum strength of 500,000 by 1935, and more than 2.75 million youths had served in the corps when the project was ended in 1942.

The administration's primary concern in the spring of 1933 was the plight of the unemployed and the survival of the nearly 6 million persons on city and state relief rolls. In response to the president's appeal, Congress approved the Federal Emergency Relief Act, signed in May 1933. It appropriated $500 million, one-half of it to be given outright to impoverished states and the balance to other states on a basis of one federal dollar for every three dollars spent by states and municipalities. Creating the Federal Emergency Relief Administration (FERA), Roosevelt appointed Harry L. Hopkins, chairman of the New York Temporary Emergency Relief Administration, as administrator.

Actually, Roosevelt regarded these measures as stopgaps to keep people from starving until recovery had set in. The administration's ace in the hole was a gigantic public works program to be launched with the NRA to stimulate depressed industries, mainly construction, not immediately affected by the main recovery program. Title II of the NIRA, which established the Public Works Administration (PWA) and appropriated $3.3 billion for the program, gave specific authorization.

The effect might have been invigorating had this huge sum been poured immediately into the economy. As it turned out, Roosevelt unwittingly prevented any such result. Fearing that Johnson was too unstable to spend the money wisely, the president separated the PWA from the NRA and gave control of the PWA to Secretary of the Interior Ickes. Ickes was a cautious, honest man, determined that not one cent of the $3.3 billion should be stolen or wasted. He insisted on scrutinizing the details of all projects. His loving care bore fruit eventually in the form of new highways, hospitals, university buildings, municipal water works, and the like. But Ickes's slow pace prevented the PWA from spurring recovery in 1933. By September, Roosevelt was facing a critical situation. The false boom of the spring and summer had ended; the PWA was mired in red tape; and millions of families confronted the coming winter with no hope of employment.

It was during this crisis that Harry Hopkins first acquired significant influence in the administration. He saw Roosevelt in early November and urged him to launch a vast new program of work relief—a kind of primitive public works on a direct basis —for some of the unemployed. Readily concurring, Roosevelt created the Civil Works Administration (CWA), appointed Hopkins as administrator, and took $400 million from PWA funds to get the program under way. Within thirty days, the CWA was a thriving concern—and a means of living for 4 million workers and their families.

It seemed for a time that Roosevelt's approval of the CWA signified capitulation to what were then considered to be radical doctrines—that it was the federal government's duty to provide work if private industry did not. In response to the advice of conservative Democrats and bitter Republican criticism of waste, Roosevelt told Hopkins in mid-January 1934 that he planned to end the CWA. Hopkins obtained an additional $450 million from Congress in February to carry the agency through the winter, but he liquidated his CWA projects in March and April. The burden of relief for the balance of 1934, therefore, fell again on the FERA, for which Hopkins had obtained an additional $500 million from Congress in February.

An experimental approach and indecision over general objectives also characterized early New Deal labor policy. Administration leaders sincerely wanted to help organized labor, and they succeeded to some degree. Incorporation of labor provisions in all NRA codes won immediate gains that organized labor in its then weakened position could not have won on its own. The forty-hour week was established by codes covering 13 million workers, while the average work week for industries fell from 43.3 hours in June 1933 to 37.8 hours in the following October. All codes, moreover, contained provisions outlawing child labor and establishing minimum wages, ranging generally from thirty to forty cents an hour. Finally, adoption of the codes stimulated a decrease in unemployment from a quarter of the work force in 1933 to a fifth in 1935 and an increase in average weekly earnings in manufacturing from $16.73 in 1933 to $20.13 in 1935.

More important to labor in the long run was Section 7a of the NIRA. It asserted that workers possessed the right to organize and bargain collectively "through representatives of their own choosing." The act also outlawed the yellow-dog contract and declared that workers should not be required to join a company union as a condition of employment. Experience soon demonstrated that Section 7a was more an affirmation than a grant of essential protection. Nonetheless, it marked an epochal turning point. For the first time, the federal government endorsed organized labor's historic objectives in general legislation.

Under the aegis of Section 7a, AFL membership increased from 2.1 million to 3 million between 1933 and 1935, while membership in all unions grew from 2.9 million to 3.7 million. A minority of employers, particularly in the building trades and the coal and garment industries, honored Section 7a. For the most part, however, management was as determined as ever to prevent unionization, and employers by the thousands defied the NRA in labor disputes and harassed it by frequent appeals to the courts. More important, employers somewhat frantically organized company unions as a foil to independent unionism. Some 2.5 million workers were organized in company unions by 1935.

The conflict between organized labor's raised expectations and management's determination to maintain the open shop resulted in a wave of bloody strikes. In response, Roosevelt in August 1933 established a mediation commission to cooperate with the NRA—the National Labor Board, composed of distinguished labor leaders and industrialists, with Senator Robert F. Wagner of New York as chairman. During the following year, the National Labor Board settled many disputes by common sense, persuasion, and ability to find a compromise. More important, a group of public leaders studied, for the first time since 1915, the whole problem of industrial relations and discovered the full extent of management's opposition to the very principle of collective bargaining. They also learned that many employers would use almost any method, including the use of labor spies and violence, to forestall unionization.

The experience convinced Senator Wagner that unionization would never occur until the federal government came strongly to organized labor's support. When an employer refused to recognize a union or to bargain in good faith, for example, there was nothing that the National Labor Board could do but appeal to the NRA and the courts for uncertain redress. Following a wave of strikes in the spring of 1934, Roosevelt abolished the National Labor Board and established the National Labor Relations Board (NLRB), a three-man commission empowered to hold elections to determine the right of unions to conduct collective bargaining. Wagner unsuccessfully tried to persuade Roosevelt and Congress to grant the new board authority to prevent unfair practices by management. Lacking such authority, the National Labor Relations Board was even less successful in settling disputes than its predecessor had been.

7. The New Deal and Agriculture, 1933–1935

Farmers everywhere were in a rebellious mood in the spring of 1933, but in no section were they more disaffected than in the corn belt of the Middle West. Their most immediate concern was the threat of foreclosure. Midwestern farm owners joined together to save their farms, either by direct action or through their state governments. The legislature of Minnesota enacted a two-year moratorium on foreclosures, while the governor of North Dakota forbade sales of farm properties. Vigilante committees threatened to shoot bank or insurance agents and went en masse to foreclosure sales to buy back properties for nominal sums. And at Le Mars, Iowa, some 600 enraged farmers dragged a foreclosing judge from his bench and beat him into unconsciousness in April 1933.

Responding quickly, Roosevelt, in March 1933, consolidated all federal agricultural credit agencies into the Farm Credit Administration. Congress provided abundant new credit shortly thereafter. In response to radical farm demands, Congress also adopted the Frazier–Lemke Farm Bankruptcy Act in June 1934; it enabled farmers to recover lost property on easy terms. These, however, were all stopgaps rather than a long-range program for agricultural recovery. The Agricultural Adjustment Act, enacted by Congress in May 1933, was easily the most sweeping agricultural legislation in the history of the country, but all its major features had long been discussed and advocated by important farm groups. The primary objective of the act was to establish and maintain such a balance between production and consumption of agricultural commodities that farm income would possess the same relative purchasing power that it had enjoyed during the stable "parity" period from 1909 to 1914. To achieve so-called parity prices, the act authorized the imposition of various production controls on major staples. The money to finance the program would come from taxes on the processing of agricultural commodities and from customs duties on certain enumerated commodities.

While farm leaders and administration spokesmen were agreeing on this domestic allotment plan, the Agriculture Department received alarming reports of bumper crops for the coming summer and autumn of 1933. In response, Secretary Wallace and George N. Peek, the new head of the Agricultural Adjustment Administration (AAA), sent agents through the South and Southwest to persuade farmers to plow under 10 million acres, or one-fourth, of the cotton crop in return for subsidies, or benefit payments. The AAA also bought 220,000 sows and over 6 million pigs for immediate slaughter. A similar destruction of part of the wheat crop was averted only by weather reports indicating that there would be drastic natural reductions in that staple.

Cotton farmers plowed under with a vengeance, but they fertilized the remaining crop so heavily that total output in 1933 actually increased by 45,000 bales over the preceding year. The Bankhead Cotton Control Act, approved in April 1934, permitted the AAA to assign marketing quotas and imposed a prohibitive tax on cotton sold in excess of the quotas. Cotton production fell in consequence to 9.6 million bales in 1934 and to 10.6 million bales in 1935, as compared with 13 million bales in 1933.

The AAA meanwhile used its vast powers in other ways to restrict production and restore prices. After the "plow under" and the slaughter of the pigs, the AAA set production goals for 1934 in the major staples and sent out 100,000 agents to persuade farmers to sign contracts. In addition, the AAA established the Commodity Credit Corporation in October to enable cotton and corn producers to borrow against their crops and hold them until prices rose to higher levels.

In these and other measures, the AAA was largely successful, until the Supreme Court called a halt in January 1936. In the case of cotton and tobacco, the effects of the AAA program were direct. Cotton production, for example, was cut one-third during the period 1933–1935; without controls and price supports, the price of cotton would not have risen much above the depression level. The effects of the AAA program on corn, wheat, and livestock are more difficult to calculate, but it seems likely that the droughts of 1933 and 1934 caused vastly greater reductions than could ever have been accomplished by crop controls. It was as if nature cooperated with the AAA to end for a time the problem of uncontrollable surpluses in the basic food commodities.

By late 1935, farmers were experiencing a noticeable improvement. Between 1932 and 1935, net farm income more than doubled, from $1.9 billion to $4.6

billion. Moderate prosperity and increased governmental credit enabled farmers not only to hold their own in the battle against bankuptcy but also, for the first time since 1920, to make some gains. For example, they reduced the farm mortgage load from $9.6 billion in 1930 to $7.6 billion in 1935. On the other hand, the benefits of the farm program went mainly to commercial farmers, not to subsistence farmers, and only rarely did they extend to tenant farmers and sharecroppers. In the South, for example, the effect of large reductions in cotton acreage was to throw about 300,000 black and white sharecroppers out of work.

In the long run, the economic results of the first AAA program were not as significant as its political implications. Representatives of the urban majority in Congress, acting on the assumption that a bankrupt agriculture could mean only an impoverished economy, converted agriculture into a subsidized industry by taxing consumers and diverting a portion of the national income to the farming minority. To be sure, the organized farmers who benefited most from the AAA program were a powerful pressure group who were almost able to impose demands on the two parties. Even so, the first AAA stemmed also from a genuine conviction of government's duty toward disadvantaged groups.

Chapter 14

—>>> «<—

Creating the Social
Welfare State,
1935–1939

Between the spring of 1934 and early 1935, the political coalition and policy objectives of the early New Deal began to come apart at the seams. In pursuing a consensual economic policy, Roosevelt confronted a growing degree of restiveness from business leaders, whose support and participation he had sought during 1933 and 1934, but who were alienated by the NRA and, in general, by the growth of federal power. On account of the opposition of conservative leaders, the possibility existed of the erosion of Democratic support and defections to the GOP in the congressional election of 1934. Simultaneously, it appeared that the early New Deal's cautious, ameliorative economic policy left unsatisfied those who favored aggressive programs of social welfare and governmental intervention on a larger scale. Indeed, it was evident by January 1935 that the administration would have to undertake measures to allay these forces of discontent or else run a serious risk of being overwhelmed by them.

Roosevelt moved with remarkable agility to assemble a new coalition and program which would bring the political situation under his control. Gradually discarding conservative advisers, he gathered a new retinue of advisers and espoused a program designed to ameliorate the distress of the masses through deficit spending, redistribution of wealth, and the most far-reaching program of social and economic legislation in American history. This was the "second" New Deal—the culmination of an earlier generation's reform objectives. In one sense, it represented a shift leftward. Whereas the early New Deal was based on technocratic confidence in the value of national planning and on the need to restrict competition through the NRA and other agencies, the second New Deal—for all its concern to legislate help for disadvantaged groups—was based, at least in practice, on the assumption that government's main regulatory duty in the economic field was to promote competition.

Actually, it is extremely risky to force either phase of the New Deal into a clear ideological framework. Although the NIRA departed radically from traditional practices in the American political economy, it represented the triumph of a movement for self-regulation in the business community itself that was at least as old as the second administration of Theodore Roosevelt. Whatever radical departures the NIRA might have implied, moreover, were more than offset by the early New Deal's conservative reinforcement of the financial sector, even though this effort also satisfied the old demand for public control over banks and the money supply.

A critical transformation took hold in the New Deal between late 1934 and early 1935. Cooperation along NRA lines between business, labor, and government had simply not worked out. Nor did this approach seem to satisfy constituencies— farmers, labor, and minorities—which were beginning to vote solidly Democratic. Thus, in a fundamental reorientation, Roosevelt redirected New Deal social and economic policy. Discarding the industrywide approach of the NRA—and, with it, assumptions about cooperation through a business-government relationship—the president now made the federal government an arbiter of conflict and competition and a guarantor of its citizens' welfare.

1. The New Deal in Transition

With the end of the worst phase of the depression in 1934, opposition to New Deal economic policy became more vocal. In particular, mainly because of the NRA, business leaders turned decisively against the administration. On the one hand, small businessmen rebelled against codes that favored big business. On the other hand, when the NRA tried to bring the code authorities under some measure of public control, the leaders of large industry made a volte-face to oppose the administration. Moreover, practically all manufacturers, large and small, resisted when the National Labor Board attempted to implement Section 7a of the NIRA.

The conservative revolt took shape with the formation of the American Liberty League in August 1934. Its leadership included conservative lawyers and Democratic politicians like Alfred E. Smith and John W. Davis, but its financial support came from industrial interests, notably the Du Pont family. It opposed New Deal bureaucracy and capricious presidential power and championed state rights, "free enterprise," and the open shop. In their zeal to turn back the tide of reform, Liberty Leaguers entered the congressional campaign of 1934 to help elect conservatives of both parties.

Roosevelt dismissed this revolt of the business community as an elitist affair, one that lacked mass appeal. Much more disturbing to him and his political advisers was the rising tide of opposition to early New Deal programs from demagogues and disgruntled reformers. The economic situation remained hopeless for sharecroppers, tenant and subsistence farmers, millions of unemployed, and—especially—old people. These desperate groups seemed willing to follow any crackpot who offered them a way out of their plight.

Dr. Francis E. Townsend of Long Beach, California, provided one such scheme in the so-called Townsend Plan. He proposed that the federal government pay $200 monthly to all unemployed persons over sixty, on the condition that they spend the money within the month. The proposal immediately attracted widespread support among the destitute aged. There were thousands of Old Age Revolving Pension, or Townsend, clubs by 1935, which claimed 5 million followers.

More disquieting to the administration were movements promoted from 1933 to 1935 by the Reverend Charles E. Coughlin and Senator Huey Pierce Long. Coughlin was a Roman Catholic priest in a Detroit suburb who began discussing politics and economic issues in radio sermons around 1930. His railings against bankers and Republican leaders were soon more popular than his religious message. Advocating a far-reaching program of industrial and financial socialization, Coughlin at first supported the New Deal. However, he soon fell out with Roosevelt over monetary policies and turned his National Union for Social Justice against the New Deal in 1935. Coughlin claimed 9 million followers—an absurdly exaggerated estimate—at the height of his influence.

A more dangerous threat came from Huey Long. He was not a mere demagogue of the antiblack, anti-Catholic variety. Coming from the piney woods section of northern Louisiana, he won political support in the 1920s because he addressed himself realistically to the needs of workers and small farmers. Elected governor of Louisiana in 1928, Long gained a seat in the United States Senate two years later. Thereafter, he continued to dominate the government of his state as completely as if he had remained at Baton Rouge. So powerful was his hold over the lower classes that he established a virtual dictatorship in 1934–1935 and could declare, "I am the law." He was the idol of the common people of Louisiana when an assassin's bullet cut short his career on September 8, 1935.

Long's significance on the national scene lay primarily in the fact that he was the chief agitator in lower-class protest against the consensual approach of the early New Deal. Long, like Coughlin, was an ardent Roosevelt supporter in 1932. But the Louisianan turned savagely against the administration and set out to win control of the Democratic party when Roosevelt refused to nationalize banks, expropriate wealth, and knuckle under to Long's patronage demands in 1933. Organizing the Share Our Wealth Society that same year, Long promised to make "every man a king." His proposed method was simple: every family would have a homestead worth $5,000 and an annual income of $2,500, financed by the confiscation of large fortunes.

Roosevelt in late 1934 and early 1935 launched a program designed to provide more security and income for the masses. This sudden leftward shift, if such it may be called, was a significant turning point in twentieth-century American politics. It occurred primarily in response to the developments just discussed: Roosevelt converted challenge into opportunity. He accepted leadership of a new coalition of farmers, workers, the aged, the lower middle classes, and the unemployed, a coalition that came into existence during the congressional campaign of 1934. Roosevelt then redirected New Deal policies to satisfy the basic aspirations of these various groups.

The catalyst for this reorientation was the congressional election of November 1934, which returned Democratic majorities in both houses. Senate and House alike were now committed to expanding the New Deal. In his annual message to Congress in January 1935, Roosevelt announced his new legislative agenda. He declared that the popular mandate was clear: the time had come to fulfill a new social mission and to subordinate profits and wealth to the general good. This he proposed to accomplish by ending the dole; putting the 3.5 million able-bodied persons on relief rolls to work in new programs of slum clearance, rural housing, rural electrification, and expanded public works; and by inaugurating a comprehensive social security program to reduce the hazards of unemployment and old age.

2. Creating the Federal Social Safety Net

Between 1935 and 1937, Congress answered Roosevelt's call by enacting a spate of laws that substantially expanded the federal government's role. Taken together, they realized the goals of social-justice reformers and established at least the framework of a welfare state.

The first item—the work relief program—came with the adoption and signing of the Emergency Relief Appropriation Act in April 1935, which provided nearly $5 billion for the fiscal year 1935–1936. Launching the new program with the establishment of the Works Progress Administration (WPA) and allied agencies in May, Roosevelt appointed Harry L. Hopkins as WPA administrator. Hopkins first transfered unemployed and indigent people to local relief rolls; then he initiated small work projects designed to put as many as 5 million jobless back to work.

Actually, the number of workers on WPA rolls never reached that large figure. The average monthly number from 1935 to 1941 was 2.1 million, and the peak of WPA employment was 3.2 million in November 1938. The agency, along with cooperating sponsors, spent $11.4 billion on some 250,000 projects. Seventy-eight percent of WPA money went for public construction and conservation; the balance was spent on community projects which—on the novel theory that even intellectuals had to eat—enrolled musicians, actors, writers, artists, and even historians.

Hopkins and his colleagues also used their broad authority to foster ambitious experiments that well exemplified the New Deal's humanitarian impulses. One of these new agencies of social reform, funded by money taken from the Emergency Relief appropriation, was the Resettlement Administration (RA), which Roosevelt established as an independent agency under Rexford G. Tugwell in the Department of Agriculture in May 1935. Another new agency was the Rural Electrification Administration (REA), established in May 1935 to provide loans and WPA labor for extension of power lines into rural areas not served by private companies. The REA made such a successful beginning that its authority and resources were greatly expanded in 1937. Still another agency was a program to benefit young people, the National Youth Administration (NYA), established as part of the WPA in June 1935. Under the NYA, some 750,000 high school, college, and graduate students were earning from $5 to $30 a month by 1939–1940 as typists, laboratory and library assistants, tutors, and the like.

All of these developments signaled the rise of Harry Hopkins's star and the triumph of the social worker over the businessman in Roosevelt's inner circle. Hopkins believed that it was government's duty to provide jobs if private industry could not and regarded the WPA not as a stopgap but as a means to fulfill society's obligations to its citizens. Roosevelt's approval of the work relief concept also committed the administration to a program of pump priming by deficit spending on what then seemed a huge scale. Although Congress increased income and estate taxes in 1935, the administration did not attempt to redistribute the national income through drastic tax increases; it paid for the WPA program mainly through borrowing.

The WPA's accomplishments were substantial. The agency greatly relieved the discontent of the millions of persons formerly on the dole, while its expenditures contributed to notable progress toward recovery between 1935 and 1940. Politically, the WPA helped strengthen the Democratic party's control over the country, although not usually in the manner that Republicans alleged. To be sure, local politicians used WPA staffs and funds, and their exploitation of these resources became so flagrant during the congressional and senatorial campaigns of 1938 that Congress intervened the following year to end it. The chief political significance of the WPA, however, was the fact that workers and their families on WPA rolls tended to support an administration that had befriended them.

Other measures adopted after 1935 more permanently altered the role of the federal government in American society. The first was the Social Security bill, prepared in 1934 by a nonpartisan Committee on Economic Security and presented to Congress in January 1935. The bill became law, with only minor amendments, in August 1935. For senior citizens, the Social Security Act provided two kinds of assistance. First, it established a nationwide system of old-age insurance, participation in which was compulsory except for public servants, domestic servants, farm and casual workers, merchant seamen, and employees of educational, religious, and philanthropic institutions. Benefit payments (from $10 to $85 a month) would begin in 1942. Second, the federal government offered to share equally with the states the burden of caring for people over sixty-five who did not qualify for the new old-age insurance program.

The Social Security Act nominally left the establishment of unemployment insurance systems to the states. Actually, it gave state governments little alternative but to cooperate. It imposed on employers an unemployment tax beginning at 1 percent of all payrolls in 1936 and rising to a permanent level of 3 percent after 1937. However, employers might pay 90 percent of the tax to approved state unemployment compensation commissions, and most of the balance paid directly into the federal Treasury would be returned to the states to finance their own systems. On the other hand, states that failed to establish unemployment compensation systems would lose all the taxes paid by employers within their jurisdiction. All states complied within two years; each provided a schedule of benefits that met minimum federal standards and provided protection for some 28 million workers. The Social Security Act also offered federal aid to the states on a matching basis for the care of the crippled, the blind, and dependent mothers and children, and for public health services. To administer the entire system, it established a nonpartisan Social Security Board.

Roosevelt and other designers of the Social Security Act knew that the new scheme was experimental and inadequate. They were also confident that the system would be strengthened and enlarged with the passage of time. The Social Security Act was indubitably one of the most important of all New Deal measures. Between

1935 and 1939, when the system was launched and strengthened, the administration and Congress effected a lasting revolution in American public policy. Discarding ingrained traditions of self-help and individual responsibility, they set the United States on a road leading to the welfare state. This was a rare—and welcome— moment of consensus.

No such unanimity prevailed in early 1935 regarding labor policy. Senator Robert F. Wagner was working almost single-handedly in Congress for passage of a labor disputes bill that would provide federal protection for unions. But Roosevelt opposed the measure because he preferred to obtain protection through renewal of the NIRA.

The Senate, under administration pressure, voted to renew the NIRA. Then it approved the Wagner bill in May 1935; a presidential veto seemed likely if the House approved the measure. On May 25, the Supreme Court declared the code system of the NIRA unconstitutional. In response, Roosevelt reversed himself on the Wagner bill (he had indicated on May 24 that he favored it), persuaded House leaders to bring it to the floor, and signed the measure in early July after speedy approval in the House.

The Wagner Act, also known as the National Labor Relations Act, reaffirmed the principles set forth in the now defunct Section 7a of the NIRA. But the Wagner Act was specific and strong where Section 7a had been vague and weak. By making the organization of company unions virtually impossible and by outlawing so-called unfair practices, it deprived employers of their most formidable antiunion weapons. By establishing a nonpartisan National Labor Relations Board (NLRB) empowered to issue cease-and-desist orders and compel obedience from employers, the act provided machinery for its own enforcement. Finally, by setting forth the explicit conditions under which unions were entitled to recognition, it threw the federal government's power behind unions that sought to compel employers to bargain in good faith. Coming at a time when the advance guard of the AFL was making plans to organize the basic industries, the Wagner Act and the NLRB made the federal government a guarantor of organized labor's right to unionize.

Work relief, Social Security, and legislation to reinforce the labor movement were only the beginning of a new program designed to increase and strengthen public control over business and industry. That the Supreme Court invalidated the NIRA just as Roosevelt and his advisers were formulating these new measures meant that they could decide what features of the NRA experiment were worth salvaging. Early in 1935, Roosevelt had approved the Connally Act prohibiting shipment of oil produced in violation of interstate compacts. With adoption of the Guffey–Snyder Coal Conservation Act in August 1935, the administration salvaged the bituminous coal code and reestablished the NRA coal code authority in a different form. Refusing to approve a general wages-and-hours bill because the measure was probably unconstitutional, Roosevelt instead supported and signed the Walsh–Healey Act in late August 1936. This legislation attempted indirectly to establish fair labor standards for manufacturing and the construction industry. Other measures preserved those sections of the NRA codes which prohibited destructive price competition; the NRA liquor code was also reenacted in this way.

To these measures for regulation were added other, more important, substantive reforms during 1935 and 1936. We have seen how the Banking Act of 1935 established comprehensive federal control over the Federal Reserve System, and how Roosevelt broke up the public utility giants and tightened Washington's control over smaller holding companies. The Federal Power Act of 1935 enlarged the jurisdiction and rate-making authority of the Federal Power Commission. The Motor Carrier Act of 1935 and the Transportation Act of 1940 brought trucking concerns and domestic water carriers under the regulation of the ICC. The Merchant Marine Act of 1936 created a new Maritime Commission authorized to foster the American merchant marine. And the Civil Aeronautics Act of 1938 established a Civil Aeronautics Authority, later called the Civil Aeronautics Board, to regulate the operation and services of airlines.

These were all bipartisan measures, and, except for the Holding Company Act, they excited little opposition. More indicative of the later New Deal's controversial social and economic agenda was Roosevelt's campaign in 1935 to revise the federal tax structure. Roosevelt conciliated his critics on the Left in June 1935 by calling on Congress to increase the upper-income and corporate tax burden. Restructuring taxation, he claimed, would restrain concentrated economic power, reduce "social unrest and a deepening sense of unfairness," and encourage the wider distribution of wealth. Congress wrote most of these suggestions into the wealth tax bill—the Revenue Act of 1935—which Roosevelt signed in August. The Revenue Act left the normal income tax unchanged but raised the surtax to the highest rates yet in American history, increased the federal estate tax to a maximum of 70 percent, and imposed a graduated tax on net corporation income.

3. The Election of 1936

Republican leaders surveyed the political scene during the early months of 1936 with what must have been considerable dismay. Not since Andrew Jackson's day had the Democratic party been so firmly entrenched or attracted such extensive popular support. Nor was the GOP leadership one that could challenge the new Democratic supremacy with much hope of success. The only serious candidate was Governor Alfred M. Landon of Kansas. Landon had survived the Democratic landslide of 1934 and had the support of William Randolph Hearst and his newspaper chain. Republican delegates assembled in Cleveland in June, named Landon on the first ballot on June 11, and then nominated Frank Knox, publisher of the *Chicago Daily News,* as his running mate. Republican orators generally denounced the New Deal, but the party platform did not threaten to destroy New Deal reforms. It did, however, propose to revise the corporate tax structure. The Republican platform also advocated revision of the Trade Agreements Act of 1934, which empowered the president to make tariff agreements (see p. 304). Republicans in 1936 reaffirmed their own reform tradition by promising to provide better relief, farm-subsidy, and labor programs.

The Democrats met in Philadelphia in June 1936 in a triumphant mood. So prevalent was the good feeling that Roosevelt and Garner were nominated by a mighty shout on the first ballot. Southern Democrats, in a moment of exhilaration —or, perhaps, intoxication—even agreed to abrogate the historic party rule that required a two-thirds majority for a presidential nomination. The Democratic platform was a frank reiteration of New Deal ideals and a recital, with emphatic endorsement, of the good works of the Roosevelt administration. Declaring that "government in a modern civilization has certain inescapable obligations to its citizens," the platform promised more rural electrification and a stronger farm program, improved public housing, additional legislation to protect workers, and vigorous enforcement of the antitrust laws. The foreign policy planks, like those of the Republican platform, reflected the then dominant isolationist temper and the popular determination to avoid, as the Democrats said, "being drawn, by political commitments, international banking, or private trading, into any war which may develop anywhere."

Both candidates conducted dignified and strenuous campaigns. Landon spoke forcefully and made it clear that he approved the basic features of the New Deal program. But he did not fire the public imagination or inspire much confidence. On the other hand, Roosevelt was at his magnificent best as a campaigner and phrasemaker in this battle. His acceptance speech was a declaration of war against "economic royalists" who had supposedly regimented and enslaved the people in an "industrial dictatorship." Roosevelt's oration was also a new call for dedication to the cause of democracy. "This generation of Americans," he concluded, "has a rendezvous with destiny. . . . We are fighting to save a great and precious form of government for ourselves and the world." Taking nothing for granted, the president stumped the country as if his election were in doubt, and the themes of social and economic democracy ran strongly throughout all his speeches.

Two developments of the campaign were significant because they indicated long-range realignments. One was the development of a vigorous political consciousness within organized labor and the participation of the major unions in an all-out effort to return the Democrats to power. The leaders in labor's first important political crusade since 1924 were George L. Berry of the AFL and John L. Lewis and Sidney Hillman, two spokesmen of the newly formed CIO (see below, pp. 275–278). They organized Labor's Non-Partisan League in April 1936, raised some $1 million, half of which came from Lewis' United Mine Workers, and temporarily turned their unions into political machines. The second significant development in 1936 was the shift of a majority of black leaders and newspapers in northern and midwestern states from the GOP to the Democratic party. In 1936, for the first time in American history, a majority of black voters supported a Democratic candidate.

It was obvious by mid-October that Landon did not have a chance, in spite of the fact that more than two-thirds of the metropolitan newspapers supported him. Even so, most observers were startled by the magnitude of the Democratic victory on November 3. Landon won 16.7 million popular votes and carried only Vermont and Maine, for a total of eight electoral votes. Representative William Lemke, radical farm leader from North Dakota, running on a Union party ticket supported by Dr. Townsend, Father Coughlin, and Huey Long's successor, the Reverend Gerald L. K. Smith, polled nearly 900,000 votes. The Socialist Norman Thomas and the Communist Earl Browder trailed far behind. In contrast, Roosevelt won 27.8

million popular and 523 electoral votes and carried huge Democratic majorities with him in the greatest sweep since 1920. The verdict of the people was unmistakable: it was an emphatic mandate for continuation of New Deal policies.

4. The Court-Packing Controversy

Roosevelt's decisive victory emboldened him to begin what was perhaps the most controversial act of his presidency—an attempt to bring the Supreme Court under his control. Although in retrospect Roosevelt's court-packing plan was a grievous political error that weakened support for his presidency and the New Deal, it reflected the high degree of frustration that he felt toward the Court, whose majority had nearly paralyzed the executive and legislative branches. Four of the justices— James C. McReynolds, George Sutherland, Willis Van Devanter, and Pierce Butler —were so consistently hostile to the expansion of federal power that they were popularly called the "Four Horsemen." In a minority were three other justices— Louis D. Brandeis, Benjamin N. Cardozo, and Harlan F. Stone—who were willing to tolerate expanded regulatory and welfare power and to a certain extent sympa- thized with the New Deal. Somewhere between the reactionaries and the progres- sives stood the chief justice, Charles Evans Hughes, and Justice Owen J. Roberts.

Before 1935, a majority of the Court seemed capable of recognizing an emer- gency when they saw one, but what soon became prodigious judicial nullification began in January 1935. In the so-called hot oil cases, *Panama Refining Company* v. *Ryan* and *Amazon Petroleum Corporation* v. *Ryan,* the Court invalidated Section 9c of the NIRA on January 7, because it conferred improper legislative authority on the president to regulate the petroleum industry. More alarming to the adminis- tration was the Court's decision, in *Railroad Retirement Board* v. *Alton Railroad,* rendered on May 6 in a five-to-four verdict, which nullified the Railroad Retirement Act of 1934. The majority alleged, first, that the government had deprived railroad companies of property without due process of law by compelling them to contribute to pensions for their employees and, second, that Congress's control over interstate commerce did not warrant such interference in labor relations. The Social Security bill then pending was also surely unconstitutional if this was true.

These two decisions constituted a kind of prelude to "Black Monday," May 27, 1935, when the Court set a new record in judicial review. In *Louisville Joint Stock Land Bank* v. *Radford,* it nullified the Frazier–Lemke Farm Mortgage Act on the ground that it deprived creditors of property without due process of law. In *Hum- phrey's Executor* v. *United States,* the majority reprimanded Roosevelt for removing William E. Humphrey, a Republican, from the Federal Trade Commission. The most important decision on this fateful "Black Monday" was rendered in *A.L.A. Schechter Corporation* v. *United States.* In this decision, all the justices agreed that the NIRA was unconstitutional, either on the ground that the statute conferred essentially legislative authority on the president, or on the ground that the corpora- tion involved in the case was engaged in intrastate commerce only.

Stunned by the *Schechter* decision, Roosevelt, in a press conference, pointed out that the court's objection to a plenary grant of legislative power to the executive could be easily overcome. The danger, he said, lay in the court's narrow view of interstate commerce as consisting only of goods in transit. How could the federal government seek to remedy *any* national economic problem if this "horse and buggy" definition of interstate commerce prevailed?

After a period of anxious waiting, the court answered the president's query in a series of epochal decisions that emphatically confirmed the Schechter doctrine. In January 1936, Justice Roberts, speaking for himself, Hughes, and the "Four Horsemen," held in *United States* v. *Butler* that the Agricultural Adjustment Act of 1933 was unconstitutional. It was a strained decision, but its meaning was clear: production of agricultural commodities was a local activity, not interstate commerce. Therefore Congress could not use the taxing power to regulate agriculture. Then an even clearer reaffirmation of the Schechter doctrine came in May 1936. Justice Sutherland, in *Carter* v. *Carter Coal Company,* rendered an opinion invalidating the Guffey–Snyder Coal Conservation Act. The mining of coal, Sutherland asserted, was obviously not interstate commerce, and Congress could not use the taxing power to regulate an industry over which it possessed no constitutional control. Having thus denied to the federal government jurisdiction over manufacturing, mining, agriculture, and labor conditions, the conservative majority next denied to states the right to regulate hours and wages. This decision, rendered by Justice Butler in *Morehead* v. *New York* ex rel. *Tipaldo* in June 1936, nullified a New York State minimum wage law for women and children by resurrecting the doctrine enunciated in *Adkins* v. *Children's Hospital* in 1923. Having wrecked several key New Deal enterprises, it seemed certain that the justices would soon invalidate the Social Security and Wagner acts. Nor was this all. Lower federal courts, engaged in a similar campaign, issued no less than 1,600 injunctions against federal administrative officials before 1937; for intermittent periods they paralyzed such important agencies as the NLRB and the SEC.

With an emphatic mandate in the election of 1936, Roosevelt concluded that the time had come to curb the Court's power. Democratic spokesmen uttered veiled threats against the Supreme Court during the presidential campaign of 1936 for overturning New Deal measures, but Roosevelt gave little indication that he supported them. Nor was there any strong hint of an impending attack in Roosevelt's annual message in January 1937, or in his second inaugural address. Not until early February, when he submitted a Judiciary Reorganization bill, did Roosevelt make his intentions clear. The measure would empower him to appoint a new federal judge whenever an incumbent failed to retire within six months after reaching the age of seventy. The number of additional judges would be limited to fifty, and not more than six of them would be named to the Supreme Court. Roosevelt explained in an accompanying message why he desired to enlarge the federal courts. He pointed to the crowded dockets and delay in judicial business caused by insufficient and infirm personnel; described the confusion created by hundreds of injunctions issued by inferior courts; and asserted that the courts needed new blood and a modern outlook. The whole plan was based on Roosevelt's assumption that he could control the huge Democratic majorities in both houses of Congress. He was consequently surprised, even stunned, when violent opposition developed in his own party, from liberals and conservatives alike.

Actually, the original Judiciary Reorganization bill was never brought to a vote in Congress, and Roosevelt might have won most of his measure if an extraordinary change in the opinions of the Supreme Court had not occurred at the height of the controversy in Congress. But such a change did occur—and with dramatic suddenness. For the rupture in his party, Roosevelt was himself in large measure responsible. In his cocksureness, he had not taken Democratic leaders into his confidence before submitting the Judiciary Reorganization bill. He allowed Postmaster General Farley to use the patronage stick too openly after the controversy had begun. Worst of all, he refused to listen to compromise proposals that might have succeeded. "All his sagacity seemed to desert him," presidential adviser Rexford Tugwell wrote of Roosevelt. "He was arrogant to those who counseled caution, disbelieving when they warned him of defeat, and neglectful until too late of their alternative suggestions." Consequently, Roosevelt no longer dominated Congress for the first time since 1933.

The Court rendered judgment on a minimum wages statute of the state of Washington in the case of *West Coast Hotel* v. *Parrish* in March 1937. Roberts had joined the "Four Horsemen" only a year before to invalidate a similar New York law. Now he joined Hughes and the liberals to approve the Washington statute in sweeping language that left room for almost any reasonable form of state wage and hours legislation. The crowning irony came when the new majority upheld the Wagner Act in *National Labor Relations Board* v. *Jones and Laughlin Steel Corporation* in April 1937. Here the issue was essentially the same as in the *Schechter, Butler,* and *Carter Coal Company* cases. Did the power of Congress to control interstate commerce include the power to control the actual production of commodities? In the *Jones and Laughlin* decision, the chief justice in effect reversed the earlier decisions without openly admitting that any change in interpretation had occurred. Congress's control over interstate commerce was absolute, Hughes declared, and included the power to encourage and protect such commerce. The peaceful movement of goods was essential to the life of the nation. Hence Congress might even prescribe the labor relations prevailing at factories in which goods were manufactured. In addition, the court approved the Social Security Act in May 1937 and upheld the compulsory features of the unemployment and old-age retirement systems.

By the end of May 1937, the threat to the New Deal had essentially ended. Justice Van Devanter retired on June 1, thus allowing Roosevelt to create a new, pro-New Deal majority. Now that the constitutional crisis was resolved in favor of broader interpretation, the advocates of compromise, Vice-President Garner and Majority Leader Alben W. Barkley of Kentucky, came forward with a new judiciary bill that denied the president power to enlarge the courts but conceded badly needed procedural reforms. The Judicial Procedure Reform Act, which Roosevelt accepted and signed in August 1937, empowered the attorney general to participate in cases involving the constitutionality of federal statutes when such cases were first tried before district courts. It also provided that when such cases went against the government they could be appealed directly to the Supreme Court and severely circumscribed the right of federal judges to stay the execution of federal laws.

5. The New Deal's Last Surge

On several notable occasions after the election of 1936, Roosevelt reiterated his conception of the federal government's new social responsibilities. In his annual message of 1937 and in his second inaugural address, he called on Congress to provide aid for the "one third of a nation ill-housed, ill-clad, ill-nourished," over whom disaster hung like a pall. "The test of our progress," he declared in his inaugural, "is not whether we add more to the abundance of those who have much; it is whether we provide enough for those who have too little."

Because of uncertainty about how the Supreme Court might react, however, Roosevelt presented his new program cautiously during the early months of 1937. On January 6, he asked Congress to consider measures for public housing, aid to tenant farmers, and broader Social Security coverage. On January 12, he submitted a plan for the reorganization of the Executive Department. On February 5, he added his plan for reorganization of the judicary. Moreover, once the Supreme Court's new position on the New Deal became apparent, Roosevelt rounded out his program. In late May, he urged Congress to "extend the frontiers of social progress" by enacting legislation establishing minimum wages and maximum hours in American industry. Finally, on July 12, he asked Congress to reestablish the AAA.

Unfortunately for Roosevelt, the Judiciary Reorganization bill consumed much of Congress' energies during the spring and early summer of 1937, disrupted the Democratic party's ranks, and gave conservative Democrats in both houses an excuse for defying presidential leadership on other issues. They combined with the Republican minority to defeat the Executive Reorganization bill by charging that it was a twin of the Judiciary Reorganization bill and another step toward dictatorship. The Senate approved the administration's wages and hours, or Fair Labor Standards, bill in July 1937, but conservative Democrats and Republicans on the House Rules Committee prevented the House from voting on the measure. Roosevelt's proposal for a new agricultural act received scarcely any attention from the lawmakers.

Even so, between January and September 1937, the first session of the Seventy-fifth Congress left a memorable record of achievement: the Judicial Procedure Reform Act; the Guffey–Vinson Bituminous Coal Act, which reenacted most of the provisions of the Guffey–Snyder Act; and, most important, the Bankhead–Jones Farm Tenancy Act and the Wagner–Steagall National Housing Act. The last two measures were landmarks in the growing role assumed by the federal government in reducing poverty.

The Bankhead–Jones Farm Tenancy Act grew out of an investigation by the president's Committee on Farm Tenancy. Its report, issued in February 1937, revealed that more than half the farmers in the South, nearly a third in the North, and one-fourth in the West were sharecroppers or tenants. Highlighting the poverty and misery of this important segment of the farm population, the report also took serious notice of a new group of the rural destitute—the hundreds of thousands of migratory farm workers and displaced cotton sharecroppers from the Southwest, the "Okies," who were moving en masse to California in search of jobs. To combat tenancy, the committee proposed that the Resettlement Administration (RA) be reorganized as the Farm Security Administration (FSA). The FSA would help enterprising tenants to be landowners, refinance and rehabilitate small farmers who were in danger of losing their lands, promote withdrawal of submarginal land, and help migratory workers. With the support of southern Democrats keenly responsive to the needs of small farmers and white tenants, the Bankhead–Jones Act, embodying the committee's recommendations, became law in July 1937.

Between 1937 and the end of the Second World War, the FSA was the sole New Deal social-welfare agency dealing with the problems of the rural poor. It established some thirty camps that accommodated from 12,000 to 15,000 migratory families and helped farmers scale down their debts. It also organized rural medical and dental care groups, sponsored cooperative leasing of land and purchase of machinery by tenants and small farmers, and carried on homestead projects already begun by the RA. The FSA had lent over $800 million in short-term rehabilitation loans to 870,000 farm families by June 1944. It also lent nearly $260 million to 41,000 families between 1937 and 1946 for the easy purchase of farms.

The Wagner–Steagall National Housing Act, approved in September 1937, was the product of years of planning and investigation by governmental agencies. Large-scale public housing became an objective of the PWA from 1933 to 1937; and the PWA Housing Division by 1937 had constructed fifty-one projects in thirty-six cities with new homes for 21,700 families. The housing program launched by the Wagner–Steagall Act of 1937, on the other hand, reflected the administration's determination to meet the housing problem comprehensively and not as part of a public works and recovery program. This measure established the United States Housing Authority (USHA) in the Interior Department, with a capital of $1 million and authority to borrow up to $500 million, increased to a total of $1.6 billion in 1940.

The USHA worked through public housing agencies in all important cities. It lent up to 100 percent of the costs of housing projects on a long-term basis, provided annual subsidies to local agencies, and established standards of cost, construction, and tenant eligibility. All told, before 1941, when the USHA turned to providing housing for defense workers, the agency lent over $750 million to local housing authorities for 511 projects with a total of 161,162 units. It was only the beginning of a long campaign to destroy slums and provide adequate housing for America's urban poor.

Health began to return to the ailing American economy between 1933 and 1936. National income rose from nearly $42.5 billion in 1933 to $49 billion in 1934, and to $57.1 billion in 1935. The indices of production, employment, and payrolls in manufacturing rose sharply between March 1933 and December 1935, and all indices of economic activity also went up during the spring of 1936. Removal of NRA restrictions on production perhaps gave one stimulus. Certainly increased farm income, enormous federal expenditures for work relief beginning in the spring of 1935, and the payment of the veterans' bonus in 1936 all had an important impact. From May 1936 to September 1937 the index of employment rose to a level higher than the peak figure in 1929. Disposable per capita income, measured in 1952 dollars, increased from $906 in 1935 to $1,048 in 1937. It had been $1,045 in 1929.

There was a speculative upsurge on the stock markets, but the upswing from 1935 to 1937 was essentially sound because it was based on increased investment and production and larger purchasing power through higher wages and public spending. Instead of welcoming the return of prosperity and making certain that the volume of credit was equal to business needs, the administration acted as if it feared prosperity. The board of governors of the Federal Reserve System, assuming that another runaway boom was in the making, increased reserve requirements of member banks drastically in 1936 and again in 1937, while Federal Reserve banks took sharp action on their own to prevent monetary and bank credit inflation. Roosevelt made plans to cut the work relief program drastically, reduce other federal expenditures, and balance the budget in 1939. Consequently, WPA rolls were reduced from 3 million to 1.5 million workers between January and August of 1937. Moreover, the onset of new Social Security taxes dampened consumer demand.

Credit restrictions, reduced federal expenditures, and other factors combined in September and October 1937 to cause a severe slump that set indices tumbling and threatened to wipe out all gains toward recovery that the country had made since 1935. There was grave danger that price rigidity, accompanied by widespread wage cutting, would accentuate the downward spiral, and that farm prices would fall to subdepression levels because of extraordinarily large production in 1937. Roosevelt therefore called Congress into special session in October 1937. Then, in a fireside chat with the nation and in a message to Congress on November 15, he presented a program to halt the recession and complete the New Deal. That program included a new and comprehensive agricultural act, legislation to abolish child labor and establish minimum wages and maximum hours, and revision of the antitrust laws to root out monopolistic control over prices.

Frightened by the prospect of deeper depression during an election year, congressional Democrats responded quickly. They began with legislation to prevent the collapse of agricultural prices. Soil conservation contracts and drought had kept farm production in 1936 at the lowest point since the First World War, except for the drought year of 1934. High prices stimulated tremendously increased plantings in 1937, however, and the return of good weather made possible the harvesting of the largest aggregate yield in American history. The new Agricultural Adjustment Act, enacted in February 1938, provided up to $500 million for soil conservation payments annually to farmers who cooperated in restricting production. In addition, marketing quotas might be applied to cotton, wheat, corn, tobacco, and rice if production exceeded normal requirements, and two-thirds of the producers voted to institute such controls.

The Second World War temporarily ended the farm problem, but there can be little doubt that the second AAA brought stability to American agriculture during the interim years 1938 to 1941. Huge surpluses threatened to depress prices to the level of 1932 when the measure went into effect. The Agriculture Department averted a rural depression in the critical years of 1938 and 1939 by vigorous action on many fronts and helped farmers to return to the near-prosperity of 1937 in 1940. Cash farm income, including governmental payments, was $9.2 billion in 1937, $8.1 billion in 1938, $8.7 billion in 1939, and $9.1 billion in 1940.

Meanwhile, the widespread wage cutting that occurred during the first months of the recession of 1937 prompted the administration to force passage of the Fair Labor Standards, or wages and hours bill, which became law in June 1938. It was the last major New Deal measure and joined the Social Security and National Labor

Relations acts to round out a comprehensive structure of the social-welfare state. The Fair Labor Standards Act embodied some of the most important goals of reformers. It established a minimum wage of 25 cents an hour, effective immediately and to be gradually increased to 40 cents. It limited the work week to forty-four hours, to be reduced within three years to forty, and provided for payment at the rate of time and a half for overtime work. It forbade shipment in interstate commerce of any goods manufactured in whole or in part by children under sixteen. Finally, it created a Wage and Hour Division in the Department of Labor to enforce the new law.

These welfare measures, however, did little to reverse the steadily worsening economic situation during the winter of 1937–1938. Roosevelt took aggressive steps that went well beyond his early recovery policies. In a special message to Congress in April 1938, he announced a loosening of credit restrictions, demanded a drastic revival of deficit spending, and called on business and labor to unite in a common war against the recession. A frightened Congress hastily responded. It made some $3 billion immediately available to expand the WPA, launched a huge public works program in conjunction with the states, and increased the activities of other agencies. Expanded bank credits and renewed "pump priming" reversed the tide almost at once. Indices of manufacturing production, payrolls, and employment started upward beginning in July and August 1938; recovery to the near-prosperity level of 1937 was almost complete by the end of 1939.

Partly in response to the recession, Roosevelt initiated during the spring and summer of 1938 the most intense antitrust campaign since the Taft administration. Thurman Arnold of the Yale Law School, an antitrust enthusiast, was appointed head of the Antitrust Division of the Department of Justice and given large new appropriations and increases in staff. To sharpen federal antitrust policy, he began within a short time 215 major investigations and 92 test cases. In addition, Roosevelt sent a special message to Congress in April 1938 calling for a thorough study of the concentration of economic power and its effect on the American system of free enterprise. Congress responded by creating the Temporary National Economic Committee (TNEC) in June 1938. It heard witnesses for three years, and its economists wrote forty-three monographs covering almost every phase of economic life. After taking mountains of testimony, the TNEC submitted a final report in March 1941 which recommended only traditional remedies such as strengthening the antitrust laws and reform of the patent system. By the time the final report was published, however, the administration was more concerned with preparation for war than with sweeping reform of the economic system.

6. The New Deal in Decline

The administration's ambitious domestic program came to an abrupt halt in the early months of 1939 as the result of developments in Europe and Asia and political reversals at home. Adolf Hitler's triumphs at Munich in September 1938 and his subsequent partition of Czechoslovakia in March 1939 convinced Roosevelt that the threat of German hegemony demanded a more aggressive foreign policy and preparation for possible conflict. Moreover, Japan's invasion of China in 1937 seemed to threaten American security in the Far East.

Vigorous assertion of American interests, however, required a radical change in the policy of strict nonintervention embodied in the neutrality legislation of 1935–1937 (see pp. 313–315). Such a reversal could not be accomplished unless Roosevelt had a strong majority in Congress, but the Democratic party was deeply divided on foreign policy. Midwestern and western Democrats strongly supported New Deal domestic policies but were determined to avoid any action that might conceivably lead to American participation in a new world war. Eastern Democrats also supported reform and, except for representatives of Irish-American districts, backed a stronger foreign policy. Although southern Democrats vociferously championed defense and cooperation with Great Britain and France, they were also increasingly suspicious of the New Deal's effect on *de jure* segregation in their region. The implications of Roosevelt's need for greater domestic support for his foreign policies were clear. In order to win solid southern support—and to combine it with a strong base in the East—the political price would be an end to the New Deal, even if that meant jettisoning midwestern and western support.

Political developments in 1938 emphasized this dilemma and revealed that the New Deal coalition was beginning to crumble. The first signs came in December 1937 and January 1938, during struggles in Congress over the proposed Ludlow Amendment and the Wagner–Van Nuys antilynching bill. The Ludlow Amendment would have required a national referendum to declare war, while the Wagner–Van Nuys bill proposed to make lynching a federal crime. Roosevelt strongly opposed the Ludlow resolution in January 1938, and the House defeated it by a vote of 209 to 188. But Roosevelt must have perceived the significance of the alignment in the vote: three-fourths of the Republicans and a majority of midwestern and western Democrats combined in support of the proposed amendment, while an overwhelming majority of southern and eastern Democrats voted against it. The conflict over the antilynching bill came to a head in the Senate at the same time. Although Roosevelt undoubtedly approved of the measure, he said no word in condemnation when southern senators prevented a vote by filibuster.

The development that finally compelled Roosevelt to make peace with the conservatives in order to build support for his foreign policy was his inability to purge conservative southern Democrats in the primary campaigns during the summer of 1938. After announcing in June that he would participate in the Democratic primaries, he actively campaigned during the next two months. Roosevelt's message was direct: conditions that made the South "the Nation's No. 1 economic problem" could be remedied only by united action in which Southerners played a leading part. As it turned out, the presidential intervention boomeranged. Although two staunch southern New Dealers, Representative Lister Hill of Alabama and Senator Claude W. Pepper of Florida, had won notable victories in earlier primary campaigns in which Roosevelt was not involved, not a single southern conservative was dislodged by the would-be purge.

The outcome of the congressional elections in November, moreover, left Roosevelt no alternative but to draw his party together. The Republicans made enormous gains in the Middle and Far West and, by winning seven seats in the Senate and eight in the House, became a formidable power in Congress for the first time since 1932. Roosevelt would desperately need southern support on foreign policy in the next Congress. He would not be able to risk driving his southern allies into a league with the Republicans by further antagonizing them on domestic issues.

Roosevelt in effect announced the end of reform in his annual message of January 1939. Asking only for deficit spending until recovery had returned, he foresaw no new reform legislation. "We have now passed the period of internal conflict in the launching of our program of social reform," he declared. "Our full energies may now be released to invigorate the processes of recovery in order to preserve our reforms." The main theme of this address, in fact, was the enormity of the totalitarian threat to religion, democracy, and international peace.

Chapter 15

->>> <<<-

The New Deal and
the American People

In the four decades after 1900, a profound metamorphosis in popular attitudes toward the federal government occurred. Rejecting a long tradition of opposition to central governmental power, most Americans now agreed that the federal government should be the most powerful organized force in their society—a guarantor of solvency to farmers, beneficent protector to workers, friend to tenant farmers and the unemployed, and regulator of businessmen and bankers.

We have noted many of these changes in agriculture, industry, finance, and politics in the preceding two chapters. Now let us look at other, and in the long run perhaps more important, effects of the New Deal. We will observe how the intellectual and political upheaval of the 1930s affected the labor movement; promoted the growth of new ideas about the development of regional resources, constitutional interpretation, and the treatment of minority groups; and stimulated the expansion and maturing of a new reform ideology.

1. Labor's Civil War

The labor movement experienced its most spectacular growth from 1933 to 1941 and finally attained its old, hitherto elusive goal: unionization of the large industries. However, this triumph was accomplished at the cost of bitter internal conflict that split the ranks of organized labor and left deep scars for years to come. Leadership in the AFL had fallen to timid men after the death of Samuel Gompers in 1924. Convinced that craft or trade unionism offered the only solid basis for the American labor movement, they abhorred the concept of industrial unionism, that is, organization of all workers in a given industry into one big union. In opposition stood an aggressive minority of AFL leaders. One was John L. Lewis, who had built his UMW into the most powerful union in the United States by 1935. Another was Sidney Hillman, a founder and president of the Amalgamated Clothing Workers. A third was David Dubinsky, head of the International Ladies' Garment Workers. These and others argued that labor's hope lay in meeting strength with strength—

by organizing big industries on a mass, or industrial, basis, and by bringing the great body of black workers into the ranks of unionized labor.

Under strong pressure from Lewis, Hillman, and Dubinsky, the AFL convention voted in 1934 to charter so-called federal unions in the automobile, cement, aluminum, and other mass industries. But the conservatives had no intention of allowing these infant unions to grow and then perhaps seize control of the AFL. In fact, no sooner were the new unions launched than the old craft unions began to raid them.

In October 1935, the struggle came to a head at the AFL convention, where Lewis demanded that craft unions should have no jurisdiction over workers in mass industries and delivered a ringing plea for a great campaign to organize unskilled workers. When the convention rejected this resolution, Lewis and the leaders of eight other AFL unions met in Atlantic City in November and formed the Committee for Industrial Organization, allegedly to help the AFL unionize the basic industries. President William Green and the AFL executive council struck back in January 1936 by ordering the CIO to disband. The rebels defiantly welcomed new allies and laid plans for unionization drives. Then the AFL executive council suspended ten insurgent unions in August 1936 and expelled them in March 1937.

Ensuing months saw a bitter struggle for the allegiance of previously unorganized workers—and CIO triumphs on almost every front. Beginning with 1.8 million members in March 1937, the new organization could claim a membership of nearly 3.75 million six months later. Peace negotiations with the AFL in October 1937 failed to yield an agreement satisfactory to Lewis. At the conclusion of these negotiations the rebel leaders finally declared their independence of the parent organization and reorganized the CIO soon afterward as the Congress of Industrial Organizations.

Meanwhile, the CIO had begun its offensive in the mass industries in June 1936 by forming the Steel Workers' Organizing Committee (SWOC) under Philip Murray, a lieutenant of Lewis in the UMW. The SWOC campaigned in the steel industry for over seven months, and discontented workers everywhere broke away from company unions to join the CIO. In the past, company managers could always rely upon the military assistance of the states and the moral support of the federal government. In that year of New Deal grace 1936, however, Washington was openly friendly to the workers, while the Democratic governor of Pennsylvania promised relief assistance if a strike should occur.

It soon became evident that the executives of United States Steel, at least, preferred surrender to a long and costly strike. Myron C. Taylor, chairman of the board, held a series of private conferences with John L. Lewis beginning in December 1936. The talks led to an agreement by officials of the corporation to recognize the SWOC. Consequently, Benjamin Fairless, president of the Carnegie–Illinois Steel Company, a United States Steel subsidiary, signed in March 1937 what was perhaps the most important contract in American labor history—important because the corporation which gave in was the same one which since 1901 had led the movement to block unionization of the basic industries. All the rest of United States Steel's subsidiaries signed similar contracts within a short time. They granted recognition, a 10 percent wage increase, the forty-hour week, and time-and-a-half pay for overtime work.

It was a significant victory. Murray and the SWOC expected the rest of the steel companies, known collectively as Little Steel, to come to terms quickly. Several of them, notably Inland Steel, made no effort to break the strike. But the leaders of the Bethlehem Steel, Republic Steel, and Youngstown Sheet and Tube companies fought back with all the force that they could command. Republic Steel officials in Massillon, Ohio, organized a small army of deputies that killed two strikers in a wanton attack in July 1937. Police in South Chicago killed ten and wounded scores of strikers at the Republic Steel plant on Memorial Day, 1937.

So violent was Little Steel's counterattack that the SWOC's momentum was almost halted. Inland Steel agreed to recognize the union in July 1937, but the other companies held out. Before the New Deal, this would probably have been the end of the story, at least until the workers organized for another bloody battle. Now, however, the workers' new ally, the federal government, went into action. A Senate subcommittee, headed by Robert M. La Follette, Jr., of Wisconsin, conducted a thorough investigation into all aspects of the strike during the spring and summer of 1938. It reported numerous violations of the Wagner Act and of the strikers' civil liberties by the steel companies, local police, and the National Guard. It also discovered that the companies maintained corps of spies and *agents provocateurs*, and it revealed that the same companies had collected arsenals of guns, tear gas, and ammunition for use against strikers. The NLRB then moved into the case on appeal of the SWOC and compelled the Little Steel companies to recognize and bargain in good faith with the SWOC in 1941. By the end of that year, therefore, the steelworkers' union, now 600,000 strong, stood triumphant throughout the entire industry.

The automobile industry became the CIO's next key target. The AFL had chartered some 100 local unions in the automobile industry in 1933 and 1934 and had launched the United Automobile Workers (UAW) in August 1935. Homer Martin, an industrial unionist and former Baptist preacher, gained control of the UAW in May 1936, took it into the CIO, and began an intensive and successful campaign to unionize workers in General Motors and Chrysler plants during the following summer and autumn.

Martin invited officials of the General Motors Corporation to a bargaining conference in December 1936. When company spokesmen declined, workers in the Chevrolet No. 1 factory in Flint, Michigan, sat down by their machines on December 30, 1936, and, within a few days, the sit-down strike had spread to other General Motors plants. There had been minor sit-down strikes before, but none so well organized and on such a spectacular scale as this one. Company officials, fearing that violence would lead to destruction of machinery, for the most part did not dare molest the occupying forces. But there was one pitched battle in January 1937, when police tried to rush Chevrolet No. 2 factory at Flint. In this melee, strikers turned back the police and retained possession of the plant.

General Motors officials called on the recently inaugurated governor of Michigan, Frank Murphy, to use the National Guard to dislodge the trespassers. But Murphy, a Democrat elected with the support of labor, sympathized with the strikers: instead of using force, he tried conciliation. Mediation conferences in

Lansing and Washington failed to bring peace. Then the corporation appealed to Circuit Court Judge Paul V. Gadola in January 1937 for an injunction ordering the strikers to leave the plants. Gadola, on the following day, signed an injunction ordering all strikers from the property of General Motors under pain of a $15 million fine and imprisonment. When the strikers defied the injunction, Judge Gadola ordered the sheriff to arrest them. The sheriff declined. Instead, he appealed to Governor Murphy, who again refused to use the National Guard and redoubled his efforts at mediation. After days of tense negotiation, General Motors finally capitulated in February 1937.

Victorious over General Motors, UAW leaders moved next against the smaller Chrysler Corporation and applied sit-down and mass picketing techniques at eight Chrysler plants in March 1937. Judge Allen Campbell of Detroit ordered the arrest of CIO leaders and 6,000 sitting strikers (they had defied his earlier injunction). The workers prepared to resist. But public opinion throughout the country by this date was growing alarmed by a wave of sit-down strikes in many branches of industry and was turning sharply against the new technique. Governor Murphy announced that he would enforce the injunction. At the same time, he succeeded in bringing Walter P. Chrysler and John L. Lewis together for high-level peace talks. The upshot was an agreement altogether favorable to the UAW. Lewis called the strikers out of Chrysler plants on March 24, and the corporation surrendered on April 6 on the same terms General Motors had recently accepted.

Henry Ford had the lowest wage scale of any of the major automobile producers in 1937. He also had the most efficient "service department"—a collection of labor spies and company police dedicated to destroying any incipient union. The UAW began an organization campaign in the Ford Motor Company soon after Chrysler capitulated, but the drive was badly managed and failed to win the workers in Ford's huge River Rouge plant. The UAW was consistently successful among smaller producers such as Packard and Hudson, however, and by September 1937 the union had over 300,000 members and boasted bargaining agreements with every automobile producer except Ford. Even this crusty old individualist surrendered to the UAW in the spring of 1940.

Meanwhile, CIO unions had won the right to bargain for workers in most of the other basic industries. An uprising of rubber workers in Akron, Ohio, in February 1936 led to formation of the United Rubber Workers Union and the CIO's rapid conquest of the rubber industry. The United Textile Workers Union organized the textile mills of the North and made a heroic but generally unsuccessful effort to penetrate the South in 1937 and 1938. Harry Bridges organized longshoremen on the Pacific Coast into a powerful CIO union. And so it went in dozens of other industries, until by the time that the United States entered the Second World War the CIO had some 5 million members, the AFL had grown to a membership of about 4.6 million, while independent unions counted an additional 1 million. By this date, 28.2 percent of all workers in nonagricultural employment were unionized, as compared to 11.5 percent in 1933. In short, labor was well on its way toward achieving the organization of all important American industries and its long-sought goal of equality with management in the determination of labor policies.

UNION MEMBERSHIP, 1930-1980

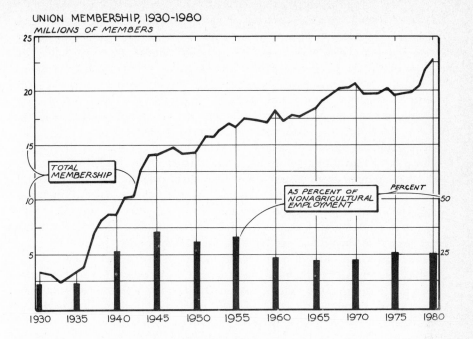

MILLIONS OF MEMBERS

2. The TVA and the Concept of the Region

No New Deal enterprise fired the imagination of progressives more than the creation and development of the Tennessee Valley Authority (TVA). The greatest hydro-electric project in American history, it harnessed the water resources of an area 40,000 square miles in size and made possible the utilization of vast quantities of electric power in a once impoverished region. It dramatically demonstrated that technology could control the primeval forces of nature and repair the damage done to the good earth during two centuries of wasteful exploitation. Even more signifi-cant was the theory behind this project. It was conceived as a regional undertaking, operated by a nonpartisan agency responsible to the people of the region as much as to its owner, the federal government. The TVA was the first really significant experiment in public planning on a regional scale.

The struggle for control of Wilson Dam at Muscle Shoals, Alabama, in the 1920s began a long political fight over hydroelectric power (see pp. 219–220). Public power enthusiasts bided their time and enlarged their objectives even while their plans for federal development were being thwarted by presidents Coolidge and Hoover. Their opportunity came with Roosevelt's election in 1932, for the new Democratic leader came out for public power projects that would serve as yardsticks for electric rates and promote the wider use of electric power.

In April 1933, Roosevelt asked Congress to establish a Tennessee Valley Author-ity, "a corporation clothed with the power of Government but possessed of the flexibility and initiative of a private enterprise," to plan for the full development of the valley's natural resources. Congress responded quickly by creating the TVA, a corporation controlled by a three-member board and endowed with sweeping authority under the general supervision of the president and Congress. TVA directors conceived their first task to be control of the Tennessee River and its tributaries to stop erosion, prevent floods, and improve navigation. The authority designed and constructed twenty new dams and improved five existing ones between 1933 and 1952, using enough material to build thirty-five Hoover or ten Grand Coulee dams. By 1978, the authority's investment stood at $6.65 billion.

The result was the completion of an extensive system of water control in one of the areas of heaviest rainfall in the United States. Once the TVA dams were completed, no more floods occurred; and TVA engineers could also greatly reduce the flood menace in the Ohio and Mississippi valleys by holding back the Tennessee and its tributaries. The TVA also created an inland waterway 652 miles long with a minimum depth of nine feet, which connected the interior of the South with the Great Lakes, the Ohio River, and the Missouri–Mississippi river systems. By 1977, more than 27 million tons of barge freight moved on the river annually.

TVA directors viewed their task, moreover, in the broader terms of preventing erosion and recovering the valley's lost fertility. The TVA thus used facilities at Muscle Shoals to produce phosphatic fertilizers it then distributed through the AAA. It also conducted a demonstration program to teach farmers how to prevent erosion and rebuild soil, and it worked with the CCC in the reforestation of hundreds of thousands of acres of gullied lands.

From a strictly legal point of view, the TVA was not established to manufacture and distribute electric power. However, if the authority should manufacture electric power as a by-product of its main activities, the act of incorporation declared, it might then dispose of it. This, of course, was said for the benefit of the Supreme Court, for there was grave doubt in 1933 whether the federal government could

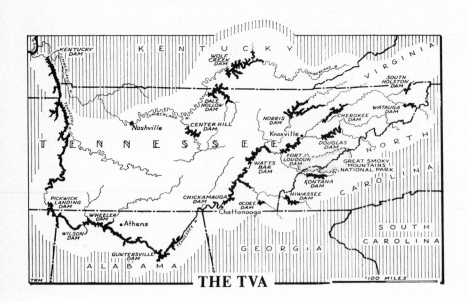

THE TVA

constitutionally engage in such activity. No sooner had the TVA begun its work than a group of stockholders in the Alabama Power Company sued to prevent that company from selling certain properties to the TVA. In deciding the case in February 1935, the federal district judge in Birmingham ruled that the TVA had no right to manufacture and sell electric power; moreover, he forbade seventeen municipalities from buying TVA power produced at Wilson Dam.

This judgment was reversed by the Supreme Court in *Ashwander* v. *T.V.A.* in February 1936. But in this decision the Court ruled only on the constitutionality of selling electricity produced at Wilson Dam. Seeing the loophole, nineteen utility companies brought suit against the TVA in May 1936, seeking an injunction to forbid the authority to produce or distribute electric power anywhere but at Wilson Dam. The companies won a temporary injunction in December 1936, but the Supreme Court summarily disposed of the case in *Tennessee Electric Power Company* v. *T.V.A.* in January 1939. The Court ruled that private companies had no right to complain of competition by the government. The leader of the utility interests, Wendell L. Willkie, president of the Commonwealth & Southern Corporation, gave up the fight after this rebuff. He sold the entire facilities of the Tennessee Electric Power Company to the TVA in August 1939 at his own price of nearly $79 million.

Commonwealth & Southern's withdrawal signaled the end of private enterprise in the utilities field in the Tennessee Valley, for numerous smaller operating companies had either already sold out to the TVA or proceded to follow Commonwealth & Southern's example. The TVA soon emerged as the largest producer of electric power in the United States. Over the period 1933–1978 total generating capacity in the valley increased from 800,000 kilowatts to 28 million kilowatts, while actual production of electricity increased from 1.5 billion to 118 billion kilowatt-hours.

President Roosevelt, in June 1937, urged Congress to plan for six additional regional authorities. He was thinking, however, more in terms of future than of immediate development. Meanwhile, the administration pushed forward in a more limited way with other regional projects. One was Hoover Dam and the All-American Canal, completed in 1936 with the aid of PWA funds at a total cost of about $165 million. Hoover Dam was producing a billion kilowatt-hours annually by the late 1970s. Another important project was the Grand Coulee Dam on the Columbia River in Washington state; the largest masonry structure in the world, it was completed in 1942 at a cost of $436 million. It had a total power capacity of nearly 2 million kilowatt-hours. A third such undertaking was the great earthen Fort Peck Dam on the Missouri River in Montana, completed in 1939 and used principally for flood control.

3. The New Deal in the Supreme Court

Although it was the last branch of the federal government to fall under New Deal influence, after 1937 the Supreme Court adopted a profoundly different approach to constitutional interpretation. Sweeping away all doubt about the constitutionality of advanced social and economic legislation, it became the chief practitioner of sociological jurisprudence—a legal approach that relied on social scientific evidence —gave a large degree of freedom to state and federal regulatory agencies, and added strong safeguards for the protection of civil liberties, labor, and minorities. This new direction in American law occurred primarily because Roosevelt, as a result of his long tenure and the advanced age of incumbent judges, was able to appoint virtually a new federal judiciary—from district courts to the supreme tribunal. By 1941, he had appointed the chief justice and seven of the eight associate justices of the Supreme Court.

Convinced that the Constitution must serve the needs of an urbanized and industrialized democracy, the members of the "Roosevelt Court" completed and clarified the changes begun by the unreformed Court in 1937. In a series of cases from 1938 to 1942 testing the constitutionality of the TVA's power operations, the Fair Labor Standards Act, the Public Utility Holding Company Act of 1935, the second Railroad Retirement Act, the second Agricultural Adjustment Act, and other measures, the Court gave Congress virtually unlimited authority under the interstate commerce clause. While accepting the principle of stringent federal regulation, the new Court also gave federal and state administrative agencies broad new freedom to act in the public interest—a reversal of the old Court's insistence on imposing judicial criteria on the regulatory agencies.

The New Deal Court made its most important contribution in the development of broad federal protection of religious, civil, and political liberty and defense against arbitrary police authority. Chief Justice Hughes had already firmly laid the basis for new safeguards in the 1930s. Decisions of that time established the doctrine that the Fourteenth Amendment meant no state could deprive a person of any of the basic rights guaranteed by the first ten amendments. Significant was the way in which the New Deal Court, with Hughes still its spokesman until his retirement in 1941, expanded the concept of basic liberties guaranteed by the Fourteenth Amendment.

To begin with, the Court reaffirmed Hughes's earlier condemnation of so-called third-degree methods—obtaining confessions by beating and torture—and applied this ban against subtler forms of torture as well. Then, too, the court majority went to the defense of Jehovah's Witnesses, a religious group that disavowed loyalty to any earthly state, ruling in 1943 that local or state authorities could not require children of Jehovah's Witnesses to salute the flag in school: such action, said the Court, violated the witnesses' religious scruples and liberty. The high bench also nullified local ordinances requiring religious groups to obtain licenses to conduct open-air services or distribute literature.

Blacks, who had most often been denied civil rights on account of race, benefited most from the Court's increased vigilance. As a result of decisions cited above, they enjoyed a larger degree of personal safety and the right to a fair trial. It was perhaps more important that the new Court began to open the gates to educational opportunities for Negroes. On this front, the Court took the first step toward abandoning the legalism which, under the "separate but equal" concept enunciated in 1896 in the *Plessy* v. *Ferguson* case, had permitted southern states to maintain racially segregated educational facilities. In *Missouri* ex rel. *Gaines* (1938), the legal validity of segregated education began to erode. Argued by lawyers from the NAACP's Legal Defense Fund, the case hinged on whether the University of Missouri Law School could deny admission to a black student even though no separate black law school existed in the state. The Court ruled that it could not, and it ordered the law school to admit the black student. Although *Gaines* did not overturn the "separate but equal" dictum, it paved the way for more ambitous legal challenges during the next two decades.

Nearly as important were decisions that freed organized labor from the restrictions imposed by the courts under the Sherman Antitrust Act. The fundamental issue was whether labor unions, in their conduct of industrial warfare, might employ methods that restrained interstate commerce. The Roosevelt Court formulated a new doctrine in *Apex Hosiery Company* v. *Leader* (1940) and *United States* v. *Hutcheson* (1945): labor unions might restrain commerce when such restraint was incidental to the achievement of legitimate objectives. The *Apex* and *Hutcheson* rulings reversed earlier decisions and gave organized labor its long-sought immunity from prosecution under the antitrust laws, except when unions sought direcily to restrain commerce through monopolistic and restrictive practices or attempted to defy the government when it was an employer.

4. Intellectuals in Turmoil

For American intellectuals, the period between the beginning of the Great Depression and the Second World War was a time of violent crosscurrents of thought and confusing challenges. Although the rebels of the Lost Generation lived on into the thirties, their revolt had lost much of its meaning by 1933. There was the tragic spectacle of F. Scott Fitzgerald, caught in the moral and cultural collapse of which he had written so poignantly. His final works, *Tender Is the Night* (1934) and *The Last Tycoon* (1941), were artistically distinguished but revealed a mind sickened by the corruption that he thought damned American life.

Ernest Hemingway and Sinclair Lewis gave further evidence of the bewilderment that confused and enfeebled the survivors of the Lost Generation. In a series of books—*Death in the Afternoon* (1932), *Winner Take Nothing* (1933), and *The Green Hills of Africa* (1935)—Hemingway violated his own literary standards and nearly renounced humane values altogether. Then, alarmed by the challenge of fascism, he replied in 1940 with his most popular novel, *For Whom the Bell Tolls*. In the place of nihilism he now substituted devotion to a cause—that of the Loyalists in the Spanish Civil War. The work of Sinclair Lewis after 1930 illustrated in a different way the dissolution of the Lost Generation. Lewis was superbly effective in exposing the absurdities of middle-class thought and manners. But after 1930 he searched for new themes and evidenced less hostility toward society. His *It Can't Happen Here* (1935) depicted the triumph of fascism in America and forecast the salvation of democracy by the middle class. Yet neither this nor his final novels, written in the 1940s, displayed the trenchant power which characterized his work during the 1920s.

In contrast, the late 1920s and 1930s saw the rise of the brightest star in the whole twentieth-century American literary constellation. He was William Faulkner of Oxford, Mississippi, who had begun to write in the 1920s but who had been culturally too isolated—or intellectually too independent—to be a member of the Lost Generation. From his lonely outpost, Faulkner sought to find the meaning of life through reconstruction of the southern past, through the heroes and villains and plain people caught in the vortex of a society in dissolution. From reading his earlier novels—such as *The Sound and the Fury* (1929), *Light in August* (1932), and *Absalom! Absalom!* (1936)—it is difficult for the layman to know whether Faulkner rejected completely the value structure of the past or used a powerful symbolism to reaffirm old values. But in a later volume—*The Unvanquished* (1938)—Faulkner began to exhibit clearer signs of the high purpose that underlay his important novels of the 1940s and 1950s.

Meanwhile, a rebirth of the social and economic novel in America occurred during the 1930s. The most loquacious and perhaps the bitterest critic of American capitalism among the fictional writers of the 1930s was John Dos Passos. In his trilogy, *U.S.A.*—*The Forty-Second Parallel* (1930), *Nineteen-Nineteen* (1932), and *The Big Money* (1936)—Dos Passos used a variety of literary techniques to reconstruct the panorama of American life from 1900 to 1929. In a second trilogy—*Adventures of a Young Man* (1939), *Number One* (1943), and *The Grand Design* (1949)—he continued the story through the depression and the New Deal. Another social novelist, John Steinbeck, protested against the injustices of an economic system that allegedly degraded workers and sharecroppers to the level of animal existence. His greatest work, *The Grapes of Wrath* (1939), movingly portrayed the odyssey of a small-farmer family, the unforgettable Joads, from Oklahoma to California.

Similar crosscurrents affected American poetical writing. Some of the old masters and practitioners of more conventional forms continued to practice in the 1930s. For example, the dean of American poets, Edwin Arlington Robinson, confirmed his supremacy during the period between the completion of his Arthurian trilogy in 1927 and his last work, *King Jasper,* published in 1935. His death in that year deprived America of her greatest poet since Walt Whitman. Robert Frost, whose reputation was already well established by 1930, continued to write with deceptive simplicity about nature and man's struggles. Carl Sandburg, another of the new poets of the earlier renaissance, affirmed his faith in American destiny in *The People, Yes* (1936). Edna St. Vincent Millay, a lyrical poet of some power who had begun her work in the early 1920s, came to full artistic maturity in the 1930s, particularly in *Fatal Interview* (1931).

These latter-day traditionalists had some followers in the 1930s. There was Stephen Vincent Benét, who continued to voice American democratic idealism in *Litany for Dictatorships* (1936), *Nightmare at Noon* (1940), and, in the year of his untimely death, *Western Star* (1943). Moreover, the challenge of depression at home and the rise of fascism abroad stimulated a brief outburst of democratic and leftist poetry in the 1930s. Muriel Rukeyser's *Theory of Flight* (1935) and *U.S. 1*

(1938); Kenneth Fearing's *Poems* (1935); and Archibald MacLeish's *Public Speech* (1936), *America Was Promises* (1939) and, as well as works by others, were poetic counterparts of popular fictional literature.

Despite these survivals of more-or-less traditional poetry, the most important fact about American poetic thought and writing in the 1930s was the growing influence of the imagist school, established by Ezra Pound before the First World War and dominated by T. S. Eliot in the 1920s and 1930s. Converted to Anglo-Catholicism in the late 1920s, Eliot turned to religious themes. His later notable poems, *Ash Wednesday* (1930) and *Four Quartets* (1943), and his plays, *Murder in the Cathedral* (1935) and *The Cocktail Party* (1950), sought to convey the meaning of life and the universe as seen from a strongly Christian, traditionalist viewpoint.

The imagist revolt had long since become a mature movement with elaborate standards by 1940. We can now see that its emphasis upon imagery, symbolism, and intellectual quality produced a new poetry which, in its attempt to recreate the complexity of human experience, often went beyond the ability of the average reader to comprehend and enjoy. But many great poets have done this. The significant contribution of the modern poets was, in the words of one historian of the school, the triumph of "sincerity over sham, naturalness over affectation, of a striking turn toward precision, analysis, and structure; of a wider range of conception and idea; of a deeper apprehension of meaning."

A host of young playwrights, notably Eugene O'Neill, created an American drama in the decade following the armistice. O'Neill's creative energies waned in the early 1930s, and leadership passed to others. Maxwell Anderson, who had made his literary debut earlier in the 1920s, turned to writing historical tragedies in poetic verse. His *Elizabeth the Queen* (1930), *Mary of Scotland* (1933), and *Valley Forge* (1934) established him as perhaps the leading American dramatist of the 1930s. S. N. Behrman and Philip Barry continued to enliven the stage with penetrating social satires that often said more than audiences understood. Marc Connelly depicted black folkways and religious thought in *The Green Pastures* (1930), one of the most beautiful plays of the decade. Thornton Wilder expressed the theme of man's survival in spite of evil, ignorance, and war in *Our Town* (1938) and *The Skin of Our Teeth* (1942).

These and a host of other playwrights depicted the foibles and follies as well as the enduring values of American life, but they were creative artists rather than social critics. Of greater significance to the political historian of the 1930s was the work of a large group who used the stage as a sounding board for all kinds of ideologies and social and political protest. There were, most notably, the leftists—Elmer Rice, John Howard Lawson, and especially Clifford Odets, the most frankly Marxian of them—who joined in the Theater Union and Group Theater to write fierce denunciations of the sins of capitalism. Some of these writers were also subsidized by the Federal Theatre Project, an enterprise of the New Deal's relief agency, the WPA. The most talented social playwright, Lillian Hellman, demonstrated great power in *The Children's Hour* and then turned to propaganda in *The Little Foxes* (1939) and *The Watch on the Rhine* (1941). Of different political faith was Robert Sherwood, who best reflected the changing temper of the non-Marxist intellectual during the 1930s. His *The Petrified Forest* (1935) reflected the pessimistic view of its day that reason was ineffectual as compared with brute force. His *Idiot's Delight* (1936) was one the most eloquent pieces of antiwar propaganda during the high tide of pacifist sentiment. In response to the challenges of nazism and communism, however, Sherwood wrote two ringing affirmations of faith in democracy—*Abe Lincoln in Illinois* (1938) and *There Shall Be No Night* (1940).

Other intellectuals were even more deeply affected by the social and political atmosphere of the depression and New Deal. More than ever before, intellectuals —political thinkers, academic scholars in various disciplines, journalists, lawyers, and the like—actively participated in the formulation and execution of policy. Thus, during the first two years of the New Deal, the brain trust wrote much of the emergency legislation, while Roosevelt summoned people like William O. Douglas of the Yale Law School and Dean James M. Landis of the Harvard Law School to head the SEC. Involvement by intellectuals in policy making occurred on a much broader scale when Roosevelt utilized the services of scholars and experts to formulate and carry out subsequent New Deal measures. A host of men and women also left university and foundation posts to launch and direct the Social Security, Farm Security, and kindred agencies.

Intellectuals did more than staff New Deal agencies. They were organized in various presidential committees on social security, farm security, executive reorganization, natural resources, the problem of southern poverty, and the like; and they issued reports that stirred thoughtful Americans to recognize the necessity for action in these fields. Sociologists and economists working with the National Resources Planning Board surveyed the problem of population redistribution and other such subjects. A large group of economists working in conjunction with the TNEC revealed the concentration of control in American industry, exposed the quasi-monopolistic practices of big business, and proposed reforms.

The 1930s were a time also when social scientists, under the impact of the depression crisis, discarded old concepts and matured new ones to justify a broad expansion of public authority. Following the trail blazed years before by the iconoclastic Thorstein Veblen, economists analyzed American economic institutions critically and without a priori assumptions about the nature of economic activity. These institutional economists taught the necessity of governmental intervention in the economy. Disciples of the British economist John Maynard Keynes, for example, evolved a theory of governmental compensatory spending to prevent or end depressions and worked out intricate mathematical formulas to buttress an otherwise common-sense theory. The institutional economists of the 1930s were collectivists to the degree that they recognized the interdependent character of the economy and the necessity for a larger measure of public participation in economic affairs.

A group of political scientists working in an allied field abandoned the ivory tower of abstract principles to discover how and why the American political system actually functioned. It was the sociologists, however, who won the largest audience and had the most significant impact on the thoughtful American public. They were learned, sophisticated, and "scientific," to be sure, but their primary purpose was to expose the unpleasant realities of American social life. The most important new developments in this field accurately reflected the major concerns of the later New Deal—the Negro, rural poverty, the South and the concept of the region. Led by

Howard W. Odum and Rupert B. Vance of the University of North Carolina, southern sociologists scrutinized their region's institutions and social structure. Moreover, Southerners joined other sociologists in a drive to understand and destroy the bases of racial prejudice. The culmination of this campaign was a collaborative study financed by the Carnegie Corporation of New York and synthesized by the Swedish sociologist, Gunnar Myrdal, in a huge volume entitled *An American Dilemma: The Negro Problem and Modern Democracy* (1944).

5. Challenges from the Left and Right

The 1930s was a decade during which liberal democracy was, in a sense, on trial. Abroad, western democracies faced an audacious threat in the rise of fascism, nazism, and militarism. In the United States, various new leaders presented alternatives to traditional democratic practices.

On one side were a crowd of fascist and Nazi-financed demagogues and their organizations, whose themes ranged from social justice to violent anti-Semitism. The Reverend Charles E. Coughlin, Catholic priest of Royal Oak, Michigan, quickly emerged as the preeminent leader of American fascism after 1935. Coughlin discarded his social justice guise in 1938, came out frankly as a pro-Nazi and anti-Semite, and formed the Christian Front in 1939 to unite the widely scattered antidemocratic organizations. The Christian Front had mobilized strong-arm gangs in cities throughout the country by the autumn of 1939, and Coughlin counted his followers by the hundreds of thousands and his audience by the millions.

Working for the same objectives and using the same anti-Semitic, anti-Communist propaganda were a group of lesser Fascist demagogues. There was, for example, William Dudley Pelley, who in 1933 organized the Silver Shirt Legion, a counterpart of Hitler's Brown Shirts. Lawrence Dennis, author of *The Coming American Fascism* and other works, was the intellectual leader and principal adviser of the Fascist groups. Huey P. Long's chief organizer and then successor, the Reverend Gerald L. K. Smith of Shreveport, Louisiana, moved to Detroit, converted the Share Our Wealth organization into the Committee of One Million, and began a campaign against Jews, blacks, and Communists. In the Northeast, Fritz J. Kuhn, a naturalized German American and veteran of Hitler's Munich beer-hall *Putsch* in 1923, formed the *Amerikadeutscher Volksbund* in 1936. As *Bundesführer,* he hailed the day when the swastika would replace the Stars and Stripes.

These and lesser prophets of fascism and religious hatred flooded America with Nazi propaganda, nurtured anti-Semitic passions, and formed an important component of the large isolationist faction after 1939. They had the support of a small but vocal element in Congress, and they reached a combined audience running into the millions. They were potentially dangerous, but they failed to subvert democracy, or to become anything more than a lunatic fringe. Most of them were sheer moneymakers rather than conspirators working under the control of the German government. Factionalism and personal rivalries prevented them from uniting. Most important, practically the entire civil and religious leadership of the United States recognized these rabble-rousers for what they were and effectively neutralized their message.

The Communist movement in the United States, on the other hand, was better organized, used the media more effectively, and was closely tied to the Soviet government. The Communist party of the United States was torn during the 1920s by an internal power struggle between Josef Stalin and Leon Trotsky then going on within the Soviet Union. Stalin, after winning absolute power in 1927–1928, called the leaders of the American section to Moscow, removed the Trotskyites, and established a party loyalist, Earl Browder, as secretary general of the party in the United States.

The purging of the Trotskyites weakened American communism just when the depression offered some opportunity to the party. Communists tried to bore within the AFL unions and were turned back. They then organized rival but successful unions in the clothing, coal, textile, and other industries. They also tried to organize the unemployed. The net effect of all these efforts was only to confirm the dominant popular conviction that communism represented an alien, un-American political ideology. Party membership, which stood at 8,000 at the beginning of the depression, was only 12,000 in 1932 and, after two years of vigorous recruiting, only 24,000 in 1934. William Z. Foster, the party's presidential candidate in 1932, polled a mere 102,991 votes.

Dominated by Stalinists, American Communists never developed an independent ideology or program. They were forced to follow tactics and a party line dictated by the Comintern, or Communist International. International communism from 1928 to 1935 was in its so-called third period, in which Stalin adhered to exaggerated notions of imminent world revolution in order to diminish Trotsky's influence. Convinced that the depression would culminate in the downfall of capitalism, western Communists declared war on long-established labor unions and democratic leaders and on reform and recovery programs.

Partly because such a policy seemed to help fascists in Europe, Stalin announced a new approach at the seventh Comintern meeting in Moscow in the summer of 1935. Hereafter Communists should take leadership in a movement to contain fascism by cooperating, in so-called Popular Front organizations, with democratic antifascist forces in political parties, labor unions, and even church groups. Quietly putting revolutionary doctrines and heroes in temporary storage, American Communists now proclaimed the slogan "Communism Is Twentieth Century Americanism," disclaimed any intention forcibly to subvert the Constitution, and made a bold bid for the friendship of old-line groups. Their chief aim after 1935 was not rapid expansion of party membership but infiltration and control of labor unions, writers' groups, Popular Front organizations with mass memberships, and, finally, the federal government itself.

Communists scored their most important successes on the labor front. To be sure, they were in no way responsible for events that led to the split of the AFL and the formation of the CIO in 1935. But Lewis, Hillman, and other CIO leaders needed thousands of trained organizers, so they accepted such support as the Communists could give without questioning Communist motives. As a consequence, Communists by 1938 controlled several major unions, including those of the electrical workers, the West Coast longshoremen, and the seamen, and were in strategic positions in the powerful UAW. Moreover, Lee Pressman and Len De Caux— fellow travelers if not party members—were highly placed in the leadership of the CIO as, respectively, general counsel and editor of the *CIO News.* Even more important, the general counsel and a member of the NLRB, Nathan Witt and Edwin S. Davis, were strong Communist sympathizers if not card-bearing party members during the critical struggle between the CIO and the AFL from 1935 to 1940.

To a large group of writers, communism either appealed with the force of a new religion or else held out the hope of genuine cooperation to halt the spread of fascism and anti-Semitism at home and abroad. Many intellectuals were sickened by the plight of the lower classes in the United States and inspired by the seeming material progress and social stability of the Soviet Union during the depression period. Hence a number of distinguished American novelists, including Sherwood Anderson, Erskine Caldwell, and Granville Hicks, publicly supported Foster for president in 1932. Moreover, left-wing writers and artists banded together in John Reed clubs to foster the creation of proletarian literature from 1932 to 1935. The John Reed clubs metaphorsed into the League of American Writers in 1935. It held annual conferences until 1939 and included a hard core of Communists and a host of momentary cooperators like Ernest Hemingway, Richard Wright, Archibald MacLeish, Upton Sinclair, and James T. Farrell. Left-wing actors also banded together in the Group Theater, Theater Union, and Theater Collective to produce plays of Clifford Odets, John Howard Lawson, Elmer Rice, and other "proletarian" playwrights.

Communists were even more ambitous in organizing more general "front" organizations. In these, distinguished non-Communist reformers lent their names and energies to Communist-controlled bodies. Three such front organizations were the American League for Peace and Democracy, which claimed an affiliated membership of over 7 million; the American Student Union, which claimed 20,000 members; and the American Youth Congress, which enjoyed the support of Eleanor Roosevelt and claimed to represent almost 5 million young people.

On the political front, Communists pursued a two-pronged campaign between 1935 and 1939: to bore into and gain control of independent non-Communist political groups, and to build a powerful machine within the federal government to influence federal policies and carry on political espionage. This campaign met with some success in both goals. The Communists put a ticket, headed by Browder, into the field during the campaign of 1936; undercover, they worked very hard for Roosevelt. Only in New York, however, did they gain any power in an important political party.

More successful was the Communist effort to establish an underground network of cells based in Washington. The leader of the principal group was Harold Ware, who had managed a large collective farm in Russia in the early 1920s. Ware organized a Communist cell soon after Roosevelt's inauguration; Ware's group included a number of party members strategically placed in various government departments and agencies. Several of the conspirators and cooperators, notably Alger Hiss, Harry Dexter White, Julian Wadleigh, and Nathan Witt, rose to positions of high responsibility and carried from their offices thousands of documents to be photographed and passed on to the head of the Soviet underground, Colonel Boris Bykov. Witt, and later John Abt, became leaders of the cell after Ware's death in an automobile accident in 1935.

The American Communist movement began to lose strength in 1937, suffered heavy blows in 1938 and 1939, and had shrunk to a hard core by 1941. The decline of American communism was partly a result of its slavish affiliation with Stalinism. In the Spanish Civil War from 1936 to 1939, many young American idealists fighting on the Loyalist side saw Communists at work, conspiring to control the Loyalist government and betraying and killing comrades-in-arms to achieve this goal. John Dos Passos, one of the most distinguished of the Popular Front novelists, was thus disillusioned by what he saw in Spain. The purges, trials, and executions from 1936 to 1938, by which Stalin eliminated his closest friends and rivals and established a ruthless monolithic dictatorship, similarly undermined American communism. The crowning disillusionment came when the Soviet government signed a nonaggression pact with Germany in August 1939. Many communists changed immediately from ardent antifascists into opponents of any form of support for Britain and France in their war against Germany.

6. Blacks and the New Deal

More than for other minorities in the United States, the 1930s was a decade of enhanced expectations among black Americans. The depression affected them more severely than any other group. In 1931, for example, Baltimore blacks composed 17 percent of the city's total population but a third of its unemployed; in Chicago, they constituted 4 percent of the city's population but 16 percent of the unemployed. On the other hand, the increased federal commitment under the New Deal to protect disadvantaged groups seemed to provide hope for their improvement. In reality, the New Deal did not directly attempt to end Jim Crow practices in the South. Nor did it bring an unqualified support for racial justice from the federal government. Yet in important respects it set in motion developments and forces that made possible future challenges to segregation and racial discrimination.

When Franklin Roosevelt became president in 1933, blacks had little political leverage among his closest advisers. The vast majority of southern blacks were disfranchised; only in northern cities did Negroes possess any real political power. Even so, blacks composed only 3 percent of the national electorate in 1940. Still more important was another political reality. When Roosevelt was elected in 1932, the large majority of voting blacks cast their ballots, as they always had, for the party of Abraham Lincoln, the Republican party. Between the presidential elections of 1928 and 1932, the percentage of blacks voting Republican either stayed the same or, in some cities, even increased. Thus in Chicago, some 75 percent of voters in black districts voted for Hoover, as, in similar districts, did 82 percent in Cleveland, 71 percent in Philadelphia, and 71 percent in Cincinnati.

Within the next four years, however, black voters moved in significant numbers into Democratic ranks. Where blacks possessed the franchise, they decisively approved of the New Deal and Franklin Roosevelt and began a new pattern of staunch allegiance to the Democratic party. The increase of Democratic strength in black districts in northern cities was nothing short of astounding. In Cleveland, between 1932 and 1936, Roosevelt increased his share of the black vote by 250 percent; in Chicago, by 132 percent; and in Philadelphia, by 157 percent.

Ironically, the shift in black support from the GOP to the Democrats was not the product of any concerted effort on the part of Roosevelt or the New Deal to support racial justice or to defy southern Democrats. Indeed, the record of the Roosevelt administration on civil rights was ambiguous. Roosevelt himself, along with perhaps most of his major advisers, was either unconcerned about promoting civil rights or hesitant to stir up a hornest's nest in the white South. A patrician in demeanor and attitudes, Roosevelt expressed a paternalistic concern for blacks but was rarely exposed to them except as domestics. On the other hand, other members of the Roosevelt administration emerged as spokesmen for more aggressive federal policies on behalf of blacks. Perhaps the most influential racial liberal was Eleanor Roosevelt. Another civil-rights advocate was Harold L. Ickes, who had been president of the Chicago NAACP in the early 1920s. He soon established himself as the administration's leading supporter of a nondiscriminatory hiring policy in federal contracts. As head of the PWA, Ickes, in September 1933, issued a general order banning racial discrimination in public works employment. When that order proved difficult to enforce, Ickes added a clause to PWA contracts with local builders requiring that they hire black skilled and unskilled workers according to a specified quota.

In other New Deal agencies and in branches of the federal government, blacks gradually acquired greater influence. Early in the Roosevelt administration, in September 1933, a group of "racial advisers" were hired in several federal departments. By 1936, an unofficial "Black Cabinet," made up of the racial advisers and other black officeholders, was formed under the leadership of Mary McLeod Bethune, a black official in the National Youth Administration who was closely associated with Eleanor Roosevelt. By monitoring hiring and financial practices in federal and New Deal agencies and often by promoting the New Deal among blacks, the Black Cabinet began to have a significant effect on the Roosevelt administration.

Black progress under the New Deal should not, on the other hand, be overstated. In many New Deal agencies, officials acquiesced in local racial practices and, in effect, condoned discrimination. In the CCC, for example, local selection agents frequently excluded blacks from their recruitment rolls. In Mississippi, only forty-six blacks, or 2 percent of the total membership of the CCC there, were enrolled in 1933. Three years later, the number of blacks enrolled in the agency had only reached 10 percent. The pattern was similar in other agencies, such as the AAA and NRA, which depended on local support and cooperation.

Perhaps the clearest evidence of the ambivalent position of the New Deal on civil rights was the fate of a federal antilynching bill. Such a statute had long been an objective of the NAACP, which began supporting it in 1919. In 1922, an antilynching bill, sponsored by Leonidas C. Dyer, a Republican from St. Louis, passed the House but expired in the Senate after a southern filibuster. After a surge of lynchings in the South during the early 1930s, the campaign for federal antilynching legislation was revived. Although Roosevelt denounced lynch law in December 1933, he refused to endorse strong legislation for fear of alienating his southern Democratic supporters. The president remained neutral when the Wagner–Costigan antilynching bill passed the House and went to the Senate in 1934; it then again encountered a southern filibuster and, despite further efforts to revive it, never passed the Congress.

On the whole, the position of Roosevelt toward black Americans was cautious and conservative and tended to follow prevailing racial attitudes rather than challenge them head on. Without any pressing political reason to advance the issue of racial equality to the top of his political agenda, Roosevelt instead attempted to satisfy both segregationists and the pioneers of the civil-rights movement. To a large extent, he was able to accomplish this seemingly impossible task. Over the long term, moreover, his administration began to reverse more than half a century of federal indifference or even open hostility toward the rights and status of black Americans.

Chapter 16

—»» «««—

The Versailles Legacy, 1920–1936

In spite of the hopes of Woodrow Wilson and other liberal internationalists, the conclusion of the First World War did not bring a new era of world stability. A new collective-security organization, the League of Nations, was established under the terms of the Versailles Treaty, yet without American support or vigorous Anglo–French backing, it never developed into anything more than an international debating society. In other respects, meanwhile, the world became a very dangerous place during the two decades following the Paris Peace Conference, for the discordant and frightening forces of nationalism, fascism, and totalitarian statism were beginning to raise their ugly faces.

Concluding a separate peace with its enemies in the First World War, the United States adapted to its new role as the world's dominant economic and strategic power hesitantly and with great difficulty. Soon after his inauguration, Harding began a retreat from the obligations of Wilsonian internationalism. He made it clear that the United States would not join the League, and he concluded separate peace treaties with Germany, Austria, and Hungary. Yet, as Harding and his successors discovered, the absence of international obligations did not change an inescapable reality: the United States was now vitally involved in world affairs, and its security depended on events transpiring outside of its own borders. As the internal problems of the Versailles security system became apparent, moreover, policy makers were forced to reconcile domestic pressures for noninvolvement with policy pressures for internationalism.

1. The Washington Conference

In the years before, during, and after the First World War, a growing Japanese–American rivalry for dominance in Asia began to crystalize. Despite the Lansing–Ishii Agreement of November 1917 (see p. 114), embittered relations existed over American attempts to thwart Japanese control of northern China and Manchuria. In 1919, as a result of the Russian Revolution, the Japanese had intervened in eastern Siberia. Partly in response to Japanese aggressiveness, American troops were also dispatched to Siberia, while Wilson put heavy pressure on Japan to withdraw its troops. At Paris, American opposition to Japanese control of Shantung Province in China and former German colonies in the western Pacific convinced the Japanese that the Americans were determined to frustrate their expansion in the Far East.

Partly because of Japanese–American tensions, moreover, a naval arms race followed the end of the war. The United States was perhaps most responsible. In 1918, 1919, and 1920, the Navy Department pressed the Wilson administration for a building program to provide the United States with naval dominance in both the Atlantic and the Pacific. In both Japan and Great Britain, leaders were alarmed. "Great Britain would spend her last guinea to keep a navy superior to that of the United States or any other Power," Prime Minister David Lloyd George had declared; and the British government in March 1921 revealed plans to resume construction on a large scale. Even more disturbing to the Japanese than the threat of new American naval construction was the stationing, by the end of 1919, of an American fleet in the Pacific nearly as powerful as the entire Japanese navy, together with plans by the Navy Department to enlarge naval bases in Hawaii and the Philippines and to fortify Guam.

As it turned out, public opinion in all three countries strongly opposed a naval arms race and, largely at the instigation of the British—who could neither afford an arms race nor desired competition with the United States—Secretary of State Charles Evans Hughes issued invitations in August 1921 to Great Britain, Japan, and six other countries with Asian interests to join the United States at a conference in Washington. By the time the conference convened, on November 12, 1921, Hughes had concluded that the only disarmament formula acceptable to the United States, Great Britain, and Japan would be one in which the powers agreed to abandon present building plans and set definite limits on capital ships. He outlined a bold plan for a ten-year holiday in the construction of capital ships, accompanied by agreement to set the maximum capital tonnage of the United States and Great Britain at 500,000 tons, and that of Japan at 300,000 tons.* This could be accomplished, Hughes said, if the United States scrapped 845,740 tons, the British 583,-375 tons, and the Japanese 448,928 tons of capital ships already built or under construction.

The Five Power Naval Treaty, signed by Great Britain, Japan, the United States, Italy, and France on February 1, 1922, forestalled a postwar naval arms race. Under this treaty, the naval powers agreed to abandon capital ship construction for ten years, to follow—with a few exceptions—Hughes's proposal for destruction of existing tonnage, and to limit auxiliary craft to 10,000 tons and aircraft carriers to 27,000 tons. The Five Power Naval Treaty also established a new stability to great power competition in the Pacific and the Far East. Japan, the United States, and Great Britain all promised not to fortify their island possessions in the western Pacific.

The Americans, meanwhile, insisted on the abrogation of the Anglo–Japanese Alliance of 1902, which obligated Britain to assume a benevolent neutrality toward Japan in the event of a Japanese–American war. Months before the Washington Conference, when the renewal of the alliance was under consideration, Hughes had

---

*Thus the ratio was 10:10:6.

brought strong pressure upon the British Foreign Office for abrogation or modification of the 1902 treaty. Japan and Great Britain were willing to abrogate their alliance, which had now seemingly outlived its original purpose of restraining Russian expansion in the Far East, provided they could obtain a new, triple alliance that included the United States. Hughes rejected this proposal and insisted upon bringing France into the new understanding. The outcome was the Four Power Treaty, presented to a plenary session of the Washington Conference on December 10, 1921. It pledged Great Britain, the United States, Japan, and France to respect each other's possessions in the Pacific and to confer if disputes among them or aggression by nonsignatories threatened the peace. The pact provided also that the Anglo–Japanese Alliance would be abrogated upon ratification of the Four Power Treaty.

Another troublesome issue in Japanese–American relations confronted in the Washington Conference was the status of China. The question of Japan's intentions toward that republic was still unanswered. Under steady Anglo–American pressure the Japanese yielded their imperialistic ambitions and approved an agreement—the Nine Power Treaty—that reaffirmed the historic American policy of the Open Door and noninterference. Signed on February 6, 1922, by representatives of the United States, Great Britain, Japan, France, Italy, China, the Netherlands, Belgium, and Portugal, it pledged the signatories to respect the sovereignty, independence, and integrity of China, and to refrain from seeking special rights and privileges in China that would impair the rights of friendly states.

Nor was this all, though it did represent the most sweeping self-denial that Japan had yet made. Hughes meanwhile had been hard at work on the Japanese and Chinese delegates to effect a direct settlement of the Shantung question. Actually, the Japanese were more reasonable than the Chinese; and the treaty concluded on February 4, 1922, conceded everything Hughes had asked—restoration of full Chinese sovereignty over Shantung and the sale by Japan to China of the Shantung Railroad. Finally, as if to demonstrate their determination to liquidate all sources of potential trouble, the Japanese promised to evacuate Siberia, conceded the American demand for special cable rights on the island of Yap, and joined the United States in abrogating the Lansing–Ishii Agreement.

Years later, the American architects of these treaties were condemned for surrendering naval supremacy and failing to obtain ironclad guarantees against future aggression. Yet naval supremacy was possible only if Americans would pay for it through an arms race—which they were not willing to do. Congress afterward refused even to maintain the fleet at the authorized treaty strength. And although the absence in the Washington treaties of any enforcement mechanism undoubtedly weakened them, enforcement would have involved the giving of guarantees that the Senate never would have approved.

The expressed determination of Americans to avoid a naval rivalry and even so much as a suggestion of binding obligations to preserve the peace were the compelling realities which shaped Hughes's approach. But by yielding, he obtained for his country parity in capital ships with Great Britain and considerable supremacy over Japan under an agreement that ended the most dangerous phase of the naval race for a decade. He cleared the air of suspicion and distrust and won the abrogation of the Anglo–Japanese Alliance. Best of all, he helped to erect a new peace structure for the Far East that seemed to make it possible for Great Britain, the United States, and Japan to live and work together in mutual trust and respect.

Yet Japanese–American relations, in spite of the good will fostered at the Washington Conference, were disrupted by a catastrophic development—congressional prohibition in 1924 of Japanese immigration to the United States. Japanese immigration had been restricted by the Gentlemen's Agreement of 1907. But when House leaders began writing a new immigration bill in 1923, there were strong demands for statutory exclusion from the AFL, the American Legion, Californians, and others. In spite of vigorous opposition from the Japanese embassy and from Hughes, the House Immigration Committee reported a bill that forbade the immigration of persons "ineligible for citizenship"—code words hateful to the Japanese. Passed by the House, the bill cleared the Senate by a vote of seventy-one to four and was signed by Coolidge in April 1924.

It is no exaggeration to say that this action virtually nullified all the progress that Hughes and Japanese leaders had made since 1921 in restoring cordial relations. "Our friends in the Senate have in a few minutes spoiled the work of years and done a lasting injury to our common country," Hughes wrote in disgust. Unfortunately, reaction in Japan justified the secretary's gloomy observation. The day upon which the immigration law went into effect was a day of national mourning, and millions in Japan thereafter nursed feelings of humiliation.

2. The United States in the World Economy

While international political developments in the early 1920s made a reversion to isolation impossible, the American people were projected into the world arena by still another force—the decline of European economic power during the war and the sudden emergence of the United States as the chief source of international capital. In 1914, American citizens invested some $3.5 billion abroad but still owed Europe a net amount of almost $3.7 billion. Because of the wartime sale of British- and French-owned American securities, the aggregate investment of foreigners in the United States was reduced from a little over $7 billion to nearly $4 billion. During the same period, private American investments abroad increased to nearly $7 billion. By 1920, therefore, foreigners owed Americans a net private debt of nearly $3 billion. In addition, European governments owed the United States more than $10.3 billion borrowed during the war and postarmistice periods.

This basic shift in the world economy required aggressive American leadership to establish stability in the postwar system of international exchange. By all measures of leadership, Americans failed badly. Instead of agreeing to mutual cancellation of all intergovernmental debts and reparations—the most disturbing factors in the postwar international economy—the United States insisted on full payment of war debts. And instead of lowering tariffs to enable Europeans to pay their debts by selling more goods, Congress increased the duties.

The result was by no means international chaos. Private bankers constructed a new system of international exchange that worked remarkably well for some time.

But given the balance-of-payments situation, the new system was bound to be entirely dependent upon the maintenance of a high level of American export of capital for successful operation. Through the annual export of about $1 billion between 1919 and 1930, American bankers and businessmen supported the huge volume of American foreign trade and the world economy as well. The fatal weakness of the system was that its maintenance depended upon a continuing flow of American dollars in the form of purchases and investments abroad.

Administrations from Wilson to Hoover worked to withdraw the federal government from the realm of international economic activity. At the same time, the State and Commerce departments worked vigorously and often successfully to protect American economic interests abroad and to expand the frontiers of American foreign trade and investments. One notable victory was the Nine Power Treaty, which for a time preserved an area of freedom for American merchants and capitalists in China. More important was Secretary Hughes's fight to break the monopoly over middle eastern oil reserves that the British, French, and Dutch governments had established at the end of the First World War. Seven American oil companies were given a quarter share in the future exploitation of oil in Iraq in 1925 as a result of Hughes's intervention. In these and other economic aspects of diplomacy, the State Department continued the well-established policy of opposing special concessions or exclusive rights for Americans, insisting only upon equal commercial opportunity abroad.

The most challenging and perplexing problem of the postwar international economy was that of war debts and reparations. During the war, the United States lent Allied governments about $7 billion; in the months after the armistice, it provided another $3.25 billion in cash and supplies. At the same time, in a complicated web of international debts, the British lent more than $4 billion to seventeen nations, while ten nations owed the French various large sums. In February 1922, Congress established a World War Foreign Debt Commission to negotiate long-term funding agreements with European debtors. The British, with their reputation for financial integrity at stake, agreed in June 1923 to pay $4.6 billion in principal and accrued interest over a sixty-two-year period at 3 percent for the first decade and 3.5 percent thereafter. When the French and Italians refused to acknowledge their indebtedness, the State Department retaliated by imposing a ban on all private loans to citizens and governments in default. Cowed by this bludgeoning, the French and Italians finally surrendered in 1925 and 1926, and in the same manner the smaller nations of Europe came to terms.

Closely tied to the debt problem was the question of war reparations. In May 1921, the Reparations Commission determined that the German Republic owed reparations of $33 billion, in addition to the total Belgian war debt and the costs of the armies of occupation. Within a year, the German government defaulted, and the French retaliated by occupying the Ruhr, the center of German industry and coal mining. Thereupon the Germans inaugurated a program of passive resistance that soon resulted in a spectacular inflation of the German currency. The German government was bankrupt by the end of 1923, and the country tottered on the brink of total economic ruin.

At the initiative of Great Britain and the United States, and with the eventual support of the French, the Reparations Commission appointed a committee in November 1923, on which two Americans, Charles G. Dawes and Owen D. Young, served unofficially. This so-called Dawes Committee submitted a plan in April 1924 that provided elaborate financial machinery to collect and distribute reparations, established a schedule of payments that Germany could bear, and arranged for a gold loan of $200 million by American bankers to the German government to stabilize the German mark on a gold standard. A new committee of experts, headed by Owen D. Young, reexamined the reparations question in 1929, set the total bill at a little more than $2 billion exclusive of interest, and provided for an end of payments by 1988.

The significant point of this complicated story is that the American government and private bankers cooperated to help establish a system of intergovernmental debt and reparations payments that worked so long as the dynamic factor in the system continued to operate. That dynamic factor was private American loans to the central government, states, municipalities, and corporations of Germany, totaling some $2.5 billion from 1924 to 1930. During the same period, Germany paid reparations under the Dawes Plan of nearly $2 billion, while the former Allies in turn paid to the United States more than $2.6 billion on their war debt accounts—about the same amount that American bankers had lent to Germany. Thus, in spite of the refusal of the State Department ever to admit the fact, payment of war debts under this complicated structure became contingent upon the payment of reparations by Germany. This in turn depended on the flow of dollars from the United States.

3. The Search for Peace, 1924–1930

In the postwar United States, a prevailing passion was the search for peace without obligations. Although a small but influential minority continued to support membership in the League, most Americans favored advancing peace through unilateral disarmament, membership in the World Court, voluntary cooperation with the League, ad hoc efforts to outlaw war, and the like.

Membership in the World Court was a project supported by both advanced and cautious internationalists, for it existed apart from the League, and membership did not involve any obligation to help enforce its decisions. Although both kinds of internationalists endorsed a resolution approving membership in 1924, bitter-end isolationists like Senator William E. Borah of Idaho forced adoption of a reservation restricting the right of the court to render advisory opinions. When the member nations refused to accept the reservation, Presidents Hoover and Roosevelt, in 1930 and 1935, again vainly urged membership in the court.

Another manifestation of the American search for peace in the 1920s was the gradual change in official policy toward the League of Nations. The State Department during the early months of the Harding administration had not only refused to cooperate with the League's nonpolitical agencies but had also failed, either accidentally or deliberately, even to acknowledge communications from the League's secretariat.

In any event, the secretary of state launched a new policy of cooperation in the spring and summer of 1922 by sending "unofficial observers" to speak for the United States in various League agencies and commissions. This policy developed rapidly, and the American government cooperated in conferences to control the traffic in arms, women, and opium, in the work of the Reparations Commission, in the League Health Organization, and in the International Labour Organization. The United States by 1930 had participated in some forty League conferences and had five permanent representatives stationed at the Geneva headquarters of the League.

Even so, there were few indications in the 1920s that the American people were willing to undertake responsibilities for preserving the peace in times of crisis. This reluctance was vividly illustrated by the peculiar American peace movement that culminated in the signing of the Kellogg–Briand Pact in 1928. American peace organizations voiced a passion for peace during the early 1920s but could not agree on the crucial issue, American membership in the League of Nations. It fell to Salmon O. Levinson, a Chicagoan interested in the peace cause, to devise a program upon which all the disparate and warring peace elements could agree—a program to outlaw war as an instrument of national policy. Levinson's crusade, begun in 1921, became more formidable when he won the support of Nicholas Murray Butler and James T. Shotwell, two officials of the Carnegie Endowment for International Peace.

Shotwell visited the French foreign minister, Aristide Briand, in March 1927. Perceiving an opportunity to draw the United States and France together in an entente, Briand in April 1927 addressed an open letter to the American public, proposing that the two countries join hands in a pact forever outlawing war between them. Reluctant to accept this special arrangement, Coolidge and his secretary of state, Frank B. Kellogg, suggested in December 1927 that France and the United States invite other powers to join them in a treaty renouncing war as an instrument of national policy.

Kellogg's counterthrust came as an alarming move to Briand, who well knew that France's security rested upon her willingness to go to war to preserve her dominant position in Europe. Negotiations went smoothly, however, once the State Department made it clear that the proposed pact should outlaw only aggressive war and not legitimate defensive efforts. Representatives of all the great powers except the Soviet Union (which later ratified) signed the Pact of Paris in the French capital in August 1928. Signers of the Kellogg–Briand Pact agreed to renounce "recourse to war . . . as an instrument of national policy." To be sure, the treaty established no enforcement machinery and would be only as effective as the signatories made it. But it was not meaningless. By outlawing aggressive war it changed international law in an important way. At the same time, it brought the United States, however tenuously, into the peace system established by the Treaty of Versailles.

The diplomacy of peace was also reflected in new efforts to further naval disarmament. Although the Five Power Naval Treaty of 1922 forestalled an arms race in battleship and aircraft carrier construction, it did not affect the building of cruisers, destroyers, and submarines. When Great Britain launched a new construction program in 1924 by laying keels for five heavy cruisers of 10,000 tons each and in the following year adopted a program for building nine 10,000-ton and seven 8,000-ton cruisers, the Japanese countered by beginning work on four heavy cruisers.

Meanwhile, the American Congress in December 1924 authorized the president to undertake construction of eight 10,000-ton cruisers. Obviously, the major naval powers by 1927 stood on the verge of another costly race that threatened to upset the balance established so auspiciously at the Washington Conference.

In response to urgings by the House of Representatives and peace organizations in the United States, President Coolidge issued a hasty call in February 1927 for a five-power naval disarmament conference to meet at Geneva that same year. Despite the refusal of the French and Italians to attend, British, Japanese, and American representatives met in Geneva from June to August 1927. But, because the British and Americans were unable to agree upon the limitation of light cruisers, the conference broke up in disagreement.

Public opinion in the United States and Britain refused to accept the Geneva failure as final, despite the passage by Congress in February 1929 of a second and larger cruiser bill. The coming to power of the Hoover administration in the United States and the Labour government under Ramsay MacDonald in Great Britain in 1929 raised new hopes for Anglo–American accord, and MacDonald and the new American ambassador, Charles G. Dawes, set to work to prepare the way for understanding. By July 1929, the two governments had agreed to establish equality in combat strength, to be determined in all categories of fighting ships.

The settlement of Anglo–American differences paved the way for a new five-power conference, which opened in London in January 1930. The American, British, and Japanese representatives readily agreed to extend the construction "holiday" on capital ships for five years and to scrap a total of nine battleships. However, Japanese insistence upon greater cruiser strength than the 10:10:6 ratio would allow threatened for a time to disrupt negotiations. In the end, the Japanese accepted a compromise by which they obtained a 10:10:6 ratio for heavy cruisers, a 10:10:7 ratio for light cruisers and destroyers, and equality in submarines. In addition, the delegates fixed a definite tonnage quota, based upon these ratios, for cruisers, destroyers, and submarines.

Coming at the end of a decade of popular agitation, the London Treaty was a striking victory for the peace movement and further evidence of the determination of the British, American, and Japanese peoples to live in close friendship. As President Hoover declared in 1930, the alternative to naval agreement was mutual "suspicion, hate, ill-will and ultimate disaster." The governments chose mutual trust instead, at least for a moment, in this, the last successful effort to preserve the peace system of the postwar era.

4. A New Latin American Policy Takes Shape

When Harding took office in 1921, relations between the United States and Latin America had reached a low point. Americans troops were sustaining a minority government in Nicaragua, while American naval commanders were running the governments of the Dominican Republic and Haiti. And the State Department and the government of Mexico, headed by Álvaro Obregón, were not even on speaking terms, even though Wilson had successfully resisted congressional pressure for military intervention in Mexico in 1919.

The Republican administrations of the 1920s were protectors of American investors at home, but they oversaw a partial breakup of formal American hemispheric control. For this phenomenon a number of factors were responsible. Most important was the end of every threat to American security in the approaches to the Panama Canal. Also important was the accidental injection of Latin American policy as an issue in the campaign of 1920. Franklin D. Roosevelt, Democratic vice-presidential candidate, indiscreetly boasted that the United States would control twelve Latin American votes in the League assembly and inaccurately bragged that he had written the Haitian constitution—a claim which provoked Harding to pledge nonintervention toward Caribbean republics. Finally, the new secretary of state in 1921, Charles Evans Hughes, and the career diplomat who headed the Latin American desk, Sumner Welles, were determined to withdraw American power as fast as circumstances would permit.

Hughes soon tested out his new policy. In the Dominican Republic, elections were held and a new government formed between 1922 and 1924. American occupation forces were gradually withdrawn after the inauguration of President Horatio Vásquez in July 1924, although the customs houses remained under American control. Similarly, in Nicaragua, Hughes withdrew the marines in August 1925. When the elected president, the Liberal Carlos Solórzano, was forced out of office by the Conservative leader, Emiliano Chamorro, the United States withheld recognition. But after the Nicaraguan Congress elected to the presidency another Conservative leader and long-time American ally, Adolfo Díaz, Secretary of State Kellogg unwisely extended recognition.

Renewed American intervention in Nicaraguan affairs followed. The exiled Liberal vice-president, Juan B. Sacasa, returned to raise a general anti-Díaz revolt. In response to frenzied appeals from Díaz, President Coolidge dispatched some 5,000 marines to suppress the uprising early in 1927, an action that evoked a storm of protest in the United States. Coolidge then sent Henry L. Stimson to Nicaragua to mediate, and, by tact and patience, Stimson persuaded the Liberals to give up the fight. In return, he guaranteed a fair presidential election—under American military supervision—and compelled Díaz to admit Liberals to his Cabinet.

The result of Stimson's mediation became apparent when the Liberals were elected to the presidency in 1928 and 1932. The United States had used military force from 1909 to 1927 to keep unpopular but pro-American conservative governments in power, in defiance of the wishes of a large majority of Nicaraguans. When Stimson offered impartiality in return for the cooperation of the Liberals, he was in effect reversing the historic policy of the State Department. American troops remained in Nicaragua to help the government suppress the popular guerilla leader, Augusto Sandino, and were gradually withdrawn from 1931 to 1933.

Setting in motion the withdrawal from the Dominican Republic and Nicaragua was easy compared with the task of reestablishing friendly Mexican–American relations. Tension between the two countries (which had been provoked by Wilsonian intervention), was increased during the war by American charges that Mexico was a hotbed of German espionage, and especially by Carranza's decree of February

1918, applying Article XXVII of the Mexican Constitution of 1917. This highly controversial provision vested the Mexican people with ownership of all subsoil rights to oil and mineral properties acquired by foreigners before 1917; it also required foreign owners of such properties to obtain new concessions from the revolutionary government. Vigorous protests from the United States and Great Britain forced Carranza to postpone implementation of the law.

A coup led by General Obregón deposed Carranza and put Obregón and a less anti-American group in power in Mexico City in April 1920. The Wilson adminis-tration left the question of the recognition of Obregón to the incoming Harding administration. By firm but cordial dealings, Secretary Hughes won all his demands and recognized the Obregón regime in 1923. The accession to the presidency in 1924 of Plutarcho Elias Calles, however, brought a more radical wing of the revolu-tionary party to power, and relations between Mexico and the United States sud-denly worsened. Calles threatened to overturn the Mexican–American agreement of 1923 by requiring American owners of oil lands to exchange their titles for fifty-year leases. He also launched a bloody campaign against the Catholic church that greatly inflamed Catholic opinion in the United States.

In early 1927, Secretary of State Kellogg foolishly charged that the Mexicans were creating a "Bolshevik hegemony intervening between the United States and the Panama Canal." At the same time, serious efforts were afoot to win Mexican friendship. In September 1927, Coolidge sent Dwight Morrow, a Morgan & Com-pany partner and a man of extraordinary tact and ability, as ambassador to Mexico City. By offering genuine friendship, Morrow won the affection of the Mexican people. By his shrewd handling of Calles, he also won a compromise settlement of the oil lands dispute, a surcease of the anticlerical campaign, and a new Mexican–American accord.

Republican leaders not only retreated from empire in the Caribbean area but also set in motion repudiation of the Roosevelt Corollary to the Monroe Doctrine, which Theodore Roosevelt had devised in 1904 to justify a policy of intervention (see pp. 107–108). Hughes began the reversal in 1923 by attempting to explain to the American people that the Monroe Doctrine was exclusively a policy of self-defense. It neither infringed on the independence of any American state, he said, nor warranted interference by the United States in the affairs of neighboring coun-tries. That such an interpretation did not imply complete American abandonment of the alleged right to intervene, however, was dramatically revealed at the Pan American Conference at Havana in January 1928. There Hughes, as head of the American delegation, stubbornly refused to yield to the vociferous Latin American demands that his country give an unequivocal pledge of nonintervention.

Even so, there were numerous signs from 1928 to 1933 that the United States could not long maintain its traditional position in face of a growing Latin American demand. President-elect Hoover made a good-will tour of Latin America in early 1929; a short time later he promised never to intervene to protect American property rights abroad. He courageously honored this promise, even when the depression set off a wave of revolutions and debt repudiations throughout Latin America. It was little wonder, therefore, that relations between the United States and Latin America were on a more cordial basis by 1933 than they had been at any time since 1901.

5. The Good Neighbor Policy, 1931–1936

Even so, much remained to done when Roosevelt came to power before relations between the United States and Latin America were put on a truly cordial footing. The Hoover administration had repudiated the Roosevelt Corollary, but it had steadfastly refused to surrender the alleged right of intervention. Tragic circumstances now presented the new Roosevelt administration with perplexing difficulties. American trade with Latin America had declined from $2.1 billion in 1929 to $574 million in 1932. The effect was to shatter Latin American prosperity and cause economic disorganization, bankruptcy, and repudiation of debts. Meanwhile, war or the threat of war raged between Paraguay and Bolivia, Colombia and Peru, and inside Cuba under the brutal dictatorship of Gerardo Machado.

These developments sorely tested the determination of Roosevelt and his secretary of state, Cordell Hull, to establish friendly Pan-American relations. The Peruvian–Colombian conflict was settled through League of Nations mediation in 1933 and 1934, and the Roosevelt administration agreed to withdraw troops from Haiti by October 1934. And, when a revolution against the Machado government broke out in Cuba in the spring of 1933, Roosevelt and Hull resisted calls for intervention.

An even more important step in Latin American relations came at the Seventh Inter-American Conference in Montevideo, Uruguay, in December 1933. There, in a historic reversal of American policy, Hull agreed to renounce any right to intervene in the affairs of Latin American states. The signing of a series of inter-American treaties then followed, the most important of which was the Convention on Rights and Duties of States. It represented a sweeping triumph for Latin American jurisprudence on such important issues as recognition of *de facto* governments, nonintervention, the equality of states and their sovereignty in dealing with foreign nationals, inviolability of territory, and territorial changes effected by forceful means.

In the months following the Montevideo Conference, the Roosevelt administration began to abide by the Convention on Rights and Duties of States by renouncing any legal basis for intervention. In May 1934, Hull signed a treaty formally abrogating the Platt Amendment and ending all special American rights in Cuba, except the right to maintain a naval base at Guantánamo. By special agreement with the Haitian government, American marines were withdrawn from Port-au-Prince in August 1934, instead of in October, as the treaty of 1933 had stipulated. Moreover, Washington allowed the Haitian–American treaty of 1916, which had made Haiti a semiprotectorate of the United States, to expire in 1936 and relinquished its control over Haiti's financial affairs. Panama and the United States concluded a treaty in 1936 that ended the American right to intervene in Panamanian affairs granted in the Panamanian–American treaty of 1903. The Dominican–American treaty of 1924, which had continued American receivership of the Dominican customs after the withdrawal of American troops and which was not to expire until 1945, was abrogated by a new treaty between the two countries in 1940, and the receivership was ended in 1941.

In the Pacific, Roosevelt endorsed a policy of decolonization of the Philippines. In 1920, Wilson had recommended full independence, but Harding favored a slower and more cautious policy. All Filipino leaders continued publicly in the 1920s to demand immediate independence—and to wonder privately whether independence was worth losing the free American market for Philippine sugar and other agricultural products. But, by 1932, worldwide depression had given greater impetus to the independence movement. Moreover, American sugar producers, cotton growers, and dairymen were determined to end Philippine competition, and, in January 1933, Congress adopted over Hoover's veto an act for Philippine independence after a ten-year transition period, provided that the Filipinos established a republican form of government. The Philippine legislature rejected the act and sought dominion status instead. But Congress was adamant, and the Filipino leaders had to accept the Tydings–McDuffie Act of March 1934. It was almost an exact replica of the Independence Act of 1933. Filipino voters and President Roosevelt subsequently approved a Philippine Constitution drafted by a constitutional convention in 1934 and 1935; Manuel Quezon became first president of the Commonwealth of the Philippines in 1935; and July 4, 1946, was set as the date for launching the Philippine Republic.

From the beginning, Roosevelt's secretary of state, Cordell Hull, was obsessed with the conviction that the United States could never find prosperity and friendship abroad unless it was willing to act like a good neighbor in economic affairs. He saw his suggestions for currency stabilization and a reciprocal trade program go unheeded for almost a year while proponents of economic nationalism had Roosevelt's ear. But he waited patiently, and Roosevelt was ready to stabilize the dollar and conclude his experiment in autarky by the end of 1933.

With the White House's blessing, therefore, Hull and his assistants set to work on a reciprocal trade bill in January 1934. It empowered the president to negotiate trade agreements, which would go into effect without congressional approval, to raise or lower existing Hawley–Smoot rates by as much as 50 percent in order to obtain concessions from other countries. All tariff reductions would apply to any nations that accorded the benefit of their lowest tariff rates to the United States. The Trade Agreements bill passed Congress easily, and the president signed the measure in June 1934. The State Department concluded its first such trade agreement with Cuba in August 1934 and began negotiations with other nations soon afterward. By the end of 1936, it had concluded agreements with Belgium, Sweden, Holland, Canada, France, Switzerland, Finland, and six Latin American nations as well.

For the most part, the Good Neighbor policy brought unspectacular results. Yet, in one case—the Mexican expropriation of American-owned land and oil properties —which exploded rather violently in the 1930s and involved the fate of holdings worth many millions of dollars—the principles of the Good Neighbor were put to a severe test.

Beginning in 1934, the government of Lázaro Cárdenas began to expropriate land belonging to American citizens in Mexico. Following the advice of the extraordinarily popular ambassador in Mexico City, Josephus Daniels, Hull refused to deny Mexico's right to expropriate, but he did put pressure on Mexico to compensate former owners. The controversy over land expropriations, heated though it threatened to become, was of minor importance compared to the storm set off when Mexico moved against the British and American oil companies.

As we have seen, the Mexicans agreed in 1928 that foreign oil companies might retain possession of properties acquired before 1917 (see p. 302). Reversing this position, Cárdenas decided to nationalize the oil industry and expropriate foreign holdings in March 1938. Claiming that their property had a potential value of $450 million, British and American oil companies protested loudly. But under pressure from Daniels—and perhaps because of President Roosevelt's direct intervention— the secretary of state began negotiations that culminated on November 19, 1941, in a general settlement of the land and oil claims, conclusion of a Mexican–American trade agreement, and a promise by the United States to help stabilize the peso and obtain loans for Mexico through the Export–Import Bank. Roosevelt, with Daniels's vital help, turned the expropriation affair to the advantage of the people of the United States. By refusing to interfere in a controversy that was essentially Mexican in character, he won the friendship of the Mexican people and a valuable ally during the Second World War. More important, he convinced most Latin Americans that there were no strings attached to the Good Neighbor policy.

6. Challenges to the Versailles System, 1931–1936

Beginning in the early 1930s, several factors—the fear and mutual suspicion arising from the Versailles settlement, the collapse of international trade, and the world depression—worked to destroy the international equilibrium. More specifically, aggressors in Europe and the Far East made a mockery of the peace structure established during the Paris Peace Conference and the 1920s, while the western democracies of Great Britain, France, and the United States appeared unable to agree on the need for or proper form of collective defense.

The first important assault upon the postwar peace structure occurred when Japan occupied Manchuria and made war on China in 1931–1932, and the western powers with interests in the Far East failed to cooperate in any effective measures to halt Japanese aggression. After their victory in the Russo–Japanese War of 1905, the Japanese colonized southern Manchuria and came to regard it as a bulwark against Russian expansion in the Far East. Two developments during the 1920s excited Japanese fears for the safety of their protectorate in Manchuria. One was the resurgence of Soviet Russia as a far eastern power after Japanese withdrawal from northern Manchuria and the Maritime Province following the Bolshevik revolution. In an undeclared war between China and Russia in 1929, Soviet armies invaded northern Manchuria and compelled the Chinese to respect the Sino–Soviet treaty of 1924 providing for joint Chinese and Russian control of the Chinese Eastern Railway that ran from Siberia to Harbin and Vladivostok. At the same time, the Soviet government began construction of a huge naval base at Vladivostok that pointed at the heart of Japan. Resurgent Russian power in the Far East made the Japanese all the more determined to reinforce southern Manchuria as a barrier against Soviet expansion.

To the Japanese, an even more alarming development was the spread of Chinese nationalism into Manchuria and the attempt of the president of China, Chiang Kai-shek, to control that province. A number of minor incidents had increased the tension to the breaking point by 1931. The Japanese army, taking control of policy out of the hands of the Japanese foreign minister, attacked and occupied Mukden, Changchun, and other Manchurian cities on September 18–19, 1931. China appealed to the League of Nations, but the British opposed strong measures against Japan and waited to see what policy the Washington government would follow. Secretary of State Henry L. Stimson, convinced by early 1932 that militarists controlled Japanese policy and that the Asian security system erected at the Washington Conference was in shambles, was eager to organize an Anglo–American defense of China—even if that meant economic sanctions or even war.

Yet Stimson was virtually powerless to act, for it was clear that, although Americans strongly condemned Japanese ruthlessness, they even more strongly opposed any measures that might conceivably lead to war. The same public spokesmen who were loudest in condemning Japan advised complete withdrawal of American forces from China. If this overwhelming popular resistance to warlike moves had not been enough, then President Hoover's determination to avoid the risk of war would have provided an insurmountable barrier to forceful action. When Stimson suggested in October 1931 that the United States might have to cooperate with the League of Nations in imposing sanctions against Japan, Hoover quipped that his "able Secretary was at times more of a warrior than a diplomat." Aware that the British would not support a strong anti-Japanese policy and convinced that Americans did not want war, Hoover vetoed Stimson's plan for economic measures in early 1932.

Instead, Hoover preferred the use of moral weapons. He suggested that Stimson should revive the doctrine of nonrecognition of territorial and political changes effected by military force, which Secretary Bryan had first enunciated in 1915 at the time of the crisis over Japan's Twenty-one Demands upon China (see p. 114). Hence Stimson issued an identical warning to Japan in January 1932. The American government, he announced, would recognize no changes in the Far East brought about by force which impaired the treaty rights of the United States and the independence and administrative integrity of China.

Less than two weeks later, the Japanese responded by invading Shanghai. Although the British foreign secretary now joined Stimson in vigorously condemning Japanese aggression, Hoover refused more emphatically than ever to support economic sanctions, and the secretary of state once again was forced to rely on moral weapons. Yet it soon became clear that moral suasion would not deter aggression. When the League in March 1932 unanimously endorsed the Bryan–Stimson doctrine of nonrecognition and then, in February 1933, called for the return of Manchuria to China, the Japanese replied by withdrawing from the League.

These are the bare facts of this episode. Their meaning is still not altogether clear. This much, at least, can be said by way of conclusion: the policy of the United States and the League of Nations was far from effective, however one views the case. If the Japanese attack on Manchuria was a gross violation of the Covenant of the League of Nations and the Nine Power Treaty, then only willingness go to war, not

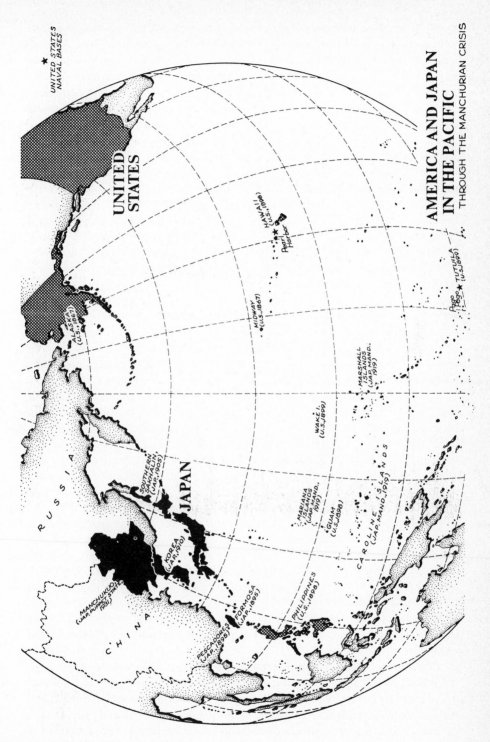

UNITED STATES
NAVAL BASES ★

UNITED STATES

AMERICA AND JAPAN
IN THE PACIFIC
THROUGH THE MANCHURIAN CRISIS

HAWAII
(U.S., 1898)
★ Pearl Harbor

PAGO PAGO ★ TUTUILA
(U.S., 1899)

ALASKA
(U.S., 1867)

MIDWAY
(U.S., 1867)

WAKE I.
(U.S., 1899)

MARSHALL
ISLANDS
(JAP. MAND.
1919)

RUSSIA

SOUTHERN
SAKHALIN
(JAP., 1905)

JAPAN

MARIANA
ISLANDS
(JAP. MAND.
1919)

GUAM
(U.S., 1898)

C A R O L I N E   I S L A N D S
(JAP. MAND., 1919)

KOREA
(JAP., 1910)

MANCHUKUO
(JAP. PUPPET STATE,
1931)

FORMOSA
(JAP., 1895)

PHILIPPINES
(U.S., 1898)

PESCADORES
(JAP., 1895)

CHINA

moral exhortation, would have sufficed to bring the Japanese to book. If the Japanese were justified in securing their hold on Manchuria, then wisdom would have demanded a policy of acquiescence. Hoover and Stimson in effect simply perpetuated a policy that had long been irrelevant to the facts of international life in the Far East. More than this, they gave a simple moral gloss to an enormously complicated situation. Without knowing it, they staked out a policy that would eventually culminate in war between their country and imperial Japan.

Meanwhile, other forces were beginning to undermine the Versailles system in Europe. In the late spring of 1931, as we have seen (see p. 237), Hoover issued a plan for a one-year moratorium on all intergovernmental debt and reparations payments. Although this move eased the strain on the international economy, the time was ripe for Hoover to propose a mutual cancellation of all intergovernmental debt and reparations. Hoover was personally willing to extend the moratorium until the worst of the depression had passed, but he regarded Europe's debts to the United States as sacred obligations and would never consent to cancel them or connect them officially with Germany's reparations debt. In this matter he, not Stimson—who wanted mutual cancellation—spoke for the vast majority of Americans and Congress. The latter voiced its emphatic opposition to any reduction or cancellation of the war debts by joint resolution in December 1931.

Because, however, Germany could not pay reparations in 1932, most of the European debtors were unable to meet their own debt payments to America. In response, representatives of the western and central European powers, meeting at Lausanne, Switzerland, in June 1932, reduced Germany's reparations obligations to $714 million and tacitly agreed that this sum would never have to be paid. However, this final settlement would go into effect only when the nations in debt to the United States and one another had reached a "satisfactory settlement" of war debt questions. Stimson urged a graceful acceptance of the inevitable, but Hoover condemned the Lausanne agreement and continued to apply diplomatic pressure on Europe.

Meanwhile, Germany ceased reparations payments altogether after the Lausanne Conference. Then, when the time for renewal of semiannual payments to the United States came in December 1932, Great Britain, Czechoslovakia, Italy, Finland, Latvia, and Lithuania met their obligations, while France, Greece, Poland, Belgium, Estonia, and Hungary defaulted. Great Britain, Italy, Czechoslovakia, Rumania, Lithuania, and Latvia made token payments in June 1933, while the remaining debtors, except Finland, again defaulted. Congress replied, in April 1934, with the Johnson Act. It forbade any American citizen or corporation to lend money to any nation in default on its debt payments to the United States. When the attorney general ruled that token payments did not meet the requirements of the Johnson Act, all of America's debtors except Finland defaulted in 1934 and afterward.

Concerning two other impediments to international economic recovery—high tariffs and unstable currencies—the situation in early 1933 appeared more hopeful. Both Hoover and the new president, Roosevelt, supported the London Conference, and European spokesmen descended on Washington in late April and early May for preliminary conversations with Roosevelt and his economic advisers. Although the Americans firmly refused to discuss suspension of war debt payments, they provided vague assurances of cooperation in lowering tariff barriers and stabilizing currencies.

Once again the United States had an opportunity to exercise bold leadership in formulating a program to repair the ravages of the depression. Once again the American government refused the opportunity, because Roosevelt had no intention of agreeing to the first necessary step—currency stabilization—unless the dollar had fallen sufficiently in value to stimulate a considerable price increase at home and an increase of American exports abroad. A large American delegation, headed by the new secretary of state, Cordell Hull, sailed for London in May 1933; but they sailed deeply ignorant of the president's intentions and divided among themselves. Hull believed that his government should agree to lower its tariffs and peg the dollar at its then present value in gold; moreover, he thought that Roosevelt agreed with him. On the other hand, a majority of the delegates opposed tariff reductions and were confused about stabilization.

As a result, the conference, which opened in London in June 1933, never made much progress. When it stalled on the war debts and currency issues, Roosevelt sent his economic adviser, Raymond Moley, to London with a tentative proposal to stabilize the dollar, then worth $4.00 to the British pound, at between $4.05 and $4.25 to the pound. But while Moley was on the high seas the dollar began to fall rapidly in value, until it reached $4.38 to the British pound on June 28. Delighted by this development, Roosevelt was convinced that further depreciation of the dollar was essential to recovery at home. He thus decided to end the agonizing debate at London by sending his "Bombshell Message" on July 3, announcing that the United States could not agree to immediate currency stabilization. Hull kept the conference alive for another three weeks, but all the delegates knew that further talk was futile.

American leadership in the movement for disarmament was considerably more vigorous than in international economic policies. Amid alarming developments in Asia and Europe, the World Disarmament Conference met in Geneva in February 1932. After months of deadlock, Hoover, in June, presented a bold plan which proposed immediate abolition of all bombers, tanks, large mobile artillery, and instruments of chemical warfare, and the reduction of all land and naval forces by approximately one-third. Hoover's proposal revived the conference; and American, British, and French leaders soon afterward promised revision of the Versailles Treaty and equality in land armaments for Germany. But these concessions came too late. Adolf Hitler became chancellor of Germany in January 1933. Roosevelt renewed Hoover's plea for action in May and promised American participation in a new collective security system, but Hitler withdrew his delegations from the World Disarmament Conference and the League in October 1933.

Another development in 1933—American recognition of the Soviet Union—at first seemed a positive step in the direction of common action to prevent aggression. Since 1917, the United States had withheld recognition because the Soviets had repudiated the czarist debts, confiscated American property, and supported world revolution. By 1933, the Soviets, who feared a Japanese attack on their Maritime Province and needed access to American trade, appeared ready to make significant policy changes. After negotiations in the autumn of 1933, an agreement was embodied in a formal exchange of notes in November 1933. In return for American recognition, the Soviet government promised to abstain from propaganda activity in the United States, to guarantee religious freedom and fair trials to Americans in the Soviet Union, and to negotiate a settlement of the czarist debt to the United States.

The Washington administration, eager to promote full economic intercourse with the Soviet Union, established an Export–Import Bank in February 1934 to facilitate exchange. Secretary Hull's bright hopes of friendship and mutual accommodation were soon blasted, however, by Russian failure to honor its pledges. Negotiations over a debt settlement failed, and the State Department blocked the extension of any credits to the Soviet Union. More damaging to Russian–American relations was the Kremlin's refusal to restrain the activities of the American Communist party. Consequently, relations between the two governments were formally correct but far from cordial before 1941.

Chapter 17

—>>> <<<—

The Coming of War, 1936–1941

The breakdown of the Versailles security system and the rise of aggressive new forms of militarism in Europe and Asia presented Americans with as serious a choice about their international position as they had ever faced. Should they resist further entanglement, allow a chaotic world to disintegrate, and establish a strong system of hemispheric defenses? Should they combat aggression by proxy—by providing material support, but not American lives, to allies or potential allies? Or, should the United States expand the tentative steps toward world involvement it began during the 1920s?

Between 1936 and 1941, American political leaders responded to the growing international crisis by experimenting with each of these very different approaches. In the process, two factors decisively affected the formulation of American foreign policy. The recollection of the First World War in particular and a pronounced antipathy toward war in general dominated public opinion in the western world and prompted its political leaders to avoid military conflicts at all costs. Another factor affecting policy making was the strong revival of isolationism. Frequently associated with domestic reform, isolationists held that the historical role of the United States lay outside of European affairs. Fueled by antiwar sentiment and isolationism, a public-opinion consensus about American foreign policy existed before 1939 that seriously limited Franklin Roosevelt's options and made him a largely passive actor in the interaction of domestic politics and international affairs.

1. The Triumph of Isolationism

Although Roosevelt realized the consequences to the United States of the breakdown of the international system in Europe and Asia, he was more often a captive of public opinion than an audacious leader. Perhaps the administration might have pursued a different course had the public been willing to approve collective action for peace. The important facts, however, were the determination of the American people to avoid international commitments and participation in all future wars, and the administration's refusal to run perhaps politically fatal risks by flouting the popular will.

As we have observed earlier, isolationism—the feeling of apartness coupled with a belief in the degeneracy of Europe and the unique virtue of American institutions and motives—was one of the oldest traditions and perhaps the dominant ideological force in American history. The American people shared the internationalist vision for a brief moment during the First World War. But events at Paris in 1919 and afterward soured American idealism and confirmed traditional beliefs about Europe's congenital perversity. Moreover, intellectuals in the 1920s nursed a nagging guilt feeling about American participation in the war and the peace conference. As European archives were opened, American historians examining the causes of the war concluded that Germany had been among the powers least responsible for the tragedy—a "new" history soon mushroomed into a cult of so-called revisionism. If Germany had not been primarily responsible for the war, these revisionists argued, then the Versailles Treaty was a monstrous fraud and injustice, and the American people had been tricked into fighting for an unworthy cause.

This belief, popular among American intellectuals during the late 1920s, was fired by sensational exposures after 1932 and spread rapidly among the American public. The House Foreign Affairs Committee, in 1933, conducted an investigation of the arms traffic and its allegedly sinister influence in world politics. In April 1934, the Senate approved a resolution for a special investigation of the munitions industry offered by Senator Gerald P. Nye, an extreme isolationist Republican from North Dakota. Nye himself was appointed chairman of the investigating committee. What ensued was not a restrained inquiry but rather a ruthless attempt to prove the old progressive thesis that wars are always primarily economic in origin. The committee's report grossly exaggerated the influence of bankers and businessmen and distorted the causes for America's entry into the First World War, but it convinced many thoughtful Americans that intervention in 1917 had been a ghastly mistake. They vowed that nothing like it would happen again.

The dominant temper of the American people in the mid-1930s was doggedly isolationist. Works by scholars, journalists, and professional pacifists expressed anti-war themes while they asserted that Americans could make their best contribution by staying out of Europe's troubles and strengthening democracy at home. High school and college students organized Veterans of Future Wars, joined pacifist movements like the Fellowship of Reconciliation, and vowed that they would not fight if the nation went to war again. A wave of pacifism also affected the clergy. It was little wonder that nearly two-thirds of the people questioned in a Gallup poll in April 1937 said that American participation in the First World War had been a mistake.

So strong was the popular feeling by 1935 that neutrality legislation of some kind was inevitable. The only question was whether Congress would take control of foreign policy out of the president's hands. Senator Key Pittman of Nevada, chairman of the Foreign Relations Committee, introduced a resolution in August 1935 prohibiting, "upon the outbreak or during the progress of war between, or among, two or more foreign States," the export of arms and munitions from the United States. It also made it unlawful for American ships to carry arms for or to any

belligerent and empowered the president to warn American citizens against traveling on belligerent ships. The president had no discretion and no authority under this
resolution to discriminate in favor of the victims of aggression. When the Senate
approved the bill, the best that Hull could do was to persuade the House to amend
the measure by limiting the life of the mandatory arms embargo provision to six
months. Thus amended, the Pittman Resolution was quickly adopted by Congress
and approved by Roosevelt with some misgivings in late August 1935.

2. The United States and World Aggression

By the mid-1930s, international stability was beginning to crumble in Europe and
Asia. In March 1935, Hitler denounced all provisions of the Versailles Treaty for
German disarmament and inaugurated conscription. The British, French, and Ital-
ian governments had the power to compel German compliance with the treaty, but
they contented themselves with verbal protests. Meanwhile, a skirmish between
Italian and Ethiopian troops in December 1934 gave Benito Mussolini the pretext
for picking a quarrel with Haile Selassie, emperor of Ethiopia. Rejecting mediation
by the League of Nations, Mussolini launched an invasion from Eritrea and Italian
Somaliland in October 1935. Roosevelt quickly applied an arms embargo, and the
State Department waited to see what the League would do. The League council,
under strong British pressure, condemned Italy as the aggressor; the League assembly then imposed economic sanctions. When the British moved their main fleet to
the Mediterranean, it seemed that a real test of the collective security system might
occur.

Britain and France, however, preferred compromise to conflict. The League's
sanctions against Italy went into effect in November. But the embargo omitted oil
and coal, resources the Italian fleet and war machine needed to function. Actually,
Roosevelt and Hull, given League leadership and cooperation, would have been
prepared to cooperate in strong measures of economic coercion. But Pierre Laval,
the French foreign minister, feared that such action would drive Italy into the arms
of Germany, and he blocked all suggestions for an oil embargo. While the League
debated, Mussolini completed his conquest of Ethiopia in May 1936.

Consultation with Democratic leaders had convinced Hull that Congress was
determined to enact permanent neutrality legislation to supplant the Pittman Resolution, which would expire in February 1936. It also led the secretary to believe that
the Senate would not give Roosevelt discretionary authority to apply the embargo
only against aggressors. Hull attempted to add provisions for a virtual embargo on
the export of essential raw materials and extension of credits to belligerents—a
provision which, in the Ethiopian crisis, would have ended shipments of oil and coal
to Italy. But the Senate Foreign Relations Committee refused even to report Hull's
measure, largely because of isolationist opposition. Instead, Congress extended the
provisions of the Pittman Resolution to May 1937 and added amendments that gave
the president discretionary power in finding that a state of war existed, prohibited
extension of war loans and credits to belligerents, required the president to apply

the neutrality legislation in the event that other nations went to war after hostilities had begun, and exempted from the resolution's provisions any American republic at war with a power outside of the Western Hemisphere.

Mussolini's successful defiance of the League revealed England's and France's fatal timidity and indecision—partly caused by the conviction that they would get no help from the United States in the event of war—and cleared the road for new assaults on the peace by Germany, Italy, and Japan. Indeed, Hitler denounced European security treaties and sent his troops into the demilitarized Rhineland in March 1936 at the height of the Ethiopian crisis. Hitler and Mussolini joined hands eight months later, on October 25, in the so-called Rome–Berlin Axis, which afterward metamorphosed into a political and military alliance between the two dictators. Then the Germans and Italians joined forces with the Japanese in the Anti-Comintern Pact of November 1936.

The Soviet leaders recognized the new coalition as a dire threat to the security of their own regime and appealed to the western democracies for strong collective action to contain fascism. The British and French, however, feared the Communist threat from within as much as the Fascist danger from without. They were obsessed by fear of a general war, which they would have to fight without even a modicum of support from the United States. And they hopefully assumed that satisfaction of legitimate German and Italian complaints would preserve the peace of Europe.

No sooner had the Ethiopian crisis ended than Europe's peace was again threatened by the outbreak of civil war in Spain. The conflict was in the beginning simply a Spanish affair—a revolt of the army, which began under General Francisco Franco, supported by large landholders, the Roman Catholic Church, and the business classes, against a Popular Front government. Soon, however, Spain became an arena in which Spanish, Italian, and German Fascists fought an incompatible coalition of democrats and Communists.

Before the civil war was internationalized, the British, French, German, Italian, Russian, and other European governments adopted a policy of seemingly strict nonintervention to prevent the Spanish cauldron from boiling over into a general war. In September 1936, representatives of the European powers established a Non-Intervention Committee in London to prevent troops or supplies from going to either side. In March 1937, the committee established a naval blockade of Spain.

While the Italians, Germans, and Russians made a laughingstock of the blockade, the Americans joined the British and French in applying a policy of nonintervention. The Neutrality Act of 1936 did not apply to civil wars, but the State Department announced a "moral" embargo against the export of arms and war materials as a means of strengthening the Non-Intervention Committee. Then, when a dealer in secondhand airplanes sought to export some 400 airplane engines to the Loyalist government in December 1936, the administration hastily requested Congress to apply the arms embargo to Spain. A joint resolution granting the president's request passed with only one dissenting vote in both houses in January 1937. It became law two days later with Roosevelt's approval. Even after the true character of the civil war became evident and a large body of opinion favorable to the Loyalists developed in the United States, the administration, fearful of alienating Catholic opinion, blocked all efforts at repeal of the joint resolution. With the open support of Germany and Italy, Franco destroyed the Spanish democracy and secured his dictatorship in 1939.

The overriding American determination to avoid entanglement in European troubles was again demonstrated in the late winter and spring of 1937, when Congress adopted a new and permanent neutrality law to supplant the temporary measure of 1936. Hull knew that he could not prevent the legislation, and so he worked quietly and to a degree successfully to win larger discretion for the executive branch of the government in the enforcement of the new statute. Approved by Congress on April 29 and signed by Roosevelt on May 1, 1937, it authorized the president to determine when a state of war existed or a civil war threatened the peace of the world. If the president should find that such an international or civil war existed, an embargo against the export of arms, ammunition, and credits would go immediately into effect. In addition, a "cash-and-carry" provision, to run for two years, empowered the president to require belligerents who purchased nonmilitary commodities in the United States to pay cash for such goods and to transport them in their own vessels.

It was a bad time for national leaders to have bound their hands. The Japanese army, after absorbing Manchuria and Outer Mongolia in 1932 and 1933, began a campaign to wrench the five northern provinces of China from the control of the Nationalist government at Nanking. At the same time, the Nationalist leader, Chiang Kai-shek, consolidated his administrative power and strengthened his armed forces in preparation for an inevitable showdown. A minor clash between Chinese and Japanese troops at the Marco Polo Bridge near Peking in July 1937 gave the Japanese army an excuse for launching full-scale war. Instead of submitting, however, the Chinese fought back; thus what the Japanese military leaders thought would be a mere incident quickly settled into a long and bloody war.

Hull circulated a note in July in which he implicitly condemned the Japanese and called upon the powers to reaffirm allegiance to the principles of international morality. Next, Roosevelt dispatched 1,200 marines to Shanghai in August to reinforce the 2,200 American soldiers already stationed in China. In order to stir public support for a stronger policy, Hull persuaded Roosevelt to include a plea for international cooperation in an address he was scheduled to deliver in Chicago in early October. But Roosevelt, going far beyond the draft prepared by the State Department, suggested that western democracies might have to cooperate to quarantine aggressors to prevent the spread of international anarchy. Although Roosevelt hoped that the slogan "Quarantine the Aggressors" would catch the public fancy, public reaction was negative.

Indeed, it soon became apparent that public opinion favored noninvolvement at all costs. Press polls revealed a two-to-one congressional majority against cooperation with the League in applying sanctions against Japan. Roosevelt beat a quick retreat from the advanced position of his quarantine address. When the Japanese in December 1937 bombed and sank the United States gunboat *Panay* and three Standard Oil tankers in the Yangtze River near Nanking, the chief reaction in the United States was a loud demand for withdrawal of all American forces in China. Meanwhile, because the British and French were equally unwilling to risk war, collective action by the western powers was impossible.

3. The Outbreak of War in Europe

During 1938 and 1939, events in Europe moved toward war. Unopposed by the British—and encouraged by British Prime Minister Neville Chamberlain's policy of appeasement—Hitler began a series of aggressive moves to expand Germany terri- tory. In 1938, he orchestrated an *Anschluss,* or union, with Austria. He then initiated a campaign for incorporation of the German-speaking Sudeten provinces of Czechoslovakia into Greater Germany.

Meeting with Hitler and Mussolini in Munich in late September 1938, Cham- berlain and the French premier, Edouard Daladier, agreed to outright cession of the Sudetenland. By a stroke of the pen, the western leaders confirmed Hitler's suprem- acy over his generals, who had opposed his recent reckless moves, and made Ger- many absolutely dominant on the Continent. The British and French leaders also weakened the attractiveness of a western alignment for the Soviets and demon- strated their own incompetence as diplomats. All that they received in return was Hitler's unctuous promise that he would make no more territorial demands in Europe, respect Czech sovereignty, and settle all future disputes by peaceful negotia- tion.

The Munich meeting, for Roosevelt, was a turning point. In late 1938 he began a reorientation of his domestic and foreign policies. Abandoning his "purge" of conservative Democrats while calling a halt to further domestic reform, he began to assemble political support for an internationalist foreign policy. Meanwhile, he initiated a new rearmament program. In May 1938, Congress—in response to Japanese denunciation of the Five Power Naval Treaty in December 1934—had authorized the expenditure of some $1 billion for naval construction. Subsequently, Roosevelt endorsed a further military buildup. In October 1938, he announced a $300 million increase in American spending for defense purposes and called upon his military advisers to plan for huge increases in aircraft production. In January 1939, he asked for $1.3 billion for the regular defense establishment and an addi- tional $525 million from Congress, most of it for airplanes.

Congress and public opinion responded favorably, for a military buildup did not necessarily mean involvement in a foreign war. At the same time, the Munich tragedy had opened the eyes of millions of Americans to the German threat, while violent anti-Jewish pogroms in Germany in November 1938 revealed the brutish character of the Nazi regime. Thus, Congress increased the military and naval budgets by nearly two thirds and authorized Roosevelt to begin accumulating stock- piles of strategic raw materials for use if war occurred.

Roosevelt also began shoring up the hemispheric defense system. At the Pan- American Conference that opened at Lima, Peru, in December 1938, Hull won Latin American support for hemispheric solidarity. Despite the opposition of Argen- tina, Hull marshaled a nearly solid Latin American opinion, conducted patient negotiations with the president and foreign minister of Argentina, and secured unanimous approval of the Declaration of Lima on Christmas Eve 1938. It reaffirmed the twenty-one American republics' determination to resist jointly any Fascist or Nazi threat to the peace and security of the hemisphere.

Roosevelt also sought to expand his foreign-policy options by seeking repeal or major changes in the Neutrality Act of 1937. When Hitler violated the Munich accord and invaded Czechoslovakia in March 1939, it had a pronounced effect upon western democracies. In Great Britain, Chamberlain was forced to abandon appeasement, and the prime minister began negotiations for treaties guaranteeing the independence and territorial integrity of countries believed to be next in Germany's line of march—Poland, Rumania, Greece, and Turkey. In Congress, Senator Pittman, with administration support, introduced a measure in March 1939 that extended the cash-and-carry provision but amended it to include arms, ammunition, and other war materials. Although Roosevelt ventured all of his prestige in the fight to obtain either passage of the Pittman bill or outright repeal of the arms embargo, both houses of Congress decisively refused during July 1939 to approve revision.

Meanwhile, Europe moved steadily toward war. The signing of the Nazi–Soviet Nonaggression Pact—whose secret provisions provided for a German and Soviet division of eastern Europe—protected Hitler against the danger of a two-front war and encouraged him to increase his demands on Poland. Chamberlain warned that Britain would go at once to Poland's aid if Germany attacked but offered to discuss the Polish question, and Roosevelt added a new appeal for peace. Hitler responded by sending his armies into Poland on September 1; two days later, Britain and France declared war on the Third Reich.

In response, Roosevelt issued an official proclamation of neutrality on September 5, 1939, and put the Neutrality Act into force. The administration also strengthened the defenses of the Western Hemisphere by arranging for a conference of the foreign ministers of the American republics, who met at Panama City in September and agreed with surprising unanimity upon common neutrality regulations and mutual consultation in the event that a transfer of territory from one European power to another threatened the security of the new world. The conference also adopted the Declaration of Panama, marking out a broad zone 300 miles wide around the Americas, excluding Canada and European colonies, into which the belligerents were forbidden to carry the war. It was, actually, only a verbal prohibition and had no practical effect.

At home, Roosevelt's primary objective was still repeal of the arms embargo provision of the Neutrality Act. Calling Congress into special session to plead earnestly for repeal on September 21, he stressed the need for neutrality by urging the prohibition of American ships from entering European war zones and the application of the cash-and-carry principle to all European purchases in the United States. Although modest and thoroughly neutral, Roosevelt's request met frenzied isolationist and pacifistic opposition. On the other side, in support of Roosevelt, was ranged a powerful new combination of southern and eastern Democrats in Congress, joined nationally by such preparationist Republicans as Stimson and Frank Knox, a vast majority of the business interests and the metropolitan press, and a large segment of the intellectual leadership of the country. It was evident by the middle of October that the tide had turned in the president's favor. When Senator Pittman introduced a new neutrality bill in September 1939 which lifted the arms embargo, applied the cash-and-carry principle, and forbade American ships to trade with belligerent countries and Americans to travel on belligerent ships, Congress approved it.

Roosevelt's policy of cash-and-carry represented an attempt to combine noninvolvement with stronger support for western democracies. In the period between the invasion of Poland and the spring of 1940—when peace on the western front prompted characterizations of a "phony war"—Roosevelt's new policy appeared to be sufficient to forestall a German victory. But all this changed on April 9, 1940, when Hitler hurled his armies in a *Blitzkrieg* (lightning war) into Denmark and Norway, and German airplanes and *panzer* (armored) divisions struck at Belgium, Holland, and northern France on May 10. Dismay swept over the American people. All Americans except a few diehard isolationists recognized that a Germany dominant in Europe would pose a dire threat to their peace and security. And now it was about to happen, the catastrophe that only a week before had seemed impossible. There was France, her demoralized armies reeling and scattering under the impact of Nazi power. There was the British expeditionary force, driven to the sea at Dunkirk and forced to undertake a nearly impossible evacuation.

The impending German conquest of Europe prompted Roosevelt to take further steps toward involvement. In April 1940, he declared that Greenland, a possession of conquered Denmark, would enjoy the protection of the Monroe Doctrine, and he furnished military supplies to and established a coastal patrol of Greenland. In May, when the British occupied Iceland, another Danish possession, Roosevelt was obviously pleased. That same month, Roosevelt requested substantial increases in military preparedness. He called for production of 50,000 aircraft a year, requested from Congress an additional $1 billion in defense expenditures, and asked for authority to call the National Guard and reserves into active service.

Meanwhile, Roosevelt had also been trying to bolster French morale and to dissuade Mussolini from joining Hitler. Mussolini was deaf to such appeals and joined the Germans by declaring war on France and Great Britain in June. This act gave Roosevelt an opportunity to express, in clear and ringing words, American policy on the European war. In an address at the University of Virginia on the same day that Italy entered the war, Roosevelt announced the end of American isolation and the beginning of a new phase of nonbelligerency. Hereafter the United States would "extend to the opponents of force the material resources of this nation."

By mid-June 1940, Roosevelt confronted a critical situation. The French, headed by a government led by the aged Marshal Henri-Philippe Pétain, surrendered to the Germans on June 22. The British prime minister, Winston Spencer Churchill, who came to power in May, had warned in repeated messages that the British Isles might be overrun unless immediate American assistance was forthcoming, and that a successor government might have to surrender the great British fleet in order to save the realm. Should the Roosevelt administration assume that the British were lost, abandon its aid to them, and prepare to defend the Western Hemisphere? Or should it strip American defenses in the hope that the British could still be saved?

Although it was clearly a high-risk policy, Roosevelt decided to gamble on Britain. In this decision he had the support of his new secretaries of war and of the navy, Henry L. Stimson and Frank Knox, whom he had appointed in June to gain Republican support for the defense effort. Roosevelt ordered the War and Navy departments to "scrape the bottom of the barrel" and turn over all available guns and ammunition to private firms for resale to Britain. In addition, officials of the War, Navy, and Treasury departments conferred with a British Purchasing Mission and promised to deliver 14,375 aircraft by April 1942. Roosevelt's decision to gamble on British survival was the most momentous of his career to this time, for he acted in the certain knowledge that war with Germany was probable if Great Britain should go down.

4. Domestic Debate and the Election of 1940

The fall of France and the seeming imminence of British defeat shocked the American people and stimulated much wild talk of an immediate German invasion of the Western Hemisphere. More significant was the way that the threat of German victory intensified a debate over American foreign policy that had been in progress since the Munich crisis. Soon after the invasion of Poland, a small but influential group who favored an anti-German policy formed the Non-Partisan Committee for Peace through Revision of the Neutrality Law, with William Allen White of Kansas as chairman. With branches in thirty states by October 1939, it was decisive in swinging public opinion behind repeal of the arms embargo provision. Quietly disbanding during the so-called phony war, the committee reorganized in May 1940 as the Committee to Defend America by Aiding the Allies. The committee had over 600 local branches within a few months and had taken leadership in a nationwide campaign to combat isolationism and stimulate public support for the government's policy of all-out aid short of war. The committee's success was reflected in a transformation of public opinion, which now favored, according to polls taken during July and August 1940, some form of aid to Britain.

Meanwhile, although isolationist ranks were considerably thinner, they were still a powerful if incongruous group by the autumn of 1940. They included pro-Nazi spokesmen like Father Coughlin, Gerald L. K. Smith, and William Dudley Pelley. A large body of midwestern businessmen joined their ranks mainly out of hatred for the New Deal. Old progressives like Senators Burton K. Wheeler and Gerald P. Nye still identified cooperation with England with the machinations of Wall Street. Many Protestant ministers and idealists had embraced a philosophy of nonresistance. The Hearst papers, the *Chicago Tribune,* the *New York Daily News,* the *Washington Times-Herald*, and other newspapers, lent editorial support to isolationist currents. Cooperating also were the Socialists, led by Norman Thomas, who still thought of war in economic terms, and the Communists, who had become suddenly indifferent about the Nazis after the signing of the Nazi–Soviet Nonaggression Pact.

The leading isolationist organization was the America First Committee, incorporated in September 1940 with Robert Wood, chairman of the board of Sears, Roebuck and Company, as national chairman. The America First movement soon included thousands of patriotic Americans who sincerely believed that defense of the Western Hemisphere and nonintervention in Europe's war were the only course of safety for the United States. But the American First Committee also had the support of all pro-Nazi groups in the country.

The debate between proponents of strong support for Great Britain and the noninterventionists did not end until Japanese bombs fell on Pearl Harbor, but it was evident that the former had won the battle for public opinion long before then. The polls showed the metamorphosis that occurred. In September 1939, some 82 percent of persons queried thought that the Allies would win; by July 1940, only 43 percent were sure that Great Britain would win. More important, the proportion of Americans who believed that a German victory would menace their security increased from 43 percent in March 1940 to 69 percent in July 1940. All through the period 1939–1941, an overwhelming majority of Americans indicated a desire to avoid active participation in the war. The important fact was that this same majority approved strong assistance to Great Britain. And by the spring of 1941, a majority favored extending such aid even if it led to hostilities with Germany.

Roosevelt, administration leaders, and the Committee to Defend America played a significant role in this erosion of isolationist sentiments, but events in Europe and the Far East from 1939 to 1941 played an even more important part. The American people, not wanting to defend obsolete neutral rights or to engage in a second crusade for democracy, supported the administration in a strong policy and accepted the risk of war.

The international crisis of 1940 had an impact no less significant on the presidential campaign of 1940. Early in the year, it seemed certain that a noninterventionist candidate—Senator Robert A. Taft of Ohio, Senator Arthur H. Vandenberg of Michigan, or young Thomas E. Dewey of New York—would become the Republican nominee. Almost at the last minute, however, Wendell L. Willkie of Indiana, utility magnate and advocate of aid to the British, entered the campaign. Meeting

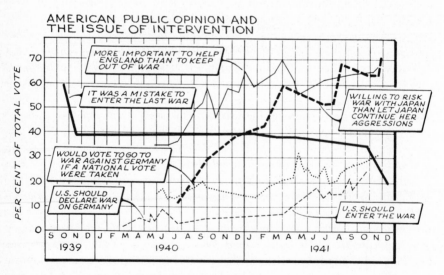

Reproduced by permission of Professor Hadley Cantril and the Public Opinion Research Project of Princeton University.

amidst the panic created by the French surrender in June 1940, the Republican convention nominated Willkie and endorsed a platform favoring "prompt" and "realistic" aid to victims of aggression.

By refusing to support another candidate and by failing to discourage efforts on his own behalf, Roosevelt probably revealed his intention to run for a third term. On July 16, 1940, he sent a message to the Democratic National Convention announcing that he had no desire to remain in office but also leaving the door open for his renomination. Although few of the party bosses wanted Roosevelt, because of his popularity there was nothing they could do except nominate him on the first ballot. The delegates, however, rebelled when the president insisted on Secretary of Agriculture Henry A. Wallace as his running mate. Roosevelt's spokesman, Harry Hopkins, was able to force the Iowan upon an unwilling party only by using the most ruthless methods.

Roosevelt delivered his acceptance speech by radio to the convention early in the morning of July 19 and then did not make another campaign address until September 11. In the meantime he concentrated on the international crisis. At Roosevelt's initiative, Congress approved larger military appropriations as well as the Burke–Wadsworth bill for selective service. In July, Roosevelt and Hull organized a conference of Pan-American foreign ministers to meet at Havana. They unanimously declared that an attack on any American republic was an attack against all of them. The most urgent necessity confronting the administration during this summer of campaign and crisis, however, was devising some legally acceptable means of transferring forty or fifty destroyers to Britain for antisubmarine operations and assistance in defense of the British Isles against the invasion that Hitler planned for mid-September.

Roosevelt found a solution through an agreement signed in Washington in September 1940. The United States gave fifty destroyers to the British government in return for a formal pledge that Great Britain would never surrender its fleet. In addition, the British government gave to the United States ninety-nine-year leases on air and naval bases on British territory in Newfoundland, Bermuda, and the Caribbean. The enhancement of hemispheric security met American statutory requirements, but Churchill insisted upon outright gift of the leases for American bases in Newfoundland and Bermuda. The destroyer-bases agreement meant an important step toward the end of formal neutrality and marked the beginning of a period of limited American participation in the war.

While Roosevelt was thus engaged, Wendell Willkie had undertaken a one-man campaign against a silent opponent. But Willkie was fatally handicapped by his own basic agreement with most of Roosevelt's domestic and foreign policies. By early October, Willkie realized that he might be defeated. In desperation, he jettisoned his progressive, internationalist advisers and began emphasizing the danger of war. As the war issue began to invigorate Willkie's campaign, Roosevelt was forced to respond. At Philadelphia in late October, he assured Americans that no secret agreement would drag the United States into war. But, at New York several days later, he warned that Americans could keep war from their shores only by stopping aggression in Europe. When the New York speech neither reversed the rising Willkie tide nor allayed the fears of Democratic politicians, Roosevelt spoke even more directly in a speech in Boston on October 30. "I have said this before, but I shall say it again and again and again," he declared in a passage he added at the last minute. "Your boys are not going to be sent into any foreign wars. . . . The purpose of our defense is defense."

It was evident by the late evening of election day, November 5, that Roosevelt had won again, although the margin of his victory was considerably smaller than it had been in 1936. He received 27.2 million popular and 449 electoral votes as compared with 22.3 million popular and 82 electoral votes for Willkie. In addition, the Democrats retained large majorities in both houses of Congress. The Socialist and Communist candidates, Norman Thomas and Earl Browder, received 100,264 and 48,579 popular votes, respectively.

5. The United States and the European War, 1940–1941

By the autumn of 1940, because of the near exhaustion of British cash reserves, the danger existed that the flow of American supplies would be cut off. Out of their total dollar resources of $6.5 billion at the beginning of the war, the British had spent $4.5 billion in the United States by November 1940. By that time they were ready to place new orders for American airplanes, armored equipment for ten divisions, and cargo ships. But the Neutrality Act of 1939 required cash payment for all supplies, and the British were nearing the end of their ability to pay. Roosevelt and Treasury officials well knew that the entire system of American aid would soon collapse unless some solution was quickly found.

In December, responding to an urgent appeal from Churchill, Roosevelt unveiled a new plan. In a fireside chat on December 29, he declared that Great Britain and the Royal Navy stood between the Western Hemisphere and German aggression and that the United States had to become "the great arsenal of democracy." In January 1941, elaborating further, he asked Congress for authority to provide military supplies "to those nations which are now in actual war with aggressor nations." These supplies, he went on, would be paid for, not in dollars, but in goods and services at the end of the war. Called the Lend-Lease bill, Roosevelt's measure was introduced in Congress in early January. The House approved the Lend-Lease bill a month later, the Senate, in March. Roosevelt signed it on March 11, 1941, and promptly asked Congress for $7 billion for lend-lease production and export. Congress complied two weeks later.

Adoption of the Lend-Lease Act converted the United States from a friendly neutral, which sometimes helped more than the rules of traditional neutrality permitted, into a full-fledged nonbelligerent, committed to pour out all its resources if need be to enable Great Britain to bring Germany to its knees. If there had ever been any doubts before that the American people would falter or reject the risk of war, those doubts were now resolved. Having committed itself to underwriting a British victory, the Washington government was not willing to watch Nazi submarines prevent the delivery of goods vital to German defeat. German depredations on British and neutral shipping from the beginning of the *Blitzkrieg* to the end of

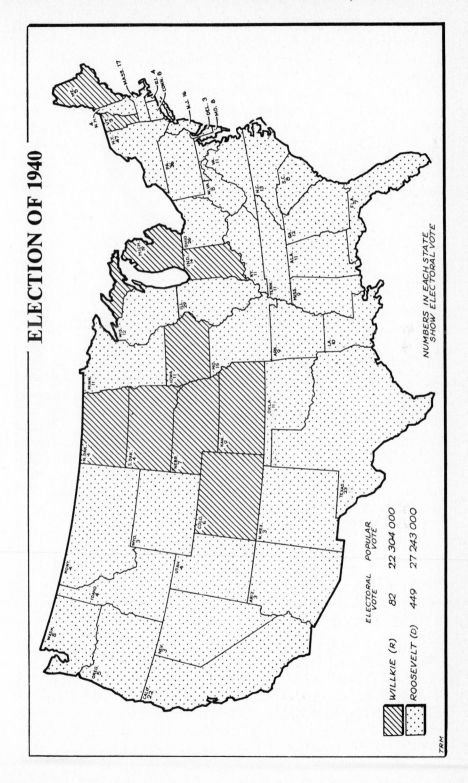

ELECTION OF 1940

NUMBERS IN EACH STATE
SHOW ELECTORAL VOTE

	ELECTORAL VOTE	POPULAR VOTE
WILLKIE (R)	82	22 304 000
ROOSEVELT (D)	449	27 243 000

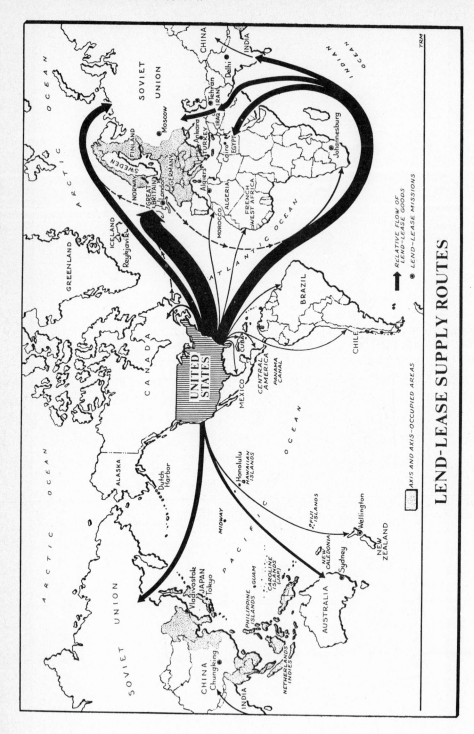

LEND-LEASE SUPPLY ROUTES

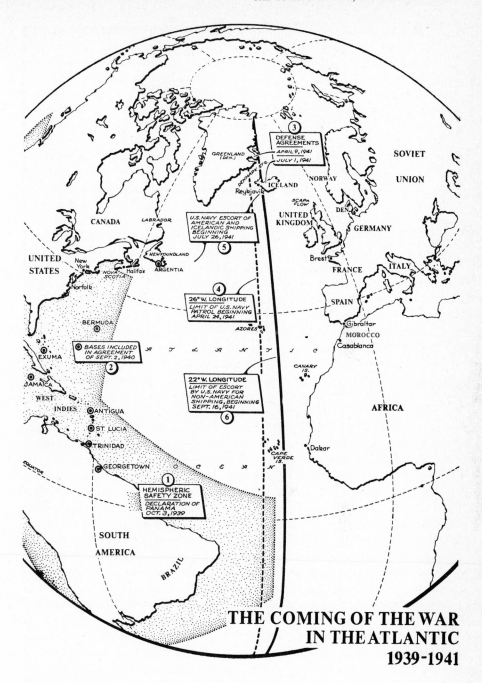

THE COMING OF THE WAR
IN THE ATLANTIC
1939-1941

1940 had been staggering enough, but the spring of 1941 witnessed an even more powerful German attack. The Nazis extended their war zone on March 25 to include Iceland and Denmark Strait between Greenland and Iceland and sent dozens of new submarines into the North Atlantic to hunt their prey in "wolf packs." They also used surface vessels in daring raids and threw a large part of their air force into the battle to choke off the stream of supplies flowing from American to British ports.

Roosevelt responded by steadily escalating American participation in the Battle of the Atlantic. In the spring of 1941, he authorized American naval yards to repair British vessels, transferred ten Coast Guard cutters to the British fleet to help in antisubmarine operations, and seized thirty Axis and thirty-five Danish merchant ships in American ports. In April, stopping short of providing naval convoys for merchantmen, Roosevelt extended the American Neutrality Patrol far out into the Atlantic—to longitude twenty-five degrees west, a line between Brazil and the west coast of Africa in the south and slightly west of Iceland in the north. American naval vessels would search out, but not attack, Nazi submarines, and they would warn British vessels of the presence of U-boats within the area between the American coast and longitude twenty-five degrees west. In addition, Roosevelt issued a proclamation on April 10 removing the area of the Red Sea from the list of war zones forbidden to American ships.

Isolationists in Congress were meanwhile pressing the charge that Roosevelt had begun an undeclared naval war by ordering American vessels in the patrol area to convoy British ships and attack Nazi U-boats. A German submarine torpedoed an American freighter, *Robin Moor,* in the South Atlantic, on May 21. Roosevelt, in a fireside chat six days later, told Americans what their navy was doing: he said that German control of the Atlantic would imperil American security, and he revealed that the Nazis were sinking ships twice as fast as British and American shipyards could replace them. The hope of victory, he continued, lay in increasing shipbuilding and in helping to reduce losses at sea. To accomplish the latter objective, he explained, "Our patrols are helping now to insure delivery of the needed supplies to Britain." He ended by warning that "all additional measures necessary to deliver the goods" would be taken, by calling upon industry and labor to redouble their efforts, and by declaring an unlimited state of national emergency.

The European war took a dramatic turn in late June 1941, when Hitler launched an attack on the Soviet Union. Roosevelt used the breathing space afforded by the German attack to strengthen home defenses and the American position in the North Atlantic. The most urgent defense necessity in the early summer of 1941 was extension of the terms of service of the 900,000 men drafted in the preceding autumn. The defense effort would have practically collapsed if the men had been allowed to go home at the end of their one-year terms. The president, therefore, permitted General George C. Marshall, army chief of staff, to ask Congress in July to extend the term of service and also to remove the provisions of the Selective Service Act of 1940 that prohibited sending draftees outside the Western Hemisphere. The Senate extended the term of service by six months in August 1941. On the other hand, the struggle in the House of Representatives was bitter and long in doubt until that body approved extension by a vote of 203 to 202.

While this controversy was in its first stage, Roosevelt moved decisively to strengthen American control of the North Atlantic sea lanes. Negotiations between Roosevelt, Churchill, and the prime minister of Iceland culminated in the occupation of Iceland by American marines in July 1941 and then the inauguration of United States naval escorts for convoys of American and Icelandic ships between America's Atlantic Coast and Iceland later that month. Thus at one stroke the character of American operations in the North Atlantic changed drastically. Henceforward the navy would not merely patrol the area between Iceland and the United States but would destroy "hostile forces" that threatened American and Icelandic shipping in that broad expanse of water.

At the same time, Roosevelt shored up the British and Soviets. In August 1941, Harry Hopkins flew to Moscow, where he learned from Stalin that the Kremlin would welcome lend-lease aid. Hopkins had earlier visited London to arrange a secret meeting between Roosevelt and Churchill, which took place when the British battleship, *Prince of Wales,* made its rendezvous with the American cruiser, *Augusta,* off Argentia, Newfoundland, on August 9. Although the British tried to obtain some commitment of American support if Japan attacked British possessions in the Far East, Roosevelt and his advisers refused to make any promises of a military or naval character. The most important work of the Argentia meeting was the approval, after some stiff argument about Great Britain's imperial policy, on August 12 of the joint declaration known as the Atlantic Charter. It was the product of careful thought and patient negotiation and recorded Anglo–American agreement as to "certain common principles" on which the two governments based "their hopes for a better future for the world." These principles were: no territorial aggrandizement, no territorial changes that did not accord with the wishes of the people involved, the right of all peoples to choose their own form of government, economic collaboration in the postwar world, and the right of all peoples to live in peace and in freedom from fear, want, and aggression.

News of the Argentia conference and the text of the Atlantic Charter were published in the press on August 15 and provoked isolationist editors and politicians to new outbursts. But the overwhelming majority of Americans believed Roosevelt's assurances that he had made no commitment to intervene actively and approved the Wilsonian aspirations embodied in the Atlantic Charter. Soon after his return from Argentia, moreover, Roosevelt set about to provide greater assistance to Russia. Although uncertain of public and congressional reaction, Roosevelt began discussions that led to an Anglo–American–Soviet conference in Moscow in late September 1941 and an Anglo–American promise to furnish $1 billion worth of aid to Russia before June 30, 1942. When Congress, while voting a new $6 billion appropriation for lend-lease production and export in October, rejected an amendment forbidding extension of aid to Russia, Roosevelt declared the Soviet Union eligible for lend-lease assistance. More significant for the immediate future, however, was Roosevelt's decision further to relieve the British position in the North Atlantic. The president decided at Argentia to allow British and allied vessels to join American convoys between the United States and Iceland. This was done unofficially before the end of August, although orders to this effect were not issued until mid-September.

While Roosevelt pondered the best way to break the news of this new policy, a German submarine attacked the destroyer *Greer* south of Iceland on September 4, after the *Greer* had joined a British airplane in trailing the U-boat. The incident gave Roosevelt the "provocation" he needed to justify a change of policy. In a radio address on September 11, he declared in seeming seriousness that the attack on the *Greer* was part of a Nazi plan to control the Atlantic, in preparation for an assault upon the Western Hemisphere. The time for active defense had come, he added; hereafter, American ships and planes would protect all ships within the area between the United States and Iceland. Moreover, he continued, he had ordered the army and navy to fire upon sight at all German and Italian war vessels in the American patrol area.

The president's speech, in effect, began an undeclared naval war against Germany—the perhaps inevitable outcome of adoption of the Lend-Lease Act and the American decision to get supplies to Great Britain. Not only did a large majority of Congress and the public approve this forward step; the majority also approved when Roosevelt finally asked Congress in October 1941 to revise the Neutrality Act of 1939. He requested permission to arm American merchantmen and indirectly suggested that Congress should permit American ships to enter war zones and belligerent ports. While debate on these proposals proceeded, a German submarine torpedoed the destroyer *Kearny* on the night of October 16–17, with the loss of eleven lives. In November, the Senate and the House voted to allow merchantmen to arm and to pass through the war zone to British ports. Meanwhile, the undeclared naval war in the North Atlantic proceeded. A submarine sank the destroyer *Reuben James* with the loss of 115 lives on October 31, but there was no such general agitation for war as had followed German attacks on American ships in early 1917.

6. Toward Pearl Harbor

During 1938 and 1939, relations between the United States and Japan remained in a state of suspended hostility. During this period Japanese military leaders pressed for an alliance with Germany to offset Soviet and American power. The Japanese army was also undertaking extensive military operations against Russian forces along the Manchurian border. The Nazi–Soviet Pact in August 1939 momentarily ended the Japanese army's hopes for an alliance with the Nazis; meanwhile, however, Japan undertook a diplomatic campaign to force the British to recognize Japanese conquests in China. The Chamberlain government surrendered to these demands in July 1939 by recognizing that the Japanese army was supreme in the areas it occupied.

The announcement of this agreement galvanized Washington's determination to establish a stronger far eastern presence. In late July, Roosevelt gave notice of the possible abrogation of the Japanese–American Commercial Treaty of 1911; after January 26, 1940, the United States might therefore deny Japan access to the source from which it obtained more than half the raw materials, especially iron, steel, and oil, for its war machine. The threat of full-scale war with Russia and economic retaliation by the United States restrained the extreme militarists in Japan and prevented the imperial government from embarking upon new conquests following the outbreak of war in Europe. Instead, the Japanese ended the border conflict with Soviet forces in September and then launched a strenuous effort to end the war in China. Moreover, the Japanese opened negotiations with the State Department in December 1939 to prevent imposition of the threatened American embargo. These talks ended in a stalemate because neither government would retreat on the basic issue of China.

By 1940, American public opinion was moving strongly toward the application of an embargo. Even so, the State Department's policy of merely threatening economic retaliation might well have succeeded had not Germany's triumph in western Europe convinced the Japanese military leaders that the power of Great Britain, France, and the Netherlands was gone, and that henceforth they would have to deal only with the United States. In July 1940, a new government came to power headed by Prince Fumimaro Konoye, with the boastful Yosuke Matsuoka as foreign minister and the ardent expansionist, General Hideki Tojo, as minister of war. This new government, as a first step toward achieving a "new order in Greater East Asia," demanded and, after some negotiation, obtained from the Vichy government the right to build airfields and station troops in northern Indochina. At the same time, the Tokyo government began negotiating an alliance with Germany following the arrival of a new German ambassador in September. A Tripartite Agreement, or Triple Alliance, between Germany, Italy, and Japan, was formally sealed in Berlin on September 27, 1940.

Washington moved cautiously, hoping to avoid provoking a Japanese thrust into the South Pacific. It imposed an embargo on the export of aviation gasoline, lubricants, and prime scrap metal to Japan in late July 1940. Then, after the Japanese occupied northern Indochina, the American government announced extension of a new $25 million loan to China in late September. It also decreed an embargo on the export of all types of scrap iron and steel to Japan. Following this action came a virtual embargo in December on the export of iron ore and pig iron, certain chemicals, certain machine tools, and other products. Churchill, in October 1940, was encouraged to reopen the Burma Road, the chief supply route between Nationalist China and the outside world. The Japanese protested, but Washington's firm stand and rumors of Anglo–American naval cooperation in the Pacific caused the Konoye government to beat a momentary diplomatic retreat.

The United States, by a policy of implicit threats, had, therefore, prevented further Japanese military adventurism. There was still the danger that the Soviet Union would strike in the North if Japan turned southward. And there was still the faint hope in Tokyo that somehow the United States might be frightened into acquiescing in Japanese plans. In order to safeguard Japan's long, exposed northern flank, Matsuoka made a pilgrimage to Berlin, Rome, and Moscow in March and April 1941. Hitler urged that Japan strike immediately at Singapore. Foreign Minister Joachim von Ribbentrop, intimating that a German–Russian conflict was no longer inconceivable, promised that Germany would attack Russia if the Soviets attacked Japan after it was involved in war with Great Britain and America. Matsuoka was pleased but not entirely satisfied by these assurances. His supreme objective—a pledge of Soviet neutrality—he obtained in Moscow on April 13, in a pact by which Japan and Russia promised to remain neutral if either power was attacked by one or more countries.

Japan, meanwhile, began secret discussions with Washington during late 1940 and early 1941. These negotiations continued off and on until mid-July 1941, when the Japanese demanded that the Vichy French government relinquish military control over southern Indochina. Washington reacted swiftly. The United States, Hull told the Japanese ambassador, Admiral Kichisaburo Nomura, could only conclude that the occupation of southern Indochina was the prelude to further Japanese conquests and could see no point in further discussions. On the following day, after Vichy had surrendered to the Japanese demand, Roosevelt received the Japanese ambassador, hinted that he was contemplating an embargo on the export of oil to Japan, and warned that a Japanese attack on the Dutch East Indies would result in serious consequences. If Japan would withdraw from Indochina, Roosevelt continued, he would support its neutralization and help Japan to find access to raw materials.

But Roosevelt was finished with parleying. He impounded all Japanese funds in the United States, closed the Panama Canal to Japanese shipping, and called the Philippine militia into active service on July 26. On August 1, he forbade the export to Japan of a number of vital materials, including oil that could be refined into aviation gasoline, while the British and Dutch governments applied similar sanctions. This decisive step put Tokyo in the dilemma of having to choose between a modified retreat or a desperate war with the United States. Although some extremists welcomed the prospect of war, the naval leaders were reluctant to risk hostilities and warned that the empire would probably be defeated in a protracted conflict. The cabinet, therefore, maneuvered to find a solution that would include both Japanese occupation of southern Indochina and peace with the United States. Further negotiations, through messages between Konoye and Roosevelt, then followed during August and September. Urging a personal meeting between Konoye and Roosevelt, the Japanese offered to withdraw from southern Indochina once the China Incident ended, to pledge no further territorial expansion, and to ignore any obligation to go to war under the terms of the Tripartite Agreement if the United States became involved in a defensive war with Germany.

Based on these terms, Roosevelt was ready to give immediate consent to the proposal for a meeting with Konoye. But Hull urged caution and insisted that the two governments agree upon the fundamental issue of China before the chiefs of state met. Despite warnings from Tokyo that only some bold stroke could restrain the war party, Roosevelt accepted the State Department's view that Japan would not attack and that a policy of continued firmness would force the imperial government to surrender. Thus Roosevelt replied in early September that he would be glad to confer with Konoye, but that basic differences, particularly on China, would have to be cleared up first.

Roosevelt's reply in the circumstances spelled the doom not only of the projected conference, but of peace as well. Whether the momentous decision was wise or foolish will be long debated by historians. Defenders of the administration have argued that agreement on important issues was impossible, and that in any event Konoye could not have forced the army to make the concessions necessary to preserve the peace. On the other hand, Roosevelt's critics have maintained that the administration rejected Konoye's invitation in order to goad Japan into attacking the United States. At least on the point of the administration's intentions, the records are full and revealing. They indicate that the president and the State Department, far from desiring war, were convinced that the Japanese could not undertake hostilities and would retreat in the face of a firm American policy.

In view of the primacy of the Nazi danger and the likelihood that the United States would soon be drawn into the European war, American policy in the Far East should perhaps have been directed at one objective only—maintenance of peace with Japan on any terms short of further Japanese aggression, this time, perhaps, in the southwestern Pacific. Such a policy might have necessitated unfreezing Japanese assets, lifting the embargo on export of oil and metals, and easing the pressure on Japan to withdraw immediately from China. There is considerable evidence that such concessions by the United States at this time—that is, early September 1941—would have enormously strengthened the Japanese moderates and might have sufficed to preserve the status quo and gain precious time.

Roosevelt and Hull were influenced by Sinophiles in the State Department to believe that Japan would not fight, and that it would not matter much if it did. Instead of making any concessions, they continued to press demands for immediate Japanese withdrawal from China—demands that were impossible in the circumstances. The time might have eventually come when the United States and Great Britain could have forced a showdown on China without having to go to war. But that time would have been after the defeat of Germany, when the two democracies were invincible, not in in the late summer of 1941, when they were weak, and when wisdom demanded a policy of delay.

7. Pearl Harbor

Analysis of events during the autumn of 1941 supports the thesis that American policy strengthened the extremists and perhaps tipped the balance in Tokyo in favor of the war party. By mid-October, Konoye, unsuccessful in his attempt to reach an accommodation with the United States, resigned and was replaced by General Tojo. The fall of the Konoye government only intensified the conflict in Tokyo between the army and the antiwar group. Both sides compromised by agreeing to further negotiation, with the proviso that preparations for an immediate attack take place if talks yielded no results by November 25.

As a consequence, negotiations proceeded anew in Washington between November 7 and December 7. The repetitious details need not be given here. It suffices to say that neither government retreated from its position on the key issue of China, and that the American leaders continued the discussions mainly in the hope of deferring the conflict that they now thought was practically inevitable. When negotiations foundered, Japanese leaders, in an imperial conference on December 1, concluded that there was no recourse but war. To responsible Japanese leaders, an uncertain war, which they really did not expect to win, seemed the only way to avoid slow economic strangulation or humiliating surrender that would spell Japan's end as a great power.

Meanwhile, Japanese preparations for probable conflict had been proceeding on the assumption that one must be prepared to fight if diplomacy fails. A carrier task force left the Kuriles on November 25 to attack the great American naval base at Pearl Harbor in Hawaii, while large army forces were poised in southern Indochina to strike at Malaya. The Washington leaders knew from intercepted messages only that the Japanese would attack somewhere soon. They recognized that an assault on the Philippines and Guam was possible, but they concluded that Tokyo would avoid such direct provocation to the United States. When news of the movement of large Japanese forces against Malaya reached Washington on December 6, Roosevelt dispatched an urgent personal appeal to Emperor Hirohito, warning that the present tension could not last much longer and urging him to take some action to dispel the threat of war.

American military and naval commanders in the Pacific had been duly but not strenuously warned that surprise attacks were likely. Like their superiors in Washington, they expected the Japanese to strike at Malaya, not at them. The commanders in Hawaii, Admiral Husband E. Kimmel and General Walter C. Short, were not overly concerned as what Roosevelt would call the "day of infamy" approached. Kimmel had concentrated virtually his entire fleet in Pearl Harbor; fearing sabotage, Short had disposed his airplanes and antiaircraft guns in such a manner as to make successful defense impossible. Neither commander had established an effective air patrol. Thus the carrier task force under Admiral Chuchi Nagumo approached Hawaii from the northwest undetected.

The first wave of Japanese airplanes attacked airfields at 7:55 A.M. on December 7, 1941, and then struck the fleet anchored in the harbor. A second wave followed at 8:50. The navy and Marine Corps were unable to get a single plane off the ground. An army fighter squadron at Haleiwa, which the Japanese overlooked, got a few planes into the air and destroyed several of the attackers. A few antiaircraft batteries were operating by the time of the second major assault. And several naval craft were able to get into action and attack Japanese submarines. Otherwise, the Japanese were unopposed and strafed and bombed at will. When the last planes turned toward their carriers at about 9:45, the great American bastion in the Pacific was a smoking shambles. Practically every airplane on the island of Oahu was either destroyed or disabled. All eight battleships in Pearl Harbor were put out of action—two of them, *Oklahoma* and *Arizona,* were destroyed or sunk. Three cruisers and three destroyers were heavily damaged or destroyed. And 2,323 men of both services were dead. The cost to the Japanese was twenty-nine airplanes, five midget submarines, and one fleet submarine.

First reports of the attack came to Washington at about two in the afternoon, while later news told of other Japanese attacks on the Philippines, Hong Kong, Wake Island, Midway Island, Siam, and Malaya, and of a Japanese declaration of war against the United States and Great Britain. After cabinet meetings in the afternoon and evening, Roosevelt called congressional leaders to the White House and reviewed the dispatches he had received. He appeared before the two houses in joint session the following day, December 8, excoriated the "unprovoked and dastardly attack by Japan," and asked Congress to recognize the obvious state of war that existed. It was done within an hour and with only one dissenting vote in the House of Representatives. Roosevelt had deliberately avoided mention of Germany and Italy in his war message, in order to leave the decision for full-fledged war for the time being to Hitler. The Pearl Harbor attack delighted Hitler, and he complied with the Japanese request for a German declaration of war against the United States on December 11. Mussolini followed suit at once. The president and Congress reciprocated during the afternoon of the same day.

Shock and indignation surged through Americans as they heard the news of the Japanese attack over their radios on the afternoon of December 7. They did not realize that their armed forces had suffered the most humiliating defeat in American history by a foreign foe; nor did they understand the desperate circumstances that impelled the Japanese to undertake a suicidal war. The American people only thought that they had been treacherously attacked. And in their anger they forgot all the partisan quarrels and debates over foreign policy that had so long divided them and resolved with firm determination to win the war that the Japanese had begun.

Chapter 18

-»>» «««-

The Second World War:
The American Home Front

Not since the dark days of the Revolution had the American people confronted so dire a military menace or so staggering a task as during the Second World War. Within a few months after Japanese bombs fell on Pearl Harbor, the ensign of the Rising Sun floated triumphantly over all the outposts and bastions of the far Pacific region, while Hitler and his armies stood poised to strike at the Middle East and join forces with the Japanese in India.

It was perhaps fortunate that the American people in December 1941 little knew how long the war would last and what the costs would be. However, they had certain advantages that made victory possible: courageous allies, unity unprecedented in American history, enormous resources and industrial capacity, superb political and military leadership, and, most important, determination to win. These factors combined from 1941 to 1945 to achieve miracles of production that made earlier American war efforts look small by comparison.

The astonishing thing, however, was the fact that Americans could engage in total war without submitting to the discipline of total war at home. To be sure, the war intensified certain social tensions and created new problems of adjustment; but most Americans took the war in stride, without emotional excitement or hysteria.

1. Manpower for War

The adoption of the war resolutions found the United States in the midst of a sizable rearmament campaign, the momentum of which was daily increasing. Congress quickly ordered the registration of all men between the ages of twenty (lowered to eighteen in 1942) and forty-four for war service and of men between forty-five and sixty-five for potential labor service. All told, draft boards registered some 31 million men, of whom 9.9 million were inducted into service. Including volunteers, a total of 15.2 million men and women served in the armed services before the end of the war—10.4 million in the army, 3.9 million in the navy, 599,693 in the marines, and 241,902 in the Coast Guard.

Because the first offensive blows could be delivered from the air, the army air forces were authorized at the outset to increase their strength to 2.3 million men and were given highest priority on manpower and materials. When the Japanese attacked Pearl Harbor the Army Air Force (AAF) had 292,000 men and 9,000 planes (1,100 of which were fit for combat). When the Japanese surrendered in August 1945, the AAF enlisted 2.3 million men and women and had 72,000 planes in service.

Thanks to the wealth, technology, and industrial and agricultural capacity of his country, the American soldier was the best-paid, best-clothed, and by 1943 the best-equipped fighting man in the world. In that year, for example, Americans achieved not only a quantitative but also a decided qualitative superiority in fighter planes and bombers. Even in areas of research in which the Germans had a head start, such as atomic fission, American scientists and engineers had won decisive advantages by 1945. On the battlefield the best American weapons were the light semiautomatic Garand rifle and the multiple-driven truck. They combined to give a superiority in firepower and mobility that the Germans were never able to overcome in spite of general equality in machine guns, mortars, rocket-launched missiles, and artillery.

In the meantime, the navy, marines, and Coast Guard had grown from relative weakness after Pearl Harbor to dimensions of gigantic strength at the time of the Japanese surrender. On December 7, 1941, the navy had a complement of 337,349 men, in addition to 66,048 in the Marine Corps and 25,336 in the Coast Guard. By the summer of 1945, the navy's manpower had increased to 3.4 million officers and men, the Marine Corps' to 484,631, and the Coast Guard's to 170,480. Before Japanese bombs disabled or sank part of the Pacific Fleet at Pearl Harbor, the navy

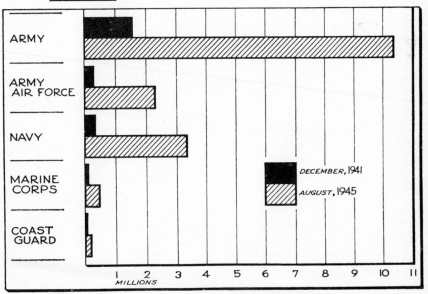

EXPANSION OF U.S. ARMED FORCES
1941-1945

had in operation some 4,500 ships, including 17 battleships, 7 fleet carriers, 18 heavy and 19 light cruisers, 200 destroyers and torpedo boats, and 114 submarines. By the end of 1945, the navy had grown to more than 91,000 ships of all sizes, including 24 battleships, 2 large cruisers, 29 fleet carriers, 73 escort carriers, 23 heavy and 45 light cruisers, 489 destroyers and torpedo boats, 500 escort vessels, and 274 submarines.

Finally, there was mobilization of women for war service. The Women's Auxiliary Corps, which grew in size to 100,000, sent 17,000 WACs overseas; the navy's counterpart, the WAVEs, numbered about 86,000 at the end of the war. There was also the Coast Guard's SPARs and the Marine Corps' Women's Reserve. Working as stenographers, clerks, technicians, cryptographers, and the like, female contingents not only performed indispensable functions but released over 200,000 men for service on the battle fronts.

Measured in human costs, the price of victory in the Second World War came high to the American people—253,573 dead, 651,042 wounded, 114,204 prisoners, and 65,834 men missing. For the men who died, however, Americans and their allies exacted a fearful retribution. Germany and Italy suffered 373,600 dead and lost 8.1 million prisoners to the Allies on the western front alone. The Japanese gave up 1.1 million battle dead in areas outside China.

For their comparatively low death lists, Americans in large measure could thank the medical corps of the several services. Although American soldiers lived and fought in deserts and jungles as well as in the temperate zones, the death rate from nonbattle causes was no higher than the rate for similar groups at home. And for the sick and wounded, there was extraordinary care, while use of sulfa drugs, penicillin, and whole blood brought such healing and relief from wounds and shock as would not have been possible a decade before. The result was to cut the rate of deaths from disease and battle wounds in half from the rate of the First World War.

2. Scientists Against Time

In the last analysis the war was won as much in the laboratory and on the testing ground as on the battlefield. American scientists at the outset of the war lagged far behind the Germans in research in atomic fission, jet propulsion, and rockets, and they were behind the British in work on jet propulsion, radar, and other electronic devices. Alarmed by the prospect of his country entering the war scientifically unprepared, Dr. Vannevar Bush, president of the Carnegie Institution of Washington, persuaded the president in June 1940 to establish the National Defense Research Committee (NDRC), with representatives from the defense departments, universities, and private industry. Then Roosevelt reorganized the government's research program in June 1941 by creating the Office of Scientific Research and Development (OSRD). Bush was director of the OSRD, with power to approve or veto all projects and to initiate research.

Bush and his colleagues had accomplished a full mobilization of scientific personnel and facilities by the autumn of 1941. Some of the most significant results of this great effort include the development of radar and electronic devices, rockets for combat use, the proximity fuse, and, finally, the atomic bomb.

It was the British who first perfected radar and put it to large-scale use during the great German air assault of 1940–1941. Radar sets in patrol planes enabled the British and American navies to bring the German submarines under control. Perhaps even more effective in antisubmarine operations was so-called sonar, or underwater sound detection apparatus, developed by the NDRC in conjunction with the Harvard Underwater Sound Laboratory. Radar in fighters enabled the air forces to launch powerful night interceptors; in bombers, it provided a generally accurate bombsight. The American armed services alone had received $3 billion worth of radar equipment and $71 million worth of Loran, a long-range navigational aid, by July 1945.

The outbreak of the war found research in the field of rocket warfare well advanced in Britain and Germany and practically nonexistent in the United States. But NDRC scientists had a sizable research program under way by the end of 1941. One of the first results was the "bazooka," a tube rocket-launcher perfected in 1942, which could be operated by two infantrymen and discharged a rocket powerful enough to destroy a tank. Subsequently, scientists developed a variety of rocket-launchers and rockets for use in land combat and antiaircraft operations, by airplanes, and in ship-to-shore bombardments. What this meant in terms of increased firepower can perhaps best be illustrated by the fact that a single fighter plane carrying rockets could discharge a salvo as heavy as a destroyer's.

Still another important wartime scientific achievement was the development, exclusively by the OSRD, of the proximity fuse. It was a miniature radio set in the head of the shell that detonated it by proximity to the target. Proximity fuses were first used by the navy against Japanese aircraft in 1943. Fearing that the Germans would recover an unexploded shell and put the fuse into production, the joint chiefs of staff did not allow ground forces in Europe to use the new weapon until December 1944. Put into use against the Germans in their Ardennes counteroffensive (see pp. 380–381), the proximity fuse compounded the effectiveness of American artillery and proved devastating against German ground troops.

The mobilization of American scientists paid numerous other dividends— among them the development of more powerful explosives and fire bombs, of DDT and other insecticides, of advanced techniques in the use of blood plasma and whole blood, of penicillin, and of new and deadly gases, which were never used. But the greatest triumph of American scientific and productive genius was the development of the atomic bomb. The perfection of this weapon marked a decisive turning point in history.

The Danish physicist Niels Bohr startled a group of American physicists assembled in Washington in January 1939 by announcing that two Germans at the Kaiser Wilhelm Institute in Berlin had recently accomplished atomic fission in uranium. Nuclear physicists had long understood the structure of the atom and known that atomic fission was theoretically possible. But the deed had now been done, and the road was open for the development of a bomb more powerful and deadly than the world had ever imagined. A real danger existed that the Nazis would produce atomic bombs and literally conquer the world. Therefore, Enrico Fermi of Columbia University, Albert Einstein of the Institute for Advanced Study, and others, persuaded Roosevelt to begin a small research program. It was not until 1940, however, that work began in earnest. By the summer of 1941, research at Columbia, California, and other universities had confirmed the possibilities of atomic fission through a chain reaction. The chief problem now was to find a fissionable element in sufficient quantity. Earlier experiments had proved that the uranium isotope, U-235, was fissionable; but, since U-235 was an infinitesimal part of uranium, the chances were remote of ever accumulating enough of the element to manufacture atomic bombs. This problem was solved by Dr. Ernest Lawrence of the University of California at Berkeley, who used a huge cyclotron, or "atom smasher," to convert the plentiful uranium element, U-238, into a new element, plutonium, which was as fissionable as U-235 and much easier to obtain in quantity.

The next objective became a chain reaction in uranium, that is, the almost simultaneous fission of the uranium atoms through a chain bombardment by neutrons. A group of physicists under the direction of Dr. Arthur H. Compton built the first atomic pile, or apparatus, under the stadium at Stagg Field of the University of Chicago. They produced the first controlled chain reaction in December 1942. Production of an atomic bomb was now possible, provided a means of production could be devised. OSRD turned the problem over to the Manhattan District of the Army Engineer Corps, headed by General Leslie R. Groves in May 1943. Drawing upon the combined resources of the OSRD, universities, and private industries, Groves pushed the project with incredible speed. Work on the bomb itself was begun in the spring of 1943 at a laboratory built on a lonely mesa at Los Alamos, outside Santa Fe, New Mexico. Here a group of American, British, and European scientists under direction of Dr. J. Robert Oppenheimer worked night and day to perfect the bomb. They began the final assembly of the first atomic bomb on July 12, 1945, and tension mounted as the fateful day of testing drew near. Nearly $2 billion had been expended in an effort which yet might fail. The bomb was moved to the air base at Alamagordo and successfully detonated at 5:30 A.M. on July 16. A searing blast of light, many times brighter than the noonday sun, was followed by a deafening roar and a huge mushroom cloud. And relief mixed with a feeling of doom filled the minds of those who watched the beginning of a new era in human history.

3. American Industry Goes to War

The story of how changing agencies mobilized the American economy for the war effort is a tale full of confusion and chaos, incompetence and momentary failure, political intrigue and personal vendetta, but withal one of superb achievement on many home fronts. Government and industry accomplished one of the economic miracles of modern times before it was too late—the production of a stream of goods that provided a high standard of living at home and also supplied the American armed forces with all and the British, French, and Russians with a large part of the resources and matériel for victory.

The task during the first period of industrial mobilization, from August 1939 until about the end of 1941, was the comparatively easy one of utilizing idle plants and men to supply the inchoate American armed forces and the British. In August 1939, Roosevelt established the War Resources Board, headed by Edward R. Stettinius, Jr., of the United States Steel Corporation, to advise the administration on industrial mobilization. It soon fell victim to labor and New Deal critics, who charged that it was dominated by Morgan and Du Pont interests.

This was, of course, the time of the so-called phony war, when Allied victory seemed assured and the necessity for total economic mobilization seemed remote. Nevertheless, the War Resources Board, before its dissolution in October 1939, prepared an industrial mobilization plan that envisaged dictatorial economic authority for a single administrator in the event that the United States entered the war. Roosevelt rejected this plan and asked the former chairman of Wilson's War Industries Board, Bernard M. Baruch, to prepare another. Baruch presented a plan that met all Roosevelt's objections to the earlier proposal and provided for gradual transition to a total war economy.

Roosevelt, for reasons still unknown, suppressed the Baruch plan and permitted the partial mobilization effort of 1939–1940 to drift aimlessly. The fall of France, however, galvanized him into action, inadequate though it was. Calling for vast new defense appropriations and the production of 50,000 planes a year, he reestablished the Advisory Commission to the old and nearly defunct Council of National Defense in May 1940. It was supposed to get defense production into high gear. In addition, Congress on June 25 authorized the RFC to finance the building of defense plants and, in the Revenue Act of October 1940, permitted businessmen to write off construction costs over a five-year period.

The Advisory Commission abdicated control over priorities to the Army-Navy Munitions Board and had lost all control of industrial mobilization by December 1940. Roosevelt still stubbornly refused to institute the kind of mobilization plan that Baruch had earlier suggested. Instead, in January 1941, he established the Office of Production Management (OPM), headed by William S. Knudsen of the Advisory Commission and Sidney Hillman of the CIO. It was directed to cooperate with the president and defense secretaries in stimulating and controlling war production. In addition, an Office of Price Administration and Civilian Supply, established in April, would work to protect consumers' interests.

The OPM went to work to improve the priorities system, to coordinate British and American orders, and especially to help automobile manufacturers prepare for conversion to production of tanks and planes. The result was a gradual shift during the spring and summer of 1941 to a wartime economy. Shortages of electric power, aluminum, steel, railroad stock, and other materials became acute. The priorities system nearly broke down, and internal bickering and public criticism mounted. Roosevelt attempted another superficial reorganization. He suspended the OPM in August 1941, but left an OPM Council. Then he created a Supplies Priorities and Allocation Board, headed by the Sears-Roebuck executive, Donald M. Nelson, and added other agencies, many of which overlapped in a confusing way. The central force in the new apparatus, however, was the Supplies Priorities and Allocations

Board. It had the power to determine and allocate requirements and supplies for the armed forces, the civilian economy, and the British and the Russians.

In January 1942, Roosevelt established a comprehensive economic mobilization by creating the War Production Board (WPB) under Donald Nelson. Nelson was an excellent technician, but he failed to meet the test of leadership. Because he continued to allow military departments to control priorities, he never established firm control over production. He permitted large corporations to dominate war production, and a near scandal ensued when the facts were disclosed by a special Senate committee headed by Harry S Truman of Missouri. Finally, Nelson allowed industrial expansion to get out of hand and occur in the wrong areas.

American industry was booming by the autumn of 1942, but chaos threatened. Alarmed by the prospect, Roosevelt brought Justice James F. Byrnes to the White House as head of the new Office of Economic Stabilization in October and gave him complete control over economic mobilization. Byrnes forced adoption of a plan that established such total control over allocation of steel, aluminum, and copper that the priorities difficulty soon vanished. Then Roosevelt, in May 1943, created the Office of War Mobilization, a sort of high command with control over all aspects of the economy, with Byrnes as director or "assistant president." Representative Fred M. Vinson of Kentucky succeeded Byrnes as head of the Office of Economic Stabilization.

4. The Miracle of Production

In spite of all its shortcomings, the American industrial mobilization did succeed far beyond any reasonable expectations. We can gain some understanding of the total achievement by considering the general performance of the American economy from 1939 through 1945. Measured by depression standards, 1939 was a relatively prosperous year. Gross national product stood at $91.3 billion—higher in real dollars than during the boom year of 1929. On the other hand, the gross national product had risen, in 1939 dollars, to $166.6 billion by 1945. Moreover, from 1939 to 1945 the index of manufacturing production increased 96 percent; agricultural production was up 22 percent; and transportation services increased 109 percent. Contrasted with the performance of the economy during the First World War, when the total national output increased hardly at all, this was a remarkable achievement.

The main engine of these increases was, of course, war production. In 1941 it was a mere trickle—only $8.4 billion in value. A year later, it totaled $30.2 billion in value and equaled that of Germany, Italy, and Japan combined. American factories by 1944 were producing twice the volume of the Axis partners. A few examples illustrate these generalizations. The American airplane industry employed 46,638 persons and produced 5,865 planes in 1939. At the peak of production in 1944, the industry employed more than 2.1 million persons and turned out 96,369 aircraft. All told, American factories from Pearl Harbor to the end of the war produced 274,941 military aircraft. Production of merchant ships, an essential ingredient of Allied victory, which had totaled only 1 million tons in 1941, rose to a peak of over 19 million tons in 1943. As the need diminished, production declined to nearly 16.5 million tons in 1944 and nearly 8 million tons from January through July of 1945. All told, from July 1940 to August 1945, American shipyards produced a total of more than 55.2 million tons of merchant shipping—a tonnage equal to two-thirds of the merchant marines of all Allied nations combined.

Perhaps most remarkable was the creation, almost overnight, of a new synthetic rubber industry. Japanese conquest of Malaya and the Netherlands East Indies deprived the United States of 90 percent of its natural rubber supply. Total imports could not exceed 175,000 tons during 1942, and the rubber shortage threatened to hobble the entire war effort. In August 1942, Roosevelt appointed a special commit-tee headed by Bernard M. Baruch to investigate and recommend. It reported a month later and warned that the war effort and civilian economy might collapse if a severe rubber shortage occurred and urged immediate construction of a vast industry to produce rubber synthetically from petroleum. Roosevelt acted immedi-ately and appointed William M. Jeffers, president of the Union Pacific Railroad, as rubber director in the WPB. Jeffers ruthlessly cut his way through the existing priorities system. By the end of 1943, he had brought into existence a synthetic rubber industry that produced 762,000 tons in 1944 and 820,000 tons in 1945.

5.   The Greatest Tax Bill in History

Federal expenditures aggregated in excess of $321.2 billion from 1941 to 1945. Some 41 percent of the money for the war effort came from tax receipts, which totaled nearly $131 billion during the fiscal years 1941–1945. The balance was raised by borrowing, which in turn increased the gross national debt from $49 billion in 1941 to $259 billion in mid-1945.

Meanwhile, the administration and Congress had revolutionized the tax struc-ture. On the one hand, the president, Congress, and a vast majority of Americans, rich and poor alike, agreed that the few should not profit from the sacrifices of the many, and that there should be no new millionaires as a result of the defense and war efforts. On the other hand, it became increasingly evident that it would be hopelessly inadequate to use the income tax as a tax principally on wealth, and that the costs of the war would have to be borne in part also by the lower and middle classes.

The administration's tax program evolved gradually in response to the need for revenues and the necessity for curbing inflation. Congress thus approved two reve-nue acts in 1940 that increased income and corporation taxes and imposed an excess profits tax graduated to a maximum of 50 percent. Congress again increased old taxes in 1941 and devised new means of finding revenue. Even so, the income tax still touched only the small minority with upper middle- and upper-class incomes. A significant departure in federal tax policy occurred in January 1942, when Roosevelt, in his Budget Message to Congress, proposed a $7 billion increase in the tax burden. After months of agonizing delay, Congress responded with the Revenue Act of 1942, approved October 21.

Described by Roosevelt as "the greatest tax bill in American history," it was designed to raise more than $7 billion additional revenue annually, a sum exceeding total federal revenues in any peacetime year before 1941. The measure increased the combined corporate income tax to a maximum of 40 percent and raised the excess profits tax to a flat 90 percent. Moreover, it increased excise taxes and levied a host of new ones, and stiffly increased estate and gift taxes. The revolutionary feature of the Revenue Act of 1942, however, was its broadening of the income tax to tap low incomes as well as to increase the burden on large ones. Only 13 million persons had paid federal income taxes in 1941; in contrast, some 50 million persons were caught in the net cast in 1942. The difficulty of collecting income taxes from 50 million persons by the conventional method of individual returns led to the adoption, in 1943, of a measure requiring employers to collect the tax by payroll deductions.

Meanwhile, personal incomes, governmental expenditures, and inflationary pressures continued to mount. The president therefore came back in his Budget Message of 1943 to demand an increase of $16 billion in the federal tax load. Treasury officials later lowered the request to $10.5 billion. Even so, congressional leaders rebelled and adopted a Revenue Act in early February 1944 that yielded additional revenue of only $2.2 billion, chiefly by increasing the excess profits tax to 95 percent and by heavy increases in excise taxes. The president replied on February 22 with a veto so stinging that his spokesman in the Senate, Alben W. Barkley of Kentucky, resigned his post as majority leader. The Senate Democratic caucus promptly and unanimously reelected Barkley, and an angry House and Senate overrode the veto

EXPENDITURES OF THE UNITED STATES GOVERNMENT, 1914–1952

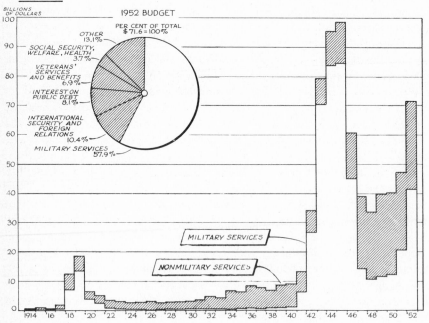

BILLIONS OF DOLLARS

1952 BUDGET

PER CENT OF TOTAL $71.6 = 100%

OTHER 13.1%

SOCIAL SECURITY, WELFARE, HEALTH 3.7%

VETERANS' SERVICES AND BENEFITS 6.9%

INTEREST ON PUBLIC DEBT 8.1%

INTERNATIONAL SECURITY AND FOREIGN RELATIONS 10.4%

MILITARY SERVICES 57.9%

MILITARY SERVICES

NONMILITARY SERVICES

by enormous majorities. From this time forward administration and congressional leaders were concerned, not with increasing the tax burden, but with simplifying the withholding system and planning for the reconversion that would soon come with the end of the war.

In retrospect, perhaps the most significant aspect of the wartime tax program was the way it reflected the nation's conviction that a war for survival should not become a war for the enrichment of the few. There could be no "swollen fortunes" when the federal income tax reached a maximum of 94 percent of total net income, to say nothing of state income and local property taxes. Indeed, the nation's top 5 percent of income receivers suffered their severest relative economic losses in the history of the country during this period. Their share of disposable income fell from 25.7 percent in 1940 to 15.9 percent in 1944. The relative status of the top 1 percent of income receivers declined even more. Their share of disposable income decreased from 11.5 percent in 1940 to 6.7 percent in 1944. And with an excess profits tax of 95 percent and corporation income taxes reaching a maximum of 50 percent, there were few cases of swollen profits. Net corporation income was $9.4 billion in 1941 and 1942, increased slightly in 1943 and 1944, and fell back to $8.5 billion in 1945.

6. Combating Inflation

Aside from the mobilization of fighting men and the maintenance of a steady flow of materials to the battle fronts, perhaps the most important problem at home was prevention of a runaway inflation that would compound the costs of the war and increase the burdens of many classes. To state the problem in its simplest terms, inflationary pressures existed after 1941 because the volume of disposable personal income greatly exceeded the supply of goods and services available for civilian consumption at the prevailing price level. Disposable personal incomes rose from $92 billion in 1941 to $151 billion in 1945, but the supply of civilian goods and services, measured in constant dollars, rose from $77.6 billion to only $95.4 billion during the same period. The danger of inflation stalked the home front because of this inflationary gap.

The most obvious weapon against inflation and the first to be tried was control of prices and rents. It will be recalled that Roosevelt, while reorganizing the defense mobilization machinery, had established an Office of Price Administration and Civilian Supply (OPA), headed by Leon Henderson, to work in conjunction with the Office of Production Management. Without any real power, Henderson was helpless to control prices during 1941. Consequently, retail prices were rising at the rate of 2 percent a month by February 1942. Roosevelt asked for new authority, and Congress responded with the Emergency Price Control Act of 1942. It empowered the price administrator to fix maximum prices and rents in special areas and to pay subsidies to producers, if that was necessary to prevent price increases. On the other hand, the powerful farm bloc denied the price administrator authority to control agricultural prices until they reached 110 percent of parity.

The OPA during the next three months launched a two-pronged campaign—to stabilize prices piecemeal, and to establish a system of rationing for tires, automobiles, gasoline, and sugar and, somewhat later, for shoes, fuel oil, and coffee. In April 1942, the OPA issued its first General Maximum Price Regulation, which froze most prices and rents at the level of March 1942. Events soon revealed large loopholes in the stabilization program, the most obvious of which was the ban on a ceiling for food prices until they reached an extraordinary level. As food prices rose steadily —they increased a total of 11 percent during 1942—organized labor redoubled its demands for pay increases that in turn would mean higher prices for manufactured products. Somehow, somewhere, the inflationary spiral had to be stopped, Roosevelt exclaimed in a special message in September 1942. "I ask Congress to take . . . action by the first of October. . . . In the event that the Congress should fail to act, and act adequately, I shall accept the responsibility, and I will act."

Congress responded swiftly if grudgingly with the Anti-Inflation Act of October 2, 1942. It empowered the president to stabilize wages, prices, and salaries at their levels on September 15. Roosevelt established the Office of Economic Stabilization on the following day, October 3, and forbade any further increase in wages and salaries without the approval of the stabilization director, James F. Byrnes. In addition, Roosevelt froze agricultural prices at their level on September 15 and extended rent control to all areas of the country.

It was a good beginning, but even rougher storms lay ahead. The OPA administrator, Leon Henderson, had never been popular with Congress and the public. Roosevelt permitted him to resign in December 1942 and replaced him with Prentiss S. Brown, former senator from Michigan. Unfortunately, business, farm, and

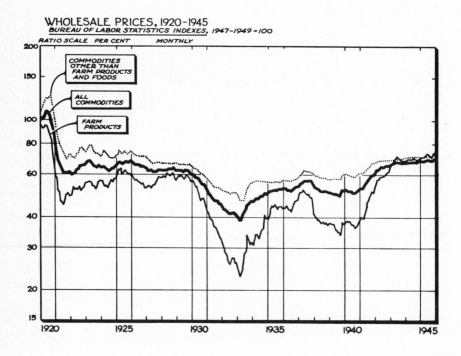

WHOLESALE PRICES, 1920–1945
BUREAU OF LABOR STATISTICS INDEXES, 1947–1949 = 100
RATIO SCALE PER CENT   MONTHLY

COMMODITIES OTHER THAN FARM PRODUCTS AND FOODS

ALL COMMODITIES

FARM PRODUCTS

labor groups took Brown's appointment as a signal for an all-out campaign against stabilization. Congress tried to open a large hole in the dike in March 1943 by approving a bill to exclude subsidy and parity payments in determination of parity levels for agriculture. But Roosevelt vetoed the measure, pointing out that it would increase the cost of living by more than 5 percent. At the same time, labor spokesmen were growing restive under a formula by which workers had been allowed a 15 percent wage increase in 1942, and were threatening to break the no-strike pledge they had given after Pearl Harbor.

Roosevelt responded to this dangerous situation by ordering, in April 1943, the stabilization agencies to "hold the line" against any further unwarranted price and wage increases. Nor was this all. When John L. Lewis called a general coal strike in May in defiance of the hold-the-line order, the president seized the coal mines and virtually ordered miners back into the pits. Moreover, the OPA began an

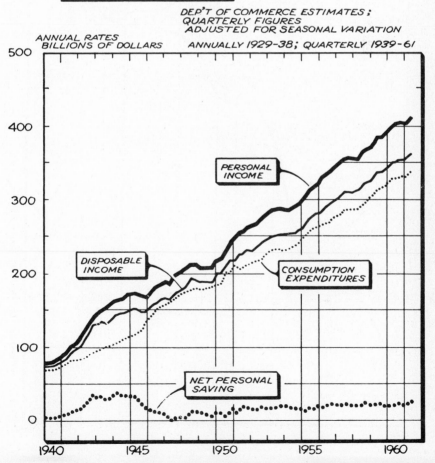

PERSONAL INCOME, CONSUMPTION, AND SAVING, 1940-1961

DEP'T OF COMMERCE ESTIMATES; QUARTERLY FIGURES ADJUSTED FOR SEASONAL VARIATION

ANNUAL RATES BILLIONS OF DOLLARS

ANNUALLY 1929-38; QUARTERLY 1939-61

PERSONAL INCOME

DISPOSABLE INCOME

CONSUMPTION EXPENDITURES

NET PERSONAL SAVING

aggressive campaign to roll back food prices. It culminated in a 10 percent reduction in the retail prices of meat, coffee, and butter in May. As a result of these efforts, the cost of living increased less than 1.5 percent between the spring of 1943 and the summer of 1945. The Consumer Price Index had increased by 28.3 percent during the entire period 1940–1945. This was a remarkable record in view of the power of organized pressure groups and inevitable public vexation at the inconveniences of direct controls.

CONSUMER PRICES
1940 – 1960

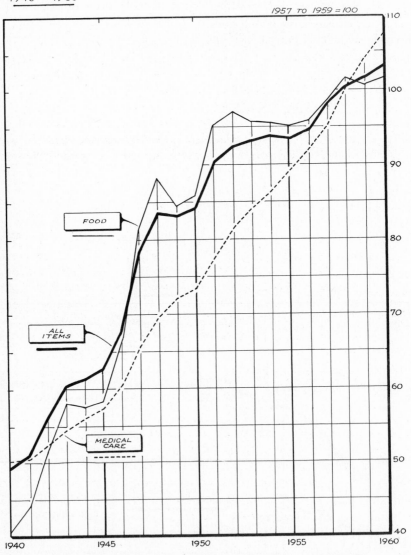

7. Workers, Farmers, and the War Effort

The nearly insatiable demands of the American and Allied war machines solved the unemployment problem almost overnight, as the number of civilian workers increased from about 46.5 million to over 53 million from 1940 to the middle of 1945. The chief factor in this expansion was the addition of about 7 million workers from the reservoir of the unemployed. To workers, the war boom brought unprecedented prosperity. Although the Consumer Price Index advanced 23.3 percent between 1941 and 1945, weekly earnings of those employed in manufacturing increased 70 percent.

It was not easy to mobilize this huge labor force, restrain labor's natural desire for higher wages, and bridle irresponsible labor leaders. Indeed, the administration never achieved comprehensive control over manpower resources. Roosevelt created the War Manpower Commission (WMC) in April 1942 and appointed former Governor Paul V. McNutt of Indiana to direct the flow of workers into war industries. The WMC gradually developed coercive measures that prohibited workers in defense industries from leaving their jobs without approval of the United States Employment Service. This system worked reasonably well, but it did not solve a more important problem—recruiting new workers and shifting workers from non-defense to war industries. One solution, of course, was national service legislation to draft men for war work. The CIO and AFL bitterly opposed such legislation, but the manpower shortage seemed so critical by the end of 1943 that Roosevelt supported a national service act in his annual message in January 1944. The House approved a labor draft bill in December 1944, but Germany collapsed before the Senate could act on the measure.

Much more important and difficult was the prevention of strikes and the reconciliation of labor's natural desires for economic advancement and union security with the general objective of winning the war without runaway inflation. This gigantic and at times nearly impossible task was entrusted to the War Labor Board (WLB), created by the president in January 1942. The WLB was established simply to settle labor disputes, but it soon discovered that mediation was impossible without a comprehensive labor policy. Inevitably, therefore, the WLB emerged as a powerful policy-making body in the war economy.

To the leaders of organized labor, the fundamental issue was protection of the right of collective bargaining. The WLB stood firm in defense of labor's rights under the Wagner Act, even the right to the closed shop when a majority of workers voted in favor of it. Moreover, it applied a compromise—the so-called maintenance of membership plan—that protected unions in rapidly expanding war plants. Union membership expanded under its aegis to nearly 15 million by the end of the war.

The thorniest problems of wartime labor administration were demands for higher wages and strikes to enforce such demands. Here the issue did not lie between labor and management—for management was usually eager to increase wages in order to hold and attract labor—but rather lay between the public interest and combined private interests. The WLB defended labor's right to enjoy a standard of living "compatible with health and decency." It also endorsed union demands for equal pay for blacks and women and the elimination of sectional differentials. On the other hand, the WLB also asserted that workers should be content to maintain and not improve their standard of living during wartime. In theory, most labor leaders concurred; the trouble was that they could never agree with the WLB on what that standard of living was. The rise in the cost of living during the early months of 1942 precipitated the first crisis. The WLB responded in July 1942, with the so-called Little Steel formula. It granted most workers a 15 percent wage increase to offset a similar increase in the cost of living since January 1941. But employers began to award pay increases that exceeded the Little Steel formula, and the president, under authority of the Stabilization Act of October 1942, empowered the WLB to forbid increases that imperiled the stabilization program.

Meanwhile, the WLB's determination to restrain wage increases had driven a minority of labor to irresponsible action. The AFL and CIO had given a no-strike pledge soon after Pearl Harbor and promised to "produce without interruption." Although responsible labor leaders kept this promise for the most part, restlessness among the rank and file of workers caused some labor strife. All told, there were 14,731 work stoppages involving 6.7 million workers and resulting in the loss of 36.3 million work days from December 8, 1941, through August 14, 1945. However, most work stoppages were short-lived, occurred in defiance of union leadership, and caused a loss of only one-ninth of 1 percent of total working time.

Even so, it was difficult for the mass of Americans to think in terms of averages when they saw workers in airplane factories and shipyards striking for higher pay or over union jurisdiction. Two major incidents—a coal strike and the near occurrence of a nationwide railroad strike in 1943—particularly alarmed the American people. John L. Lewis refused to appear before the WLB and called a general coal strike in May 1943. Roosevelt seized the mines, but the miners struck again in June because the WLB would not break the Little Steel formula and grant high wage increases. Miners returned to work when Roosevelt threatened to ask Congress to draft them, but Lewis forced the administration to surrender by threat of a third strike.

Lewis's cynical defiance of federal authority was more than Congress would tolerate. In June 1943, in hot resentment it approved and reenacted over Roosevelt's veto the Smith-Connally, or War Labor Disputes, Act. It empowered the president to seize any struck war plant and required unions to wait thirty days before striking and to hold a secret vote of the workers before a strike was executed. More indicative of the rising antilabor sentiment was the enactment by many state legislatures of laws to prevent certain union practices and to subject unions to a measure of public regulation. In a number of states, these laws forbade the closed shop, mass picketing, secondary boycotts, and the like, and required unions to file financial reports and obtain licenses for labor organizers.

For agriculture, the war boom brought new problems but also a stability and prosperity unknown since 1919. Net cash income from farming increased from $2.3 billion to $9.5 billion from 1940 to 1945, or by more than 300 percent. Two factors —increased production and higher prices, both of them stemming from vastly increased demands at home and abroad—restored agriculture to its long-sought position of parity in the American economy. Agricultural prices more than doubled between 1940 and 1945. During the same period, the index of all farm production rose from 108 to 123, while increases in food crops were even more spectacular. Incredible though it sounds, this expansion was accomplished in spite of a declining farm population and without any significant increase in acreage planted and harvested. It was, rather, the product of greater use of machinery, more productive hybrid crops, and fertilizers and insecticides.

8. Public Opinion and Civil Liberties During the War

Never before had Americans gone to war with such determination and unity. Significant opposition to the war effort simply did not exist after the Pearl Harbor attack, mainly because Communists rallied to the defense and war efforts after the Germans attacked Russia. And because disloyalty was rare, there were no volunteer leagues of patriots, no committees of public safety, no high-powered propaganda campaigns and war madness. This is not to say that the government abandoned control over news and expressions of opinion, or that it was not ready to act ruthlessly to suppress dangerous dissent. For example, the Justice Department at Roosevelt's command convened a special grand jury in Washington in July 1941 and laid before it and two succeeding grand juries voluminous evidence on the far-flung network of Nazi and Fascist organizations in the United States. The upshot was the indictment under the Smith Act* of thirty leading seditionists for conspiring to establish a Nazi government in the United States and to incite disloyalty among the armed forces. The trial proceeded for more than seven months in 1944 until the judge died, apparently a victim of the badgering of defense attorneys. The seditionists were indicted a second time in 1945, and government attorneys rushed to Germany to obtain new evidence. However, the Circuit Court of Appeals of the District of Columbia ended the fiasco in November 1946 by dismissing the indictment on the ground that the government's proceedings were a travesty of justice.

The government was scarcely more successful when it tried to imprison individual champions of nazism and opponents of the war. The critical test arose when the Justice Department invoked the Espionage Act of 1917 against a man named Hartzel, who published a diatribe against American participation in the war in 1942 and mailed copies to army officers. The Supreme Court, in *Hartzel* v. *United States* (1944), made enforcement of the Espionage Act virtually impossible by declaring that the government had to prove specific intent to obstruct the war effort before it could obtain convictions under the law. Again, when the government obtained the conviction of twenty-four leaders of the German-American Bund for violating the Espionage Act, the court reversed the conviction on the ground of insufficient evidence of criminal intent.

Actually, the government knew that the assorted crackpots who made up the Bund and other pro-Nazi organizations were no menace, for the FBI had penetrated these groups and placed their leaders under surveillance. Espionage and sabotage, however, were different matters, and the Justice Department moved swiftly and

*Enacted in 1940, it forbade persons to advocate the violent overthrow of the government of the United States.

sternly in dealing with them. The FBI broke a small Nazi espionage ring in 1938, destroyed the major Nazi network in 1941, and was prepared to move against potential spies and saboteurs on the eve of American entrance into the war. The FBI had taken more than 1,700 enemy aliens into custody within less than three days after the Pearl Harbor attack. By such effective countermeasures the Justice Department completely destroyed the elaborate German intelligence and sabotage systems, with the results that not a single known act of sabotage was committed in the United States after December 7, 1941.

Deprived of its underground in America, the German high command resorted to audacious plans. It trained two teams of saboteurs—composed of Germans who had lived in America and American citizens of German descent—and sent them by submarines in May 1942 to destroy the American aluminum industry and blow up bridges and railroad facilities. One team landed on Long Island, the other on the Florida coast. The eight invaders were captured almost immediately by the FBI, tried by a special military commission, sentenced to death, and executed on August 8. The father of one of the saboteurs, Hans Haupt of Chicago, was also convicted of treason for hiding his son and given life imprisonment. Another German American, Anthony Cramer, was convicted of treason for assisting one of the saboteurs.

The one great blot on the administration's otherwise excellent civil liberties record during the war was the detention and forced removal of Japanese Americans from the West Coast to internment camps in the interior. It was the greatest single violation of civil rights in American history. The issue was not the arrest of Japanese subjects who were potential saboteurs, for they were rounded up immediately after the Pearl Harbor attack. It was the loyalty of some 41,000 Japanese ineligible to citizenship and 71,000 Nisei, or American citizens of Japanese ancestry. The general staff declared the West Coast a theater of war in the panic following December 7, 1941, and newspapers and political leaders in California began a widespread campaign for removal of all Japanese Americans, whether citizens or not. The demand was taken up in Washington by the congressional delegations from the Pacific Coast states, and was seconded by the commanding general on the West Coast, John L. De Witt. On February 19, 1942, Roosevelt authorized the army to take control. General De Witt soon afterward ordered removal of *all* Japanese Americans from an area comprising the western third of Washington and Oregon, the western half of California, and the southern quarter of Arizona. Some 110,000 Japanese and Nisei were ruthlessly ejected from their homes and herded into temporary stockades surrounded by barbed wire. They were then transported to ten relocation centers established by the War Relocation Authority in western deserts and the swamplands of Arkansas. Eventually some 18,000 persons suspected of disloyalty were confined in a camp at Tule Lake, California, while the remainder were allowed to find new homes or go to colleges in the Midwest and East. Some 36,000 chose resettlement during the war.

The most disappointing aspect of the whole affair was the Supreme Court's refusal to vindicate the principle of civilian supremacy or defend elementary civil rights. A divided court, in *Korematsu* v. *United States* (1944), apologetically approved the evacuation on the ground that military leaders were justified in taking extreme measures against persons on account of race to protect national security, even though the situation was not serious enough to justify the imposition of martial law. The meaning of the decision was clear and foreboding: in future emergencies no American citizen would have any rights that the president and army were bound to respect when, *in their judgment,* the emergency justified drastic denial of civil rights.

9. Blacks and the Home Front

The Second World War was a time of unrest and new striving on America's troubled frontier of black-white relations. There were race riots and national discriminations like the continued segregation of nearly a million blacks in the armed services and the separation of black and white blood in Red Cross blood banks. Racial tensions rose to the danger point in the South, as blacks acquired a measure of financial independence and social self-respect. Nonetheless, Negroes emerged from the war with a larger measure of self-esteem and economic and political power than they had ever enjoyed.

The most dangerous racial tensions developed in industrial areas outside the South, as a result of the sudden immigration of nearly 1 million southern blacks in search of jobs and new social opportunities. There were numerous minor clashes in many cities, and New York escaped a major race riot in early 1944 only because of the quick action of its mayor and police force. Tensions flared into large-scale rioting in Detroit, home of Gerald L. K. Smith and other Negro-baiters. A fight between a black and a white man in June 1943 led to other clashes. Soon mobs of whites were roaming the black section, killing and burning as they went. By the time that federal troops had restored order, twenty-five blacks and nine whites had been killed.

This was the dark side of an otherwise bright picture, for the Second World War was a time also of progress for American blacks. Blacks in the South enjoyed greater acceptance and security and larger political and economic opportunities than ever before. Lynching, long the extreme form of southern race control, became almost a historic phenomenon. The number of Negroes thus put to death declined from five in 1942 to one in 1945. A distinguished body of southern leaders, black and white, met in Atlanta in 1944 and organized the Southern Regional Council to combat prejudice and misunderstanding. Equally significant was the growth during the war of an advanced equalitarian movement outside the South. This campaign assumed the proportions almost of a crusade against Jim Crow and won many triumphs, the most important of which was a growing concern for civil rights by the major parties.

Blacks made greatest progress during the war, in both the North and the South, on the economic front. Of all groups they had suffered most during the depression and profited least from New Deal measures. Nor did the defense boom of 1940–1941 bring relief, as employers stubbornly refused to hire black workers. The administration moved slowly, until A. Philip Randolph, president of the Brotherhood of Sleeping Car Porters, called upon 50,000 blacks to march on Washington to protest. Randolph called off the threatened march; but he did so only after Roosevelt, in June 1944, issued Executive Order 8802. It directed that blacks be admitted to job training programs, forbade discrimination in work on defense contracts, and established a Fair Employment Practices Committee to investigate charges of discrimination on account of race.

The FEPC made progress slowly and performed its most effective service during 1942 and 1943 by conducting hearings on discrimination in most of the large cities of the country. It worked even more vigorously when Roosevelt, in May 1943, reorganized the agency, expanded its budget, and directed that antidiscrimination clauses in contracts be enforced. The FEPC established fifteen regional offices, heard some 8,000 complaints, and conducted thirty public hearings from 1943 to 1946. The results were unexpectedly successful. Nearly 2 million Negroes were at work in aircraft factories, shipyards, steel mills, and other war plants in the South and elsewhere by the end of 1944.

The millennium had not come for American blacks when the war ended. To men of good will, however, the steady enlargement of economic, social, and political opportunities for blacks during the war years was perhaps the most encouraging development on the American home front. Blacks in 1945 could look forward to a postwar era full not only of struggle but also of hope for a new era in which they might stand erect as free men and women and citizens of the great democracy.

Chapter 19

—»» ««—

The Second World War: Diplomatic and Military Aspects

The American people were destined to play a leading and decisive role in the military operations that brought victory for the United Nations in 1945. In this chapter we will follow the Allies on the long and tortuous road from near defeat to victory. Since the war was won not only in the factory and on the battlefield but also around the conference table, we will also relate how Roosevelt and Churchill forged the bonds of Anglo-American unity, drew the Russian leaders into close association, and gave such an effective demonstration of allied cooperation in wartime as the world had rarely seen before.

1. The Formation of the Grand Alliance

American and British leaders gathered in Washington soon after the Pearl Harbor attack to lay plans for combined conduct of the war. Liaison with the Russians would come later, as soon as circumstances permitted. Prime Minister Winston Churchill arrived in Washington on December 22, 1941, for a week of conferences known by the code name of ARCADIA. These discussions continued on the military level until January 14, 1942. This was a time when Allied military fortunes were at their lowest ebb since the fall of France, but negotiations proceeded smoothly and yielded complete agreement on all important points. These were American production goals for 1942 and 1943, pooling of Anglo–American munitions and their disposal by a joint Munitions Assignment Board, and immediate establishment of a Combined Chiefs of Staff in Washington and a combined British, American, and Dutch command in the Pacific. ARCADIA's most important work was reaffirmation of the earlier staff decision to defeat Germany first since that nation was the stronger enemy and possessed industry and manpower superior to that of the Japanese. The Allies planned major offensives against the Continent first, with holding operations in the Pacific until Nazi power had been subdued.

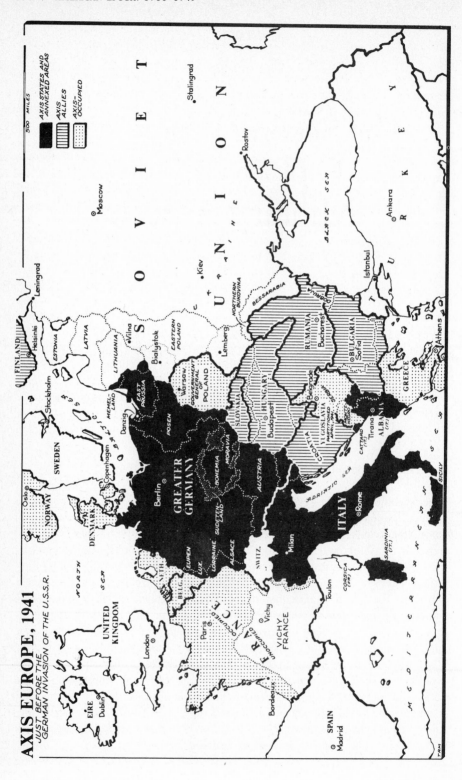

AXIS EUROPE, 1941
JUST BEFORE THE GERMAN INVASION OF THE U.S.S.R.

500 MILES

AXIS STATES AND ANNEXED AREAS

AXIS ALLIES

AXIS-OCCUPIED

On the diplomatic level, moreover, Roosevelt and Churchill worked in complete harmony for the formation of a grand coalition of the Allies. The fruit of their labor was the Declaration of the United Nations, signed at the White House on New Year's Day, 1942, by Roosevelt, Churchill, Maxim Litvinov for the USSR, and representatives of twenty-three other nations. The signatory powers reaffirmed the principles set forth in the Atlantic Charter, pledged their full resources to the defeat of the Axis nations, and promised one another not to make a separate peace.

The most uncertain link in the new Allied chain was Russia. By vigorous cooperation, the USSR could hasten victory and help lay the groundwork for postwar cooperation. By making a separate peace, on the other hand, Russia could postpone the hope of Allied victory perhaps indefinitely. The president's and the prime minister's most pressing diplomatic problem during early 1942 was Russian territorial ambitions in Europe and a Russian demand that Britain and the United States guarantee those ambitions in advance. The Kremlin presented the first installment of its demands during a visit of Foreign Secretary Anthony Eden to Moscow in December 1941. Josef Stalin, the Soviet dictator, then requested Great Britain's immediate approval of Russia's absorption of the Baltic states and parts of Finland, Poland, and Rumania. He warned, moreover, that conclusion of a British–Soviet alliance would depend upon British endorsement of these territorial claims.

The issue came to a head when the Soviet foreign minister, Vyacheslav Molotov, arrived in London in May 1942 to press Russian territorial and military demands. Churchill and Eden had been strengthened by a warning from Washington that the United States might publicly denounce any Anglo–Russian agreement conceding Stalin's ambitions. They stood firm and persuaded Molotov to sign a general twenty-year Treaty of Alliance that included no reference to boundaries.

2. The Low Point: 1942

Axis victories were so swift and far-reaching during the first six months of 1942 that it seemed that the United Nations might lose the war before they could begin fighting. The Japanese, following air attacks on British and American possessions on December 7, launched seaborne invasions of Hong Kong, Malaya, the Philippines, and lesser islands. They were free to roam and strike almost at will, for the once mighty Anglo–American Pacific naval power was nearly gone by the end of 1941. Guam fell on December 11, 1941; Wake Island, on December 23; Hong Kong, on Christmas Day. Meanwhile, Japanese forces pressed forward in conquest of Malaya, Burma, and the Philippines. Singapore, the great British naval base in the Far East, surrendered on February 15, 1942, to a Japanese force that came down from the north through Malaya. Most of Burma fell in March and April 1942, while Ceylon and India were threatened by a large Japanese naval force that momentarily controlled the Indian Ocean and the Bay of Bengal in April.

In the Philippines, General Douglas MacArthur, with a force of 19,000 American regulars, 12,000 Philippine Scouts, and 100,000 soldiers of the new Philippine army, fought a desperate delaying action. When Japanese troops threatened Manila,

MacArthur declared the capital an open city, moved to Corregidor, and withdrew his troops into Bataan Peninsula for a hopeless but gallant last stand. MacArthur was transferred to Australia in March 1942. His successor, General Jonathan Wainwright, continued the fight from Corregidor and other forts off the tip of the peninsula and held out there until disease, starvation, and superior enemy forces made further resistance impossible. He surrendered on May 6, 1942.

Meanwhile, large new Japanese forces were poised in Malaya and the Philippines by the end of December 1941 to strike at Borneo, the Celebes, New Guinea, and the Dutch East Indies. Only the small American Asiatic Fleet and a few Dutch and British cruisers stood athwart the path of Japanese conquest of the Indies. In the Battle of Macassar Strait, January 1942, American destroyers executed a daring night attack against a Japanese convoy and forced it to turn back. But in the subsequent engagements, known as the Java Sea campaign, the Allies lost their entire naval force, except for four American destroyers. By the end of March 1942, the Japanese were in possession of the East Indies, had pushed into New Britain and the Solomon Islands, and were in position to strike at Port Moresby, the Allied base in southern New Guinea, and at Australia itself. In little more than three months, the Japanese had gained control of a vast area which extended from the Gilbert Islands in the Central Pacific west and south through the Solomons and New Guinea to Burma. India and Australia lay virtually undefended.

Events almost as catastrophic for the Allies were transpiring in the Atlantic, on the eastern front in Russia, and in North Africa. German submarines came perilously close to winning the Battle of the Atlantic during 1942, when Allied and neutral shipping losses aggregated nearly 8 million tons. "The disaster of an indefinite prolongation of the war," to quote Churchill's phrase, threatened to upset Allied plans for military operations.

Meanwhile, the Germans had mounted a large offensive to drive through North Africa, cut the Suez Canal, and penetrate Arabia and the Middle East. General Erwin Rommel, the "Desert Fox," opened the campaign in Libya in May 1942. The British, after several sharp defeats, retreated to El Alamein in Egypt, only seventy-five miles from Alexandria, to regroup and reinforce their shattered Eighth Army. The German lines were overextended by July 1, and Rommel's Afrika Korps was too exhausted to press the offensive.

These reversals during the spring and summer of 1942 had a nearly fatal impact on the Grand Alliance, when the hard-pressed Russians demanded assistance in the form of a second front in the West. The issue first arose prominently when Molotov arrived in Washington in late May 1942 for conferences mainly of a military nature with Roosevelt and his advisers. Stalin wanted, Molotov declared, an Anglo–American invasion of western Europe strong enough to draw forty German divisions from the eastern front. Without a second front in 1942, he continued, Germany might deal the USSR a crushing blow. Roosevelt turned to General Marshall for an answer. Marshall replied that there were enough men and supplies for the undertaking. The chief problem was to obtain adequate shipping for an expeditionary force without cutting off supplies to the Soviet Union.

Molotov returned to Moscow with a virtual promise that the United States would launch a cross-Channel invasion in 1942. The Germans drove deeper into

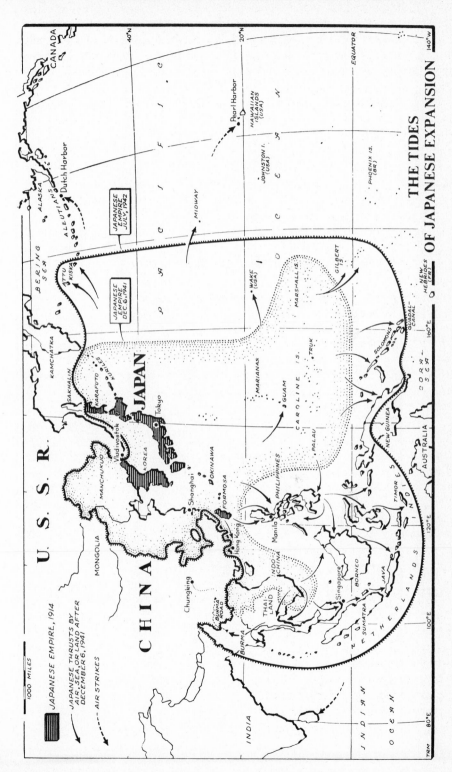

THE TIDES OF JAPANESE EXPANSION

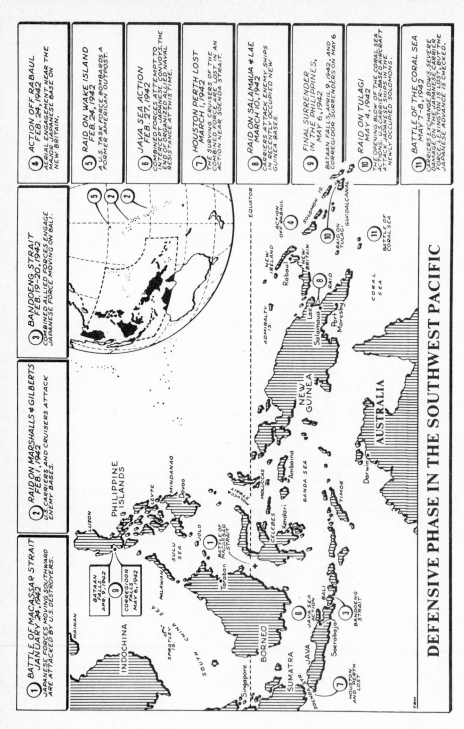

DEFENSIVE PHASE IN THE SOUTHWEST PACIFIC

① BATTLE OF MACASSAR STRAIT
JANUARY 24, 1942
JAPANESE FORCES MOVING SOUTHWARD ARE ATTACKED BY U.S. DESTROYERS.

② RAID ON MARSHALLS & GILBERTS
FEB. 1, 1942
U.S. CARRIERS AND CRUISERS ATTACK ENEMY BASES.

③ BANDOENG STRAIT
FEB. 19–20, 1942
COMBINED ALLIED FORCES ENGAGE JAPANESE FORCE MOVING ON BALI.

④ ACTION OFF RABAUL
FEB. 24, 1942
AERIAL ENGAGEMENT NEAR THE NEW BRITAIN.

⑤ RAID ON WAKE ISLAND
FEB. 24, 1942
A U.S. TASK FORCE BOMBARDS A FORMER AMERICAN OUTPOST.

⑥ JAVA SEA ACTION
FEB. 27, 1942
COMBINED FORCES ATTEMPT TO INTERCEPT JAPANESE CONVOYS. THE END OF ORGANIZED ALLIED NAVAL RESISTANCE AT THIS TIME.

⑦ HOUSTON PERTH LOST
MARCH 1, 1942
THE SURVIVING CRUISERS OF THE COMBINED FORCE ARE LOST IN AN ACTION NEAR SOENDA STRAIT.

⑧ RAID ON SALAMAUA & LAE
MARCH 10, 1942
CARRIERS ATTACK ENEMY SHIPS IN RECENTLY OCCUPIED NEW GUINEA BASES.

⑨ FINAL SURRENDER
IN THE PHILIPPINES,
MAY 6, 1942
BATAAN FALLS, APRIL 9, 1942, AND CORREGIDOR SURRENDERS ON MAY 6

⑩ RAID ON TULAGI
MAY 4, 1942
THE OPENING BLOW OF THE CORAL SEA ACTION. U.S. CARRIER AIRCRAFT ATTACK JAPANESE SHIPS IN THE NEWLY OCCUPIED SOLOMONS.

⑪ BATTLE OF THE CORAL SEA
MAY 7–8, 1942
CARRIERS EXCHANGE BLOWS. SEVERE DAMAGE ON THE JAPANESE CARRIER FORCE. LEXINGTON IS LOST, BUT THE JAPANESE ADVANCE IS CHECKED.

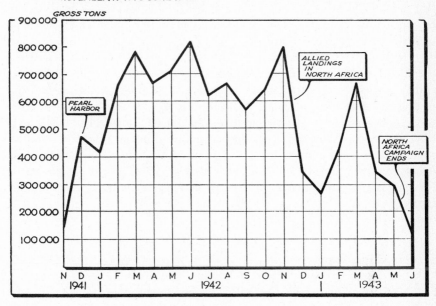

MERCHANT SHIPS SUNK
BY GERMAN SUBMARINES
NOVEMBER 1941 *TO JUNE* 1943

southeastern Russia and penetrated the Caucasus, and the pressure from Moscow for relief in the West increased. At this point Roosevelt and his advisers began to consider the feasibility of an Anglo–American thrust at the northern coast of France, known by the code name SLEDGEHAMMER, as a means of averting total disaster in eastern Europe. This was the issue that dominated the conferences among Roosevelt, Churchill, and their chiefs of staff that began in Washington during June 1942. Churchill stubbornly opposed any limited diversionary attempt. He admitted that the British would have six or eight divisions available for an invasion by September. They would participate if the Americans could guarantee the success of the undertaking. But were there not other ways, perhaps an invasion of North Africa, in which combined Anglo–American forces could attack more successfully? In the midst of these heated deliberations came news of Rommel's threatened drive into Egypt. It diverted the conferees' attention from the coast of France to the imperiled area, enabled Churchill to drive home his arguments for a North African invasion, and caused him to hurry home to face his critics in the House of Commons.

The president and his military staff moved swiftly to bolster British defenses in Egypt during the last week of June 1942. But this crisis soon passed, and Roosevelt decided to have the issue of the second front determined once and for all. He sent Harry Hopkins, General Marshall, and Admiral Ernest J. King, American naval commander, to London in mid-July. They joined General Dwight D. Eisenhower, now commander of the European theater of operations, and other Americans in London on July 18 for preliminary conferences. Marshall and Eisenhower were enthusiastic for an invasion of France, which they contemplated beginning on a limited scale until a large offensive could be mounted. But British staff officers refused to budge from their adamant opposition. And American naval officers agreed that a cross-Channel operation in September or October would be dangerous. Informed of the stalemate, Roosevelt replied that his spokesmen should now insist upon offensive operations somewhere, preferably in North Africa. When it seemed that the conferees would also postpone decision on GYMNAST, as the North African operation was then called, Roosevelt replied that plans must be made at once, and that landings in North Africa should occur no later than October 30, 1942. Churchill agreed, and there now remained only the task of preparing for TORCH—the new code name of the North African operation—and the unpleasant job of telling Stalin why his western Allies could not open a second front in France in 1942. All apprehensions about a premature second front were confirmed in August. A commando raid by a force of 5,000 men, mainly Canadians, against Dieppe, on the French coast, was a disaster. The strongly entrenched Germans inflicted nearly 3,000 casualties.

3. The Tide Turns

Events of the autumn of 1942 began for the first time to bring some hope to the embattled United Nations. The American navy and marines finally stemmed the onrushing tide of Japanese conquest and began their slow and painful progress on the road to Tokyo. The Anglo–American Allies began a campaign in North Africa that ended the Nazi threat to the Middle East and culminated in an invasion of Sicily and Italy in 1943. The Russians finally held firm on the banks of the Volga and then began a counteroffensive that would not cease until Soviet armies had captured Berlin.

The American Pacific Fleet, commanded by Admiral Chester W. Nimitz, had regrouped and given evidence of its valor and power even during the high tide of Japanese expansion. A spectacular blow came in April 1942, when United States Army medium bombers under Colonel James Doolittle took off from the carrier *Hornet* to raid Tokyo. But the most decisive engagement during this defensive phase was the Battle of the Coral Sea, in early May 1942, when planes from *Lexington* and *Yorktown* turned back a large Japanese force moving around the southeastern coast of New Guinea to attack Port Moresby.

The Japanese, shocked by the raid on Tokyo and unaware that the planes had come from a carrier, concluded that the Americans had launched the attack from one of the outlying islands in the Central Pacific. To avoid repetition of this air attack, they decided to extend their perimeter and sent a large armada and invasion force against Midway Island, an outpost guarding the Hawaiian Islands, in a bold bid to cut American communication lines in the Pacific and perhaps establish bases in the islands themselves. Warned of this attack by intercepted Japanese code messages, Nimitz had moved his carriers and cruisers into the Central Pacific, and one of the most decisive battles of the Pacific war raged with incredible fury from June 3 to June 6, 1942. Dive bombers and B-17s from Midway joined with dive bombers and torpedo planes from *Enterprise, Hornet,* and *Yorktown* to sink four Japanese carriers, a heavy cruiser, and three destroyers, and to damage one heavy cruiser and two destroyers. In contrast, the Americans lost only *Yorktown* and a destroyer. The Battle of Midway not only removed the threat to the Hawaiian Islands but also restored the balance of naval power in the Pacific. It was, moreover, convincing proof of the importance of air power, for warships in this battle, as in the Battle of Coral Sea, did not exchange a single salvo during the engagement.

Now it was the Americans' turn to go on the offensive. The Japanese had recently moved into the southern Solomon Islands and were building an airfield on Guadalcanal, which imperiled the Allied position in the entire South Pacific and the line of communication to Australia. Assembling a large force of warships, transports, and marines in New Zealand, Admiral Robert L. Ghormley attacked Tulagi and Guadalcanal in the Solomons in August and soon won control of Tulagi and the airfield on Guadalcanal. At the same time, Japanese cruiser and destroyer force surprised the Allies and sank four cruisers and damaged other ships in the Battle of Savo Island in one of the most humiliating defeats ever suffered by the United States Navy. The Japanese did not know what damage they had done, and they withdrew without attacking the Allied transports. But they soon returned with troops, and the battle raged on Guadalcanal and for control of the air and seas in the area of the Solomons during the next six months. The issue was long in doubt, as the Japanese enjoyed an advantage in land-based aircraft from their base in Rabaul on New Britain Island. However, the American navy won control of the seas in a number of violent battles. Then American army forces, relieving the battle-weary First Marine Division, gradually overcame the enemy on Guadalcanal. The Japanese withdrew in early February 1943.

In the meantime, Allied planners and diplomats had been at work preparing TORCH, the offensive in North Africa under General Eisenhower. The British Eighth Army opened an offensive against Rommel's forces at El Alamein in late October 1942, and three great Anglo–American convoys converged west of Gibraltar soon afterward. Two weeks later, they struck simultaneously at Oran and Algiers in Algeria and Casablanca on the Atlantic coast of French Morocco. They encountered heavy French resistance only around Casablanca. Marshal Henri-Philippe Pétain, head of the Vichy French government, severed diplomatic relations with the United States on November 9 and called upon his forces in North Africa to resist. But Pétain's deputy in North Africa, Admiral Jean Darlan, took control when the Germans invaded unoccupied France on November 11. He concluded an armistice agreement with the Allied supreme commander, General Eisenhower, that recognized Darlan's control and promised the cooperation of some 50,000 French colonial troops in North Africa.

During the two weeks following the conclusion of the Darlan agreement, American and British units from Algiers engaged in a race with the Germans for control of Tunisia, then occupied by small French forces. The Germans reached the province in large numbers first and poured additional men, tanks, and planes into North Africa, and the ensuing campaign became a crucial test of strength. Fighting began in earnest in February 1943. It mounted in intensity as General Sir Bernard Montgomery's British Eighth Army in the East and Eisenhower's combined armies in the

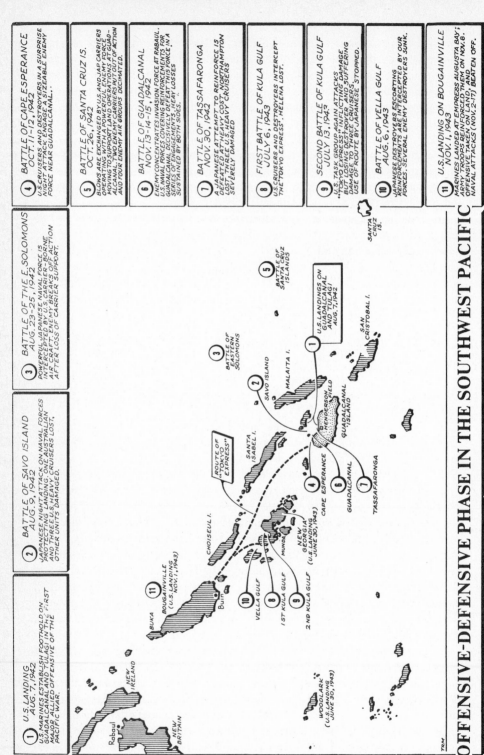

OFFENSIVE-DEFENSIVE PHASE IN THE SOUTHWEST PACIFIC

(1) U.S. LANDING
AUG. 7, 1942
U.S. MARINES ESTABLISH FOOTHOLD ON GUADALCANAL AND TULAGI IN THE FIRST MAJOR ALLIED OFFENSIVE OF THE PACIFIC WAR.

(2) BATTLE OF SAVO ISLAND
AUG. 9, 1942
JAPANESE NIGHT ATTACK ON NAVAL FORCES PROTECTING LANDING. ONE AUSTRALIAN AND THREE U.S. HEAVY CRUISERS LOST, OTHER UNITS DAMAGED.

(3) BATTLE OF THE E. SOLOMONS
AUG. 23–25, 1942
POWERFUL JAPANESE NAVAL FORCE IS INTERCEPTED BY U.S. CARRIER-BORNE AIRCRAFT. ENEMY BREAKS OFF ACTION AFTER LOSS OF CARRIER SUPPORT.

(4) BATTLE OF CAPE ESPERANCE
OCT. 11–12, 1942
U.S. CRUISERS AND DESTROYERS IN A SURPRISE NIGHT ATTACK ENGAGE A SIZEABLE ENEMY FORCE NEAR GUADALCANAL.

(5) BATTLE OF SANTA CRUZ IS.
OCT. 26, 1942
BLOWS ARE EXCHANGED BY U.S. AND JAP CARRIERS OPERATING WITH A POWERFUL ENEMY FORCE MOVING TO SUPPORT LAND OPERATIONS AT GUADALCANAL. TWO ENEMY CARRIERS PUT OUT OF ACTION AND FOUR ENEMY AIR GROUPS DECIMATED.

(6) BATTLE OF GUADALCANAL
NOV. 13–14–15, 1942
ENEMY CONCENTRATES INVASION FORCE AT RABAUL. U.S. NAVAL FORCES COVERING REINFORCEMENTS FOR GUADALCANAL DECISIVELY DEFEAT THIS FORCE IN A SERIES OF ENGAGEMENTS. HEAVY LOSSES SUSTAINED BY BOTH SIDES.

(7) BATTLE OF TASSAFARONGA
NOV. 30, 1942
A JAPANESE ATTEMPT TO REINFORCE IS DEFEATED AT HEAVY COST. NORTHAMPTON LOST, THREE U.S. HEAVY CRUISERS SEVERELY DAMAGED.

(8) FIRST BATTLE OF KULA GULF
JULY 6, 1943
U.S. CRUISERS AND DESTROYERS INTERCEPT THE TOKYO EXPRESS. HELENA LOST.

(9) SECOND BATTLE OF KULA GULF
JULY 13, 1943
U.S. TASK GROUP AGAIN ATTACKS "TOKYO EXPRESS," INFLICTING DAMAGE. WHILE LOSING DESTROYER AND SUFFERING DAMAGE TO OTHER CRUISERS. USE OF ROUTE BY JAPANESE STOPPED.

(10) BATTLE OF VELLA GULF
AUG. 6, 1943
JAPANESE DESTROYERS ESCORTING REINFORCEMENTS ARE INTERCEPTED BY OUR FORCES. SEVERAL ENEMY DESTROYERS SUNK.

(11) U.S. LANDING ON BOUGAINVILLE
NOV. 1, 1943
MARINES LANDED AT EMPRESS AUGUSTA BAY; ARMY TROOPS REINFORCED THEM ON NOV. 8. OFFENSIVE TAKEN ON LAND, AND NAVAL ATTACKS (NOV. 2–17) BEATEN OFF.

West gradually closed the jaws of a gigantic vise on the Germans. The result was a complete Allied victory, signaled by German surrender on May 12, which cost the Axis fifteen divisions, and 349,206 men killed and captured, 250 tanks, over 2,300 airplanes, and 232 ships. In contrast, the Allies suffered 70,000 casualties in a campaign that seasoned their troops and opened the Mediterranean once again to Allied shipping.

In the meantime, Roosevelt, Churchill, their political advisers, and the American and British chiefs of staff had met at Casablanca for a full-dress conference in January 1943. Two decisions—both arrived at reluctantly by the Americans—were reached: to invade Sicily in order to secure complete control of the Mediterranean and advanced air bases and to defer the invasion of France at least until 1944. General Marshall argued strenuously for a cross-Channel invasion in 1943, but without success.

The work of the conference completed, Roosevelt and Churchill held a joint press conference at Casablanca in which they reviewed their work and looked forward to victories ahead. But more important was Roosevelt's declaration, made after previous consultation with Churchill, that the Allies would insist upon the unconditional surrender of the Axis enemies. "It does not mean the destruction of the population of Germany, Italy, and Japan," Roosevelt explained, "but it does mean the destruction of the philosophies in those countries which are based on conquest and the subjugation of other people." It was, as one critic afterward said, one of the "great mistakes of the war." It hardened the German popular will to resist and shut the door to negotiations by an anti-Hitler faction. Worse still, it virtually precluded a negotiated settlement of the Pacific war, the one conflict that might have been terminated by negotiation.

4. The Allies On the Offensive

The decisive turning point of the European war in 1942–1943 occurred when the Russians held Stalingrad from September to November 1942 against furious German attacks. Then the Russians launched a counteroffensive that destroyed or captured a large German army in the blazing city in February 1943. From this point on, the Soviet armies pressed forward along the entire length of the eastern front. By October 1943, the Red armies had driven deep into the Ukraine and stood on the eastern bank of the Dnieper River, poised for a winter offensive that would drive through the Ukraine into Rumania.

The year 1943 also witnessed the turning of the tide in the Battle of the Atlantic. The Germans had more than 100 U-boats constantly at sea by the spring of 1943. But the Anglo-American Allies had finally found the means of victory—aggressive offense through new methods of detection, air patrols both from land bases and escort carriers, and fast destroyers and destroyer escorts to protect the convoys. The turning point came from March through May 1943, when U-boat sinkings in the Atlantic declined from 514,744 tons in March to 199,409 tons in May, and the number of submarines destroyed rose from 12 to 40. Allied shipping losses had

THE DATES NEAR THE CAPITAL CITIES ARE THE DATES OF FINAL CAPTURE
BOUNDARIES AS OF JULY 1, 1944

AXIS STATES AND ANNEXED AREAS

AXIS ALLIES

TERRITORY ACQUIRED BY U.S.S.R., 1939 TO JUNE 22, 1941

THE WAR AGAINST GERMANY IN THE EAST, 1941-1945

declined to 29,297 tons by May 1944, and not a single Allied ship was torpedoed in the summer of 1944. And for decreasing results the Germans paid such a high price—237 submarines sunk in 1943, 241 in 1944, and 153 during the first four months of 1945—as to make their underseas campaign a useless drain on resources and manpower.

Allied power increased so swiftly in the Pacific from March 1943 to March 1944 that the two major commanders in the area, Admiral Nimitz and General MacArthur, were able not only to overwhelm or neutralize the Japanese bastions in the Central and South Pacific, but also to launch new offensives that pierced the outer perimeter of Japanese defenses.

The objective of the first great offensive was Rabaul on New Britain Island, the most important Japanese air and naval base in the Southwest Pacific area. The Allied attack was two-pronged. First came a tortuous drive up the New Guinea coast from Port Moresby to Hollandia by American and Australian ground forces, paratroops, and the American Fifth Air Force and Seventh Fleet—all under MacArthur's general command. The enemy had been cleared from the eastern part of New Guinea by February 1944. Meanwhile, American and New Zealand ground forces and strong air and naval forces under Admiral William F. Halsey began a drive in June 1943 through the central and northern Solomon Islands that had carried to New Georgia and Bougainville by November 1943, and to Green Island by February 1944. Finally, with the occupation of the Admiralty Islands north of New Guinea in late February 1944, Rabaul was cut off from communication with the Japanese base of Truk, and its encirclement was complete. Thereafter, Allied commanders were content to reduce Rabaul to impotence through aerial bombardment, without attempting to capture it.

While Allied forces under MacArthur thus secured their hold on the South Pacific, the forces under Admiral Nimitz launched two major offensives in the Central Pacific that cracked the outer rim of Japanese defenses in that area. A new Central Pacific Force, including marine and army units, under the command of Admiral Raymond A. Spruance, attacked Tarawa and Makin islands in the Gilberts in late November 1943. Makin was lightly garrisoned and fell quickly to army troops; but the Second Marine Division, which invaded Tarawa after an inadequate bombardment, met fierce resistance from Japanese marines and had to fight for every inch of ground until the last defenders were wiped out on November 24. Striking next at the Marshall Islands, army and marine divisions rooted out Japanese defenders on Kwajalein, Roi, Namur, and Eniwetok between February 1 and 19, 1944. Next the American navy steamed into the enemy's interior defenses in daring raids against Truk and Saipan in the Marianas, only 1,350 miles from Tokyo, in February 1944.

Meanwhile, the Allies began a major Mediterranean campaign when a huge Anglo-American armada disgorged 160,000 troops, 600 tanks, and 1,800 guns on the beaches of Sicily in July 1943. The British Eighth Army, under General Montgomery, and the American Seventh Army, under General George S. Patton, had routed the Italian and German defenders and overrun the island by mid-August. It was an important turning point, for a group of Italian conspirators persuaded King Victor Emmanuel to connive at the deposition and arrest of Mussolini on July 25 and

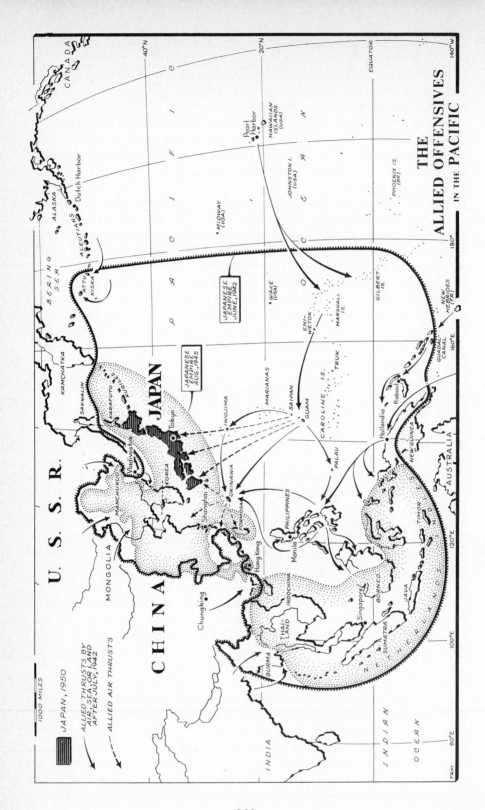

THE
ALLIED OFFENSIVES
IN THE PACIFIC

JAPANESE
EMPIRE
JUNE, 1942

JAPANESE
EMPIRE
AUG., 1945

JAPAN, 1950

ALLIED THRUSTS BY
AIR, SEA, OR LAND
AFTER JULY, 1942

ALLIED AIR THRUSTS

1000 MILES

366

formed a new government under Marshal Badoglio. He proceeded to open negotiations looking toward the surrender of Italy.

This sudden turn of events raised new perplexities for Roosevelt and Churchill —whether to negotiate with the Badoglio government, as Eisenhower and other Allied leaders requested, or to demand unconditional surrender in accordance with the Casablanca declaration. The situation was so uncertain that the president, the prime minister, and their respective entourages met in Quebec on August 17, 1943, for a conference known by the code name of QUADRANT.

The new Italian government made secret contact with the Allies. The Italians were eager to surrender but insisted that the Allies protect Rome, the king, and the government from the Germans, who had meanwhile taken control of most of Italy. Roosevelt and Churchill agreed to send an airborne division to capture the airfields around Rome, and the armistice was signed on September 3. By the time that preparations for an airborne assault on Rome were completed, however, the Germans had surrounded the city in force and seized the airfields. A German parachute force rescued Mussolini on September 12, 1943, and he then established a new Fascist government at Lake Como under German protection.

Meanwhile, the British Eighth Army crossed the Straits of Messina on September 3 and began the invasion of the Italian mainland in an operation called AVALANCHE. A week later a British airborne division seized the large Italian naval base at Taranto, while the United States Fifth Army, under the command of General Mark Clark, landed in the Gulf of Salerno south of Naples. The Fifth Army occupied Naples on October 7 in spite of furious German counterattacks and pushed northward to the Volturno River. Meanwhile, British forces had cleared the central and eastern sections of the Italian boot. Allied forces had pushed to a winter line south of Cassino by January 1, 1944.

A long and bloody campaign for Italy still impended, but the Italian surrender and successful invasion of Italy yielded large dividends to the Anglo-American Allies. It brought the surrender of the Italian fleet and guaranteed complete Allied control of the Mediterranean. It gave the Allies advanced air bases from which to bomb the Balkans and Central Europe. It consumed some of Hitler's best divisions. Most important, it gave the British and Americans the incalculable advantage of being on the offensive.

5. The Soviets and the Grand Alliance

The QUADRANT conferees at Quebec turned to other urgent problems after they approved final arrangements for the Italian surrender. They reaffirmed May 1, 1944, as the date for OVERLORD, the long delayed cross-Channel invasion. Hull and Eden discussed postwar plans for Germany and approved the draft of a Four Power Declaration—to be submitted to the coming conference of foreign ministers in Moscow—pledging America, Great Britain, Russia, and China to cooperate in the establishment of an effective postwar security organization. The conference was over on August 24, and Churchill accompanied Roosevelt back to Washington and

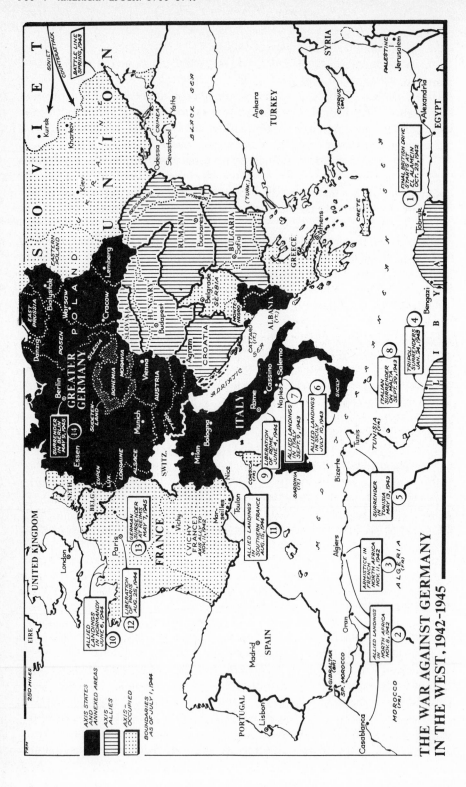

THE WAR AGAINST GERMANY
IN THE WEST, 1942–1945

stayed with him intermittently during the next three weeks. During this time the Badoglio government surrendered, and the Allies began their invasion of the Italian mainland.

Soon afterward, in October 1943, Secretary Hull made the arduous air journey to Moscow for the conference of foreign ministers that opened in the Russian capital. Before this time, no one in Washington or London knew what Russian postwar ambitions were, except for the territorial demands that Stalin had outlined to Eden in December 1941. In Moscow, Hull, Molotov, and Eden discussed immediate and postwar problems, with so little disagreement that future accord seemed assured. They completely endorsed an American plan for the postwar treatment of Germany. It called for the unconditional surrender of Germany by whatever government exercised power at the end of the war. An Inter-Allied Control Commission would supervise the surrender and occupation of Germany by Soviet, American, and British troops. It would undertake to destroy all vestiges of nazism and encourage establishment of a democratic government and the restoration of freedom of religion, speech, the press, and political activity. Moreover, Germany should be denied a standing army and general staff and prohibited from manufacturing any war materials or aircraft of any kind. Finally, Germany should be required to pay reparations in goods, equipment, and manpower, but not in money. The conferees agreed, moreover, that Austria should be reconstituted an independent nation and regarded as a liberated and not an enemy state, while Hull persuaded Stalin and Molotov to sign the Four Power Declaration. In addition, at a state dinner on October 30, Stalin told Hull the welcome news that Russia would join the war against Japan after the defeat of Germany.

Despite differences over Poland, the Moscow Conference was a resounding success. No one in the West knew absolutely whether Russia would cooperate in the postwar era, but such cooperation now seemed at least possible. As one milestone along the road to Allied unity, the conference prepared the way for the next—a personal meeting of the Big Three.

Roosevelt had long wanted to meet with the Russian leader, and he had invited Stalin before the Moscow Conference to join him and Churchill at Ankara, Baghdad, or Basra in Iraq. Stalin replied that he would go only to Teheran, since he could maintain personal control over his high command from the Iranian capital. The president agreed and left Hampton Roads on the new battleship *Iowa* in November 1943 for the long journey to Cairo. There he conferred with Churchill, Chiang Kai-shek, Lord Louis Mountbatten, Allied commander in Southeast Asia, and General Joseph W. Stilwell, American commander in the China area and adviser to Chiang. Most of these discussions revolved around an Allied drive in Burma to open supply lines to China, and a Chinese offensive in northern China.

Roosevelt and his party next flew from Cairo to Teheran. During the subsequent days, the Big Three thrashed over practically all outstanding military and political problems, including military operations in Italy and American plans for offensive operations in the Pacific. Stalin again promised that Russia would join the war against Japan after Germany's surrender.

The Russians were most concerned about OVERLORD and seemed desperately anxious to pin Roosevelt and Churchill to a definite time and place for the great invasion. Stalin pressed Roosevelt to name a supreme commander for OVERLORD, and, on his return from Teheran, the president chose Eisenhower for this position.

The Big Three also discussed the future of Germany and plans for postwar collaboration. They now seemed to favor partition. Stalin emphasized the danger of future German resurgence. Roosevelt outlined his plan for a future United Nations organization, which would assume responsibility for preventing wars and aggression. During all these conversations, Roosevelt became convinced that he had broken through the wall of suspicion and distrust surrounding Stalin, won Russian trust and friendship, and laid the basis for fruitful collaboration in the future. His feeling was well expressed in the concluding sentences of the Declaration of Teheran, issued on December 1: "We came here with hope and determination. We leave here, friends in fact, in spirit, and in purpose."

6. The European Air War, 1940–1945

After the failure of the German air blitz against England in 1940–1941, the British gained air superiority. The RAF Bomber Command conducted a limited number of night raids against selected industrial and transportation targets in Germany from 1940 to early 1942. Results were so unsatisfactory that the new chief of the Bomber Command, Sir Arthur Harris, executed a complete change in British bombing tactics—from the target system to mass bombing of industrial areas in order to disrupt the German economy and lessen the will of the German people to fight. The first 1,000-plane RAF raid, against Cologne on May 30, 1942, signaled the beginning of the new campaign. It was followed in 1942 by others against centers in the Ruhr, Bremen, Hamburg, and other German cities. This was only a small beginning, for less than 50,000 tons of bombs fell on Axis Europe in 1942, and German war production and civilian morale were not visibly impaired.

Meanwhile, the United States Eighth Air Force had established bases in England in early 1942 and joined in the air war in August 1942. The offensive power of the Eighth Air Force grew and was reinforced by the Ninth Air Force and the Fifteenth Air Force, and the Americans became a powerful factor in the air campaign during the summer of 1943. While the British continued their devastating night attacks, the Americans used their heavier armored Flying Fortresses and Liberators in daring daylight raids. However, extremely heavy losses in a raid on Schweinfurt in October 1943 convinced American commanders that further large daylight operations had to await production of long-range fighters to protect the bombers. All told, American and British bombers dropped 206,188 tons of bombs on European targets in 1943.

A new phase in the air campaign began in February 1944. The arrival in England of substantial numbers of long-range American fighters made resumption of daylight raids possible. The introduction of radar bombsights had already greatly increased the accuracy of night bombing. And there was a use of increasingly heavy bombs and a rapid build-up of the Eighth and Fifteenth Air Forces. The Americans first began a systematic campaign to destroy the German aircraft industry. Then the attack shifted in March to French and Belgian marshaling yards, railroads, and bridges. And, after the invasion of France, the American and the British air forces began a coordinated and relentless round-the-clock assault upon German synthetic oil and chemical plants. Some 8,000 to 9,000 Allied planes turned to the task of paralyzing the German transportation system in February 1945. Finally, the air forces joined the advancing Allied armies in April in reducing the German nation to utter impotence and ruin.

The overall dimensions of the Anglo-American air effort in Europe stagger the imagination: 1,442,280 bomber and 2,686,799 fighter sorties, which dropped 2,-697,473 tons of bombs on Germany and Nazi-occupied Europe. This effort cost the Allies some 40,000 planes and 158,000 personnel. All told, Allied bombs dropped on Germany killed 305,000 people and wounded 780,000 others, destroyed or damaged 5.5 million homes, and deprived 20 million persons of essential utilities. By the beginning of 1944, according to a poll taken by the Strategic Bombing Survey immediately after the war, some 77 percent of the German people were convinced that the war was lost; and by May 1945 most Germans had lost all will to continue the uneven struggle.

7. Toward Victory In Europe

General Dwight D. Eisenhower, supreme commander of the Allied Expeditionary Forces, arrived in London in January 1944, with orders from Roosevelt and Churchill to "enter the continent of Europe and, in conjunction with the other Allied Nations, undertake operations aimed at the heart of Germany and the destruction of her armed forces." The Combined Chiefs of Staff and various technical staffs in Great Britain and the United States had been hard at work on OVERLORD since 1942. Planning for the actual invasion and subsequent operations continued in Eisenhower's London headquarters after January 1944.

The appointed time now approached rapidly. The great invasion armada was delayed by a sudden storm and put out to sea early in the morning of June 6. The Germans expected the invasion to come in the Pas de Calais area, where the English Channel is narrowest. Instead, the Allies struck at five beaches along a sixty-mile stretch of the Cotentin Peninsula in Normandy. First there were furious air and naval bombardments of the invasion area and beaches. Next came the landing of three airborne divisions behind the German lines a few minutes after midnight on June 6. Finally, the seaborne troops hit the beaches at 7:30 in the morning. German resistance was generally light; but American invaders met a fierce defense on Omaha Beach and suffered heavy casualties.

The German commanders, Field Marshals Rommel and Karl von Rundstedt, mistook the Normandy invasion as a screen for a larger invasion in the Pas de Calais. They were not able to bring up their reserve divisions in time to prevent the Allies from securing and capturing a bridgehead in Normandy. Within two weeks after D day, the Allies had landed more than 1 million troops with enormous quantities of supplies in a broad sector along the Normandy coast. They had also captured

Cherbourg, Caen, and St. Lô, "eaten the guts out of the German defense," and were poised for a grand sweep through northern France.

The battle of the breakthrough began on July 25, with a lightninglike thrust by General Patton's Third Army into Brittany and a breakthrough to Avranches and Falaise by the American First Army and the British Second Army. Soon the battle for Normandy turned into the battle for France. The German Seventh Army in the area between Falaise and Argentan was under orders to stand firm. It was surrounded and partially destroyed or captured during a furious battle from August 19–23. The Allies completed the liberation of France in their own version of lightning warfare while the surviving German armies moved back to their Siegfried line. The American Seventh Army invaded southern France on August 15 and joined the race for the German frontier. Paris fell to French and American troops ten days later. By mid-September, American and British armies had captured Brussels and Antwerp, occupied Luxembourg, and crossed the German border at Aachen.

The Allies were on the move on other fronts as well. They had tried vainly to break the German lines in southern Italy. Then they tried to turn the German flank on January 22, 1944, by landings at Anzio and Nettuno on the Italian western coast, only thirty-six miles from Rome. This effort failed. But the British Eighth Army and the American Fifth Army pushed northward in the spring, joined the beleaguered divisions on the Anzio beachhead, and captured Rome on June 4, 1944. Under heavy Allied pressure and harrassment, the Germans pulled back to their Gothic line, which ran across Italy some 150 miles north of Rome. There they managed to stabilize the fighting around September 1, 1944.

Meanwhile, the Russians, during the spring of 1944, began offensives along the entire eastern front fully as important in the Allied strategy as the Anglo-American sweep across France. One Russian drive on the northern sector forced Finland to sue for peace on August 25. The greatest Russian offensive, however, opened on June 23 to coincide with the Anglo-American drive in the West. Soviet armies captured the German stronghold of Vitebsk and then broke through to the Baltic on August 1. Five Russian armies in the central sector rolled into Poland, reached the Vistula River in late July, captured Warsaw on January 17, 1945, and reached the Oder River, only forty-five miles from Berlin, the following month. Farther to the south, two Red armies overran Rumania in August 1944. Then they marched into Bulgaria, captured Belgrade on October 20, and entered Budapest in February 1945.

It was obvious to almost everyone by the autumn of 1944 that the German military situation was hopeless. Germany was now a beleaguered fortress awaiting final destruction because her fanatical master preferred complete destruction to unconditional surrender. Some high German officers, foreseeing inevitable ruin under Hitler's leadership, in cooperation with certain anti-Nazi groups, perfected plans to take control of the German government and assassinate Hitler. Their agent left a time bomb in Hitler's headquarters on July 20, 1944. Thinking Hitler dead, the conspirators proceeded to take first steps to seize control of the army and government. As it turned out, Hitler was only injured by the bomb's blast. With the support of loyal troops he rounded up the opposition, executed about 5,000 after drumhead trials, and sent another 10,000 enemies to concentration camps. In consequence, the war would proceed to its bitter end.

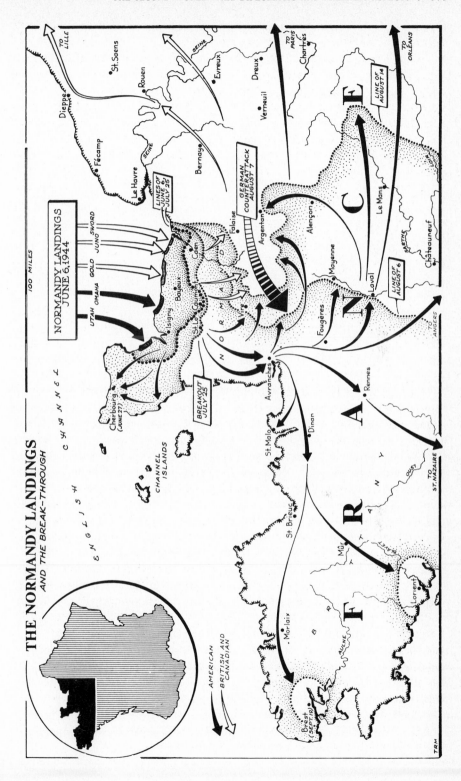

THE NORMANDY LANDINGS
AND THE BREAK-THROUGH

NORMANDY LANDINGS
JUNE 6, 1944

100 MILES

ENGLISH CHANNEL

CHANNEL ISLANDS

AMERICAN
BRITISH AND CANADIAN

Dieppe
St. Saens
Rouen
Fécamp
Le Havre
Evreux
Dreux
SEINE
Bernay
Verneuil
TO LILLE
TO PARIS
Chartres
TO ORLEANS
LINE OF AUGUST 14

LINES OF JUNE 6, JULY 25
GERMAN COUNTERATTACK AUGUST 7
Falaise
Argentan
Alençon
Le Mans
Châteauneuf
SARTHE

UTAH OMAHA GOLD JUNO SWORD
Caen
Bayeux
Isigny
St. Lo
Caumont
NORMANDY
Mayenne
Fougères
Laval
LINE OF AUGUST 6
TO ANGERS

Cherbourg (JUNE 27)

BREAKOUT JULY 25

Avranches
St. Malo
Dinan
Rennes
TO ST. NAZAIRE

St. Brieuc
Dinan
BRITTANY

Morlaix
Mûr
Lorient
Brest (SEPT. 19)
FRANCE
BLAVET
AULNE
OUST
VILAINE

TRM

8. The Campaign and Election of 1944

Meanwhile, partisan politics had persisted in the United States. The Republicans made a hard fight to win control of Congress in 1942. They failed, but they made such sweeping gains in the elections on November 3 that a GOP victory in 1944 seemed at least possible. The Democrats elected 222 and the Republicans 209 members to the House—a Republican gain of 47 seats. The Republicans, moreover, gained 9 seats in the Senate. Actually, what occurred in the federal and state elections in November 1942 was not merely a Republican revival but also a strong conservative upsurge. The significance of the upheaval became apparent after the organization of the Seventy-eighth Congress in January 1943, when many southern Democrats joined Republicans to form a majority coalition and seize control of legislative policy. This coalition gave the president aggressive support in all matters relating to war and postwar policies. In domestic matters, however, it proceeded as fast as it could to destroy certain parts of the New Deal.

Wendell L. Willkie was still titular head of the GOP, but he had no support among party leaders and had become so closely identified with the Roosevelt administration as to lose his status as leader of the opposition. He withdrew from the preconvention campaign after suffering an impressive defeat in the Wisconsin presidential primary in April 1944. Meanwhile, Willkie's chief rival, Governor Thomas E. Dewey of New York, was fast emerging as the new Republican leader. The presidential nomination went to him on the first ballot when the Republican National Convention met in Chicago on June 26, with the vice-presidential nomination going to Governor John W. Bricker of Ohio. The convention adopted a platform that was aggressively internationalistic and essentially progressive in tone. It roundly condemned the Roosevelt administration's alleged inefficiency, waste, excessive centralization, and destruction of private enterprise. However, it made it clear that Republicans had no fundamental quarrel with Democrats on domestic issues. On the contrary, it promised to strengthen the New Deal's labor, social security, and agricultural programs. All in all, it was the most significant endorsement of the Roosevelt policies yet written.

There never was much doubt that the Democrats would nominate Roosevelt for a fourth term, and he was willing to accept even although he had recently suffered from cardiac failure, hypertension, and hypertensive heart disease. On July 11, the president announced that he would accept renomination, and his announcement settled the matter when the Democratic National Convention opened in Chicago on July 19.

In view of Roosevelt's precarious health and poor chances of serving out a fourth term, the crucial struggle revolved around the nomination of a vice-presidential candidate. This battle was bitter and created divisions in the party that persisted for years afterward. Vice-President Henry A. Wallace enjoyed the support of the advanced progressive wing and large elements in the CIO. But he was almost unanimously opposed by party bosses, Southerners, and many moderates who suspected that he was temperamentally unfit for the presidency and hopelessly inept at political leadership. Roosevelt endorsed Wallace publicly but refused to insist upon his nomination. In fact, the president had apparently promised the succession to Byrnes and actually tried to obtain the nomination for the South Carolinian.

The president's plans, however, were upset on the eve of the convention by a newcomer in high Democratic councils, Sidney Hillman, a vice-president of the CIO and former codirector of the defense effort. Alarmed by the rising tide of antilabor sentiment and the failure of workers to go to the polls in 1942, Hillman organized the Political Action Committee (PAC) of the CIO in 1943. His purpose was not only to rally workers and progressives but also to win new bargaining power for labor within the Democratic party.

Hillman used his power in a spectacular way at the Democratic National Convention. He virtually vetoed Byrnes's nomination by warning the president that the South Carolinian was unacceptable to labor and northern blacks. The president concluded that his assistant must give way to a compromise candidate. He therefore declared that either Senator Harry S Truman or Justice William O. Douglas would be an agreeable running mate. And he agreed with Hillman that the PAC should shift its support from Wallace to Truman when it became obvious that Wallace could not be nominated. In any event, Roosevelt declared in his final instructions to National Chairman Robert E. Hannegan that the party managers had to "clear it with Sidney," that is, had to win Hillman's approval for any vice-presidential candidate.

The issue was actually settled during the three days before the convention opened in Chicago on July 19, 1944. Hillman declared that he would fight Byrnes's nomination to the bitter end, and the president on July 17 asked the South Carolinian to withdraw. Byrnes's withdrawal narrowed the field to Wallace, who still enjoyed the PAC's seeming support, and Truman, upon whom administration and party leaders had finally agreed. During the balloting for the vice-presidential nomination on July 19 and 20, Wallace led on the first ballot and Truman won on the third, as the leaders had planned. The convention had nominated the president on the first ballot a short time before. The Democratic platform promised continuation of progressive policies at home and vigorous American leadership abroad in the postwar era.

Dewey campaigned hard under tremendous handicaps during the ensuing summer and autumn. He was beaten before he started—by smashing Allied victories in Europe and the Pacific, a general reluctance to change governments in the midst of the world crisis, and above all by his own general agreement with basic administration policies. This latter handicap forced him to make criticisms that could only sound captious. Dewey's chief advantage was Roosevelt's failing health and a growing suspicion that perhaps the president was incapable of managing affairs of state. This suspicion increased after Roosevelt's address at Bremerton, Washington, on August 12, during which he was halting and ineffective because he was suffering at this very time from an attack of angina pectoris. However, Roosevelt, his health substantially recovered, came back in a speech before the Teamsters' Union in Washington on September 23 that convinced millions of voters that he was still the champion campaigner. He followed this masterpiece with strenuous tours and speeches in Chicago, New York, Wilmington, Delaware, and New England.

This aggressive campaign gave Roosevelt the initiative that he had seemingly lost. He also recovered lost ground by committing himself squarely to a full resumption of progressive policies in the postwar era. Almost as decisive was the PAC's success in getting workers to the polls. In the election on November 7, Roosevelt received 25,602,505 popular and 432 electoral votes; Dewey, 22,006,278 popular and 99 electoral votes. The Democrats lost one seat in the Senate, but they gained twenty seats in the House, all but four of them in the large cities, and captured governorships in Ohio, Massachusetts, Missouri, Idaho, and Washington. The most important outcome of the election was not the continuation of Democratic control but rather the fact that Americans of both parties were now irrevocably committed to assume the leadership in world affairs that they had so often rejected before 1941. For better or for worse, there could be no turning back on the high road to international responsibility.

9. The Yalta Conference

The rapid progress of Allied and Russian armies raised the possibility that the war in Europe might end before the three great powers had come to definitive agreement on plans for future collaboration. Indeed, there was little evidence that the American leaders yet knew even their own minds on the most important aspect of postwar planning—a policy for the control of Germany. More disturbing, however, were signs of growing Allied dissension that threatened to split the Grand Alliance and prevent organization of a postwar United Nations. British, American, and Russian delegates met at Dumbarton Oaks in Washington in September 1944. They agreed on a basic structure for a United Nations but could not agree upon certain fundamental aspects of voting procedure. Following this, the State Department and the British Foreign Office engaged in heated controversies over the organization of a new Italian government and the methods and objectives of British intervention in Greece. The most dangerous potential source of trouble was Russian policy in eastern Europe, especially in Poland.

Roosevelt's thoughts inevitably turned toward another meeting of the Big Three to discuss matters that could be settled only on the highest level. Churchill and Stalin were agreeable, although Stalin insisted that he could not leave Russia because he was personally directing the Russian armies. The three leaders soon agreed upon Yalta in the Crimea as the place and early February 1945 as the time of the conference.

The Yalta meeting would obviously be the last Big Three conference before the surrender of Germany, and the president and the new secretary of state, Edward R. Stettinius, Jr., went to unusual effort, first, to formulate an American program and, second, to come to firm agreement with the British before the Big Three met. Stettinius took his staff to Marrakech in French Morocco for a briefing session in

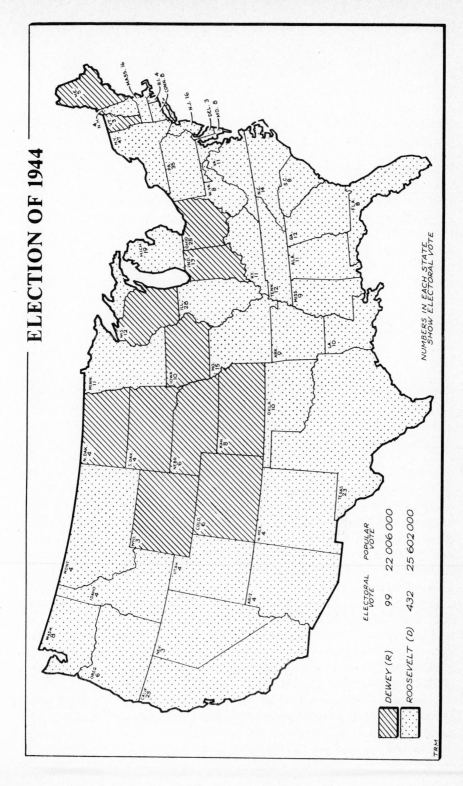

ELECTION OF 1944

NUMBERS IN EACH STATE
SHOW ELECTORAL VOTE

	ELECTORAL VOTE	POPULAR VOTE
DEWEY (R)	99	22 006 000
ROOSEVELT (D)	432	25 602 000

TRM

January 1945, and they then went to Malta for conferences with Churchill and Eden.

The Anglo-American-Russian conferees assembled at Yalta on February 3 and 4, 1945, for the opening of the conference called ARGONAUT on the latter day. The Big Three discussed almost every conceivable problem related to the future of Europe, Asia, and the United Nations from February 4 through 11. In addition, the foreign ministers and military and naval leaders of the three powers worked behind the scenes to smooth out minor differences and lay the groundwork for major understandings. Without following the conferees in their long deliberations, let us now summarize their major agreements and decisions.

Germany   The discussions relating to Germany revolved around the questions of dismemberment, reparations, future Allied control, and French participation in the Inter-Allied Control Commission. The conferees approved dismemberment in principle and agreed to consider details in future negotiations. However, they agreed that northern East Prussia, including Königsberg, should go to Russia; that Poland should annex the southern half of East Prussia; that Russia should annex certain former eastern Polish provinces; and that Poland should receive territory in eastern Germany as compensation. As for reparations, the Russians proposed exacting a total of $20 billion, half of which should be paid to the USSR. Roosevelt and Churchill would not approve any fixed sum. But they agreed to accept the Russian proposal as the basis for future negotiations and to establish a reparations commission with headquarters in Moscow. The Russians withdrew their objection to French participation in the occupation of Germany, and Stalin agreed also that France should have a seat on the Control Commission. As the several occupation zones had already been drawn by the European Advisory Commission in London, there was no discussion of this matter at Yalta.

The Governments of Poland and Eastern Europe   The crucial question was Poland's political future. Stalin and Molotov said quite frankly that they would not tolerate a Polish regime unfriendly to the USSR. As they pointed out, the Germans had twice within twenty-five years used Poland as the corridor for attacks against Russia. They insisted that Great Britain and the United States recognize a provisional Polish government in Lublin that Russia had sponsored and recognized. Roosevelt and Churchill adamantly refused. Then Stalin suggested that the Lublin government be enlarged to include some of the leaders of the Polish government-in-exile that the western powers supported and which was now in London. Roosevelt and Churchill again refused. Stalin finally agreed that the Lublin government should be reorganized to include Polish democratic leaders at home and abroad, and that free elections should be held at an early date to determine the future government of the country. Roosevelt made it clear that the British and American ambassadors in Warsaw would judge whether this pledge had been honestly kept.

The three powers pledged themselves to assist the peoples of other so-called liberated countries of eastern Europe to establish, through free elections, democratic governments responsive to popular will.

Churchill and Eden had had conferences with Stalin in Moscow over the future of the Balkans in October 1944 in which they agreed that Russia should have predominance in Rumania and Bulgaria, that Britain should have predominance in Greece, and that the two countries would share responsibility in Yugoslavia and Hungary.

The Yalta agreements were to supersede the Churchill-Stalin agreement.

The Organization of the United Nations   The Russians conceded practically everything for which Americans had contended at the Dumbarton Oaks Conference in discussions at Yalta over organization of the United Nations. First, they accepted the American formula for voting in the Security Council. Second, the Soviets withdrew their demand for sixteen votes in the General Assembly and received in return additional representatives and votes for the Ukraine and White Russia. Third, Stalin agreed to Roosevelt's proposal that all nations at war with Germany by March 1, 1945, might become members of the United Nations.

The Far East   By a secret agreement between the Americans and Russians, which Churchill approved but did not help make, and which was not published until February 1946, Stalin agreed to bring Russia into the war against Japan within two or three months after the surrender of Germany. In return, Roosevelt approved the transfer of the Kurile Islands from Japan to Russia, recognized Russian control of Outer Mongolia, and agreed that Russia should recover all rights and territory lost at the end of the Russo-Japanese War. Finally, Stalin agreed to recognize Chinese sovereignty over Manchuria and to conclude a treaty of friendship and alliance with the Nationalist government of China.

Millions of words have since been spoken and written about the Yalta agreements. Critics have called them base appeasement of Russia, betrayal of Poland and eastern Europe to Soviet imperialism, and useless surrender to communism in the Far East—all by a mentally incompetent president who was hoodwinked by the wily Stalin. Defenders have replied that the agreements were necessary and realistic.

The charge that Roosevelt was mentally incompetent is most easily disposed of. Roosevelt was obviously tired at Yalta and exhausted afterward by the strain of the grueling sessions and of his long journeys. But there is no evidence that he was not in full possession of his mental faculties during the conference itself. The consensus of historical judgment rather emphatically supports the conclusion that Roosevelt and Churchill achieved nearly everything that circumstances permitted. They undoubtedly knew the risks they were running in the agreements on Poland and eastern Europe. They knew also that they had no alternative but to accept a compromise and to hope that the Russians would honor it. The Russians were already in eastern Europe. The United States and Britain might conceivably have driven them out, but neither the Anglo–American peoples nor soldiers would have tolerated even the suggestion of a long and bloody war to save Poland or Rumania from Communist domination. These were the two prime historical realities with which Roosevelt and Churchill had to reckon, and from which Stalin could benefit, at Yalta. The Anglo–American leaders obtained important concessions from Stalin in spite of their weak bargaining positions. Future conflicts with the Soviet Union developed, not because the Russians honored the Yalta agreements, but precisely because they violated them.

We now know that Roosevelt concluded the secret far eastern agreement with Stalin because he and his military advisers believed that the Japanese would not surrender unconditionally without invasion and occupation. Moreover, no one yet knew whether the atomic bomb would explode or what damage it would do. Acting on the advice of his military advisers, Roosevelt made the agreement with Stalin, he thought, in order to prevent the death of perhaps 1 million American men in bloody campaigns in Japan and on the Asiatic mainland. To avert this catastrophe, the president virtually let Stalin name his own price for Soviet participation. Actually, Soviet far eastern policy was neither determined nor defined at Yalta. It is a fair assumption that the Russians would have entered the war against Japan and reestablished themselves as a major far eastern power whether the Americans liked it or not.

Critics of the Yalta agreements tend to forget that the Russians also made substantial concessions. They agreed to participate in a United Nations that would certainly be controlled by the Anglo–American bloc; to give France a share in the control of Germany; and to respect the integrity of the peoples of eastern Europe. They seemed determined to act reasonably and to meet Churchill and Roosevelt halfway on all important issues. Roosevelt and Churchill, therefore, acted in the only manner that was historically possible.

10. Victory in Europe

The British and American armies approached the Siegfried line in September 1944. Eisenhower made an effort to turn the northern flank of the German defenses by landing three airborne divisions to capture bridges across the Meuse, Waal, and Rhine rivers. This effort failed when the British First Airborne Division was unable to hold a bridge across the Rhine at Arnhem, and the Allies were denied the opportunity to make a rapid drive across the north German plain. Instead, they brought up reinforcements for a winter campaign through the heavy German defenses manned by armies now regrouped and strengthened.

While American and British armies were probing along the length of the Siegfried line, Hitler laid plans for one final gamble—a counteroffensive through the weak center of the Allied lines in the Ardennes Forest. This, he hoped, would split the enemy's forces and carry to Liège and perhaps Antwerp. Bad weather in late November and early December enabled von Rundstedt, the German commander, to bring up his forces in secret. They struck furiously in the Ardennes on December 16 and scored heavily until Allied counterattacks forced them to withdraw. The Battle of the Bulge, as the German offensive is commonly known, was over by January 1945. Hitler's gamble had cost him his last reserves of aircraft and some of his best divisions.

In fact, the German army in the west was so weakened by ruinous losses in the Ardennes counteroffensive that it could no longer prevent the Allied armies from advancing to the Rhine. Forces under Field Marshal Montgomery captured Cleves, in the north, on February 12. Cologne fell to the American First Army on March 6. Troops of the French First and the American Third and Seventh armies had cleared the Saar and Palatinate areas in the south by March 25. Meanwhile, American troops, by an unbelievable stroke of good luck, captured the Ludendorff Bridge across the Rhine at Remagen on March 7 before it could be demolished. They quickly established a bridgehead on the other side of the river.

Anglo–American armies were now poised along the Rhine for a final drive into the heart of Germany, and Russian armies were massed on the Oder River for an assault upon Berlin. But new tensions between the western democracies and Russia gave warning of troubled times ahead. For one thing, the Russians, in February 1945, had imposed a Communist government on Rumania. For another thing, Anglo–American negotiations with a German general for surrender of German forces in Italy had caused Stalin to address a letter to Roosevelt virtually accusing him and Churchill of treacherously negotiating for surrender of all German forces in the west so that British and American armies could occupy Berlin before the Russians.

Even more ominous were Russian actions in Poland. The Russians had not only refused to honor the Yalta agreement to reorganize the puppet Lublin government, but they had also refused to allow American and British observers to enter Poland and had proceeded to liquidate the leaders of the democratic parties in that unhappy country. It was plain that Stalin would tolerate no Polish government that he could not completely control; indeed, he admitted as much in correspondence with Churchill. The Polish dispute was nearing the point of open rupture by mid-March, but Roosevelt was now so weak that he had lost his grasp and could not take leadership in opposing Soviet violations of the Yalta agreements. Actually, Poland was irretrievably lost to Soviet domination, as Stalin's blunt replies to Churchill's vigorous protests revealed.

Poland was lost, but not yet Prague and Berlin, if the Allies resolved to act quickly and send their armies hurtling across Germany. Churchill perceived clearly enough that "Soviet Russia had become a mortal danger to the free world." He pleaded all through April and early May with his American colleagues to push as rapidly as possible toward the two central European capitals. Even more important, he proposed that the Allies stay in force on this forward eastern line until the Russians had honored earlier promises.

The reasons for the failure to attempt to seize strong outposts in Central Europe can best be seen in an account of military and political events. The combined Anglo–American armies began their crossing of the Rhine on March 24. Montgomery's forces in the north and Omar N. Bradley's in the center had converged by April 1 to encircle the Ruhr and trap more than 250,000 German troops. General Montgomery was all for driving straight to Berlin. But Eisenhower, for what seemed to be sound military reasons, decided to drive from the Kassel–Frankfurt area to the Elbe in order to split the German forces and prevent them from retreating to the Bavarian mountains. Eisenhower would then turn his armies directly to the north and southwest of the Elbe. In late March, Eisenhower relayed this decision to Stalin,

ALLIED OFFENSIVES TO THE RHINE
1944-1945

who approved it. At this point, Churchill appealed personally to Roosevelt to join him in ordering Eisenhower to use his main forces in a drive to capture Berlin.

When the vanguard of the American army reached the Elbe, only fifty-three miles from Berlin, the Russians stood on the banks of the Oder, thirty to forty miles from the German capital. Churchill now redoubled his pleading, but his voice was no longer heard in Washington. Roosevelt was tired and unable to stand any longer at the helm. He wanted rest and recovery, not a new quarrel with the Russians. He went to Warm Springs, Georgia, early in April to renew his strength before opening the San Francisco Conference of the United Nations on April 25. On April 12 he complained of a terrific headache, lost consciousness, and died at 4:35 P.M. of a massive cerebral hemorrhage.

Roosevelt's growing weakness and death came at a fateful time in the history of the world. The new president, Harry S Truman, had been utterly unprepared by his predecessor. Eisenhower had submitted a plan for further action to the Combined Chiefs of Staff on April 7. He proposed pushing through to the Elbe near Leipzig and then turning northward to the Baltic coast in order to prevent the Russians from occupying any part of the Danish peninsula. He added that he saw no point in making Berlin a military objective, but that he would cheerfully accept the decision of the Combined Chiefs of Staff on this matter. The military leaders did not discuss the question of Berlin. President Truman supported Eisenhower's proposal. Even Churchill agreed on April 19 that the Anglo–American forces were "not immediately in a position to force their way into Berlin." Eisenhower informed Stalin of this plan on April 21, adding that he intended to send forces not only northward but also southward into the Danube Valley. He sent General Patton into Bavaria on the following day.

Even at this date Eisenhower could have captured Prague with ease, and Churchill pleaded for action that "might make the whole difference to the postwar situation in Czechoslovakia." Eisenhower in response decided to send Patton into Prague and so informed the Soviet high command. But he called Patton back after receiving a vehement protest from Stalin. Thus, while the Americans waited, the Russians occupied Prague on May 9.

Meanwhile, Hitler remained in Berlin, confident that a miracle would yet save the Third Reich. He was heartened by Roosevelt's death and certain that the western Allies and Russia would soon turn against each other. But *Götterdämmerung* was near. Marshal Georgii K. Zhukov began a massive offensive across the Oder on April 15 that reached the suburbs of Berlin a week later. American and Russian troops met on the Elbe near Torgau on April 27. Italian partisans captured and shot Mussolini on the following day. Hitler married his mistress, Eva Braun, in his bunker in Berlin and appointed Admiral Karl Doenitz his successor on April 29. He committed suicide on the next day, and his body was burned in the garden of the Reich chancellery.

Nothing remained but to end the war as quickly as possible. Nearly 1 million German troops in northern Italy and Austria surrendered on May 2. Two days later, German troops in northwest Germany, Holland, Schleswig–Holstein, and Denmark laid down their arms. Then Colonel General Alfred Jodl surrendered unconditionally the remnants of the German army, air force, and navy at Eisenhower's headquarters at Rheims at 2:41 A.M. on May 7. All hostilities ceased at midnight May 8, 1945.

11. Victory in the Pacific

American ground, naval, and air power in the Pacific was overwhelmingly preponderant by the early summer of 1944. The American navy was now five times stronger than the imperial fleet. The time had come to close in on the stronghold of the enemy's inner ring. Admiral Raymond A. Spruance with a huge force of ships, aircraft, and troops moved against the strongly held Marianas, about 1,350 miles south of Tokyo. After a bitter struggle, in which the Japanese fought fanatically, the three principal islands in the group—Saipan, Tinian, and Guam—fell before the overpowering assault. While Americans were invading Saipan, a large Japanese force of 9 aircraft carriers, 5 battleships, and other ships sailed from the Philippines to intercept the invaders. In June 1944, over 500 Japanese airplanes attacked and slightly damaged a battleship and 2 carriers. But the Japanese lost 402 airplanes and pilots, the core of their naval aviation, and pursuing American submarines and aircraft caught up with the Japanese fleet. They sank 3 Japanese carriers and 2 destroyers and severely damaged 1 battleship, 4 carriers, and other craft in the first Battle of the Philippine Sea. American naval and ground forces then attacked the western Caroline Islands in September. They overpowered fierce resistance on Peleliu, Angaur, and Ngesebus islands and neutralized the main Japanese garrisons on the islands of Babelthuap and Yap.

While Admiral Nimitz's forces were clearing the Central Pacific route to the Philippines, farther in the Southwest Pacific General MacArthur was making final preparations for an invasion of those islands. First came an Allied drive in April and May 1944 that cleared the northern coast of New Guinea; next, amphibious offensives against Wakde, Biak, Noemfoor, and other islands off the northwestern coast of New Guinea that cleared the lower approaches to the Philippines. Finally, the capture of Morotai Island in September put the Southwest Pacific forces within striking distance. As prelude to an invasion, land-based bombers and planes from carriers of the Third Fleet scourged Japanese airfields and installations in Mindanao, Luzon, and Formosa during September and October. These operations practically destroyed Japanese air power in the area and disrupted Japanese sea communications. Then Americans returned in October to redeem their pledge to liberate the Philippines—with an invasion of Leyte Island by the Sixth Army, the Seventh Fleet under Admiral Thomas C. Kinkaid, and the Third Fleet under Admiral Halsey.

The Japanese admirals well knew that American conquest of the Philippines would spell the doom of the empire, because it would cut communication between Japan and Indochina, Malaya, and the East Indies. They made one last desperate effort to destroy the American invaders in Leyte Gulf. The three naval engagements that ensued between October 24 and 25—the battle of Surigao Strait, the battle off Samar, and the battle off Cape Engaño, collectively known as the Battle for Leyte Gulf—ended disastrously for the Japanese. In this greatest naval battle in history, the Japanese lost practically their entire fleet—three battleships, four carriers, nine cruisers, and eight destroyers.

The threat of Japanese naval intervention was forever ended, and MacArthur could now press forward with his overwhelming campaign in the Philippines. While the invasion of Leyte was at its height, MacArthur launched an attack against Mindoro in December and then attacked Luzon from Lingayen Gulf in early January 1945. Not until July, however, were the Japanese rooted out of the mountains of northern Luzon and out of Mindanao and dozens of smaller islands. All told, Japan lost over 400,000 men and 9,000 planes in the entire Philippines campaign.

The American conquest of the Marianas, western Carolines, and Philippines blasted the inner rim of Japanese defenses, cut communications between the home islands and Indochina, Malaya, and the East Indies, and reduced the Japanese navy to the size of a single task force. Equally important, it afforded advanced bases from which to bomb the empire. Indeed, the air war against Japan had already begun in June 1944, when a force of large new B-29 Superfortresses of the Twentieth Air Force, operating from bases in China, attacked steel works in Kyushu. The Twentieth Air Force made subsequent raids on Japan and Manchuria, but its operations were limited because all its supplies and bombs had to be flown over the Himalayan Hump from India. A massive B-29 attack became possible only with the capture of Saipan in the Marianas. The capture of Iwo Jima later yielded bases for American fighter planes and fighter-bombers that joined in the increasing aerial assault. All told, American planes dropped about 160,000 tons of bombs on the Japanese home islands from November 1944, when the bombardment from the Marianas began, to September 1945, when the war ended.

Although the tonnage of bombs dropped on Japan was about one-ninth of that dropped on Germany, the physical destruction in Japan almost equaled that in Germany. American bombs killed 330,000 Japanese civilians and injured nearly 500,000; moreover, they destroyed 2,510,000 buildings and 40 percent of the built-up areas of sixty-six cities. The effects on the Japanese war economy were equally devastating. Air attacks by July 1945 had reduced the productive capacity of Japanese oil refineries by 83 percent, aircraft engine plants by 75 percent, electronics and communication equipment plants by 70 percent, and munitions factories by some 30 percent. For a nation with an industrial capacity only 10 percent that of its chief enemy, these losses were fatal.

Let us now turn back to the last phase of the relentless American drive by land and sea toward Japan. While MacArthur was bringing the Philippines campaign to its climax, marine divisions invaded Iwo Jima, 750 miles south of Japan, on February 19, 1945. The Japanese defenders had made the island virtually one vast pillbox. They fought so courageously that the Iwo Jima operation was the bloodiest in the history of the United States Marine Corps. However, the entire island, with its two airfields, was in American hands by March 16. Next came a larger attack, beginning April 1, by marine and army forces against Okinawa, a large island in the Ryukyus only 350 miles southwest of Japan. The Japanese and American leaders both knew that the fall of Okinawa would spell the early doom of the empire. The defenders, therefore, fought fanatically during the battle that raged from April 1 to June 21 and lost nearly 111,000 dead and 9,000 prisoners. The most spectacular aspect of

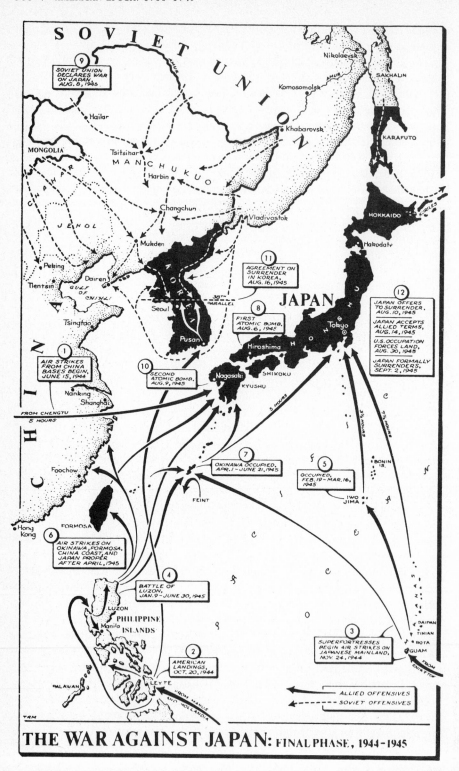

THE WAR AGAINST JAPAN: FINAL PHASE, 1944–1945

the defense was the unrelenting and often effective Kamikaze, or suicide, attacks by Japanese aircraft against American warships and transports. All told, the Japanese lost some 4,000 aircraft, 3,500 of them in Kamikaze attacks, during the Battle of Okinawa.

By this time the main question was whether Japan would collapse internally before the Americans had launched their final invasion of the island empire. We have noted the terrible devastation wrought by the Superfortresses from Saipan. They were joined in February 1945 by thousands of planes of the Third Fleet and in April by fighter-bombers from Iwo Jima and Okinawa. American battleships and heavy cruisers joined in the attack in mid-July by shelling steel works, synthetic oil plants, and other industrial targets on the mainland and by heavy attacks upon Japanese shipping. But Japan was suffering most from a combined sea, air, and mine blockade that had reduced her once large merchant fleet to ineffectiveness and deprived her people of food and her industries of vital raw materials.

Indeed, it had been evident to certain Japanese leaders since the autumn of 1943 that they were fighting a losing battle, and that the imperial government should seek peace, even at the cost of giving up China, Korea, and Formosa. In July 1944, soon after the American invasion of the Marianas, a moderate group led principally by the naval chieftains forced Tojo to resign and establish a new cabinet under General Kuniaki Koiso. An important element in the new government, led by Navy Minister Mitsumasa Yonai and allied with officials in the imperial court, were determined to end the war as quickly as possible. The emperor threw his full support to the peace party in February 1945. After the invasion of Okinawa on April 8, he appointed Baron Kantaro Suzuki as premier and ordered him to end the war. Suzuki, however, did not control the army, which was determined to fight to the bitter end and threatened to revolt if the cabinet moved for peace. Thus the cabinet began secret discussions in May with the Russian ambassador, Jacob Malik, looking toward Russian mediation. In addition, the emperor appealed directly to the Soviet government in June and July to help to arrange peace talks with the United States.

This was the situation when Truman, Churchill, Clement Attlee, soon to be Churchill's successor, and Stalin met at Potsdam on July 17, 1945, for the last conference of the Big Three. Truman almost certainly knew about the Japanese peace overtures even before the Potsdam Conference met; in any event, Stalin soon gave full information about them. Truman was not inclined to take the overtures seriously. He did not trust the Japanese, and his military advisers believed that Japan would not surrender until Allied forces had invaded and occupied the islands. He therefore approved a discouraging Soviet reply to Tokyo.

Meanwhile, word had come to the American leaders at Postdam on July 16 that an atomic bomb had been exploded in New Mexico. Knowing that the bomb was a reality (there were materials on hand to assemble two additional bombs at once), and that its use might avert the necessity of a long and bloody campaign, Truman now concentrated on a public warning to Japan. It was the Potsdam Declaration, issued on July 26 under Truman's, Churchill's, and Chiang Kai-shek's signatures. It promised stern justice to Japanese war criminals and enforcement of the Cairo Declaration stripping Japan of all conquests. But it also held out the hope of generous treatment of a Japan purged and reformed. "The alternative for Japan," it concluded, "is prompt and utter destruction."

The leaders of the Suzuki government in Tokyo agreed to accept the Potsdam Declaration but could not persuade the army leaders to surrender. When Suzuki declared on July 28, only for home consumption, that the Potsdam Declaration was "unworthy of public notice," President Truman and his advisers took this as a refusal and decided to use the atomic bomb. The decision was made largely on military grounds. The Japanese were doomed, to be sure, but they still had large supplies of weapons and an army of 2 million in the home islands. An invasion would surely have succeeded only at great human costs on both sides.

Thus a lone B-29 flew over Hiroshima on August 6 and dropped the first atomic bomb used in warfare. It leveled 4.4 square miles of the city and killed between 70,000 and 80,000 persons. On the same day, President Truman announced the news to the world and warned the Japanese that if they did not surrender they could expect "a rain of ruin from the air, the likes of which has never been seen on this earth." Still the Japanese army refused to surrender. Then, on August 9, news came to Tokyo that Russia had entered the war, and that the Americans had dropped a second atomic bomb on Nagasaki. When hurried conferences failed to yield agreement to accept the Potsdam ultimatum, the emperor made the decision for peace. The cabinet informed Washington on the following day that it accepted the Potsdam terms, provided that the status of the emperor would not be changed. The military and naval chieftains balked when Washington replied on August 11 that the emperor must be subject to the supreme commander of the Allied powers. But the emperor insisted, and the Suzuki government formally accepted the Allied demands on August 14. The emperor at once prepared records of an imperial rescript ordering his armed forces to surrender; and the cabinet, after suppressing an insurrection of army fanatics, sent emissaries to General MacArthur to arrange the details of surrender. A great Allied fleet entered Tokyo Bay on September 2. Soon afterward Foreign Minister Mamoru Shigemitsu and a representative of the imperial general staff signed articles of surrender on board the battleship *Missouri*. General MacArthur and representatives of the Allied powers accepted on behalf of their respective governments.

Suggested Additional Reading

1. American Politics, 1900–1945

A. THE PROGRESSIVE TRANSFORMATION

On the background to reform, see Sidney Fine, *Laissez Faire and the General Welfare State* (1956); Harold U. Faulkner, *Politics, Reform, and Expansion, 1890–1900* (1959); John L. Thomas, *Alternative America: Henry George, Edward Bellamy, Henry Demarest Lloyd, and the Adversary Tradition* (1983); and Stephen Skowronek, *Building a New American State: The Expansion of National Administrative Capacities, 1877–1920* (1982). Among the general, synthetic works on progressivism are Eric F. Goldman, *Rendezvous with Destiny* (1952); Richard Hofstadter, *The Age of Reform* (1955); Robert H. Wiebe, *The Search for Order* (1967); Samuel P. Hays, *The Response to Industrialism, 1885–1914* (1957); John W. Chambers II, *The Tyranny of Change: America in the Progressive Era, 1900–1917* (1980); and Arthur S. Link and Richard L. McCormick, *Progressivism* (1983).

Several works illustrate the regional variety of progressive political reform along with its common, national characteristics. These include Ru.sel B. Nye, *Midwestern Progressive Politics* (1951); C. Vann Woodward, *Origins of the New South, 1877–1913* (1951); Jack T. Kirby, *Darkness at the Dawning: Race and Reform in the Progressive South* (1972); Richard L. McCormick, *From Realignment to Reform: Political Change in New York State, 1893–1910* (1981); Evan Anders, *Boss Rule in South Texas: The Progressive Era* (1982); David L. Carlton, *Mill and Town in South Carolina, 1880–1920* (1982); and Dewey W. Grantham, *Southern Progressivism: The Reconciliation of Progress and Tradition* (1983).

Other state studies supplement the foregoing: Ransom E. Noble, Jr., *New Jersey Progressivism Before Wilson* (1946); George E. Mowry, *The California Progressives* (1951); Spencer C. Olin, Jr., *California's Prodigal Sons: Hiram Johnson and the Progressives, 1911–1917* (1968); David P. Thelen, *The New Citizenship: Origins of Progressivism in Wisconsin, 1885–1900* (1972); Carl H. Chrislock, *The Progressive Era in Minnesota, 1899–1918* (1971); Richard M. Abrams, *Conservatism in a Progressive Era: Massachusetts Politics, 1900–1912* (1964); Albert D. Kirwan, *The Revolt of the Rednecks: Mississippi Politics, 1876–1925* (1951); Raymond H. Pul-

i

ley, *Old Virginia Restored: An Interpretation of the Progressive Impulse* (1968); and Charles Granville Hamilton, *Progressive Mississippi* (1978).

It is impossible to comprehend progressivism without understanding its roots in the urban polity. A wide variety of studies of urban and municipal reform and reformers are now available. Three classics by a muckraker are Lincoln Steffens, *The Shame of the Cities* (1904), *The Struggle for Self-Government* (1906), and *The Autobiography of Lincoln Steffens* (1931). For general works on municipal reform, see Frank M. Stewart, *A Half Century of Municipal Reform: The History of the National Municipal League* (1950); Bradley R. Rice, *Progressive Cities: The Commission Government Movement in America, 1901–1920* (1977); Martin J. Schiesl, *The Politics of Efficiency: Municipal Administration and Reform in America, 1880–1920* (1977); and Jon C. Teaford, *Unheralded Triumph: City Government in America, 1870–1900* (1984). For case studies of urban reform, see Melvin G. Holli, *Reform in Detroit: Hazen S. Pingree and Urban Politics* (1969); Zane Miller, *Boss Cox's Cincinnati: Urban Politics in the Progressive Era* (1968); William D. Miller, *Memphis during the Progressive Era, 1900–1917* (1957); Joel A. Tarr, *A Study in Boss Politics: William Lorimer of Chicago* (1971); David C. Hammack, *Power and Society: Greater New York at the Turn of the Century* (1982); Carl V. Harris, *Political Power in Birmingham, 1871–1921* (1977); and David Paul Nord, *Newspapers and New Politics: Midwestern Muncipal Reform, 1890–1900* (1981).

Valuable sources for the history of state and local political reform are biographies of progressive leaders. They include Alpheus T. Mason, *Brandeis: A Free Man's Life* (1946); Dewey W. Grantham, *Hoke Smith and the Politics of the New South* (1958); William Larsen, *Montague of Virginia: The Making of a Southern Progressive* (1965); Robert F. Wesser, *Charles Evans Hughes: Politics and Reform in New York, 1905–1910* (1967); Nancy J. Weiss, *Charles Francis Murphy, 1858–1924: Respectability and Responsibility in Tammany Politics* (1968); Robert M. Crunden, *A Hero in Spite of Himself: Brand Whitlock in Art, Politics, and War* (1969); William D. Miller, *Mr. Crump of Memphis* (1964); J. Joseph Huthmacher, *Senator Robert F. Wagner and the Rise of Urban Liberalism* (1968); and William F. Holmes, *The White Chief: James Kimble Vardaman* (1970).

The literature on social reform is voluminous. Robert M. Crunden, *Ministers of Reform: The Progressive Achievement in American Civilization, 1889–1920* (1982), and Robert H. Bremner, *From the Depths: The Discovery of Poverty in the United States* (1956), are excellent general accounts. They should be supplemented by Roy Lubove, *The Professional Altruist: The Emergence of Social Work as a Career, 1880–1930* (1965) and *The Struggle for Social Security, 1900–1935* (1968); Allen F. Davis, *Spearheads for Reform: The Social Settlements and the Progressive Movement, 1890–1914* (1967); Paul S. Boyer, *Urban Masses and Moral Order in America, 1820–1920* (1978); Leroy Ashby, *Saving the Waifs: Reformers and Dependent Children, 1890–1917* (1984); and Steven J. Diner, *A City and Its Universities: Public Policy in Chicago, 1892–1919* (1980).

A profusion of specific studies of social reform in a variety of areas are now available. On progressive education, Lawrence A. Cremin, *The Transformation of the School: Progressivism in American Education, 1876–1957* (1961), and David B. Tyack, *The One Best System: A History of American Urban Education* (1974), are the standard accounts. Two more recent studies are David John Hogan, *Class and Reform: School and Society in Chicago, 1880–1930* (1985), and William A. Link, *A Hard Country and a Lonely Place: Schooling, Society, and Reform in Rural Virginia, 1870–1920* (1986). On child labor reform, see Walter I. Trattner, *Crusade for the Children* (1970); Jeremy P. Felt, *Hostages of Fortune: Child Labor Reform in New York State* (1965); and David L. Carlton, *Mill and Town in South Carolina, 1880–1920* (1982). Samuel P. Hays, *Conservation and the Gospel of Efficiency: The Progressive Conservation Movement, 1880–1920* (1959); Samuel Haber, *Efficiency and Uplift: Scientific Management in the Progressive Era* (1964); and Mark Haller, *Eugenics: Herditarian Attitudes in American Thought* (1963), treat different dimensions of social reform. Two important studies of other urban social reforms are Dominick Cavailo, *Muscles and Morals: Organized Playgrounds and Urban Reform, 1880–1920* (1981) and Martin V. Melosi, *Garbage in the Cities: Refuse, Reform, and the Environment, 1880–1980* (1981).

A central part of social reform, social purity campaigns, is the subject of several studies. James H. Timberlake, *Prohibition and the Progressive Movement, 1900–1920* (1963), should be supplemented by Norman H. Clark, *Deliver Us From Evil: An Interpretation of American Prohibition* (1976), and H. Austin Kerr, *Organized for Prohibition: A New History of the Anti-Saloon League* (1985). For two other approaches to prohibition, see Perry R. Duis, *The Saloon: Public Drinking in Chicago and Boston, 1880–1920* (1983), and Jack S. Blocker, Jr., *Retreat from Reform: The Prohibition Movement in the United States, 1890–1913* (1976). Other dimensions of social purity reform are detailed in Mark Thomas Connelly, *The Response to Prostitution in the Progressive Era* (1980), and Ruth Rosen, *The Lost Sisterhood: Prostitution in America, 1900–1918* (1982).

Several recent studies have substantially expanded our understanding of public health reform: John Ettling, *The Germ of Laziness: Rockefeller Philanthropy and Public Health in the New South* (1981); Stuart Galishoff, *Safeguarding the Public Health: Newark, 1895–1918* (1975); Judith Walzer Leavitt, *The Healthiest City: Milwaukee and the the Politics of Health Reform* (1982); and David J. Rothman, *Conscience and Convenience: The Asylum and Its Alternatives in Progressive America* (1980). But see especially Gerald N. Grob, *Mental Illness and American Society, 1875–1940* (1983), the second in a monumentally important three-volume series.

B. NATIONAL REFORM, 1901–1913

Arthur M. Schlesinger, Jr., ed., *History of U.S. Political Parties* (4 vols., 1973), and Schlesinger, Fred L. Israel, and William P. Hassen, eds., *History of American Presidential Elections* (4 vols., 1971), are basic. Robert C. Hilderbrand, *Power and the People: Executive Management of Public Opinion in Foreign Affairs, 1897–1921* (1981), and George Juergens, *News from the White House: The Presidential–Press Relationship in the Progressive Era* (1981), both examine the growth of presidential power through the media. George E. Mowry, *The Era of Theodore Roosevelt, 1900–1912* (1958), is a concise political history. Gabriel Kolko, *The Triumph of Conservatism: A Reinterpretation of American History, 1900–1916* (1963), and

James Weinstein, *The Corporate Ideal in the Liberal State: 1900–1918* (1968), offer Marxist interpretations of the period. For other valuable general studies, see Horace S. and Marion G. Merrill, *The Republican Command, 1897–1913* (1971); James Holt, *Congressional Insurgents and the Party System, 1909–1916* (1967); and Norman Wilensky, *Conservatives in the Progressive Era: The Taft Republicans of 1912* (1965).

Biographical accounts are another essential source. Henry F. Pringle, *Theodore Roosevelt, a Biography* (1931), long the standard, has been supplanted by William H. Harbaugh, *Power and Responsibility: The Life and Times of Theodore Roosevelt* (1961). Edmund Morris, *The Rise of Theodore Roosevelt* (1979), a richly documented portrayal and the first in a multivolume biography, carries the story to 1901. Other important biographical studies include Henry F. Pringle, *The Life and Times of William Howard Taft* (2 vols., 1939); John Morton Blum, *The Republican Roosevelt* (1954); Williard B. Gatewood, Jr., *Theodore Roosevelt and the Art of Controversy: Episodes of the White House Years* (1970); and John Milton Cooper, Jr., *The Warrior and the Priest: Woodrow Wilson and Theodore Roosevelt* (1983). On the important subject of Roosevelt's attitudes toward race, see Thomas G. Dyer, *Theodore Roosevelt and the Idea of Race* (1980). On Roosevelt and conservation, see Paul Russell Cutright, *Theodore Roosevelt: The Making of a Conservationist* (1985).

For studies of other political leaders, see Richard W. Leopold, *Elihu Root and the Conservative Tradition* (1954); Merlo J. Pusey, *Charles Evans Hughes* (2 vols., 1951); John A. Garraty, *Henry Cabot Lodge* (1953); Francis B. Simkins, *Pitchfork Ben Tillman* (1944); Paul W. Glad, *The Trumpet Soundeth: William Jennings Bryan and His Democracy, 1896–1912* (1960); Paolo E. Coletta, *William Jennings Bryan: Political Evangelist, 1860–1908* (1964); Kendrick A. Clements, *William Jennings Bryan: Missionary Diplomatist* (1982); and Robert W. Cherny, *A Righteous Cause: The Life of William Jennings Bryan* (1985).

Other studies treat the legislative issues and political conflicts in the early twentieth-century national government. Frank W. Taussig, *Tariff History of the United States* (1931), remains the standard work on that subject, as does Hans Thorelli, *The Federal Antitrust Policy* (1954), on his subject. Historians, vigorously debating federal regulatory policy, have sharply criticized both its motivations and consequences. Gabriel Kolko, *Railroads and Regulation, 1877–1916* (1965), maintains that large industries, even railroads themselves, were behind legislation to strengthen the ICC. In contrast, another study, Albro Martin, *Enterprise Denied: Origins of the Decline of American Railroads, 1897–1917* (1971), argues that federal regulation effectively crippled an efficient, well-managed enterprise. Sidney Ratner, *Taxation and Democracy in America* (1967), treats the transformation of fiscal policy. The subject of conservation and its political consequences is treated in Elmo P. Richardson, *The Politics of Conservation: Crusaders and Controversies, 1897–1913* (1962); Alpheus T. Mason, *Bureaucracy Convicts Itself: The Ballinger–Pinchot Controversy of 1910* (1941); and James R. Penick, *Progressive Politics and Conservation: The Ballinger–Pinchot Affair* (1968).

For the rise and decline of the Socialist party, see David A. Shannon, *The Socialist Party of America: A History* (1955); Donald D. Egbert and S. Persons, eds.,

Socialism and American Life (2 vols., 1952); Howard Quint, *The Forging of American Socialism* (1953); Ira Kipnis, *The American Socialist Movement, 1897–1912* (1952); James Weinstein, *The Decline of Socialism in America, 1912–1925* (1967); and the excellent biography, Nick Salvatore, *Eugene V. Debs: Citizen and Socialist* (1982).

C. THE WILSON ERA

The best general account of the Wilson presidency is Arthur S. Link, *Woodrow Wilson and the Progressive Era* (1954). Two recent studies of the early twentieth-century growth of presidential power are Hilderbrand, *Power and the People,* and Juergens, *News from the White House,* already cited. For more specialized studies of domestic politics and policy making, see Louis Filler, *Appointment at Armageddon: Muckraking and Progressivism in the American Tradition* (1976); Henry Parker Willis, *The Federal Reserve System* (1923), and J. Laurence Laughlin, *The Federal Reserve Act* (1933); John D. Clark, *The Federal Trust Policy* (1931) (on the writing of the Clayton and Federal Trade Commission bills); and Stephen B. Wood, *Constitutional Politics in the Progressive Era: Child Labor and the Law* (1968). George B. Tindall, *The Emergence of the New South, 1913–1945* (1967), discusses the relationship of the South to Wilsonian policies. A. L. Todd, *Justice on Trial: The Case of Louis D. Brandeis* (1964), is a good account of the fight over the confirmation of Brandeis's appointment to the Supreme Court. On the preparedness controversy, see Michael Pearlman, *To Make Democracy Safe for America: Patricians and Preparedness in the Progressive Era* (1984).

The American home front during the war is treated by Robert H. Ferrell, *Woodrow Wilson and World War I, 1917–1921* (1985); Seward W. Livermore, *Politics Is Adjourned: Woodrow Wilson and the War Congress, 1916–1918* (1966); David M. Kennedy, *Over Here: The First World War and American Society* (1980); George Q. Flynn, *Lewis B. Hershey, Mr. Selective Service* (1985); Frederick Palmer, *Newton D. Baker: America at War* (2 vols., 1931); and Daniel R. Beaver, *Newton D. Baker and the American War Effort, 1917–1919* (1966). Arthur S. Link, ed., *The Impact of World War I* (1969), reprints some of the significant articles on this subject. Bernard M. Baruch, *American Industry in War* (1941), and Robert D. Cuff, *The War Industries Board: Business–Government Relations during World War I* (1973), discuss the problems of industrial mobilization. For special studies, see Alexander D. Noyes, *The War Period of American Finance, 1908–1925* (1926); Charles Gilbert, *American Financing of World War I* (1970); Walker D. Hines, *War History of American Railroads* (1928); Edward N. Hurley, *The Bridge to France* (1927); Frank M. Surface and R. L. Bland, *American Food in the World War and Reconstruction Period* (1931); George Creel, *How We Advertised America* (1920); James R. Mock and C. Larson, *Words That Won the War: The Story of the Committee on Public Information, 1917–1919* (1939); Stephen Vaughn, *Holding Fast the Inner Lines: Democracy, Nationalism, and the Committee on Public Information* (1979), a highly revisionist study; George T. Blakey, *Historians on the Home-Front: American Propagandists and the Great War* (1971); Carol S. Gruber,

Mars and Minerva: World War I and the Uses of Higher Learning in America (1975); Frank L. Grubbs, Jr., *The Struggle for Labor Loyalty: Gompers, the A. F. of L. and the Pacifists, 1917–1920* (1968); Valerie Jean Conner, *The National War Labor Board: Stability, Social Justice, and the Voluntary State in World War I* (1983); Melvin I. Urofsky, *Big Steel and the Wilson Administration* (1969); Joan M. Jensen, *The Price of Vigilance* (1968); and H. C. Peterson and Gilbert C. Fite, *Opponents of War, 1917–1918* (1957).

On demobilization and postwar politics and problems, see Mark Sullivan, *Our Times: The United States, 1900–1925* (6 vols., 1926–1935), Vols. V and VI; Frederick Lewis Allen, *Only Yesterday, an Informal History of the Nineteen-Twenties* (1931); William E. Leuchtenburg, *The Perils of Prosperity, 1914–1932* (1958); and Preston W. Slosson, *The Great Crusade and After, 1914–1928* (1930). James R. Mock and E. Thurber, *Report on Demobilization* (1944), is the most detailed account of that subject. On the race riots of 1917–1920, see Elliott M. Rudwick, *Race Riot at East St. Louis* (1964); Charles F. Kellogg, *NAACP: A History, Volume I: 1909–1920* (1967); William M. Tuttle, Jr., *Race Riot: Chicago in the Red Summer of 1919* (1970); and Arthur I. Waskow, *From Race Riot to Sit-In* (1966). David Brody, *Labor in Crisis: The Steel Strike of 1919* (1965), is superb. For civil liberties during the war and the Red Scare, see Zechariah Chaffee, Jr.'s, *Free Speech in the United States* (1941); Robert K. Murray, *Red Scare: A Study in National Hysteria, 1919–1920* (1955); Stanley Coben, *A. Mitchell Palmer: Politician* (1963); Theodore Draper, *The Roots of American Communism* (1957); William Preston, Jr., *Aliens and Dissenters: Federal Suppression of Radicals, 1903–1933* (1963); Robert L. Friedheim, *The Seattle General Strike* (1964); and Woodrow C. Whitten, *Criminal Syndicalism and the Law in California, 1919–1927* (1969).

William T. Hutchinson, *Lowden of Illinois* (2 vols., 1957); Frank Friedel, *Franklin D. Roosevelt: The Apprenticeship* (1952); James M. Cox, *Journey Through My Years* (1946); Robert K. Murray, *The Harding Era: Warren G. Harding and His Administration* (1969); and Randolph C. Downes, *The Rise of Warren Gamaliel Harding, 1865–1920* (1970), are all informative about the presidential campaign of 1920. But see especially the fine general study by Wesley M. Bagby, *The Road to Normalcy: The Presidential Campaign and Election of 1920* (1962).

The most voluminous and often best literature on the Wilson era are the biographies and memoirs of the leaders of that period. Arthur Walworth, *Woodrow Wilson* (1958), is a good personal biography. Two insightful studies of Wilson's political personality are Cooper, *The Warrior and the Priest*, already cited, and Edwin A. Weinstein, *Woodrow Wilson: A Medical and Psychological Study* (1981). Arthur S. Link, *Wilson: The Road to the White House* (1947), *Wilson: The New Freedom* (1956), *Wilson: The Struggle for Neutrality, 1914–1915* (1960), *Wilson: Confusions and Crises, 1915–1916* (1964), and *Wilson: Campaigns for Progressivism and Peace, 1916–1917* (1965), cover Wilson's public career from 1902 to 1917. Arthur S. Link, *Woodrow Wilson, a Brief Biography* (1963); John M. Blum, *Woodrow Wilson and Politics of Morality* (1956); and John A. Garraty, *Woodrow Wilson* (1956) are brief biographies. Arthur S. Link et al., eds., *The Papers of Woodrow Wilson* (1966–), has now reached the Paris Peace Conference. An indispensable but sometimes unreliable source is Charles Seymour, ed., *The Intimate Papers of*

Colonel House (4 vols., 1926–1928). For biographies of persons active in the Wilson era, see John M. Blum, *Joe Tumulty and the Wilson Era* (1951); Friedel, *Franklin D. Roosevelt: The Apprenticeship,* already cited; Monroe L. Billington, *Thomas P. Gore: The Blind Senator from Oklahoma* (1967); C. H. Cramer, *Newton D. Baker, a Biography* (1961); Margaret L. Coit, *Mr. Baruch* (1957); Jordan A. Schwarz, *The Speculator: Bernard M. Baruch in Washington, 1917–1965* (1981); Coben, *A. Mitchell Palmer,* just cited; Lawrence W. Levine, *Defender of the Faith, William Jennings Bryan: The Last Decade, 1915–1925* (1965); Paolo E. Coletta, *William Jennings Bryan, Progressive Politician and Moral Statesman, 1909–1915* (1969), and *William Jennings Bryan: Political Puritan, 1915–1925* (1969); Richard Lowitt, *George W. Norris: The Persistence of a Progressive* (1971); Evans C. Johnson, *Oscar V. Underwood: A Political Biography* (1980); and Ronald Steel, *Walter Lippmann and the American Century* (1980).

D. THE SUPREME COURT AND ECONOMIC POLICY, 1900–1920

Charles Warren, *The Supreme Court in United States History* (2 vols., 1937); William F. Swindler, *Court and Constitution in the Twentieth Century* (2 vols., 1969–1970); Alfred H. Kelly and W. A. Harbison, *The American Constitution* (1963); and Paul L. Murphy, *The Constitution in Crisis Times, 1918–1969* (1972), are excellent surveys. John E. Semonche, *Charting the Future: The Supreme Court Responds to a Changing Society, 1891–1920* (1978), is a significant reappraisal. Louis B. Boudin, *Government by Judiciary* (2 vols., 1932), focuses on the Supreme Court and social and economic legislation. Biographies of leaders in the court for this period include Pusey, *Charles Evans Hughes,* and Mason, *Brandeis,* both cited earlier; Max Lerner, ed., *The Mind and Faith of Justice Holmes* (1943); and Kathryn Griffith, *Judge Learned Hand and the Role of the Federal Judiciary* (1973). David Wigdor, *Roscoe Pound: Philosopher of Law* (1974), is an excellent biography of the founder of sociological jurisprudence.

E. THE POLITICS AND PROBLEMS OF THE 1920s

For general histories, see Murray, *The Harding Era;* Eugene P. Trani and David L. Wilson, *The Presidency of Warren G. Harding* (1977); Donald R. McCoy, *Calvin Coolidge: The Quiet President* (1967); George E. Mowry, *The Urban Nation, 1920–1960* (1965); John D. Hicks, *Republican Ascendancy, 1921–1932* (1960); Leuchtenburg, *The Perils of Prosperity;* Paul A. Carter, *The Twenties in America* (1975) and *Another Part of the Twenties* (1977); Burl Noggle, *Into the Twenties: The United States from Armistice to Normalcy* (1974); Sullivan, *Our Times,* Vols. V and VI. John Braeman et al., eds., *Change and Continuity in Twentieth-Century America: The 1920s* (1968), includes some good essays on various developments during the decade.

Valuable for Republican politics and policies of the period are Samuel H. Adams, *Incredible Era: The Life and Times of Warren Gamaliel Harding* (1939), a scathing account; Andrew Sinclair, *The Available Man: The Life Behind the Masks of*

Warren Gamaliel Harding (1965); Francis Russell, *The Shadow of Blooming Grove: Warren G. Harding and His Times* (1968); William A. White, *A Puritan in Babylon* (1938), a biography of Coolidge; Herbert Hoover, *Memoirs* (3 vols., 1951–1952), Vol. II; Robert H. Zeiger, *Republicans and Labor, 1919–1929* (1969); and Donald L. Winters, *Henry Cantwell Wallace as Secretary of Agriculture, 1921–1924* (1970).

William H. Harbaugh, *Lawyer's Lawyer: The Life of John W. Davis* (1973), is a biography that tells much about the politics of the 1920s. For the Democratic and liberal politics of the period, see also David Burner, *The Politics of Provincialism: The Democratic Party in Transition, 1918–1932* (1968); Frank Friedel, *Franklin D. Roosevelt: The Ordeal* (1954); Oscar Handlin, *Al Smith and His America* (1958); Matthew and Hannah Josephson, *Al Smith: Hero of the Cities* (1969); Richard O'Connor, *The First Hurrah: A Biography of Alfred E. Smith* (1970); Edmund A. Moore, *A Catholic Runs for President: The Campaign of 1928* (1956); Allan J. Lichtman, *Prejudice and Old Politics: The Presidential Election of 1928* (1979); D. Joy Humes, *Oswald Garrison Villard: Liberal of the 1920's* (1960); Arthur Mann, *La Guardia Comes to Power, 1933* (1965); Howard Zinn, *La Guardia in Congress* (1959); and Le Roy Ashby, *The Spearless Leader: Senator Borah and the Progressive Movement in the 1920s* (1972). J. Joseph Huthmacher, *Massachusetts People and Politics, 1919–1933* (1959), and Franklin D. Mitchell, *Embattled Democracy: Missouri Democratic Politics, 1919–1932* (1968), are pioneering state studies. James W. Prothro, *The Dollar Decade: Business Ideas in the 1920's* (1954), tells us much about the conservative politics of the period.

There is an abundant specialized literature on the problems of the postarmistice decade. Theodore Draper, *The Roots of American Communism* (1957) and *American Communism and Soviet Russia During the Formative Period* (1960), are superb contributions. Major aspects of postwar intolerance and bigotry are treated by Arnold S. Rice, *The Ku Klux Klan in American Politics* (1962); David M. Chalmers, *Hooded Americanism: The First Century of the Ku Klux Klan, 1865–1965* (1965); Charles C. Alexander, *The Ku Klux Klan in the Southwest* (1965); Kenneth T. Jackson, *The Ku Klux Klan in the City, 1915–1930* (1967); Robert Alan Greenberg, *Hooded Empire: The Ku Klux Klan in Colorado* (1981); Walter Lippmann, *American Inquisitors* (1928); and Howard K. Beale, *Are American Teachers Free?* (1936). The facts and significance of the greatest legal cause célèbre of the 1920s are related in Felix Frankfurter, *The Case of Sacco and Vanzetti* (1927); G. Louis Joughlin and E. M. Morgan, *The Legacy of Sacco and Vanzetti* (1948); David Felix, *Protest: Sacco–Vanzetti and the Intellectuals* (1965); and Roberta Strauss Feurlicht, *Justice Crucified: The Story of Sacco and Vanzetti* (1977). Norman F. Furniss's *The Fundamentalist Controversy, 1918–1931* (1954), is judicious, but see also Willard Gatewood, Jr., *Preachers, Pedagogues, and Politicians: The Evolution Controversy in North Carolina* (1966); Richard Hofstadter, *Anti-Intellectualism in American Life* (1963); and Ray Ginger, *Six Days or Forever? Tennessee v. John Thomas Scopes* (1958). For the origins of the twentieth-century prohibition movement, see Timberlake, *Prohibition and the Progressive Movement,* already cited; Peter H. Odegard, *Pressure Politics, the Story of the Anti-Saloon League* (1928); and H. Austin Kerr, *Organized for Prohibition: A New History of the Anti-Saloon League* (1985). The failure of the "noble experiment" is recounted by Herbert Asbury, *The Great*

Illusion, an Informal History of Prohibition (1950); Norman H. Clark, *The Dry Years: Prohibition and Social Change in Washington* (1965) and *Deliver Us from Evil: An Interpretation of American Prohibition* (1976); Alan Everest, *Run Across the Border: The Prohibition Era in Northern New York* (1978); and David E. Kyvig, *Repealing National Prohibition* (1979). John Kobler, *Capone: The Life and World of Al Capone* (1971), is a racy biography of one of prohibition's chief beneficiaries.

Burl Noggle, *Teapot Dome: Oil and Politics in the 1920's* (1965), is excellent. For three major legislative issues of the 1920s—tariff, taxes, and federal policy toward the electric power industry—see Taussig, *Tariff History of the United States;* Ratner, *Taxation and Democracy in America* (1967); and George W. Norris, *Fighting Liberal* (1945). Judson King, *The Conservation Fight: From Theodore Roosevelt to the Tennessee Valley Authority* (1959), is highly antagonistic toward private utilities. Preston J. Hubbard, *Origins of the TVA, the Muscle Shoals Controversy, 1920–1932* (1961), is a superb scholarly account of the greatest single power fight of the 1920s, but see also Lowitt, *George W. Norris: The Persistence of a Progressive.* The farm problem, the revival of insurgency, and the Progressive party of 1924 are amply treated in Nye, *Midwestern Progressive Politics;* Theodore Saloutos and John D. Hicks, *Agrarian Discontent in the Middle West, 1900–1939* (1951); Saloutos, *Farmer Movements in the South, 1865–1933* (1960); and Gilbert C. Fite, *George N. Peek and the Fight for Farm Parity* (1954). See also James H. Shideler, *Farm Crisis, 1919–1923* (1957); Robert L. Morlan, *Political Prairie Fire: The Nonpartisan League, 1915–1922* (1955); and Kenneth C. Mackay, *The Progressive Movement of 1924* (1947). Clarke A. Chambers, *Seedtime of Reform: American Social Service and Social Action, 1918–1933* (1963), provides one answer to the question: what happened to the progressive movement in the 1920s?

For the Supreme Court between 1920 and the court packing controversy of 1937, see the following general surveys, all of them cited earlier: Warren, *The Supreme Court in United States History;* Swindler, *Court and Constitution in the Twentieth Century;* Kelly and Harbison, *The American Constitution;* and Murphy, *The Constitution in Crisis Times, 1918–1969.* Again, Boudin, *Government by Judiciary,* focuses on the Supreme Court and social and economic legislation. Alpheus T. Mason, *The Supreme Court from Taft to Warren* (1958), and *William Howard Taft, Chief Justice* (1965), cover the 1920s.

F. HERBERT HOOVER AND THE GREAT DEPRESSION

For brief and objective surveys of the Hoover period, see Hicks, *Republican Ascendancy;* Leuchtenburg, *The Perils of Prosperity;* and Mowry, *The Urban Nation,* all already cited. The first volume of a multivolume biography, George H. Nash, *The Life of Herbert Hoover: The Engineer, 1874–1914* (1983), treats Hoover's early career. Arthur M. Schlesinger, Jr., *The Age of Roosevelt: The Crisis of the Old Order, 1919–1933* (1957)—the first volume in a monumental series noted more fully below—marks the beginning of a reevaluation of the Hoover administration, as do David Burner, *Herbert Hoover, the Public Life* (1979); Joan Hoff Wilson, *Herbert Hoover: Forgotten Progressive* (1975); Martin L. Fausold, *The Presidency of Herbert*

C. Hoover (1985); Harris G. Warren, *Herbert Hoover and the Great Depression* (1959); Albert U. Romasco, *The Poverty of Abundance: Hoover, the Nation, the Depression* (1965); Gene Smith, *The Shattered Dream: Herbert Hoover and the Great Depression* (1970); and Jordan A. Schwarz, *The Interregnum of Despair: Hoover, Congress, and the Depression* (1970). Herbert Hoover, *Memoirs* (3 vols., 1951–1952), Vol. III, concedes nothing to his critics.

For vivid accounts of the impact of the depression on American life, thought, and politics, see Clarence J. Enzler, *Some Social Aspects of the Depression* (1939); Dixon Wecter, *The Age of the Great Depression, 1920–1941* (1948); Frederick Lewis Allen, *Since Yesterday: The Nineteen-Thirties in America* (1940); Bernard Sternsher, ed., *Hitting Home: The Great Depression in Town and Country* (1970); and Roger Daniels, *The Bonus March: An Episode of the Great Depression* (1971). Broadus Mitchell, *Depression Decade* (1947), analyzes the causes and problems of the depression in a general way, but the following are more useful for specific aspects: Elmus R. Wicker, *Federal Reserve Monetary Policies, 1917–1933* (1966); Milton Friedman and Anna J. Schwartz, *A Monetary History of the United States, 1867–1960* (1963); John Kenneth Galbraith, *The Great Crash* (1955); Brookings Institution, *The Recovery Problem in the United States* (1936); Charles S. Johnson et al., *The Collapse of Cotton Tenancy* (1935); Maurice Levin et al., *America's Capacity to Consume* (1934); and Edwin G. Nourse et al., *America's Capacity to Produce* (1934). Josephine C. Brown, *Public Relief, 1929–1939* (1940), is good on Hoover's relief policies.

G. FRANKLIN D. ROOSEVELT AND AMERICAN POLITICS

The literature on the era of Franklin Roosevelt is constantly growing. A basic source for the entire New Deal period is Samuel I. Rosenman, ed., *The Public Papers and Addresses of Franklin D. Roosevelt* (13 vols., 1938–1950). The best introduction is Schlesinger's multivolume *The Age of Roosevelt*, which is both excellent history and great literature. He has published *The Crisis of the Old Order, 1919–1933* (1957), *The Coming of the New Deal* (1958), and *The Politics of Upheaval* (1960). William E. Leuchtenburg, *Franklin D. Roosevelt and the New Deal, 1932–1940* (1963), and Albert U. Romasco, *The Politics of Recovery: Roosevelt's New Deal* (1983), are both excellent surveys. Much more critical of Roosevelt is Paul K. Conkin, *The New Deal* (1967). Samuel Lubell, *The Future of American Politics* (1952), and John M. Allswang, *The New Deal and American Politics: A Study in Political Change* (1978), shrewdly analyze the impact of the New Deal on party loyalties and the party structure, while Matthew Josephson, *Sidney Hillman: Statesman of American Labor* (1952), is useful for understanding the New Deal's impact on labor politics. Huthmacher, *Senator Robert F. Wagner*, already cited, is significant for the entire New Deal period.

Useful specialized studies are Harold F. Gosnell, *Champion Campaigner* (1952); Thomas H. Greer, *What Roosevelt Thought* (1958); Bernard Bellush, *Franklin D. Roosevelt as Governor of New York* (1955); A. J. Wann, *The President as Chief Administrator: A Study of Franklin D. Roosevelt* (1968); Max Freedman, ed.,

Roosevelt and Frankfurter: Their Correspondence, 1928–1945 (1968); and Richard Polenberg, *Reorganizing Roosevelt's Government: The Controversy over Executive Reorganization, 1936–1939* (1966). No thoughtful student should ignore Edgar E. Robinson's conservative critique, *The Roosevelt Leadership, 1933–1945* (1955). For Roosevelt's third-term nomination and campaign, see Bernard F. Donahoe, *Private Plans and Public Dangers: The Story of FDR's Third Nomination* (1965), and Herbert S. Parmet and Marie B. Hecht, *Never Again: A President Runs for a Third Term* (1968).

There are numerous biographies of Roosevelt. Frank Freidel's study has reached the first months of the New Deal. The volumes that have been published include *Franklin D. Roosevelt: The Apprenticeship* (1952); *Franklin D. Roosevelt: The Ordeal* (1954); *Franklin D. Roosevelt: The Triumph* (1956); and *Franklin D. Roosevelt: Launching the New Deal* (1973). Geoffrey C. Ward, *Before the Trumpet: Young Franklin Roosevelt, 1882–1905* (1985), is the first volume of a multivolume biography. Robert E. Sherwood, *Roosevelt and Hopkins* (1948), is a fascinating biography of Harry L. Hopkins, Roosevelt's closest adviser from 1935 to 1945. Rexford G. Tugwell, *The Democratic Roosevelt* (1957) and *FDR: Architect of an Era* (1967), are important studies by a contemporary, while James M. Burns, *Roosevelt: The Lion and the Fox* (1956), is a superb study of Roosevelt the political leader. Joseph P. Lash, *Eleanor and Franklin* (1971), and *Eleanor: The Years Alone* (1972), constitute the definitive life of Mrs. Roosevelt.

Some of our best sources for the New Deal era are the memoirs of Roosevelt's contemporaries. Among the best of these are Samuel I. Rosenman, *Working with Roosevelt* (1952); Frances Perkins, *The Roosevelt I Knew* (1946); Eleanor Roosevelt, *This Is My Story* (1937) and *This I Remember* (1949); Raymond Moley, *After Seven Years* (1939) and *The First New Deal* (1966); Cordell Hull, *Memoirs* (2 vols., 1948); and Harold L. Ickes, *Secret Diary* (3 vols., 1953–1954).

H. ASPECTS OF THE NEW DEAL

There are many very good studies of financial reform, fiscal policies, and the problem of recovery. A general discussion is available in Harvard Sitkoff, ed., *Fifty Years Later: The New Deal Evaluated* (1985). Of major significance, because they cut across all the New Deal period, are John M. Blum, ed., *From the Morgenthau Diaries: Years of Urgency, 1938–1941* (1965) and *From the Morgenthau Diaries: Years of War, 1941–1945* (1967). For those who want a briefer version, there is John M. Blum, *Roosevelt and Morgenthau: A Revision and Condensation of the Morgenthau Diaries* (1970). A major revisionist study is Mark H. Leff, *The Limits of Symbolic Reform: The New Deal and Taxation, 1933–1939* (1984). For another major work, see Beatrice Bishop Berle and Travis Beal Jacobs, eds., *Navigating the Rapids, 1918–1971: From the Papers of Adolf A. Berle* (1973). Also useful is Patrick J. Mancy, *"Young Bob" La Follette: A Biography of Robert M. La Follette, Jr., 1895–1953* (1978). Norman D. Markowitz, *The Rise and Fall of the People's Century: Henry A. Wallace and American Liberalism, 1941–1948* (1973), is overly partial to its subject, so one should also see John M. Blum, ed., *The Price of Vision:*

The Diary of Henry A. Wallace, 1942–1946 (1973). Other valuable studies of New Dealers are Peter H. Irons, *The New Deal Lawyers* (1982), and Graham White and John Maze, *Harold Ickes of the New Deal: His Private Life and Public Career* (1985).

Ferdinand Pecora, *Wall Street Under Oath* (1939), and J. T. Flynn, *Security Speculation* (1934), argue the need for financial reform. Marriner S. Eccles, *Beckoning Frontiers: Public and Personal Recollections* (1951), tells the story of the writing of the Banking Act of 1935, while Marion L. Ramsay, *Pyramids of Power: The Story of Roosevelt, Insull, and the Utility Wars* (1937); Michael E. Parrish, *Securities Regulation and the New Deal* (1970); and Ralph F. de Bedts, *The New Deal's SEC: The Formative Years* (1964), cover the Public Utility Holding Company Act of 1935 and the effort to regulate the securities exchanges.

Friedman and Schwartz, *A Monetary History of the United States,* is the best source for New Deal fiscal policies, but see also G. Griffith Johnson, Jr., *Treasury and Monetary Policy* (1939); John Kenneth Galbraith and G. Griffith Johnson, Jr., *The Economic Effects of the Federal Public Works Expenditure, 1933–1938* (1940); John A. Brennan, *Silver and the First New Deal* (1969); Robert Lekachman, *The Age of Keynes* (1966); Herbert Stein, *The Fiscal Revolution in America* (1969); Marion Clawson, *New Deal Planning: The National Resources Planning Board* (1981); and Robert M. Collins, *The Business Response to Keynes, 1929–1964* (1981).

Ellis W. Hawley, *The New Deal and the Problem of Monopoly: A Study in Economic Ambivalence* (1966), is the best analysis of the NRA, but also useful are Bernard Bellush, *The Failure of the NRA* (1975); Leverett S. Lyon et al., *The National Recovery Administration* (1935); Merle Fainsod and L. Gordon, *Government and the American Economy* (1959); and Thomas E. Vadney, *The Wayward Liberal: A Political Biography of Donald Richberg* (1971). For the work of the RFC, see Jesse H. Jones, *Fifty Billion Dollars: My Thirteen Years with the RFC, 1932–1945* (1951). Otis L. Graham, Jr., *Toward a Planned Society: From Roosevelt to Nixon* (1976), is the best general study of that subject.

For general surveys of New Deal relief and public works programs, see Mitchell, *Depression Decade;* Brown, *Public Relief, 1929–1939;* and Sherwood, *Roosevelt and Hopkins.* Searle F. Charles, *Minister of Relief: Harry Hopkins and the Depression* (1963), is more detailed. For various aspects of the New Deal relief program, see Bonnie Fox Schwartz, *The Civil Works Administration, 1933–1934: The Business of Emergency Employment in the New Deal* (1984); John A. Salmond, *The Civilian Conservation Corps, 1933–1942: A New Deal Case Study* (1967); Jane De Hart Mathews, *The Federal Theatre, 1935–1939: Plays, Relief, and Politics* (1967); William F. McDonald, *Federal Relief Administration and the Arts* (1969); Marlene Park, *Democratic Vistas: Post Offices and Public Art in the New Deal* (1984); Paul K. Conkin, *Tomorrow a New World: The New Deal Community Program* (1959); Bernard Sternsher, *Rexford G. Tugwell and the New Deal* (1964), which covers relief and many other matters; and William W. Bremer, *Depression Winters: New York Social Workers and the New Deal* (1984).

For the background of the Social Security Act, see Lubove, *The Struggle for Social Security,* and David Nelson, *Unemployment Insurance: The American Experi-*

ence, 1915–1935 (1969). The writing of the Social Security Act and subsequent developments are well recounted in Perkins, *The Roosevelt I Knew;* Edwin E. Witte, *Development of the Social Security Act* (1962); Arthur J. Altmeyer, *The Formative Years of Social Security* (1966); Theroon F. Schlabach, *Edwin E. Witte: Cautious Reformer* (1969); and Charles McKinley and R. W. Frase, *Launching Social Security: A Capture-and-Record Account, 1935–1937* (1971). Daniel S. Hirshfield, *The Lost Reform: The Campaign for Compulsory Health Insurance in the United States from 1932 to 1943* (1970), and Charles O. Jackson, *Food and Drug Legislation in the New Deal* (1970), deal with related subjects. A radical approach to New Deal legislation is Francis Fox Piven and Richard A. Cloward, *Regulating the Poor: The Functions of Public Welfare* (1972), which views the various New Deal initiatives as instruments used to assuage a disgruntled populace.

A large literature exists on the subject of agrarian problems and policies. Saloutos and Hicks, *Agrarian Discontent in the Middle West, 1900–1939;* Saloutos, *The American Farmer and the New Deal* (1982); and Fite, *George N. Peek and the Fight for Farm Parity,* should be supplemented by Murray R. Benedict, *Farm Policies of the United States, 1790–1950* (1953); Frederick H. and Edward L. Schapsmeier, *Henry A. Wallace of Iowa: The Agrarian Years, 1910–1940* (1968); Richard S. Kirkendall, *Social Scientists and Farm Politics in the Age of Roosevelt* (1966); and Robert J. Morgan, *Governing Soil Conservation: Thirty Years of the New Decentralization* (1966).

John L. Shover, *Cornbelt Rebellion: The Farmers' Holiday Association* (1965), is excellent for the general farm crisis. The writing of the AAA and subsequent policies is treated in William D. Rowley, *M. L. Wilson and the Campaign for the Domestic Allotment* (1970), and Van L. Perkins, *Crisis in Agriculture: The Agricultural Adjustment Administration and the New Deal, 1933* (1969). For the impact of the AAA on two major crops, see Anthony J. Badger, *Prosperity Road: The New Deal, Tobacco, and North Carolina* (1980), and Robert E. Snyder, *Cotton Crisis* (1984). On southern agriculture in general, see Pete Daniel, *Breaking the Land: The Transformation of Cotton, Tobacco, and Rice Cultures Since 1880* (1985). See also David E. Conrad, *The Forgotten Farmers: The Story of Sharecroppers in the New Deal* (1965); Donald H. Grubbs, *Cry from the Cotton: The Southern Tenant Farmers' Union and the New Deal* (1971); and Louis Cantor, *A Prologue to the Protest Movement: The Missouri Sharecropper Roadside Demonstration of 1939* (1968). Sidney Baldwin, *Poverty and Politics: The Rise and Decline of the Farm Security Administration* (1968), is excellent. Clyde T. Ellis, *A Giant Step* (1966), tells the story of the REA, while Dean Albertson, *Roosevelt's Farmer: Claude R. Wickard in the New Deal* (1961), is useful for the latter stages of New Deal farm policy. Nathan Straus, *Seven Myths of Housing* (1944), surveys the New Deal's housing program.

On the South, the regions and states, and the TVA, Rupert B. Vance, *All These People, the Nation's Human Resources in the South* (1945), is comprehensive, as is V. O. Key, Jr., *Southern Politics in State and Nation* (1949). Tindall, *The Emergence of the New South,* already cited, is excellent for the impact of the New Deal on the South. See also Frank Friedel, *F.D.R. and the South* (1965); Thomas A. Krueger, *And Promises to Keep: The Southern Conference for Human Welfare,*

1938–1948 (1967); Paul E. Mertz, *New Deal Policy and Southern Rural Poverty* (1978); Wilma Dykeman and James Stokely, *Seeds of Southern Change: The Life of Will Alexander* (1966); Wilma Dykeman, *Prophet of Plenty: The First Ninety Years of W. D. Weatherford* (1962); and Chester M. Morgan, *Redneck Liberal: Theodore G. Bilbo and the New Deal* (1985). Howard W. Odum and H. E. Moore, *American Regionalism* (1938), developed the concept of the region. Richard Lowitt, *The New Deal and the West* (1984), is a pioneering work. For the impact of the New Deal on cities and states, see James T. Patterson, *The New Deal and the States: Federalism in Transition* (1969); Robert E. Burke, *Olson's New Deal for California* (1953); Francis W. Schruben, *Kansas in Turmoil, 1930–1936* (1969); Ronald L. Heinemann, *Depression and New Deal in Virginia: The Enduring Dominion* (1983); and Bruce M. Stave, *The New Deal and the Last Hurrah: Pittsburgh Machine Politics* (1970).

For the TVA, see C. Herman Pritchett, *The Tennessee Valley Authority: A Study in Public Administration* (1943); David E. Lilienthal, *TVA: Democracy on the March* (1953) and *The Journals of David E. Lilienthal: The TVA Years, 1939–1945* (1965); Thomas K. McCraw, *TVA and the Power Fight, 1933–1939* (1970); Wilmon H. Droze, *High Dams and Slack Waters: TVA Rebuilds a River* (1965); and John R. Moore, ed., *The Economic Impact of the TVA* (1967). Richard Lowitt, *George W. Norris: The Triumph of a Progressive* (1978), is the third and final volume of his biography of the father of the TVA.

There is still no general study of political opposition to the New Deal, or of the Republican party in the 1930s, but Donald R. McCoy, *Landon of Kansas* (1966); Donald B. Johnson, *The Republican Party and Wendell Willkie* (1960); Warren Moscow, *Roosevelt and Willkie* (1968); and Ellsworth Barnard, *Wendell Willkie: Fighter for Freedom* (1966), fill in many gaps. A full biography of Roosevelt's opponent in the election of 1940 is Steve Neal, *Dark Horse: A Biography of Wendell Willkie* (1984). Lubell, *The Future of American Politics,* analyzes the causes of the GOP's weakness during this period. Morton Keller, *In Defense of Yesterday: James M. Beck and the Politics of Conservativism, 1861–1936* (1959), describes the conservative Republican reaction to the New Deal, while Otis L. Graham, Jr., *An Encore for Reform: The Old Progressives and the New Deal* (1967), tells about widespread disenchantment among old Wilsonians. Even more revealing are George Wolfskill, *Revolt of the Conservatives, a History of the American Liberty League, 1934–1940* (1962), and George Wolfskill and John A. Hudson, *All but the People: Franklin D. Roosevelt and His Critics, 1933–1939* (1969). For the beginnings of effective congressional opposition, see James T. Patterson, *Congressional Conservatism and the New Deal: The Growth of the Conservative Coalition in Congress, 1933–1939* (1967); David L. Porter, *Congress and the Waning of the New Deal* (1980); and John Robert Moore, *Senator Josiah William Bailey of North Carolina* (1968).

We now have a number of excellent studies of non-Communist left-wing opposition to the New Deal: T. Harry Williams, *Huey Long* (1969); Allan P. Sindler, *Huey Long's Louisiana* (1956); Donald R. McCoy, *Angry Voices: Left-of-Center Politics in the New Deal Era* (1958); David H. Bennett, *Demagogues in the Depression: American Radicals and the Union Party, 1932–1936* (1969); Charles J. Tull, *Father*

Coughlin and the New Deal (1965); and Alan Brinkley, *Voices of Protest: Huey Long, Father Coughlin, and the Great Depression* (1982).

Egbert and Persons, eds., *Socialism and American Life*, already cited, and Harvey Klehr, *The Heyday of American Communism: The Depression Decade* (1984), are the best surveys of the rise and decline of communism in the United States in the 1930s. But see also John P. Diggins, *Up from Communism: Conservative Odysseys in American Intellectual History* (1975); Vivian Gornick, *The Romance of American Communism* (1977); Earl Latham, *The Communist Controversy in Washington: From the New Deal to McCarthy* (1966); Frank A. Warren III, *Liberals and Communism: The "Red Decade" Revisited* (1966); Wilson Record, *The Negro and the Communist Party* (1951); Ralph L. Roy, *Communism and the Churches* (1960); Robert W. Iverson, *The Communists and the Schools* (1959); Daniel Aaron, *Writers on the Left* (1961); and Richard H. Pells, *Radical Visions and American Dreams: Culture and Social Thought in the Depression Years* (1973). Recent revisionist accounts have attempted to portray the Communist party as possessing both grass-roots support and a degree of independence from Moscow. See Paul Lyons, *Philadelphia Communists* (1982); Mark Naison, *Communists in Harlem During the Depression* (1983); Harvey A. Levenstein, *Communism, Anticommunism and the CIO* (1981); and Maurice Isserman, *Which Side Were You On? The American Communist Party during the Second World War* (1982). For the decline of the Socialist party during the New Deal period, see Shannon, *The Socialist Party of America: A History;* Murray B. Seidler, *Norman Thomas: Respectable Rebel* (1967); Bernard K. Johnpoll, *Pacifist's Progress: Norman Thomas and the Decline of American Socialism* (1970); and W. A. Swanberg, *Norman Thomas: The Last Idealist* (1976).

The best study of the Supreme Court controversy and the New Deal court is Leonard Baker, *Back to Back: The Duel Between FDR and the Supreme Court* (1967); but see also Samuel Hendel, *Charles Evans Hughes and the Supreme Court* (1951); Pusey, *Charles Evans Hughes;* Mason, *Brandeis: A Free Man's Life* and *Harlan Fiske Stone* (1956); and Murphy, *The Constitution in Crisis Times.* For the New Deal court, see C. Herman Pritchett, *The Roosevelt Court* (1948); J. Woodford Howard, *Mr. Justice Murphy: A Political Biography* (1968); and Gerald T. Dunne, *Hugo Black and the Judicial Revolution* (1977).

I. THE HOME FRONT DURING THE SECOND WORLD WAR

For general studies of the home front during the Second World War, see Allan M. Winkler, *Home Front U.S.A.* (1986); Richard Polenberg, *War and Society: The United States, 1941–1945* (1972); John M. Blum, *V Was for Victory: Politics and American Culture During World War II* (1976); and Geoffrey Perrett, *Days of Sadness, Years of Triumph: The American People, 1939–1945* (1973). Jack Goodman, ed., *While You Were Gone: A Report on Wartime Life in the United States* (1946), contains some interesting essays. Alan S. Milward, *War, Economy, and Society, 1939–1945* (1977), surveys the impact of the war on the American economy in a worldwide setting.

Donald M. Nelson, *Arsenal of Democracy* (1946), is an official history of industrial mobilization, while Eliot Janeway, *The Struggle for Survival* (1951), is extremely critical of the administration. Harold G. Vatter, *The U.S. Economy in World War II* (1985), is a general account. Nelson Lichtenstein, *Labor's War at Home: The CIO in World War II* (1982), treats organized labor's response. Frederick C. Lane et al., *Ships for Victory* (1951), is excellent for the shipbuilding program; E. R. Stettinius, Jr., *Lend-Lease, Weapon of Victory* (1944), is good for the export of war materials; James P. Baxter III, *Scientists Against Time* (1946), is a superb account of American scientific achievement during wartime; and Leslie R. Groves, *Now It Can Be Told* (1962), is the story of the Manhattan Project by its director. Walter Wilcox, *The Farmer in the Second World War* (1947) is excellent, while Randolph E. Paul, *Taxation for Prosperity* (1947), recounts wartime tax struggles with commendable objectivity. Herman M. Sowers, *Presidential Agency OWMR* (1950), is especially good on plans for reconversion of the wartime economy. Davis R. B. Ross, *Preparing for Ulysses: Politics and Veterans during World War II* (1969), is also a good study. Dorothy S. Thomas et al., *The Spoilage* (1946), Roger Daniels, *Concentration Camps, U.S.A., Japanese Americans and World War II* (1972), and Peter H. Irons, *Justice at War* (1983), are scholarly studies of the wartime mistreatment of Japanese Americans.

2. The United States and its World Relations, 1900–1945

A. GENERAL

Samuel F. Bemis and Robert H. Ferrell, eds., *The American Secretaries of State and Their Diplomacy* (17 vols., 1927–1967); Foster R. Dulles, *America's Rise to World Power, 1898–1954* (1955); George F. Kennan, *American Diplomacy, 1900–1950* (1951); Norman A. Graebner, ed., *An Uncertain Tradition, American Secretaries of State in the Twentieth Century* (1961); Robert E. Osgood, *Ideals and Self-Interest in America's Foreign Relations* (1953); Selig Adler, *The Isolationist Impulse* (1959); H. C. Allen, *Great Britain and the United States* (1955); William Appleman Williams, *The Roots of the Modern American Empire* (1969); Julius W. Pratt, *Challenge and Rejection: The United States and World Leadership, 1900–1921* (1967); E. Berkeley Tompkins, *Anti-Imperialism in the United States, 1890–1920* (1970); Sondra R. Herman, *Eleven Against War: Studies in American Internationalist Thought, 1898–1921* (1969); and Warren F. Kuehl, *Seeking World Order: The United States and International Organization to 1920* (1969), are good surveys for readers seeking background. Charles Chatfield, *For Peace and Justice: Pacifism in America, 1914–1941* (1971), is excellent on the peace movement in the twentieth century. However, the best general work is Richard W. Leopold, *The Growth of American Foreign Policy* (1962).

B. IMPERIALISM, 1900–1914

Julius W. Pratt, *America's Colonial Experiment* (1950), is a splendid survey of the rise and fall of the American colonial empire. It may be supplemented by Edward

J. Berbusse, *The United States in Puerto Rico, 1898–1900* (1966); David A. Lock-miller, *Magoon in Cuba: A History of the Second Intervention, 1906–1909* (1938); Allan Reed Millett, *The Politics of Intervention: The Military Occupation of Cuba, 1906–1909* (1968); W. Cameron Forbes, *The Philippine Islands* (2 vols., 1928); Glenn A. May, *Social Engineering in the Philippines: The Aims, Execution, and Impact of American Colonial Policy, 1900–1913* (1980); Stuart Creighton Miller, *"Benevolent Assimilation": The American Conquest of the Philippines, 1899–1903* (1982); and Charles C. Tansill, *The Purchase of the Danish West Indies* (1932).

We lack any good general study of American relations with Europe from 1900 to 1914. Howard K. Beale, *Theodore Roosevelt and the Rise of America to World Power* (1956); Richard H. Collin, *Theodore Roosevelt, Culture, Diplomacy, and Expansion* (1985); Walter V. and Marie V. Scholes, *The Foreign Policies of the Taft Administration* (1970); John A. Garraty, *Henry Cabot Lodge* (1953); Richard W. Leopold, *Elihu Root and the Conservative Tradition* (1954); Philip C. Jessup, *Elihu Root* (2 vols., 1938); Henry F. Pringle, *Theodore Roosevelt, a Biography* (1931) and *The Life and Times of William Howard Taft* (2 vols., 1939); William H. Harbaugh, *Power and Responsibility: The Life and Times of Theodore Roosevelt* (1961); and Tyler Dennett, *John Hay* (1933), are all valuable for the diplomacy of the Roosevelt–Taft period. Bradford Perkins, *The Great Rapprochement: England and the United States, 1895–1914* (1968); Charles S. Campbell, Jr., *Anglo–American Understanding, 1898–1903* (1957); Richard R. Heindel, *The American Impact on Great Britain, 1898–1914* (1940); Alexander E. Campbell, Jr., *Great Britain and the United States, 1895–1903* (1961); Lloyd C. Gardner, *Safe for Democracy: The Anglo–American Response to Revolution, 1913–1923* (1984); Clara E. Schieber, *The Transformation of American Sentiment Toward Germany, 1870–1914* (1923); and H. G. Nicholas, *The United States and Britain* (1975), are excellent particular studies.

In contrast to the paucity of general works on American–European relations from 1900 to 1914 stands a large body of general literature dealing with the United States and the Far East during the same period. A. Whitney Griswold, *The Far Eastern Policy of the United States* (1938); Edwin O. Reischauer, *The United States and Japan* (1965); and John K. Fairbank, *The United States and China* (1958), are the best surveys, but Kennan, *American Diplomacy, 1908–1950,* and Louis J. Halle, *Dream and Reality: Aspects of American Foreign Policy* (1958), make some provocative observations. For important monographs on Japanese–American relations, see Raymond A. Esthus, *Theodore Roosevelt and Japan* (1966); Tyler Dennett, *Roosevelt and the Russo–Japanese War* (1925); John A. White, *The Diplomacy of the Russo–Japanese War* (1964); Eugene P. Trani, *The Treaty of Portsmouth: An Adventure in American Diplomacy* (1969); Thomas A. Bailey, *Theodore Roosevelt and the Japanese–American Crises* (1934); and Charles E. Neu, *An Uncertain Friendship: Theodore Roosevelt and Japan, 1906–1909* (1967). For special studies on Chinese–American relations, see Herbert Croly, *Willard Straight* (1924); Paul A. Varg, *Missonaries, Chinese, and Diplomats* (1954) and *The Making of a Myth: The United States and China, 1897–1912* (1968); Jerry Israel, *Progressivism and the Open Door: America and China, 1905–1921* (1971); Thomas J. McCormick, *China Market: America's Quest for Informal Empire* (1967); Charles Vevier, *The United States and China, 1906–1913* (1955); and Nemai S. Bose, *American Attitude and Policy to the Nationalist Movement in China (1911–1921)* (1970). L. Ethan Ellis,

Reciprocity, 1911 (1939), relates Taft's ill-fated effort to win a reciprocal trade agreement with Canada. The most concise survey of Wilson's far eastern policy before 1917 is in Arthur S. Link, *Woodrow Wilson and the Progressive Era* (1954), but see also his *Wilson: The New Freedom* (1956), and *Wilson: The Struggle for Neutrality, 1914–1915* (1960).

C.   THE UNITED STATES AND LATIN AMERICA, 1900–1920

Samuel F. Bemis, *The Latin American Policy of the United States* (1943), and Lester D. Langley, *The Banana Wars: An Inner History of American Empire, 1900–1934* (1983), are general surveys. For works on the United States and the Caribbean, see Wilfrid H. Callcott, *The Caribbean Policy of the United States, 1890–1920* (1942); Dexter Perkins, *Hands Off: A History of the Monroe Doctrine* (1941), *The Monroe Doctrine, 1867–1907* (1937), and *The United States and the Caribbean* (1947); Howard C. Hill, *Roosevelt and the Caribbean* (1927); Dana G. Munro, *Intervention and Dollar Diplomacy in the Caribbean, 1900–1921* (1964); David Healy, *Gunboat Diplomacy: The United States Navy in Haiti, 1915–1916* (1976); Dwight C. Miner, *The Fight for the Panama Route* (1940); and William D. McCain, *The United States and the Republic of Panama* (1937), are good for the Panama incident. Link, *Woodrow Wilson and the Progressive Era, Wilson: The New Freedom, Wilson: The Struggle for Neutrality, 1914–1915, Wilson: Confusion and Crises, 1915–1916* (1964), and *Wilson: Campaigns for Progressivism and Peace, 1916–1917* (1965), have the best accounts of Wilson's Caribbean and Mexican policies. For specialized works on the United States and Mexico, see Howard F. Cline, *The United States and Mexico* (1953); Peter Calvert, *The Mexican Revolution, 1910–1914: The Diplomacy of Anglo–American Conflict* (1968); Kenneth J. Grieb, *The United States and Huerta* (1969); Robert E. Quirk, *An Affair of Honor: Woodrow Wilson and the Occupation of Veracruz* (1962) and *The Mexican Revolution, 1914–1915: The Convention of Aguascalientes* (1960); Clarence E. Clendenen, *The United States and Pancho Villa* (1961); and Friedrich Katz, *The Secret War in Mexico: Europe, the United States, and the Mexican Revolution* (1981).

D.   THE FIRST WORLD WAR AND AMERICAN INTERVENTION

Among the general studies, Charles Seymour, *American Diplomacy During the World War* (1934), and *American Neutrality, 1914–1917* (1935); Ernest R. May, *The World War and American Isolation* (1959); Patrick Devlin, *Too Proud to Fight: Woodrow Wilson's Neutrality* (1974); and Edward H. Buehrig, *Woodrow Wilson and the Balance of Power* (1955), are the best. Charles Seymour, ed., *The Intimate Papers of Colonel House* (4 vols., 1926–1928), includes materials indispensable to understanding Wilson's policies. Link, *Woodrow Wilson and the Progressive Era,* is a useful summary, but see particularly Link's much fuller account in *Wilson: The Struggle for Neutrality, 1914–1915, Wilson: Confusions and Crises, 1915–1916,* and *Wilson: Campaigns for Progressivism and Peace, 1916–1917,* and the same author's

Wilson the Diplomatist (1957 and 1963) and *Woodrow Wilson: Revolution, War, and Peace* (1979).

Special studies on this subject abound, and we will mention only a few: Karl E. Birnbaum, *Peace Moves and U-Boat Warfare* (1958), is one of the best monographs in modern diplomatic history; Joseph P. O'Grady, ed., *The Immigrants' Influence on Wilson's Peace Policies* (1967), begins in the period 1914–1917; Laurence W. Martin, *Peace Without Victory: Woodrow Wilson and the British Liberals* (1958), is useful for the entire period 1914–1919; H. C. Peterson, *Propaganda for War* (1939), overrates the influence of Allied propaganda; George S. Viereck, *Spreading the Germs of Hate* (1930), is excellent for German propaganda in the United States; and Carl Wittke, *German–Americans and the World War* (1936), is the standard work on that subject. Kathleen Burk, *Britain, America, and the Sinews of War, 1914–1918* (1985), discusses the crucial subject of credit and war finance.

Osgood, *Ideals and Self-Interest in America's Foreign Relations,* and John Milton Cooper, Jr., *The Vanity of Power: American Isolationism and the First World War* (1969), present incisive analyses of American reactions to the challenges of the war. For the preparedness controversy and the peace movement from 1914 to 1917, see Hermann Hagedorn, *The Bugle That Woke America* (1940), a study of Theodore Roosevelt and the preparedness crisis; Michael Pearlman, *To Make Democracy Safe for America: Patricians and Preparedness in the Progressive Era* (1984); Elting E. Morison, *Admiral Sims and the Modern American Navy* (1942); Hermann Hagedorn, *Leonard Wood* (2 vols., 1931); Peter Brock, *Pacifism in the United States* (1968); Charles Chatfield, *For Peace and Justice: Pacifism in America; 1914–1921* (1971); and Link, *Wilson: Confusion and Crises, 1915–1916.*

Almost all the biographies and memoirs cited in preceding sections have chapters on the background of America's first intervention in Europe. To these should be added Robert Lansing, *War Memoirs of Robert Lansing* (1935); Burton J. Hendrick, *The Life and Letters of Walter H. Page* (3 vols., 1922–1926); John Milton Cooper, Jr., *Walter Hines Page: The Southerner as American, 1855–1918* (1977); Ross Gregory, *Walter Hines Page: Ambassador to the Court of St. James* (1970); and Stephen Gwynn, ed., *Letters and Friendships of Sir Cecil Spring Rice* (2 vols., 1929).

E. AMERICAN PARTICIPATION IN THE FIRST WORLD WAR

General works include Edward M. Coffman, *The War to End All Wars: The American Military Experience in World War I* (1968); Harvey A. DeWeerd, *President Wilson Fights His War: World War I and the American Intervention* (1968); and Robert H. Ferrell, *Woodrow Wilson and World War I, 1917–1921* (1985). The best summaries of military operations are John J. Pershing, *Final Report* (1919), and Leonard P. Ayres, *The War with Germany* (1919). John J. Pershing, *My Experiences in the World War* (2 vols., 1931), and James G. Harbord, *The American Army in France, 1917–1919* (1936), are candid memoirs by two American commanders. The definitive biography of General Pershing is Frank E. Vandiver, *Black Jack: The Life and Times of John J. Pershing* (2 vols., 1977). On the American naval contribution, see Thomas G. Frothingham, *The Naval History of the World War* (3 vols., 1924–1926), and Elting E. Morison, *Admiral Sims and the Modern American Navy* (1942).

F. THE WAR, THE PARIS PEACE CONFERENCE, AND THE TREATY FIGHT

We are now beginning to have an excellent literature on American diplomacy during the period of belligerency and the Paris Peace Conference. Among the general works, the following are excellent: W. B. Fowler, *British–American Relations, 1917–1918: The Role of Sir William Wiseman* (1969); Arno J. Mayer, *Political Origins of the New Diplomacy, 1917–1918* (1959); Harry R. Rudin, *Armistice, 1918* (1944); Louis L. Gerson, *Wilson and the Rebirth of Poland* (1953); Victor S. Mamatey, *The United States and East Central Europe, 1914–1918* (1957); George F. Kennan, *Russia Leaves the War* (1956), *The Decision to Intervene* (1958), and *Russia and the West under Lenin and Stalin* (1961); Betty Miller Unterberger, *America's Siberian Expedition, 1918–1920* (1956); Klaus Schwabe, *Woodrow Wilson, Revolutionary Germany, and Peacemaking, 1918–1919* (1985); Carl P. Parrini, *Heir to Empire: United States Economic Diplomacy, 1916–1923* (1969); David F. Trask, *The United States in the Supreme War Council* (1961); Arthur S. Link, ed., *Woodrow Wilson and a Revolutionary World, 1913–1921* (1982); and A. Lentin, *Lloyd George, Woodrow Wilson, and the Guilt of Germany: An Essay in the Prehistory of Appeasement* (1985).

The early American movement for a League of Nations is described by Ruhl J. Bartlett, *The League to Enforce Peace* (1944). For background on the Paris Peace Conference, see Lawrence E. Gelfand, *The Inquiry: American Preparations for Peace, 1917–1919* (1963). The best single volume on the Paris Peace Conference is Inga Floto, *Colonel House in Paris* (1980). R. S. Baker wrote *Woodrow Wilson and World Settlement* (3 vols., 1922) in collaboration with Wilson. Sympathetic to Wilson are N. Gordon Levin, Jr., *Woodrow Wilson and World Politics: America's Response to War and Revolution* (1968); Paul Birdsall, *Versailles Twenty Years After* (1941); Herbert Hoover, *The Ordeal of Woodrow Wilson* (1958); and Seth P. Tillman, *Anglo–American Relations at the Paris Peace Conference* (1961). Thomas A. Bailey, *Woodrow Wilson and the Lost Peace* (1944), is more critical of Wilson. Arno J. Mayer, *The Politics and Diplomacy of Peacemaking: Containment and Counterrevolution at Versailles, 1918–1919* (1967), and John M. Thompson, *Russia, Bolshevism, and the Versailles Peace* (1966), highlight the Russian problem. Russell H. Fifield, *Woodrow Wilson and the Far East* (1952), relates Wilson's struggles with the Japanese at Paris.

The indispensable source on Wilson and the problems of the peace conference is Arthur S. Link et. al., eds., *The Papers of Woodrow Wilson* (1966–), beginning with Vol. 53.

The best accounts of the treaty fight in the United States are Ralph Stone, *The Irreconcilables: The Fight Against the League of Nations* (1970); Thomas A. Bailey, *Woodrow Wilson and the Great Betrayal* (1945); and Denna F. Fleming, *The*

United States and the League of Nations, 1918–1920 (1932). John M. Blum, *Joe Tumulty and the Wilson Era* (1957 and 1963); Richard W. Leopold, *Elihu Root and the Conservative Tradition* (1954); John A. Garraty, *Henry Cabot Lodge* (1953); and William C. Widenor, *Henry Cabot Lodge and the Search for an American Foreign Policy* (1980), all discuss the treaty fight. The chapter on Wilson in Bert E. Park, M.D., *Fit to Lead? The Impact of Illness on World Leaders* (1986), emphasizes the effect of disease on Wilson's behavior at Paris and during the treaty fight.

G. THE SEARCH FOR ISOLATION, 1921–1932

The most comprehensive general histories of American foreign policy during this period are Denna F. Fleming, *The United States and World Organization, 1920–1933* (1938), and L. Ethan Ellis, *Republican Foreign Policy, 1921–1933* (1968), but see also the briefer Selig Adler, *The Uncertain Giant: 1921–1941, American Foreign Policy between the Wars* (1965). Studies of secretaries of state include Merlo J. Pusey, *Charles Evans Hughes* (2 vols., 1951); L. Ethan Ellis, *Frank B. Kellogg and American Foreign Relations, 1925–1929* (1961), which is also the best general work on the foreign policies of the second Coolidge administration; Robert H. Ferrell, *Frank B. Kellogg-Henry L. Stimson* (1963); Richard N. Current, *Secretary Stimson* (1954); and Elting E. Morison, *Turmoil and Tradition: A Study of the Life and Times of Henry L. Stimson* (1960).

The postwar naval race, the Washington Naval Conference, Japanese–American tension, and Russian–American relations from 1920 to 1933 are discussed by Thomas H. Buckley, *The United States and the Washington Conference* (1970); Harold and Margaret Sprout, *Toward a New Order of Sea Power* (1940); Griswold, *The Far Eastern Policy of the United States;* Akira Iriye, *After Imperialism: The Search for a New Order in the Far East, 1921–1931* (1965); Merze Tate, *The United States and Armaments* (1948); Rodman W. Paul, *Abrogation of the Gentlemen's Agreement* (1936); Robert P. Browder, *The Origins of Soviet–American Diplomacy* (1953); William A. Williams, *American–Russian Relations, 1781–1947* (1952); and Peter G. Filene, *Americans and the Soviet Experiment, 1917–1933* (1967). Robert H. Ferrell, *Peace in Their Time* (1952), is a fine account of the American peace crusade of the 1920s and the negotiation of the Kellogg–Briand Pact. For American international economic policy during the 1920s, see Herbert Feis, *The Diplomacy of the Dollar, First Era, 1919–1932* (1950); Parrini, *Heir to Empire;* Stephen J. Randall, *United States Foreign Oil Policy, 1919–1948: For Profits and Security* (1985); and Joan Hoff Wilson, *American Business and Foreign Policy* (1971). For a study of the spread of American dominance and its effect in Europe, see Frank Costigliola, *Awkward Dominion: American Political, Economic, and Cultural Relations with Europe, 1919–1933* (1984). The best general work on the foreign policy of the Hoover administration is Robert H. Ferrell, *American Diplomacy during the Great Depression* (1957). Works on the Manchurian crisis are cited in the following section.

H.   THE UNITED STATES AND EUROPEAN DISORDER, 1931–1936

One of the basic sources is Edgar B. Nixon, ed., *Franklin D. Roosevelt and Foreign Affairs* (3 vols., 1969), which covers the period 1933–1937. The best general survey for the Roosevelt era is Robert Dallek, *Franklin D. Roosevelt and American Foreign Policy, 1932–1945* (1979), while Howard Jablon, *Crossroads of Decision: The State Department and Foreign Policy, 1933–1937* (1983), is also valuable. The literature on the first important challenge to the postwar treaty structure—Japan's invasion of Manchuria in 1931—is voluminous and many-sided in interpretation. Among the general works, Richard W. Leopold, *The Growth of American Foreign Policy* (1962); Ferrell, *American Diplomacy in the Great Depression;* Griswold, *The Far Eastern Policy of the United States;* Fleming, *The United States and World Organization, 1920–1933;* and Council on Foreign Relations, *The United States in World Affairs, 1931–1933* (3 vols., 1932–1934), are most useful. Hoover defends his failure to take stern action in his *Memoirs* (3 vols., 1951–1952), Vol. III, while Stimson explains his differences with Hoover frankly in Henry L. Stimson and M. Bundy, *On Active Service in War and Peace* (1948).

Specialized studies of the Manchurian crisis are Robert Langer, *Seizure of Territory: The Stimson Doctrine* (1947); Sara R. Smith, *The Manchurian Crisis, 1931–1932* (1948); Reginald Bassett, *Democracy and Foreign Policy, the Sino–Japanese Dispute, 1931–1933* (1952); Armin Rappaport, *Henry L. Stimson and Japan, 1931–1933* (1963); and Justus D. Doenecke, *When the Wicked Rise: American Opinion-Makers and the Manchurian Crisis of 1931–1933* (1984).

The shifting pattern of Roosevelt's international policies comes out clearly in Raymond Moley, *After Seven Years* (1939), and Cordell Hull, *Memoirs* (2 vols., 1948). But see also Lloyd C. Gardner, *Economic Aspects of New Deal Diplomacy* (1964); R. L. Buell, *The Hull Trade Program* (1938); Herbert Feis, *The Changing Pattern of International Economic Affairs* (1940); Richard N. Kottman, *Reciprocity and the North Atlantic Triangle, 1932–1938* (1968); and Julius W. Pratt, *Cordell Hull, 1933–1944* (1964), which is, of course, useful for the entire period.

Cordell Hull, *Memoirs,* Sumner Welles, *The Time for Decision* (1944), and Irwin F. Gellman, *Good Neighbor Diplomacy: United States Policies in Latin America, 1933–1945* (1979), are basic sources for the Good Neighbor policy. Edward O. Guerrant, *Roosevelt's Good Neighbor Policy* (1950), is a brief analysis, but see also Bryce Wood, *The Making of the Good Neighbor Policy* (1961), and Samuel F. Bemis, *The Latin American Policy of the United States* (1943). E. David Cronon, *Josephus Daniels in Mexico* (1960), is excellent for Mexican–American relations in the 1930s.

Other important works for this period are Arnold A. Offner, *American Appeasement: United States Foreign Policy and Germany, 1933–1938* (1969); Brice Harris, Jr., *The United States and the Italo–Ethiopian Crisis* (1964); John P. Diggins, *Mussolini and Fascism: The View from America* (1972); Richard P. Traina, *American Diplomacy and the Spanish Civil War* (1968); and Douglas Little, *Malevolent Neutrality: The United States, Great Britain, and the Origins of the Spanish Civil War* (1985). Robert Dallek, *Democrat and Diplomat: The Life of William E. Dodd*

(1968), is particularly good on German–American relations during the early years of the Roosevelt administration. See also Beatrice Farnsworth, *William C. Bullitt and the Soviet Union* (1967), on Roosevelt's early ties with Russia, and Joan Hoff Wilson, *Ideology and Economics: U. S. Relations with the Soviet Union, 1918–1933* (1974).

There is no general history of the antiwar crusade of the 1930s, but the volumes of *The United States in World Affairs* for the years 1934 to 1939 contain a wealth of information on public opinion, as do Adler, *The Isolationist Impulse,* already cited, Thomas A. Bailey, *The Man in the Street* (1948), and Eileen Eagan, *Class, Culture, and the Classroom: The Student Peace Movement of the 1930s* (1981). More specialized are Ralph B. Levering, *American Opinion and the Russian Alliance, 1939–1945* (1976); Warren I. Cohen, *The American Revisionists: The Lessons of Intervention in World War I* (1967); John K. Nelson, *The Peace Prophets: American Pacifist Thought, 1919–1941* (1967); and Manfred Jonas, *Isolationism in America, 1935–1941* (1966). For the enactment of the neutrality legislation, see James M. Seavey, *Neutrality Legislation* (1939), and Elton Atwater, *American Regulation of Arms Exports* (1941).

I. ORIGINS OF THE SECOND WORLD WAR

The body of literature on the background of American participation in the Second World War is immense. The two outstanding works on the subject are William L. Langer and S. E. Gleason, *The Challenge to Isolation, 1937–1940* (1952) and *The Undeclared War, 1940–1941* (1953). Other general works are Dallek, *Franklin D. Roosevelt and American Foreign Policy;* James M. Burns, *Roosevelt: The Soldier of Freedom* (1970); Robert A. Divine, *The Reluctant Belligerent: American Entry into World War II* (1965); T. R. Fehrenbach, *F.D.R.'s Undeclared War, 1939 to 1941* (1967); and James V. Compton, *The Swastika and the Eagle: Hitler, the United States, and the Origins of World War II* (1967). Robert E. Sherwood, *Roosevelt and Hopkins* (1948); and Winston S. Churchill, *The Gathering Storm* (1948) and *Their Finest Hour* (1949), are invaluable sources. See also Charles A. Beard, *American Foreign Policy in the Making, 1932–1940* (1946) and *President Roosevelt and the Coming of the War, 1941* (1948), critical studies worthy of serious consideration. Specialized works relating to the United States and Europe from 1938 to 1941 are Alton Frye, *Germany and the American Hemisphere, 1933–1941* (1967); John M. Haight, *American Aid to France, 1938–1941* (1970); Philip Goodhart, *Fifty Ships That Saved the World* (1965); Warren F. Kimball, *The Most Unsordid Act: Lend-Lease, 1930–1941* (1969); Theodore A. Wilson, *The First Summit: Roosevelt and Churchill at Placentia Bay, 1941* (1969); and David Reynolds, *The Creation of the Anglo–American Alliance: A Study in Competitive Cooperation* (1982).

Relations with Japan during the 1930s to 1941 are traced by Griswold, *The Far Eastern Policy of the United States*; Dorothy Borg, *The United States and the Far Eastern Crisis of 1933–1938* (1964); Waldo H. Heinrichs, Jr., *American Ambassador: Joseph C. Grew and the Development of the United States Diplomatic Tradition* (1966); and Joseph C. Grew, *Turbulent Era, a Diplomatic Record of Forty Years,*

1904–1945 (2 vols., 1952). The Langer and Gleason volumes and Gordon W. Prange, *At Dawn We Slept: The Untold Story of Pearl Harbor* (1981), contain the best accounts of events leading to the rupture in Japanese–American relations, but see also Manny T. Koginos, *The Panay Incident: Prelude to War* (1967); John Toland, *The Rising Sun: The Decline and Fall of the Japanese Empire, 1936–1945* (1970); Herbert Feis, *The Road to Pearl Harbor* (1950); Paul W. Schroeder, *The Axis Alliance and Japanese–American Relations, 1941* (1958); Robert J. C. Butow, *Tojo and the Coming of the War* (1961); and Roberta Wohlstetter, *Pearl Harbor: Warning and Decision* (1962). Insightful essays on various aspects of Japanese and American foreign policies are contained in Dorothy Borg and Shumpei Okamoto, eds., *Pearl Harbor as History* (1973).

For the debate over American intervention, we now have adequate studies for both the internationalists and the isolationists: Walter Johnson, *The Battle Against Isolation* (1944); Mark L. Chadwin, *The Hawks of World War II* (1968); Donald J. Friedman, *The Road from Isolation: The Campaign of the American Committee for Non-Participation in Japanese Aggression, 1938–1941* (1968); Wayne S. Cole, *America First, the Battle Against Intervention, 1940–1941* (1953); and Manfred Jonas, *Isolationism in America, 1935–1941* (1966).

J. THE DIPLOMACY AND CONDUCT OF THE SECOND WORLD WAR

The best and most revealing source on the Anglo–American wartime relationship is Warren F. Kimball, ed., *Churchill and Roosevelt: The Complete Correspondence* (3 vols., 1984). Dallek, *Franklin D. Roosevelt and American Foreign Policy, 1932–1945;* Burns, *Roosevelt: Soldier of Freedom;* and Herbert Feis, *Churchill, Roosevelt, and Stalin* (1957), are the best one-volume accounts, but see also Churchill's magisterial *The Grand Alliance* (1950), *The Hinge of Fate* (1950), *Closing the Ring* (1951), and *Triumph and Tragedy* (1953); John S. D. Eisenhower, *Allies: Pearl Harbor to D-Day* (1982); Sherwood, *Roosevelt and Hopkins;* and W. Averell Harriman and Elie Abel, *Special Envoy to Churchill and Stalin, 1941–1946* (1975). Akira Iriye, *Power and Culture: The Japanese–American War, 1941–1945* (1981), is a reconsideration of the Pacific War. Other general studies are Robert A. Divine, *Roosevelt and World War II* (1969); Gaddis Smith, *American Diplomacy During the Second World War* (1965); Christopher Thorne, *Allies of a Kind: The United States, Britain, and the War Against Japan* (1978); and William Roger Louis, *Imperialism at Bay: The United States and the Decolonization of the British Empire, 1941–1945* (1978), a monumental study.

For more specialized works, see Mark A. Stoler, *The Politics of the Second Front: American Military Planning and Diplomacy in Coalition Warfare, 1941–1943* (1977); Herbert Feis, *The China Triangle* (1953); Paul A. Varg, *The Closing of the Door: Sino–American Relations, 1936–1946* (1973); E. J. Kahn, Jr., *The China Hands: America's Foreign Service Officers and What Befell Them* (1975); John L. Snell, ed., *The Meaning of Yalta* (1956); Keith Eubank, *Summit at Teheran: The Untold Story* (1985); Stephen E. Ambrose, *Eisenhower and Berlin: The Decision to Halt at the Elbe* (1967); Robert A. Divine, *Second Chance: The Triumph of Interna-*

tionalism in America during World War II (1967); Herbert Feis, *Between War and Peace: The Potsdam Conference* (1960), *Japan Subdued* (1961), and *From Trust to Terror: The Onset of the Cold War, 1945–1950* (1971); Frank D. McCann, Jr., *The Brazilian–American Alliance, 1937–1945* (1973); Robert J. C. Butow, *Japan's Decision to Surrender* (1954); and William L. Neumann, *After Victory: Churchill, Roosevelt, Stalin, and the Making of the Peace* (1969). Gabriel Kolko, *The Politics of War: The World and United States Foreign Policy, 1943–1945* (1969), challenges, not always successfully, and rarely without bias in favor of the Soviet Union, many traditional assumptions about relations between the western Allies and the Soviet Union and about Soviet policies.

The sad story of the Roosevelt administration's failure to do much to help European Jews in danger of extermination is related in David S. Wyman, *Paper Walls: America and the Refugee Crisis, 1938–1941* (1968); Henry L. Feingold, *The Politics of Rescue: The Roosevelt Administration and the Holocaust, 1938–1945* (1970); Arthur D. Morse, *While Six Million Died* (1968); and Saul S. Friedman, *No Haven for the Oppressed: United States Policy Toward Jewish Refugees, 1938– 1945* (1973).

Winston S. Churchill, *The Grand Alliance* (1950), *The Hinge of Fate* (1950), *Closing the Ring* (1951), and *Triumph and Tragedy* (1953), give brilliant accounts of all major military operations. Good general works are Martha Byrd Hoyle, *A World in Flames: The History of World War II;* Chester Wilmot, *The Struggle for Europe* (1952); Charles B. MacDonald, *The Mighty Endeavor: American Armed Forces in the European Theater in World War II* (1969); Ronald Schaffer, *Wings of Judgment: American Bombing in World War II* (1985); and Gary R. Hess, *The United States at War, 1941–1945* (1985). The Department of the Army's Office of Military History has published numerous volumes in its large and generally excellent series, *U. S. Army in World War II.* Samuel E. Morison, *History of the United States Naval Operations in World War II* (15 vols., 1947–1962), is definitive, but see Gordon Prange, *Miracle at Midway* (1982) and Walter Lord, *Incredible Victory* (1967), on the Battle of Midway. Kent Roberts Greenfield, ed., *Command Decisions* (1959), contains a number of brilliant analyses of crucial military events and also reveals how considerations of military strategy affected diplomacy. Greenfield, *American Strategy in World War II: A Reconsideration* (1963), is another provocative assessment. For British perspectives on Anglo–American strategic planning and operations, see Michael Howard, *The Mediterranean Strategy in the Second World War* (1966) and John Keegan, *Six Armies in Normandy* (1982).

For American military and naval leaders, see Alfred D. Chandler, Jr., Stephen E. Ambrose, and Louis Galambos, eds., *The Papers of Dwight D. Eisenhower: The War Years* (9 vols., 1970, 1978); Stephen E. Ambrose, *The Supreme Commander: The War Years of General Dwight D. Eisenhower* (1970) and *Eisenhower: Soldier, General of the Army, President-Elect, 1890–1952* (1983); Dwight D. Eisenhower, *Crusade in Europe* (1948); Forrest C. Pogue, *George C. Marshall* (3 vols., 1962– 1973); William Raymond Manchester, *American Caesar, Douglas MacArthur, 1880–1964* (1978); Gavin Long, *MacArthur as Military Commander* (1969); D. Clayton James, *The Years of MacArthur*, Vol. I (1970); Douglas MacArthur, *Reminiscences* (1964); H. Essame, *Patton: A Study in Command* (1976); E. B. Potter,

Nimitz (1976); Henry H. Arnold, *Global Mission* (1949); Omar N. Bradley, *A Soldier's Story* (1951); Ernest J. King and W. M. Whitehill, *Fleet Admiral King* (1952); William D. Leahy, *I Was There* (1950); and Henry H. Adams, *Witness to Power: The Life of Fleet Admiral William D. Leahy* (1985). Richard F. Haynes, *The Awesome Power: Harry S. Truman as Commander in Chief* (1973), is a significant study of the military power inherent in the office of the presidency.

3. Social and Economic Trends, 1900–1945

A. DEMOGRAPHIC CHANGES AND WEALTH

The handiest references for general economic and social data are U.S. Bureau of the Census, *Historical Statistics of the United States, Colonial Times to the Present* (1976), and *Statistical Abstract of the United States* (published annually). Warren S. Thompson, *Population Problems* (1953), is an excellent survey. The best sources for decennial demographic changes are the summary volumes of the census.

There are a number of excellent studies of wealth, income, and income distribution. For discussions in the broad context of economic development, see Harold U. Faulkner, *The Decline of Laissez Faire, 1897–1917* (1951); George Soule, *Prosperity Decade: From War to Depression, 1917–1929* (1947); and Broadus Mitchell, *Depression Decade* (1947). Milton Friedman and Anna J. Schwartz, *A Monetary History of the United States, 1867–1960* (1963), is a monumental study. Robert F. Martin, *National Income in the United States, 1799–1938* (1939), is an excellent statistical summary. Charles B. Spahr, *An Essay on the Present Distribution of Wealth* (1896); Wilford I. King, *The Wealth and Income of the People of the United States* (1915); and Wesley C. Mitchell et al., *Income of the United States . . . 1909–1919* (2 vols., 1921–1922); President's Conference on Unemployment, *Recent Economic Changes in the United States* (2 vols., 1929); and Robert J. Lampman, *The Share of Top Wealthholders in National Wealth, 1922–1956* (1962), discuss income distribution from the late 1890s to 1960. Simon Kuznets, *Capital in the American Economy* (1961), and Raymond W. Goldsmith, *The National Wealth of the United States* (1962), are general studies. Louis Galambos and Barbara Barrow Spence, *The Public Image of Big Business in America, 1880–1940* (1975), is an excellent study of popular attitudes toward economic conglomerations, while Steven L. Piott, *The Anti-Monopoly Persuasion: Popular Resistance to the Rise of Big Business in the Midwest* (1985), discusses it as a political issue. A study of responses to industrialization in one state is David P. Thelen, *Paths of Resistance: Tradition and Dignity in Industrializing Missouri* (1986).

B. INDUSTRY AND FINANCE

A groundbreaking and now-standard work is Alfred D. Chandler, Jr., *The Visible Hand: The Managerial Revolution in American Business* (1977). W. Eliot Brownlee, *Dynamics of Ascent: A History of the American Economy* (1979); Stuart Bruchey, *Growth of the Modern American Economy* (1975); Faulkner, *Decline of*

Laissez Faire, 1897–1917; Soule, *Prosperity Decade: From War to Depression, 1917–1929;* Broadus Mitchell, *Depression Decade,* all just mentioned; Harold F. Williamson, ed., *The Growth of the American Economy* (1957); and Glen Porter, *The Rise of Big Business, 1860–1910* (1973), include chapters on the growth of industry from 1900 to 1920. Thomas C. Cochran, *The American Business System, 1900–1950* (1957), is a thoughtful analysis. Interesting also among the general studies are Alan R. Raucher, *Public Relations and Business, 1900–1929* (1968), and Morrell Heald, *The Social Responsibilities of Business: Company and Community, 1900–1960* (1970). The government's influence upon the economy is surveyed by Merle Fainsod and L. Gordon, *Government and the American Economy* (1959); Gerald D. Nash, *United States Oil Policy, 1894–1964* (1968); Ari and Olive Hoogenboom, *A History of the ICC* (1976); Albro Martin, *Enterprise Denied: Origins of the Decline of American Railroads, 1897–1917* (1971); and William H. Becker, *Dynamics of Business–Government Relations: Industry and Exports, 1893–1921* (1981).

For general developments in the late nineteenth century and from 1900 to 1920, see also Thomas C. Cochran and W. Miller, *The Age of Enterprise* (1942); Edmund E. Day and W. Thomas, *The Growth of Manufactures, 1899 to 1923* (1928); Solomon Fabricant, *The Output of Manufacturing Industries, 1899–1937* (1940); John W. Kendrick, *Productivity Trends in the United States* (1961); and David A. Hounshell, *From the American System to Mass Production, 1850–1932: The Development of Manufacturing Technology in the United States* (1984).

For the growth of particular industries, see Harold F. Williamson and Arnold R. Daum, *The American Petroleum Industry, 1850–1899: The Age of Illumination* (1959); Williamson et al., *The American Petroleum Industry: The Age of Energy, 1899–1959* (1963); Harless D. Wagoner, *The U. S. Machine Tool Industry from 1900 to 1950* (1968); Arthur M. Johnson, *The Development of American Petroleum Pipelines and Public Policy, 1906–1959* (1967); Nannie M. Tilley, *The R. J. Reynolds Company* (1985); Alfred S. Eichner, *The Emergence of Oligopoly: Sugar Refining as a Case Study* (1969); Erik Barnouw, *A Tower in Babel: A History of Broadcasting in the United States, Volume I: to 1933* (1966) and *The Golden Web: A History of Broadcasting in the United States, Volume II: 1933–1953* (1968); and John B. Rae, *Climb to Greatness: The American Aircraft Industry, 1920–1960* (1968).

The great work on the rise of the modern supercorporation is Chandler, *The Visible Hand,* but Henry R. Seager and C. A. Gulick, Jr., *Trust and Corporation Problems* (1929), is still useful. See also Arthur F. Burns, *The Decline of Competition* (1936); Ralph L. Nelson, *Merger Movements in American Industry, 1895–1956* (1959); Naomi R. Lamoreaux, *The Great Merger Movement in American Business, 1895–1904* (1985); Adolph A. Berle, Jr., and G. C. Means, *The Modern Corporation and Private Property* (1932); G. Warren Nutter, *The Extent of Enterprise Monopoly in the United States, 1899–1939* (1951); Louis Galambos, *Competition and Cooperation: The Emergence of a National Trade Association* (1966); Federal Trade Commission, *The Merger Movement* (1948); Thurman W. Arnold, *The Bottlenecks of Business* (1940); Wallace H. Hamilton, *Antitrust in Action* (1940); and Corwin D. Edwards, *Maintaining Competition* (1949).

Frederick Lewis Allen's racy *The Lords of Creation* (1935), gives special attention to the financial leaders during this period. Indispensable general works for the serious student are George W. Edwards, *The Evolution of Finance Capitalism* (1938); Margaret G. Myers, *A Financial History of the United States* (1970); and Vincent P. Carosso, *Investment Banking in America: A History* (1970). For specialized studies, see C. A. E. Goodhart, *The New York Money Market and the Finance of Trade, 1900–1913* (1969); Cedric B. Cowing, *Populists, Plungers, and Progressives: A Social History of Stock and Commodity Speculation, 1890–1913* (1965); Louis D. Brandeis, *Other People's Money, and How the Bankers Use It* (1914), which summarizes the findings of the Pujo committee in 1913; Henry L. Staples and Alpheus T. Mason, *The Fall of a Railroad Empire* (1947), the story of J. P. Morgan and the New Haven Railroad; William Z. Ripley, *Main Street and Wall Street* (1927); Ferdinand Pecora, *Wall Street Under Oath* (1939); J. T. Flynn, *Security Speculation* (1934); S. E. Harris, *Twenty Years of Federal Reserve Policy* (2 vols., 1933); and Elmus R. Wicker, *Federal Reserve Monetary Policy, 1917–1933* (1966).

Excellent surveys and special studies of the technological revolution are Elting E. Morison, *From Know-How to Nowhere: The Development of American Technology* (1974); John W. Oliver, *History of American Technology* (1956); Leonard S. Silk, *The Research Revolution* (1960); George Wise, *Willis R. Whitney, General Electric, and the Origins of U.S. Industrial Research* (1985); Leonard S. Reich, *The Making of American Industrial Research: Science and Business at G.E. and Bell* (1985); Hugh G. Aitken, *The Continuous Wave: Technology and American Radio, 1900–1932* (1985); Harry Jerome, *Mechanization in Industry;* and David A. Hounshell, *From the American System to Mass Production, 1850–1932: The Development of Manufacturing Technology in the United States* (1984).

Biographies are often the most tangible form of economic history for the general reader. Frederick Lewis Allen, *The Great Pierpont Morgan* (1949), and Lewis Corey, *The House of Morgan* (1930), reveal different points of view about the great financier. Allan Nevins, *Study in Power: John D. Rockefeller, Industrialist and Philanthropist* (2 vols., 1953), is as much a history of the American oil industry as a biography of its master builder, just as his *Ford, the Times, the Man, the Company* (1954), tells the saga of the automobile industry. For the leaders in iron, steel, and tobacco, see Joseph Frazier Wall, *Andrew Carnegie* (1970); Ida M. Tarbell, *The Life of Elbert H. Gary* (1925); and Robert F. Durden, *The Dukes of Durham, 1865–1929* (1975).

C. AMERICAN WORKERS, 1900–1945

There are brief discussions in Faulkner, *Decline of Laissez Faire, 1897–1917;* Soule, *Prosperity Decade;* Philip Taft, *Organized Labor in American History* (1964); and Henry Pelling, *American Labor* (1960). Other general works for the period are John R. Commons et al., *History of Labour in the United States* (4 vols., 1918–1935); Philip Taft, *The A. F. of L. in the Time of Gompers* (1957); and Foster Rhea Dulles and Melvin Dubofsky, *Labor in America: A History* (1984).

A number of recent studies, known broadly as the "new" labor history, have transformed our understanding of twentieth-century labor. Several valuable general works are Harvey Braverman, *Labor and Capital: The Degradation of Work in the Twentieth Century* (1974); Melvyn Dubofsky, *Industrialism and the American Worker*, 2d ed. (1984); Richard Edwards, *Contested Terrain: The Transformation of the Workplace in the Twentieth Century* (1979); Edwards et al., *Segmented Work, Divided Workers* (1982); James R. Green, *The World of the Worker: Labor in Twentieth Century America* (1980); Herbert Gutman, *Work, Culture, and Society in Industralizing America: Essays in American Working-Class and Social History* (1976); and David Montgomery, *Workers' Control in America: Studies in the History of Work, Technology, and Labor Struggles* (1979).

For more specialized studies, also see John Bodnar, *Workers' World: Kinship, Community, and Protest in an Industrial Society, 1900–1940* (1982); Bodnar, Roger Simon, and Michael P. Weber, *Lives of Their Own: Blacks, Italians, and Poles in Pittsburgh, 1900–1960* (1982); David Alan Corbin, *Life, Work, and Rebellion in the Coal Fields: The Southern West Virginia Miners, 1880–1922* (1981); James E. Cronin and Carmen Siriannia, eds., *Work, Community, and Power: The Experience of Labor in Europe and America, 1900–1925* (1983); Stephen Meyer III, *The Five Dollar Day: Labor Management and Social Control in the Ford Motor Company, 1908–1921* (1981); Katherine A. Harvey, *The Best-Dressed Miners: Life and Labor in the Maryland Coal Region, 1835–1910* (1969); Daniel Nelson, *Frederick Taylor and the Rise of Scientific Management* (1980) and *Managers and Workers: The Origins of the Factory System in the United States, 1880–1920* (1975); Sanford M. Jacoby, *Employing Bureaucracy: Managers, Unions, and the Transformation of Work in American Industry, 1900–1945* (1985); Michael P. Weber, *Social Change in an Industrial Town: Patterns of Progress in Warren, Pennsylvania, from the Civil War to World War I* (1976); and Roy Rosenzweig, *Eight Hours for What We Will: Workers and Leisure in an Industrial City* (1983). A pioneering study of rural workers is available in Cletus Daniel, *Bitter Harvest: A History of California Farm-workers, 1870–1941* (1981).

Daniel T. Rodgers, *The Work Ethic in Industrializing America, 1850–1920* (1978), is magnificient on the transformation of attitudes toward work. For detailed and specialized studies of unionization, union politics, and labor struggles, see Melvyn Dubofsky, *When Workers Organize: New York City in the Progressive Era* (1968); Lewis L. Lorwin, *The American Federation of Labor* (1933); Leo Wolman, *The Growth of American Trade Unions, 1880–1923* (1924); Marguerite Green, *The National Civic Federation and the American Labor Movement, 1900–1925* (1956); David Brody, *Steelworkers in America: The Nonunion Era* (1960); Marc Karson, *American Labor Unions and Politics, 1900–1918* (1958); and Melvyn Dubofsky, *We Shall All Be One: A History of the Industrial Workers of the World* (1969). See also Louis Adamic, *Dynamite, the Story of Class Violence in America* (1934); Bruno Ramirez, *When Workers Fight: The Politics of Industrial Relations in the Progressive Era* (1978); Robert L. Tyler, *Rebels in the Woods: The IWW in the Pacific Northwest* (1968); Samuel Yellen, *America Labor Struggles* (1936); Stanley Buder, *Pullman: An Experiment in Industrial Order and Community Planning, 1880–1930* (1967); and George S. McGovern and Leonard F. Guttridge, *The Great Coalfield War* (1972), on the Colorado coal strike of 1913–1914.

Excellent for labor during the 1920s, the Great Depression, and the New Deal era are Irving Bernstein, *The Lean Years: A History of the American Worker, 1920–1933* (1960) and *Turbulent Years: A History of the American Worker, 1933–1941* (1970); but see also James O. Morris, *Conflict Within the AFL: A Study of Craft Versus Industrial Unionism, 1901–1938* (1958); Walter Galenson, *The CIO Challenge to the AFL: A History of the American Labor Movement, 1935–1941* (1960); Sidney Fine, *The Automobile Under the Blue Eagle: Labor, Management, and the Automobile Manufacturing Code* (1963) and *Sit Down: The General Motors Strike of 1936–1937* (1969); Jerold S. Auerbach, *Labor and Liberty: The La Follette Committee and the New Deal* (1966); David Brody, *The Butcher Workmen: A Study of Unionization* (1964); Joel I. Seidman, *American Labor from Defense to Reconversion* (1953); and John Barnard, *Walter Reuther and the Rise of the Auto Workers* (1983).

For specialized studies on hours and working conditions, see Albert Rees, *Real Wages in Manufacturing, 1890–1914* (1961); Solomon Fabricant, *Employment in Manufacturing, 1899–1939* (1942); and Robert M. Woodbury, *Workers' Health and Safety* (1927).

All the general and many of the specialized studies cited above include discussions of the development of public policy and judicial interpretation concerning labor unions. For judicial interpretation, the following monographs are excellent: Felix Frankfurter and N. Greene, *The Labor Injunction* (1930); Edward Berman, *Labor and the Sherman Act* (1930); Charles O. Gregory, *Labor and the Law* (1946); and Elias Lieberman, *Unions Before the Bar* (1950). Arthur S. Link, *Woodrow Wilson and the Progressive Era* (1954) and *Wilson: The New Freedom* (1956), discuss the labor policies of the Wilson administration; but for labor during the First World War, see Henry F. Pringle, *The Life and Times of William Howard Taft* (2 vols., 1939); Alexander M. Bing, *War-Time Strikes and Their Adjustment* (1921); and Valerie Jean Conner, *The National War Labor Board: Stability, Social Justice, and the Voluntary State in World War I* (1983). Concerning public policy during the New Deal, Carroll R. Daugherty, *Labor Under the N.R.A.* (1934), is a contemporary survey, which should be supplemented by Robert Ziegler, *Organized Labor and the New Deal Dispensation* (1986). Another useful account is Irving Bernstein, *A Caring Society: The New Deal, The Worker, and the Great Depression: A History of the American Worker, 1933–1941* (1985). Robert R. R. Brooks, *When Labor Organizes* (1937) and *Unions of Their Own Choosing* (1939), survey the impact of the Wagner Act. J. Joseph Huthmacher, *Senator Robert F. Wagner and the Rise of Urban Liberalism* (1968), is excellent on the writing of labor's charter of liberties.

The history of the labor movement since 1900 is writ large in the memoirs and biographies of its leaders. Samuel Gompers, *Seventy Years of Life and Labor* (2 vols., 1925), is one of the great autobiographies in American literature, but see also Bernard Mandel, *Samuel Gompers: A Biography* (1963). Nick Salvatore, *Eugene V. Debs: Citizen and Socialist* (1982), treats the major left-wing labor leader of his generation. Elsie Gluck, *John Mitchell, Miner* (1929), and Hyman Weintraub, *Andrew Furuseth: Emancipator of the Seamen* (1959), illuminate the careers of two leaders. James A. Wechsler, *Labor Baron: A Portrait of John L. Lewis* (1944), Saul

D. Alinsky, *John L. Lewis: An Unauthorized Biography* (1949), and Melvyn Dubofsky, *John L. Lewis: A Biography* (1977), present different portraits of the stormy petrel of the twentieth-century labor movement. Matthew Josephson, *Sidney Hillman: Statesman of American Labor* (1952), is an important if uncritical contribution, while Charles A. Madison, *American Labor Leaders* (1950), is also useful. Robert L. Tyler, *Walter Reuther* (1973), and John Barnard, *Walter Reuther and the Rise of the Auto Workers* (1983), treat the most important American labor leader since John L. Lewis. David Dubinsky and A. H. Raskin, *David Dubinsky: A Life with Labor* (1977), provides another interesting portrait of the labor movement in the interwar years through the eyes of one of its leaders.

D. IMMIGRATION AND ITS IMPACT

Carl Wittke, *We Who Built America* (1939); George M. Stephenson, *History of American Immigration, 1820–1924* (1926); Maldwyn Allen Jones, *American Immigration* (1960); and Philip Taylor, *The Distant Magnet: European Immigration to the U.S.A.* (1971) are surveys. Louis Adamic, *From Many Lands* (1940), and Oscar Handlin, *The Uprooted* (1951), highlight the impact of the uprooting upon the immigrants and their contributions to American life. Two excellent recent syntheses are Alan M. Kraut, *The Huddled Masses: The Immigrant in American Society, 1880–1921* (1982), and John Bodnar, *The Transplanted: A History of Immigrants in Urban America* (1985). Good specialized studies are Humbert S. Nelli, *The Italians in Chicago, 1880–1930* (1970); John M. Allswang, *A House for All Peoples: Ethnic Politics in Chicago, 1890–1936* (1970); Rowland T. Berthoff, *British Immigrants in Industrial America, 1790–1950* (1953); Theodore Saloutos, *They Remember America: The Story of the Repatriated Greek–American* (1956); Carl Wittke, *The Irish in America* (1956); and William I. Thomas and Florian Znaniecki, *The Polish Peasant in Europe and America* (2 vols., 1927).

Also useful are John Higham, *Send These to Me: Jews and Other Immigrants in Urban America* (1975); John W. Briggs, *An Italian Passage: Immigrants to Three American Cities, 1890–1930* (1978); Virginia Yans-McLaughlin, *Family and Community: Italian Immigrants in Buffalo, 1880–1930* (1977); Jack Chen, *The Chinese of America* (1980); Josef Barton, *Peasants and Strangers: Italians, Rumanians, and Slovaks in an American City, 1880–1950* (1975); Thomas Kessner, *The Golden Door: Italian and Jewish Immigrant Mobility in New York City, 1880–1915* (1977); John Bodnar, *Immigration and Industrialization: Ethnicity in an American Mill Town, 1870–1940* (1977); Michael J. Piore, *Birds of Passage: Migrant Labor and Industrial Societies* (1979); Richard L. Ehrlich, ed., *Immigrants in Industrial America, 1850–1920* (1977); Donna R. Gabbacia, *From Sicily to Elizabeth Street: Housing and Social Change among Italian Immigrants, 1880–1930* (1984); Olivier Zunz, *The Changing Face of Inequality: Urbanization, Industrial Development, and Immigrants in Detroit, 1880–1920* (1982); Judith E. Smith, *Family Connections: A History of Italian and Jewish Immigrant Lives in Providence, Rhode Island, 1900–1940* (1985); and Robert Anthony Orsi, *The Madonna of 115th Street: Faith and Community in Italian Harlem, 1880–1950* (1985).

Most of the works on immigration policy reflect the controversial aspects of the issue, but Roy L. Garis, *Immigration Restriction* (1927), and William S. Bernard, *American Immigration Policy* (1950), are thorough and objective. John Higham, *Strangers in the Land, Patterns of American Nativism, 1860–1925* (1955), concentrates on nativism in the twentieth century. A pioneer study of anti-Semitism in higher education is Marcia G. Synnott, *The Half-Opened Door: Discrimination and Admissions at Harvard, Yale, and Princeton, 1900–1970* (1979). Roger Daniels, *The Politics of Prejudice: The Anti-Japanese Movement in California and the Struggle for Japanese Exclusion* (1962), and Stuart Creighton Miller, *The Unwelcome Immigrant: The American Image of the Chinese, 1785–1882* (1969), both deal with anti-Asian sentiment. Another study which examines ethnocultural conflict is Ronald H. Bayor, *Neighbors in Conflict: The Irish, Germans, Jews, and Italians of New York City, 1919–1941* (1978).

4. Social and Intellectual Trends, 1900–1945

A. SOCIAL TRENDS

Daniel J. Boorstin, *The Americans: The Democratic Experience* (1973), is a fascinating discussion of many recent social changes within the larger context of the period since the Civil War. Harold U. Faulkner, *The Quest for Social Justice, 1898–1914* (1931); Preston W. Slosson, *The Great Crusade and After, 1914–1928* (1930); Lloyd R. Morris, *Postscript to Yesterday* (1947); and Frederick Lewis Allen, *The Big Change: America Transforms Itself, 1900–1950* (1952), are excellent general surveys emphasizing manners and ideas. Mark Sullivan, *Our Times: The United States, 1900–1925* (6 vols., 1926–1935), contains a wealth of social history, as does Walter Lord, *The Good Years: From 1900 to the First World War* (1960). Most helpful for understanding prewar social and intellectual currents is Henry F. May, *The End of American Innocence: A Study of the First Years of Our Own Time, 1912–1917* (1959). See also Nathan G. Hale, Jr., *Freud Comes to America* (1971); John C. Burnham, *Psychoanalysis and American Medicine, 1894–1918* (1967); Dorothy Ross, *G. Stanley Hall: the Psychologist as Prophet* (1972); Richard Weiss, *The American Myth of Success: From Horatio Alger to Norman Vincent Peale* (1969); and James Harvey Young, *The Medical Messiahs: A Social History of Health Quackery in Tentieth-Century America* (1967). The best general survey of urbanization is Charles N. Glaab and A. Theodore Brown, *A History of Urban America* (1976), but see also Zane L. Miller, *The Urbanization of Modern America* (1973). The subject of childhood in American history is at an early stage of exploration. Joseph F. Kett, *Rites of Passage: Adolescence in America 1790 to the Present* (1977), is the best and most comprehensive study, but also useful are Fred Hechinger and Grace Hechinger, *Growing Up in America* (1975); Robert H. Bremner et al., *Children and Youth in America* (4 vols., 1974); and David Nasaw, *Children of the City: At Work and at Play* (1985).

Aspects of the rise of mass commercial culture are treated in the following: Gunther P. Barth, *City People: The Rise of Modern City Culture in Nineteenth Century America* (1980); MacDonald Smith Moore, *Yankee Blues: Musical Culture and American Identity* (1985); Charles C. Alexander, *Ty Cobb* (1984); Benjamin Arthur, *Actors and American Culture, 1880–1920* (1984); Lewis A. Erenberg, *Steppin' Out: New York Nightlife and the Transformation of American Culture, 1890–1930* (1981); Stuart Ewen, *Captains of Consciousness: Advertising and The Social Roots of Consumer Culture* (1976); Peter Levine, *A. G. Spalding and the Rise of Baseball: The Promise of American Sport* (1985); Lary May, *Screening Out the Past: The Birth of Mass Culture and the Motion Picture Industry* (1981); Donald J. Mrozak, *Sport and American Mentality, 1880–1910* (1983); Daniel Pope, *The Making of Modern Advertising* (1983); Daniel Horowitz, *The Morality of Spending: Attitudes Toward the Consumer Society in America, 1875–1940* (1985); Steven A. Reiss, *Touching Base: Professional Baseball and American Culture in the Progressive Era* (1980); Robert Sklar, *Movie-Made America: A Social History of American Movies* (1975); Harold Seymour, *Baseball* (2 vols., 1960–); David Q. Voigt, *American Baseball* (3 vols., 1966–1983); and Joseph H. Odelson, *The Great Television Race: A History of the American Television Industry, 1925–1941* (1982).

The following works illuminate social and intellectual trends of the 1920s and 1930s: President's Committee, *Recent Social Trends in the United States* (2 vols., 1933); Dixon Wecter, *The Age of the Great Depression, 1929–1941* (1948); Frederick Lewis Allen, *Only Yesterday, an Informal History of the Nineteen-Twenties* (1931) and *Since Yesterday: The Nineteen-Thirties in America* (1940); Robert S. and Helen M. Lynd, *Middletown* (1929) and *Middletown in Transition* (1937); Guy Alchon, *The Invisible Hand of Planning: Capitalism, Social Science, and the State in the 1920s* (1985); James W. Prothro, *The Dollar Decade: Business Ideas in the 1920's* (1954); Sigmund Diamond, *The Reputation of the American Businessman* (1955); Harold E. Stearns, *America Now* (1938); Ruth Linquist, *The Family in the Present Social Order* (1931); Foster R. Dulles, *America Learns to Play* (1940); G. J. Stigler, *Domestic Servants in the United States, 1900–1940* (1946); and David L. Cohn, *Combustion on Wheels, an Informal History of the Automobile Age* (1944).

B.   CURRENTS OF AMERICAN THOUGHT

Herbert W. Schneider, *A History of American Philosophy* (1946); Merle Curti, *The Growth of American Thought* (1964); and Ralph H. Gabriel, *The Course of American Democratic Thought* (1956), discuss important developments since the 1890s. Henry S. Commager, *The American Mind* (1950), James B. Gilbert, *Work Without Salvation: America's Intellectuals and Industrial Alienation, 1880–1910* (1977), and T. J. Jackson Lears, *No Place of Grace: Antimodernism and the Transformation of American Culture, 1880–1920* (1981), are also general in scope.

For specialized studies, see Morton White, *Social Thought in America* (1949); Joseph Dorfman, *The Economic Mind in American Civilization* (5 vols., 1946–1959); Sidney Hook, *John Dewey* (1939); Donald B. Meyer, *The Positive Thinkers* (1966); R. Wilson Jackson, *In Quest of Community: Social Philosophy in the United States, 1860–1920* (1968); John Tipple, *The Capitalist Revolution: A History of American Social Thought 1890–1919* (1970); John P. Diggins, *The Bard of Savagery: Thorstein Veblen and Modern Social Theory* (1978); and Arthur A. Ekirch, Jr.,

Ideologies and Utopias: The Impact of the New Deal on American Thought (1969). Harold E. Stearns, ed., *Civilization in the United States* (1922); Joseph Wood Krutch, *The Modern Temper* (1929); and Walter Lippmann, *A Preface to Morals* (1929), voice the intellectual discontent of the 1920s.

C. AMERICAN EDUCATION

Of all major fields of American history, the history of education is most neglected. Among the general surveys, Ellwood P. Cubberly, *Public Education in the United States* (1934); Stuart G. Noble, *A History of American Education* (1938); David B. Tyack, *The One Best System: A History of American Urban Education* (1974); Edgar W. Knight, *Education in the United States* (1951); Erwin V. Johanning-meier, *Americans and Their Schools* (1980); and Paul E. Peterson, *The Politics of School Reform, 1870–1940* (1985), are the best. Isaac L. Kandel, ed., *Twenty-Five Years of American Education* (1924), has excellent chapters on developments during the first two decades of this century, but see especially his thoughtful *American Education in the Twentieth Century* (1957). Lawrence A. Cremin, *The Transformation of the School: Progressivism in American Education, 1876–1957* (1961), is excellent social history, but see also William A. Link, *A Hard Country and a Lonely Place: Schooling, Society, and Reform in Rural Virginia, 1870–1920* (1986); Selwyn K. Troen, *The Public and the Schools: Shaping the St. Louis System, 1838–1920* (1975); and David John Hogan, *Class and Reform: School and Society in Chicago, 1880–1930* (1985). Laurence R. Vesey, *The Emergence of the American University* (1965), is superb.

Among the specialized studies, President's Committee, *Recent Social Trends in the United States,* is very informative about developments in the 1920s. David Tyack, Robert Lowe, and Elisabeth Hansot, *Public Schools in Hard Times: The Great Depression and Recent Years* (1984); Malcolm W. Wiley, ed., *Depression, Recovery, and Higher Education* (1933); Isaac L. Kandel, *The End of an Era* (1941); and Hollis P. Allen, *The Federal Government and Education* (1950), are useful for the depression and the impact of federal aid in the 1930s. Isaac L. Kandel, *The Impact of the War upon American Education* (1948), is a good source for the period of the Second World War.

D. AMERICAN RELIGIOUS INSTITUTIONS AND THOUGHT

Sydney E. Ahlstrom, *A Religious History of the American People* (1972), and James W. Smith and A. Leland Jamison, eds., *Religion in American Life* (4 vols., 1961), are the best introductions. The two bibliographical volumes in the latter are particularly helpful. William W. Sweet, *The Story of Religion in America* (1939); Winthrop S. Hudson, *Religion in America* (1973); Robert T. Handy, *A Christian America: Protestant Hopes and Historical Realities* (1971); Martin E. Marty, *Righteous Empire: The Protestant Experience in America* (1970); Jerald C. Brauer, *Protestantism in America* (1953); and Clifton E. Olmstead, *History of Religion in the United States* (1960), cover the period, but more detailed are Herbert W. Schneider,

Religion in Twentieth Century America (1952), and Willard Sperry, *Religion in America* (1945). Other useful specialized works are Thomas T. McAvoy, *A History of the Catholic Church in the United States* (1969); John T. Ellis, *American Catholicism* (1956); Will Herberg, *Protestant, Catholic, Jew* (1955); Nathan Glazer, *American Judaism* (1957); Joseph L. Blau, *Judaism in America* (1976); Melvin L. Urofsky, *American Zionism from Herzl to the Holocaust* (1976); Naomi W. Cohen, *American Jews and the Zionist Idea* (1975); Winthrop S. Hudson, *American Protestantism* (1961); and Kenneth K. Bailey, *Southern White Protestantism in the Twentieth Century* (1964). William G. McLoughlin, Jr., *Modern Revivalism* (1959) and *Billy Sunday Was His Real Name* (1955), are superb on twentieth-century revivalism. Gerald B. Smith, ed., *Religious Thought in the Last Quarter-Century* (1927), and Arnold S. Nash, ed., *Protestant Thought in the Twentieth Century* (1951), are both very useful. Charles A. Braden, *These Also Believe* (1949), is an account of the sects along the frontier of Protestantism. Norman F. Furniss, *The Fundamentalist Controversy, 1918–1931* (1954), should be supplemented by Ernest R. Sandeen, *The Roots of Fundamentalism: British and American Millenarianism, 1800–1930* (1970). George Marsden, *Fundamentalism and American Culture: The Shaping of Twentieth-Century Evangelicalism, 1870–1925* (1980), is a pioneering venture in cultural history, now the definitive work on the subject.

Excellent for the awakening of the church's social conscience in the progressive era are Charles H. Hopkins, *The Rise of the Social Gospel in American Protestantism, 1865–1915* (1940); Aaron I. Abell, *The Urban Impact on American Protestantism, 1865–1900* (1943); Henry F. May, *Protestant Churches and Industrial America* (1949); Aaron I. Abell, *American Catholicism and Social Action* (1960); Herbert A. Wisbey, Jr., *Soldiers Without Swords: A History of the Salvation Army in the United States* (1955); Charles H. Hopkins, *History of the Y.M.C.A. in North America* (1951); Jacob Henry Dorn, *Washington Gladden: Prophet of the Social Gospel* (1967); Dores R. Sharpe, *Walter Rauschenbusch* (1942); and Ronald C. White, Jr., and C. Howard Hopkins, *The Social Gospel: Religion and Reform in Changing America* (1976).

Robert Moats Miller, *American Protestantism and Social Issues, 1919–1939* (1958); Paul A. Carter, *The Decline and Revival of the Social Gospel, 1920–1940* (1956); and David J. O'Brien, *American Catholics and Social Reform: The New Deal Years* (1968), are excellent for the Social Gospel during the 1920s and beyond. For American religious thought during this period, see Donald B. Meyer, *The Protestant Search for Political Realism, 1919–1941* (1960). For biographies of two important Protestant figures in the interwar period, see Richard Wright Fox, *Reinhold Neibuhr* (1985), and Robert Moats Miller, *Harry Emerson Fosdick: Preacher, Pastor, Prophet* (1985).

E. AMERICAN WRITING

For significant work in fiction, poetry, and drama, see the relevant sections in this volume. The following list includes only general works and omits critical studies of individual writers.

The basic general history is Robert E. Spiller et al., *Literary History of the United States* (1963), which contains discussions of virtually every American writer worthy of mention, lengthy essays on major writers, and a good bibliography. For general works on fiction, see Leon Howard, *Literature and the American Tradition* (1960); Willard Thorp, *American Writing in the Twentieth Century* (1960); Frederick J. Hoffman, *The Modern Novel in America, 1900–1950* (1951); and Marcus Klein, *Foreigners: The Making of American Literature, 1900–1940* (1981), all valuable surveys. For more specialized studies, see Walter F. Taylor, *The Economic Novel in America* (1942); Walter B. Rideout, *The Radical Novel in the United States, 1900–1954* (1956); Alfred Kazin, *On Native Grounds* (1942); Malcolm Cowley, *Exile's Return: A Literary Odyssey of the 1920's* (1951); John W. Aldridge, *After the Lost Generation* (1951); Leo Gurko, *The Angry Decade* (1947); and F. Garvin Davenport, Jr., *The Myth of Southern History: Historical Consciousness in Twentieth-Century Southern Literature* (1970). Alan S. Downer, *Fifty Years of American Drama, 1900–1950* (1951), and Louise Bogan, *Achievement in American Poetry, 1900–1950* (1951), cover the main currents in their respective fields. James O. Young, *Black Writers of the Thirties* (1973), is excellent on that subject.

F.   AMERICAN BLACKS

The best guide to the subject is James W. McPherson et al., *Blacks in America: Bibliographical Essays* (1971). Rayford W. Logan, *The Negro in American Life and Thought: The Nadir, 1877–1901* (1954) and *The Betrayal of the Negro from Rutherford B. Hayes to Woodrow Wilson* (1965); C. Vann Woodward, *The Strange Career of Jim Crow* (3d rev. ed., 1974); Joel Williamson, *The Crucible of Race: Black–White Relations in the American South Since Emancipation* (1984); and William Toll, *The Resurgence of Race: Black Social Theory from Reconstruction to the Pan–African Conferences* (1979), provide background discussions for twentieth-century developments. General histories abound, but the best are John Hope Franklin, *From Slavery to Freedom: A History of American Negroes* (5th ed., 1980); August Meier and E. M. Rudwick, *From Plantation to Ghetto: An Interpretive History of American Negroes* (1976); and Lawrence W. Levine, *Black Culture and Black Consciousness: Afro–American Folk Thought from Slavery to Freedom* (1977). Other useful general volumes are Gunnar Myrdal, *An American Dilemma* (2 vols., 1944), a massive, penetrating study; Arnold M. Rose, *The Negro in America* (1948), an abridgment of Myrdal's volumes; E. Franklin Frazier, *The Negro Family in the United States* (1939) and *The Negro Church in America* (1973); Charles S. Johnson, *Patterns of Negro Segregation* (1943); John Hope Franklin and Isidore Starr, *The Negro in Twentieth Century America: A Reader on the Struggle for Civil Rights* (1967); S. P. Fullinwider, *The Mind and Mood of Black America: 20th Century Thought* (1969); August Meier and E. M. Rudwick, eds., *The Making of Black America* (2 vols., 1969); August Meier and E. M. Rudwick, *Along the Color Line: Explorations in the Black Experience* (1976); August Meier, *Negro Thought in America, 1880–1915* (1963); Francis L. Broderick and August Meier, eds., *Negro Protest Thought in the Twentieth Century* (1970); and Talcott Parsons and Kenneth B. Clark, eds., *The Negro American* (1966).

For the biography of a major black leader of his generation, see Louis R. Harlan, *Booker T. Washington: The Making of a Black Leader, 1856–1901* (1972) and *Booker T. Washington: The Wizard of Tuskegee, 1901–1915* (1983). For black movements and militancy and blacks in politics during the first two decades of the twentieth century, see Charles F. Kellogg, *NAACP: A History, Volume I: 1909–1920* (1967); Nancy J. Weiss, *The National Urban League, 1910–1940* (1974); Robert L. Jack, *History of the National Association for the Advancement of Colored People* (1943); Walter White, *A Man Called White* (1949); Arvarh E. Strickland, *History of the Chicago Urban League* (1966); John Hope Franklin, *George Washington Williams: A Biography* (1985); E. David Cronon, *Black Moses: The Story of Marcus Garvey* (1955); W.E.B. Du Bois, *Dusk of Dawn* (1940) and *The Autobiography of W.E.B. Du Bois* (1968); Francis L. Broderick, *W.E.B. Du Bois: Negro Leader in a Time of Crisis* (1959); Shirley Graham, *Du Bois, His Day Is Marching On: A Memoir of W.E.B. Du Bois* (1971); Andrew Buni, *Robert L. Vann of the Pittsburgh Courier: Politics and Black Journalism* (1974); Stephen R. Fox, *The Guardian of Boston: William Monroe Trotter* (1970); Jervis Anderson, *A. Philip Randolph* (1973); Margaret L. Callcott, *The Negro in Maryland Politics, 1870–1912* (1969); and Henry L. Moon, *Balance of Power: The Negro Vote* (1948). William B. Hixson, Jr., *Moorefield Storey and the Abolitionist Tradition* (1972), is an excellent account of a white leader of the early civil rights movement.

The following is an incomplete list of specialized studies: Edwin S. Redkey, *Black Exodus: Black Nationalist and Back-to-Africa Movements, 1890–1910* (1969); John D. Weaver, *The Brownsville Raid* (1970); Gilbert Osofsky, *Harlem: The Making of a Ghetto* (1966); Seth M. Scheiner, *Negro Mecca: A History of the Negro in New York City, 1865–1920* (1965); Allan H. Spear, *Black Chicago: The Making of a Ghetto, 1890–1920* (1967); Louis R. Harlan, *Separate and Unequal: Public School Campaigns and Racism in Southern Seaboard States, 1901–1915* (1958); John Dittmer, *Black Georgia in the Progressive Era, 1900–1920* (1977); George C. Wright, *Life Behind a Veil: Blacks in Louisville, Kentucky, 1865–1930* (1985); David R. Colburn, *Racial Change and Community Crisis: St. Augustine, Florida, 1877–1980* (1985); Thomas Cripps, *Slow Fade to Black: The Negro in American Film, 1900–1942* (1977); Daniel J. Leab, *From Sambo to Superspade: The Black Experience in Motion Pictures* (1975); Claude H. Nolen, *The Negro's Image in the South: The Anatomy of White Supremacy* (1967); Thomas F. Gossett, *Race: The History of an Idea in America* (1963); I. A. Newby, *The Development of Segregationist Thought* (1969) and *Jim Crow's Defense: Anti-Negro Thought in America, 1900–1930* (1965); and David M. Reiners, *White Protestantism and the Negro* (1965). Louise V. Kennedy, *The Negro Peasant Turns Cityward* (1930), and Ira DeA. Reid, *The Negro Immigrant* (1939), are both excellent for the black migration from the South during and after the First World War. Walter White, *Rope and Faggot* (1929), and Arthur F. Raper, *The Tragedy of Lynching* (1933), are both good on lynching in the twentieth century. Morton Sosna, *In Search of the Silent South: Southern Liberals and the Race Issue* (1977), and John T. Kneebone, *Southern Liberal Journalists and the Issue of Race, 1920–1944* (1985), are excellent for the beginnings of southern white liberal attitudes toward race. John B. Kirby, *Black Americans in the Roosevelt Era* (1980), and Nancy J. Weiss, *Farewell to the Party of Lincoln: Black Politics in the Age of FDR* (1983), both discuss the complex relationship between blacks and the New Deal.

Other excellent studies are Nathan I. Huggins, *Harlem Renaissance* (1972) and *Voices from the Harlem Renaissance* (1976); Wayne Cooper, ed., *The Passion of Claude McKay* (1973); Judith Stein, *Race and Class: The World of Marcus Garvey* (1985); Robert A. Hill, ed., *The Papers of Marcus Garvey* (1983–); Dan T. Carter, *Scottsboro: A Tragedy of the American South* (1969); Raymond Wolters, *Negroes and the Great Depression* (1970); Horace R. Cayton and George S. Mitchell, *Black Workers and the New Unions* (1939); Walter B. Weare, *Black Business in the New South: A Social History of the North Carolina Mutual Life Insurance Company* (1973); Herbert R. Northrup, *Organized Labor and the Negro* (1944); Robert L. Zangrando, *The NAACP Crusade Against Lynching, 1909–1950* (1980); and Dominic J. Capeci, Jr., *Race Relations in Wartime Detroit: The Sojourner Truth Housing Controversy of 1942* (1984).

G. WOMEN AND THE FAMILY, 1900–1945

The field of women's history has benefited from a growing number of new studies on the roles of women in the family and in the work force. The best general studies of those subjects are Carl F. Degler, *At Odds: Women and the Family from the Revolution to the Present* (1980); Alice Kessler-Harris, *Out to Work: A History of Wage-Earning Women in the United States* (1982); Susan Estabrook Kennedy, *If All We Did Was to Weep at Home: A History of Working-Class Women in America* (1979); Linda K. Kerber and Jane DeHart Mathews, eds., *Women's America: Refocusing the Past* (2d ed., 1986); Glenda Riley, *Inventing the American Woman*, Vol. 2 (1986); and Anne Firor Scott, *The Southern Lady: From Pedestal to Politics, 1830–1930* (1970) and *Making the Invisible Woman Visible* (1984).

For studies of women and the family during the progressive era, consult David M. Katzman, *Seven Days A Week: Women and Domestic Service in Industrializing America* (1978); Susan Levine, *Labor's True Women: Carpet Weavers, Industrialization, and Labor Reform in the Gilded Age* (1984); Elaine Tyler May, *Great Expectations: Marriage and Divorce in Post-Victorian America* (1980); Barbara Melosh, *The Physician's Hand: Work, Culture, and Conflict in American Nursing* (1982); Leslie Woodcock Tentler, *Wage-Earning Women: Industrial Work and Family Life in the United States, 1900–1930* (1979); and Mari Jo Buhle, *Women and American Socialism, 1870–1920* (1981). Two recent studies of women during the interwar period are Winifred D. Wandersee, *Women's Work and Family Values: 1920–1940* (1981), and Susan D. Becker, *The Origins of the Era: American Feminism Between the Wars* (1981). The changing role of women during the Second World War is the subject of Karen Anderson, *Wartime Women: Sex Roles, Family Relations, and the Status of Women During World War II* (1981); D'Ann Campbell, *Women at War with America: Private Lives in a Patriotic Era* (1984); and Maureen Honey, *Creating Rosie the Riveter: Class, Gender, and Propaganda during World War II (1984).*

Index

ABOUT THE AUTHORS

—————— ⇢⟫ ⟪⇠ ——————

ARTHUR S. LINK, who received his B.A. and Ph.D. from the University of North Carolina, is the George Henry Davis '86 Professor of American History at Princeton University and Director and Editor of *The Papers of Woodrow Wilson*. He has held Rockefeller, Guggenheim, and Rosenwald fellowships, in addition to memberships at the Institute for Advanced Study. He has been the Harmsworth Professor of American History at Oxford University and has lectured in South America, Japan, Western Europe, and Poland. Two of his many books have been awarded The Bancroft Prize, and he has received eight honorary degrees. He is a member of and has been an officer of many professional societies and is a past president of the Southern Historical Association, the Association for Documentary Editing, the Organization of American Historians, and the American Historical Association.

WILLIAM A. LINK received his B.A. from Davidson College and M.A. and Ph.D. from the University of Virginia. He has taught at the University of Virginia and at the University of North Carolina at Greensboro, where he is associate professor of history. He is the author of *A Hard Country and a Lonely Place: Schooling, Society, and Reform in Rural Virginia, 1870–1920* (Chapel Hill: University of North Carolina Press, 1986).

WILLIAM B. CATTON received his B.A. and M.A. from the University of Maryland and his Ph.D. from Northwestern University. He has taught at Northwestern University, the University of Maryland, Princeton University, and at Middlebury College, where he was Charles A. Dana Professor of American History, Chairman of the Division of the Social Sciences, and Historian in Residence. Currently he is Professor Emeritus. He is coauthor, with Bruce Catton, of *Two Roads to Sumter* and *The Bold and Magnificent Dream: America's Founding Years 1492–1815*.

A NOTE ON THE TYPE

————————— →≫ ≪← —————————

This book is set in Electra, a typeface designed by W.A. Dwiggins. This face cannot be classified as either modern or old-style. It is not based on any historical model, nor does it echo any particular period or style. It avoids the extreme contrasts between thick and thin elements that mark most modern faces, and attempts to give a feeling of fluidity, power, and speed.

This version of Electra, (called Avanta), was set on a *VideoComp 570* PAGESETTER by ComCom, a division of Haddon Craftsmen.

Printed and bound by R.R. Donnelley & Sons, Harrisonburg, Va.